Inventing the
Modern Yiddish Stage

Inventing the Modern Yiddish Stage

Essays in Drama, Performance, and Show Business

Edited by Joel Berkowitz and Barbara Henry

Wayne State University Press, Detroit

© 2012 by Wayne State University Press, Detroit, Michigan 48201.
All rights reserved. No part of this book may be reproduced without formal permission.
Manufactured in the United States of America.

16 15 14 13 12   5 4 3 2 1

Library of Congress Cataloging-in-Publication Data

Inventing the modern Yiddish stage : essays in drama, performance, and show business/
edited by Joel Berkowitz and Barbara Henry.
p. cm.
Includes bibliographical references and index.
ISBN 978-0-8143-3504-8 (pbk. : alk. paper) — ISBN 978-0-8143-3719-6 (e-book)
1. Theater, Yiddish—Congresses. 2. Yiddish drama—History and criticism—Congresses.
3. Judaism and literature—Congresses. I. Berkowitz, Joel, 1965– II. Henry, Barbara J., 1965–
PN3035.I59   2012
792.089'924—dc23

2011050451

∞

Grateful acknowledgment is made to the Driker family for the generous support
of the publication of this volume.

Further support of the publication of this book was given through the generosity of the
Bertha M. and Hyman Herman Endowed Memorial Fund.

Designed by BookComp, Inc.
Typeset by BookComp, Inc.
Composed in Times New Roman and Helvetica Neue

Contents

List of Illustrations, vii
Note on Transliteration, ix

Introduction, 1
Joel Berkowitz and Barbara Henry

Part I. Origins, Influences, and Evolution

1. Between Two Worlds: Antitheatricality and the Beginnings of Modern Yiddish Theatre, 27
Jeremy Dauber

2. The Salon and the Tavern: Yiddish Folk Poetry of the Nineteenth Century, 40
Alyssa Quint

3. Jacob Gordin in Russia: Fact and Fiction, 64
Barbara Henry

Part II. Toward a Jewish Stage

4. Translations of Karl Gutzkow's *Uriel Acosta* as Iconic Moments in Yiddish Theatre, 87
Seth L. Wolitz

5. "Cosmopolitan" or "Purely Jewish?": Zygmunt Turkow and the Warsaw Yiddish Art Theatre, 116
Mirosława M. Bułat

6. From *Boston* to *Mississippi* on the Warsaw Yiddish Stage, 136
Jeffrey Veidlinger

Part III. Authors, Actors, and Audiences

7. *Patriotn* and Their Stars: Male Youth Culture in the Galleries of the New York Yiddish Theatre, 161
Nina Warnke

8. Liquor and Leisure: The Business of Yiddish Vaudeville, 184
Judith Thissen

9. "Gvald, Yidn, Buena Gente": Jevel Katz, Yiddish Bard of the Río de la Plata, 202
Zachary M. Baker

Part IV. Recoveries and Reconstructions

10. Reconstructing a Yiddish Theatre Score: Giacomo Minkowski and His Music to *Alexander; or, the Crown Prince of Jerusalem*, 225
Ronald Robboy

11. Sex and Scandal in the *Encyclopedia of the Yiddish Theatre*, 251
Faith Jones

12. Joy to the Goy and Happiness to the Jew: Communist and Jewish Aspirations in a Postwar *Purimshpil*, 275
Annette Aronowicz

13. No Raisins and Almonds in the Land of Israel: A Tale of Goldfaden Productions Featuring Four Hotsmakhs, Three Kuni-Lemls, Two Shulamits, and One Messiah, 295
Donny Inbar

Notes on Contributors, 321
Bibliography, 325
Acknowledgments, 367
Index, 371

List of Illustrations

Frontispiece to *Der beyzer marshalik: satirishe folkslider fun Yitskhok Yoel Linetski* (The vexed wedding jester: Satirical folk poetry by Yitskhok Yoel Linetski) features an etched image of a westernized Jew and a religious Jew in a tense encounter, 47

Cover to *Der shiker, oder di makhloyke tsvishn Reb Trinkman un dem shnaps* (The drunkard: or the debate between Reb Drinker and the whiskey), 53

Luba Rymer in *Uriel Acosta*, 88

Zygmunt Turkow and an unidentified actress in *Uriel Acosta*, 121

"A farblondzheter patriot" (A lost *patriot*). A fan of David Kessler's mistakenly wanders into Boris Thomashefsky's "People's Theatre" and receives a "trimming" by Thomashefsky's *patriotn*, 162

Jevel Katz in the early 1930s, 203

Boris and Bessie Thomashefsky, c. 1890, 226

Zalmen Zylbercweig, editor of the *Leksikon fun yidishn teater* (Encyclopedia of the Yiddish theatre), 252

Keni Liptzin, photographed in an unidentified Gordin role, 255

A Yiddish theatre audience, New York, 1920s, 263

Mordechai (Oscar Fessler) does battle with Haman (Leon Szpigelman) in the original 1946 Paris production of *Homens mapole*, 280

King Ahasuerus (Moshe Kineman) and the Herald (Yashar [Jakub Aronowicz]) in the original Paris production of *Homens mapole*, 1946, 283

Ensemble photograph of a revival of *Homens mapole* features the original Fessler production's characteristic triangular, hamentash shape on stage. Paris, 1948 or 1949, 284

Ha-mekhashefa (The sorceress), by Avrom Goldfaden, produced in Hebrew at the Ohel Theatre, Palestine, 1946, 297

Shulamit, by Avrom Goldfaden, produced in Hebrew at the Ohel Theatre, Israel, 1957, 306

Shoshana Damari as Shulamit, Do-Re-Mi Theatre production of Avrom Goldfaden's *Shulamit*, Israel, 1957, 307

Cover image: Haman conducts Mordechai on horseback down "Ahasuerus Boulevard" in *Homens mapole*

Note on Transliteration

For the romanization of Yiddish words and names, we have adopted, with some modifications (described below), the transliteration system established by the YIVO Institute for Jewish Research. That system phonetically reproduces the pronunciation of words in "standard" Yiddish, with the following correspondence to the Latin alphabet:

a	'a' as in 'father'
ay	'i' as in 'wine'
e	'e' as in 'bed'
ey	'a' as in 'gate'
i	'i' as in 'sit'
o	similar to 'o' in 'born'
oy	'oy' as in 'boy'
u	similar to 'oo' in 'book'
dzh	'j' as in 'jury'
kh	'ch' as in 'Bach' or 'chutzpah'
tsh	'ch' as in 'cheer'
zh	'j' as in the French 'je'

We have made three exceptions to this rule:

1. No attempt has been made to standardize non-standard Yiddish orthography. For example, when a newspaper or journal used the spelling *Idish* rather than *Yidish* in its title, we reproduce the original title—thus, *Idishe tsaytung* rather than *Yidishe tsaytung*.

2. When Yiddish names or words have a commonly accepted Latin transcription, we have used that; e.g., Maurice Schwartz, not Moris Shvarts. The exception to this is in the romanization of book titles in the endnotes and bibliography. In these sections, we follow the YIVO system for the title, followed by an English translation: e.g., *Moris Shvarts un der yidisher kunst teater* (Maurice Schwartz and the Yiddish Art Theatre).
3. When transliterating lines of dramatic dialogue or song texts, we have on rare occasions departed from the pronunciation considered normative by YIVO, and followed the dialect clearly dictated by the text. For example, under the YIVO system, the refrain of Avrom Goldfaden's song "Rozhinkes mit mandlen" ("Raisins and Almonds"), discussed in Chapter 13, would end, *Shlof-zhe yidele shlof* (Sleep, Yidele, sleep). Since, however, that line is clearly meant to rhyme with *baruf* two lines earlier, the line needs to be pronounced, *Shluf-zhe yidele shluf*, which is how we have transcribed the line.

Our transcription of Hebrew phonetically follows modern Israeli pronunciation. We use "*kh*" for the sound made by the Hebrew letters *khet* and *khaf*. The definite article *ha* and "and" (*ve* or *u*, depending on the next letter), which are always attached to another word, are always followed by a hyphen; e.g., . . . *ve-ha-te'atron* (. . . and the theatre). Vowels that appear sequentially in English, but that would be pronounced as separate syllables in Hebrew, are separated by an apostrophe, as in *te'atron* (theatre) in the previous example.

We have capitalized only the first words of all Hebrew and Yiddish titles, with the exception of people's (including dramatic characters' names, which are always capitalized: thus, for example, *Der yidisher kenig Lir* (the Jewish King Lear). Russian names, titles, and terms are rendered according to the system used by the United States Board on Geographic Names, with one modification, in that the letter *ë* is rendered as *yo*. Words and names that include a soft sign have been transliterated as '. Words including a hard sign have been rendered as ". Pre-revolutionary orthography has been updated to reflect modern Russian usage. Capitalization reflects Cyrillic convention.

Introduction

Joel Berkowitz and Barbara Henry

The book of Genesis opens with two creation stories. Not to be outdone, the annals of the Yiddish stage add several more. They tend to be variations on a theme, but anyone trying to find out how the modern Yiddish stage developed is likely to come across an account that reads something like this:

Before the 1870s (the creation myths collectively suggest), *there was no theatrical performance to speak of in the Yiddish-speaking world, aside from crude amateur entertainments associated with the winter holiday of Purim and a small handful of plays that circulated among intellectuals. That all changed suddenly in the autumn of 1876, when poet and composer Avrom Goldfaden was invited to perform his own compositions at Shimen Mark's Green Tree Café in Jassy, Romania. The evening was a fiasco for reasons that vary among different accounts, including Goldfaden's own, which he would publish just a few months before his death in 1908. The failed performance had a silver lining, however. It taught Goldfaden valuable lessons about his audience's taste, which he proceeded to accommodate in a series of plays of varying length, tailor-made for the two performers who constituted the playwright's and the Yiddish theatre's first troupe. The professional Yiddish theatre was born, thanks to the efforts of Goldfaden, the "father of the Yiddish stage."*

While this creation myth has some basis in fact, it recasts and oversimplifies the genesis of the modern, and indeed the pre-modern, Yiddish theatre. In doing so, it erases a centuries-old Yiddish performance tradition, including earlier efforts in modern times to assemble a professional company in much the same way that Goldfaden would ultimately do.[1] The absence of a premodern Yiddish stage makes for a tidier legend, accompanied by an untainted paternity test. Yet not only does the creation myth run contrary to extensive historical evidence of a wide variety of performance forms reaching back into medieval central Europe,[2] it also relies on a limited understanding of how performance traditions develop in any culture. If an account of the origins of, say, Western drama were to claim that Aeschylus invented Greek tragedy out of whole cloth, any sensible reader would be skeptical, if not downright dismissive. Yet something about the way that the Yiddish theatre has been perceived by insiders and outsiders, creators and audiences, and contemporaries and successors, seems to encourage the persistence of this charming but ahistorical myth of origins.[3] To this day, despite a continuing stream of new scholarship that enriches and refines our understanding of Yiddish theatre history, in some circles, the legend lives on, usually embellished with colorful anecdotes about scenery-chewing divas, breathlessly naïve audiences, and outrageous off-stage antics.

As a consequence of the reluctance to complicate nostalgic legends of the Yiddish stage by a deeper consideration of its performance practices, dramatic texts, artists, and day-to-day business, there is little understanding, outside a small circle of specialists, of the role that Yiddish theatre played in the wider context of modern Jewish life and culture. Far from being a marginal activity, the Yiddish stage was central to the cultural experience of millions of Jews. It was also an international phenomenon, whose audiences could be found in eastern and western Europe, North and South America, South Africa, and Australia. But despite its reach and influence, the Yiddish stage remains curiously compartmentalized, largely removed from most people's conceptions of modern Jewish history. Yet the Yiddish theatre, in all its forms and phases, was intimately bound up with that history, and reflected the totality of modern Jewish experience in a popular art form.

That myth should continue to trump fact will, perhaps, not come as too great a shock, particularly since the myth-makers of the Yiddish stage—notably, actors, playwrights, and other theatre personnel, as well as journalists who frequently relied on the memoirs of these individuals for their own writings—manufactured self-serving legends by the barrelful and then recycled them for decades. These retellings went largely unchallenged by scholars, who had not yet "discovered" the Yiddish theatre as a subject of academic scrutiny or historical value.

The mythology of the Yiddish stage, and perhaps even more strikingly, its practitioners' and theorists' conscious attempts to construct that mythology, highlight another important characteristic of this theatrical culture: its striking self-consciousness. Faith Jones, who writes in Chapter 11 about Yiddish commentators working in the early twentieth century, notes the "obsessive activity on the part of so many people to fully document and describe a form of cultural expression that had, at that point, operated on a mass scale for only a few decades." Remarkable as this was, it had already been going on for some time—to the very dawn of modern Yiddish drama at the tail end of the eighteenth century. At that moment, when dramatists were just beginning to lay the foundation of the modern Yiddish repertoire, they simultaneously raised questions about its nature and direction. To what extent should it replicate pre-existing Jewish performance forms? To what degree should it follow the footprints of drama being written in other European languages? What was its role beyond entertainment? The first modern Yiddish plays bear the hallmarks of these questions, which would continue to reverberate throughout the history of the Yiddish theatre in the nineteenth and twentieth centuries. From almost the inception of the modern Yiddish stage, the people who created it, as well as the audiences and critics who beheld it, entered into an ongoing debate over the nature of their theatrical culture and the direction they felt it should take.

To a certain extent, the very public, provocative, and occasionally dangerous nature of live theatre has meant that it is always concerned on some level with how it is seen not only by its creators and its audience, but by the states and societies that support, tolerate, or discourage its practice. The self-critical and self-conscious tendencies of the Yiddish stage were in part necessitated by the particular challenges it faced, exigencies that were little known to comparable theatrical cultures in England, France, or Germany. Yiddish companies and playwrights could count on no financial support from courts or kings; its actors underwent no recognized form of professional training. The very language of the Yiddish repertoire was often regarded as unfit for high dramatic art, and in the most densely populated Jewish territories in eastern Europe, the Pale of Settlement, Yiddish plays were subject to censorship far more rigorous than that imposed on Russian-language productions.[4] In the ideologically loaded atmosphere of Jewish eastern Europe, in the infancy of the professional Yiddish theatre—a time that gave rise to Zionism, extensive Jewish participation in socialist and other radical politics, and the counterbalancing reinvigoration of traditional Jewish belief and practice—the very act of attending a Yiddish play amounted to making a public declaration of one's Jewishness and support of a Jewish art, which might be construed in some corners (both Jewish and Gentile) as a provocation. Disapproval from religious authorities within the Jewish community itself presented another stumbling block. Add to all of this the financial insecurity of any theatrical enterprise, the combustible personalities that often coalesce around collaborative endeavors, and the ever-present anxiety within Jewish communities that the Yiddish stage might present non-Jewish onlookers with an unfavorable image of Jews and Jewish culture, and one has a small idea of the unique challenges that faced the nascent Yiddish theatre. Western European theatre might have had to wrangle with the fluctuating support and suppression of church and state, with the prescriptions of critics and the proscriptions of censors, and with the caprices of popular taste, but it very rarely had to examine the legitimacy of its very existence or defend that existence to forces both within and outside its own community, as did the Yiddish stage.

Despite the difficulties that the Yiddish theatre encountered in its establishment and conduct, it proved an extraordinarily precocious student. Its history is astonishingly compressed, leaping in just one generation from the work of untrained, if sometimes brilliant, performers in Romania and southern Russia in the 1870s to a global phenomenon that could boast, at least among a handful of its elite actors, figures who could hold their own with the great contemporary luminaries of the stage. This compression posed considerable challenges, forcing theatre artists to reckon with changes in repertoire, music, acting styles, and performance practices that might in other cultures take generations to unfold. But it also gave Yiddish playwrights, actors, and other theatre personnel a bird's-eye view of the development of European theatre and drama that would not have been available to writers, performers, and others working within theatrical traditions that evolved more gradually. When the modern professional Yiddish theatre entered the scene around 1880, it could survey the totality of the European theatrical landscape. The European stage's stirring melodramas, Shakespearean classics, lavish operas, neoclassical veterans, romantic warhorses, earnest realist dramas, and bread-and-butter staples of farces, revues, and one-night wonders had unfolded over centuries. The Yiddish theatre, latecomer that it was, could import its European neighbors' most proven, desirable, and profitable features. Of course, what one artist or audience desired, another might disdain—a fact that would itself animate the evolution and reception of the modern Yiddish stage.

Within one generation, Yiddish playwrights, actors, directors, and designers of the early 1900s ventured increasingly often, and with more and more success, into the great artistic experiments of the age. Expressionism, symbolism, constructivism, and other avant-garde movements were eagerly taken up by Yiddish theatre artists. The plays they wrote and the productions they mounted also tackled the socio-political issues and events of the era, both within the Jewish world and beyond, which did not lack for wars, controversial political movements, migrations, and religious reforms.

The unusually accelerated pace at which the modern Yiddish theatre developed helped lend it its distinct character. Its infancy involved a curious, fascinating mixture of the kinds of crude plays, performances, and audience reactions one might expect to find at such an early juncture, alongside more ambitious offerings from individuals who were acutely conscious of their theatre's deficiencies and aspired to much greater artistry and even social engagement, almost from the moment that the first Yiddish troupes formed. In some cases, both of these impulses went to war within the same individual, Avrom Goldfaden (1840–1908) being exhibit A.[5] Born to a well-educated, reasonably prosperous artisan who educated his sons in both Jewish texts and traditions, and modern, secular subjects, Goldfaden achieved modest renown in Hebrew, and then Yiddish, lyric poetry before turning his hand to playwriting. His first forays into the latter field—a two-person dramatic dialogue, but more significantly, a full-length comedy, *Di mume Sosye* (Aunt Sosia)—were published in his third book, *Di yidene* (The Jewish woman, 1869). *Di mume Sosye* mimicked, quite skillfully, earlier comedies of the *Haskalah*, or Jewish Enlightenment, which in turn relied heavily on conventions that prevailed in eighteenth- and nineteenth-century Continental bourgeois comedy. Goldfaden's characters were deftly drawn, his plot brisk and artfully constructed, and his message neatly packaged. The young playwright's bona fides for entering the world of the Jewish intellectual salon were abundantly in evidence.

There were just a couple of problems, though. Goldfaden was born at the wrong time and place for this to happen. Such salons were all but non-existent in mid- to late-nineteenth-century eastern Europe as Goldfaden was coming of age there. And just as important, to the extent Goldfaden might have contributed to or founded such a salon, it is hard to imagine a scenario in which writing for like-minded intellectuals would have enabled him to earn a living. Predecessors in this arena like Aaron Halle Wolfsson, Solomon Ettinger, Goldfaden's teacher Avrom Ber Gottlober, and others, earned their livelihoods as educators, community leaders, or physicians; their literary efforts tended to be extracurricular ones. With brief flirtations with fields as diverse as Jewish education, medicine, and haberdashery, Goldfaden seemed headed down a parallel road; that is, earning a living by day and writing poetry or drama in his own time. But his destiny would be different.

Much of Goldfaden's contribution to the birth of the professional Yiddish stage is shrouded in legend, but there is no doubt that he possessed a genius for tapping into audience tastes, particularly in his extremely fecund period of the mid-1870s to the early 1880s. Goldfaden's upbringing and education allowed him to draw upon multiple literary, musical, and theatrical traditions simultaneously; his great talent manifested itself not only in his ability to synthesize these raw materials into something whole, but in his creating, at his best, works that were far from derivative and spoke to audiences in powerful ways. In this sense, he created a significant portion of the Yiddish theatre's "classical" tradition. This repertoire included plays that would not only be wildly popular in their time and in later periods, but that would both influence other works and be adopted and adapted in endless ways to speak to ever-changing aesthetic, social, and political sensibilities.

"Second-generation" Yiddish playwrights like Jacob Gordin (1853–1909) would acknowledge and react to the foundational Yiddish plays of Goldfaden. Given the accelerated pace of Yiddish theatrical development, it might be assumed that their works, having an established Yiddish repertoire from which to learn, and an audience already schooled in the ways of the Jewish stage, might have undergone a marked increase in dramatic sophistication. Yet second-generation playwrights (who were chronologically more Goldfaden's contemporaries than his "sons") often struggled to match Goldfaden's originality, and their plays rarely enjoyed the popularity and longevity of Goldfaden's work. Second-generation playwrights, moreover, found their basic financial circumstances little altered from those in which Goldfaden had functioned.[6] While the Yiddish stage expanded to North America by the 1890s, thereby increasing performance opportunities for Yiddish actors, playwrights, and impresarios, and allowing for the establishment of a genuinely international Jewish theatre culture, Gordin still had to maintain a profile as a New York journalist in order to supplement his earnings as a playwright. Financial exigencies, not surprisingly, considerably compromised Gordin's oft-stated ambition to improve the Yiddish repertoire. This he approached through the strategic appropriation of non-Jewish source materials, the use of vernacular Yiddish dialogue, and by addressing overtly, even stridently, political themes in his plays. But aspiring to aesthetic achievements and social relevance always needed to be tempered by audience tastes and their constant demand for new plays. Gordin's audience was relatively small, and their tastes—when they could be enticed to try something other than broad comedies and elaborate spectacles—were less inclined to grim, gritty realism. Gordin cannily obliged them by melding the melodramatic tradition of the Goldfaden era with a superficially realistic mise-en-scène. The result, as playwright Dovid Pinski would proclaim in 1909, was an improvement on what he dismissed as the "circus pantomime" level of works by the first generation of Yiddish playwrights. But for Pinski (who earned some of his critical bona fides earning a Ph.D. in comparative literature from Columbia), this new phase of Yiddish drama nevertheless still "straddled the divide between art and trash."[7]

Pinski's harsh characterization of Gordin's work—one shared by many a critic, then and since—typifies the severity and seriousness with which Yiddish theatre professionals and critics generally regarded their art. Yiddish theatre was rarely given a pass based on its youth and inexperience, and its shortcomings as it developed formed the subject of countless newspaper editorials, stage-curtain speeches, and journal articles. Again, the compressed development of the Yiddish stage made itself felt here; many a Yiddish critic clearly wanted this culture to skip the teething pains that naturally came with the emergence of a young, unpolished theatrical culture. Could not this gifted Jewish child simply move right on to more mature stages, perhaps skipping the rebelliously experimental teenage years entirely? This desire for an even more accelerated growth process was a phenomenon apparent even in Goldfaden's time, and it was a trope that never disappeared from the rhetoric of Yiddish critics.[8] Certainly Yiddish playwrights and actors were guilty, more than a few times, of pandering to juvenile tastes, to Moyshe, their disparaging collective name (actually Yiddish for Moses) for the Yiddish audience. The fact, however, that this pandering went on in every other language, in every other culture, in every other time, and in every other place in which theatre was performed, was largely overlooked in pained reviews of the latest popular-theatre offerings. More was expected from the Jewish stage, just as more was expected from the Jewish audience. Yiddish theatre was not alone in being least appreciated by many of the people closest to it. And there was much to appreciate, as was sometimes pointed out by contemporary non-Jewish commentators, and has been explored for decades by scholars, journalists, and the occasional novelist, poet, or filmmaker. The essays that follow explore various facets of this Yosl-come-lately to the modern theatre, which rapidly blossomed into a global phenomenon that branched out in numerous artistic directions and addressed all the major historical and social forces that swept through the modern Jewish world of the past couple of centuries.

This book takes as a primary focus a fundamental characteristic of the modern Yiddish stage: its relentless and far-ranging capacity for self-invention. From its genesis at the end of the eighteenth century, modern Yiddish drama was consciously constructed, in terms of both form and content, to serve the goals of the Haskalah, and it served a variety of artistic, political, and other agendas as Yiddish drama and theatre continued to evolve. While Yiddish theatre is better known as a vehicle for popular entertainment than as a medium for political engagement (though these two categories are by no means mutually exclusive), its creators would continually reshape its orientation in response to changing social and political conditions, as this book will demonstrate. Examples of this self-fashioning could be found wherever one turned in Yiddish theatrical culture. It was reflected in playwrights' and performers' consciously crafting personae not only for the stage, but elsewhere in public (and even private) life, and in the ongoing tug-of-war among artists/entertainers, critics, and audiences to influence the Yiddish dramatic and musical-theatre repertoire. Self-fashioning tendencies were evidenced in production choices and in the staging of those works; they emerged in fundamental frictions that were acutely felt in the Yiddish theatre, such as the tensions between a text-based dramatic culture and a performance-oriented theatrical culture, and between an emphasis on home-grown, Jewish-inflected performance traditions and an embrace of the wider Western tradition. The urge to accommodate and cultivate standards of decorum and self-presentation emerges in a persistent self-consciousness that had Yiddish commentators constantly comparing the Yiddish stage to its Western counterparts, usually to the detriment of the former. Also much in evidence was a comparable awareness among managers and artists of what their counterparts were performing, not just across the street or around the corner, but across national borders, to other parts of the Yiddish-speaking world; and, of course, in the never-ending effort to have the last word, to tell the story of the Yiddish stage, its repertoire, and its personnel, according to the agendas of the chroniclers.

The chapters here begin at the roots of modern Yiddish drama and performance and span a century and a half, to beyond the heyday of the Yiddish stage that was all but eradicated by the Nazi Holocaust. Taken chronologically, they begin in eastern Europe in the nineteenth century and then follow the great migration that took millions of Jews elsewhere—most of them westward, to and through western Europe and on to the Americas, with a much smaller but culturally and historically significant number emigrating to what is present-day Israel. Each chapter takes its own distinct approach to its subject, with authors examining the Yiddish theatre from the perspectives of theatre history, comparative literature, cultural studies, critical biography, musicology, and related fields. Chapters take us through various countries and regions: Poland and the Russian empire, France, the United States, Argentina, and Palestine/Israel. Readers will spend time with notable individuals and troupes; meet creators, critics, and audiences; sample different dramatic genres; and learn about issues that preoccupied artists and audiences alike. What ties these disparate essays together is how they illuminate the fascinating story of the modern Yiddish stage as a phenomenon that was constantly inventing and reinventing itself, and simultaneously examining and questioning these very processes.

Each chapter is accompanied by an appendix consisting of primary material, much of it available here in translation for the first time. It is our hope that these materials—previously available only in Yiddish, Russian, Polish, and German—will enrich readers' appreciation of the issues explored in the chapters and may be used in the classroom as supplementary teaching texts.

The varied subjects of the chapters, and their approaches to the material, are reflected in the diversity of the appendices themselves. Two feature non-textual materials: rare illustrations, in the case of Alyssa Quint's appendix on Goldfaden, and reconstructions of musical notation that draw on disparate archival sources, in the case of Ronald Robboy's appendix on composer Giacomo Minkowski. Appendices such as Seth Wolitz's tables, which illustrate key differences among the original German text of Karl Gutzkow's *Uriel Acosta* and its four Yiddish translations, and Donny Inbar's detailed chronology of Goldfaden productions in Palestine and Israel, synthesize and organize the wide-ranging material discussed in their corresponding chapters.

The majority of appendices offer full texts and translations of materials discussed in the chapters, as in the case of Zachary Baker's song lyrics by Jevel Katz, and Mirosława Bułat's contemporary reviews of the interwar Varshever Yidisher Kunst-Teater. Jeremy Dauber, Annette Aronowicz, Jeffrey Veidlinger, and Barbara Henry offer translated texts—introductions, essays, and letters—by the writers and directors discussed in their respective chapters. A different sort of correspondence can be found in Faith Jones's translation of the full set of fiery exchanges among three major players in the world of Yiddish theatre history and criticism: Zylbercweig, Shatzky, and Mukdoyni. Nina Warnke's translations from the memoirs of Yiddish actresses, on the vociferous fan culture of New York's Yiddish theatre, is complemented by the appendix to Judith Thissen's chapter on the changing fortunes of the Yiddish stage in the same period.

Taken as a whole, the appendices offer a relatively unfiltered opportunity for the reader to encounter primary documents relating to the creation and interpretation of Yiddish theatre, drama, and performance in the nineteenth and twentieth centuries. They help readers better appreciate the issues explored in corresponding chapters, and can be used in the classroom, with instructors helping to guide students through the many nuances suggested by these fascinating documents.

Opening chapters take readers back to moments in the nineteenth century, when pioneering dramatists were in the position to make conscious choices about the directions in which they would take Yiddish drama and theatre. In Chapter 1, Jeremy Dauber finds the anonymous creators of two foundational texts of modern Yiddish drama asking what role drama should play in Jewish society, and finds in the plays *Di genarte velt* (The deceived world) and *Di hefker-velt* (The topsy-turvy world) an ambivalence about the very idea of performance. These plays were written, after all, at a time when no mechanism was yet in place to stage Yiddish plays professionally, and the only tradition of performing plays in Yiddish was limited to a short period on and around Purim each year. The same traditionalism that gave rise to those conditions in the first place also engendered a suspicion about performance in everyday life, and by extension, on stage, that goes back at least as far as Plato, who would have barred poets (which included playwrights) from his ideal Republic because, in Plato's view, poets lie. While lovers of theatre and drama might argue that playwriting and acting are founded on revealing deep truths, such activities are, by a certain definition, forms of lying. Dauber's chapter gives us just one example of the types of deep-seated attitudes in Jewish society that needed to be overcome if professional Yiddish theatre troupes were ever to get off the ground.

Alyssa Quint, in Chapter 2, explores further manifestations, several decades after those Dauber examines, of the relationship between dramatic script and performed event in an emergent secular Yiddish culture. Quint's chapter assesses the rise of the folk poet in Yiddish-speaking society in nineteenth-century eastern Europe, and illustrates the two divergent paths, broadly speaking, that such figures were able to take: the "highbrow" path of the literary salon, or the "low" road of the tavern, a venue inextricably linked to the genesis of modern Yiddish theatre, whose first troupes frequently performed in taverns, wine gardens, and similar informal entertainment venues, rather than the more formal types of spaces offered by traditional theatre buildings. As in any other theatrical culture, form followed function; that is, certain types of dramas—almost invariably bourgeois comedies—tended to be written for Yiddish literary salons. By contrast, material written for the rough-and-tumble world of tavern performances—not only early professional plays, but also poems, songs, and monologues—bear the distinct marks of that environment, including broad humor, lively rhymes, and an inclination to focus more on action, songs, and jokes than on nuanced character development or sophisticated ideas.

The Yiddish theatre, as it developed, would draw on both of these inheritances. From the "high" road, Yiddish theatre inherited the aspiration to use drama to address social problems, and perhaps also the restless spirit of aesthetic experimentation that would ultimately prevail in many an individual and company. And from the so-called "low" road—a term that we use as a reference point for how many commentators viewed popular Yiddish theatre, rather than a pejorative judgment on such material, which has many beauties of its own—Yiddish theatre was bequeathed a boisterous spirit that gave it a freewheeling give-and-take with its audiences, as well as a different sort of experimentation: the ever-present impulse to find the right combination of performance ingredients to keep Moyshe happy, at least until the next performance.

If we stay with the road metaphor for a moment longer, it would be more accurate to modify contemporaries' frequent articulation of highbrow versus lowbrow by seeing Yiddish drama and performance as a network of intersecting paths: some headed straight toward lofty aesthetic and social goals; others clearly diverted toward, well, diversion; but many others possessing qualities that could both impress critics and literati while pleasing a wider public. It was not uncommon, as with many theatre companies in any culture, for theatre troupes to offset the likely financial losses incurred by aesthetically ambitious productions by alternating them with crowd-pleasers that would restore the box office to the pink of health. Yet contemporary commentators tended to describe the Yiddish theatre in Manichean terms: *kunst* (art) versus *shund* (trash); "better" or "literary" plays versus those designed to please Moyshe; plays and productions to which one could proudly welcome the *umes ha-oylem*—literally, the "nations of the world," the non-Jewish public—versus the cultural equivalent of dirty laundry that would, in the eyes of many a critic, both debase the theatre-going Yiddish-speaking public and bring it disgrace in the eyes of its non-Jewish (as well as Jewish but non-Yiddish-speaking) neighbors.

This mixture of artistic impulses could be seen in the work of two important figures who star in their own chapters in this collection, Y. Y. Lerner and Jacob Gordin. Gordin, more than any other single playwright, is associated with a new wave of American Yiddish playwrights who, beginning in the early 1890s, sought to infuse performances with some of the spirit of dramatist-heroes like Henrik Ibsen and Maxim Gorky. Yet even Gordin was no Gordin; that is, he was by no means the aesthetic purist and ethical crusader that he made himself out to be in many of his critical essays about drama, or his Yiddish manifestos of the early 1890s in which he promises to reform the Yiddish stage. Gordin, with a wife, many children, and a stomach, tempered his high-mindedness with a spirit of compromise that helped make him a popular playwright, albeit one received with decided ambivalence by critics (some of whom, like the labile Abraham Cahan, strew rose petals in his path at first, but later turned on him, took the rose petals back, and publicly burned them in vitriolic anti-Gordin polemics in the Yiddish newspapers).

In Chapter 3, Barbara Henry reveals a side of Gordin that has hitherto been all but unknown: his earliest literary efforts, in Russian fiction rather than the Yiddish drama for which he would become world-famous. Gordin's talent for creating vibrant, memorable dramatic characters skillfully tailored to the talents of his star and supporting actors made him a sensation on the Yiddish stage. Behind the scenes, he displayed a similar knack for fashioning personae of his own. The one who, as a young man, signed on to various utopian causes expressed, in his Russian fiction and polemical writing, what Henry characterizes as a "deeply conflicted and divided loyalty to Jewish culture." His attacks on Jewish texts and traditions, couched in the language of an ideological reformer, at the very least bordered on, if not fully crossed over into, anti-Semitism. Yet Gordin's life and career show that there are second acts in the lives of Yiddish artists. Soon after his arrival in America, though his reputation preceded him, Gordin would reinvent himself in several ways at once: as a Yiddish writer, as a playwright, and as a kind of aesthetic sheriff of the Bowery, then the crucible of Yiddish theatre in New York. And though Jacob Gordin would continue to be famous, or in some circles infamous, for his critiques of Jewish tradition, these came in a far gentler and more nuanced form than they had from the pen of the Russian writer Yakov Gordin and his alter egos writing under various noms de plume.

In the annals of the Yiddish stage, the work of Y. Y. Lerner has tended to be concealed in the shadows of better-known contemporaries like Goldfaden and Gordin. (The fact that Lerner ultimately converted to Christianity, particularly when his Yiddish plays so effectively champion Jewish characters being persecuted by both Jewish and Christian authorities, undoubtedly contributed to contemporary and later critics minimizing his place in the pantheon.) Certainly the latter two were far more prolific, but Lerner has not been given his due. In his crusade to reform Yiddish drama, which predated Gordin's, Lerner tilted his lance directly at Goldfaden, by using physically and morally misshapen characters like Goldfaden's wildly popular, eponymous Shmendrik and Kuni-Leml as symbols of all that was wrong with the low aesthetic level of the first generation of professional Yiddish plays. By contrast, Lerner crowed,

> I produced several historical plays, in which noble heroes took the place of "lunatics" and "cripples," and instead of dark, ugly scenes, one could behold enlightened and uplifting portraits of the holy past. My hope that simple folk did not easily let themselves be diverted from the proper path [. . .] did not deceive me, and with great joy I was shown with what friendly warmth people embraced serious drama, with what pleasure they would listen to every idea, how eagerly they would devour every word. [. . .] One must admit that the Yiddish stomach can also digest fresh, clean dishes, as long as they are prepared well.[9]

In service of this more refined Yiddish diet than others were catering to, Lerner created a small but notable body of drama, the most successful being his version of Karl Gutzkow's German drama, *Uriel Acosta*, a rare example of a foreign import's becoming a staple of the Yiddish repertoire.

In his detailed comparison of Gutzkow's original German text with translations by four Yiddish translators, Seth Wolitz, in Chapter 4, guides us through the process of refashioning this German drama of ideas for audiences situated in four different times and places. Wolitz powerfully demonstrates the critical role of the translator in shaping the sensibility of the translation. And since Lerner's version of *Uriel Acosta* in particular was in the repertoire of countless troupes and performers, Wolitz shows us how Gutzkow, via Lerner, helped shape the sensibilities of Yiddish performers and audiences. Wolitz's chapter also contains, as it were, a surprise ending. The passage from Lerner quoted above might appear to be wishful thinking: from all that has been written about the low tastes of early Yiddish audiences, wasn't Lerner gilding the lily? Wolitz's meticulous analysis suggests not. At least not entirely, in any case, for in Wolitz's view, Lerner was at least as successful, aesthetically speaking, as any later Yiddish translators who took upon themselves the challenge of rendering Gutzkow's German verse into a Yiddish suited to the stage. Those later translations were products, like Lerner's, not only of the individual translators' skills and sensibilities, but of the ethos of the Yiddish theatre in interwar Poland, Depression-era New York, and Communist Romania at three different historical moments.

Translators of literature share a fundamental challenge: capturing and rendering the form and spirit of a text written in one language into a version that is understandable and pleasing to readers of another. Seth Wolitz's dissection of *Uriel Acosta* and its four Yiddish incarnations turns up fascinating examples of the particular challenges at play when translators reworked a text by a non-Jewish writer, in a non-Jewish language, but replete with Jewish characters and subject matter into a Jewish language and milieu, for an almost entirely Jewish audience. Looking at parallel passages from these five works in the appendix to Wolitz's article, we may be able to imagine the translators' minds at work: shall I hew closely to Gutzkow's text here, or betray the literal meaning in service of some other principle? Shall I seize or forgo opportunities to Judaize my material more than it already is? Comparable questions constantly preoccupied creators of Yiddish theatrical performances, regardless of whether or not translation was an issue. As Polish theatre historian Mirosława Bułat shows in Chapter 5, the choice of either having plays and productions speak directly to Jewish sensibilities or having them address more universally familiar stories, characters, and ideas was central to the development of the repertoire of the Varshever Yidisher Kunst-Teater (VYKT, Warsaw Jewish Art Theatre). Under the leadership of actor/director Zygmunt Turkow, the company, in several different stages, offered a fairly balanced mixture of original Yiddish plays and translations from other European languages, as well as a number of stage adaptations of novels by Yiddish authors like Sholem Asch and Sholem Aleichem, and fiction by French (Dumas, Hugo) and Russian (Dostoevsky, Andreev) writers.

Turkow would come to characterize VYKT as "a European theatre in the Yiddish language,"[10] a description that is more complex than it may appear at first glance. Turkow's descriptor signals his theatre's outward-looking orientation, its "European" sympathies, suggesting that Yiddish is simply the company's language of communication. If that were the entire story of VYKT, however, its repertoire would likely have looked quite different: its major productions would presumably have consisted primarily of the translations of notable plays from other languages, with the occasional Yiddish classic—Ettinger's *Serkele* or Goldfaden's *Tsvey Kunileml*. Bułat explores the implications of VYKT's having served two masters: the pan-European and the specifically Yiddish.

Between the two world wars, a period that VYKT spanned almost in its entirety, Warsaw was one of the leading centers of Yiddish theatrical activity, along with New York and Moscow, and at least the equal of those other cultural capitals in this regard. The city was rich in Jewish cultural organizations, including numerous Yiddish theatres, from mainstream venues playing a fairly traditional repertoire to cabarets and small art theatres that often presented more daring or unconventional fare. A prominent example of the latter type of troupe was Yung Teater (Young Theatre), the focus of historian Jeffrey Veidlinger in Chapter 6. Yung Teater's ethos, as articulated by its founder and director, Dr. Mikhl Weichert, oriented the company decidedly in the direction of a universalist rather than a particularist approach to its subject matter:

> Yung Teater will first of all produce modern dramatic creations, both Yiddish and European; modern life with its peculiar rhythm, with its ideas and slogans, will find a living echo in the performances of Yung Teater. Yung Teater takes its first step into the public without outside help, propelled by its own striving and deep devotion to theatrical performance, believing in the creative strength of that part of the Jewish masses for whom theatre is not simply entertainment, but rather a medium for the struggle for human and social liberation.[11]

In the spirit of this statement, many of the company's productions dramatized fictional and non-fictional instances of gross injustice, from Georg Büchner's haunting *Woyzeck* to documentary-style treatments of two notorious, contemporary travesties of justice, the Sacco-Vanzetti and Scottsboro affairs.

Yung Teater was remarkably ambitious—socially, politically, and aesthetically. In the spirit of earlier, socially-committed ensembles, the troupe drew its performers from the ranks of non-actors, who studied intensively in its studio and who were transformed into performers from the ground up. As Veidlinger writes, the studio school "taught not only theatre skills, but also general studies. Classes included dance, music, make-up, costume, stage design, phonetics, dialectology, history of European theatre, history of Yiddish theatre, Jewish history, acoustics, psychology, hygiene, sexual education, physiology, and physical education; many were taught by Warsaw's leading Jewish luminaries [...] The goal was not only to train students in the theatrical arts, but also to endow them with a general humanistic education." The company's approach to theatrical production was total as well, and in many ways ahead of its time, for Yung Teater often practiced what, decades later, would become known as environmental theatre, which broke down traditional barriers between actor and audience and used every inch of available space within the performance venue to tell its story.[12] Thus, with its distinct combination of holistic actor training, political content, and innovative production choices,

Yung Teater helped lead the way in fashioning a truly avant-garde Yiddish theatre in the vibrant but troubled interwar period.

Though Weichert found brilliant ways to break down the "fourth wall" separating onstage action from audience in a proscenium theatre, Yiddish audiences were notorious for crossing these borders, albeit for very different reasons. If one is to believe numerous legends from the annals of the Yiddish stage of spectators too unsophisticated to recognize certain basic theatrical conventions, we can accept tales of audience members offering to feed actors whose characters complained of hunger, clothe freezing characters, and all but adopt lonely ones. Not all the drama of the Yiddish theatre involved interactions with actors on the stage, however; much transpired, as theatre historian Nina Warnke relates, offstage and in the house as well. Much has already been said here about Moyshe, held in such low regard by Yiddish playwrights and performers, but whose high regard was essential to their livelihood. Moyshe was famous for being opinionated, vociferous, boisterous, and less than refined. He was not particularly known for his machismo, though Warnke's Chapter 7 demonstrates a decidedly testosterone-fueled side of the New York Yiddish stage in the early twentieth century. Heated arguments, on rare occasions leading to violence, were known to erupt in American theatres, often exposing fissures of social class, education levels, and political sensibilities within the audience. A number of observers have cited references by Yiddish writers and cartoonists to squabbles between various factions in the Yiddish theatre, but Warnke's study gives us the first genuine chronicle of the exact nature and scope of such battles, illustrating how closely the Yiddish stage was connected with Jews' own self-presentation. As individual actors acquired an almost-totemic significance for their *patriotn*—most passionate fans—the glamour and mystique of stars like David Kessler or Jacob Adler appeared to offer an alternative identity to the narrower range of traditional Jewish male roles. Actors might play the parts of pious scholars or union bosses, romantic leads or dashing scoundrels, tragic heroes or comedians. Their mobile natures had in previous centuries led to actors' characterization as inconstant and untrustworthy, but in twentieth-century Jewish immigrant New York, the actor's essential volatility and capacity for self-creation now appeared a virtue, a quality to be prized and emulated.

Countless books and articles have been written about how eastern European immigrants to America refashioned both their own beliefs and practices and their newly adopted land, often by working out the balance between Jewish traditions and American values in fiction, poetry, music, theatre, and other artistic and intellectual endeavors. Much less attention has been paid to a similar process that unfolded south of the equator, where a smaller influx of Yiddish-speaking Jews led to the formation of important and sometimes sizable Jewish communities throughout Latin America.[13] In terms of Yiddish theatre, by far the most noteworthy of these was the one that developed in Buenos Aires, where figures like Vilna-born troubadour Jevel Katz, the focus of Judaica librarian Zachary Baker's Chapter 9, made a name for himself. This description gives a sense of Katz's versatility as a performer, and of the serio-comic nature of his compositions:

> Katz toured widely, entertaining his audiences with a medley of monologues, humoresques, couplets, parodies, nostalgic songs, and satires, in which he provided his own accompaniment on guitar, mandolin, harmonica, and accordion. Katz performed upwards of six hundred and fifty original compositions. He also acted in Yiddish plays and was featured on radio programs. Katz's themes of nostalgia, privation, and struggle tugged at his audiences' heartstrings, though he also leavened his lyrics with copious doses of comic relief.

Katz belongs to a long tradition of Yiddish minstrels and troubadours dating back to the Middle Ages, giving Yiddish speakers in communities throughout central and eastern Europe (and in more modern times, other parts of the world) forms of public performance even though theatre per se was generally proscribed.

Such performers, like Katz, also frequently commented in their compositions on both local issues and concerns, and much broader ones. Katz's work commingled Jewish imagery and subject matter with deeply Argentinean ones; after all, writes Baker, Katz was

> a product of twentieth-century Vilna—a city that was steeped in the traditions of the Gaon, the Haskalah, the Jewish labor movement, Zionism, and Yiddishism. At the same time, Katz's Argentine parodies and satirical songs, with their intensely local frames of reference, struck a profound chord with his audience, whose members had been set adrift by the tempestuous tides of twentieth-century Jewish history. These songs helped to anchor immigrants in their new surroundings, even as they underscored their very marginality in Argentina.

The language of Katz's compositions—primarily Yiddish, but sprinkled with a playful and inventive Spanish—itself reflects this shuttling back and forth in his work between eastern European roots and Argentinean surroundings.

Katz's ability to sum up his audience's situation as eastern Europeans transplanted to a new environment in Latin America made him wildly popular, and provides a further example of Yiddish performers' ability to fashion circumstance into theatrical and musical material. For Katz and his audience, the critical circumstance was their uprooting from eastern Europe and relocation to the Argentinean milieu, a process echoed in the experiences, and the art, of transplanted Jewish communities around the world. Although often overshadowed in popular memory by the drama of their flight from persecution, these epic journeys and new lives begun in very different places clearly presented social, linguistic, and cultural challenges to immigrant Jews everywhere. Yet everyday economic challenges also played just as pivotal a role in both initiating migrations and shaping their trajectories and outcomes. Market forces have usually been given short shrift in analyses of the development of Yiddish theatre, cinema, and popular entertainment, a gap that Judith Thissen has begun to fill through her doctoral dissertation and a number of articles and book chapters focusing on the business side of American Yiddish entertainment in the early twentieth century.[14]

In Chapter 8 of this volume, Thissen chronicles "specific local conditions that spurred the exceptionally rapid transformation of the Jewish immigrant entertainment business in New York City." Examining such evidence as real estate documents of sales and leases, liquor regulations and other laws, advertisements, and seating capacities, Thissen lays out the conditions behind the rise and ultimate decline of venues that housed vaudeville performances. As theatrical entrepreneurs have done in many countries and cultures, theatre owners on New York's Lower East Side responded innovatively to an ever-changing business climate, altered by such factors as demographic shifts, legal requirements, and the changing nature and format of entertainment itself, particularly with the advent of cinema. The very existence of Yiddish vaudeville, Thissen notes, was due in large measure to a "surplus of Jewish immigrant performers, which resulted in a desperate struggle for jobs and constant search for new opportunities to make a living on the stage." Thissen's work is the first to offer concrete documentation and analysis of the Yiddish theatre's engagement in ongoing, market-driven reinventions of itself, changes that paralleled and informed other forms of theatrical self-fashioning. Moyshe, it appears, was not just a consumer; he was also a creator.

While owners and managers tailored their offerings to a complex variety of factors and artists geared their work to overlapping and diverging ones, chroniclers of the Yiddish stage helped regulate, consciously or unconsciously, how the Yiddish theatre was viewed by contemporaries and (as they were acutely conscious) by posterity. Librarian, historian, and literary scholar Faith Jones explores a particularly dramatic example of this effort in Chapter 11: a no-holds-barred dust-up among three heavyweights of Yiddish theatre history and dramatic criticism. The controversy revolved around an entry in Zalmen Zylbercweig's (1894–1972) six-volume *Encyclopedia of the Yiddish Theatre*, by far the largest reference work on the history of the Yiddish stage. The controversy pitted Zylbercweig first against prominent historian Jacob Shatzky (1893–1956), and before long, also against noted theatre critic Alexander Mukdoyni (Alexander Kappel, 1878–1958), both of whom took issue with a handful of entries in the *Encyclopedia*, but also with Zylbercweig's very approach to documenting the history of the Yiddish stage. In 1928, Shatzky took Zylbercweig harshly to task for purported inaccuracies and other editorial missteps, including this intriguing comment about a period in the life of Keni Liptzin, "Regarding her employment in Smile [Ukraine] there are various versions. Some say that she worked there as a seamstress; but certain actors report that her employment was of a completely different kind."[15] In tone and in length, Shatzky's reaction to the implication here that Liptzin may have worked for a time as a prostitute was all out of proportion to his objections to the incipient encyclopedia's other purported shortcomings. His reaction ignited a vicious exchange of charges and counter-charges that would appear in the Yiddish press for another eight years, with Mukdoyni joining the fray in 1931 and echoing many of Shatzky's often ugly characterizations of Zylbercweig's unfitness as an editor.

This long episode might appear on the surface to be little more than a rather childish public display of three large but fragile egos, but Jones makes a compelling case for its broader significance. At the start of his poison-pen campaign, Shatzky introduced questions about Zylbercweig's legitimacy as the curator of a project as ambitious as the *Encyclopedia* by scoffing at the young editor's inclusion of various details such as the payment of a Goldfaden-era actor in tobacco, not to mention the controversial allusion to Keni Liptzin's possible employment, a subject that Zylbercweig raises without any trace of value judgment. Shatzky and Mukdoyni would proceed, in further chapters of this controversy, to denigrate Zylbercweig's skills by questioning both details he proposed to include and his methodology, such as his extensive use of oral history. Though the *Encyclopedia* has many flaws as a reference work, Jones makes an eloquent case for its many virtues as well, including Zylbercweig's admirable even-handedness when handling the information that comes his way—in other words, one of the very characteristics that gets him in trouble with Shatzky and Mukdoyni in the first place. In the process, Jones also opens up her discussion to questions of women's sexuality in relation to the Yiddish stage. The long association between the theatre and sexual transgression is familiar to students of theatre history, but less so to students of the Yiddish stage, arising as it did out of a traditional, conservative culture. Jones's chapter provides a powerful example of how gender informed the way that chroniclers of the Yiddish theatre attempted to shape how its history was told.

Where Zalmen Zylbercweig ultimately chose to suppress a hint of one star's sexual activity, actor Boris Thomashefsky (1866–1939) took quite the opposite tack in discussing his own amorous adventures. Indeed, in his 1937 memoirs, Thomashefsky chronicles one sexual episode after another with such relish, and often in such detail, that this facet of his life often overshadows his illustrious stage career and the significant contributions he made to the Yiddish stage as a performer, director, manager, and composer. One of the productions that helped launch Thomashefsky to stardom was the 1892 operetta *Aleksandr, oder der kroynprints fun yerusholayim* (Alexander, the crown prince of Jerusalem), with a libretto by Joseph Lateiner and music by Giacomo Minkowski. Thomashefsky devotes several pages of his memoirs to the play—or rather, all too characteristically, primarily to what it did for his love life. Describing the play's successful run in New York for two years, the actor writes, "They say that I was so handsome in the lead role of Alexander that anyone who saw me in that role simply fell in love with me."[16] Not content to leave it at that, Thomashefsky proceeds to suggest that his performance, and/or his pulchritude, literally drove at least one spectator insane. During one performance, the actor writes, he was so captivated by a beautiful young woman sitting in the first row that he could not take his eyes off her, and she returned his gaze. As this went on, the woman grew increasingly restless, until she leapt to her feet during the performance and cried, "Give me the king!" and started ripping off her clothes and repeatedly calling out for Thomashefsky—or for Alexander, perhaps. The girl's family and theatre staff, Thomashefsky continues, escorted her from the theatre, and she spent the next year in a mental institution, where she fortunately made a full recovery.[17]

The story of *Alexander*, in Thomashefsky's hands, grows more salacious a moment later, when we reach perhaps the oddest and most disturbing moment in the entire memoir, with Thomashefsky treating the reader to a description of the loge set aside expressly for the purpose of romantic trysts he would have with lovers from the audience *during* performances. These were of course timed to coincide with periods when his character was not on stage, though rather inevitably, we learn of moments when his romantic entanglements led to missed cues. To the audience's astonished delight, but not to the surprise of cast and crew, of course, Alexander would join a musical number from up in the loge rather than on stage.

Given the time and energy Thomashefsky spends on such stories, at the expense of any significant details about the production, historians of the Yiddish theatre often need to turn elsewhere for meaningful performance-related evidence. Musicologist Ronald Robboy does just that to unravel the story of *Alexander* not told by Thomashefsky—or anyone else, for that matter. In Chapter 10, Robboy introduces us to the hitherto all but unknown composer of the work, Giacomo Minkowski, surveys highlights of his varied musical-theatre career, unpacks the plot of *Alexander*, and most important, explains Minkowski's accomplishment in creating a musical vehicle suited to the formidable talents of Thomashefsky and his fellow performers. In so doing, Robboy helps demystify a substantial but poorly understood facet of Yiddish theatre history: the story of its music. Robboy assesses this Yiddish theatre score on its own merits, rather than as just an adjunct to stage legends or as a lesser entity than the libretto it accompanied.

The collection's final two chapters take the reader far afield from the other entries, both geographically and chronologically. Annette Aronowicz, in Chapter 12, offers a close reading of Paris-based playwright Haim Sloves's (1905–1988) dark comedy, *Homens mapole* (*Haman's Downfall*), completed in 1940, but performed primarily from 1945 to 1949), one of a number of plays from World War II and the immediate postwar period in which Sloves would grapple, directly or indirectly, with the Holocaust, its aftermath, and its implications for both Jewry and mankind in general. Aronowicz's chapter belongs to a much larger project on Communist lawyer-cum-playwright Sloves's life, career, and fascinating body of plays and essays.

The Holocaust decimated Yiddish culture and wiped out millions of those who spoke it. The vibrant cultural scene of many an eastern European city and town, which once abounded with Yiddish theatres, publishing houses, art studios, and literary salons, was laid waste, its fortunes never to be restored after the war. At best, Yiddish culture was given isolated, attempted revivals, often under the auspices of Communist regimes eager to make a show of their commitment to cultural diversity, but these efforts at reviving Yiddish culture were a pale shadow of its former self. Yet despite this near-complete annihilation of Yiddish culture in its lands of origin, a small but important cadre of Yiddish playwrights—some of whom were at least as well known for their contributions to other literary genres—continued to produce important work after the war, and some of that work grappled with the Holocaust and its fallout. The elder statesmen among these writers included H. Leivick (1888–1962) and Dovid Pinski (1872–1959), both of whom began their lives and literary careers in eastern Europe but made their way to New York City as young men, and continued to be active as writers and critics beyond mid-century. Leivick, at least as well known for his lyric poetry as for his dramas (many of which he called, aptly, "dramatic poems" rather than plays), grappled with the Holocaust repeatedly in his poetry and drama after the war.[18] Kadia Molodowsky (1894–1975), a peripatetic writer who moved from Poland to New York in 1935, published and edited major works of Holocaust poetry,[19] and though far better known for her poetry than for her work in other genres, published an accomplished historical drama based on the life of the Portuguese-born philanthropist and community leader Doña Gracia Mendes Nasi (1510–1569).[20]

Sloves had published a monograph in French on French-Soviet relations, but did not publish drama, or in Yiddish, before the Holocaust. After the war, he published a small but distinguished body of dramas, a number of which entered the repertoire of notable theatre troupes. Some of these works commented directly on the Holocaust;[21] others, like Molodowsky's play, drew upon Jewish traditions to comment obliquely but recognizably on contemporary events. Sloves twice turned to the *purimshpil*, the typically raucous, irreverent dramatic form dating back to medieval times, for darkly comic material that commented on current events.[22] Annette Aronowicz's chapter pays close attention to textual details, but also displays a broad and deep understanding of Sloves's life and career, and his work's place in the wider context of literary and political activity in postwar Paris. Aronowicz decodes *Homens mapole*'s deft rhymes and comic inventiveness, which belie a seriousness of purpose befitting Sloves's lifelong Communist allegiances.[23]

Donny Inbar's survey and analysis of productions of Goldfaden's plays in Palestine and Israel in Chapter 13 brings us back, in a sense, to the founding figure of the modern Yiddish stage, but also intersects with other chapters that illustrate important milestones in the development of the Yiddish theatre well into the twentieth century. The story of Yiddish in Israel is a curious and in many ways discouraging one, for Palestine, and later, the state of Israel, would often prove far from hospitable to the *mame-loshn*, or mother tongue, of so many of its founders and leaders. Caught in an often-acrimonious language battle, Yiddish fell victim to a sensibility that saw the promotion of anything but Hebrew—and not just Hebrew, but Hebrew pronounced in a particular fashion—as anathema to the Zionist ethos. Despite its substantial population base and the continuing influx of native speakers from eastern Europe, Yiddish became marginalized in Israeli culture, but would nevertheless continue to exert its presence.[24]

Though Yiddish was often tainted, in the Zionist sensibility, by associations with the vulnerability of Jews in the Diaspora (a neutral-sounding word that elides the deeply negative associations of the Hebrew/Yiddish word *galut/goles*), Inbar's discussion demonstrates that Goldfaden, in Yiddish and in Hebrew translation, was alive in Israel, if not always well. Indeed, it is telling that Inbar's chapter begins with efforts to sabotage a Yiddish performance of Goldfaden's operetta *Shulamis* in 1914, reminiscent of stories of German Jews in New York finding different sorts of subterfuge to undermine a production of Goldfaden's *Di kishefmakherin* (The sorceress) over three decades earlier. (Readers may want to pause a moment to ponder the significance of the American episode, which reportedly revolved around a bribe paid to the lead actress to feign illness and thereby abort the performance, while the Tel Aviv performance was disrupted by a stink bomb planted by Zionists antagonistic to Yiddish.)

Yet, according to Inbar, Goldfaden's plays nevertheless entered the theatrical mainstream in Israel. They enjoyed numerous translations into Hebrew, productions by major companies, and successful films. And as had been the case in eastern Europe, Goldfaden's plays continued to have the ability to generate iconic moments. In one fascinating example, Inbar documents how Abraham Levinson, translating an important phrase from an aria in *Di kishefmakherin* into Hebrew, a language with very different rhythms and cadences than those of Yiddish, came up with a phrase that would not only become a "Goldfaden trademark" in Israel, it would arguably become "the trademark of Yiddish theatre itself for Israeli audiences."

Inbar's chapter also documents continuity, albeit not always of the smoothest kind, of Yiddish theatrical production that spans virtually all of the twentieth century. Israel would be a safe haven in some ways, but troubled waters in others, for maintaining a Yiddish theatrical presence. Israeli society erected its own barriers against the Yiddish language, and the culture that it begat, thus keeping Yiddish from ever reaching full flower there, in spite of an ongoing infusion of talented Yiddish-speaking performers who continued to immigrate to Israel long after the Holocaust, and visiting performers who might have immigrated had the working conditions for Yiddish actors been more favorable.

The modern Yiddish stage came into being on the cusp of one of the most eventful periods in all of Jewish history. Its very existence was made possible by the Jewish Enlightenment that emerged in central Europe in the late eighteenth century, and moved eastward into the Russian empire through much of the nineteenth. Drama—specifically satire—would become an important weapon in the enlighteners' campaign to combat Jewish beliefs and behaviors that they saw as benighted, superstitious, fanatical, and insular. And the plays they wrote continued a tradition that was by then well entrenched in Yiddish drama: drawing inspiration from both Jewish and non-Jewish sources to stimulate, provoke, entertain, and enlighten a Yiddish-speaking audience.

That tradition would continue in Yiddish drama and performance for many decades to come, as would its vigorous engagement with the key issues, ideas, people, and events of the day, particularly as they affected the lives of Jews who lived in, or traced their ancestry to, eastern Europe. The essays in this volume, surveying examples of Yiddish theatre and drama in eastern and western Europe, North and South America, and Palestine/Israel, address the massive demographic shifts of the modern Jewish world, engagement with radical social and political movements, adaptation to new countries and cultures, persecution and near-annihilation, and the settling of territory that would become a Jewish state. The modern Yiddish stage would track all of these changes and be shaped by them. The ongoing give-and-take among all artists and entertainers, owners and companies, and audiences and critics, would create a theatrical culture that creatively intermingled Jewish and Gentile influences, high and low, performed and textual, deliriously comical and devastatingly tragic, and was subject, at every turn, to a fierce and relentless spirit of invention, re-invention, and discovery.

Notes

1. If anything, Goldfaden's ability to accomplish what predecessors had failed to do—most notably, establish a theatre troupe stable enough to set the professionalization of the Yiddish theatre in motion—makes his achievements more remarkable rather than less so.

2. Seminal studies of the origins of Yiddish drama and performance include Ahuva Belkin, *Ha-purim shpil: iyunim ba-te'atron ha-yehudi ha-amami* [The purimshpil: Studies in Jewish folk theatre] (Jerusalem: Mosad Bialik, 2002); Evi Bützer, *Die Anfänge der jiddischen purim shpiln in ihrem literarischen und kulturgeschichtlichen Kontext* [The beginnings of the Yiddish purimshpil in literary and cultural context] (Hamburg: Helmut Buske Farlag, 2003); Max Erik, *Di geshikhte fun der yidisher literatur fun di eltste tsaytn biz der haskole tkufe* [The history of Yiddish literature from olden times to the Haskalah period] (Warsaw: Kultur-lige, 1928); Ariela Krasney, *Ha-badkhan* [The wedding jester] (Ramat Gan: Bar-Ilan University Press, 1998); Ezra Lahad, "Ha-badkhanim" [The jesters], *Bama* 95–96 (1983): 43–68; W. Staerk, "Die Purim-komödie *Mekhires Yoysef*" [The Purim comedy *The sale of Joseph*], *Monatsschrift für Geschichte und Wissenschaft des Judentums*, 30 (1922): 294–299. Yitskhok Shiper, *Geshikhte fun yidisher teater-kunst un drame* [The history of Yiddish theatre art and drama], 3 vols, (Warsaw: Kultur-lige, 1923–1928); and Khone Shmeruk, *Makhazot mikra'im be-yidish, 1697–1750* [Yiddish biblical plays, 1697–1750] (Jerusalem: Israel Academy of Sciences and Humanities, 1979).

3. As recently as 2007, journalist Stefan Kanfer told Terry Gross, host of National Public Radio program *Fresh Air*, that the first professional Yiddish acting troupes operating in Romania in the mid-1870s "developed a theatre out of nothing almost overnight." *Fresh Air*, January 2, 2007, http://www.npr.org/templates/story/story.php?storyId=6710019.

4. For the definitive analysis of the censorship of Yiddish plays in Tsarist Russia, see John D. Klier, "'Exit, Pursued by a Bear': Russian Administrators and the Ban on Yiddish Theatre in Imperial Russia," in Joel Berkowitz, ed., *Yiddish Theatre: New Approaches* (Oxford, UK: Littman Library of Jewish Civilization, 2003), 159–174.

5. Countless sources on Yiddish theatre touch on Goldfaden's life and work in some way, including numerous memoirs by actors and other theatre personnel whose careers intersected with his. Major studies on the artist's biography and career include S. Bilov and A. Veledinsky, Introduction to Goldfaden, *Geklibene dramatishe verk* [Selected dramatic works] (Kiev: Melukhe-farlag, 1940), 3–64; Donny Inbar, "A Closeted Jester: Abraham Goldfaden Between *Haskalah* Ideology and Jewish Show Business" (Ph.D. thesis, Graduate Theological Union, 2007); *Leksikon fun der nayer yidisher literatur* [Encyclopedia of the new Yiddish literature] (New York: Congress for Jewish Culture, 1958), 2:77–87; Nakhman Mayzel, *Avrom Goldfaden: der foter fun yidishn teater* [Avrom Goldfaden: Father of the Yiddish theatre] (Warsaw: Farlag Groshn-bibliotek, 1935); Nokhem Oyslender and Uri Finkel, *A. Goldfadn: materyaln far a biografye* [A. Goldfaden: Materials for a biography] (Minsk: Institut far Vaysruslendisher Kultur, 1926); Yitskhok Perkof, *Avrom Goldfadn: mayne memuarn un zayne brif* [Avrom Goldfaden: My memoirs and his letters] (London: Jouques Print Works, 1908); Alyssa Quint, "The Botched Kiss: Abraham Goldfaden and the Literary Origins of the Yiddish Theatre" (Ph.D. thesis, Harvard University, 2002); Yankev Shatski, ed., *Goldfaden-bukh* [Goldfaden book] (New York: Idisher Teater-Muzey, 1926) and *Hundert yor Goldfadn* [A hundred years of Goldfaden] (New York: YIVO, 1940); Yitskhok Turkow-Grudberg, *Goldfaden un Gordin* (Tel Aviv: S. Grinhoyz, 1969); Zalmen Zylbercweig, *Avrom Goldfaden un Zigmunt Mogulesco* (Buenos Aires: Farlag Elisheva, 1936); and Zylbercweig, ed., *Leksikon fun yidishn teater* [Encyclopedia of the Yiddish theatre] (New York: Farlag Elisheva, 1931), 1:275–367.

6. For assessments of Gordin's life and work, see, *i.a.*, Joel Berkowitz, *Shakespeare on the American Yiddish Stage* (Iowa City: University of Iowa Press, 2002); Jacob Gordin, *Ale shriftn* [Complete writings], 4 vols. (New York: Hebrew Publishing Co., 1910); Jacob Gordin, *The Jewish King Lear: A Comedy in America*, trans. and ed. Ruth Gay (New Haven, CT: Yale University Press, 2007); Yisrael Gur, "Goldfaden ve-Gordin" [Goldfaden and Gordin], *Bama* 87–88 (1981): 189–204; Barbara Henry, "Jacob Gordin's Dialogue with Tolstoy: *Di Kreytser Sonata* (1902)," in Edna Nahshon, ed., *Jewish Theatre: A Global View*, 25–48 (Leiden: Brill, 2009); "Tolstoy on the Lower East Side: *Di Kreytser Sonata*," *Tolstoy Studies Journal* 17 (2005): 1–19; *Rewriting Russia: Jacob Gordin's Yiddish Drama* (Seattle and London: University of Washington Press, 2011); Beth Kaplan, *Finding the Jewish Shakespeare: the Life and Legacy of Jacob Gordin* (Syracuse, NY: Syracuse University Press, 2007); Kalmen Marmor, *Yankev Gordin* (New York: YKUF, 1953); Leonard Prager, "Of Parents and Children: Jacob Gordin's *The Jewish King Lear*," *American Quarterly* 18 (Autumn 1966): 506–516; Turkow-Grudberg, *Goldfaden un Gordin*; Morris Winchevsky, *A tog mit Yankev Gordin* [A day with Jacob Gordin] (New York: M. Mayzel, 1909); and Zalmen Zylbercweig, *Di velt fun Yankev Gordin* [The world of Jacob Gordin] (Tel Aviv: Farlag Elisheva, 1964).

7. Dovid Pinski, *Dos idishe drama: eyn iberblik iber ir antviklung* [Yiddish drama: A survey of its development] (New York: S. Drukerman, 1909), 57.

8. Nina Warnke provides an astute reading of this phenomenon in "The Child Who Wouldn't Grow Up: Yiddish Theatre and Its Critics," in Joel Berkowitz, ed., *Yiddish Theatre*, 201–216.

9. Y. Y. Lerner, Prologue to Karl Gutzkow, *Uriel Akosta*, 3rd. ed., (Warsaw: A. Glinka, 1903), 1–2.

10. M. K. [Mojżesz Kanfer], "Teatr Goldfadenowski—teatrem żydowskim: Z rozmowy z Zygmuntem Turkowem" [Goldfaden's theatre—Jewish theatre: From an interview with Zygmunt Turkow], *Nowy Dziennik*, April 20, 1939.

11. Cited in Yosef Glikson, "Yung teater," [Young Theatre], in Itzik Manger, Jonas Turkow, and Moyshe Perenson, eds., *Poyln*, vol. 1 of *Yidisher teater in eyrope tsvishn beyde velt-milkhomes* [Yid-

dish theatre in Europe between the two world wars] (New York: Alveltlekher Yidisher Kultur-kongres, 1968), 127.

12. The definitive study of this phenomenon is Richard Schechner's *Environmental Theater* (New York: Hawthorn Books, 1973).

13. The vibrant, multifaceted environment of Yiddish performance in Latin America—most notably Buenos Aires—has been has been the subject of a number of books and articles in Spanish and Yiddish, but far less in English. See Jacob Botoshanski, *Nokh der forshtelung: groteskn un bilder funem idishn aktyorn-lebn* [After the performance: Grotesques and images from the lives of Yiddish actors] (Buenos Aires: Farlag Shlayfer, 1926); Nora Glickman, "Max Berliner and Cipe Lincovsky: Two Great Actors of the Yiddish/Spanish Theatre in Argentina," *Modern Jewish Studies* 14 (2004): 50–56; Sylvia Hansman and Susana Skura, "Curatorship, Patrimonialization, and Memory Objects: Exhibition of Yiddish Theater Posters Created in Argentina," *Modern Jewish Studies* 14 (2004): 57–86; Sylvia Hansman, Susana Skura, and Gabriela Kogan, *Oysfarkoyft, Localidades Agotadas: Afiches del Teatro Ídish en la Argentina* [Sold out: Argentinian Yiddish theatre posters] (Buenos Aires: Del Nuevo Extremo, 2006); Shmuel Iris, *Ot azoy hot men geshpilt teater* [That's how theatre was performed] (Buenos Aires: A Gezelshaftlekher Komitet, 1956); Max Klos, *Baym shayn fun rampe-likht* [By the glow of the footlights] (Buenos Aires: Stilos, 1972); A. Mide, *Epizodn fun yidishn teater* [Episodes from the Yiddish theatre] (Buenos Aires: Asociacion judeo argentina de estudios historicos, 1954); Bentsion Palepade, *Beyn hashmoshes* [At dusk] (Buenos Aires, 1951); Palepade, *Zikhroynes fun a halbn yorhundert idish teater* [Memoirs of a half-century of Yiddish theatre] (Buenos Aires, 1946); Shmuel Rozhansky, ed., *Gedrukte vort un teater in argentine* [The printed word and theatre in Argentina] (Buenos Aires, 1941); Susana Skura and Leonor Slavsky, "El teatro idish como patrimonio cultural judío argentino" [The Yiddish theatre as Argentinian cultural legacy], in Ricardo Feierstein and Stephen A. Sadow, eds., *Encuentro: Recreando la Cultura Judeoargentina* 2, 41–50 (Buenos Aires: Editorial Milá, 2004); M. Zakin, G. Gelman, and Victor Kohn, eds. *30 yor ift* [30 years of IFT] (Buenos Aires: IFT [Argentinian Yiddish People's Theatre and Art Society], 1962).

14. See Judith Thissen, "Film and Vaudeville on New York's Lower East Side," in Barbara Kirshenblatt-Gimblett and Jonathan Karp, eds., *The Art of Being Jewish in Modern Times*, 42–56 (Philadelphia: University of Pennsylvania Press, 2007); "Jewish Immigrant Audiences in New York City, 1905–14," in Melvyn Stokes and Richard Maltby, eds., *American Movie Audiences: From the Turn of the Century to the Early Sound Era*, 15–28 (London: BFI Publishing, 1999); "'Leshono habo' bimuving piktshurs* (Next year at the moving pictures): Cinema and Social Change in the Jewish Immigrant Community," in Richard Maltby, Melvyn Stokes, and Robert C. Allen, eds., *Going to the Movies: Hollywood and the Social Experience of Cinema*, 113–129 (Exeter: University of Exeter Press, 2008); "Moyshe Goes to the Movies: Jewish Immigrants, Popular Entertainment, and Ethnic Identity in New York City (1880–1914)," (Ph.D. thesis, University of Utrecht, 2001); and "Reconsidering the Decline of the New York Yiddish Theatre in the Early 1900s," *Theatre Survey* 44 (November 2003): 173–197.

15. Yankev Shatski, "A muster fun a teater-leksikon" [An example of a theatre encyclopedia], in *Teater mozaik* [Theatre mosaic], ed. Zalmen Zylbercwieg (New York: Biderman, 1941), 68–69. Originally published in *Literarishe bleter* (Warsaw) 28 (1928).

16. Boris Thomashefsky, *Mayn lebns-geshikhte* [My life story] (New York: Trio Press, 1937), 281.

17. Ibid., 281–283.

18. Leivick's Holocaust-related plays are *Maharam fun rotenburg* [The Mahara'm (Hebrew acronym for Moreynu Ha-rav Rav Meir—Our Teacher Rabbi Meir) of Rotenburg], (New York: H. Leyvik Jubilee Fund of the CYCO Press, 1945) and *In di teg fun Iyov* [In the days of Job] (New York: CYCO, 1953). Leivick also published a volume of Holocaust-related poetry, *In treblinke bin*

ikh nit geven [I was not in Treblinka] (New York: H. Leyvik Jubilee Fund of the CYCO Press, 1945), and a work of non-fiction, *Mit der sheyres-hapleyte* [With the "saving remnant" (i.e. Holocaust survivors)] (New York: CYCO, 1947).

19. See Molodowsky's own poetry collection, *Der meylekh Dovid aleyn iz geblibn* [King David alone remained] (New York: Papirene brik, 1946), and the magnificent anthology of Yiddish Holocaust poetry she edited, *Lider fun khurbn, t."sh.–t.sh"h* [Poems of the Holocaust, 1940–1945] (Tel Aviv: Farlag Y. L. Perets, 1962).

20. *Nokhn got fun midber* [After the God of the desert] (New York: Papirene Brik, 1949).

21. See *Nekome-nemer* [Avengers] (Paris: Oyfsnay, 1947), and *Tsen brider zenen mir gevezn* [Ten brothers were we] (Paris: Oyfsnay, 1965).

22. *Homens mapole* [Haman's downfall] (Paris: Oyfsnay, 1949), and *Di Yoynes un der valfish* [The Jonahs and the whale] (Paris: Oyfsnay, 1953).

23. See also Annette Aronowicz, "Haim Sloves, the Jewish People, and a Jewish Communist's Allegiances," *Jewish Social Studies* 9 (Fall 2002): 95–142.

24. For sources on the ambivalent place of Yiddish in Palestine under the British Mandate, see Yael Chaver, *What Must Be Forgotten: the Survival of Yiddish in Zionist Palestine* (Syracuse, NY: Syracuse University Press, 2004) and Arye Leyb Pilovsky, *Tsvishn yo un neyn: yidish un yidish literatur in erets-yisroel, 1907–1948* [Between yes and no: Yiddish and Yiddish literature in the land of Israel, 1907–1948] (Tel-Aviv: Veltrat far Yidish un Yidisher Kultur, 1986). For additional sources on Yiddish theatre in Palestine and Israel, see Joshua Fishman, "Yiddish in Israel: the Press, Radio, Theatre, and Book Publishing," *Yiddish* 1 (1974): 4–23; Boris Kotlerman, ed., *Te'atron yidish: sifrut tarbut u-le'umiyut* [Yiddish theatre: Literature, culture, and nationalism] (Ramat-Gan: Bar-Ilan University Press, 2009); Ezra Lahad, "Ha-badkhanim be-yisrael (mavo ve-bibliografia)" [Jesters in Israel (introduction and bibliography)], *Tatslil* 11 (1980): 51–58; Olga Levitan, "Ha-te'atron ha-erets-yisraeli ba-shanim 1904–1914: ben ivrit le-yidish" [Theatre in Eretz, Israel, 1904–1914: Between Hebrew and Yiddish], *Bama* 172 (2005): 42–58; Levitan, "Theater in the Land of Israel: Between Hebrew and Yiddish (1904–1914)," *Theatralia* 7 (2005): 139–150; Rachel Rojanski, "The Struggle for a Yiddish Repertoire Theatre in Israel, 1950–1952," *Israel Affairs* 15 (January 2009): 4–27; and Diego Rotman, "Ha-te'atron yidish be-yisrael, 1948–1988" [Yiddish Theatre in Israel, 1948–1988], *Zemanim* 99 (2007): 38–45.

PART I
Origins, Influences, and Evolution

CHAPTER 1

Between Two Worlds: Antitheatricality and the Beginnings of Modern Yiddish Theatre

Jeremy Dauber

The early history of the Yiddish theatre offers a tantalizing instance of a marked shift from one form of theatrical culture to another. If by the nineteenth century's end a full-fledged secular Yiddish theatrical culture revolving around professional performance had been firmly established in eastern Europe, it diverged markedly from its origins in a text-centered, reading-oriented dramatic culture at the century's beginning. A full study of the dynamics of this transformation would necessitate discussing numerous causal factors, including, among others, the availability of professional actors, rates of acculturation, and degrees of cultural permeability.[1] By studying two Yiddish Enlightenment (Haskalah) dramas from the first decades of the century, the anonymous *Di genarte velt* (The deceived world) and Israel Ber Levinson's *Di hefker-velt* (The topsy-turvy world), this chapter will focus on one particular ideological and thematic element of the process, an element that complicated this theatrical transformation—a marked opposition to theatricality itself.

These two dramatic works—respectively representing early examples of the literary projects of the Galician and the Russian Enlightenment movements—are deeply influenced by the aesthetic and ideological positioning of their foundational predecessor, the Prussian (often referred to as the "Berlin") Haskalah. As is now well known, the Haskalah was hardly a monolithic movement; however, much of the scholarship attending to local variations in *maskilic* (that is, Haskalah-related) patterns of thought and activity has been located in the historical, rather than the literary, sphere.[2] My hope is that further studies of maskilic literature will continue to focus on local variation in conjunction with overarching patterns of influence and ideology; this chapter, indeed, is premised on the understanding that the centrality of this literary and dramatic trope of antitheatricality in early eastern European

Yiddish drama cannot be understood without combining local and global maskilic contexts.

Western literary and dramatic thought is saturated with the tension between written drama and performed theatre, with notable expressions of the antitheatrical impulse by dramatists, critics, and potential audience members alike.[3] The Berlin Haskalah, however—the attempt by mid-eighteenth-century Jews to prove their suitability for social and political emancipation into general, non-Jewish society—had its own unique constellation of considerations with respect to staging theatre; a brief review of these is relevant to our concerns here.[4]

Prussian maskilim, on the one hand, hoped to demonstrate their political and social bona fides through aesthetic accomplishment, particularly by means of their mastery of contemporary German literary genres and the dramatic genre central to that culture. Theoretically, maskilic attitudes toward drama and theatre could simply mimic contemporary Prussian ones. The resulting work they produced could range along the spectrum of "dramatic" output—from philosophical dialogues intended only for reading (like the philosophical work of Moses Mendelssohn, or Aaron Halle-Wolfssohn's *Sikha b'erets ha-khayim* (Conversation in the land of the living), to full-fledged dramas quite possibly intended for performance, such as Wolfssohn's *Laykhtzin un fremelay* (*Silliness and Sanctimony*) or Isaac Euchel's *Reb Henokh, oder vos tut men damit?* (Reb Henokh, or what can one do about it?).[5] Their range was conditioned, if not fully shaped, by the dynamics of a theatrical or antitheatrical bias attendant in that majority culture; however, three additional factors unique to the Jewish community affected both practical and aesthetic maskilic considerations. The first was the still significant traditionalism among some of the maskilim and, more to the point, the Jewish audience they intended to persuade of their Enlightenment ideas. Such traditionalism manifested itself in a strongly felt interdiction against theatrical performance, with certain festive exceptions, particularly related to the holiday of Purim. Second, and perhaps more important, was the maskilic perception of those "exceptional" performances, the Purim plays themselves, as regressive, unsophisticated displays of boorishness inimical to the Enlightenment project of displaying Jews' cultured and *salonfähig* (salon appropriate) nature.[6] Maskilic attempts to solve or circumvent this problem generally manifested themselves in the creation of "refined" Purim plays such as Wolfssohn's *Laykhtzin un fremelay*, rather than in eliminating theatrical activity entirely. This was perhaps a concession to the twin demands of traditional audiences' (as well as their own) desire to continue Jewish practice, and the maskilic need to compete in the German aesthetic enterprise on all generic fronts. Still, it is hardly unreasonable to suggest that some trace of antitheatrical bias unique to the Jewish situation continued to exist in such settings.

Such bias, I would argue, was narrowed and concretized within the dramatic sphere itself to account for the third factor: the maskilic strategy of presenting the Ostjude (eastern European Jewish) population in Prussia as an obstacle to successful acculturation.[7] This was obviously an issue unique to the Jewish community, and could take dramatic form in representations of the Ostjude as a villain, often as a religious hypocrite, as in the case of *Laykhtzin un fremelay*'s Reb Yoysefkhe, whose character is modeled directly on Molière's Tartuffe. But the Ostjude's villainy lay also in his theatricality, and the masking that hypocrisy necessarily entails. Such masking is directly at odds with maskilic efforts to present the "normative" and "normalizing" Prussian Jewish community as precisely who they seem to be, in an effort to conquer external suspicion of Jewish duplicity, bad faith, or hidden agendas in their Enlightenment efforts. Whether the dramatist agrees or not that the *theatre* mimetically represents social norms or characters in general,[8] his presentation of the Ostjude, and in Wolfssohn's case a specifically Hasidic Ostjude,[9] as the apotheosis of what we might call "internal theatricality" within the play—Reb Yoysefkhe's shifting of his identity, his language, his character, profound shifts unique to his character within the play[10]—opens several possibilities for the dramatist-cum-ideologue. It allows the identification of the Ostjude with problematic activities within the Jewish tradition, such as uncultured or boorish tendencies aesthetically antithetical to those championed by acculturation-minded Prussian Jews, and an immoral stance predicated on false identity that stands in contradistinction to the "honest" constitution of the potential maskilic member of Prussian society.

This antitheatricality, despite its unusual sources and reasoning, nonetheless speaks of the maskilim's general social and aesthetic accord with the norms of the larger co-territorial culture, especially given the lesser dissonance of Prussian maskilic activity within a rapidly changing and modernizing socioeconomic milieu. The Galician and early Russian Haskalah, however, were both deeply influenced by the ideological positions and aesthetic products of the Berlin Haskalah, but operated in substantially different milieus. The result is a markedly different calibration of the emphasis on the role of theatre and performance, in life as in art.

Unlike in Prussia, none of the Galician and early Russian maskilic dramatic works bear any suggestion of having been performed during their first few decades of composition, but were rather circulated in manuscript.[11] This difference speaks of substantial discrepancies in social and ideological background, and disjunctions affecting the eastern European maskilim as they attempted to apply the aesthetic and ideological dicta of the Berlin Haskalah to their own local circumstances. In contrast to the Jews of Berlin, eastern European Jews had few, if any, theatrical examples to follow aside from the demonized Purim plays. Unlike the Prussians, they had little access to friendly printing presses, to comparatively organized networks of like-minded individuals, and certainly to an increasingly friendly (though admittedly still skeptical) population. Exactly the opposite, in fact: the popularity of Hasidism was exploding in the region, contributing to the Galician (and, to a slightly lesser extent, Russian) Haskalah's explicit and vitriolic anti-Hasidic character.[12] The increasing power of Hasidism certainly had its effect on the persecution of maskilic individuals and activities. An 1815 ban of excommunication against the maskilim in Lemberg, for example, substantially affected the composition of *Di genarte velt*, as we will see later in this chapter. The reach of Hasidic power necessitated the transmission of written maskilic material, including dramatic material, in *samizdat* form, thus further depressing any possibility of open performance.[13] It also contributed to maskilic perceptions of a Jewish social and economic system as being increasingly overtaken by a constituency whose anti-rationalist ideologies and beliefs were precisely antithetical to those of the Haskalah.[14]

Resulting anti-Hasidic critiques by Galician and Russian maskilim—critiques which, following the literary aesthetics of the Berlin Haskalah, took the form of dramas as well as works in other genres—were conditioned by both positive and negative characteristics of theatrical deceit and unmasked honesty essential to the Berlin Haskalah's own models of portraiture. But in an "Ostwelt" where the theatrical Ostjude was no longer an external irruption who catalyzed the play's action, but a representative of the empowered majority, maskilic dramatists were forced to elevate the localized antitheatrical bias of the earlier period to reflect a society permeated with those problematic tendencies. Theirs was a *generally* flawed society: deeply hypocritical, secretive, not what it seems to be. In short, it was "theatrical" in the worst ways.

Such portraiture was undesirable in the Prussian maskilic context, where efforts were focused on representing a society that was rapidly converging on the ideal; in western Europe, localized, negative theatricality was a temporary regression, a problem to be overcome. In eastern Europe, conversely, such theatricalized society, inherently saturated with ethical, aesthetic, and religious problems, required revolutionary transformation. The resulting deconstructive tensions—how, after all, does one use the theatrical medium to decry a theatrical society?—are balanced by maskilic awareness of the impossibility of performing these texts theatrically. In other words, they too advance the *dramatic* form, but do so by decrying the centrality of the *theatrical* act as an ethically ruinous feature of the world at large, which befits the fact that these are, themselves, dramatic texts not meant to be performed. In doing so, they seem to turn their inability to create performed texts into a Pyrrhic victory—but, paradoxically and even somewhat unintentionally, they open the door for a later history of performed Yiddish theatre by continuing to privilege and value the dramatic form as an "acceptable" vehicle for maskilic discourse.

A closer look at two seminal maskilic dramatic texts—particularly their employment of the central trope of "world" (*velt*)—which, in its Hebraic analogue *oylem*, would become the Yiddish term of choice for a theatrical audience—permits examination of this process in more detail.

Both *Di genarte velt* and *Di hefker-velt*, in the best traditions of the rationalist Haskalah, set out to investigate and critique the corrupting and aberrant forces that have diverted social reality from its potential optimal state. The results are virtual taxonomies of anti-*Bildung* processes. In the religious society of maskilim and their opponents alike, such investigations naturally have metaphysical and theological overtones. More important for our purposes, the dynamic of "corruption and aberration" also takes on a strong theatrical dimension, one that thwarts reform by boggling the minds and eyes of a credulous society (or audience). These dramatic maskilic works pull back the curtain; in revealing these deceptions, the maskilim attempt to present an image of a pure, uncorrupted, normative world. In doing so, they hope their attempt to show how things truly are, and how things could be but are not, provides the impetus for the readers' sympathies to swing toward the authors' desired goals. But as time goes on, they become increasingly skeptical of the practical possibility of achieving such an outcome.

The anonymous author of the early nineteenth-century Galician play *Di genarte velt*, "the first maskilic comedy in eastern European Yiddish,"[15] explicitly correlates disguise, moral corruption, reform, and unmasking in his introduction to the play, which he describes as "the best mirror in the world," accentuating his ultimately mimetic enterprise.[16] He writes:

> Our holy Talmud says, *mefarsemin et ha-khaneyfim mipney khilul ha-shem*, that is, it is proper to reveal the shame of false people, who disguise themselves (*farshteln zikh*) and who say that they are pious, but in truth they are great evildoers; they bow down to the ground and blaspheme to high heaven. Such men disgrace God's name in the world, and through them it emerges that even someone who is in truth an honest Jew can become ashamed. One must not be ashamed, but rather one must openly let the world know that they are swindlers and that their piety is pure deception (*batrigeray*). So says our Talmud, and this is in truth the main purpose of this small volume. . . . Concerning them [these deceivers] it is a great *mitsve*[17] to tear the false masks off these people's faces. (51)[18]

Such an emphasis on unmasking deceivers and pious hypocrites strongly evokes the Prussian maskilic context we have discussed, and indeed numerous points of comparison between *Di genarte velt* and *Laykhtzin un fremelay* seem to confirm Viner's supposition that the author of the former had read the latter.[19] Setting the play's action on the holiday of Purim—thus linking its reformed dramatic identity to the problematized theatrical tradition,[20] the play's lack of any performance tradition, and indeed the emphasis placed on reading the work[21]—reinforces the structural basis of the problematic nature of performance itself. Given the Galician Haskalah's vitriolic anti-Hasidism, the play's particularly anti-Hasidic construction of this theatrical conceit is hardly surprising. Such critique strongly echoes the Galician maskil Joseph Perl's (1773–1839) characterization of Hasidism as a mystificatory, deceptive movement in his *Über das Wesen der Sekte Chassidim* (On the nature of the Hasidic sect, 1816) where he suggests that Hasidic leaders, charlatans to a man, engage in theatrical ceremony and trumpery, which has the effect of disguising their corrupt and avaricious natures from their credulous followers.[22]

Indeed, the play's action—which presents a hypocritical Hasidic character, the *melamed*, striving for educational, romantic, and economic dominance in a merchant household, only to be unmasked and discredited at play's end—once more models the maskilic wish-fulfillment fantasy in a manner analogous to the ideals of the Prussian Haskalah.[23] Beyond that, however, it also offers an assessment of the present world's problems and crises as aberrations that stem from a surfeit of theatricality that threatens to impose its false image of reality on reality itself. This constitutes a real discrepancy with *Laykhtzin un fremelay*, as other discussions—more or less tangentially related to the "hypocrisy unmasked" plot[24]—begin to suggest the authorial desire to effect a more unusual concern about theatre.

Most meaningful for our purpose is the ongoing discussion between the *melamed* and the maskilic figure, known as the Shrayber (writer), concerning the possibility and frequency of miraculous action (56–57). The conversation is first and foremost a maskilic dig at the Hasidic propensity to ascribe wonders to their rebbes, itself the premise for many a maskilic satire.[25] By contrast, the writer's position—which, not surprisingly, minimizes the miraculous—echoes maskilic traditionalism by presenting the enlightened figure as a defender of Jewish law.[26] "Law" is cast in opposition to Hasidic preference for *minhag* (custom); the latter is presented here not only as an antinomian institution that places its own values above those of sacred law, but one which will—vitally for our purposes—reshape the world to the custom-making group's imagination in theatrical fashion, through performance or belief. Custom, in the Hasidic sense, is inherently, ontologically, dangerous, as it threatens to present the world as it is not.

Maskilic sentiment, accordingly, is expressed by the desire to "naturalize" the Hasidic term *minhag* by employing it in an earlier, classically "purer" context: the Talmudic phrase *olam ke-minhago noheg* (the world goes according to its regular process).[27] Such insistence on, and commitment to, the natural order of the world that Hasidic practice and philosophy rejects explains the play's presentation of the Hasid as disproportionately material (he is a glutton and highly licentious). But it also serves as a leading metaphor for opposition to the unnatural, corrupting influence that spreads through society, best expressed in the Shrayber's[28] complaints about increasing social problems. If reality ceases to matter, he argues, then so does knowledge. And training, experience, and skill—the bywords of the new Haskalah movement—are by extension also undervalued. These infectious aberrations, where people claim expertise (and job titles) that they lack the ability to perform, allow for an epidemic expansion of "disguise" to everyday social and economic life, not just to theatrical Hasidic individuals (76–77, 100). This universalizing trend ends, in *Di genarte velt,* with an optimistic unmasking.

Israel Ber Levinson's *Di hefker-velt,* however, illustrates how such triumphant claims become increasingly complicated. *Di hefker-velt* can be seen as the application of Galician maskilic mentalities to Russian contexts. Levinson (1788–1860), a major figure of the Russian Haskalah, spent most of 1812 to 1820 in Galicia, originally seeking treatment for his nervous condition. While there, he visited many local maskilic centers, meeting (and in some cases befriending) the local movement's leaders, most notably Joseph Perl and Nachman Krochmal (1785–1840).[29]

Viner raises the strong possibility that Levinson was directly familiar with *Di genarte velt*.[30] Aside from thematic similarities (to be discussed in more detail later in the chapter), and correspondences in the plays' Purim-oriented intent,[31] the dramatic works share similarities in processes of composition, dissemination, and their having no history of being staged. Like *Di genarte velt,* Levinson's work was published decades after its composition, although it circulated extensively in manuscript.[32] It also shares an unfinished appearance and its conscious design is as a dramatic but not theatrical work—it was to be read, not performed.[33]

The plot, such as it is, consists of a discussion between Zerach and Faytel, two average Volhynian Jews, and a visitor from *Raysn*.[34] The latter receives, in tones combining offended horror and cynical resignation, a stinging critique of contemporary life in the Pale of Settlement. Zerach's and Faytel's primary charge is the crushing exploitation of the poor by the rich, who maintain their power through rigged elections, the levying of crippling taxes that are disproportionately distributed and applied, and the threat of conscription—a system they regularly abuse and manipulate to protect the wealthy—to keep potential objectors in line.[35] The religious and moral leadership and authorities who could conceivably mount an opposition are either terrified, absent, ignorant, or corrupt themselves—if not some combination of the above (51, 59).

Levinson's critique, following in the footsteps of the Shrayber and Soykher in *Di genarte velt,* expands his purview to society at large, and also takes on Hasidism.[36] Most important, it presents falsehood, hypocrisy, and deception as symptoms of the aberrant nature of the present society (65), an aberration that is "objectively" confirmed by the external observer. Such transformation of characters into "objective" spectators for societal theatrical activity is confirmed by the trio's observation of a theatrical, dramatically dressed (complete with red parasol!), constantly performing figure who continually attempts to give the impression of business activity and acumen when in reality lacking anything of the sort (60–61). This and other types of falsehood—concretized in the play in the often-discussed phenomenon of false oaths (50, 57)—creates a false picture of the world not as it is in reality, but in the malicious imagination of the oath-takers. The *effects of their deceptions,* however, expand to have actual and forceful consequences. Such falsehood does more than dupe the world; it actually reshapes it so fundamentally that there is little hope of its returning to its natural path, the desired *olam ke-minhago noheg* model of *Di genarte velt*. Such radical doubt—not only about the world's current status, but also its future—is expressed most powerfully by Levinson's use of the title phrase *hefker-velt*, topsy-turvy world, an allusive Yiddish phrase, retextualized by its current circumstances.[37]

The phrase may allude to, if not have its origins in, a Talmudic narrative from BT Pesakhim 50a, describing one Rav Yosef, the son of Rabbi Yehoshua ben Levi, who slipped into a comatose state.[38] After his return to consciousness, his father asked him:

> What did you see [in the next world]? He said to him: 'I saw an inverted world (*olam hafukh ra'iti*)! The uppermost are below and the lowly are above.' He said to him: 'My son, you have seen a clear world (*olam barur ra'ita*). 'And how are we [Torah scholars] there?' 'Just as we are regarded here, so are we regarded there. And I heard them saying, 'fortunate is he who comes here and his learning is in his hand.' And I also heard them saying, 'those executed by the government no other person can stand in their enclosure.'

Though the Yiddish phrase is sufficiently familiar that its roots—or particular conceptual provenance—are not necessarily extrusive, Levinson's continued insistence on the trope of otherworldly visitation within the text itself—particularly, though not solely, through ironic references that the Hasidim go *me'akhorey ha-pargod* (behind the Heavenly curtain, 64) to get their information—may well be sufficient to alert us to a retextualization process.[39] (As the author of the *Te'udah be-yisroel*, one of the Russian Haskalah's more allusive and learned polemics, Levinson's familiarity with classical texts in general and this text in particular seems likely.)[40]

This ur-text for the topsy-turvy or inverted world boasts features highly relevant to Levinson's (and our) discussion. It casts the current world as corrupted, aberrant, inverted, dislocated from an ultimately fixed position of rightness, one that is visible and mimetically "clear." The text of the inverted world reconceptualizes corruption from given social institutions into a universal condition with metaphysical resonances; the observers of these processes operate from a radically and deeply disempowered position, for Rav Yosef is comatose or dead, and the observer from *Raysn* is a stranger without power other than to observe and criticize. Despite the positive valence attributed to such observers,[41] the situation's repair (or arrival of that observer's vindication) is not for this world, which is too far gone, but is deferred to some utopian, metaphysically distant one.

This last point, appearing clearly in the Talmudic source, is present only by implication in *Di hefker-velt,* which itself offers no solutions at all, either theological, rationalistic, or metaphysical. It may be taken as a reflection of the text's status as a very early expression of maskilic ambivalence about the reformist's ability to achieve genuine social change, despite his certainty of the rightness of his cause.[42]

Such ambivalence is well-known, of course, in much Russian maskilic literature more generally.[43] More directly, though, it questions the possibility of theatricality more powerfully than ever—and casts doubt on the plays' ability to perform the act of unmasking that is so optimistically and ardently expressed in the introduction to *Di genarte velt*. Such actions may be theatrically possible, but they fail to reflect the world as it is: a world where theatricality and masking never go away.

In short, early Galician and Russian maskilic dramas are at least powerfully ambivalent and perhaps even firmly deconstructive on the very role of the theatrical enterprise. Perhaps this was, to coin a phrase, making a vice out of necessity, a genuine expression of religious feeling, or simply an anguished reflection of how they conceived the lived omnipresence of theatricality within their milieu. But whichever combination of these motives it may have been, the resulting ideologically complex heritage they left their successors may help us further illuminate the decidedly mixed emotions surrounding the modern Yiddish theatre's origins.

Appendix

Introduction to *Di genarte velt*, reprinted from M. Viner, ed., *Di genarte velt* (Moscow: Melukhe-farlag, 1940), 51–52.

Our holy Talmud says, *mefarsemin et ha-khaneyfim mipney khilul ha-shem*, that is, it is proper to reveal the shame of false people, who disguise themselves and who say that they are pious, but in truth they are great evildoers; they bow down to the ground and blaspheme to high heaven. Such men disgrace God's name in the world, and through them it emerges that even someone who is in truth an honest Jew can become disgraced. One must not be ashamed, but rather one must openly let the world know that they are swindlers and that their piety is pure deception. So says our Talmud, and this is in truth the main purpose of this small volume. It shows us how the world can at times become deeply deceived. There are people who lack a single virtuous attribute and commit all sorts of sins; however, they put one over on the world and say they are good and pious; and whoever looks upon their God-fearing faces thinks that they are surrounded by flights of angels. This is terribly bitter, since as soon as the world takes one of them to be pious, he can do what he will; he can steal and swindle and swear falsely, and can lead people to disaster—and no one will dare to speak a word against him; in fact, people will look to speak up on his behalf. Concerning them it is a great *mitsve* to tear the false masks off these people's faces and to show the swindle to the world. This little book teaches us that one should not rely on the pious countenance, but should investigate diligently, with intelligence, before taking someone to be truly pious. It also teaches us that the deceiver's end is dark and bitter, and that his falsehood must in time be revealed. It also teaches us ethics and wisdom, how a man should conduct himself. And whoever will read this little book will have great pleasure in doing so. It may happen that some individuals will get angry when they read it. To them I say: if the shoe fits, then wear it; if you don't eat garlic, then your breath won't stink. Do you understand what I mean?

Notes

I am extremely grateful to Barbara Henry and Joel Berkowitz for their detailed and thorough comments on a draft of this chapter; I am also indebted to the insightful comments from the conferees of the "Yiddish Theatre Revisited" conference—especially those of Seth Wolitz and Alyssa Quint.

1. Many of these aspects have been discussed elsewhere, to greater or lesser extent; see especially Joel Berkowitz, ed., *Yiddish Theatre: New Approaches* (Oxford, UK: Littman Library of Jewish Civilization, 2003).

2. For discussion of these topics more generally and historical sources on the Prussian and Galician Haskalah in particular, see my *Antonio's Devils: Writers of the Jewish Enlightenment and the Birth of Modern Hebrew and Yiddish Literature* (Palo Alto, CA: Stanford University Press, 2004).

3. For some general considerations, compare Jonas Barish, *The Antitheatrical Prejudice* (Berkeley: University of California Press, 1981); for relevant essays in a more historically circumscribed period, see the special issue of *The Eighteenth Century* on "Theater and Theatricality," 43, no. 2 (Fall 2002).

4. For more detail, see the introduction in Joel Berkowitz and Jeremy Dauber, trans. and eds., *Landmark Yiddish Plays* (Albany: SUNY Press, 2006).

5. These last plays were most likely intended for reading aloud in salons, but a more elaborate performance—at least within the context of the schoolroom—was likely.

6. Wolfssohn's complaint about the traditional Purim plays he saw around him expresses it best: "On the days of Purim . . . youths arise and joke in front of us with filthiness and frivolity . . . which, upon hearing it, sickens the soul of any listening enlightener." See the discussion of Wolfssohn in *Antonio's Devils*, esp. 178–187.

7. On this phenomenon, compare Steven E. Aschheim, *Brothers and Strangers: The East European Jew in German and German Jewish Consciousness, 1800–1923* (Madison: University of Wisconsin Press, 1982).

8. Wolfssohn may have felt that it did, at least in part; in his introduction to *Laykhtzin un fremelay*, Wolfssohn speaks about the three different types of people that he finds in the society he sees around him: the falsely enlightened, the traditionalist fanatics, and well-meaning but perhaps foolish Everymen (in the Hebrew version of the introduction, he compares these types to three shepherds, in a nod to the pastoral dialogue tradition championed by his idol Mendelssohn). Wolfssohn continues, "Should any reader, man or woman, find themselves portrayed here, and then come to the conclusion to improve themselves, then I will have achieved my goal, which was to unite pleasure and utility." Cited by B. Gorin, *Di geshikhte fun idishn teater* [History of the Yiddish theatre] (New York: Literarisher farlag, 1918), 1:74.

9. Reb Yoysefkhe is referred to specifically as a Hasid by three characters in the play; see Act 1, Scene iv.

10. Though Markus, the maskilic hero of the piece, briefly pretends to be a customer at the brothel where Yetkhen has been imprisoned, I see this less as Wolfssohn's indicating that theatricality is an essential and universal component of the entire enterprise (though we, in a postmodern age, may reasonably derive that lesson) than as a stand-in for the maskilic necessity of instrumental engagement in problematic and problematized activities to achieve noble goals. Such efforts may admittedly result in deconstructive outcomes (see my "Looking Again: Representation in Nineteenth-Century Yiddish Literature," *Prooftexts* 25 (Fall 2005): 276–318, for a discussion of the phenomenon) but a historicized analysis of the dynamics as they pertain to the Berlin Haskalah and Wolfssohn's play suggest the conscious awareness of such a scenario is unlikely.

11. Classic sources on the Galician and Russian Haskalah include Simon Dubnow, *History of the Jews in Russia and Poland*, 3 vols., (Philadelphia: Jewish Publication Society, 1916–1920) and Ra-

phael Mahler, *Hasidism and the Jewish Enlightenment: Their Confrontation in Galicia and Poland in the First Half of the Nineteenth Century* (Philadelphia: Jewish Publication Society, 1985); for some fine recent scholarship on the period, see Shmuel Feiner, *The Jewish Enlightenment*, trans. Chaya Naor (Philadelphia: University of Pennsylvania Press, 2002) and Benjamin Nathans, *Beyond the Pale: The Jewish Encounter with Late Imperial Russia* (Berkeley: University of California Press, 2002), as well as the essays collected in Shmuel Feiner and David Sorkin, eds., *New Perspectives on the Haskalah* (London: Littman Library of Jewish Civilization, 2001).

12. On the phenomenon more generally, see Mahler.

13. Such a mode of transmission was not uncommon in contemporary eastern Europe; I mean to focus here not only on the outcome, but on the Hasidic cause.

14. Recent research on the early spread of Hasidism has only further developed the model of viewing the increase of Hasidic influence as a complex social and economic process, rather than a largely charismatic/religious/ideological one (though of course these types are hardly separable). Compare Glenn Dynner, *Men of Silk: The Hasidic Conquest of Polish Jewish Society* (New York: Oxford University Press, 2006).

15. For details on the provenance, publication history, and potential authorship of the play (including the possibility of female authorship), see Khone Shmeruk, "Nusakh bilti yadua shel ha-komediya ha'anonimit 'di genarte velt'" [Unknown version of the anonymous comedy 'The deceived world'], *Kiryat Sefer* 54 (1979): 802–816, which includes an appendix containing an expanded introduction and more complete ending of the play taken from an 1865 edition, apparently based on a different manuscript—one unknown to Meir Viner, who based his edition of the play on a defective Lemberg 1863 edition. Viner suggests the maskilic author's anonymity derives at least in part from anxiety about the fall 1815 *kherem* (excommunication decree) leveled against Enlightenment leaders in Lemberg. See Viner, "Di yidishe literatur baym onheyb funem 19tn yorhundert," in M. Viner, ed., *Di genarte velt* (Moscow: Melukhe-farlag, 1940), 3–47, 32. On the ban more generally, see Mahler, 73–76.

16. *Di genarte velt*, 49. Further references to page numbers will appear in the body of the text. For further authorial emphasis on truthfulness, see the expanded introduction in Shmeruk, 811.

17. (Hebrew/Yiddish): Literally, commandment; colloquially often translated as "good deed."

18. A similar point is made in the expanded introduction (Shmeruk, 810): "Our world is extremely deceived; the greatest scoundrels and the worst people swindle the world and persuade it that they are good and pious." See also, in a very different context, my discussion of the original introduction in "What's So Funny About the Yiddish Theater? Comedy and the Origins of the Yiddish Drama," in Justin Cammy, Dara Horn, Alyssa Quint, and Rachel Rubinstein, eds. *Arguing the Modern Jewish Canon: Essays on Literature and Culture in Honor of Ruth R. Wisse* (Cambridge, MA: Harvard University Press, 2008), 535–550.

19. On the (numerous) other points of comparison between the two plays, see Viner, 34–36; for a summary of the somewhat complex and frantic plot, revolving around the Yiddish dramatic staples of arranged marriages, orphans, inheritances, and insolent servants with secrets, see 34. On reading the play, Shloyme Ettinger compared it to *Tartuffe*, the same comparison often made about *Laykhtzin un fremelay*; see Shmeruk's comments on 802.

20. The title page of the 1865 edition explicitly suggests the work was designed for Purim; see Shmeruk, 805.

21. See Shmeruk, 804–805, on the relation of the expanded introduction to the conceptualization of the work as a read, not performed, piece.

22. A. Rubinstein, ed., *Über das Wesen der Sekte Chassidim* [On the nature of the Hasidic sect] (Jerusalem: Israel Academy of Sciences and Humanities, 1977). All critics agree that the author of *Di genarte velt* was intimately acquainted with Perl's Galician maskilic circle; though *Über das Wesen*

was, at that point, still unpublished, the author would almost certainly have been familiar with the substance of the argument, if not indeed a manuscript version of the work itself. Though hardly necessary to note these claims' subjectivity and bias, contemporary Zaddikism certainly did boast ceremonies and modes that could be considered theatrical; compare the discussion in Israel Bartal, "Le'an halakh tseror ha-kesef? Ha-bikoret ha-maskilit al hebeteha ha-kalkali'im shel ha-khasidut" [Where did the bundle of money go?: Maskilic criticism of Hasidic economic perspectives], in Menakhem Ben-Sasson, ed., *Dat ve-kalkala* [Religion and economics] (Jerusalem: Zalman Shazar, 1995), 375–385.

23. His hypocrisies abound; they begin, notably, with his hasty exit from evening prayers ending the Fast of Esther so he can get an illegal head start on the community's food! (60)

24. On the centrality of this aspect of the plot to the play as a whole, see Viner, 42.

25. For a notable case in point, see Joseph Perl, *Megale temirin* [*Revealer of Secrets*] (Vienna: Anton Strauss, 1819).

26. On maskilic traditionalism, compare Viner, 36–37 and Edward Breuer, "Between Haskalah and Orthodoxy: The Writings of R. Jacob Zvi Meklenburg," *Hebrew Union College Annual* 66 (1996), 259–287.

27. See BT Avoda Zara 54b.

28. His complaints are often accompanied or echoed by those of the Soykher, the merchant paterfamilias, who serves as an externalized, observing, judging figure slightly detached from the struggles of the Hasidim and the maskilim.

29. For biographical details on Levinson, "The Mendelssohn of the Russian Jews," especially his various maskilic works, programmatic *Te'uda be-yisroel* [Testimony in Israel, 1828] and his important anti-blood libel polemic *Efes damim* [No blood, 1838], see *Leksikon fun der nayer yidisher literatur* [Encyclopedia of the new Yiddish literature] (New York: Alveltlekher Yidisher Kultur-kongres, 1956–1981), 5:306–309.

30. See Viner, 43–44.

31. Note the references to a Purim-shpil in *Di hefker velt*, 49 and 63. Page numbers are taken from the play's appearance in Shmuel Rozhanski, ed., *Nusekh haskole* [Haskalah style] (Buenos Aires: Ateneo Literario en el IWO, 1968), 49–66, and will subsequently appear in the body of the text.

32. Though Levinson wrote *Di hefker-velt* in 1830, it remained unpublished until after his death three decades later, appearing most prominently in Sholem Aleichem's *Dos yidishe folksbibliotek* [The Jewish people's library] in 1888. Levinson's early biographer and publisher, Duber Natanson, writes of "several reasons" for the failure to publish the play, perhaps including Levinson's reticence, not uncommon among maskilim, to be identified publicly as a Yiddish writer, though the manuscript circulation may vitiate this theory. See *Dos yidishe folksbibliotek* 1 (1888), 125.

33. The manuscript is itself unfinished, and so, therefore, is the printed version, although Natanson says it lacks only one page.

34. The definition of *Raysn* is somewhat varied; compare Harkavy's note (in his *Yiddish Hebrew-English Dictionary*, 477), which suggests that though the word's general sense is simply "Russia," Polish Jews used the term to refer to a specific Polish/White Russian [i.e., present day Belarus] province also known, ironically, as *Shvartzrusland*. Other intimations in the text (see 49) suggest he comes from Lithuania.

35. See 52–56 for the most detailed description of the process; for more on taxes, see 61–62.

36. The Hasidic rebbes are considered by Faytl, at least, to have authoritarian force in the society, though Zerach has a slightly different perspective; see 51–52. They have also attacked potential reformers; see, 63–65 for more detail on Hasidic activity.

37. On this phenomenon, see *Antonio's Devils*, chapter 2, esp. 56.

38. Compare Rashi and Rabbi Chananel's commentaries ad loc, which claim he actually died.

39. Beyond this, the references to false oaths having no atonement in "this world or the next" (50) and its direct linkage to the first mention of the words *hefker-velt* (50) and *farkerte velt* (51) also suggest the extension of the polemical issues to the metaphysical sphere.

40. Such retextualization also seems more plausible given a likely intended audience of a more limited, elite group of maskilic readers rather than—or in addition to—a polemic for the masses, allowing the suggestion that the intended audience would also have understood the text. For other references, with a greater or lesser degree of explicitness, to the Talmud, see 51 and 57.

41. See esp. 52, for the praise of sages and learned types.

42. Such ambivalence is clearly apparent in the authorial stand-in's (i.e., the visitor's) reactions and comments in the play.

43. Examples range from J. L. Gordon's "Le-mi ani amel?" [For whom do I toil?] to the Haskalah's death-knell, S.Y. Abramovitch's *Di klyatshe* [The mare].

CHAPTER 2

The Salon and the Tavern: Yiddish Folk Poetry of the Nineteenth Century

Alyssa Quint

This chapter is a historical treatment of Yiddish poems, sketches, skits, and songs that in their day were referred to as "folk poetry," a cultural composite of a phenomenon that peaked in popularity among eastern European Jewish audiences in the second half of the nineteenth century. "Folk poetry" (in Yiddish, the terms *folksdikhtung* and *folkslider* were used interchangeably) refers to a wide variety of cultural moments. At times, Yiddish folk poetry resembled the European art song of the same period, with its simple rhyme scheme set to a specific melody and intended for performance in intimate spaces, either by the poets who composed them or other entertainers.[1] The public performance of folk poetry (in Yiddish, *kupletn, forshtelungen*) also referred to dramatic sketches set to music in tavern settings and performed in a cabaret-like format, or in less-refined spectacles, which might have been enjoyed in the same way Russians took in Gypsy songs or peasant music in *pogrebki* (cellar restaurants).[2] On the level of literary genre, elaborate folk poetry (longer than a conventional poem with two or more speaking parts) resembles contemporary Russian-language *kartiny*, literary sketches of everyday life. And, as published items, some of the folk poetry appeared to be Yiddish equivalents of *pesenniki*, small, cheaply printed song booklets of lyrics, minus the music, that were popular with Russian readers. In this chapter, I examine examples of folk poetry in its late nineteenth-century cultural-historical context in an attempt to appreciate the variegated nature of their composers, their contemporary consumers, and the works themselves.

Many previous scholars, folklorists, and ethnomusicologists especially, have shed light on the segment of this material insofar as it became "folklorized"—poetry, that is, detached from its authors in its oral transmission and changed into multiple unattributed variations.[3] My work builds on the work of Chana and Yosef Mlotek, who have reconnected these songs to their verifiable composers and fleshed out the lives of the composers, as well as the work of Leo Wiener who, over a century ago, instinctively relied on a formalist approach to Yiddish folk poetry, analyzing it for its content, as well as its rhyme and meter. Here, some discussion is likewise given over to the poetry itself, albeit with a greater emphasis on its ideological hue and the reference it makes to its context. Moreover, when historical sources permit, I consider the folk poetry as both of and for the refined salons of the educated and the bourgeoisie as well as of and for the tavern.

The Folk of Folk Poetry

Yiddish folk poetry is far from an uncomplicated example of folk culture, yet there is something undeniably folk-like about it. At one end of the spectrum there are examples of folk poetry composed by entertainers who had little in the way of formal education and wrote as a kind of bohemian gadfly or member of the underclass. At the other end, a large segment of published folk poetry offers stylized literary material produced by a class of educated, multilingual writers, whose works self-consciously focus on the daily lives of the Jewish working class, and deploy narrative voices of simple, pious Jewish men and women. Such composers deployed the word "folk" often, and worked off the energy of what they considered "the masses." The subtitles of two volumes published by the educated maskil and founder of the Yiddish theatre, Avrom Goldfaden, illustrate this phenomenon: *Dos yudele: yudishe lider af prost yudishe shprakh* (The little Jew: Jewish folk songs in the simple Yiddish language, 1866) and *Di yidene: farsheydene gedikhte un teater in prost yudishen* (The Jewess: A collection of varied poetry and dramatic writings in crude Yiddish, 1869). The latter was named in Russian "lyrical-epic and dramatic writings" to underscore the untutored hybridization that Goldfaden associated with folk poetry. And yet, with his invocation of the lyric and epic poem—in print—Goldfaden sought out the attention of a sophisticated audience.

The "folk" question of folk poetry takes on a dynamic circularity driven by its themes and different audiences. Less slippery is the fact that by the 1880s the bundle of incidental genres amassed under the folk-poetry rubric grew into an exemplary Yiddish culture in the eyes of the Yiddish literary establishment (such as it was): more than experimental or aesthetically remarkable, folk poetry was lauded for its accessibility and its catholic appeal. Its exaggerated privileged status in the eyes of, for example, Jacob Dinezon (1856–1919) and Sholem Rabinovitch (Sholem Aleichem) is particularly obvious when compared with their dim views of the Yiddish theatre's arguably more formidable achievements. Dinezon characterizes folk poetry as the product of "undistilled inspiration," and "the unadulterated incarnation of Jewish nationalist sentiment" in his seminal essay, "Di yidishe shprakh un ir shrayber" (The Yiddish language and its writer). He believed it to be the most evolved area of Yiddish literary culture:

> In addition to stories, dramas, comedies and ethical literature in Yiddish, we have, from a variety of talented men, many poems, epic poems, and songs in our national language; when the famous European literatures boast of their folk poets, our literature can be even more boastful about our folk poets [. . .] the masses, the readers themselves, for whose benefit the books were written . . . listen to what they have to say . . . [and] open their hearts to the songs thousands of miles apart from one another [. . .] thousands not even knowing to whom they belong, but knowing their content well and taking them as their own, becoming as one. Because the folk poets, to whose hearts they were first born, were moved by divine spirit to write them down not for themselves but for their people, for their brothers and sisters, whom they love as their own lives and for whom they sacrifice their efforts.
>   . . . Yiddish possesses writers as well as books that have established a good and proper name among their Jewish readers . . . how speedily and how well the people received them and sang them in the salons and in the dilapidated houses, at a celebration, in the company of friends, and in a sad state all alone.[4]

While Dinezon waxes poetic (and Romantic, and populist) about the poet in Yiddish literary culture, he leaves the accomplishments of the Yiddish theatre unmentioned. This might strike the observer as an accidental oversight, if the same erasure of the theatre did not also mark *Shomers mishpet* (*The Trial of Shomer*, 1888), Sholem Aleichem's famous attempt at carving out what is tasteful and appropriate for Yiddish.[5] In his attack on the popular pulp fiction writer Shomer (Nokhem Shaykevitsh, 1849–1905), Sholem Aleichem in fact singled out the theater's founder, Goldfaden, as one of the four finest Yiddish writers—but without a single reference to the twelve operettas he had penned and staged by this point! For Sholem Aleichem, it was Goldfaden's folk poetry alone that earned him this distinction.

Variables beyond aesthetics are also at work in Dinezon's and Rabinovitsh's evaluations. Where good feelings were apparently engendered by Yiddish folk poetry, Yiddish theatre stoked resentment among the acculturated and sophisticated class of Russian Jews for its mocking depictions of Jews. The intelligentsia considered such portraits humiliating and unproductive. The association of the Yiddish theatre with lewdness, display, and deception (alongside their anxieties about the theatre that touched more particularly on their own minority status as Jews) mirrors the "antitheatrical prejudice" that is explored in Jonas Barish's classic work of the same title.[6] Though there was substantial overlap in material between the theatre and folk poetry performance, the latter lent itself to a diversity of performance possibilities; in the tavern, for example, material that played for laughs there took on an earnest tone when presented in the salon—each fit the desires of its particular audience. The parlor audience *imagined* their rough-hewn counterparts recalling and singing anew the songs they heard in their charming *shtetl* taverns—just as Dinezon does. The fantasy of sharing a cultural experience with one's "simple traditional brethren of the shtetl" was itself a large part of the appeal of the folk-poetry experience for its enlightened salon audience. The proceedings of a London-based concert held in 1901 are revealing in this respect:

> Now I must remind you that there are concert rooms in the East End as well as in the West End of London. Yet being composed by Jews, in a Jewish dialect and expressing a Jewish sentiment, [certain "Hebrew" (sic) melodies] fully merit our sympathetic attention. The folk-song of our Jüdisch-Deutsch speaking brethren contains a rich store of beautiful and characteristic melody such as that exquisite last movement in the duet to which we have been listening. . . .[7]

In contrast—when the venue allowed it—the theatre often forced the enlightened audience into an encounter with the actual tavern performer as well as his ragtag audience. They sat in the same theater. Non-Jews were also known to attend (though we do not know in what numbers). The idea that non-Jews might take in a theatre experience and formulate opinions about Jews based on these visits was deeply unsettling for the Jewish bourgeois taste-maker still unsure of his place in non-Jewish society. In contrast, the versatility of its consumption rescued folk poetry from accruing such a bad reputation, and made it the perfect showpiece for the new, modern Yiddish culture. This chapter tracks the rise and fall of Yiddish folk poetry with both the circular question of "folk" and its tavern/salon versatility in mind.

Broder Singers: the Roots of Popular Secular Yiddish Entertainment

Broder Singers, the first secular Jewish entertainers in eastern Europe, began appearing in the first decades of the nineteenth century in the wake of modernizing trends among Russian Jews.[8] In his *Encyclopedia of Yiddish Literature,* Zalmen Reisen singles out Berl Broder Margulies (ca. 1817–1868) as the first known folk poet. An entertainer who hired himself out to tavern-keepers, he is credited with assembling the first traveling troupe of Yiddish performers, who modeled themselves after Viennese café-chanteurs. Itinerant Yiddish entertainers were called Broder Singers possibly because of Berl Broder's prominence among them, or for the city of Brody, where they first performed. By the beginning of the nineteenth century, an increasing number of Russian-Jewish merchants began expanding their business operations, traveling westward to the biannual Leipzig markets. Along the way, they would stay overnight in Brody at lodges with taverns. To attract customers, tavern-keepers provided their patrons with entertainers who performed one-act improvisations, or sang Yiddish songs, sometimes accompanied by a piano or a violin. Competition among increasing numbers of Broder Singers forced them eastward across the border into the Russian empire and Romania, where they found more venues in cities with growing Jewish populations. Although the phenomenon has never been quantified, scholars assert that by the 1850s, Broder Singers appeared regularly in commercial centers as residents or itinerants, spreading their songs among their listeners, swapping materials with other entertainers, inspiring new folk poetry, and all the while attracting new performers.[9]

By the 1850s, Broder Singers expanded their audience beyond traveling merchants. Yiddish entertainers secured acts in the well-appointed homes of wealthy Jews, local wedding halls, and outdoor amphitheatres,[10] but the taverns of country inns, the city "wine cellars," and coffeehouses and tea gardens were their most habitual venues.[11] Odessa, the largest Jewish settlement in the Ukraine, boasted taverns where "the dessert of the Yiddish folksong and vaudeville (vodevil) was a necessity, without which no tavern could exist."[12] As Ashkenazic folk performance evolved, it moved into more sophisticated locations:

When the folk singers found the wine cellar and taverns too provincial, they transferred their performances to the "gardens" (the Yasha Hant-garten in Lemberg, Edelhofer's garden in Vienna and similar gardens in Romania). Amid the greenery, restaurant owners built permanent stages with an orchestra pit on the side (hammered dulcimer, violin, and at times a drum, a clarinet and less frequently a piano). The audience would sit at tables along the avenue.[13]

Berl Broder is also closely associated with the founding genre of folk poetry that is designated by its first line, "Ikh bidne" (I, wretched), in which the singer adopts the persona of various shtetl characters, each of whom describes his or her particular hardships.[14] His routines are evocative of commedia dell'arte's reliance on a stock of "masks," in which the performer relies on exaggerated grimaces and gesticulations to communicate a given persona.[15] In "Dos lid fun dem shames" (The sexton's song), for instance, a synagogue sexton (*shames*) describes the thankless job of waking shtetl residents for morning prayer services:

Ikh krumer shames
Mayn getsayg iz der krumer shtekn.
Mayn lebn vert mir nimes
Az ikh darf uf shteyn vekn.
Far tog iz bay yedn der bester shlof,
Er iz zeyer gezunt un git

Af mir iz oysgegangen eyn gots shtrof
Fun dem tam veys ikh nebekh nit.[16]

(I, hunchbacked sexton
My crooked staff is the tool of my trade.
I despair of my life
When I must rise early to earn a living.
At dawn everyone gets the best sleep
So good, apparently, and so sweet
With God's curse I am constantly faced:
And such sleep I will never taste.)

Although the poem on the page evinces a solemn tone, the historical record shows that the performers played the texts with a sense of irony. We must laugh, for instance, because the sexton's grievance is so trifling—who would imagine that a man who occupies the miserable position of a sexton and abides by the strict dictates of God's law cannot muster more than such a modest longing than to sleep late? Or is his grievance a comment on human nature—the only thing he cannot have is what he wants more than anything? The dominant trait of these sketches is Broder's understated but unequivocal affection for his subject, expressed more explicitly in a folk poetry convention that I call the "poet's declaration of love to his people." In a poem that reveals a poetic persona with something of a modern edge, Broder emerges from beneath his gallery of adopted personae to assure his audience that his ironic depictions mean no offense or condescension:

Ikh broder Berl
Ikh shray tsu ale mentshn.
Hert oys verter vi perl
mit kheyn zol mir got bentshn.

Dos zogt men nokh yeder shtrofe.
Ikh Berl fun brod
Ikh bin di kleynste berye
Ikh dank dir un loyb dir ziser got
fun dir iz mayn yeshue.

Mayne libe gute brider
hert mikh nor tsu
un mayne sheyne lider
un oykh tsu der sheyner melodye.[17]

(I, Broder Berl
I shout to every man.

Hear my pearly words
With charm, may God bless me.

So says every strophe.
I, Berl from Brody
I am the tiniest creature
I thank you and love you sweet God
You are my salvation.

My beloved good brothers,
Listen to me
And my lovely songs
And to the lovely melody, too.)

Broder pleads his modesty with an irrepressible boldness and love for his vocation and the people to whom it is devoted. With an equal measure of exuberance, Broder displays his devotion to God. And he inserts himself into the frame of the poem: "I, Broder Berl," "I Berl from Brody," "I, Berl Broder"—a presence that emerges as another touchstone of the body of Yiddish folk poetry under discussion. The frequent presence of the subject in the poetic text legitimizes the growing role of the individual writer in the modernizing Ashkenazic culture. Thus, the first conventions of the genre materialized.

"Ikh bidne" songs evolved into tableaux or, in Yiddish, the genre of *farshteln zikh* (literally, "masquerading"),[18] a Yiddish performance tradition that required actors to appear in costume even as one was still expected to put on stage make-up (*grimirn*) and perform a kind of pantomime, "which was done in the most primitive ways." The tableaux also implied a more developed sketch or one-act play format that often had a prose portion. A *badkhn* of Zembin, for instance, was most famous for his act as a priest—he would drape himself with a tablecloth as if it were a priest's habit and use the hammer of the dulcimer player for a cross. The instrumentalist Yeshayahu Muravanshik would dress as a peasant woman and together the two performers would play out a scene in which the peasant comes to the priest to confess her sins.[19] A number entitled simply "Der goy" (The Gentile) solidified the reputation of David the Badkhn from Bober: "David would dress up as a peasant, fold his beard, and together with his gait, his movements, and his accent, perform a monologue in which he tried to convey the naiveté, crudeness, and idiocy of a peasant as he tries to explain his visit to a Jewish Passover Seder."[20] Moshe Marekhovski, the Boslever Marshalik, known for his talent for mimicry and his beautiful voice, and who later acted on the Yiddish stage, did a Rip Van Winkle routine in which he acted as if he were just resurrected from the dead and no longer recognized the world he sees before him. The most iconic act—recorded in a number of memoirs and found in many songbooks—played out encounters of

Frontispiece to *Der beyzer marshalik: satirishe folkslider fun Yitskhok Yoel Linetski* (The vexed wedding jester: Satirical folk poetry by Yitskhok Yoel Linetski) features an etched image of a westernized Jew and a religious Jew in a tense encounter. The image is labeled "Dos bagegenish" (the encounter). (From the library of the YIVO Institute for Jewish Research, New York.)

the *daytsh* (literally "German," a common name for a modern Jew) and the Hasid, in which both fall victim in equal measure to the actors' parodying effects.[21]

Sometimes the Hasid and *daytsh* would spar over the proper traditions to follow on Yom Kippur. Israel Grodner, a prodigiously talented Broder Singer, conceived of an act in which cursing between the two characters escalates into a brawl until they reach their limit of violence and break into dance: the "*daytsh* dancing a Hasidic dance and the Hasid dancing a Russian Kamarinsky."[22]

The Classic Folk Poets—Zbarzher, Gordon, and Zunser—and the Earlier Oral Dissemination of their Work

After becoming an established folk poet, Berl Broder was visited by a young maskil named Velvl Zbarzher-Ehrenkrants (1826–1883). This is the only known contact between Broder and the classic folk poets—Zbarzher, Mikhl Gordon (1823–1890), and Elyokum Zunser (1836–1913). All of them acquired a measure of Enlightenment education but differed considerably in temperament. Born in Zbaraz, Galicia in 1826, Zbarzher, a published Hebrew poet by the mid-1850s, discovered his talents as a folk poet singing to friends in a tavern in the Romanian city where he made his living as a tutor.[23] Reputation and word of mouth made his appearances in taverns and private homes a full-time vocation; the esteem he earned among the maskilic literati—despite his reportedly uncouth behavior—was enhanced by his Hebrew publications.[24] Gordon grew up with strong ties to Vilna's Enlightenment intelligentsia—a community that epitomized the Hebrew-centered version of the Haskalah. A good friend of Hebrew poet Mikhah Yosef Lebensohn (1828–1852), Gordon was "der groyser Mikhl" to Lebensohn's "kleyner Mikhl." At age twenty, Mikhl Gordon married the sister of Hebrew poet and publicist Judah-Leib Gordon (1831–1892).[25] On a whim, he began composing Yiddish songs to entertain friends.[26] Elyokum Zunser, also of Vilna, composed works for his performances at weddings as a sophisticated wedding jester or badkhn. Notwithstanding differences among the three men, their folk poetry demonstrates mutual influence and common artistic purpose.

Zunser, the most widely celebrated folk poet and most successful career wedding jester, reminds us that while the very first folk singers wandered eastward into the Russian empire from western cities like Brody, the entertainer was a new and secular version of the existing tradition of the wedding jester.[27] The wedding jester—comparable to "poetry slammers" of our day—improvised songs that might playfully riff on the name of the bride or a remarkable wedding gift the couple received from a prominent guest.[28] He was often the enfant terrible of the community, priding himself on his iconoclasm and often compensated for his work with alcohol instead of money.[29] The persona of the badkhn may also be the point of origin of the Jewish bohemianism that came to be associated with Zbarzher, the patron saint of Yiddish entertainers. The tavern's stage offered the wedding jester a new venue, a reason to expand his repertoire by composing his own poetry or seeking out published songbooks. As Roskies explains, the popular entertainers represented "the appearance of native talent, unencumbered by Jewish learning, pedigree, or ideology who spread good cheer beyond weddings and Purim to the rest of the calendar year."[30]

One genre of folk poetry the classic poets cultivated in particular is philosophical in content and temperament. Although philosophical poetry might have less bearing on the development of the theatre, it enriched the Yiddish folk poetry genre with European conventions and character and a profoundly secular orientation. In his wide-ranging discussion of nineteenth-century Yiddish folk poems, Leo Weiner classified these works as *memento mori* and *memento vivere*, or "reminders of death and life," in which objects became "excuses to meditate on the vanity of life [and] the inconstancy of fortune." In "Der freylekher mentsh" (The contented),[31] the poet considers himself far happier than most men since he is too clever to harbor expectations of happiness that life's experience may disappoint. "I never expected happiness / I accept my fate as it is given / Sometimes the field receives sun, sometimes rain / I never worry and take things as they come."[32] Weaving the same fatalism into many of his poems, Zunser compares life philosophically to a train and to a theatre, exploring the limits of the analogy in fresh and creative ways. Another variation on *memento mori* is "Tsu dem tsen rubl bilet" (To the ten-ruble note), in which Zunser implores his ten-ruble note to reveal the string of narratives that propelled it from hand to hand: "You, ten-ruble note, will you not tell / "What time has made of you? And into which hands you fell / Before you were brought to me?"[33] In a casual and unstrained style, Zunser's ordinary object is infused with an untappable reservoir of human experience. In the poet's hands, however, the ten-ruble note yields its stories, becoming a symbol of the currency and the communicability of the poet's songs themselves. Zbarzher's gold watch, in his poem of the same title "Der goldener zeyger," complains that it must be everybody's slave and is discarded when it can no longer work, while the narrator argues that it complains unjustly, "since it enjoys the privilege of being worn by fine ladies and gentlemen, of never growing old [and] of being clad in gold and precious stones."[34] The common reader took to these songs even when they had little to do with Jewish culture per se, and their composers made no effort to hew to a traditional Jewish worldview. But the poets found that in their native tongue and song, they spoke directly to the experience of their audience. Despite scholars' emphasis on the discomfort maskilim experienced in writing Yiddish, the folk poets' compositions never feel pinched or hampered by the Yiddish language in which they are written, as they tackle new forms and subjects. At the same time, they fulfilled an emerging maskilic imperative to Europeanize Jewish literature.

Of the three, Gordon was the virtuoso composer of *kartines* or sketches, the most elaborately dramatic folk-poetry genre. Much of his work touching on Jewish life employs the entertainer's emblematic audience-pleasing strategy of double-edged meaning that sought to navigate issues of acceptable and unacceptable change. Gordon's popular song "Di bord" (The beard), for instance, presents a traditional Jewish female narrator who implores her husband to tell her what compelled him to shave off his beard: "Did it do you any harm? Did it demand to be fed?"[35] The irony cuts both ways: we laugh at her because she has invested too much significance in his beard, and we laugh with her because she correctly identifies her husband's shaving as an exaggerated gesture of rejection. Gordon's dramatic poem "Der get" (The divorce), penned while he was a bookkeeper for Baron Ginzburg in the progressive Russian city of Poltava, plays out a familiar scenario as it comments on the changing character of the Yiddish language. It describes a traditional Jewish woman who demands that a traveling merchant instruct her wayward husband, Zhargon (a commonly used term for the Yiddish language), to grant her a divorce. "They say that he walks around in a short coat / Gentile fashion, prêt-à-porter / He wears no hat the entire day / And when you speak to him he says 'it is allowed.'"[36] In a cleverly self-reflexive mode, the poem points out that Yiddish has "changed its ways a little" ("*a bisl andersh gevorn*") and argues implicitly that just as the Jew can modernize without the threat of surrendering his overall character, so can the Yiddish language. In the understated mode typical of the folk poet, Gordon emancipates Yiddish and communicates to his audience that the hysterical reaction of the wife is unwarranted.

A poem that indicates its suitability for the stage is "Der litvak" (The Litvak), in which a Jewish Lithuanian (or Litvak), confident that his training in Torah has prepared him for the world, approaches a (probably acculturated Jewish) government contractor for a job:

Otkupshtik. Sholem aleykhem yunger man
Vuhin fort ir, un fun van?

Litvak. Ikh for fun lite, fun gants vayt
Ikh kum aroys fun groyse layt
Ikh bin gekumen tsu zayn a sluzhitil
Ikh vil nor zayn a glavner upravitil.

Otkuptshik. An upravatil, in glavnem kantor
Vi kent ir zayn in dem ershtn yor?

Litvak. Farshteyt ir, ikh bin a ben toyre
Dertsu bin ikh a meyvn, af shnit skhoyre
Ikh vel kenen zayn, in otkup a sluzhitil,
Ikh vil nor zayn a glavner upravitel.

(The contractor. Welcome, young man
Where do you travel, and from where?

LITVAK. I travel from Lithuania, from quite a distance
I was born into an important family
I want to become a civil servant
I shall settle for nothing less than chief governor.

THE CONTRACTOR. How can you become a governor
in the head office in your very first year?

LITVAK. Try to understand, I am a learned man,
And also an expert in dry goods
I could be a civil servant as a leaseholder
But I shall only settle on being a chief governor.[37])

The poem plays on subtle distinctions of class, region, and education that organize the worldview of the young man: the government contractor is aghast at the provincial Jew's attitude of self-importance, which the audience knows he inherited from his native Jewish-Lithuanian culture and merchant class. The poem's macaronic quality attests to the mixture of cultures, modern and traditional, Russian and Jewish, and exemplifies the idiomatic, tongue-in-cheek, and vernacular hue of the genre. Finally, the moral of the tale is the urgency of Jewish adaptability and the need to meet the Russian on his own terms.

To the debate as to whether popular culture is associated with radical expression—the voice of the underclass—or if it reinforces the status quo and is a conservative, tempering force, folk poetry is an example of the latter—at least vis-à-vis Jewish authority. Folk performances occasionally displayed a subversive attitude toward Russian authority, but in general they functioned ideologically to absorb the trauma and challenge of the Haskalah and modernity. Compared to Jewish Enlightenment dramas that promote refined and cosmopolitan lifestyles that depended upon a merchant income, folk poetry could easily be interpreted by a traditional audience as reinforcing the values of the shtetl—or at least not challenging them. By wearing traditional dress and sidelocks, Broder Singers visually communicated to their audience that they shared its worldview. Such visual cues had the potential to mediate or undermine the weight of criticism in a dramatic sketch by Gordon, which were often directed against traditionalists. Even the word badkhn on the songbooks that Zunser began publishing in 1862 renders them "kosher," or non-threatening. The bond of trust itself became the subject of Broder's declaration of love to his audience. In a foreword from one of Zunser's earliest collections, for instance, he offers himself as the target of the audience's aggression: "Stand with humility before pious Jews / Do not be proud toward the enlightened of our people / Do not forget that a wedding jester has created you / And that these days it is he who is hated by both sides."[38] This was the tone and modality of secular—and yet in some ways traditional and conservative—nineteenth-century Yiddish folk poetry.

The Folk Poetry Narrative: *Dos yudele* (*The little Jew*), *Di bord* (*The beard*), *Mikal no'am* (*The staff of beauty*), and the Growth of Highbrow Yiddish Folk Poetry

Zunser's songbooks (which he began publishing later than their oral dissemination in 1862) inspired "a legion of imitators" who fed a full-blown phenomenon of folk poetry publishing that unfolded over the next two decades."[39] According to Ginsburg and Marek's index compiled in 1901 (but which is undoubtedly not comprehensive), in the ten years between 1866 and 1876, Jewish publishing houses in Odessa, Vilna, Zhitomir, and Warsaw cumulatively published around forty such songbooks, and the numbers mounted into the early 1880s. Most resembled the Russian-language *pesenniki*, song booklets also produced at roughly the same time, in part by sophisticated writers emulating naïve folk forms. Like the *pesenniki*, the Yiddish poetry booklets (*bikhlekh*) were "cheaply produced collections of texts from songs that had achieved widespread musical popularity and that often presented the texts as poems, without printed music."[40] The remarkable number of such songbooks published—at a time when prominent Yiddish writers still faced difficulty in publishing longer Yiddish works—had to do, in part, with economics: the songbooks asked little effort of the censor, their diminutive size made them inexpensive to produce and to purchase, and their content appeared less provocative to publishers who worried about sullying their reputation in the eyes of a still pious Jewish mass readership. Multiple reprints of so many of the songbooks, especially those of Zunser, suggest that they were just as important as, say, the chapbooks of Isaac Meir Dik (1814–1893), as a brand of modern literature making inroads into the otherwise conservative Russian-Jewish readership.[41] But the relative accessibility of poetry, and the pre-existing culture of entertainment that the printed songbooks tapped into, inspired other *badkhonim* to publish their work. Eventually, Jewish men from diverse socioeconomic and educational strata wrote folk poetry, engaging in a common desire to entertain and to enlighten through a broadened Yiddish culture. Avrom Fishzon, brought up on the authorless sacred texts of the Jewish tradition, recalls the thrill of penning his first Yiddish rhymes: "There was something about taking the pen in my hand; I felt that I would find what I was looking for."[42] Maskil and badkhn Avigdor Barkhiye Ruf published his clever versified epic *Der shiker: oder di makhloykes tsvishn Reb Trinkman un dem shnaps* (The drunkard: or the debate between Reb Drinker and the whiskey) in 1871.[43] The well-known memoirist Pauline Wengeroff reports that she encouraged the wedding jester Alexander Sender Fidleman to publish his compositions, which he did in 1873 under the title *Shirey asaf* (Songs of harvest). And wedding jesters or folk singers known only as Mordkhe Mane, Peysekh Eliyohu the Badkhn, or Khonen Badkhn also enjoyed the benefits of seeing their songs in print.[44] As Leo Wiener pointed out over a century ago, the songs are some of the first examples of indi-

Cover to *Der shiker, oder di makhloyke tsvishn Reb Trinkman un dem shnaps* (The drunkard: or the debate between Reb Drinker and the whiskey) (Warsaw, 1871). (From the library of the YIVO Institute for Jewish Research, New York.)

vidual poetic consciousness modeled after that of European poets, and were put into practice not by enlightened intellectuals, but by those with little European education.

Folk poetry remained a dominant secular genre of popular literature among eastern European Jews for decades, and as such it suffered all the vicissitudes to which dominant forms are exposed. As Wiener explained it, Zunser's imitators "make no efforts toward innovation and identify themselves as traditional on their works' title page."[45] Linetski reacted harshly to the plunge in literary quality:

> Greetings, poets, song-makers, and badkhonim! What, no thanks for the verse I included in *The Polish Lad*'s wedding? You're not worth the dirt you tread on! You're happy for your rhymes to gush from your shirtsleeves! But do you know how much effort it costs me before I live to craft a proper rhyme? I have since caught on to how you operate: don't bother with the beginning, don't bother with the middle, as long as the end is skillfully crafted. . . . That is your only aspiration! . . . The whole book should be vacant and flat save for the rhyme on the very last page . . .[46]

A sufficient number of poets took the genre seriously enough and, possessing the self-consciousness of literary innovators, continued to express the vitality of the form in their compositions.

Goldfaden was one such innovator in his first folk poetry volume, *Dos yudele* (The little Jew), published in 1866. While the songs of these self-described maskilim evince little self-consciousness of the kind educated men might express in taking up a relatively primitive literary form, the belated print editions of their songs are heavy with self-reflection. Participating in a Yiddish culture that appeared different from a didactic culture from atop but one inspired (if not originating) from the folk, "below," demanded intellectual rationalization in the eyes of its first authors.

In Goldfaden's case, the oral circulation of his Yiddish folk poetry had already earned legitimacy in the world of the crown teachers' seminary in the city of Zhitomir.[47] Although he only collated the songs for his first Yiddish songbook, Goldfaden had published some of them as early as 1862 in *Kol mevaser* (The heralding voice), a newspaper commonly believed to have reached the masses.[48] The cultivation of Hebrew language and literature remained the creative focal point of the seminary's faculty and students, but the output of Yiddish songbooks by seminarians claimed at least an unofficial space in the seminary's cultural life. Fellow student and Hebrew critic Avraham Paperna recalls that alongside the Hebrew poetry that won him the special attention of the seminary instructors, Goldfaden wrote Yiddish songs.[49] Students of the seminary sang them so often that they eventually caught on among Zhitomir residents and carried over to the countryside. He writes, "this is the way Goldfaden, still sitting on the school bench, became a popular and beloved folk singer."[50] Goldfaden was not alone in his attraction to Yiddish folk creativity. During his final year at the seminary (1866), he met the newly appointed instructor, Avrom Gottlober (1811–1899), fifty-five years old at the time, who regularly hosted musical soirées. During the summer months, Goldfaden toured the provincial market towns gathering folk tunes he and Gottlober would later match to their own Yiddish verse.[51] Interestingly, despite Gottlober's commitment to Hebrew, he consistently wrote Yiddish plays, songs, stories, and poems beginning in the 1840s.[52] Along with his colleagues, Goldfaden was also a regular guest at the home of Meir Varshavski, father of Mark Markovich Varshavski (1848–1907), a well-known composer of songs, including perhaps the most famous Yiddish song, "Aleph beys," better known for its first line, "Oyfn pripetshik" ("By the Hearth").[53] With Odessa, Zhitomir was perhaps the most vibrant hub of Yiddish activity in the 1860s.[54] Goldfaden distinguished himself as a promising Hebrew poet and published his Hebrew *Tsitsim u'frakhim* (Blossoms and flowers, 1865) and his Yiddish *Dos yudele* in quick succession.

The blend of maskilic and popular elements of *Dos yidele* makes it difficult to gauge the book's potential audience. Was it intended for his colleagues, perhaps as a challenge to the orthodoxy of the Hebraist Haskalah?[55] Or was *Dos yidele* meant to signify Goldfaden's return to "the people" who had embraced his songs? Perhaps both. Goldfaden's dedication of the booklet (using the Hebraic *seyferl*, rather than the Yiddish *bikhele*) is to his "Loyal and worthy, beloved and dear, mother Khana Rivke," and the affected naiveté with which he designates the book's table of contents ("This is how the songs in this book are called"), suggest that Goldfaden equated Yiddish with a traditional audience. But his footnotes, which include citations from a Russian-language study, seem to target a learned one.

"Dos pintele yid" (The essence of a Jew) refashions the literary convention of "the folk poet's declaration of love to his audience" into something epic in scale and sophisticated—even benignly superior—in tone. It is also a more sympathetic recasting of the Haskalah ideology of which Goldfaden's work became emblematic.[56] If it yields an overarching idea, it is that the irreducible essence of the Jew binds all Jews together, whether *daytsh* or Hasid. And yet, this is offered only tentatively. We are never sure if Goldfaden—responsible for popularizing (if not coining) the term *dos pintele yid* that grew so popular that it became part of the Yiddish lexicon—truly subscribes to it himself. At least there is palpable ambivalence about it in this poem. Goldfaden roams freely into areas of religious folk history and modern history, and intersperses bits of dialogue into the narrative. In its first section, for example, Goldfaden gives voice to a number of characters, including an anti-Semite: "Little Israel? . . . You are still alive? . . . We thought you already died!" and then reassures Yekele, "among noblemen you are just as noble." But the subsequent section repudiates this triumphal tone and proceeds with a traditional jeremiad. "Only woe to the sheep that has strayed from his shepherd / Not just one sacrifice has been brought to your altar."[57] Goldfaden's ruminations on "the essence of a Jew" turn on what he conceives of as the many paradoxes the Jew embodies: persecuted, but also self-persecuting; expelled from every place he goes, but finding his rest everywhere; always entreated, but asking nothing of anyone. But the poem only grazes issues of a philosophical-historical kind, and there is no sense that Goldfaden has worked through the quandary that the poem has marked out.

The "working through" of Goldfaden's radical yet desultory poetic manifesto occurs two and three years later in the works of Gordon and Zbarzher, who articulate a viable ideological bridge to folk poetry in more precise terms. Even if their songs resembled those of Zunser (they were often confused by the public), Zbarzher's and Gordon's introductions to their published work reconceived the station of the folk poet specifically for their cosmopolitan colleagues—something with which neither Broder nor Zunser bothered. Either responding to the interest maskilic audiences already took in the orally circulating Yiddish folk poetry, or following in the footsteps of Goldfaden, Zbarzher and Gordon expanded on their Yiddish literary project by justifying it in Hebrew! Zbarzher and Gordon describe their personal and ideological journey to composing Yiddish verse. They turned to Yiddish verse after shedding many aspects of traditional life and adopting a more modern and bourgeois outlook, from the clothes they wore, to the languages they spoke, to the books they read. In his foreword to the first and second volumes of *Mikal no'am* (The staff of beauty), Zbarzher calls on maskilim to recognize the historical necessity of Yiddish literature and invokes Friedrich Schiller's *Über naïve und sentimentalische Dichtung* (*Naïve and Sentimental Art*, 1845). Comparing his idea of naïve art to the work of the Hebrew poets who try but fail to recapture the ancient artistic sensibility, Zbarzher observes: "their words (*melitsim*) are inadequate . . . they cannot conjure up the immediate realities of our pleasure and delight."[58] Zbarzher explains that literature depends on an audience not only for readers but also to sustain the expressive value of its language. Finally, Gordon's rediscovery of Yiddish, poignantly rendered in his Hebrew introduction to his first Yiddish songbook, *Di bord un dertsu andere sheyne yidishe lider* (The beard and other beautiful Yiddish songs, 1868), is a mystical parable narrated by a collection of songs who have been abandoned by their father.[59] A kind stranger clothes them in fresh white garments and returns them to their father. Before they part, the mysterious man reveals his name to be Ger Dal Mikh, Ani—a Hebrew-Yiddish acrostic of Mikhl Gordon's name that means something like "I am a Poor Stranger." Gordon sees himself at once separated from the songs but as someone who rescues them from their abandoned state and beautifies them with new clothing. The poetic "I," the Jewish people, and aesthetic purity represented in the white clothing are united through an act of paternal kindness. Along with Goldfaden's *Dos yidele*, Zbarzher's and Gordon's discussions of Yiddish are not rationalizations of "a Yiddish literature for the masses," but of a literary culture that is both high-minded and that needs an audience as both a source and target of his aesthetic aspirations.

The songbooks of intellectual authors evidence an interest in certain values of civic society and their poetry tends to be longer and denser. S. Bernstein's songbook "Magazin far yidishe lider far dem yidishn folk" (A store of Yiddish songs for the Jewish people), for instance, included an encomiastic poem by his close friend, veteran folk poet Gordon.[60] S.Y. Abramovitsh's allegory *Dos yidele* (The little Jew) is an epic poem in 4000 verses. Similarly, Linetski's collection *Dos mishlakhes:*

kartines fun yudishn lebn (The plague: tableaux from Jewish life) included his drama *Di vibores* (The elections)—a masterpiece of Yiddish folk poetry. It portrays a group of rough-hewn guildsmen and councilmen exchanging their opinions over drinks in a local tavern about an upcoming election. Although focused on common Jewish workmen and craftsmen, *Di vibores* is so dense and literary, so deft in its depiction of the thick Yiddish street patois—including curse words, Ukrainianisms, and twisted quotations from the Bible—it could not have been intelligible to the majority of Yiddish readers. Moreover, Linetski introduced the work with an essay (obviously directed at maskilim), "Der kurtszeiker shrayber" (The shortsighted writer), that called for an ideologically re-orientated literature that accounted for the dire social and economic circumstances of its readers:

> It is high time we take our eyes in our hand and take a look at ourselves! Enough with the Hasid, with the small-shtetl community member (*balebos*), calling on them for good institutions, and to arrange reforms in their communities. Every community member, pitiful members of one or another guild, runs around night and day with a headache and a heart ache to pull together a scrap of bread for his wife and children and with his sweat and tears he manages only a half a bite . . .[61]

A poem in the deceptively sophisticated songbook of Zhitomir seminary graduate Moshe Danzig (1830–1906), *Di litvetshke: farsheydene yidishe lider af prost yidisher shprakh* (The litvak woman: a variety of Yiddish songs in Yiddish, 1870) turns its lens onto maskilic cultural life. The rather oddly titled "Der kukuk," for instance, describes the exchange between two maskilim who avidly follow the literary activity of the Hebrew poets: "Mr. Star hurried from Vilna / And Mr. Kukuk met him / Welcome Mr. Star! How are you, brother? / What's the word on Gottlober's *Splendor to the Sons of Perception*?" Mr. Kukuk proceeds to inquire after the reception of Avraham Dov Lebensohn's 1867 play *Emet ve-emunah* (Faith and truth) and the Hebrew poetry of Y. L. Gordon.[62] Adopting the popular trope of a casual meeting between two Jews, Danzig blends the faux-naïf mode of the folk poet with references to high-minded Hebrew poetry. Goldfaden's Yiddish imaginative world began with *Dos yudele,* to whom he strained to make himself intelligible, but maskilim eventually envisioned themselves in their Yiddish work, a transition that reflects how much they integrated the Yiddish language into their cultural life, and how much the poetry was directed at themselves and not just "the little Jew."

Conclusion

Folk poetry survived as folksongs for generations, but the tavern culture that generated it faded quickly.[63] Yiddish performance sprang from the folk poets and performers, replacing the tavern and absorbing its actors, musicians, and audience, and contributing to the cultivation of a more sophisticated audience that grew more curious about Russian, German, and Polish theatre. Following attempts by the Russian government to limit performances of the Yiddish theatre after 1883, opportunities to see Yiddish performances grew more scant.[64] It seems, anyway, that neither audience nor actor returned to the tavern. By the close of World War I, when actor Yitskhok Turkow-Grudberg began to research the folk poetry culture for a play to be based on Goldfaden's life during his pre-theatre years, he could cull information only from the memories of a few elderly men.[65] "If only you could have been here some twenty years ago," Linetski had said to Granovsky about the vibrant performance culture in Odessa by the turn of the century.[66] In a sense, we see in the folk poetry culture a brief era in which all the stars aligned, so to speak: high culture was in sync with low culture, performance was in sync with print. Neither was a perfect reflection of the other, but each worked off the other's energy, as each dimension met with some measure of commercial success. Two Yiddish cultures grew up alongside one another—the one of the salon and the one of the tavern—and the "openness" between them was policed by creative operations and excisions that ultimately transformed or re-packaged the works as they traveled from one side to the other of the invisible divide. Not surprisingly, these changes were unconscious when traveling from "high" to "low" and fraught with consciousness when traveling from "low" to "high." Broder Singers, traveling entertainers, and moonlighting choristers pillaged the work of the highbrow intelligentsia, and maskilim elevated "the little Jew" into literary masterpieces.

Notes

1. European composers had been setting poetry to melodies inspired by folk music of their particular countries since the eighteenth century; the trend became more popular throughout the nineteenth century. They intended art songs for performance before smaller gatherings for which opera did not allow. For a discussion of the art song, see A. L. Bacharach and J. R. Pearce, eds., *The Musical Companion* (New York: Harcourt Brace Jovanovich, 1977), 473–490.

2. For a detailed social portrait of the popular singer in Paris, see Charles Rearick's "Song and Society in Turn-of-the-Century France," *Journal of Social History* 22 (Autumn 1988): 45–63. On *pogrebki*, see Robert Whittaker, "The *Ostrovskii-Grigor'ev* Circle, alias, the 'Young Editors' of the *Moskvitianin*," *Canadian-American Slavonic Studies* 24 (Winter 1990): 385–412. I am grateful to Barbara Henry for pointing out this article to me.

3. Y. L. Cahan, *Yidishe folkslider mit melodyes fun Y. L. Kahan; tsunoyfgenumen un fun dos nay aroysgegebn durkh Maks Vaynraykh* [Yiddish folk poetry with melodies by Y. L. Cahan; collected and reprinted by Max Weinreich] (New York: YIVO, 1957). Folklorist Yehuda Leib Cahan (1881–1957) collected variants of many of the songs that were first produced by folk poets and that with time, were folklorized. My argument here is not that there is no such thing as a Yiddish folk song but that this is (if not entirely) a separate phenomenon from "folk poetry." For scholarship on the Yiddish folk song, see, as well, Eleanor Gordon Mlotek's learned article, "International Motifs in the Yiddish

Ballad," in *For Max Weinreich on His Seventieth Birthday; Studies in Jewish Languages, Literature, and Society* (The Hague: Mouton Publishing, 1964), 209–228.

4. Jacob Dinezon, "Di yidishe shprakh un ir shrayber" [The Yiddish language and its writer], *Hoyzfraynt* [Home companion] 1 (1888): 12–13, 16.

5. (Berdichev: Jacob Sheftil). See Justin Cammy's annotated translation, *The Judgment of Shomer*, in *Arguing the Modern Jewish Canon: Essays in Honor of Ruth R. Wisse* (Cambridge, MA: Harvard University Press, 2008), 129–185.

6. See Jonas Barish, *The Antitheatrical Prejudice* (Berkeley: University of California Press, 1981).

7. F. L. Cohen, "Hebrew Melody in the Concert Room" in *Jewish Historical Society of England* 2 (1894–1895): 12.

8. My account draws from a variety of sources including "Broderzingers un folkzingers" in Zylbercweig, *Leksikon fun yidishn teater* [Encyclopedia of the Yiddish theatre] (New York: Farlag Elisheva, 1931), 1:216–236.

9. The Broder Singer's itinerant nature was one of his distinguishing features, in contrast to wedding jesters, Purim jesters, or cantors, all of whom were relatively more local and settled.

10. Nokhem Oyslender draws attention to an announcement he discovered in three consecutive issues of the *Varshever yidishe tsaytung* [Warsaw Jewish newspaper] of 1867 that advertise a performance by Broder Singers in a garden café called the Bavaria. See "Varshever mekhabrim in di 50er-60er yorn" [Warsaw writers in the 1850s and 1860s], in Chone Shmeruk and Chava Turniansky, eds., *Yidishe literatur in nayntsntn yorhundert: zamlung fun yidisher literatur-forshung un kritik in ratn-farband* [Nineteenth-century Yiddish literature: A collection of Yiddish literary research and criticism in the Soviet Union] (Jerusalem: Magnes, 1993), 244.

11. Soviet historian A. Margolies published statistics of Jewish liquor-lease holders in the year 1849 that show hundreds of drinking establishments owned by Jews in the city of Berdichev alone. It is impossible to say how many existed, but a typical reference to their "ubiquity" is the following: "When Velvl Zbarzher . . . declaimed and sang his songs in the tea-houses and in the rich private homes . . ." Shlomo Bickel, *Rumenye: geshikhte, literatur-kritik, zikhroynes* [Romania: history, literary criticism, memoirs] (Buenos Aires: Poalei Zion Farlag, 1961), 103. Similarly, Fishzon describes all the men he dined with as "frequent spectators of the shows that regularly played in the restaurants and wine-cellars." Avrom Fishzon, "Fuftsik yor yidishe teater" [Fifty years of Yiddish theatre], *Morgn zhurnal* [Morning journal], February 13, 1925. References to specific cities and even names of such wine cellars, mostly in memoiristic literature, include Brody, Leipzig, Kremenchug, Vienna, Jewish-populated cities of Romania, Berdichev, Nikolaev, Warsaw, and Odessa.

12. Y. Reminik, "Di ershte trit funem yidishn teater" [The Yiddish theatre's first steps], *Der hamer* [The hammer], February 1928, 52.

13. Jacob Mestel, *Undzer teater* [Our theatre] (New York: YKUF), 13. The prospect of a better livelihood drew choristers and cantors to join the ranks of the entertainers and perform in private homes. See, for instance, M. Teplitski, "Zikhroynes fun mayn lebn" [Memoirs of my life], *Literarishe bleter* [Literary pages] (September 8, 1931), 45. Eventually, these performers moonlighted in the taverns where, in order to remain competitive, they avoided synagogue music for "more secular and piquant songs." See E. Lifschutz, "Merrymakers and Jesters among Jews (Materials for a Lexicon)," *YIVO Annual of Jewish Social Sciences* (1952), 44.

14. He eventually collected his songs and tableaux in *Shirey zimra* [Songs] (Zhitomir: Y. H. Baksht, 1865).

15. See B. Gorin, *Geshikhte fun idishn teater* [History of the Yiddish theatre] (New York: Literarisher farlag, 1918), 144–149, and Wiener, 80.

16. Berl Broder, *Shirey zimra* [Songs] (Warsaw: Y. Unterhendler, 1882), 16–17. The collection (not the original edition) is subtitled, "Thirty authentic Broder songs in pure Yiddish, each song sung

beautifully for every class of men. One learns from them much wisdom, they express accurately the character of everyone and they are of great amusement to read."

17. Ibid., 40–41.

18. Rubin, *Voices of a People*, 258.

19. Zylbercweig, *Leksikon,* 1:136.

20. Zylbercweig, *Leksikon,* 1:135.

21. Linetski's *Der beyzer marshalik* [The vexed wedding jester] has an illustration of the *daytsh* and a traditional Jew on its cover—one of the few illustrated title pages among the songbooks. See my appendix for a sampling of songbook covers.

22. Israel Berkovitsh, *Hundert yor yidish teater in rumenye 1876–1976* [One hundred years of Yiddish theatre in Romania, 1876–1976] (Bucharest: Kriteryon, 1976), 31.

23. Before turning to Yiddish, Zbarzher published twice in Hebrew: *Kokhevey yitskhak* [Stars of Isaac] (1848)—an adaptation of a fable—and *Khazon le-mo'ed* [The time has come] (1855), a collection of anti-Hasidic satirical songs. His fame was widespread in Moldavia and Bessarabia, where he performed. Shlomo Bikel, *Yahadut rumenye* [The Jews of Romania], trans. K. A. Bartini (Tel Aviv: Lahav, 1978), 64–65. His most famous Hebrew poem is about a pogrom in Romania. It was published in *Ha-shakhar* [The dawn], the journal of Hebraist maskil Peretz Smolenskin, a friend of Zbarzher who helped support him financially and who lamented his devotion to Yiddish. For more biographical information, see Khane Mlotek, "*Velvl Zbarzher: tsu zayn hundertstn yortsayt*" [Velvel Zbarzher: on the hundredth anniversary of his death], *Tsukunft* 89 (January–February, 1983): 1.

24. See Mlotek, 2 and Roskies, 95–97. Zbarzher's appearances drew audiences mostly from the communities of Romanian or Polish "Ostjuden" of Vienna. On Saturday nights, Zbarzher would play the popular Edelhoffers Tavern in Vienna, which later became a Yiddish theatre venue in the 1890s. See *Naye tsayt* [New times], April 5, 1924.

25. Reisen, *Leksikon*, 1:511.

26. Jacob Shatzky quoted in Zylbercweig, *Leksikon*, 2:129. Poets like I. L. Peretz and Shimon Frug singled out Gordon's work as a particular inspiration in their own writing, while critic Shmuel Niger argued that even Gordon's propagandistic poetry achieves great clarity and concentration of expression. Niger, "Fun tsaytungen un zhurnaln" [From newspapers and magazines], *Bikher velt* [Book world] (Warsaw: Kultur Lige, 1923), 411. For more on Gordon, see Mlotek and Mlotek, *Perl fun der yidisher poezye* [*Pearls of Yiddish Poetry*] (Tel Aviv: Farlag Y. L. Perets, 1974), 18–19 and M. Pines, *Di geshikhte fun der yidisher literatur* [The history of Yiddish literature] (Warsaw: B. Shimin, 1911), 101–115. For biographical details on Gordon, see Dinezon's memoirs published in "Di ershte yidishe drame" [The first Yiddish drama], *Pinkes: a fertlyoriker zhurnal far yidisher literaturgeshikhte, shprakhforshung, folklor un bibliografye* [Pinkes: a quarterly journal on Yiddish literary history, language research, folklore, and bibliography] 2 (1929), 145–167. Dinezon and Gordon were childhood friends.

27. Zylbercweig discretely catalogues some twenty "jesters" who performed at weddings and later in the theatre, and forty "Broder Singers and folk singers" who mostly performed in taverns and sometimes composed original material. But the categories, in practice, were very fluid. See *Leksikon,* 1:216–236 and 1:132.

28. See Ariela Krasney's *Ha-badkhan* [The wedding jester] (Ramat Gan: Bar-Ilan University, 1998). For a literary representation of the badkhn, see the last scenes of Aksenfeld's 1840s drama *Man un vayb, shvester un bruder* [Man and wife, sister and brother].

29. See Lifschutz, 44. On their social status, see S. M. Ginsburg and P. S. Marek's introduction to *Evreiskaya narodnaya pesnya v Rossii* [The Jewish folksong in Russia] (St. Petersburg: Redakstiya "Voskhoda," 1901), x–xv.

30. Roskies, 94.

31. Wiener was the first to apply this term to these songs. Zunser was very fond of this genre. See *Elyokum Tsunzers verk: kritike oysgabe* [Elyokum Zunser's work] (New York: YIVO, 1964), 72–93.

32. Velvl Zbarzher, "Ikh hob keyn mol af glik geklert / Ikh bin tsufridn vi es iz mir bashert / Dem feld iz a mol di zin a mol regn git / Ikh nem oykh on vi mir iz, ikh zorg keyn mol nisht." *Mikal no'am (ha-khadash)* 3 [The (new) staff of beauty], 123. Zbarzher published his works in Yiddish with a Hebrew translation in four volumes under the complete title, *Mikal no'am: kolel shirey am (folks lider) be-lashon ha-meduberet ben ha-yehudim be-artsot polin le-moldoviya im he'ateket lashon ivrit* [The staff of beauty: including folksongs in the vernacular of the Polish and Moldavian with Hebrew translation] (Vol. I, Vienna: Berl Luria, 1865; Vols. II–IV, n.p.: Lemberg, 1869, 1873, 1878).

33. "Du, tsener-bilet, kenstu mir nit zogn / Fun der tsayt, vos me hot dir gemakht? / Vosere hent hobn dir ibergetrogn / Biz me hot tsu mir gebrakht?" *Elyokum Zunsers verk*, 1:250–252.

34. Wiener, 78.

35. Mikhl Gordon, *Di bord un dertsu andere sheyne yidishe lider fun a groysn khosid* [The beard and other beautiful Yiddish songs from a great Hasid] (Zhitomir: Shadav, 1868), 22–24.

36. Ibid., 24–25.

37. Ibid., 60–63.

38. Elyokum Zunser, *Kol rina* (Vilna: Dvorzets, 1867), 8.

39. In the absence of sales records from this period, a book's popularity may be judged by a print run, since printers were very conservative, had a "print on demand" approach, and tried hard to anticipate the number of buyers for the hundred copies printed. Although we have little publishing information to rely upon, a list compiled by Sholem Aleichem in "Bibliografye: a rester fun ale zhargonishe bikher vos zaynen opgedrukt inem yor 1888" [Bibliography: A roster of all the Yiddish books that were published in the year 1888], *Folksbibliotek* [The people's library] 2:137, shows that Zunser, over two decades into his publishing career, was outdoing most of his Yiddish-writing maskilic contemporaries. Wiener confirms that the badkhonim were "the most potent factors in the dissemination of the songs of the [maskilic folk poets] long before they were accessible in printed form" (Wiener, 92).

40. Thomas P. Hodge, *A Double Garland: Poetry and Art Song in Early Nineteenth Century Russia* (Evanston, IL: Northwestern University Press, 2000), 244. On the upswing in literacy within the general Russian population, see Jeffrey Brooks's *When Russia Learned to Read: Literacy and Popular Literature (1861–1917)* (Princeton, NJ: Princeton University Press, 1985; rpt. Evanston, IL: Northwestern University Press, 2003).

41. On I. M. Dik, see David Roskies's chapter on him in his book *A Bridge of Longing: the Lost Art of Yiddish Storytelling* (Cambridge, MA: Harvard University Press, 1995), 56–98. "Ayzik-Meyer Dik and the Rise of Yiddish Popular Literature," Ph.D. thesis, Brandeis University, 1975.

42. Avrom Fishzon, "Fuftsik yor yidish teater," Oct. 17, 1924.

43. Avigdor Barkhiye Ruf, *Der shiker: oder di makhloyke tsvishn Reb Trinkman un dem shnaps* [The drunkard: or the debate between Reb Drinker and the whiskey] (Warsaw: Tipografiya Yu. Lebenson, 1871). Ruf's dates are unknown. He was active on the literary scene through the 1850s and 1860s. I am grateful to Eddy Portnoy for bringing this work to my attention.

44. Including reprints of his songbooks, Mordkhe Mane the Badkhn published eight songbooks between 1872 and 1877. See *Bibliograficheskii ukazatel'* [Bibliographical guide], in Shaul Ginsburg and Peysakh Marek, *Evreiskie narodnye pesni v Rossii* [Jewish folksongs in Russia] (St. Petersburg: Voskhod, 1901), i–xiv.

45. Wiener, 93.

46. *Dos mishlakhes: kartines fun yudishn lebn* [The plague: tableaux from Jewish life] (Zhitomir: n.p., 1875), 6.

47. A song found among his papers by scholar A. R. Malachi is marked, "my first song written at Zhitomir, 1859." In a story he told David Zilberbush, Goldfaden referred to Yiddish songs he penned

as a child which were then sung by an apprentice in his father's workshop. See his article, "Goldfadn materyaln" [Goldfaden materials], *YIVO Bleter* [YIVO journal] 1946 (XV): 328–351.

48. *Dos yudele: yudishe lider af prost yudesher shprakh* [The little Jew: Jewish folksongs in the simple Yiddish language] (Zhitomir: Boksht, 1873). This is an important point to keep in mind when exploring the influence of the earlier folk poets on Goldfaden. Zbarzher began publishing his work only two years earlier (in Lemberg) and Zunser published his first work in the same year as Goldfaden. There is no doubt that their songs had gained substantial currency long before they were published.

49. See Shatzky's separate inventory of his songs in his general inventory, "Goldfaden's shafn" [Goldfaden's creations], in *Goldfaden-bukh* [Goldfaden book] (New York: Jewish Theatre Museum, 1926), 84–85. Shatzky also drew up a separate inventory of a collection of Goldfaden's poetry in manuscript (found relatively late) that includes their publication information, information on discrepant versions, as well. "An Unpublished Collection of Goldfaden's Poems" [Yiddish], in *Hundert yor goldfadn* [Goldfaden: A centenary], ed. Yankev Shatski (New York: YIVO, 1940), 95–106. Oyslender discusses one of these early poems, "Der marsh fun meshikhn: a troym-bild" [The messiah's steps: A dream scene], (dated to December 14, 1865, Zhitomir and published in *Kol mevaser* in 1870) in the Birobidzhan-based *Forpost* [Wagon post], 2 (1938): 99–105.

50. "Di ershte yidishe drame," [The first Yiddish drama], *Pinkes*, 2 (1929), 187–188.

51. S. L. Tsitron, *Dray literarishe doyres* [Three literary generations] (Vilna, Warsaw: S. Sreberk, 1922), 314. The popularity of the songs Gottlober adapted or reshaped was still in evidence in Russia thirty years later. See Z. Suditski, "Vegn folk iberarbetungen fun gotlobers lider" [On folk adaptations of Gottlober's songs], in *Di yidishe literatur in nayntsntn yorhundert* [Yiddish literature in the nineteenth century] (Kiev: Melukhe-farlag far di natsyonale minderhaytn in U.S.R.R, 1935), 289–304.

52. Zinberg, *The History of Jewish Literature*, trans. and ed. Bernard Martin, (Cleveland, OH: Press of Case Western Reserve University, 1972–1978), 160. See Zinberg for a biography of Gottlober and other biographical sources, 158–169. On Gottlober's creative bilingualism, see Shmuel Verses's *Ben lashon le-lashon* [Between language and language] (Jerusalem: Magnes Press, 1996).

53. Mark Varshavski became a lawyer and, for many years, did nothing more with his compositions than sing them to pass the time on the train. When Sholem Aleichem discovered his talents through a friend, he ushered Varshavski's work to publication. See his introduction to *Yidishe folkslider* [Jewish folksongs] (New York: Hoypt Ferkoyf, 1918). They also toured together; Sholem Aleichem performed his monologues and Varshavski sang and played the piano. See Nakhmen Meisel's *Noente un eygene: fun Yankev Dinezon biz Hersh Glik* [Our own: From Yankev Dinezon to Hersh Glik] (New York: YKUF, 1957), 35–53.

54. The Hebrew publishing house in Zhitomir in the 1860s and 1870s published many of the Yiddish songbooks under discussion. See the index of original publication provided by Ginsburg and Marek, "Bibliograficheskii ukazatel'," *Evreiskie narodnye pesni*, i–xiv.

55. The status of Hebrew and Yiddish for Goldfaden and his colleagues is a complex question that does not yield simple answers. An introduction to an edition of *Tsitsim u'frakhim* (Cracow: Bedefus Yosef Fisher, 1892) in which Goldfaden rejects Hebrew for Yiddish as a move from maskilic elitism to an embrace of the common folk, seems to resolve this question: "The spirit of the new is upon us and we must set our gaze on languages of nations that are living today and not to resurrect the dry bones [of Hebrew] and to tell this dead language 'Live!' when it has no breath in its midst." But it is problematic since it was only published as an introduction to the 1892 edition of his Hebrew work, not its initial run in 1865. Whether or not Goldfaden simply thought twice of publishing it in 1865 or wrote these words to retroactively capture his sympathies renders them unreliable as historical testimony.

56. Shmuel Niger describes Goldfaden as the first to express an unfettered nationalist impulse in his poetry. "The superstition, the orthodoxy, the silly traditions, the fanaticism, and all the other reli-

gious issues that claimed such an important place in the Hebrew Haskalah literature—Goldfaden has little interest in." Shmuel Niger, "*Di lider fun Avrom Goldfadn*" [The poetry of Avrom Goldfaden], *Tsukunft* 3 (March 1926): 150–154.

57. *Dos yidele*, 8.

58. *Mikal no'am*, 3:49.

59. Gordon published this songbook under the pseudonym "a great Hasid." *Di bord un dertsu andere sheyne yidishe lider fun a groysn khosid* (Zhitomir: Shadav, 1868), 4–5.

60. This collection enjoyed four reprintings, in Warsaw in 1880 and 1884, and in Berdichev in 1888 and 1891.

61. *Dos mishlakhes*, 50–51.

62. *Di litvetshke: farsheydene lider datsu eyn lid "Di litvetshke"* [The Lithuanian Jewess: a variety of poems including one entitled "The Lithuanian Jewess"] (Odessa: Beilinson, 1870), 31–33. A year earlier, Danzig published the songbook *Der litvak: farsheydene lider datsu eyn lid "Der litvak"* [The Lithuanian Jew: a variety of poems including one entitled "The Lithuanian Jew"] (Odessa: Beilinson, 1869); I have not been able to locate a copy of it.

63. The first generation of folk singers—Broder, Zbarzher, and Gordon—died in relative obscurity. See Roskies, Chapter 6. For folk poetry of the 1880s, see Wiener's chapter, "Poetry in the Eighties in Russia."

64. See John Klier, "'Exit, Pursued by a Bear': Russian Administrators and the Ban on Yiddish Theatre in Imperial Russia," in Joel Berkowitz, ed., *Yiddish Theatre: New Approaches* (Oxford, UK: Littman Library of Jewish Civilization, 2003), 159–174.

65. Zygmunt Turkow, *Shmuesn vegn teater* [Conversations on the theatre] (Buenos Aires: Unzer bukh, 1950), 167. Turkow appeared in a three-act comedy entitled *Di broder zinger* that depicted the interaction of the folk singers with shtetl residents and actual acts by the most famous folk singers, like Yankevke der Vilner, Moyshe Taykh, Moyshe Kop, and those whose fame would grow even greater when they became actors on the Yiddish stage, like Finkel, Grodner, and Goldshteyn. *Di broder zinger* was composed by poet Yisroel Ashendorf and musician Shloyme Prizament in 1938, and performed the same year in Lemberg. Turkow assisted in collecting historical materials about Broder Singers in small shtetls and even stumbled upon a tavern that still had Brodersinger-like performances.

66. See his book of memoirs about the famous author, *Yitskhok Yoel Linetski un zayn dor, derinerungen: tsu zayn hundert yorikn geburtstog* [Isaac Joel Linetsky and his generation, memories: On his 100th birthday] (New York: Farlag "Kolegn," 1941).

CHAPTER 3

Jacob Gordin in Russia: Fact and Fiction

Barbara Henry

A man stands aboard a ship bound for New York and gazes at the wintry, gray Atlantic. Sea winds whip the blackening clouds, waves crash against the hull of the old steamer and flood its decks with sheets of icy water. But the man grips the railings, eyes fixed on the horizon. The persecution he has suffered, the silencing he has endured, the sacrifices he has made for his ideals will not have been in vain. His eyes are alight with hope for the possibilities that await him on the other side of the sea, far from his Russian homeland.

This man is not Jacob Gordin.

This is not the "reformer" of the American Yiddish stage, whose plays excited and enraged hundreds of thousands of theatergoers and set off torrents of debate in the Yiddish press. This is not Jacob Gordin, the tireless social activist, journalist, and educator. This man is not Jacob Gordin, but he'd like you to think that it is.

The hero of *Der shvimender orn* (The floating casket, 1892) is a Russian Jew bound for New York on the steamship *Devonia*.[1] But there the similarities end. Gordin's literary creation has devoted his life to the cause of Russian revolution. He has suffered censorship, arrest, exile, and the distrust of both his own people and those whose liberation he serves. Health broken but spirit unbowed, Gordin's hero sets off for America, but dies en route. His body is put in a wooden casket and set upon the waves, final resting place unknown.

Gordin's story appeared in the inaugural issue of *Di tsukunft* (The future) in 1892 as "Di shvimende trune (a fantazye)."[2] Despite the parenthetical title, the tale draws deliberate parallels between the life of its hero and that of Yakov Gordin—a Russian writer with rumored revolutionary connections, lately become Jacob Gordin—a Yiddish writer with rumored revolutionary connections. The story is one of the earliest articulations of Gordin's fictive biography, and while it veers widely from the historical record, in one respect it remains true to the circumstances of the writer's immigration. The passage from Russia, a journey across water with mythic connotations of transformation and rebirth, did mark the death of one Jacob Gordin, and the birth of another.

But who was Yakov Gordin before he became Jacob Gordin? The latter's elision of the former was so successful that the specifics of his life and work in Russia have largely eluded four biographers: names are garbled, dates uncertain, events muddled and occasionally fabricated.[3] Clarification was hindered for most of the twentieth century by Soviet-era restrictions on Jewish research, but the mystery of the first thirty-eight years of Gordin's life also reflects his own efforts to shape the narrative of his Russian past into both a story of origins and a blueprint for the future. That future, as a quasi-socialist intellectual and splenetic "reformer" of the Yiddish theatre, derived its authority in part from the reputation that Gordin had earned as an activist, journalist, and prose writer in his native Russia. The usual accounts of this career, however, are both strikingly uniform and surprisingly sketchy, and offer little beyond the naming of a few newspapers and some dark mutterings about Russian censorship.

What was the nature of Gordin's life and literary work in his homeland? Was he really fleeing tsarist persecution? Or was he, as his detractors argued, eager to hide something in his past?[4] What connection did Gordin's Russian writing have to his Yiddish drama? This chapter assesses Gordin's work as a prose writer and journalist in his last decade in Russia, when many of the formal and thematic preoccupations that informed his Yiddish dramaturgy and journalism took shape. It also examines the circumstances of Gordin's emigration—both actual and poetic—which provided a key element in his dramatic method. The very process of creating a fictional past—of imposing creative control on events and individuals by rendering them as a literary narrative—helped to shape Gordin's playwriting strategy itself. The malleability of all texts—personal, sacred, literary, historical—and their eternal availability for revision and renewal is a leitmotif of all Gordin's Russian and Yiddish writing, and was fundamental to his playwriting method.

When Gordin arrived in New York in July of 1891, he was already a mature writer with short stories, one novel, and innumerable journalistic credits to his name—and to those of his many pseudonyms. Whether traveling the Pale of Settlement as "Yakov Mikhailovich," castigating scenery-chewing actors as "Yan," reporting on local elections as "N. N.," or strolling the sunny streets of Odessa as "Ivan Kolyuchii," Gordin employed a multiplicity of contrasting voices that echoed the combustive diversity of southern Russia itself. The Gordin whose voice is familiar from the Lower East Side newspaper and theatre worlds—advocating realism, women's emancipation, and armchair socialism in tones that ranged from the magisterial to the irascibly magisterial to the witheringly magisterial—is less marked in Russian. In short stories, feuilletons, theatre reviews, parodies, travelogues, and editorials, the Russian Gordin can be mercurial, ferocious, melancholy, and often hilarious. In his Russian writing, Gordin gives full vent to his reservations and embrace, distaste and defense, love for and frustration with his native people and his native land.

Indeed, the protean and contradictory nature of Gordin's Russian writing makes it challenging to extract a consistent view of either the writer or the positions for which he argued. Gordin's Russian writing is fractured, heterogeneous, and polyphonic. He inhabits personalities Russian, Ukrainian, and Jewish; humorous and solemn; satirical and earnest; peasant, middle class, and intellectual. While this literary strategy indicates a natural talent for playwriting, the elusiveness of Gordin's own biographical voice suggests that this play of "masks" is also a kind of blind, one that permits a freer negotiation of the otherwise fraught borders between Russian and Jewish worlds. Indeed, the difficulty of maintaining these multiple literary identities becomes increasingly evident in Gordin's writing in the late 1880s and early 1890s.

Although Gordin's biographers credit him with a writing career that began in the 1870s, articles that can be confidently ascribed to him date only to 1881, when he emerged controversially in public view.[5]

The occasion for Gordin's notice in 1881—both by the press and the tsarist police—was as the founder of the Spiritual-Biblical Brotherhood (Dukhovno-bibleiskoe Bratstvo), in the city of Elisavetgrad (today Kirovohrad, Ukraine).[6]

A quasi-religious sect that dreamt of establishing its own agrarian commune, the Brotherhood was dedicated to the reform of Jewish economic and religious life. This was to be accomplished by a return to what they believed was an ancient, biblical Judaism, before rabbinic tradition had "distorted" the faith. The Brotherhood's preference for Jewish antiquity was paralleled by a belief that only by returning to the land could Jews restore the dignity that had been theirs in biblical times. The Brotherhood urged Russian Jews to abandon "exploitative" commercial occupations, and take up "productive" labor like farming instead.[7]

The Brotherhood's arguments were not particularly original. Karaite Jews, who based their religious practices and textual interpretation solely on the Tanakh, had rejected the Talmud at least as early as the eighth century.[8] In addition, the Brotherhood's "back to basics" approach and insistence on reconciling Judaism with modernity, reason, and science, differed little from the emphases of the Berlin Haskalah. Even the Brotherhood's practical recommendations for reform of Jewish economic life echoed the humane utilitarianism of the Haskalah in its Germanic incarnation. A profound sympathy for Christianity, especially for Protestant rationalists' insistence on returning to the early scriptural foundation of the faith, also informed the Brotherhood's thinking on the "Jewish Question." Because the Brotherhood managed to merge the liberal Jewish establishment's view (that Russian Judaism was ripe for reform) with those of the tsarist government (that mercantile Jews exploited Christians, and that this was condoned by the mysterious Talmud), the Brotherhood might have found sympathy with any number of institutions.[9] Any good will that either the liberal Jewish community or press might have borne Gordin's fledgling movement evaporated, however, in the summer of 1881.

It was then that Gordin published an intemperate "Letter to Russian Jewry" only two months after the start of the devastating pogroms of the spring of 1881[10] (see the appendix to this chapter). This monumentally insensitive letter excoriated Jews for provoking Christian violence, and although Gordin would deeply regret having published it, the damage was done.[11] For the next decade, he was locked in an antagonistic relationship with the Jewish public and press. Both regarded the Brotherhood as being more intent on currying favor with the tsarist government and earning privileges for themselves than with any larger program for Jewish renewal.[12]

A significant portion of Gordin's writing from this period cannot be separated from his activities on behalf of the beleaguered Brotherhood. Even when Jews are not the explicit object of a work's interest—as in one of Gordin's earliest works of fiction, "Tipy shtundistov" (Stundist types), written for St. Petersburg's *Nedelya* (The week) in 1884—the Brotherhood is the implicit subject.[13] The Stundist stories offer Gordin a vehicle for making veiled criticisms of his own rabbinical opponents through an exploration of the power of dissident faiths to challenge conventional spiritual and secular powers.

Stundism was a Christian evangelical movement that had its roots in the faiths of German Lutherans and Mennonites who immigrated to the Russian empire in the late eighteenth century. Stundist sects varied in their emphases, but were typically hostile to ritualized worship and clerical hierarchies, eschewed alcohol and tobacco, and earned their livelihood by agriculture or artisanry.[14] Gordin's own high regard for the sober, literate Stundists is well documented, and his admiration is plainly evident in "Tipy shtundistov."[15]

Gordin prefaces the stories with a note that points to their existence somewhere between his characteristic mode of fact and fiction, observation, and invention:

> Having had the opportunity to observe personally the evolution in southern Russia of the Stundists—the quintessence of Russian dissidence—I wished to acquaint the reader with those types who are most inclined to be drawn to the beliefs of Stundism. With that goal I have conceived an entire series of short sketches. In each sketch I offer the brief characteristics of the given individual, and attempt to capture the moment in his life when a striving towards something different, something new, is born in him. It seems to me that even given the artlessness of my essays, they are not devoid of a certain interest.[16]

The narrator himself, "Yakov Gordin," assumes the role of a scholarly outsider, gathering information for his readers but remaining something of a cipher himself. While his surname makes clear to Russian readers that the narrator is Jewish, the Ukrainian-speaking Stundists take him for an intellectual of gentle birth, and address him using the Polish honorific, *pan*. Gordin's narrator shifts easily between the roles of Russian observer and Ukrainian translator, tour guide and voyeur, and between peasant testimony and his own commentary.

The first story, "Ivan Chaika," concerns the spiritual awakening of a devout Russian Orthodox believer, who still manages to spend a good portion of his life at the local tavern. There he meets a Stundist orphan girl, Paraska. One night, Ivan pauses before her window and sees her praying. The sincerity and simplicity of Paraska's prayer exposes all of Ivan's rituals and expensive icons for what they are—a performance of piety that conceals the vacuity of his beliefs. Struck by the purity of Paraska's faith, Ivan converts, and weathers further crises with the help of his Stundist brother-in-law. They read the Bible and remain firm in their faith, which empowers them to seek their own answers in the sacred text.

Another convert, Okhrem Chilchuk, joins the Stundists after a life of crime. After the murder of his partner—of which he is, by implication, guilty—Chilchuk falls prey to a fever worthy of Dostoevsky's homicidal Raskolnikov. One winter night there is a knock on the door; it is a neighboring Stundist, bearing a worn copy of the New Testament. In a scene that recalls Raskolnikov's reading of the Bible with the saintly prostitute Sonia, Chilchuk and the Stundist read the Gospels together. The candle burns late into the night in the hut. Today, as the narrator tells us, Chilchuk is upstanding and sober.

The most accomplished Stundist story concerns a retired military man, the eponymous Panas Pantilimonovich Tolyupa, who is introduced with something like stage directions:

Panas Pantilimonovich is a retired non-commissioned officer, a sailor in the Black Sea fleet. He served in the Crimean campaigns and was awarded distinguished medals for bravery. His face is stern and oval, and elongated by a pair of scraggly dark brown sideburns, which look as if they were stuck onto his emaciated cheeks.[17]

Tolyupa lives on a pittance with his wife and is locked in an eternal battle with the government to secure a better pension. He observes all of the arbitrary bureaucratic regulations, makes pilgrimages to the district administrators, and submits petition after petition to gain audiences with officials of ever higher rank. The tsarist bureaucracy, which masks the state's indifference to the fate of little men with arcane ritual and capricious demands for sacrificial offerings, is clearly a secular arm of the official church itself.

Tolyupa is finally given leave to petition St. Petersburg directly; but when he receives a negative answer months later, he is unperturbed, for he has undergone a conversion. In the midst of his frantic petitioning, Tolyupa took a train trip that led him to an isolated stop, a *polustanok*—shorthand for "existential nowhere." There a stranger gave him a copy of the New Testament, which Tolyupa then read for the first time.

As with the previous story, this one also evokes a classic work of Russian literature, Alexander Pushkin's *Stantsionnyi smotritel'* (*The Postmaster*), from *Povesti Belkina* (*The Tales of Belkin*, 1830). As in Pushkin's story, the "road" plays a crucial role—both the actual road that Tolyupa treads in fruitless pursuit of temporal justice, and the metaphoric one that leads him to the lonely station that is the site of his rebirth. The road's prominence suggests that it is Tolyupa who is the prodigal returned "home" to the Stundist creed. His faith in the Orthodox church falls by the wayside as he abandons his case with the state that is its ally.

In terms of Gordin's development as a writer for the theatre, the penultimate Stundist story is the most intriguing. The titular Antip Bosoi is a miller—a suspect profession because it depends upon the labor of others for its own profit. Bosoi spends his idle hours seeking out entertainments, what the narrator calls "scenes" (*stsenki*). Folk tales, epic songs, dancing, popular tunes, and even barroom brawls are Bosoi's only real interest in life.[18]

When hiring his thresher out to a Stundist village, Bosoi begins to attend their prayer meetings out of idle curiosity. Though initially impressed with the passion and simplicity of their service, after a year their "scenes" begin to bore him, and Bosoi leaves.

While the Stundists do not appeal to lowbrow audiences like Bosoi, they themselves are not without art and music: Gordin is at pains in each Stundist story to highlight the prominence that hymns and congregational singing play in attracting members to the creed. Their spiritual songs take the place of popular ditties, and spiritual reading supplants pagan folktales and fantastical epics. Gordin implies a strict artistic hierarchy, with preference for the functional over the "merely" entertaining. In this, he appears to have much in common with distinctions that Lev Tolstoy will draw in *Chto takoe iskusstvo?* (*What is Art?*, 1897), between "good" art (useful, spontaneous, and comprehensible) and depraved entertainments that merely satisfy our lust for aesthetic pleasure and distraction. This is not a distinction, however, that Gordin upholds with any regularity elsewhere. Indeed, his championing of the corrective, edifying forces of art is confined almost exclusively to works that relate to the Spiritual-Biblical Brotherhood's ideals, and is markedly absent elsewhere. Gordin's Russian writing tends to compartmentalize the ethical and the entertaining, while his Yiddish plays strive to merge the two.

Gordin's last "Stundist" story addresses a theme that emerges with particular force in Yiddish dramas such as *Safo* (1900) and *Elisha ben Avuya* (1906)—that of the radical visionary who is rejected and expelled by the community for refusing to conform to repressive custom. "Petr Kukuev and Roman Kirichenko" relates the conflict of the former, an intolerant military man, and the latter, a peaceful, conciliatory peasant. Kukuev is arrogant, but is respected in the community for his superlative knowledge of the Bible and the tidiness of his home. Yet Kukuev's chief delight is in censuring his brethren for their interest in "frivolous" subjects like natural sciences. Roman Kirichenko's call to respect reason and science as also being God's creation invites Kukuev's wrath. The story ends with Kirichenko tearfully taking his leave of the community.

The story is less about Stundism than it is a repackaging of the criticisms that Gordin's Spiritual-Biblical Brotherhood made of rabbinic Judaism. The hidebound Kukuev is an Orthodox rabbi in Stundist clothes. Although respected for his encyclopedic knowledge of sacred texts, he does not live by what he professes. Maintaining outward order in his own affairs but despising those of lesser learning, Kukuev uses his erudition as a weapon. Roman Kirichenko is an idealized stand-in for the Brotherhood's reformers—he objects to Kukuev's tyranny, but does so with measured criticism, appeals to reason, and eloquent pleas for understanding and love. When Kirichenko objects to the sect's departing from its own founding beliefs, the anti-ritual crusader is shown the door. He departs, and the reader must infer that his loss will ultimately be a greater one for the community that must make its way without him.

The transparency of Gordin's allegory of the conflict of his sect with the arbiters of rabbinic Judaism highlights the crucial role that his Russian fiction plays in the proselytizing schemes of the Spiritual-Biblical Brotherhood. For a sect that frequently disseminated its views through the press, fiction had a necessarily productive function. Because of this, stylistic and thematic elements familiar from Gordin's Yiddish plays—an irrepressible didacticism, intertextuality, the centrality of the "book," the treachery of one's "own," a distaste for unproductive art as well as unproductive work—are also marked in this early story cycle. Poised between invention and reportage, the stories offer a fluid exploration of the blurred lines that divide fact from fiction and fiction from propaganda.

"Tipy shtundistov" also highlights Gordin's intense concern with the processes of self-transformation, represented as spiritual awakenings, edification, *embourgeoisement*, and immigration, with occasional forays into the supernatural. But as interested as Gordin is in human beings' attempts to exceed their origins and limitations, whether social, intellectual, or physical, he is even more interested in their failure to do so.

The short-story cycle "Evreiskie siluety" (Jewish silhouettes, published between 1885 and 1891 in *Nedelya*'s prestigious literary supplement, *Knizhki nedeli* (Booklets of the week), is typical of Gordin's fixation on the urge towards self-transformation. The stories vary greatly in quality. In addition to lyrical and sensitive portraits of Russian Jews caught between Slavic and Jewish worlds, "Evreiskie siluety" also includes programmatic, Judeophobe caricatures of Jews as exploiters and social climbers. The stories speak of a deeply conflicted and divided loyalty to Jewish culture, which makes agonizing claims on Jews who are drawn to the Slavic Christian world around them.

Failure typically attends the efforts of the characters in "Evreiskie siluety" to conceal or downplay their origins in the hope of integrating into Russian society, as the irremediable fact of Jewishness can never be obscured or denied for long. Gordin's Jews are typically undone in abrupt and public turns of events: a humble Jewish mother's embarrassing appearance at a fancy party, a schoolyard taunt that reveals a hidden ethnic identity, a murderous pogrom mob that finds a convert not quite Orthodox enough. Gordin's Jewish characters' "gentility" is insubstantial and impermanent, an illusory performance that frequently yields fatal results. While traditional Jewish piety is never advocated for Gordin's Jewish characters, neither is conversion an option, and apostates invariably meet nasty ends. All measures are temporary, conditional, and subject to violent revision, and only the rapprochement of the Spiritual-Biblical Brotherhood's approach to faith and economics would appear to offer any safety. An enlightened community of rational individuals composed of Jews and non-Jews alike is the only refuge from the arbitrary terrors of Russian-Jewish life.

Both "Tipy shtundistov" and "Evreiskie siluety" are more polished and ideologically consistent than the writing that comprised the majority of Gordin's Russian work. Most of his writing was done for the regional *Elisavetgradskii vestnik* (The Elisavetgrad courier) and *Odesskie novosti* (The Odessa news). In many respects, Gordin's writing for the periphery is superior to that of the center, for he is a gifted sketch artist, skillful at turning out evocative and energetic outlines that capture the movement and vitality of his subjects. Gordin's more premeditated Petersburg stories tend to bring out his most ponderous tendencies.[19]

It was with the *Elisavetgradskii vestnik* that Gordin enjoyed his longest professional association. From mid-1885 to June of 1886, Gordin contributed regularly to the Elisavetgrad paper; from June of 1886 to late summer the following year he spent much of his time in Odessa and contributed almost daily to *Odesskie novosti*. Thereafter Gordin returned to Elisavetgrad, and seems to have been running the *Elisavetgradskii vestnik* almost single-handedly until mid-summer, 1890, when his bylines gradually disappear from the paper.

The reason for Gordin's disappearance in 1890 may well be connected with the retirement of Kherson *gubernia* governor Alexander Semyonovich Erdeli in early June 1890.[20] While not quite the imperial protector of legend, Erdeli was a popular governor of decidedly liberal cast, who had, in 1885, shown Gordin apparent favor by authorizing the legalization of the Spiritual-Biblical Brotherhood.[21] In 1891, the *Elisavetgradskii vestnik* itself ceased publication; its demise may well have figured in Gordin's decision to immigrate to the United States in June of that year.

Gordin's best-known literary creation for the provincial press was "Ivan Kolyuchii" (Ivan the sting), who made his first appearance in 1886. He was typically credited with theatre reviews, satirical feuilletons, humorous editorials, parodies, and the occasional travelogue.[22] The comic personae of Ivan Kolyuchii and his shadow-twin, "Alfei," are quite distinct from other pseudonyms used by Gordin, each of which was keyed to a particular journalistic form.

Editorials and crusading denunciations of regional woes were the province of "Yakov Mikhailovich" and "Yakov Gordin," whose prolix, stentorian tones are echoed in much of Gordin's Yiddish journalism. These two voices are largely interchangeable, and are charged with reporting on local politics and regularly deploring the condition of transportation in Kherson province. These are Gordin's only Jewish literary personae, and their comparative verbal reticence stands in marked contrast to the freedom and whimsy enjoyed by the ethnic Russians Ivan Kolyuchii and Alfei.

The classically anonymous Latin letters "N. N." and "N." are attached frequently to Gordin's stories for *Knizhki nedeli*, and to a motley variety of local news articles and opinion pieces for the *Elisavetgradskii vestnik*.[23]

"Yan," whose name "I am N" alludes to these other literary identities, is a theatre reviewer and rarely ventures beyond the confines of Melpomene's and Thalia's temple. Yan is a rigorous critic with an encyclopedic knowledge of European and Russian drama, and is sharply disapproving of actors, writers, and entrepreneurs who forget that they serve the muses first and mammon second.

One of the last of Gordin's pseudonyms to emerge is that of "Evpatii Kolovrot," who appears first in August, 1889, and has his last outing in February, 1890. This short-lived creation is a boor who cares only for food, drink, money, and parties. Kolovrot's moronic reports on lavish dinners, sleazy business dealings, and Elisavetgrad social events are some of the bitterest columns Gordin crafted. As a concentration of the very worst vices of middle-brow Russian society, Kolovrot testifies to a darkening tone in Gordin's Russian writing, and to a mounting frustration with the insular character of provincial Russian life. Curiously, though, Kolovrot also points to a parallel expansion in Gordin's range of literary voices. Kolovrot's preening and prurient tone is communicated through a rich use of slang and sickening diminutives, which had previously found little expression in Gordin's work. Kolovrot's wheedling and knowing asides, his absolute conviction that satisfying the senses is the sole purpose of life, would re-emerge in dramatic villains like Joel and Vladimir Trakhtenberg, the malevolent libertines of *Khasye di yesoyme* (Khasye the orphan, 1903).

Yakov Gordin, Man of the Theatre

The *Elisavetgradskii vestnik* served a city that was an important commercial center with a population that was estimated at around 60,000, almost a third of it Jewish.[24] Although the newspaper enjoyed a reputation for liberal sympathies, it seems to have gone to some length to avoid creating an impression of its favoring Jewish readers.

Typical of the paper's reluctance to endorse Jewish interests was its disinclination to review Yiddish plays, although advertisements and a column of Gordin's own suggest that Yiddish theatre was common enough in Elisavetgrad, even after the May Laws of 1882 restricted its performance.[25] Even though a Yiddish touring company took out a large, front-page advertisement in the paper for its final performance of Goldfaden's *Shulamis* on October 15, 1887, the *Elisavetgradskii vestnik* declined to review it. In an editorial decision that has just the whiff of a snub, the paper offered instead a lengthy discussion of a puppet show.[26]

Acid reference to Goldfaden appears in a travelogue for the *Odesskie novosti* that same year by "Yakov Mikhailovich," who reported on a Jewish widow, Esther Polinskaya, who was paid by the city of Elisavetgrad to foster a number of orphans. Her care was substandard, and the city filed a lawsuit against her. Gordin's article disparages Polinskaya's haute-bourgeois home décor, ungrammatical Russian, pretentious friends and dubious musical taste for "the *great* works of the grand master—Goldenfaden [*sic*]."[27]

Further evidence of distaste for Yiddish theatre appears in a feuilleton of January, 1889, in which "Ivan Kolyuchii" takes a moonlight stroll around Elisavetgrad. Pausing by the Kuzmitsky theatre, the city's principle venue, he notes its philo-Semitic tendencies:

> There are no Sunday matinees for general audiences, but on Saturdays there are . . . Well, no doubt the theatre administration means well. But why stage only *The Jewess, Rachel, Joseph the Magnificent, Haman's Ear*? I suppose it'll get to the point that it'll be more *interesting* to have plays with titles like *The Patriarchs and the Circumcision, Moishe and the High Holidays, Rivke and the Gefilte Fish* . . .[28]

Ivan Kolyuchii's dismissal of the artistic potential of Yiddish theatre—even as he evinces enough knowledge of it to parody its repertoire—contrasts sharply with the sympathy and critical interest he lavishes on popular Ukrainian-language theatre, then getting its start in Elisavetgrad.[29] Indeed, both Yan and Ivan Kolyuchii offer dozens of lengthy reviews and analyses of the Ukrainian theatre, and Gordin himself enjoyed friendly personal relations with the first company's actor-manager, Mark Lukich Kropivnitsky (1841–1910).[30] Popular Ukrainian theatre suffered many of the same problems as Yiddish theatre of the period—official repression, stringent censorship, and a lack of playwrights and repertoire—but Gordin's reviewers seem not to have seen any parallels between the two.[31]

Misgivings about Jewish theatre are extended to Jews in the theatre, in a review by Yan of a Russian-language production of *The Merchant of Venice* in December of 1888. Among the vast audience for the play, Yan sees Elisavetgrad's own Jewish moneylenders, and wonders if they are here for the same reason that Socrates was reportedly drawn to watch a play in which he was mocked by Aristophanes:

[. . .] to laugh at himself and to remedy his failings—if the comedy offer just evaluation of those failings. Can our usurers have come with this goal in mind? I confess that no matter how I try, I cannot find traits in common between the Jew of Venice and our Elisavetgrad Shylocks.[32]

Yan's view of Shylock is a sympathetic one.[33] In the Venetian moneylender he sees:

[. . .] a strong, pensive man, whose love of money proceeds from recognition of its power and might. It can provide a measure of security for the inequity of his existence, it can humble his enemies and vanquish his persecutors. He treasures every kopeck because he sees financial capital as an instrument of vengeance, and not just a means of obtaining the pleasures and conveniences of life.[34]

Yan will not grant Shylock's noble rage at injustice to the Jews of Elisavetgrad, however. Shylock's human dignity is pushed beyond endurance—but as for the local Jews:

Our Shylocks already know how to get what they need out of life; their way of life costs society dearly, because they desire only to avail themselves of all the pleasures and comforts achieved by man in our enlightened age. It is neither anger nor a sense of vengeance that guides them, but pursuit of easy profit; they do not strive for strength and might, for these are of no material consequence; it is not insulted human dignity that speaks in them, for they are ready to subordinate and humiliate themselves further still for the sake of money. . .[35]

Yan's remarks recall the Spiritual-Biblical Brotherhood's accusations that Jews' "exploitative" professions were at the root of their suffering in Russian society. But his preference for a sympathetic, wronged Shylock is at odds with the functional and instructive view of art advanced in "Tipy shtundistov." That Yan should prefer a noble Shylock indicates just how far Gordin's literary personae diverge both from each other, and from the didactic preferences of their creator.

These divergent opinions are so marked a feature of Gordin's Russian writing as to affect even the appraisal of realism in the arts. Although the advancement of stage realism is a campaign with which Gordin is most famously and fractiously identified in the American Yiddish theatre, realism as an artistic mode is found sorely wanting by Ivan Kolyuchii. Of an 1889 production of Tchaikovsky's opera, *Evgenii Onegin*, Ivan sighs:

Realism has already conquered one region of the arts—it holds near-absolute sway in creative literature—and we have already more or less made our peace with this. But to allow it to enter the lofty realm of the plastic arts, into the realm of wondrous sounds and harmony, would be just too much. Give mankind a chance every now and then to remove himself from this vulgar and senseless life. Let him escape with the poet to the cloudless heights, to a world of fantasy and imagination. Just for a moment, let him glimpse a life poetic, colorful and lavishly appointed. Instead of customary vulgarity and coarseness let him see noble images and marvelous visions. There is too much prose already in the lives of men.[36]

It is difficult to reconcile Ivan Kolyuchii's remarks with those of Gordin the Yiddish playwright, who declared that under proper tutelage, his American audience would come to "expect from the drama not a gilded falsehood but the real, bare truth of life."[37] Indeed, the very multiplicity of the pseudonyms created by Gordin—Ivan Kolyuchii the flâneur, Yan the romantic idealist, Alfei the clown, Kolovrot the vulgarian, Yakov Mikhailovich the stern Jewish voice of reason— is symptomatic of the porousness of identity that Gordin's writing addresses. But verbal, formal, and ethnic fluidity appears to come at no small price. The frequency of violent endings and tragic compromises in "Evreiskie siluety" among Jewish characters who attempt to cross boundaries and blur identities suggests the inherent danger of the exercise. But the cost to a writer who sustains half a dozen different distinct narrative voices also seems to be increasingly taxing, if Gordin's columns in the summer of 1889 are to be judged as evidence.

At this time, the Spiritual-Biblical Brotherhood received a much-needed injection of cash due to the contributions of two new members, Isaak Fainerman (1863–1925) and Anatolii Butkevich (1859–1942).[38] Acolytes of Lev Tolstoy, Fainerman and Butkevich had the financial support of one of Tolstoy's most impassioned followers, Arkadii Alekhin (1854–1918), who organized one of the first Tolstoyan agrarian colonies on his estate of Shevelovo, in Smolensk province in 1889.[39] With Alekhin's support, the Brotherhood hoped to finally purchase land of its own for an agrarian commune. Gordin, however, wanted to focus the organization's energies and resources on a workshop that the Brotherhood had recently opened in Elisavetgrad, for training young Jews as artisans. He was also less than excited about the increasingly Tolstoyan cast that the Brotherhood's teachings were taking, and had many personal conflicts with the outspoken Fainerman.[40]

Perhaps because of these complications, the fault-line between the many professional roles that Gordin played—as religious activist, editor, journalist, and creative writer—began to emerge.

A two-part article by Ivan Kolyuchii in June of 1889, entitled, "Dovol'no! Dovol'no!" (Enough! Enough!) finds Ivan at a circus performance. Despite his distaste for the circus' "repulsive" exploitation of animals and child performers, Ivan is inexplicably drawn to the "disgusting, appalling" show.[41] It's like alcohol, muses Ivan: something to deaden the senses, escape from the pressures of work.

Because for public figures like Ivan, who "give everything to what they believe in," he has little to show for it:

> This is our misfortune, that every avenue of social action is blocked to us. No matter what the scope of your vitality, what kind of overwhelming strengths you sense in yourself, no matter how wonderful and lofty your strivings, however honest and noble your convictions—you will not overcome the apathy that surrounds you. You will not inspire the confidence of others—those who believe only in a life of force, the power of the whip, the sincerity of fools and cretins, and the capacities of mediocrity . . .[42]

Ivan is a lonely bachelor and has only his work for comfort, which he characterizes thus:

> What are the duties of a clown? He presents our reality in somewhat exaggerated form, he offers an occasionally successful parody; he bravely shades and underlines our own weaknesses and the ridiculous aspects of our lives. Society forgives him his rude mockery because it is for their pleasure that he turns somersaults, falls to the ground, gets slapped, rubs his nose in the dirt, takes kicks and blows.[43]

Ivan Kolyuchii's feuilletons grow increasingly opaque, and the veiled complaints about life in Elisavetgrad and the futility of action continue. But still he tries to rally: in an address to his fellow writers, Ivan cries: "Do not be frightened by the indifference surrounding you, do not take people for impenetrable battleships, do not let their apathy seem insurmountable."[44]

But the mood grows steadily bleaker. In a "Letter to readers," in December of 1889, Ivan Kolyuchii effectively describes Gordin's own use of varied literary personae, and offers a clue to the strategy behind it. Their multiplication is not described, of course, as a response to official censorship, which is often the source pinpointed by Gordin's biographers. Rather, the proliferation of pseudonyms is treated as a kind of elaborate fan dance to attract a reader's attention:

> In order to please you, to make you hear us out, to pique your interest, attract your attention, our literary fraternity employs various ways and means. Some of us appear before you dressed as jesters; some clown and play the fool for you, others drape themselves in the togas of moralists, a third will appear in the garb of a prophet, a fourth in the role of a popular trendsetter. . . They all have but one goal—to please you, to gain your approval.[45]

But now Ivan wonders if his own efforts and those of his literary fraternity have had any effect. He notes, "tomorrow I will depart the stage, to be replaced by another, and you won't even notice my absence—it makes no difference to you whether I've fallen ill, or died, or succumbed to some misfortune, whether I am silent for a short time or forever."[46] Perhaps his writing only temporarily disturbs the "stagnant and fetid swamp" of his surroundings, and all the frantic energies of his and these other "representatives of the printed word" are doomed merely to create eddies that dissolve into nothingness.[47] Ivan cannot reconcile himself to a life of passivity: "There is no intelligent human life outside of ideas, outside of progress, outside of hope for a better and brighter future."[48]

In the ensuing months, Gordin's articles appeared infrequently in the pages of the *Elisavetgradskii vestnik,* and vanished altogether by mid-1890. Less than a year later, the newspaper itself ceased publication.

There is no arrest order for Yakov Gordin in his police file. On the contrary, six months passed before the tsarist police even noticed that he had left the country. It was not until February of 1892 that an order was circulated for Gordin's arrest—should he try to return to Russia.[49] The police, it seems, were only too happy to have Jacob Gordin leave Russia; their only fear was that he—an official annoyance, whose decade-long surveillance had netted the regime nary a single antigovernment plot or conspirator—would return.

The absence of an official arrest order does not mean that Gordin would not eventually have run afoul of the police, who had, after all, stepped up observation of the Brotherhood since Isaak Fainerman joined its ranks. But the absence of any evidence that Gordin was under threat, coupled with the fact that members of the Brotherhood who actually *had* violated tsarist law were never arrested either, suggests that neither Gordin nor his followers were ever under any threat whatsoever.[50] Nor was Fainerman, who had a lengthy police file, or Butkevich, who actually had served prison time on two separate occasions, threatened either. Well after Gordin's emigration, the former members of the Spiritual-Biblical Brotherhood continued to live in Ukraine, where some of them established a successful dairy collective.[51]

The closing of the *Elisavetgradskii vestnik,* difficult economic conditions in southern Russia itself after two years of failed harvests, the splintering of the Spiritual-Biblical Brotherhood, and the increasingly despondent tenor of Gordin's writing suggests that creative and economic factors, and not political ones, motivated his leaving Russia.

What did he leave behind? Gordin left a fractured literary persona, and a selective literary assimilation into Russian culture. Fiction and journalism had been the principle vehicles through which Gordin crossed borders, blurred distinctions, and eluded the limitations imposed by faith, class, and ethnicity. It was through fiction that he would manage one more self-invention when he reached New York. It would be the most successful of all: when Yakov Gordin became Jacob Gordin, Yiddish playwright, journalist, and tireless cultural activist on the Lower East Side.

The half-dozen personae inhabited by Yakov Gordin, Russian writer—Ivan Kolyuchii, Alfei, Yan, N.N., Evpatii Kolovrot, and Yakov Mikhailovich—did not die on the passage to America, but were themselves transformed. They were reborn in plays that relentlessly try to resolve fractures in families, customs, languages, and cultures through recourse to the accelerated action of plot, and the corrective forces of psychological realism. Jacob Gordin's becoming a Yiddish playwright was the logical outlet for the literary style that he developed as a Russian writer. For it was only there, on the Yiddish stage, that the many divided identities and loyalties that Gordin created and explored might be reconciled—if not in fact, then in fiction.

Appendix

Jacob Gordin, Letter to the editor, *Yuzhnyi krai* (Southern border), and reprinted in *Russkii evrei* (The Russian Jew) 27, July 2, 1881: 1042–1047.

Brother Jews!
Each of us probably knows that in order to rid oneself of a hellishly painful toothache the most appropriate course of action is to pull the ailing tooth out by its roots. In order to deaden this harsh pain, doctors destroy the nerves. . .

We Jews have a moral sickness that causes us more pain, torment, and suffering than the very worst physical ailments: our evil habits, which are deeply ingrained in our life.

You have seen, my brothers, what kind of horrifying dramas have played out in recent days before your very eyes; how mercilessly and vilely they have mocked your property, and more importantly, your human dignity. You have seen how defenseless, isolated, helpless, and despised by all you are: no one took pity on you; no one extended a hand of friendship. . . Unfortunate brothers, do not think that I have the ill intention of rubbing salt in your wounds only in order to call forth new agonies; do not think that this is not painful to me as well. Woe is me! I am pained for you, and because of you. . . Did not my heart bleed when I saw you—insulted, degraded, beaten, robbed, expelled from your homes? Could I be calm when you, my brothers, blood of my blood and flesh of my flesh—were in boundless grief? But what happened has passed, and you, my brothers, should think about the future. Consider—why does no one respect you, or love you, or pity you. The lowest levels of Russian society wait only for an opportunity to fall upon you; the merchants would like to see you torn to pieces; and the aristocracy look upon your fall with indifference. Why have these different segments of Russian society, which have no obvious common interests, hate you with such unanimity and like-mindedness? Can it really be only religious hatred? Our greed for money, our insatiability, cupidity, pursuit of profit, our importunacy, abrasiveness, our inordinate strutting and extravagance, our slavish and stupid imitation of the arrogant and unbridled Russian gentry, our usury, tavern-keeping, middle-man dealings and all our other misdeeds cause the Russian people to take up arms against us; they rouse the envy of the merchants and the contempt of the ruling classes. Certainly there are among you people who are honest, hard-working and modest in their desires, but they are lost amid the mass of swindlers who day and night think of nothing but money and profit and have no other interests or needs in life.

The sad events of recent days give me the right to remind you, brothers, that now is the time to extract the rotten teeth with which you have bitten others, and which have again and again caused you unbearable pain and suffering. My dear brothers, your nerves, the nerves of your everyday affairs and occupations have been destroyed for a time; gather your courage and pull these rotten teeth—usury, bootlegging, middle-man dealings and all other exceedingly dishonest and immoral pursuits—from your mouth once and for all, and make of yourselves honest, industrious people, who live their lives in such a way as to render the least harm to others. Remember the words of our great singer of Psalms: "a man who is wealthy but not wise is like a beast that asks for forgiveness."[52] I know that now you are in despair, bitter, pained; that you suffer. . . Come to us, beloved brothers, come! Impatiently awaiting you is a spiritual family of good, tender, and receptive people. Come, our arms are outstretched and words of comfort await you from God's own sacred Torah (holy texts). We love you passionately and sincerely, although sometimes we speak the bitterest truth, because you are our brothers and we wish with all our heart and soul to comfort, calm, and soothe you. Believe that in our brotherly bosom you will find ease! Because where—where else, can you hear words of comfort and edification?

You will say that we, the spiritual biblists, are few in number, that we are unknown, without wealth or power. Yes, now there are few of us, but we are rich in spirit, strong in our striving towards better things, powerful in our feelings and known for our good aspirations. We wish to serve not Moloch, but God's truth and the brightest, highest reason. Brothers, can it really be that this God comforts you not, and will not reward you a hundredfold with spiritual and moral wealth?

I call to all of the noble and vital forces of Jewry with this entreaty: brothers, awaken! Take up the good cause! Serve your people! With a brave hand throw off the accretion of centuries! Enough of pale tradition's gleaming, enough boasting of your senile solidity; better we draw from the fresh and life-giving source of modern life; better we be fresh, healthy, morally flourishing people! Renewal, renewal! Give your people what life, time, science, and mankind's duty demand! Give them firm moral convictions and rational beliefs, and with these you will return to them spiritual peace, and elevate them in the eyes of those closest to them. . .

A Biblical Brother

Notes

1. Gordin embarked on the *Devonia* in Glasgow, Scotland, and arrived in New York on July 27, 1891. (*New York Passenger Lists, 1820–1957*. Year: *1891*; Arrival: *New York, United States*; Microfilm serial: *M237*; Microfilm roll: *M237_572*; Line: *41*; List number: *1112*. Provo, UT: The Generations Network, 2006). Available online through Ancestry.com (accessed October 17, 2005).

2. "Di shvimende trune (a fantazye)" [The floating coffin (A fantasy)], *Tsukunft* 1 [The future] (January 1, 1892), 44–47. Reprinted, with altered title, in *Yankev gordins ertseylungen* [Jacob Gordin's stories] (New York: The International Library Publishing Co. 1909), 2, 197–204.

3. There are accounts of Gordin's life in Russia in Kalmen Marmor, *Yankev Gordin* [Jacob Gordin] (New York: YKUF, 1953) and Zalmen Zylbercweig, *Di velt fun Yankev Gordin* [The world of Jacob Gordin] (Tel Aviv: Hadfus "Orli," 1964). Both Marmor and Zylbercweig are generally very good on the organization of Gordin's Spiritual-Biblical Brotherhood, but confused on Gordin's fiction

and journalism in Russian. Beth Kaplan's biography contains valuable family information; see *Finding the Jewish Shakespeare: The Life and Legacy of Jacob Gordin* (Syracuse, NY: Syracuse University Press, 2007), 8–33. See also Melech Epstein, *Profiles of Eleven* (Detroit: Wayne State University Press, 1965), 135–158; Bernard Gorin, *Di geshikhte fun idishn teater* [History of the Yiddish theatre] (New York: Literarisher farlag, 1918); Yitskhok Turkow-Grudberg, *Goldfaden un Gordin. Eseyen un biografyes* [Goldfaden and Gordin. Essays and biographies] (Tel Aviv: "Urli," 1969); Morris Winchevsky, *A tog mit Yankev Gordin* [A day with Jacob Gordin] (New York: M. Mayzel, 1909); Zalmen Zylbercweig, *Leksikon fun yidishn teater* [Encyclopedia of the Yiddish theatre] (New York: Farlag "Elisheva," 1931), 1:392–461. See also Gordin's own discussion of how he became a Yiddish playwright, "Erinerungen fun Yankev Gordin" [Reminiscences of Jacob Gordin], *Di idishe bine* [The Yiddish stage] 1, (1897), unpaginated; and *Suvenir tsu Yankev Gordins tsen-yerikn yubileyum* [Souvenir of Jacob Gordin's ten-year anniversary] (New York: 1901), 3. The last has the most complete listing of newspapers and journals in which Gordin published.

4. The Russian-born rabbi and popular East Side lecturer Zvi Masliansky's (1856–1943) memoirs, *Maslianskis zikhroynes: fertsig yor lebn un kemfen* [Masliansky's memoirs: Forty years of life and struggle] (New York: Farlag Zerubavel, 1924) reportedly refer to Gordin's Spiritual-Biblical Brotherhood as a "new Christian sect." (Zylbercweig, *Di velt fun Yankev Gordin,* 89.) The description is echoed in the conservative press's accusations against Gordin; Nina Warnke notes that in 1901, "In order to vilify Gordin further, the conservative *Tageblatt* [Daily paper] accused him of having founded a sect in Russia in order to 'convert Jews to Christianity,' a reference to his Biblical Brotherhood which rejected all Rabbinic texts and advocated Jewish farming. In fact, the paper claimed, he had to flee to America because incensed Jews drove him out of Russia and now he continued his destructive work among the immigrants." ("Reforming the New York Yiddish Theater: The cultural politics of immigrant intellectuals and the Yiddish Press, 1887–1910," Ph.D. thesis, Columbia University, 2001, 168). Moyshe Leyb Lilienblum (1843–1910), who knew Gordin in Odessa, and was his most ferocious antagonist in the old world, did not cease his repudiation of Gordin even after the latter's death. For a discussion of Lilienblum's remarks on Gordin in "Iberige shvokhim" [Excessive praise], (*Fraynd* 127, 1909), see Morris Winchevsky, "Gordin un Lilienblum" [Gordin and Lilienblum], *Tsukunft* 8 (August 1909), 447–455.

5. Zylbercweig argues that Gordin's early articles were unsigned "for political reasons" (*Di velt fun Yankev Gordin*, 77). But Russian newspaper articles of the period rarely carried bylines, and articles that did, such as feuilletons and editorials, were typically signed with pseudonyms. None of these can be linked conclusively to Gordin.

6. For accounts of the Spiritual-Biblical Brotherhood, see Emmanuel Ben-Sion (Yakov Priluker), *Evrei-reformatory: "Novyi izrail" i dukhovno-bibleiskoe bratstvo: Opyt sotsial'no-religioznoi reformy evreistva i novoi postanovki evreiskogo voprosa v rossii* [Jewish reformers: "New Israel" and the Spiritual-Biblical Brotherhood: An experiment in Jewish socio-religious reform and a new formulation of the Jewish question in Russia] (St. Petersburg: Tipografiya i khromolitografiya A. Transhelya, 1882); N. Bukhbinder, "Iz istorii sektantskogo dvizheniya sredi russkikh evreev. Dukhovno-bibleiskoe bratstvo" [From the history of the sectarian movement among Russian Jews. The Spiritual-Biblical Brotherhood], *Evreiskaya starina* [Jewish antiquity] 11 (1918), 238–264; Lev Burshtein, "K istorii 'Dukhovno-bibleiskogo bratstve'" [Toward a history of the "Spiritual-Biblical Brotherhood"], *Perezhitoe* [The past] 1 (1908): 38–41; John D. Klier, "From Elisavetgrad to Broadway: The Strange Journey of Iakov Gordin," in Marsha Siefert, ed., *Extending the Borders of Russian History: Essays in Honor of Alfred J. Rieber* (Budapest and New York: Central European University Press, 2003), 113–125; Ezekiel Lifschutz, "Jacob Gordin's Proposal to Establish an Agricultural Colony," in Abraham J. Karp, ed., *The Jewish Experience in America; Selected Studies from the Publications of the American Jewish Historical Society* (Waltham, MA: American Jewish Historical Society, 1969), 252–264; Venyamin Portugalov, *Znamenatel'nye dvizheniya v evreistve* [Significant

movements in Jewry] (St. Petersburg: Tip. M. A. Khana, 1894); Aleksandr S. Prugavin, "Dukhovno-bibleiskoe bratstvo. (Ocherk evreiskogo religioznogo dvizheniya), gl. 1–3" [The "Spiritual-Biblical Brotherhood" (A study of a Jewish religious movement), chs. 1–3], *Istoricheskii vestnik* [Historical courier] 11 (November, 1884): 398–410; 12 (December, 1884): 632–649.

7. "Dukhovno-bibleiskoe bratstvo" [The Spiritual-Biblical Brotherhood], *Odesskii vestnik* [Odessa courier], November 14, 1882.

8. See Nathan Schur, *History of the Karaites* (Frankfurt am Main: Peter Lang, 1992); Joseph Solomon ben Moses Lutski and Philip E. Miller, *Karaite Separatism in Nineteenth-Century Russia: Joseph Solomon Lutski's Epistle of Israel's Deliverance* (Cincinnati, OH: Hebrew Union College Press, 1993).

9. On the political and cultural context of Gordin's Brotherhood, see John D. Klier, *Imperial Russia's Jewish Question, 1855–1881* (Cambridge: Cambridge University Press, 1995); Jonathan Frankel, *Prophecy and Politics: Socialism, Nationalism, and the Russian Jews, 1862–1917* (Cambridge: Cambridge University Press, 1981); Steven J. Zipperstein, *The Jews of Odessa: A Cultural History, 1794–1881* (Stanford, CA: Stanford University Press, 1986); Sergei I. Zhuk, *Russia's Lost Reformation: Peasants, Millennialism, and Radical Sects in Southern Russia and Ukraine, 1830–1917* (Washington, D.C.: Woodrow Wilson Center Press, 2004).

10. The letter, signed by a "Biblical Brother," was published first in the Khar'kov newspaper *Yuzhnyi krai* [Southern border] in early June. *Russkii evrei* [Russian Jew] reprinted the letter, with acid commentary, on July 2, 1881. It also appeared in *Razsvet* [The dawn] on June 19, 1881. See also follow-up commentary on the letter in *Russkii evrei*, July 8, 1881, and *Voskhod* [The rising], July 7, 1881: 33–48.

11. In September 1881, St. Petersburg's *Nedelya* [The week] published an interview with Gordin that noted, "We spoke with him about his conduct, and he himself admitted to us that he had made a rude and unfortunately irremediable error. The remaining 'brothers' with all their strength insisted on the moral purity of their leader. But thanks to his error, he was decidedly unpopular among the majority of the population, and this, to a significant degree, hindered the development and expansion of the tenets of the new faith." ("Nam pishut: Iz Elisavetgrada (Khersonskoi gubernii)" [They write to us: From Elisavetgrad (Kherson province)], *Nedelya*, September 27, 1881.)

12. Even five years on, Gordin remarked on the hostile reception he continued to receive from the Jewish papers. See Yakov Gordin, "Fel'eton. K voprosu o 'dukhovno-bibleiskom bratstve' [Feuilleton. On the question of "the Spiritual-Biblical Brotherhood"], *Odesskie novosti* [Odessa news], June 22, 1886.

13. Yakov Gordin, "Tipy shtundistov" [Stundist types], *Nedelya*, April 6, 1884; May 13, 1884; August 26, 1884.

14. For studies of Stundism in Russia and Ukraine, see John Brown, *The Stundists: The Story of A Great Religious Revolt* (London: James Clark, 1893); Frederick Cornwallis Conybeare, *Russian Dissenters* (Cambridge, MA: Harvard Theological Studies, 10, 1921); A. L. Klibanov, *Istoriya religioznogo sektantstva v rossii: 60-e gody XIX v.–1917 g.* [A history of religious sectarianism in Russia: 1860s–1917] (Moscow: Nauka, 1965); Sergei Zhuk, *Russia's Lost Reformation*.

15. See Marmor, 25–29; Zylbercweig, *Di velt fun Yankev Gordin*, 86–89. A reporter from *Nedelya* who covered the Spiritual-Biblical Brotherhood's anniversary celebration in 1884 also noted their close relations with Elisavetgrad's Stundists ("Nam pishut: Iz Elisavetgrada" [They write to us: From Elisavetgrad], *Nedelya*, January 15, 1884). The two sects' connections were the subject of considerable anxiety for the Tsarist police. See "Ob obshchestve Elizavetgradskom 'Dukhovno-bibleiskom bratstve,'" GARF (Gosudarstvennyi Arkhiv Rossiiskoi Federatstii) [On the Elisavetgrad society "The Spiritual-Biblical Brotherhood"] (Moscow) Fond 102, 3-e deloproizvodstvo, opis' 87, 1889, ed. khr. 606 (1, 2) ed. khr. 2, listok 57.

16. Yakov Gordin, "Tipy shtundistov," *Nedelya*, April 6, 1884.

17. Yakov Gordin, "Tipy shtundistov," *Nedelya*, May 13, 1884.

18. Yakov Gordin, "Tipy shtundistov," *Nedelya*, August 26, 1884.

19. The most egregious example of this is Gordin's only published novel, *Liberal i narodnik* [The liberal and the populist], which appeared in *Knizhki nedeli* in 1886 (8:29–94; 9:1–90). Somewhere between a parody of Ivan Turgenev's (1818–1883) *Dvoryanskoe gnezdo* [*A Nest of the Gentry*, 1858] and an ideological tract in the tradition of Nikolai Chernyshevsky's *Chto delat'?* [*What is To Be Done?*], the book weds a society tale to what might best be described as a Socialist *Bildungsroman* of awakening feminist and class consciousness. The sole bright spot is its villain, an effete, pseudo-liberal poseur who loses the object of his romantic interest to a square-jawed, flinty-eyed, Hegel-reading blacksmith.

20. Erdeli had a lengthy tenure in office and retired in 1890 due to health reasons. ("Vysochaishie Prikazy: Po Ministerstvu Vnutrennykh Del, 7-go sego iyunya" [Supreme Commands: Ministry of Internal Affairs, June 7], *Pravitel'stvennyi vestnik* [Government courier], June 9, 1890).

21. Erdeli granted the Brotherhood the right to gather and to appoint their own rabbi ("Ob obshchestve Elizavetgradskom Dukhovno-bibleiskom bratstve," GARF, 60); Marmor, 44; Zylbercweig, *Di velt fun Yankev Gordin*, 98. Beth Kaplan reports an even more fanciful legend of the identity of Gordin's "protector"—that he was a "cousin of the tsar." (Kaplan, 31)

22. The first article signed by "Ivan Kolyuchii" is a review of a Ukrainian play, "Neskol'ko mnenii i zametok o komedii 'Razumnyi i duren'" [A few opinions and observations on the comedy 'Clever and stupid'], *Elisavetgradskii vestnik*, April 25, 1886.

23. N. N.—"Nomen nescio," "I do not know the name."

24. See Aleksandr Pashutin's *Istoricheskii ocherk g. Elisavetgrada* [A historical study of the city of Elisavetgrad] (Elisavetgrad: Lito-Tipografiya Br. Shpolyanskikh, 1897), available as a facsimile at www.library.kr.ua/elib/pashutin/index.html. See also Viktor Petrakov and Valerii Mashkovtsev, *Malen'kii Parizh: Elisavetgrad v staroi otkrytke* [Little Paris: Elisavetgrad in old postcards] (Moscow: "Pinakoteka," 2004), 13; 174.

25. For the specifics of the tsarist government's restrictions on Yiddish theatre, see John Klier, "'Exit, Pursued by a Bear': Russian Administrators and the Ban on Yiddish Theatre in Imperial Russia," in Joel Berkowitz, ed., *Yiddish Theatre: New Approaches* (Oxford, UK: Littman Library of Jewish Civilization, 2003), 159–174.

26. Gordin cannot be charged with disdaining to review *Shulamis*, however, as he was in Odessa.

27. Yakov Mikhailovich, "Fel'eton. Po nashim yuzhnym palestinam" [Feuilleton. Around our southern Palestines], *Odesskie novosti*, March 11, 1887.

28. Ivan Kolyuchii, "Progulka po Elisavetgradu" [A stroll around Elisavetgrad], *Elisavetgradskii vestnik*, January 29, 1889.

29. Dramatic theatre had existed in Ukraine since the late sixteenth century as Latin "school drama" performed by seminarians. Professional, vernacular Ukrainian dramatic theatre of the late nineteenth century is largely unrelated to "school drama."

30. An 1887 report on the Spiritual-Biblical Brotherhood noted that Kropivnitsky had promised to help secure a ten-thousand ruble loan for its purchase of land. "Fel'eton. Prazdnovanie godovshchiny 'Dukhovno-bibleiskogo bratstva' v Elisavetgrade" [Feuilleton: Celebration of the anniversary of the 'Spiritual-Biblical Brotherhood' in Elisavetgrad], *Odesskie novosti*, January 10, 1887.

31. Eight years later, however, in a June, 1897 lecture on "Jewish Theatre in New York," for the Society of Russian Students, Gordin would argue that Yiddish theatre in Russia drew most of its repertoire and music from the Ukrainian theatre, and that the audience for Ukrainian theatre was itself composed largely of Jews. See the Jacob Gordin Papers, YIVO Institute for Jewish Research, Box 7, folder 108. Sections of this lecture also appear in a two-part article published in *Der teglikher herald* [Daily Jewish herald] entitled "Dos yidishe teater in 19tn yorhundert" [The Yiddish theatre in the nineteenth century]. See clippings in the Jacob Gordin Papers, Box 11, folder 194.

32. Yan, "Teatr" [Theatre], *Elisavetgradskii vestnik*, December 6, 1888.

33. Sympathetic portrayals of Shylock gained currency with Henry Irving's interpretation in the late 1870s. See Alan Hughes, "Henry Irving's Tragedy of Shylock," *Educational Theatre Journal* 24 (October, 1972), 248–264; Richard Foulkes, "The Staging of the Trial Scene in Irving's *The Merchant of Venice*," *Educational Theatre Journal* 28 (October, 1976), 312–317. For discussion of Jewish interpretations of Shakespeare's problematic character, see Joel Berkowitz, *Shakespeare on the American Yiddish Stage* (Iowa City: University of Iowa Press, 2002), 172–205.

34. Yan, "Teatr" [Theatre], December 6, 1888.

35. Ibid.

36. Ivan Kolyuchii, "*Evgenii Onegin* na elisavetgradskoi stsene" [*Evgenii Onegin* on the Elisavetgrad stage], *Elisavetgradskii vestnik*, June 4, 1889.

37. "Interesting Symposium on Modern Drama—Methods of Philanthropic Work," *Jewish Assembly Summer Supplement* 29 (July 29, 1904), 1. Gordin's remarks were made in a paper entitled, "The Jewish Drama and Its Effect in America." YIVO, Jacob Gordin Papers, Box 11, folder 193.

38. Fainerman was also the author of a monograph on Tolstoy. See Isaak Fainerman, *Lev Tolstoy o evreyakh* [Lev Tolstoy on the Jews] (St. Petersburg: Knizh. Izd. "Vremya," 1908).

39. Tolstoy himself did not finance any of the communes, colonies, or societies that were established in his name or on the basis of his ideas. Nor did he even support their establishment in principle. His followers did not have as many reservations.

40. Gordin's police file reports that he was anxious about Fainerman's publicly calling the tsarist regime "tyrannical," and that he did not approve of Fainerman's scheme to purchase land in a shtetl to establish the Brotherhood's long-delayed agrarian commune. When Fainerman proceeded anyway, and leased land in the town of Glodossy in the autumn of 1889, Gordin did not join the settlement. (GARF, 21; 25)

41. Ivan Kolyuchii, "Dovol'no! Dovol'no!" [Enough! Enough!], *Elisavetgradskii vestnik*, June 11, 1889.

42. Ivan Kolyuchii, "Razgovory" [Conversations], *Elisavetgradskii vestnik*, July 9, 1889.

43. Ibid.

44. Ivan Kolyuchii, "Pis'mo Ivana Poslednego" [A letter from Ivan the Last], *Elisavetgradskii vestnik*, August 13, 1889.

45. Ivan Kolyuchii, "Pis'mo k chitatelyam" [A letter to readers], *Elisavetgradskii vestnik*, December 17, 1889.

46. Ibid.

47. Ibid.

48. Ibid.

49. GARF, 90–6. Reports dating from January 26, 1892 allege that Gordin would attempt to return to Russia in March of that year, using an American passport registered to "James Gordin." By February 4, the threat of Gordin's return led the Ministry of Internal Affairs to circulate notices to all border checkpoints and ports to be on the alert for Gordin, and to arrest him should he materialize. He never did.

50. Two members of the sect, Rozalia Fainzilberg, who was Jewish, and Evgenii Gar, who was Russian Orthodox, had married according to the Brotherhood's rites, which did not require either partner to forswear the religion of their birth. This was in blatant violation of Russian law, which recognized no civil marriage, and forbade marriages between Orthodox Christians and members of other faiths. Fainzilberg and Gar moved to St. Petersburg after the closing of the Brotherhood, and were kept under watch of the local police, but were never arrested.

51. See Jacob Gordin Papers, Box 9, folders 178, 179.

52. Possibly a paraphrase of Psalm 49, verse 20: "A man who has riches without understanding is like the beasts that perish." *The Holy Bible: New International Version, containing the Old Testament and the New Testament* (Grand Rapids, MI : Zondervan Bible Publishers, 1978).

PART II

Toward a Jewish Stage

CHAPTER 4

Translations of Karl Gutzkow's *Uriel Acosta* as Iconic Moments in Yiddish Theatre

Seth L. Wolitz

"The translator is never neutral in the translation process but is always involved in the process of textual production."[1]

"Were the author of *Uriel Acosta* to rise up from the grave and look about and see what an Acosta the great Rafalesco had created on stage . . . he [the play's author, Karl Gutzkow] would have given his fullest assent."[2] Thus does Sholem Aleichem humorously imitate the pompous style of contemporary Yiddish theatre critics and reviewers applauding the unknown "wandering stars" (*oyfgeyende shtern*) of the young Yiddish theatre. Sholem Aleichem consciously titled the first chapter of Part II of *Blondzhende shtern* (*Wandering Stars*, 1909–1910) "Uriel Acosta," for he could count on his readers to know this famous German drama and to imagine a fine young actor playing the tragic Uriel, the noblest role on the emerging Yiddish stage. Celebrated Yiddish actor Jacob Adler (1855–1926) devoted a whole chapter of his memoirs to "My First Great Role: Uriel Acosta," in which he too underlines both the importance of this play for Yiddish-speaking audiences and its role in his career.[3] Indeed, Adler's competitor, David Kessler (1860–1920), also prized this role, as did Avrom Morevski (1886–1964) of the Vilna Troupe and Solomon Mikhoels (1890–1948) of Moscow's State Yiddish Theatre (GOSET).[4] No foreign play in the Yiddish repertoire held the Yiddish stage for as long as Karl Gutzkow's (1811–1878) *Uriel Acosta*, the text of which was first published in 1847.[5] Indeed, one could argue that no Jewish play written in the Yiddish tongue ever garnered such theatrical interest throughout the Yiddish-speaking world as did this imported work, which became "assimilated" into the repertoire.

Luba Rymer in *Uriel Acosta*. (From the archives of the YIVO Institute for Jewish Research, New York.)

    This play serves an iconic role in the history of Yiddish theatre and culture. The work embodies that culture's secular aspirations, and celebrates the integrity and uniqueness of the individual, as well as his right to claim a communal identity without being shackled to its religious authority or enforced traditions. In its Yiddish dress, the play argued for the legitimacy of aesthetic expression allied to great ideas. But just as important, the role played by the play's various Yiddish translators became crucial for the new culture and for its theatre, as translation opened the gates to the best of Western drama. Translations of *Uriel Acosta* into Yiddish reflect various cultural and ideological stages in the development of Yiddish culture and theatre, and testify to a conscious interplay of translator, audience, cross-cultural exchanges, and external realities. They illuminate a fascinating passage from a German theatre tradition to a Yiddish one, when this young theatre sought to define its own unique attributes while absorbing the secular theatrical ambience of an admired, neighboring, Gentile high culture. They serve as sites of contesting discourses between a foreign text and its domestication into Yiddish culture. These re-workings re-appropriate what seem to be Jewish thematics in the original German, and demonstrate an intensive urge to Judaize the Gentile text.

And what a subject they offer: as a Marrano, a "secret" Jew who continued to practice despite a forced conversion to Christianity, Uriel Acosta returns to his people with fresh ideas, only to be rejected and excommunicated. He is a proto-*maskil*, the first enlightened Jew, a victim of religious fanaticism that blocks the right of mankind to freedom of thought and independent reasoning. Gutzkow's play even extends the legitimacy of free choice to romantic love, not only for men but also for women! Would eastern European Jewish audiences read parallels to their own condition in this historical drama set in Amsterdam, 1640, among the Sephardim? The continuous success of *Uriel Acosta* suggests that audiences did sense parallels between its meanings and implications and their own reality.

As a *speculum mundi*, or "mirror of the world," the play corresponds to what Joergen Schroeder defines as a bourgeois family drama (*privates bürgerliches Trauerspiel*) become societal historical drama (*öffentliches Geschichtsdrama*).[6] Gutzkow places the onus of religious fanaticism on the rabbinical court that condemns the freethinking Uriel Acosta. But the play also opened the floor for commentary and objections by a German Christian audience, who were similarly invited to question their own faith and its religious magistrates. (Not for nothing was the play forbidden in Austria for ten years!) The Yiddish audience also placed the onus for religious fanaticism upon the rabbinic court (*beys din*) of Amsterdam—but their condemnation carried greater weight, for in so doing the audience is judging its own native institution. Thus for its Yiddish translators, the play provided a means of advancing their maskilic ideology, which advocated liberation from the religious *kehillah* and the initiation of intellectual and social freedoms. Yet each generation of translators reflects a different intentionality.

There are four extant Yiddish translations. Yehuda Yoysef Lerner's (1847–1907) translation, performed at the Mariinsky Theatre in Odessa in 1881, was first published there in 1885 and was widely performed.[7] The second translation, Avrom Morevski's 1920 version, was published in Warsaw and performed there by the Vilna Troupe in 1922.[8] The third, Dovid Hofshteyn's (1889–1952) translation of the play, was done around 1939 and transcribed in Moscow, and performed by Artef in

New York City in December 1939.[9] The fourth and last translation, by Israel Bercovici (1921–1988), was performed at the Yiddish State Theatre in Bucharest in 1968, where Bercovici served as both director and dramaturg.[10]

Lerner's translation was used continually up to World War I, and it is to this version that Sholem Aleichem alludes. Lerner's translation transformed the original and led to a new and very Jewish interpretation, which in turn projected itself back upon the German original for the Yiddish-speaking world. Stylistically, Lerner molded the play according to his time and age, revealing brilliantly his understanding of his target audience.[11]

De Silva's opening lines in Gutzkow's German verse are in iambic pentameter, while Lerner's is a prose translation. The difference in tone appears immediately:

De Silva
Ihr denkt, Ihr kämt mir wieder so davon?
Nein, Nein, Die Schwelle ist einmal betreten—
Nun auch geblieben, Ben Jochai!—Endlich
Daheim! Ein Arzt—o vielgeplagter Stand!
Entschuldigt mich, wenn Ihr habt warten müssen!
(*Nachdem er während dieser Worte seinen Hut abgelegt hat, reicht er
    Jochai die Hand*)
Willkommen denn in Amsterdam![12] (Act I, sc. i, lines 1–6)

(So you think you can just leave again?
No, no you crossed the threshold—
Now you must stay, Ben Jochai—
Home, at last! A doctor—that put-upon estate!
Pardon me if you had to wait!
(*After taking off his hat while speaking these words, he offers Jochai his
    hand.*) Welcome, then, to Amsterdam!

De Silva
Azoy ir hot shoyn gor tsayt nit?
Neyn, azoy gikh geyt ir fun mir nit avek,
Ikh hob oyf zikh afile a bisl lang gelozst varten.
Veyst dokh, az a dokter iz shtendig bay zayen
Khoylim in di hent, neyn? Vos-zhe makht ir? Zeyen mir aykh vider bay unz?
Ot hot ir fun mayn zayt a heysn sholem-aleykhem.

Against Gutzkow's formal verse, Lerner's prose creates eastern European Jewish intimacy with the use of Hebrew elements, *afile* [I, 3], *khoylim* [I, 5] and the Slavic enclitic, *zhe*, a verbal signifier of intimacy: *vos-zhe,* as in lines five and six. To reach his Yiddish-speaking audience, which is barely initiated into the conventions of European theatre, Lerner goes out of his way at the very beginning of the play to create a comfort level and intimacy his audience can immediately accept. Remember, these first audiences were being asked to watch something totally out of their world-view: Sephardic Jews of 300 years earlier, dressed in Rembrandtian costume! To hear these Sephardim speaking Yiddish, the *mame-loshn*, in a register that was at once intimate and elevated, was a revelation for them. Lerner used all of his verbal skills to guarantee his audience's attention and to lend dignity to a language that, at the time, was customarily belittled as a *zhargon*—"jargon." In *Uriel Acosta*, Lerner offered a simultaneous initiation into secular Western theatre, world history, national consciousness-raising, and anti-clericalism. Lerner's translation of the German play not only captivated his audience, but established *Uriel Acosta* as the most successful foreign play in the Yiddish repertoire both in eastern Europe and beyond.

But translations usually last only a generation, and new translations of successful plays always attempt to replace the older one by declaring their greater "faithfulness," lucidity, and elegance. A new version will typically argue for its own greater accuracy of language and understanding of characters and situations.

Thus Avrom Morevski, a professional actor who had played Uriel Acosta in Russian, decided that the Lerner text was dated. Lerner's translation was not in verse and removed many of Gutzkow's allusions to Greek and Roman mythology and history, as well as to Christianity. Having largely memorized the Russian verse translation, Morevski decided to render a more valid translation for an audience that was much more sophisticated than the previous generation. Morevski did not, however, forget to take an occasional peek at Lerner's version. Morevski's translation does prove that Yiddish can be put into iambic pentameter and seek a higher "Western" tone, and it does hew closer to the original, word for word. But Morevski is no poet, and Gutzkow's powerful end-stopping German iambic pentameter is often lost in Morevski's enjambments.

De Silva
Ihr denkt, Ihr kämt mir wieder so davon?
Nein, Nein, Die Schwelle ist einmal betreten—

De Silva
Ir meynt, ir vet shoyn vider fun mayn hant
farshvindn? Kh'vel nisht lozn: zent ir shoyn—[13]

The importance of Morevski's translation lies in his freedom to translate Gutzkow's allusions to Greek mythology, Christian iconic images, and European legends. Morevski felt his verse translation would not only be closer to Gutzkow, but would mark the line between the haphazard world of early Yiddish drama and his professional modern Yiddish theatre, now fully a part of the European theatrical world, but retaining its unique Jewish cultural sensibility. The Vilna Troupe, with

Morevski as one of its stars, exemplified this status and appreciated a new translation for the post–World War I Yiddish theatre.

Dovid Hofshteyn's version has yet to be studied in terms of its genesis. That it was composed in the period from 1937 to 1939 seems certain, for historical dramas with noble endings and working-class heroes who defy obscurantists and people's enemies were *de rigueur* on the Socialist Realist stage, and especially in the State Yiddish Theatre (GOSET) in Moscow. But I have found no reference to its being prepared for any Moscow performance. *Uriel Acosta* had been performed continually in a version of Lerner's text as adapted by Alexander Granovsky, but it enjoyed less popular success, despite Mikhoels's love of the role. Jeffrey Veidlinger mentions Hofshteyn's presence at the Moscow Yiddish theatre, but makes no reference to this verse translation.[14] Hofshteyn's version appears to be the basis of the Artef production in New York in 1939, as Edna Nahshon has noted, but she does not discuss the provenance of this mysterious Hofshteyn translation.[15]

The text reveals a master poet in full control of his (slightly *daytshmerish*, i.e., Germanized Yiddish) verse. Due to Soviet insistence on a de-Hebraicized Yiddish, Hofshteyn is hampered, as was Shmuel Halkin in his reworking of Goldfaden's plays, by the absence of the Hebraic strain that gave Lerner its juicy, Jewish intensity. In Hofshteyn's translation, iambic pentameter generally dominates, but the poet strays from it now and then for effect. Like Gutzkow, he knows how to make full use of the end-stopping line, which reveals how much weaker the Morevski version really is on an aesthetic level. But Hofshteyn's *Uriel* in tone at least seems closer to a Soviet *Alexander Nevsky* than a Yiddish Uriel Fefferkorn. In short, the three translations reflect the state of Yiddish culture between 1881 and 1940.

Astonishingly, Romanian Yiddish director Israel Bercovici's version of 1968 provides a loose iambic pentameter translation, but his Yiddish register seeks a clear, almost folkic Yiddish, and a streamlining of the dialogues away from the nineteenth-century rhetorical flourishes and nuanced intellectual argumentations of Gutzkow's original. His post-war Romanian audience had little Hebraic learning and he too had to conform to the realities of the Ceaușescu Communist regime. Compare, for example, Part I, lines 7–12 in the Bercovici version and the Gutzkow German (Act I, lines 11–16).

De Silva
Drückt'ich den Abschiedskuss auf eines Jünglings
Noch ungefurchte Stirn. Ihr kehrt zurück
Als Mann! Ja mehr, ich lese, Ben Jochai,
Auf dieser Stirne Sorgen—hat die Heimat
Die neue, Euch, den reichsten Erben Hollands
Stiefmütterlich Laune wohl begrüsst?[16]

([Sixteen months ago] I pressed a farewell kiss
on the still-unfurrowed brow of a young man.

You return, a man! The more I read the worries on your brow, Ben Jochai,
Has your new homeland greeted you, Holland's wealthiest heir,
In a stepmotherly fashion?)

De Silva
Hot aykh dos naye faterland
Nisht oyfgenumen gut, Ben Yokhay?[17]

Bercovici cuts the text to the bone, leaving off the high elegant rhetoric of the original, and follows Morevski's lines 16 and17: "hot aykh dos naye foterland nisht gut / getrofn, Ben-Yokhay?" Lerner's version is just as folkic, but expatiates on the German with richer intimacy (lines 12–15): "Fun a frish yunger mentshikl un atsind zey ikh . . . vos iz dos azoyns?" (From a still green youngster, you have become now a serious mature man . . . What does this mean?) Bercovici has reduced these versions to his lines 9–11: "Glaykh nekhtn ersht, ikh hob a kind gezegnt / un itst shteyt er far mir a man mit dayges oyfn ponim." (It seems just yesterday, I said good-bye to a child / and here before me stands a man with a knitted brow.) Bercovici's translation seeks easy accessibility and to maintain pace in the plotting, sacrificing the nuances of Gutzkow's arguments and poetic stylistics. Lerner and Bercovici come closest to re-creating a Yiddish register, whereas Morevski and Hofshteyn seek a higher "poetic" register, but not one that approaches Gutzkow's elevated German tone.

In German-speaking states of the 1840s, *Uriel Acosta* carried much cultural and philosophical baggage related to contemporary issues of German liberalism, the Jewish question (Gutzkow was not necessarily philo-Semitic), and the right of tolerant expression, as noted by Jonathan Skolnik.[18] In the Yiddish world, these themes are refigured in the treatment of not only the returning Jew, Uriel Acosta, who bears his subaltern condition in the belief that truth is on the side of the underdog. But more important, the drama that ensues between Uriel Acosta's plea for tolerance and individual interpretations of faith and reason not only heralds the coming of Spinoza and his great heresy, but echoes the contemporary existential condition of his newly secularizing, eastern European Jewish audience. They faced both the stridency of a traditional internal authority—the rabbinate—and the coercive religious, linguistic, political, and economic schemes of the tsarist regime.

Gutzkow's play was part of the German theatrical canon throughout the latter part of the nineteenth century. It belongs to a class of historical plays that dominated much of nineteenth-century romanticism with their strong, lonely, neurotic heroes representing originality and high nobility. The play's traditional five acts are constructed in iambic pentameter blank verse on the neoclassical triangular love plot of two male rivals. Uriel, the new man, and his rival, Ben Yokhay, the traditionalist, both seek the hand of Judith, herself caught between belief, love, and duty. The play follows the *pièce bien faite* structure of exposition, development, crisis, peripeteia, and dénouement, with well-placed *coups de théâtre*. Exterior scenes alternate with interior ones, day scenes with night, and grand scenes with intimate ones. Uriel Acosta's dilemma, trapped as he is between loyalty to his philosophical truths and loyalty to his love, Judith, hurtles him along in classic order to his tragic end. Gutzkow completely mastered the neoclassical tragic form and showed his respect to German classicism with a serious intellectual tone in Uriel's debate with De Silva and the rabbis on the place of reason in religion. The playwright borrows scene structures from all the French classic playwrights, but deftly uses them to his own ends. Gutzkow echoes Shakespeare's *Romeo and Juliet* for the last scene and even borrows a scene from the Hebrew Bible, reversing blind Isaac's mistaking Jacob by having the blind Esther, mother of Uriel Acosta, recognize him by touching his arms. If our age has little pleasure in this highly artificial construct, in which the love affair serves as the action line upon which the higher concerns of the play are presented, that is pure *Zeitgeist*. All of Europe from 1600 to World War I enjoyed a type of theatre now relegated only to opera.

Gutzkow's *Uriel Acosta* was translated and performed in many European languages and countries, and was considered both a theatrical masterpiece and a strong defense of intellectual freedom. It was even performed in German in the 1860s in New York's Stadt Theatre and translated into English there in 1860.[19] In Russia, Pyotr Veinberg (1831–1908) translated the play in 1880 into a poetic Russian using iambic pentameter blank verse; this version enjoyed many performances by leading Russian actors, as Jacob Adler noted in his memoirs.[20] Veinberg's Russian translation would directly influence most of the three Yiddish translations. So important a canonical play was *Uriel Acosta* that it was translated into Hebrew by Sholom Rubin in 1856 and re-translated into Hebrew in 1875. A new version was done in Jaffa in 1905 that mixed the translations of Rubin, Veinberg, and Lerner; a final version was prepared in 1930 for the Habima production.[21] *Uriel Acosta*'s scene of a hero's recanting a truth before a religious body, even when he knows he is right, is an allusion to Galileo's apocryphal phrase and condition, "And still it revolves around the sun," and would eventually be superseded by the twentieth-century epic theatre of Brecht's *Galileo*. At its birth in the late 1870s, the Yiddish theatre was a latecomer to the circle of admirers of *Uriel Acosta*.

In Odessa in 1881, Y. Y. Lerner rented the Mariinsky theatre to perform Yiddish plays. His troupe would not offer those "vulgar" Goldfaden productions of comic operas like *Shmendrik* and *Di tsvey Kuni-Leml*; Lerner wanted high-quality plays. Yiddish drama was in its infancy, so Lerner took it upon himself to find plays that his public would accept and enjoy, especially plays being performed on Gentile stages. This led him to translate works that were considered "modern" classics but had a Jewish angle: *Uriel Acosta* and the Halévy opera *La Juive* (1835), which were staples of the central and eastern European repertoire.

Lerner understood that his Jewish public in 1881 would not catch allusions to Greek mythology, Christian imagery, or Western legends; nor would they follow arguments derived from ancient or Western philosophical traditions. With such limitations, Lerner faced the task of creating a translation that nevertheless would affect his audience in performance. In this he succeeded; Goldfaden was allegedly envious of his rival's success, and set about immediately to create his own *Uriel Acosta*, adding his own music but cribbing Lerner's translation and camouflaging it with Germanisms instead of Hebraisms.[22]

Adler mentions that his troupe performed *Uriel Acosta* in Łódź, Poland in 1882, with a new translation based on Veinberg's Russian text, as translated into Yiddish by Yisroel Rosenberg, who was the head of the troupe in Łódź.[23] But Lerner's masterful translation continued to set the standard, and was published and republished and used for all productions even after other translations became available.

Lerner, better than Morevski or Hofshteyn, recognized that the high tone of the German verse and the putative aristocratic condition of the rich Amsterdam Jews— a condition that Gutzkow created to conform to generic definitions—would seem artificial to his audience. Still, Lerner did not want to disturb the diegesis of the original text. Thus the translation states that it is "iberzetst un aranzhirt" (translated and arranged)—but not "farbesert" (improved, as legend has other Yiddish versions of classic Western dramas claimed to be). Lerner maintains the Gutzkow text on the levels of structure, plot, and action, as all the subsequent versions do. There is some clipping here and there of verses, but no reshuffling of scenes or events. What is really *aranzhirt* is not on the level of diegesis, but of discourse. Lerner's public was at the beginning of Westernization, and still adhered to a Jewish civilization and to its ethnic and ethical perspectives.[24] Lerner's perspective was that of a Yiddish-speaking, modernizing Jew who had a *kheyder* education, knew his key midrashic and Talmudic materials, and possessed a solid memory of the Tanakh.

Lerner changed the entire tonality of Gutzkow's play by replacing the elevated register of German classicism with a Yiddish tone that did not reduce the personages to caricatures, but rendered the distant, cold Sephardic figures believable and normative *balebatishe yidn* (upstanding Jews) in Ashkenazic eastern European terms. Dare I say, he "Slavicized" and Judaized his characters, a feat realized entirely on the level of discourse. Lerner invented a Yiddish that was recognized almost immediately by his contemporaries as conforming to character and making them kinetic and believable. He rendered Sephardic personages in an Ashkenazic speech and tone that audiences in Odessa or Warsaw or anywhere in the Yiddish-speaking world felt spoke to them. Lerner reached his target audience not in the learned genre of Western tragedy, but on their own local Jewish terms. *Aranzhirt* for Lerner meant recreating the original textual diegesis and constructing an equivalent tone, discourse, and psychological perception of the characters within a Yiddish cultural context. Lerner's translation is a masterpiece of recreation no less than Wieland's prose translations of Shakespeare. Just as Edgar Allan Poe's verse is more alive in Baudelaire's and Mallarmé's translation than in his own English clangings, so too does Lerner's Yiddish *Uriel Akosta* outlive even its German progenitor.

Lerner did remove foreign allusions that were unknown to his audience and sought Jewish equivalents where possible. Most Greek mythological allusions are absent; the term "Midas touch" (*Midas-hand*) disappears in circumlocution, but a swirling Greek zodiac with its astral figures becomes in Lerner a *dreydl* covered with powerful Hebrew letters. Christian allusions are underlined according to context. What constitutes an elevated tone in Gutzkow, as in "Die Söhne Davids ehrt, aus deren Stamm / Sein Heiland, der ein Jude war, entsprossen (and honors the sons of David from whose source sprang their Savior, who was a Jew),"[25] is nationalized and sharpened in the Yiddish: "Zey muzn koved legyn oyf unz vos zeyer erleyzer shtamt aroys fun unzer folk" (They should grant us honor, for from our folk stems their savior).[26] Eastern European Jews may well have known Christological genealogy, but Lerner takes Gutzkow's normative allusion and makes it a point of honor: the Dutch would not dare contravene. The European Christian legend of Ahasuerus, the Jewish cobbler who insulted Christ and was condemned to wander forever over the earth, a nomad—a key European interpretation of the Jew—becomes in Lerner's Yiddish only a wanderer, a *na-venad*. Lerner taps into these emotional, resonant elements with equivalent Jewish allusions that render the formal tone of Gutzkow's language a more folkic, Yiddish style.

The opening lines of the play in German exhibit good-natured, elegant irony (Gutzkow, verse 1–3). The Yiddish is far more sarcastic, teasing, and simpler in tone. The pride of being a doctor in both cases is underlined, but the German speaker appears more courteous and formal: "entschuldigt mich wenn Ihr habt warten müssen!" (Do forgive me that you were forced to wait!) In the Yiddish, attention shifts to the use of *khoylim* (patient). The Yiddish doctor respects the sick human being who comes before the healthy interlocutor. De Silva's use of the Hebrew-derived word, rather than the Germanic *kranke*, dignifies the patient, and is quickly followed in Lerner's Yiddish by an intensification of welcome and intense *yidishlekh* warmth: "Vos-zhe makht ir?" This could not exist in the German verse, where it would be out of keeping with the elevated, ironic register. But in Yiddish, the use of the emphatic *zhe* enclitic appears as verbal caress: "How are you? Really!" The next sentence reinforces their allegiance in the private office. The German stage business of removing one's hat and extending a hand underscores the semiotic intentions of Western gentlemanly behavior. The Yiddish employs an idiomatic expression: "Ot hot ir fun mayn zayt a heysn sholem-aleykhem." This might be loosely translated, "A hearty welcome home! What a sight for sore eyes!," but it is also the verbal equivalent of a handshake. To intensify the power of hearing the powerful emotional idiom, *sholem-aleykhem* on stage and in Dutch costume, Lerner carefully placed this term in the last syllables of the opening dialogue. The use of *sholem-aleykhem* turns the scene into a Jewish one, an intimate one, shifting it from the Sephardic to the Ashkenazic. Likewise the German iambs, "Willkommen denn in Amsterdam" (Welcome, then, to Amsterdam), are grandiloquent but emphasize place, whereas Lerner insists on Jewish intimacy and thus a Jewish space: to be among one's own is to be truly at home. By not only translating Gutzkow's words, but culturally transplanting them, Lerner's version brings the distant events and characters depicted in this drama closer to his late nineteenth-century eastern European Jewish audience.

When one compares the *sholem-aleykhem* lines in Morevski's version, which follow closely the German directions, the s*holem-aleykhem* emerges not only in a broken line but without emotion. The next line (Morevski, Part I, line 7) "Ir zayt vider shoyn mit undz" (You're with us once again) is "filler," and the sentence is enjambed clumsily with "In Amsterdam" in line eight. Hofshteyn's effective opening verse is closest to the original German but adds the Yiddish humor—"ir meynt ir dreyt zikh vider fun mir oys?" (What's this, you're turning around and leaving me again?)—of affection with a hint of dominance in a fine end-stopping line that sparkles with phonic rhyme play: *Ir / Ir / mir*; *meynt, dreyt,* and strong rhythmic iambics ending on *oys*. The text of the first dialogue teems with Germanic-origin words—*endlekh, inderheym, antshuldikt*—but this underscores how absent—due to Soviet pressure—the Hebrew element is but for the word *reshus*. The tone sought is formal, but with a Yiddish intimacy that depends on its *daytshmerish* quality, the consciously German-derived vocabulary that is distinct to Hofshteyn's verse style. It is quite removed from Lerner's preference for Slavic syntactical enclitics, but without a Slavic-derived vocabulary. Hofshteyn clearly had Morevski's translation before him; I also suspect he had Lerner's and certainly Veinberg's and the Gutzkow original, for Hofshteyn was comfortable with German.

The Bercovici rendering of the first six lines of Part one underscores that he probably had not only the Lerner and Morevski texts but, I suspect, the Hofshteyn as well.

De Silva
Ir pruvt shoyn vider zikh aroystsudreyen?
Ikh vel nish lozn. Ir muzst blaybn.
Antshuldikt vos kh'hob aykh gelozst azoyfil vartn.
Ir veyst vi shver es iz tsu zayn an artist. (*Bay di verter tut er oys zayn hut un git di hant Yokhayn*)
Zayt bagrist! Ot zent ir nokhamol in amsterdam.
Yokhay
Zayt bagrist![27]

"Antshuldikt" [l, 3] and "Zayt bagrist" [l, 5] are borrowings, and Bercovici simplifies the sentences and makes them very clear, using a more oral Yiddish vocabulary than a literary register, and syntactically, the sentences almost all appear parallel in structure. This *Dramaturg* translated with performance in mind and with an audience that had limited religious culture. What we see before us with this last translation, then, is the continuous evolution of Yiddish language and culture at four stages of its nearly one-hundred-year professional theatrical existence.

When we watch De Silva elaborate to Ben Yochai why Holland is good to the Jews, we see an intelligent, serious presentation, well elaborated and rich in fully reasoned organization.[28] Gutzkow reflects the inheritance of both French classicism and the German penchant for dealing with significant matters in long exposition, a custom still practiced on continental stages but out of favor on the English-speaking boards. Amsterdam, and Holland in general, were the only places in the West in the seventeenth century where Jews were tolerated and given internal self-governance inside the Republic. De Silva's thesis is that the Dutch, as civilized people who had experienced the Spanish yoke like the Jews, would not turn against the Jews without serious reason. The style of his delivery in German is of the highest elegance and tone.

Lerner elects to underline the content and its meaning in terms of traditional Jewish educational training. For Morevski and certainly Hofshteyn, however, this *yidishlekh* performance is embarrassing, for it underlines the distance between the Jewish traditional world and the modern Yiddish world of the twentieth century. But I submit that Lerner, in fact, has performed a masterful translation from one civilization to another, making comprehensible the Gentile world to eastern European Jewry. Unashamedly, Lerner takes Gutzkow's first two lines and gives them a powerful Jewish image by using a Hebraic religious reference: "Tsveytns shteyt far unz vi a malekh mogn dos eygene blut" (Secondly, their own blood protects us as a guardian angel), the understanding being that the Dutch have shed their own blood to make Holland free. The use of the *malekh mogn*—guardian angel—is Lerner's addition. It strengthens this religious image of security—so dear to the traditional Jewish world—by invoking the hidden hand of God for his audience. And Lerner goes further still: not only has this blood of the Dutch people created a new, free land—Holland—but Lerner even provides a prooftext that this new people also base their culture and faith on old Jewish texts—the Hebrew Bible—and thus they must act morally by accepting the word of God, as did the Jews escaping Egypt. Together now, the Dutch and the Jews have escaped from Spain's grip, and Israel now lives in their land: "V'otem yodatem es nefesh ha-ger!"—"And the stranger shalt thou not oppress" (Seeing ye were strangers in the land of Egypt; Exod. 23:9). The Dutch will protect the Jews, for Lerner's De Silva uses medieval Jewish educational methodology that shows the circular reality of history and the truth of the Tanakh. The Dutch have learned like Israel of yore: "Dos folk vos hot aleyn ibergetrogn avdes, vet nit baroybn kheyres andere mentshn, iber narishe farurteyle." (A people who have themselves experienced slavery will not rob other men of their freedom based on foolish prejudices.) What we see is the exact message of the German original, conveyed in the highest register of Yiddish and in distinctively Yiddish cultural terms—which would never be seen again. The Bercovici translation cuts the text down to a basic folkic Yiddish with none of the biblical and specifically Jewish cultural allusions. Compare Lerner's re-creation in Yiddish to the original German of Gutzkow: "Denn jedes Volk, das selbst erfahren hat, / Wie weh die Knechtschaft tut, wird Brüder nicht /Aus einem blinden Vorurteil verfolgen." (Then each people who themselves have experienced what pain slavery inflicts will not persecute brothers out of blind prejudice.)[29] Lerner has wrought a masterful transcultural experience by placing it in strictly Jewish traditional terms that would win his public over to the seriousness of the cause of liberty.

These lines, moreover, would have found an obvious echo with any Russian Jew in the reactionary, oppressive Russia of Alexander III (1881–1894). Gutzkow's last lines, 7–9, present the argument that the Dutch should not turn their swords to enslaving other people, for they are too noble.

De Silva
Der Niederländer schuf aus seinen Ketten Schwerter—
Und aus den sieggekrönten Schwertern wieder
Für andere Dulder Sklavenketten schmieden,
Das wahrlich tut kein edeldenkend Volk.[30] (Act I, sc.i, lines 60–3)

(The Dutchman made swords from his own chains
And then, from his victorious swords, forged slave-chains once more
For other sufferers,
Truly, such is not done by any right-thinking people)

De Silva
Holand hot zikh fun keytn gemakht shverdn,
Un vet farbaytn di eygene shverdn
Vos zaynen shoyn beadekt gevorn mit koved,
Oyf keytn far umgliklekhe fartribene yidn.[31]

Lerner, making sure his public fully appreciates the metaphoric play of beating chains into swords and vice versa, with their allusions to Isaiah, underscores that the swords that brought the Dutch freedom would never turn into handcuffs or chains upon unfortunate expelled Jews ("oyf keytn far umgliklekhe fartribenen yidn"). Why does Lerner press the general into the particular here? Lerner understood that the suffering alluded to was argued as a good general law in the German text, but he wanted De Silva's inductive thinking to be exact, unsparing, and deductive for his own audience: the Dutch would not make *Jews* suffer more in their sad condition. The powerful Yiddish words, "umgliklekhe fartribene yidn," would have immediately touched every Jew in the audience, and created a shared community at once religious and secular, bound together by history. Lerner uses the text not just to praise the Dutch, but to make the Jews in the theatre feel and share the condition of the Sephardim on their own Ashkenazic terms and experiences.

Lerner goes beyond the concerns of Gutzkow's German text to reach for another vision, a wider one, of a Jewish life and a new secular world of beauty freed from angst. Holland appears—in apposition to contemporary Russia—as a special place: a republic, a modern state with an open stock market, with freedoms, the only fly in the ointment being the religious fanatics, "our" rabbis. I underscore the use of Hebrew elements, *avdes, kheyres* and *koved*, to uncover how Lerner's discourse reveals his literary skill and deft use of high register Hebrew words that raise the discourse level to a more elegant and scholarly level than Morevski's *shklaveray* [1, 5] or Hofshteyn's Germanized *knekhktshaft* [1, 4] or Bercovici's simple *farshklaft* [1, 3]. Morevski and Hofshteyn have come closer in imitating the original German text, but Lerner has re-created the text as an artwork in distinctly Jewish cultural terms.

The richness of Lerner's Yiddish underscores the power and aesthetic originality of literary Yiddish, a language of no less dexterity or art than the German original. And the proof lies in its comparison to the poetry of Hofshteyn, which has a certain noblesse but which reflects its subaltern status by seeking merely to ape the German. Compared to the Lerner text, Bercovici's rendering is almost primitive in its reduction of the German to a folkic Yiddish, without any of the rich religious and cultural allusions that Lerner supplies in abundance.

The richness of Lerner's *Uriel Acosta* is evident in a comparison of its rendering of Gutzkow's Act 4, scene vi:

Uriel
O leugnet ihr
Das Sonnenlicht durch diese matten Kerzen?
Sagt ihr, die Sterne glaubten das, was wir?
Unsterblich dünkt ihr euch in eurem Wahn?
Ihr Eintagsfliegen, sommernachtgeboren
Und wie ein Nichts im ew'gen Raum verloren!
Un Worte fesselt ihr den Geist, an Worte
Den ew'gen Gott, an diese ird'sche Schöpfung,
Die euer Auge kaum begreifen kann?
Wir wollen Freiheit von den alten Joch!
Nur die Vernunft sei das Symbol des Glaubens!
Und wenn wir zweifeln, Wahrheit aufzufinden,
So ist es besser, neue Götter suchen,
Als mit den alten, statt zu beten, fluchen![32]

(Oh, do you try to deny
The sun's light with these dim candles?
Do you mean to say that the stars believe as we do?
Do you think yourselves immortal in your delusions?

Mayflies, you, born of a summer's night
And lost like a nothing in eternal space!
And do words chain the spirit to words
And eternal God to this earthly creation
That your eye barely comprehends?
We wanted freedom from the ancient yoke!
Only reason was to be the symbol of faith!
And when we doubt, and find the truth,
Thus it is better to seek new gods
Than to curse the old one instead of praying.)

Uriel
Ir meynt, naronim, az mit di kleyne likhtlekh kont ir
Fardunklen dos groyse likht? Ir zent azoy vi fligelekh
Vos vern in zumer-nakht geborn un take bald farlorn.
Tsum sof vilt ir unzer gayst, unzer groysn frayen nefesh,
Tsukoven tsu falshe toyte oysyes, vos zenen bay aykh tayere
Fun dem emesn lebedikn got? Neyn, genug tsu zayn knekht!
Di kroyn fun der emeser emune . . . darf zayn der farshtand,
Un dort vu s'iz do a sofek, iz glaykher tsu zukhn brokhes baym
Nayem, eyder lebn baym altn mit kloles un kharotes.

Lerner's affective use of the Hebrew elements intensifies and makes dramatic in his Yiddish prose the German tirades, without the need of the iambic pentameter, and it refocuses Gutzkow's concerns into a distinctly Jewish cultural consciousness. When Uriel Acosta casts off recanting and emerges as his own self, Gutzkow gives Uriel these Cornelian-styled end-stopping lines: "Nur die Vernunft sei das Symbol des Glaubens!" (Only reason can be the symbol of belief!) Lerner exploits the familiar metaphor and analogy of a crown to heighten and concretize in Jewish terms a symbol of esteem, noblesse, and power with the no less powerful: "Di kroyn fun der emeser emune, darf zayn der farshtand." (The crown of true belief should be reason.) The Hebrew-derived *emune* effectively translates *Glaubens*, whereas *Vernunft* in the Yiddish is not just an act of reasoning but *farshtand*, understanding, the end result that Lerner mediates in Jewish terms as the most desirable. These differences are in fact cultural differences, and Gutzkow's underwhelming esteem for Judaism comes through in "So ist es besser neue Götter suchen, / Als mit den alten statt zu beten, fluchen!" (Thus is it better to seek new gods / Than to curse the old one instead of praying.) Lerner's Yiddish employs the Hebraic elements (here italicized) with idiomatic exactness: "Un dort, vu s'iz do a *sofek*, iz glaykher tsu zukhn *brokhes* baym nayem eyder leben baym altn mit *kloles* un *kharotes*." (And there where there is a doubt, it is more rational to seek blessings from the new god than to live with the old one with curses and regrets.) Note

Lerner's love of assonance in *kloles / kharotes*, typical of old-style, oral Yiddish. The rhetorical style is Yiddish, and not at all Germanic.

Now we can truly recognize the difference of cultures in translation. Gutzkow's Santos shouts out in German: "Nur deinen Dämon hast du losgebunden!" (You have only set loose your Demon!)[33] And Gutzkow's Uriel replies: "Den Dämon! Ja, de Santos, meinen Dämon! / Ich glaub'an euern Gott, Gott Adonai . . ." (Yes, de Santos, my Demon! I believe in your God, God Adonai . . .)[34] But Lerner changes the German *Dämon*, meaning both "demon" and "possessing an evil spirit," and finds the distinct Jewish equivalent with a twist. The possession is demonic but belongs to a Jewish folkloric perspective, and is introduced into the body from without, inverting De Santos's remark:

DE SANTOS. Nor a dibek redt dir oys!
URIEL. A dibek gefint ir in mir?
Neyn! Itst bin ikh ayerer!
Ayer got din ikh, er, vos iz an *el kanoy venoykem*, . . .

(DE SANTOS. Only a dybbuk spews forth from you!
URIEL. Is it a dybbuk you find in me?
No! Now I am one of yours!
I serve Him, your God, who is a vengeful and vindictive God . . .)

What Lerner has done is make Santos's devastating remark go to the heart of the Yiddish cultural territory of the mind and emotion, to the spiritual-world threat of the world beyond, represented in Yiddish folk life with the invading *dibukim*. To have evaded the word *shed*, the normative word for demon as Bashevis Singer uses it, or Bercovici's Germanic *tayvl* (lines 18, 20), and pounce instead on *dibek* (dybbuk), defines the art of Lerner. A *shed* would be adequate, and *tayvl* more than adequate; both are personifications of abstract conceptions of evil. But the word *dibek* sends a frisson through an audience. A dybbuk is truly an invasion and possession by the darkest forces, which render one mad; it is the spirit of another being who had died an untimely death and inhabits you against your will. This is what the German wants and what Lerner finds within religiously oriented, traditional Yiddish culture: a powerful equivalent that would shock his audience emotionally because it stems from within their own cultural parameters.

But Lerner does not stop there. He uses Yiddish irony more thickly than the German by implying that the God Santos worships is the *Dämon*, the Devil. Invoking the classical Biblical image by using the Hebrew *El kanoy venoykem,* a vengeful and vindictive God, Lerner has his Yiddish-speaking Uriel state both in irony and blasphemy that he now believes in this Jewish God. Lerner's Uriel mocks the rabbis in Yiddish far more brutally than does Gutzkow's Uriel in German. The Hebrew component of Yiddish—normative, familiar, but retaining elements of the sacral and elevated—makes Lerner's version of the tragedy more powerful and meaningful to his public, who in 1881 still drew their emotional understanding more from Jewish religious tradition than from Western cultural allusions.

Where the Morevski (lines 17–18) and Hofshteyn (lines 16–17) translations of *Dämon* as *deymon* only prove how Yiddish culture might seem closer now to the West, Lerner's artistry and unashamed use of traditional cultural references to establish a new aesthetic experience achieved the level of *art*, something that neither Morevski's nor Hofshteyn's translations attained. Nor could they imagine, abide, or even accept the accomplishment of Lerner, who created a level of rich Yiddish discourse the equal of any other. Conversely, to be modern in the fullest sense of the term is to be European, and was the obsession of Morevski and Hofshteyn, and this vision informs their translations, which imitate the original as much as possible.

> GUTZKOW: Den Dämon! Ja, de Santos, meinen Dämon!
> MOREVSKI: [l.18] Der deymon mayner! Yo, de Santos, yo!
> HOFSHTEYN: [l.17] Der deymon mayner! Yo, de Santos, yo!
> BERCOVICI: [l. 19–20] Dem tayvl / Yo, de Santos, yo, dem tayvl!

How weak, how sadly Western Morevski, Hofshteyn, and even Bercovici sound after the pure Yiddish traditional cultural voice of Lerner:

> DE SANTOS: Nor a dibek redt dir aroys!
> URIEL: A dibek gefint ir in mir? Neyn, itst bin ikh ayerer! Ayer got din ikh!

It is not surprising that Yiddish audiences never warmed to the newer translations; they were just that, translations (*Traduttore, traditore*); but Lerner has left us a unique Yiddish jewel.

The final lines of the drama spoken by De Silva in Gutzkow's German iambics are lofty and noble, bringing closure to the tragic events.

De Silva
O stört di Schauer dieser Stunde nicht!
Zwei Zeugen eines Glaubens, der die Welt
Verachtet! Richtet nicht, denn wie wir hier
Erstarrt vor Schrecken stehn, die wahren Mörder
Des stummen Paares sind wir! O geht hinaus
Und predigt: Schonung, Duldung, Liebe!
Und was der wahre Glaube? Ach! Der Glanz
Der alten Heiligtümer, seh' ich schwindet.
Glaubt, was ihr glaubt! Nur überzeugungsrein!
Nicht was wir meinen, siegt, de Santos! Nein!

(*Er schlägt aus Herz*)
Wie wir es meinen, das nur überwindet.
(*Die Gruppe bleibt. Der Vorhang fällt.*)³⁵ (Act V, sc.vi, lines 2013–23)

[Do not disturb this hour's awe!
Two witnesses of a faith that the world
Despises! Do not judge, for as we stand here
Frozen in fear, we are the true murderers
Of the silent pair! Leave now
And preach mercy, tolerance, love!
And what of the true faith? Alas! I see the luster
Of the ancient holy sites is fading.
Believe what you will! Only be true to your convictions!
It is not what we mean that will prevail, de Santos! No!
(*He beats his chest*) Only how we mean it will prevail.
(*The group remains on stage. The curtain falls.*)]

Morevski's and Hofshteyn's translations are adequate in their Yiddish iambics; Bercovici's appears serviceable but without any noblesse. Lerner's rendering, though, is of an entirely different cast. Here Lerner throws in his traditional learning and its didactic means to communicate the most intense ethical teaching of the drama, raising the work to its highest poetic potential. He uses biblical allusions to underscore the events witnessed, and produces a cathartic affect from the *Trauerspiel*. The very last words—in Hebrew and in Ashkenazic pronunciation—are a quotation from the Bible: "Mir meynen oyf zey b'emes zogn: ha-ne'ehovim ve-ha-ne-imim be-khayeyhem u-ve-moysam loy nifradu." (We may truly say of them: even in their death they were not divided (2 Sam.,1:23) (lines 9–10).) These lines are found nowhere in the original German but are the perfect Yiddishizing of Gutzkow's play in this cross-cultural effort. These words serve as an *El mole rakhamim* —"God Full of Mercy," the quintessential Jewish death prayer. Appealing to God to receive the deceased in His mercy at a Jewish gravesite, the phrase imparts to the scene even greater solemnity, fusing the secular with the sacred.

But Lerner is also a man of the theatre, and in the grand style of the nineteenth century, he wants a final grand scene. Whereas the original concludes with Gutzkow's stage direction, *Die Gruppe bleibt. Der Vorhang fällt* (The group remains on stage. The curtain falls.), and Morevski, Hofshteyn, and Bercovici follow this explicitly in their translations, Lerner maintains the coda in his style: the curtain indeed falls but rises for a final tableau. "The assembled sing Psalms," typical of a Jewish burial setting, but Lerner adds "*bengalishes fayer*" (Bengal fire), small fireworks set off down stage, representing a sort of *coup de théâtre*. This addition heightened the theatricality for a comparatively naïve audience, but it also deepened its irony, for the last act was supposed to be a happy one, with a wedding and fireworks. Instead, the tragedy concludes with a shock of fireworks against burial prayers. Lerner, we see, was no mere translator, but a true man of the theatre. As Maria Tymoczko and Edwin Gentzler remark, "translators, as much as creative writers and politicians, participate in the powerful acts that create knowledge and shape culture."[36]

Lerner went beyond Gutzkow and the other translators because he used translation to forge a potentially new eastern European Jewish secular culture. He removed his audience to Amsterdam of 1640 and offered a new perspective on themselves and their shared condition with world Jewry. This is quite different from the original Goldfaden style of depicting the immediate contemporary middle- and lower-class world of eastern European Jewry—before he too passed into historical representation—a change effected by Lerner. Lerner opened the new Yiddish stage to world drama and showed how through the invention of this new aesthetic space, Yiddish theatre, *Uriel Acosta* proffered a new image of the modern Jew.

In short, this play demands the closest of interpretations, for each new translation is indeed an act of will to shape this play for the realities of the contemporary Yiddish-speaking audiences for whom it is intended. In its Yiddish garb, it opens Western themes of philosophical truth, love, and meaningful relations with the Other. With its tragic voice of a man who is ultimately rejected by both religious communities, it leapt to the Yiddish audience with a dramatic power and ethical calling that expressed a new vision, Western secularism, and revealed the power of dramatic art to help reshape the life styles and thinking of the Yiddish speaking public.

Uriel Acosta's tragic example established a template for newly developing Jewish theatrical audience after 1881. The Jewish perspective applauded the sensitive Gentile writer who created the play on Jewish and universal themes, and its performance in Yiddish both consciously and unconsciously reinforced the new secular Yiddish culture. A shared universe becomes possible via humanistic expression, despite the victimization of Uriel Acosta himself. Truth will triumph and the stage gave the new secular Jews a route to their participation in the general Enlightenment of Europe. Jews were co-equals in the new world of truth. This German play, therefore, is a superb example of a trans-cultural passage that marked Yiddish theatre for most of its existence as it absorbed the world's classic plays.

These four translations illustrate the evolution and displacement of Yiddish culture over almost 100 years: from a still distinct modernizing Jewish civilization of Lerner's rendering in Odessa in 1881, to Morevski's accommodation to modern Western cultural norms in Warsaw in 1920, to Hofshteyn's Communist-shaped translation in wartime Moscow and New York in 1939 and 1940, and finally to Bercovici's impoverished, debilitated Yiddish folk culture version in Bucharest in 1968. This most remarkable non-Jewish play by the German writer Karl Gutzkow, *Uriel Acosta*, was absorbed as a central Yiddish repertory piece—and *faryidisht*. It reflects in its translations the tragic picture of Yiddish theatrical cultural evolution in time and space, place and displacement.

Appendix

Act I

Karl Gutzkow, *Uriel Acosta* (1847). Trauerspiel in Fünf Aufzügen

De Silva:
1. Ihr denkt, Ihr kämt mir wieder so davon?
2. Nein, Nein, Die Schwelle ist einmal betreten—
3. Nun auch geblieben, Ben Jochai!—Endlich
4. Daheim! Ein Arzt—o vielgeplagter Stand!
5. Entschuldigt mich, wenn Ihr habt warten müssen! (*Nachdem er während dieser Worte seinen Hut abgelegt hat, reicht er Jochai die Hand.*)
6. Willkommen denn in Amsterdam!

Uriel Akosta, far di yidishe stsene iberzetst un aranzhirt fun Y. Y. Lerner. St. Petersburg 1888.

De Silva:
1. Azoy ir hot shoyn gor tsayt nit?
2. Neyn, azoy gikh geyt ir fun mir nit avek,
3. Ikh hob oyf zikh afile a bisl lang gelozst varten.
4. Veyst dokh, az a dokter iz shtendig bay zayn
5. khoylim in di hent, neyn? Vos-zhe makht ir? Zeyen mir aykh vider bay unz?
6. Ot hot ir fun mayn zayt a heysn sholem-aleykhem.

Uriel Akosta, tragedye in finf aktn. Yidish fun Avrom Morevski, Warsaw, 1919.

De Silva:
1. Ir meynt, ir vet shoyn vider fun mayn hant
2. farshvindn? Kh'vel nisht lozn: zent ir shoyn—
3. mayn shvel ariber, muzst ir shoyn do blaybn....
4. nisht nemt far umgut, vos kh'hob aykh gelozst
5. vartn: aykh iz dokh gevis bakant,
6. vi shver es iz tsu zayn an artist
7. (*aropnemendig bay di verter zayn hut, derlangt er Ben Yokhayn di hent*) Sholem-
8. aleykhem! Ir zent vider shoyn mit unz
9. In amsterdam.

Uriel Akosta, Dovid Hofshteyn, iberzetsung, typescript; no date.

De Silva:
1. Ir meynt, ir dreyt zikh vider fun mir oys?
2. Neyn, neyn ir zayt mayn shvel ariber, blaybt ir!
3. Nu, Ben Yokhay, endlekh inderheym!
4. Antshultdikt vos ir hot gedarft do varten:
5. a dokter is dokh nit in eygenem reshus.
6. (er nemt op di hut, derlangt Ben Yokhayn di hent)
7. Bagrist iz ayer kumen
8. Tsu unz in amsterdam.

Karl Gutskov, *Uriel Akosta*, tragedye in 5 aktn, Yisroel Bercovici, typescript, 1968.

De Silva:
1. Ir pruvt shoyn vider zikh aroystsudreyen?
2. Ikh vel nisht lozn. Ir muzst blaybn.
3. Antshuldikt vos kh'hob aykh gelozst azoyfil vartn.
4. Ir veyst vi shver es iz tsu zayn an artist.
5. (bay di verter tut er oys zayn hut un git di hant Yokhayn)
6. Zayt bagrist! Ot zent ir nokhamol in amsterdam.

Jochai:
7. De Silva,
8. Ich dank Euch!

Ben Yokhay:
7. Un ikh dank aykh defar funem
8. tifn hartsen.

De Silva:
9. Die fremde Sonne hat Euch schnell gereist.
10. Un in dieser Stelle, hier, vor meinen Büchern
11. Drückt'ich den Abschiedstuß auf eines Jünglings
12. Noch umgefurchte Stirn. Ihr kehrt zurück
13. Als Mann! Ja mehr, ich lese, Ben Jochai,
14. Auf dieser Stirne Sorgen— hat die Heimat
15. Die neue, Euch, den reichsten Erben Hollands Stiefmütterlich Laune wohl begrüßt?

De Silva:
9. Oyf der zun, in der fremd, hot ir a vaks sheynem geton.
10. Ot ersht nit lang oyf dem eygenem ort, hob ikh
11. baym zegenen gekisht a reynem kloren zorglozn
12. shtern. Fun a frish yunger mentshikl, un atsind
13. ze ikh nor far mir a geelterten, an ernstn mentshen.
14. Oyf dem eygenem shtern ze ikh shoyn a slied fun makhshoves, fun zorgen.
15. Zogt-zhe mir, Ben Yokhay, vos iz dos azoyns? Hot ir baym heym kumen dos tsveyte faterland gefunen vi a kalte shtifmuter?

Ben Yokhay:
10. Sholem-aleykhem!
11. Hot ir zikh farendert! Gor nisht der,
12. Vos iz fun unz far tsvey yorn avek!
13. Vi gikh ir zent gevorn tsaytig unter
14. fremder zun! Ikh hob dokh do aleyn
15. Gekusht a kind in shtern, gor on kneytshn,
16. zorgloz, tsart un mild, un itster shteyt
17. far mir a mentsh mit dayges un geshtalt—
18. hot aykh dos naye foterland nisht gut getrofn, Ben Yokhay?

Ben Yokhay:
9. ... kh'dank aykh!

De Silva:
10. Vi ir hot zikh geendert! Gornit der.
11. Tsurik mit anderhalbn yor tseshayd zikh...
12. Di fremde zun hot shnel aykh rayf gemakht
13. Oyf otdem ort far mayne bikher do
14. hob ikh gekusht dem shtern fun a ingling,
15. Un itst—Ikh ze a man. Af ayer shtern
16. Itst hayen zikh zorgn. Ben Yokhay, meglekh
17. Di naye heym hot aykh, dem zun fun rakhste layt
18. in Holand nit bagegnt vi geherik un hot aykh vi a shtif-muter bagrist.

Ben Yokhay:
7. Zayt bagrist!

De Silva:
8. Ah, vi ir hot zikh farendert?
9. Gornisht der vos iz fun unz far tsvey yorn avek!
10. Glaykh nekhtn ersht, hob ikh a kind gezegnt
11. Un itst shteyt er far mir a man mit dayges oyfn ponim.
12. Hot aykh dos naye faterland
13. Nisht oyfgenumen gut, Ben Yokhay?

Part 2, Act I, sc. i (lines 54–63)

Gutzkow:

De Silva:
1. Und anderntheils spricht immer noch für uns
2. In diesem Dünenland das Blut, aus dem
3. Die junge Freiheit der Provinzen sproßte.
4. Denn jedes Volk, das selbst erfahren hat,
5. Wie weh die Knechtschaft tut, wird Brüder nicht
6. Aus einem blinden Vorurteil verfolgen.
7. Der Niederländer schuf aus seinen Ketten Schwerter—
8. Und aus den sieggekrönten Schwertern wieder
9. Für andre Brüder Sklavenketten schmieden,
10. Das wahrlich tut kein edeldenkend Volk.

Lerner:

De Silva:
1. Tsveytns shteyt far unz vi a malekh mogn
2. dos eygene blut,
3. vos hot fun holand gemakht a yunges frayes land. "V'atem yodatem es nefesh ha-ger"!
4. Dos folk vos hot aleyn ibergetrogn avdes,
5. vet nit baroybn kheyres andere mentshen,
6. iber narishe blinde farurteyle.
7. Holand hot zikh fun keyten gemakht shverdn,
8. un vet farbayten di eygene shverdn
9. vos zaynen shoyn bedekt gevorn mit koved,
10. oyf keyten far umgliklekhe fartribene yidn.

Morevski:

De Silva:
1. Un tsveytns shtitst
2. unz nokh dos blut, vos hot dem kheyres do
3. gebrakht, in yunger holand's republik.
4. Dos folk, vos hot aleyn gefilt oyf zikh
5. Dem shvern yokh fun sklaveray, vet zikh
6. nisht nemen yogn gor umzist di brider
7. velkhe voynen tsvishn im atsind.
8. Az holand hot fun keyten zikh a shverd
9. Geshmidt hot fun keytn, mit rum badekt
10. a keyt bashafn fundosnay far di,
11. Vos voynen do bay ir—dos vet a folk, vos shetst zayn vort, nisht ton oyf keyn shum fal.

Hofshteyn:

De Silva:
1. Un tsveytns redt far unz ot do dos blut
2. Fun velkhn es shprotst do yunge frayhayt funem land.
3. A folk, vos hot aleyn gefilt oyf zikh
4. dem shvern yokh fun knekhtshaft unterdrikung,
5. vet keynmol, keymol mentshn nit farfolgn
6. bloyz tsulib farurteyln blinde vilde.
7. Di niderlender hot fun keytn zayne,
8. a shverd a sharfe oysgeshmidt. Un itst
9. ven ot di shverd is shoyn mit zig gekroynt,
10. iz zol men zi in keytn nokhamol
11. farvandlen far a folk a tsveytn? Neyn
12. neyn, keynmol vet a folk azoy nit ton!

Berkovici:

De Silva:
1. Tsveytns...shtitst unz oykh dos blut
2. Vos hot geflosn do far holands-frayhayt.
3. A folk vos iz aleyn geven farshklaft
4. Vet aykh an ander folk nisht geyn farshklafn.
5. In oysland iz men aykh geven mekane
6. Vos ir fort aher aheym tsurik.

Part 3: Act 4, s. vi (lines 1696–1718)

Gutzkow:

Uriel:
1. O leugnet ihr
2. Das Sonnenlicht durch diese matten Kerzen?
3. Sagt ihr, die Sterne glaubten das, was wir?
4. Unsterblich dünkt ihr euch in eurem Wahn?
5. Ihr Eintagsfliegen, sommernachtgeboren
6. Und wie ein Nichts im ew'gen Raum verloren!
7. Un Worte fesselt den Geist, an Worte
8. Den ew'gen Gott, an diese ird'sche Schöpfung,
9. Die euer Auge kaum begreifen kann?
10. Wir wollen Freiheit von den alten Joch!

Lerner:

Uriel:
1. Ir meynt, naronim, as mit di kleyne likhtlekh kont ir
2. Ferdunklen dos groyser likht? Ir zent azoy vi fligelekh
3. Vos veren in zumer-nakht geboren un take bald farloren.
4. Tsum sof vilt ir unzer gayst, unzer groysen frayen nefesh,
5. Tskoven tsu falshe toyte oysyes, vos zenen bay aykh tayere
6. Fun dem emesn lebediken got? Neyn, genug tsu zayn knekht!
7. Di kroyn fun der emeser emune…darf zayn der farshtand,
8. Un dort vu s'iz do a sofek, iz glaykher tsu zukhn brokhes baym
9. Nayem, eyder leben baym alten mit kloles un kharotes.

Morevski:

Uriel:
1. Naronim! Meynt ir
2. gotes shayn mit ayere menores
3. tsu farshteln do? Ir meynt di shtern
4. gloybt oykh, vi du? Umshterblekh halt ir
5. zikh aleyn—ir, flign un a finster
6. zumer-nakht geboyren un baginen
7. shoyn farshvunden! Ir vilt mit oysyes shmidn
8. Gayst! Un oysies shmidn ir got aleyn!
9. Dem himl vilt ir opgebn der erd,
10. vos ayer oyg banemen iz nisht feyig….

Hofshteyn:

Uriel:
1. Naronim! Mit likhtlekh ayere meynt ir
2. di shayn fun zun farleshn?
3. Ir meynt, di shtern veln aykh dos gloybn?
4. Umshterblekh halt ir zikh, ir flign,
5. In fintserer zumer-nakht geboyrn,
6. un vi gornit in roym in eybikn farloyrn.
7. Ir vilt farfintstern di velt,
8. Vos ayer oyg banemen iz nit feyik.
9. Hay!, genug! Bafrayung zukhn mir fun yokh,

Berkovici:

Uriel:
1. Bakumen ir vilt di zunen-shayn
2. Mit ot di tunkle likht?
3. Ir zogt, di shtern gloybn dos vos mir?
4. Un ayer vanzin, rekhnt ir
5. Ir zent umshterblekh?
6. Ir zent nisht mer vi zumer-flign
7. Vos yaven zikh arum dem lompn-shayn
8. Un mitn tog farshvindn zey, vi nisht-geven!
9. Mit verter lang fargliverte
   …

Part 3: Act 4, s. vi (cont.)

Gutzkow

Uriel:
11. Nur die Vernunft sei das Symbol des Glaubens!
12. Und wenn wir zweifeln, Wahrheit aufzufinden,
13. So ist es besser, neue Götter suchen,
14. Als mit den alten, statt zu beten, fluchen!

Santos:
15. Du glaubst du hast den Denker dir befeit?
16. Nur deinen Dämon hast du losgebunden.

Lerner

De Santos:
10. Nor a dibek ret dir aroys!

Morevski

Uriel:
11. Zol zayn der simbol fun amune seykhl—
12. vayter nisht! Un do vu zukhendig
13. dem emes, tsveyflen mir in zikh aleyn,
14. do zoln beser naye nemen giltn
15. eyder mit alte geter shiltn!

Santos:
16. Meynst du host bafrayt dem denker—neyn!
17. In dir redt mer nisht, vi dayn deymon itst!

Hofshteyn

Uriel:
10. Zol seykhl zayn der simbol fun der gloybn!
11. Un khotsh mir tsvayflen dem emes tsu gefinen,
12. Fort beser iz es naye geter zukhn
13. Vi in'em nomen fun di alte mentshn
14. Tsu farshteln.

Santos:
15. Meynst, du host bafrayt dem denker daynem—Neyn!
16. Dayn deymon hot zikh do aroysgevizn!

Bercovici

Uriel:
10. Ir vilt dem gayst un keytn shmidn
11. Un got aleyn ir pentet mitn ort;
12. Ir vilt zey beyde tsukoven tsum erdishn
13. Vos ayer oyg kon koym bagrayfn.
14. Bafrayen veln mir zikh fun dem altn yokh!
15. Nor dos gevisn zayn zot [zol?] der simbol fun gloybn!

Santos:
16. Du meynst du host in dir bafrayt dem denker?
17. Host nor dem tayvl nokhgegebn.

Part 3: Act 4, sc. vi (cont.)

Uriel:
17. Den Dämon! Ja, de Santos, meinen Dämon!
18. Ich glaub' an euerm Gott, Gott Adonai,
19. Den Gott der seinen Feind zertritt die Ton!
20. Den Gott, dem Feuer aus dem Munde geht!
21. Den Gott, der Rache übt ins dritte Glied!
22. Ich bin ein Mensch wie dieser Gott des Zorns,
23. Und will ihm dienen, eurem Gott der Rache!
(Er fürzt fort.)

De Silva:
24. Soweit ist est gekommen!

Uriel:
11. A dibek gefint ir in mir? Neyn! Itst bin ikh ayerer!
12. Ayer got din ikh! Er, vos iz an el kanoy vnoykem, vos tret mit di fis di faynd, vos ferfolgt
13. zey biz dem driten dor—er iz mayn got, im din ikh! (er loyft aroys)

De Silva:
14. Got iz mayn eydes, ikh bin in dem khilel hashem nit shuldig!
(der forhang falt)

Uriel:
18. Der deymon mayner! Yo! De Santos, yo!
19. Mayn deymon redt in mir fun itster on!
20. In dir nor gloyb ikh, groyser adonay,
21. In got vos tret vi laym, di faynd; in got
22. vos fayert, vi blits; in got vos nemt
23. nekome bizn dritn dor avek.
24. Ikh bin aleyn aza min fayer-got
25. un din fun haynt dem groysn el nekome.
(antloyft)

Uriel:
17. Der deymon mayner! Yo, de Santos, yo!
18. mayn deymon redt in mir fun itster on!
19. In dir nor gloyb ikh, groyser adonay,
20. in got, vos tret, vi laym, di faynd; in got,
21. vos dunert...in got, vos nemt nekome
22. bizn driten dor.
23. Ikh bin aleyn aza min fayer-got,
24. Un ikh din din haynt dem groysn got fun der nekome!
(antloyft)

De Silva:
25. Vi vayt er iz avek! Kh'volt derfun
26. kriye raysn, dem kop mit ash badekn, derfar,
27. vos oykh mayn hant hot tsugerirt zikh tsu dem unrekht.

Uriel:
18. Dem tayvl!
19. Yo, De Santos, yo, dem tayvl!
20. Ikh gloyb in ayer got
21. In dem got vos farnikhtet zayne faynt,
22. Dem got vos redt mit fayer,
23. Dem got vos nemt nekome biz in dritn dor!
24. Ikh bin a mentsh, vi ayer got, fun tsorn,
25. Im vil ikh dinen, ayer got,
26. Got fun nekome! (op).

De Silva:
27. Vi tif er iz gezunken!

Part 4: Act 5, sc. v (lines 2012–2023)

Gutzkow :

De Santos:
1. Der Glaube siegt, zwei Opfer sind gefallen.

De Silva:
2. O stört die Schauer dieser Stunde nicht!
3. Zwei Zeugen eines Glaubens, der die Welt
4. Berachtet! Richtet nicht, denn wie wir hier
5. Erstarrt vor Schrecken stehn, die wahren Mörder
6. Des stummen Paars sind wir! O geht hinaus
7. Und predigt Schonung, Duldung, Liebe!

Lerner :

De Santos:
1. Tsvey korbones hot unzere heylige emune tsugenumen!

De Silva:
2. Genug, rebi, nit tist un nit do darfen mir reden ver es hot rekht…"kol dmay akhikha tsoakim."* Tsvey mentshen
4. zenen gefalen fun unzere hent…
5. Zeyer toyt vayzt unz oyf eyn ander leben: nit faynd hoben,
6. nit roydefn yenem ad lekhayim,
7. nor frayndshaft libe darf unz farbinden un ale far unz,

Morevski:

De Santos:
1. Di emune hot gevonen tsvey korbones…

De Silva:
2. Shtiler, Santos, nisht farshtert
3. Di shoyderhafte sheynkayt fun der sho.
4. Tsvey eydes fun emune, vos't di velt
5. Farakht! Nisht mishpet zey…mir muzn shtumen,
6. Vorum zey derharget hobn mir.
7. Ruft oys: geduld, rakhmones, libe…vos iz.

Hofshteyn:

De Santos:
1. Gefaln tsvey korbones ober der gloybn unzere— Er hot gezigt.

De Silva:
2, 3. Nit shtert dem shoyder fun der sho ot der!
4. Tsvey eydes fun a gloybn vos di velt farakhtet,
5. Nit mishpet zey. Fargliverte fun shrek
6. mir shteyen do di merder fun dem por—dos zenen mir.
7. Ir geyt aroyf oyf dem balemer un ir preydikt: Rakhmones, libe, tolerants? Un vos iz oyf der vor? A falsher glants!

Berkovici (page 76, manuscript):

De Santos:
1. Di emune hot gezigt! Der gloybn hot gezigt! Tsvey korbones zenen gefaln!

De Silva: (Halt im tsurik. Kukt tsu Menashen, tsu Yudisn un tsum aroysgang)
2, 3. Shtert nisht dem tsiter fun dem itsitkn moment.
4. Tsvey eydes fun a gloybn, vos di velt farhast.
5. Urteylt nisht, vayl vi ir shteyen do, dertsiterte fun shrek,
6. Zayt visn, az di merder emese fun ot dem por.

8. Und was der wahre Glaube? Ach! Der Glanz
9. Der alten Heiligtümer, seh'ich schwindet.
10. Glaubt, was Ihr glaubt! Nur überzeugungsrein!
11. Nicht was wir meinen, siegt, de Santos! Nein!

Er schlägt aus Herz.)

12. Wie wir es meinen, das nur überwindet.

(Die Gruppe bleibt. Der Vorhang fällt.)

---

8. der heyligster gloybn... Der toyt fardekt allding!
9. Mir meynen oyf zey b'emes zogn:
10. ha-ne'ehovim ve-ha-ne'imim be-khayeyhem u-ve-moysam loy nifradu.**

(Der forhang falt.)

(Ale zingen a kapitl thilim. Bengalishes fayer, der forhang falt.)

*kol dmay akhikha tso'akim. Full citation: Genesis 4:10. "And He said: 'What hast thou done? the voice of thy brother's blood crieth unto Me from the ground."

** hana'ahavim ve-ha-ne'imim be-khayeyhem u-ve-motam lo nifradu. Full citation: 2 Sam. 1:23. Saul and Jonathan, the lovely and the pleasant, in their lives, even in their death they were not divided.

---

8. Di emune shloyme? Es farlirn
9. Zeyer glants di alte kedoyshim. Rebi,
10. Gloybt in vos ir vilt, nor ernst, reyn,
11. Nit vos mir gloybn, dos iz unzer vert.

(Di grupe blaybt. Der forhang falt.)

---

8. A, heyliktimer alte! Kh'zey vi ir farshvindt vi shtoybn!
9. Gloybt vos ir gloybt! In ibertsaygung zayt nor reyn!
10. Nit vos mir gloybn, zigt, o neyn!
11. Nor viazoy mir trogn es dem gloybn!

(Forhang.)

---

8. Dos zaynen mir!
9. Geyt aroys un predikt vegn gloybn,
10. Vegn libe!
11. Zogt aykh vos ir vilt, De Santos!
12. Nisht vos mir meynen, zigt!
13. Nor viazoy mir meynen.
14. Dos geher tsu eybikayt!

(Di grupe blaybt un es falt der forhang.)

Notes

1. Maria Tymoczko and Edwin Gentzler, *Translation and Power* (Amherst: University of Massachusetts Press, 2002), xxviii.

2. "Akh, ven Karl Gutskov, der farfaser fun Uriel Akosta, zol oyfshteyn fun keyver un a kuk ton vos far eyn Akosta ot der Rafalesko hot im geshafn . . . !" Sholem Aleykhem, *Blondzhende shtern* (New York: Hebrew Publishing Co., 1920), 98. The passage is from Chapter 41, entitled "Uriel Akosta," in the beginning of part two of the novel, 97–99.

3. Jacob Adler, *A Life on the Stage, A Memoir*, trans. Lulla Rosenfeld (New York: Knopf, 1999), 199–209; Edna Nahshon, *Yiddish Proletarian Theatre: the Art and Politics of the Artef, 1925–1940* (Westport, CT: Greenwood Press, 1998), 195.

4. Dalia Kaufman, "'Uriel Akosta' l'Karl Gutzkov al ha-bima ha-yehudit (1881–1921) [Karl Gutzkow's *Uriel Acosta* on the Jewish stage (1881–1921)]," in Mordechai Altshuler, ed., *Ha-te'atron ha-yehudi be-vrit ha-mo'atsot* [Jewish theatre in the Soviet Union] (Jerusalem: Center for Research and Documentation of Eastern European Jewry, The Hebrew University), 205–224. This study is essential for establishing the rapport between the Yiddish, Hebrew, and Russian translations done between 1881 and 1921, and for noting the critical receptions of these translations and productions. Of special importance is Kaufman's study of Granovsky's productions in Petrograd in 1919 and in Moscow in 1922, with Mikhoels as Uriel Acosta. Kaufman underlines how this play affected the art of Mikhoels, who had never performed in a distinctly non-Jewish Western play before this production.

5. Karl Gutzkow, *Uriel Acosta. Trauerspiel in fünf Aufzügen*, edited with introduction and notes by S. W. Cutting and A.C. von Noé (New York: Henry Holt & Co., 1910). All subsequent German citations are from this edition.

6. Jürgen Schröder, *Geschichtsdramen: die "deutsche Misere": von Goethes Götz bis Heiner Müllers Germania?: eine Vorlesung* [Historical dramas: The "German misery": From Goethe's Götz to Heiner Müller's *Germania?*: A lecture] (Tubingen: Stauffenburg, 1994), 17.

7. Kaufman, 205; Zalman Zylbercweig, *Leksikon fun yidishn teater* [Encyclopedia of the Yiddish theatre] (Warsaw, 1931), 2:1167. I am using Lerner's translation of *Uriel Akosta, a tragedye in fnf akten fun Karl Gutskov far di yidishes tsene iberzetst un aranzhirt fun Y. Y. Lerner* [Uriel Acosta: A tragedy in five acts by Karl Gutzkow, translated and adapted for the Yiddish stage by Y. Y. Lerner] (St. Petersburg: Levi, 1888), but I have also consulted a later edition that contains Lerner's introduction (Warsaw: Glinka, 1903).

8. Zylbercweig 2:1260. The edition used in this article is from Morevski's translation of *Uriel Acosta* (Warsaw: Brider Levin-Epshteyn un shutfim, 1919).

9. Hofshteyn's version was never published. A complete copy of the working script can be found in the Artef Papers in the archives of the YIVO Institute for Jewish Research in New York.

10. Bercovici's version exists only in manuscript; I obtained a copy from the University of Potsdam, which bought Bercovici's entire library from his widow. Karl Gutzkow, *Uriel Akosta*, tragedye in fnf aktn, yidish [Uriel Acosta: A tragedy in five acts, Yiddish], trans. Yisroel Bercovici, typescript 1968, in the Universität Potsdam, Universitätsbibliotek, Archiv, Samlung Bercovici no. 1417, w 27 [incomplete] and manuscript no. 1417, w 248 [complete]. For further information on Berkovici, see Elvira Grözinger, *Die jiddische Kultur im Schatten der Diktaturen: Israil Bercovici-Leben und Werk* [Yiddish culture in the shadow of the dictatorship: Israil Berkovici, life and work] (Berlin: Philo, 2002).

11. See Appendix, translations spreadsheet, Part I, Act I.

12. Gutzkow, 9.

13. Morevski, *Uriel Akosta*.

14. Jeffrey Veidlinger, *The Moscow State Yiddish Theater: Jewish Culture on the Soviet Stage* (Bloomington: Indiana University Press, 2000).

15. Nahshon, 195–196.

16. Gutzkow, 9–10.

17. Karl Gutzkow, *Uriel Akosta, tragedye in finf aktn, yidish* [Uriel Acosta: Tragedy in five acts, Yiddish], typescript, 1968. Universität Potsdam, Universitätsbibliothek, Archiv, Samlung Bercovici no. 1417, w 27; and manuscript no. 1417, w 248. trans. Israel Bercovici [Yisroel Berkovitsh] Act I, scene one, typescript 1.

18. Jonathan Skolnik, "Writing Jewish History between Gutzkow and Goethe: Auerbach's *Spinoza* and the Birth of Modern Jewish Historical Fiction," *Prooftexts* 19 (May 1999): 108–109.

19. Nahshon, 194.

20. Adler, 201.

21. See Kaufman.

22. Kaufman, 207.

23. Adler 200.

24. Lerner's approach belongs to the group of contemporary theorists called functionalists who conceive of translation as an action, *Botschaftsträger*, a message transmitter, with a specific cross-cultural communication goal. The source text's spirit is to be passed on by *Dolmetschen*—interpretation—rather than constrained to the word-for-word method of Morevski. See Edwin Gentzler, *Contemporary Translation Theories* (Clevedon, UK: Multilingual Matters, 2001), 71. The specific term of *Botschaftsträger* comes from Justa Holz-Mänttäri, *Translatorisches Handeln: Theorie und Methode* (Helsinki: Suomalainen Tiedeakatemia, 1984).

25. Gutzkow, Act I, sc. i, lines 53–4, 11.

26. Lerner, 7.

27. Bercovici, 1.

28. See Appendix, Part II, Act I, sc. i, Gutzkow, lines 1–10, beginning "Un anderntheils spricht..."

29. Gutzkow, Act I, sc. i, lines 57–59, 11.

30. Gutzkow, 11.

31. Lerner, Act II.

32. Gutzkow, Act IV, sc. vi, lines 1696–1708, 86–87.

33. Gutzkow, Act IV, sc. vi, line 1711, 87.

34. Ibid., lines 1712–1713.

35. Gutzkow, 102.

36. Tymoczko and Gentzler, eds., *Translation & Power*, xxi. I agree with their position: "Translation is not an act of faithful reproduction, but rather a deliberate and conscious act of selection, structuration and fabrication—and even in some cases of falsification, refusal of information, counterfeiting and the creation of secret codes. In this way, translators, as well as creative writers and politicians, participate in the powerful acts that create knowledge and shape culture."

CHAPTER 5

"Cosmopolitan" or "Purely Jewish?": Zygmunt Turkow and the Warsaw Yiddish Art Theatre

Mirosława M. Bułat

What is a "true" Jewish theatre? Is it one that treats Jewish experience and culture as unique, independent entities? Or is the Jewish theatre part of a larger, universal culture, no less concerned with eternal human verities than the art of any other nation? The eternal question of Jewish particularity and universality was posed anew in connection with the success of the ambitious Vilner Trupe (Vilna Troupe) in Łódź, Poland in 1930. The local Yiddish newspaper *Folksblat* (People's newspaper) posed two key questions to members of the ensemble, which achieved wide renown ten years before through its production of *Der dibek* (*The Dybbuk*).[1] First, should Jewish theatre be *reyn-yidish* (purely Jewish) or *veltlekh* (worldly and cosmopolitan)? Second, was it time for *di kapote* (traditional Jewish garb and folklore) to be eliminated from the Jewish stage, and if so, was that even possible? The question was not an isolated one, as in 1928, a similar survey of Yiddish/Jewish theatre directors and activists had been conducted by the Warsaw daily *Der moment* (The moment).[2]

One popular notion held that Jewish theatre should present exclusively Jewish topics and plays. Another maintained that the "Jewishness" of the theatre should not be based on external appearances or the use of ethnic elements, but should concentrate instead on achieving a high artistic standard and a modern, progressive approach. The eminent Jewish theatre director, Mikhl Weichert (1890–1967), articulated a third view: that "every theatre where Jewish artists play for a Jewish audience in Yiddish is a Jewish theatre, exactly as every theatre where German artists play for a German audience in German is a German theatre."[3]

But a question of "Jewishness" in the theatre created by Jews and for Jews warrants attention not only as a theoretical problem, but also as a practical one. Drawing on examples from specific productions, I will examine the artistic evolution of the interwar Polish Yiddish director Zygmunt Turkow (1896–1970), whose work exemplifies two different concepts of the "Jewish/Yiddish theatre."

Zygmunt Turkow hailed from Warsaw.[4] His contacts with the theatre world were not limited to the Yiddish stage, as he had studied in several Polish drama schools, and his initial forays onto the stage were made in Polish theatres. At the same time, however, Turkow was interested in Yiddish literature, and he wrote and translated plays into Yiddish, and took part in amateur performances in Hebrew and Yiddish. Avrom Yitskhok Kaminsky's (1867–1918) theatre was the first professional Yiddish theatre in which Turkow began acting. Between 1917 and 1918, while the country was still under German and Austrian occupation, Turkow participated in a great tour of Poland by the theatrical company of Esther-Rokhl Kaminska (1870–1926) and her daughter, Ida Kaminska (1899–1980), whom he married in June 1918. In 1919, Turkow even performed in Russian for a short time in Kharkiv, Ukraine, before returning to Warsaw in 1920.

Zygmunt Turkow's attitude toward Jewish theatre was not static, but evolved in two distinct stages. He discussed the progressive transformation that he experienced both in interviews and in his memoirs. Reviews by eminent critics published in respected periodicals also testify to his personal exploration of Jewish theatre.[5] I will illustrate these distinct periods in Turkow's career through discussion of selected productions prepared by the director for four theatre ensembles. The first period is connected to Turkow's activities involving the Tsentral Teater in Warsaw, where he was appointed director in 1921. In 1924, the name of the company was changed to the Varshever Yidisher Kunst-Teater (the Warsaw Yiddish Art Theatre; Yiddish acronym—VYKT; I will refer to it as "the first VYKT"). It ceased to exist in 1925 because of substantial financial losses and the death of the celebrated actress (and Turkow's mother in-law) Ester-Rokhl Kaminska. In 1926, Zygmunt Turkow resurrected the theatrical company ("the second VYKT"), which continued along its initial guidelines as a "European theatre in the Yiddish language" until 1928. The evolution of the director's views on Jewish theatre became clear, however, only in 1938, when a new company was formed under the same name, "the third VYKT."

A European Theatre in Yiddish

In 1939, Zygmunt Turkow summarized the earliest phase of his activities in the first and second VYKTs as follows:

> VYKT was actually a European theatre in the Yiddish language. At that time we believed that the Jewish theatre needed European plays, and we were convinced that it was necessary to open the windows wide in order to let in European air. [. . .] In 1924 I staged [Avrom] Goldfaden's comedy *The Two Kuni-Lemls,* and a few years later *The Tenth Commandment* [1926]. Never-

theless, both these plays by Goldfaden were staged in a European way, so to speak, in a mode completely different from Goldfaden's theatre. I staged [Shloyme] Ettinger's *Serkele* [1923] in a very similar mode along with other Jewish works.[6]

The first VYKT's repertoire included a number of original plays in Yiddish that were by that time already classics: *Serkele* by Shloyme Ettinger (September 25, 1923[7]), *Der priziv* (The conscript) by S. Y. Abramovitsh, with a prologue by Yekhezkel-Moyshe Neyman (December 25, 1923); *Tevye der milkhiker* (*Tevye the Dairyman*) by Sholem Aleichem (1859–1916) (March 14, 1924); *Di tsvey Kuni-Leml* (*The Two Kuni-Lemls*) by Avrom Goldfaden (April 20, 1924); and the contemporary play *Motke ganev* (*Motke the Thief*) by Sholem Asch (1880–1957) (April 17, 1922). The second VYKT took into its repertoire Goldfaden's classic play *Loy sakhmoyd (Dos tsente gebot)* (Thou shalt not covet [the tenth commandment]) (October 19, 1926) and two contemporary Yiddish plays, *In goldn land* (In the golden land) by Yankev Pat (1890–1966) (December 25, 1926) and *Der oytser* (*The Treasure*) by Dovid Pinski (January 19, 1927). Although a detailed description of each of these plays is not possible here, I have selected productions that, according to both reviewers and the director himself, best illustrate the diversity of his work and his approach to the matter of "Jewishness" and "Europeanness" in the Yiddish theatre.

Shloyme Ettinger's (ca. 1800–1860) *Serkele* (1820s), one of the first Yiddish comedies of manners, was written before professional Yiddish theatre came into being. The plot revolves around a Jewish Cinderella named Hinde, who is raised by her wicked aunt, Serkele. Hinde's aunt not only deprives her of her inheritance from her father (who is pointedly named David Gutherts, or Goodheart), but also accuses Hinde's only ally, her fiancé, of theft. Fortunately, Gutherts, who was missing and presumed dead, reappears in time to protect his daughter and her beloved. Turkow's approach to the production of this play, combined with the fresh ideas of his set designer, Moyshe Apelbaum, attracted the notice of spectators and critics:

> Mr. Zygmunt Turkow, whose extraordinary directorial talent blossoms more and more—presented in *Serkele* an extremely interesting and original stylization of the folk genre. He interpreted *Serkele* as a folk tale illustrated with typical pictures. The first scene depicted a cover of Ettinger's book. After the book is opened, the pages form sidewalls and the play begins in the midst of the scenery—pictures adjusted perfectly to the primitive style by Mr. Apelbaum.[8]

Der priziv (1884), by S. Y. Abramovitsh (1836–1917), illustrates another of the novel approaches characteristic of Turkow's work. *Der priziv* was originally a comedy in three acts, intended for reading, not performance. Turkow inserted a *purimshpil*, a traditional Jewish amateur performance given at Purim, into the production. A typical feature of this amateur performance is the presence of the *for-redner* (announcer) or *aynshrayer* (crier), a character who introduces the play and the performers; however, in Turkow's purimshpil, one critic reported, the *aynshrayer* resembled a stock character from the Commedia dell'Arte, because his costume was completely alien to the style of the purimshpil.[9] (Unfortunately, the reviewer does not specify which Commedia character the *for-redner* resembled.) Turkow's invocation of the Commedia may have been connected with numerous contemporary European and Russian theatre artists drawing inspiration from the Commedia dell'Arte; the purimshpil was regarded as a kind of Jewish Commedia, in that it was not based on a dramatic script and incorporated improvised scenes. Apelbaum's scenery for this production consisted of two-dimensional furniture painted on the walls, in contrast to the three-dimensional objects and actors' bodies. This idea was considered controversial, yet it is worth mentioning here as an interesting experiment, another attempt to create specific, individual, modern scenery for an old Yiddish play.

For his production of *Di tsvey Kuni-Leml*, by Avrom Goldfaden (1840–1908), Turkow continued his theatrical explorations by stylizing traditional Yiddish works and drawing upon recent movements in European theatre. A Warsaw reviewer characterized the director's approach as follows:

> It is called a 'shpil' [play] in Yiddish. And indeed, there is only play here. The words play, barrel organs play in a lively fashion—and the actors spin like marionettes. Play for play's sake, not for the sake of some deeper "feeling" or solving a grave problem. Playing theatre. Theatre as a form of play—joyful amusement for actors and audiences as well.
>
> Nothing more was Mr. Turkow's intention. This talented, intelligent, unusually inventive director loves theatre toys. Encouraged by the success of his stylization experiment in Ettinger's *Serkele*, he has decided to stylize Goldfaden. He has reduced everything to the simple and naïve contours of a toy. [. . .] He has put the theatre in the toybox.[10]

The critic does not condemn Turkow's staging as an empty and idle experiment, disrespectful to tradition, but emphasizes the director's contributions to Yiddish theatre:

> The latest production should be regarded as a triumph of the director's art. Nothing happens spontaneously here; everywhere the director's conception reveals itself—in every scene, in the group composition, in dances and songs—in the coordinated rhythm of the play, in the stylized costumes, in the details of the stage choreography. This beautiful toy demanded a great deal of effort, the director's high sophistication and feeling for style.[11]

In his passion for modernizing traditional Yiddish plays, Turkow's greatest divergence was in his staging of Goldfaden's *Loy sakhmoyd (Dos tsente gebot)* (ca. 1894) in 1926. A moralizing comedy showing the consequences of lust, the play depicts a progressive German Jew, Ludwig, who succumbs to Satan's provocations and leaves his wife Matilda, a refined modern lady, in order to seduce pious Frume. In turn, Frume's husband, a kind-hearted Polish Jew named Perets, has, in a moment of weakness, an affair with Matilda. A trial takes place in the world to come, under the leadership of the Good Spirit.[12] As a result, order is restored.

The personified abstractions of good and evil spirits prompted the director to use a composite (or simultaneous) setting. Designer Józef Śliwniak's set accommodated all places of action (Heaven, Hell, Earth, the inn at the crossroads, a street in Berlin, an apartment interior), and was on the stage from the play's outset.[13] Turkow situated all the acting space on concentric scaffolding, the geometrical shape of which critics associated with Suprematism, a style much in vogue at the time.[14] Construction pieces had been used as scenery in the Soviet Yiddish theatre as early as 1922, but Śliwniak's design was a novelty in the Yiddish theatre in Poland.[15] It transformed not only the theatrical space, but the movements of actors as well, and gave the director the opportunity to create interesting arrangements of stage elements and diversified spatial relations between the actors. The production was enriched by the addition of interludes by the contemporary Jewish poet Moyshe Broderzon (1890–1956),[16] whose poetry included references to headphones, sound waves, and contemporary politics. Turkow's innovations in his 1926 production were in line with similar modernizations of Goldfaden's works staged in the Soviet Jewish theatre by Alexander Granovsky, and by Maurice Schwartz in the Yiddish Art Theatre in New York in 1924 and 1925, in productions of Goldfaden's *Di tsvey Kuni-Leml* and *Di kishefmakherin* (The sorceress), respectively. Though still a novelty in the Polish Yiddish theatre, his work was received with admiration:

> The play [. . .] was submitted to very interesting treatment by the director, implementing the most recent staging practices of the extremist style. [. . .] it has to be said that the risky attempt was made with unique artistic restraint. In such extreme experiments it is very easy to exaggerate, since the borderline is not clearly defined. The high cultural level of the director and the actors helped to avoid such deformations. This risky operation was performed in concentration and silence, and the principles of harmony were not transgressed even once.[17]

One month later,[18] Maurice Schwartz presented a modernized version of the same play at the Yiddish Art Theatre in New York.[19]

Despite his directorial and scenic innovations, the first phase of Zygmunt Turkow's career is primarily recognized in the history of the Yiddish theatre in Poland

Zygmunt Turkow and an unidentified actress in *Uriel Acosta*. (From the archives of the YIVO Institute for Jewish Research, New York.)

for his enriching the repertoire of Yiddish theatre with plays translated from other languages. This is especially true for the Tsentral Teater and the first VYKT. The Tsentral Teater staged Molière's *L'Avare* (Der karger; *The Miser*, translated by Arn Aynhorn, directed by and starring Z. Turkow; August 16, 1921) and *L'Amour médecin* (Di libe als doktor; *Love's the Best Doctor*, translated by Z. Turkow and I. Kaminska; March 17, 1922); Alexander Ostrovsky's *Bez viny vinovatye* (Umshuldike shuldike; *Guilty Innocents*, May 19, 1923); a dramatization of Leonid Andreev's *Rasskaz o semi poveshennykh* (Zibn gehangene; *The Seven Who Were Hanged*, translated by Sz. Kranc, Cwi-Hersz Daszewski, Z. Turkow; May 1923); Nikolai Gogol's *Revizor* (Der revizor; *The Government Inspector*, translated by Zusman Segalovitsh; 1922); *Der lasterhafte Herr Tschu* (Der zindiker her Tschu; *The Lascivious Mr. Chu*) by Julius Berstl (November 21, 1923), and *Koniec Mesjasza* (Shabtse Tsvi; The end of the Messiah) by Jerzy Żuławski (January 1924). The second VYKT staged dramatizations of Victor Hugo's *Notre-Dame de Paris* (Der glokn-tsiyer fun noterdam; *The Hunchback of Notre Dame*, May 6,1925) and *Les Misérables* (translated as Der giber in keytn; The hero in chains); *Les Loups* (Velf; *The Wolves*) by Romain Rolland (November 24, 1926), and a dramatization of Dostoevsky's *Brat'ya Karamazovy* (Di brider Karamazov; *The Brothers Karamazov*).

Not all of Turkow's *veltlekh* (worldly and cosmopolitan) productions enjoyed equal success. Ostrovsky's *Bez viny vinovatye* (first published in Russian in 1883), a sentimental melodrama set in the milieu of provincial Russian actors, was a failure. Even E. R. Kaminska could not find her way to act the role of a Russian actress. The director regarded this production as part of the ensemble's "transitional repertoire," whose function was to give the troupe time to prepare their "flagship" performances.[20] Polish playwright Jerzy Żuławski's *Koniec Mesjasza* (1906), about the messianic pretender, Sabbatai Zevi, was meant to be just such a production, but contrary to Turkow's expectations, the production found little success in Warsaw. In his memoirs, written in Israel after the Second World War, the director attributed this failure to the play's presentation of the weakness and defeat of the title character, in contrast to the Jewish public's preference for glorified national heroes. The first part of the drama, full of messianic hopes and appeals for freedom, moved audiences, but the second part, depicting the downfall of Sabbatai and his movement, disappointed them.[21] However, in the same book the director mentions the great success of the play in Łódź, Galicia, and Przemyśl. According to discriminating spectators in Kraków, the VYKT's production stood comparison with the Polish version presented in the local theatre. In Grodno, Turkow's staging of *Koniec Mesjasza* drew the attention even of Christian audiences.[22]

On the other hand, Turkow's stage adaptation of the story *Rasskaz o semi poveshennykh* (1908) by Leonid Andreev, about the martyrdom of Russian revolutionaries who attempted to assassinate a Tsarist minister prior to 1905, was received with admiration both in the capital and on the tour. A Warsaw critic wrote:

The production of *The Seven* in the 'Centralny' theatre is a real [historical] event in Warsaw theatrical life. I must admit that for me it was simply unexpected. Never yet have I seen a play staged so perfectly in the Jewish theatre. I venture to maintain that in *The Seven* the highest standard of the Yiddish theatre art has been achieved so far.[23]

Andreev's work was suggested to the director by the prompter Sz. Kranc and the actor Cwi-Hersz Daszewski, who had seen an adaptation of the story in a Russian theatre in Odessa, where it enjoyed great success. Turkow, who had taken a liking to Andreev's story in his school years, introduced the play to the "transitional repertoire." Contrary to the director's expectations the performance, using a script that Turkow himself had reworked considerably, appeared to be a great triumph. In Warsaw and other towns of the former Congress Poland, the play evoked the political terror and oppression of Russian rule, and drew attention to similarly alarming phenomena in their contemporary situation.[24] In eastern Galicia, which bordered Soviet Russia, the play satisfied curiosity about this country, so close geographically and yet so mysterious, "alien," and even "exotic" because of its political isolation. The artistic form of the performance also contributed significantly to its success, however. Group scenes were ingeniously staged and were presented as tableaux that emerged from the darkness before being plunged back into it before the curtain fell. Instead of elaborate, realistic settings, multi-purpose, neutral curtains provided the actors with nondescript backgrounds. The places of action were non-specific, allusive, and stylized. The staging received enthusiastic reviews both in the Jewish and Polish press. It aroused interest among Polish artists, including the eminent director and theatre manager Arnold Szyfman. As a sign of recognition, Turkow was even invited to stage and perform in Andreev's work in a Polish theatre in Warsaw, but he rejected the proposal.[25]

Der lasterhafte Herr Tschu, a play by German author Julius Berstl (1883–1975), performed by Alexander Granach (1890–1945) in the Volksbühne in Berlin, constituted an immense challenge both for the director and the actors because of its plot and Chinese setting. The play tells the story of a Mandarin, Tshu-Yuen-Vay, whose punishment after death for all his sins and deceits is to live his life again as a poor tailor. Turkow made this already difficult work even more cumbersome; instead of focusing on the human drama of a man hurled from the heights of success into destitution, Turkow decided to imbue the scenery, actors' performance, and even intonation and enunciation with Chinese characteristics. Turkow managed to interest the Chinese consul in Warsaw, who provided the director with materials and guidelines concerning Chinese life, details of garments, typical movements, phonetics, and music.[26] The effect was best achieved in the scenery designed by Moyshe Apelbaum, which consisted of multipurpose bamboo screens adorned with gods and demons from Chinese mythology, and were moved in full view of the audience. The lighting was provided by numerous colorful lanterns made of crepe paper.[27] While the sets and the lighting were appreciated by critics, the actors did not receive glowing reviews:

> Only half of the plan was executed. There was Chinese movement, Chinese mimicry; the entire visual aspect of the performance was rendered according to Mr. Turkow's idea. But the [Chinese accent] failed completely. The whole idea was rather unfortunate and it weakened the dramatic tension. The actresses made more effort to speak in a melodious but shrill tone of voice and they wasted too much energy on achieving the results.[28]

The play *Les Loups* (1898), which explores the subject of human rights, belongs to Romain Rolland's (1866–1944) cycle of dramas on the French Revolution. Stage designer Władysław Zew (Khayim Volf) Weintraub's stylized scenery drew its inspiration from old French engravings and employed a system of projected masks (or actors' illuminated masked faces—the review is ambiguous[29]) with the help of props that were used as spotlights. Writing for the Polish-language Zionist daily *Nasz Przegląd* (Our review), critic Jakub Appenszlak (1894–1950), himself a writer, translator, chair of the Jewish Association for the Advancement of Fine Arts, and a co-founder of the Jewish Theatre Society (1923), had high praise for the theatre's artistic level.[30] "The beautiful play by Rolland was staged by the Yiddish

Art Theatre appropriately and with the utmost care, as in a serious *European* theatre."[31] By stressing the "European" character of the production—manifest not only in the choice of the play, but in the admirable artistic quality of the production itself—the reviewer clearly intends this as a compliment to the director and his ensemble. Turkow's desire to create "a European theatre in Yiddish" is characterized in even greater depth by the same critic in his review of *Der lasterhafte Herr Tschu*:

> For Mr. Zygmunt Turkow, the director of the Tsentral Theatre, the most important objective is to provide evidence that the Jewish stage is able to reenact any artistic style and genre, that nothing is impossible. Just like a pilot breaking records for height, endurance, speed, and complicated air maneuvers, so is Mr. Turkow constantly breaking records with his theatrical company. This differentiates Mr. Turkow from D. [David] Herman, who is striving to create a Jewish national style in the theatre and a national repertoire. The repertoire of Mr. Turkow is international, multi-colored, and sometimes even gaudy. Mr. Turkow's experiments deserve the highest respect. They broaden the horizon of the Jewish theatrical scene, and they constitute definite visual proof in contradiction to the view that Yiddish as a literary language lacks maturity, and that only a strictly specified and severely limited repertoire is suitable for Jewish theatre. On the other hand, not all of these experiments are entirely successful, which should not be a surprise as there is such an immense gulf between certain genres that even the most perfect of the imitative arts is not enough to bring them closer together.[32]

What should be considered Turkow's accomplishments at this phase of his career? What had the director learned by this point? At the very center of his contemporary interests were issues related to the integration of staging, directing, and acting. Turkow demonstrated the courage of an experimenter and originality in his approach to the works of Jewish and European dramatic literature. He possessed a perfect feeling for various styles, and demonstrated his ability to collaborate with designers and composers to create a unified theatrical concept. As a director, he learned how to influence actors with his ideas, use lighting effects and stage movement, and arrange group scenes in an innovative manner.[33] By introducing European works into the VYKT repertoire, he made it possible for Jewish audiences to become acquainted with recent works of literature, and demonstrated the flexibility and expressive potential of Yiddish. Turkow also improved the quality and range of acting in the Yiddish theatre.[34] The scope of his repertoire was reflected in the diverse and difficult parts his actors were asked to play, which included roles as traditional and progressive Jews, Russian revolutionaries, French aristocrats, and Chinese characters, to good and evil spirits in tragic, comic, and grotesque roles. The strength of Turkow's overall vision ensured, moreover, that the most vital aspect of his theatre was not the individual creation of each actor but their work as an ensemble.

During this first phase, the Jewish theatre was understood to be a "European theatre in Yiddish." Turkow was less interested in the traditions of Yiddish theatre per se, and the problem of a separate style of Jewish theatre. Moreover, he made little effort to understand and satisfy the specific needs and tastes of the Jewish audience—a preference that had serious consequences, particularly in terms of box-office.

What happened after the dissolution of the second VYKT and before the founding of the third VYKT? Until 1929, Turkow traveled with his company through Poland and Romania. Afterwards, he worked for the German film industry in Berlin as a director's assistant for the film company UFA. Subsequently, Turkow toured Poland, Latvia, Belgium, and France. In Warsaw, he performed at the Kaminsky Theatre and at the Eliseum and for a short time in the Vilna Troupe. What changed his perception of and approach to the "Jewish theatre"? One can only rely on Turkow's own words:

> After that, my journeys around the world started and I began to understand the sense of Jewish life better: Jewish life is still shaped moment to moment, it is constantly changing, moving from utter despair to exaggerated happiness. Jewish theatre cannot be different from Jewish life; it has to embrace the depth, the lightness, the thoughtfulness, and the liveliness. Jewish theatre has to be full of music, singing and dancing, full of tears and songs. And such is Goldfaden's theatre.[35]

Goldfaden appears here as a sign of Turkow's readiness to establish contact with the traditions of Yiddish theatre, as a means of coming closer to and fulfilling the needs of Jewish audiences in a period of growing fascism, anti-Semitic tendencies, attacks on Jewish values, and depressing poverty. Turkow's (and Goldfaden's) art, aside from reflecting his maturity and artistic homecoming, was intended to raise the spirits of Jews in their struggles with an uncertain future. These were the director's objectives when he revived VYKT in 1938 in Lwów (Lviv).

In Search of a Jewish Theatrical Style

Was Turkow's Goldfaden really the theatre of Goldfaden? It seems unlikely. Apart from the revivals of Andreev's *Zibn gehangene*, Hugo's *Der glokn-tsiyer fun noterdam*, dramatizations of Sholem Asch's contemporary novel *Onkl Mozes* (*Uncle Moses*), and Sholem Aleichem's novel *Blondzhende shtern* (*Wandering Stars*), the 1938 season included only three productions based on the works of "the father of Yiddish theatre." Turkow staged Goldfaden's *Shulamis* and *Bar Kokhba*, as well as

Di broder zinger (The Broder singers)—a musical based on the work of Goldfaden and others, in 1939. Nevertheless, in this period Turkow's reputation rested primarily on these last three plays and the dramatization of Sholem Aleichem's novel, which dominated the repertoire and attracted the notice of both the press and the public.

Blondzhende shtern chronicles the challenges of the first Yiddish itinerary theatrical companies in the second half of the nineteenth century. Mark Razumny's (1896–1988) adaptation of the novel consisted of three acts and twenty-two scenes, with a subheading that described the play as a "musical comedy." In fact, it was a comedy of characters enriched with dramatic scenes, as well as dancing and singing interludes. The final result was vaudeville in its purest European form.[36] The first act retained Sholem Aleichem's characteristic laughter interwoven with tears, while the second and third acts brought to mind a melodrama with a happy ending. The play differed considerably from the novel, especially in the treatment of the character of Hirsh-Ber Holtsman, or "Hotsmakh." Sholem Aleichem presented him in a satirical fashion, whereas in Razumny's version, and especially in Turkow's performance, Hotsmakh acquired a tragic dimension, accentuating the timeliness of the issues raised. The constant grave economic difficulties facing Yiddish troupes, the almost insurmountable hardships that Yiddish actors had to bear, and the humiliations they had to suffer to ensure the survival of their national stage all resonated deeply. The sets designed by Lipski and produced by Zygmunt Balk were far from naturalistic. They had a fragmentary character and an atmosphere redolent of decadence and ephemerality, of the temporariness of life and happiness. Henryk Halperin's (1896–?) music was in the spirit of the operetta: popular, catchy, mawkish, and enriched by folk songs, as well as by Gypsy and Hungarian motifs. Act III also included a religious song, *Kol nidre*, based on the prayer that serves as the centerpiece of the liturgy of the Yom Kippur service. The performers were professional singers with well-trained voices: Didye Epstein sang baritone (formerly of the Opera of Breslau); Albert Feller sang tenor; and Luba Lewicka sang coloratura soprano. They were accompanied by an orchestra conducted by the distinguished violinist S. Rozengart. The choreography was by Bella Katz, who directed a well-known dance school in Lwów.

The first of the three Turkow productions based on the works of Goldfaden, which exemplify the director's search for a specific Jewish theatrical style, was *Shulamis; oder, bas yerusholayim* (Shulamis; or, the daughter of Jerusalem, 1881). Originally a biblical operetta that stressed the importance of keeping one's vows and promises, in Turkow's interpretation it became a "historical pastoral in three acts (six scenes)."[37] Turkow chose this play because he believed that Goldfaden had great sensitivity to the needs of the audience, as well as the capacity to fulfill those needs. In the 1930s, the theatre was a source of spiritual support and a diversion from the painful reality of the times, just as it had been during Goldfaden's lifetime:

Another period, another milieu [in order] to escape from gray reality and lead [the audience] to the splendor of the Eastern landscape, and to show them Jews—not those miserable [creatures] with care-wrinkled foreheads, not those stooping, pale youths from stuffy *kheyders* and not even our craftsman, our Jewish proletarian struggling desperately to maintain his uncertain position [. . .]—but Jewish peasants, Jewish shepherds, and Jews free from worries, human beings challenging their fate and withstanding their fate as only free people can.

These people hate cities, with the rotten air of their narrow streets, as much as they have a natural love for their fields, meadows, herds, and the boundless skies over the mountains. These people speak a different language, somehow more beautiful and melodious. Through singing, they express their joy and singing is the expression of their sorrow. But above all, they love holidays because the whole atmosphere around them is festive.

And it is precisely into this atmosphere that I want to lead our harried, careworn Jew and make him forget his misery. Let him smile, let him breathe more freely; let him leave the theatre singing, let him later recall at work the melodious Goldfaden songs.[38]

Moreover, the play was performed at a time when anti-Jewish attacks were frequent, lending urgency to the director's desire to emphasize universal values introduced by Jews into human ethics and culture. In his memoirs, Turkow quotes a statement that he made before the play's premiere:

We present a Yiddish play that contains powerful examples of exalted human ethics; a play that possesses the strongest element of ancient Greek and Shakespearean tragedy: Fatum, the Finger of God [*etsba Elohim*], which punishes sins mercilessly, but simultaneously possesses the element of Jewish ethics; and forgiveness for the penitent, which the ancient Greek and Shakespearean mentalities did not achieve.[39]

Turkow was also encouraged by the purely artistic values of the work: its theatricality, lively action, melodious folk music, and interesting roles for versatile actors who could act as well as sing and dance. The director also had the opportunity to include group and crowd scenes, ballet interludes, spoken as well as singing parts for the choir, and ample room for ingenious scenic and lighting effects.

Turkow's intentions manifested themselves not only in the choice of this play, but in the changes that he made to the original text. Avisholem, a rich soldier in the original work and the lover of the play's heroine, was presented in Turkow's version as an ordinary shepherd who refused on principle to keep slaves because he sensed in it the danger of his future country's own enslavement. Turkow transformed

Avisholem's friend Khananye, a peripheral character in the original play, into an exponent of justice. A traditionally comic character, Avisholem's black-skinned servant Tsingitang acquired some tragic attributes, expressing the protests of non-white peoples against repression. Fryc Kleinman's (1897–1943) archaically stylized scenery was a combination of static relief elements and dynamic colorful forms. Bella Katz based her choreography on the dances of the people living in areas neighboring Palestine. Shloyme Pryzament's (1889–1973) music was so reminiscent of Goldfaden's compositions that his interludes were hard to distinguish from "the original." In this production, Turkow combined qualities regarded as being both "progressive" and "European" with those associated with the traditional Jewish theatre. The director's and the painter's individual, innovative approach to scenery and choreography was regarded as evidence of the former, while the celebration of Jewish values, Jewish folk music, and the very centrality of music and dance to the production itself was considered traditionally Jewish.

The same holds true with regard to Turkow's second "Goldfaden production" in the third VYKT—*Di Broder Zinger*, although few sources are available to confirm it. Subtitled a "joyous Goldfaden play in three acts and seven scenes," the term "play" (*shpil*) pointed to the production's humorous and grotesque elements, as well as to its use of satirical songs full of allusions to contemporary events. The text was compiled for the stage by the poet and playwright Yisroel Ashendorf (1909–1956). He drew some of his best ideas from two little-known and "past their prime" comedies by Avrom Goldfaden—*Ni me, ni be, ni kukuriku* (Neither this, nor that, nor cock-a-doodle-doo) (between 1876 and 1878) and *Der dibek* (The dybbuk, not to be confused with S. An-sky's play of the same title). Ashendorf also included songs of actual Broder Singers, such as Velvl Zbarzher.[40] The resulting production had a pronounced social message, glorifying the first Yiddish performers.

In the shtetl of Fanativke ("Fanatictown," and also reminiscent of Sholem Aleichem's "Kasrilevke"), Jews are anxiously awaiting a rabbi. He is to arrive by train, which in itself is considered quite the sensation. The train indeed arrives, but instead of the expected guest, a troupe of *komediantshikes* (little comedians, clowns), with the jolly name of "Broder Singers," disembark. They head straight for the tavern. Finally, the shtetl aristocrat, Yokl, brings the "venerable rabbi" and starts preparations for the rabbi's wedding to his daughter. Meanwhile, the daughter, beautiful Malkele, has already managed to fall in love with one of the Broder Singers. Luckily for her, the rabbi is denounced by his three (!) wives and has to leave Fanativke in disgrace. The girl marries the "artist" and joins his troupe to carry Jewish songs to the world.

The music was composed by Shloyme Pryzament, an expert on the repertoire of the Broder Singers.[41] The set and costumes were designed by Fryc Kleinman, and Bella Katz's choreography included Hasidic and "satanic" dances. Little is known about the specifics of music, stage set, or choreography.

Goldfaden's *Bar Kokhba (der zun fun dem shtern); oder, Di letste teg fun yerusholayim* (Bar Kokhba [the son of the star]; or, the last days of Jerusalem, 1883) was originally a tragic opera in four acts with a prologue, about a first-century Jewish revolt against the Romans; however, the director and the author of the adaptation transformed it into a "historical folk opera."[42] Ashendorf was chosen by Turkow to rework the play and, in the end, was responsible for much of the adaptation's unique themes and perspectives. Ashendorf's text depicted a cross-section of the entire community, and introduced representatives of different social groups as well as the historical character of Rabbi Akiva, the spiritual leader of the uprising. Ashendorf also changed the title hero's character from that of a strongman who snaps his chains and tames a lion, into a true military commander. An eminent reviewer Mojżesz Kanfer described the adaptation thus:

> Ashendorf prepared above all an exciting and dynamic spectacle. The main hero himself is not simply a strongman, as Goldfaden depicted him, but grows into a national hero, who is aware of his task and his historical mission. Although the most beautiful scene when Bar Kokhba fights with the shades of his unintended victims somehow surprises us with its Hamlet-like quality, it surpasses the terms of the work itself, which Goldfaden called a historical folk opera, [. . .] [B]ut the character himself is comprehensible to us as a representative of youth that will never put up with the existing state of affairs, that will always rebel against any attempt at compromise suggested by the older generation, even in good faith. Similarly, Papus, the main instigator of the plot, is also no longer only a clown, but in Ashendorf's interpretation is imbued with the humanity of a suffering human creature. Instead of a clown amusing Goldfaden's audiences to tears with cheap comic effects, we saw something akin to Shylock's brother, complaining this time not as a Jew about social injustice, but as a miserable cripple about characteristically human injustice, which blocks his road to happiness. Finally, the powerful closing scene with its contemporary feel ends this spectacle on a note of historical pathos [. . .] Yet let me finally [. . .] state that Ashendorf, with all his controversial innovations, managed nevertheless Goldfaden's primitive magic, which moves us once again with the rhythm of folk song.[43]

Yet it was the director who was credited with the powerful finale, woven out of all the previous theatrical effects. To produce it, Turkow drew upon the skills and techniques he mastered when he experimented with production styles in the Tsentral Teater, as well as with the first and second VYKT. The discriminating reviewer from Kraków noted with satisfaction that:

> Zygmunt Turkow [. . .] did not overlook any motif, creating for us a whole coordinated with exceptional artistic precision. First of all, he turned out to

be a master of mass scenes, capable of evoking a range of moods. [. . .] Nothing here moves on its own, but everything is subordinated to the iron will [of the director], which shows the way and determines the rhythm. We sense this will from the first scene until the last, and sometimes it feels as if the actor's every step, every movement of the crowd was planned by the director. [. . .] And [. . .] the director did not always have first-rate actors at his disposal, [. . .] singers are not always good actors, and yet we did not feel any [. . .] dissatisfaction in this respect.[44]

Fryc Kleinman's scenery discarded representational settings for stylized, synthetic pieces that did not imitate reality, but hinted at it; one reviewer, himself an artist, made note of their clear and functional forms.[45] Plain, austere blocks suited the heroic tone of the spectacle perfectly. For example, in the prison scene the heavy cylinder of the mill, placed center stage, created the mood of overwhelming pressure, constraint, and toil. It was surrounded by precipitous forms that served to isolate the prisoners from the outside world and to emphasize their tragic situation. The two sides of the armed conflict were also contrasted through color; Jewish rebels were associated with white, and Romans with gaudy colors and gold. Rabbi Akiva wore a costume adorned with a *tallis* motif. Suits of armor worn by warriors looked monumental and glamorous, and suggested the fighters' power and confidence. In contrast to metallic armor and weapons, as well as royal crimson and gold, the crowd of the war victims in Bar Kokhba's hallucination attracted spectators' attention with its ghastly shade of gray.

All of the Goldfaden performances of the third VYKT were extremely popular not only in Lwów, but proved equally so on tour in Kraków and Warsaw.

In the second phase of Zygmunt Turkow's artistic evolution, the director had a sense of mission. He perceived his work as a sort of vocation, serving not art in general but Jewish art and culture specifically. Turkow endeavored to create a distinct Jewish theatrical style, inspired by his particular vision of Avrom Goldfaden's works. The objective of this theatre was to answer the needs of the Jewish public through the creation of a modern *folks-shpil*, one that synthesized drama, comedy, operetta and dance, and drew directly on Turkow's experiences in the first phase of his work with the VYKT.

The evolution of Zygmunt Turkow's ideas concerning Jewish theatre was based on his creative activity in three VYKT theatrical companies. His initial pursuit of a "European," "progressive," and "international" repertoire—one supposedly alien to the particularity of the traditional Yiddish repertoire—in fact proved inseparable from the evolution of that Yiddish repertoire.[46] His adapting the European repertoire, distinctly Russian ideas about actors' versatility and plasticity, and Soviet Constructivist and Suprematist visual elements into an unmistakably Jewish theatrical work is evidence not of these multiple sources' incompatibility, but of their fertile confluence. The "universal" and the "particular," the "worldly" and "purely

Jewish," do not exist in some ideological or aesthetic opposition, but are crucial to the survival and evolution of each.

Appendix

Jakub Appenszlak, "Żydowski teatr artystyczny: *Dziesiąte przykazanie (Łoj sachmojd)*" [Jewish art theatre: *The tenth commandment (Loy sakhmoyd)*], *Nasz Przegląd* [Our review], October 21, 1926.

(A. Goldfaden's performance in three acts (seven scenes), with a prologue and interludes. The interludes: M. Broderzon. Staging: Zygmunt Turkow. Scenery and costumes: Józef Śliwniak. Dances: Maria Ambrożewiczówna. Musical illustrations: Józef Kamiński.)

The other day, the Jewish Theatre opened in the refurbished Kaminski Theatre building on Oboźna St. [Warsaw]. It is managed by Ida Kaminska and Zygmunt Turkow. The opening ceremony became a solemn expression of national culture. On the occasion, representatives of our artistic and literary associations emphasized in their speeches the importance of regaining such a significant cultural institution, dedicated by Warsaw's Jews to the cult of true art.

Since the opening ceremony coincided with the fiftieth anniversary of the Jewish theatre's establishment, the managers of the new stage celebrated the memory of the father of our vagrant stage, Abraham Goldfaden, by commencing the season with a production of his play, *The Tenth Commandment*. The play is in the nature of a social and moral allegory, poignantly naïve in its presentation of the consequences of the sin of lust, and it was submitted to a very interesting treatment by the director, using the most recent staging practices in the extremist style. Although we could argue whether this old Goldfaden play was suited to such an experiment, or if a simple stylization of the original would have been adequate (similar to the one Turkow had produced in his production of *Serkele*), nevertheless it has to be said that this risky venture was undertaken with unique artistic restraint. In such extreme experiments it is very easy to exaggerate, since the borders are not clearly defined. The high cultural level of the director and the actors helped to avoid such deformations. This risky operation was performed in concentration and silence, and the principles of harmony were not transgressed even once.

The goal of transposing Goldfaden's drama into a miracle play with modern staging was made for the first time in a Jewish theatre in Russia. Concentrating the action within a merry miracle-play structure was supported by Goldfaden's setting elements of this comedy of adultery within the context of the eternal conflict between heaven and hell, good and evil spirits, and the devil and the angel.

Such powerful strife is reflected in small episodes of the human comedy. When Satan has the upper hand, Ludwig, a German Jew and a "progressive" old fox, covets "his neighbor's wife," the wife of an honest Polish Jew, Perets. Perets, however, turns his affection towards Ludwig's beautiful wife, the fashionable Matilda. The protagonists switch places. However, Perets feels ill-at-ease in Matilda's lounge in Berlin, and Ludwig is driven crazy by Frume's (Perets's wife's) piety. This deadlock is resolved by a "din toyre," a tribunal in the world to come chaired by the Good Spirit. Finally, each protagonist returns to his or her place.

That omnipresence of good and evil spirits determines the decorative strategy of the set design in a form characteristic of medieval miracle plays, the so-called "composite (or simultaneous) setting" where particular scenes of the action were distributed on a stage scaffold composed as a concentric set. The medieval miracle play was integrated with the most recent and modern "suprematism," or pure geometric decorative form, in the staging of *The Tenth Commandment*. That part of the performance was excellently and uniquely composed by the set designer Józef Śliwniak, who created a compact stage structure, with "heaven, hell and earth," and many levels of action, as well as a central frame used as a type of situational set, indicating the place of action (an inn at a crossroads, a Berlin street, interiors, etc.). Such a complex machine became the location for movement, speech, dance and song, for natural and supernatural comic protagonists, who fell into an abyss or emerged from the underworld. Broderzon's interludes updated the play's content, adding modern touches like radio earphones, radio waves (with music composed by Józef Kamiński), and political references. There were definitely too many of those political ideas and allusions, which sometimes changed the performance into a variety show. I am not sure whether that happened accidentally or resulted from the recent introduction of the "Azazel" into the Yiddish theatre, after the "Dybbuk" was chased out . . .[47]

The cast excellently performed their roles under Turkow's direction. Miss Ida Kaminska, playing the Good Spirit, displayed her seraphic charm, and she sang one of her songs with real finesse. Mr. Lipman acted the part of the showy Satan. Mr. Melman presented himself as a finely schooled actor, with serious ambitions to become "the first romantic lead" of the Yiddish stage. Mr. Lederman revealed strong comic powers. Matilda's coquetry was well expressed by Shoshana, while Frume's small-town conservatism was skillfully characterized by Miss Altbaum.

H.R., "Mała recenzja teatralna" [A short theatre review], *Nowy Dziennik* [New journal], May 19, 1939.

Of course, I am not a professional critic and I know that I owe the publication of this short review only to exceptional circumstances. And it's just such an exceptional circumstance represented by the performance of *Shulamis* at the Jewish Theatre, which pleased us enormously. We have to admit that we do not fully understand Yiddish, though we can understand any language when people sing as beautifully as they did in *Shulamis*. Such songs go straight to our hearts even when sung by a nightingale that sings a completely strange "nightingalese."

In addition, there were funny scenes acted in such a way that only dead people could fail to appreciate them. We especially liked the Negro characters who seemed to have legs made of chewing gum and who danced as if they had no bones. And in the last act, two luscious would-be husbands created such explosive tensions that you wouldn't even have needed dynamite! Especially the one with the beard and side-curls that looked like sausages, playfully bent upwards: that guy earned his paycheck. And when both of them introduced themselves to the bride's father and listed off their assets, you did not have to understand exactly what they were saying. It was enough to listen to the tone of their voices and see how they moved. What incredibly cool jokers!

The group scenes, dances, and songs were very beautiful. What I didn't like, though, was that the shepherds were wearing leather vests that buttoned up the back. Okay, you could only see this if you had eyesight as good as mine, and they had to have buttons to get into the costumes. But then, I have to make some objection for this to be a real review. What was really true, though, was that we all liked the performance, although we were ashamed that we understood so little Yiddish.

H.R.

(on behalf of our whole school)

Notes

1. See Mikhl Weichert, "Yidishkayt in teater" [Jewishness in the theatre], *Literarishe bleter* [Literary pages] 35 (1930), 654–655. I was not able to confirm this information elsewhere. Yechiel Szeintuch's bibliography does not mention *Folksblat* (see Yechiel Szeintuch, *Preliminary Inventory of Yiddish Dailies and Periodicals Published in Poland Between the Two World Wars* (Jerusalem: The Hebrew University of Jerusalem—Center for Research on the History and Culture of Polish Jews, 1986).

2. See "'Yidish teater' oder 'teater oyf yidish': undzere ankete tsvishn yidishe rezhisorn" ['Yiddish/Jewish theatre' or 'a theatre in Yiddish': Our survey of Jewish directors], *Moment*, December 2, 9 and 16, 1928. See Hebrew University of Jerusalem, *Index to Yiddish Periodicals*, http://jnul.huji.ac.il/iyp/ (accessed April 23, 2007).

3. Weichert, "Yidishkayt in teater," 654–655.

4. On Z. Turkow, see Zalmen Zylbercwejg, ed., *Leksikon fun yidishn teater* [Encyclopedia of the Yiddish theatre] (Warsaw, Farlag Elisheva 1934), 2:868–870.

5. See Zygmunt Turkow, *Di ibergerisene tkufe: fragmentn fun mayn lebn* [The interrupted era: Fragments of my life] (Buenos Aires: Tsentral-farband far poylishe yidn in argentine, 1961).

6. M. K. [Mojżesz Kanfer], "Teatr Goldfadenowski—teatrem żydowskim: Z rozmowy z Zygmuntem Turkowem" [Goldfaden's theatre—Jewish theatre: From an interview with Zygmunt Turkow], *Nowy Dziennik* [New daily] April 20, 1939.

7. In parentheses I provide the dates of the premieres in the Tsentral Theatre or in the VYKT.

8. Jakub Appenszlak, "Teatr 'Centralny' (Warszawska Żydowska Trupa Dramatyczna): *Serkele, czyli Rocznica śmierci brata*" ['Tsentral' Theatre (Warsaw Yiddish dramatic troupe): *Serkele, or, the anniversary of a brother's death*], *Nasz Przegląd* [Our review], October 27, 1923.

9. See Appenszlak, "Teatr 'Centralny': *Pobór*" ['Centralny' Theatre: The conscript], *Nasz Przegląd*, December 28, 1923.

10. Appenszlak, "Teatr Centralny: *Dwaj Kuni Lemel*" [Centralny Theatre: *The Two Kuni-Lemls*], *Nasz Przegląd*, April 22, 1924.

11. Ibid.

12. In Yiddish, the *yeytser tov* (good inclination) in each person is in ongoing competition with the *yeytser hore* (evil inclination), not unlike the competing angel and devil on many a Christian character's shoulders.

13. In the German theatre, a composite setting [*Einheitsdekoration*] was used by Ludwig Berger (1892–1969) earlier in his staging of William Shakespeare's *Measure for Measure* (Berlin, Volksbuehne, 1918; see Julius Bab, *Das Theater der Gegenwart* [The theatre of the present], Polish edition titled *Teatr współczesny: Od Meiningeńczyków do Piscatora* [Modern theatre; from Meiningen to Piscator] trans. Edmund Misiołek, (Warsaw: Państwowy Instytut Wydawniczy, 1959), 261.

14. Suprematism was a style of abstract art created by Russian painter Kazimir Malevich (1878–1935). It limited forms to five basics: square, quadrangle, straight line, circle, and cross. At the beginning the combinations of these primary geometric forms were flat and static; later they suggested space and motion; and from the years 1924–1926, three-dimensional compositions were also created.

15. For the staging of Goldfaden's *Di kishefmakherin* (The sorceress), directed by Alexander Granovsky (1880–1937) in Moscow's State Jewish Theatre (known by its Russian acronym GOSET) in 1922, the stage designer Isaac Rabinovich suggested a two-level wooden scaffold, with twenty-five ladders and stairs leading to the stage from behind and around it. See Lois Adler, "Alexis Granovsky and the Jewish State Theatre in Moscow," *The Drama Review* 3 (1980), 35.

16. Moyshe Broderzon (1890–1956) was a Yiddish poet and playwright who spent 1914–1918 in Moscow, working with avant-garde Jewish artists and writers. After returning to Łódź in December 1918, he became a co-founder of Yung Yidish—a group of writers and artists. In 1922, he became a co-founder of the puppet theatre Khad-gadye. Four years later Broderzon collaborated with Azazel in Warsaw, providing texts for this first *kleynkunst* theater in Poland.

17. Jakub Appenszlak, "Żydowski teatr artystyczny: *Dziesiąte przykazanie (Łoj sachmojd)*" [Jewish art theatre: The tenth commandment (Loy sakhmoyd)], *Nasz Przegląd*, October 21, 1926. See the whole review in the Appendix.

18. According to Zalmen Zylbercweig, Turkow's production had its premiere on November 18, 1926 (*Leksikon fun yidishn teater*, 3:2341). Turkow's memoirs err in stating that M. Schwartz's production of *Dos tsente gebot* preceded his own (Turkow, *Di ibergerisene tkufe*, 190).

19. On modernized versions of Goldfaden's plays performed in the United States, see Joel Berkowitz, "The Tallis or the Cross? Reviving Goldfaden at the Yiddish Art Theatre, 1924–26," *Journal of Jewish Studies* 50 (Spring 1999), 120–138.

20. See Turkow, *Di ibergerisene tkufe*, 60, 61–62.

21. Ibid., 89–90.

22. Ibid., 101, 138, 122, 108, 141 respectively.

23. Jakub Appenszlak, "*Opowieść o siedmiu powieszonych* w Teatrze 'Centralnym'" [*The Seven Who Were Hanged* at the 'Centralny' Theatre], *Nasz Przegląd*, June 2, 1923.

24. See Turkow, *Di ibergerisene tkufe*, 62–64.

25. Ibid., 66.

26. Ibid., 88.

27. Ibid., 88–89.

28. Appenszlak, "Scena żydowska: Teatr Centralny: *Grzeszny Czu*" [Jewish stage: Tsentral Theatre: *The Lascivious Mr. Chu*], *Nasz Przegląd*, November 27, 1923.

29. See Appenszlak, "Żydowski Teatr Artystyczny: *Wilki*" [Yiddish Art Theatre: *The Wolves*], *Nasz Przegląd*, November 26, 1926.

30. *Nasz Przegląd* regularly published articles on Jewish, Polish, and European literature, music, and fine arts, as well as theatre and film reviews.

31. Ibid. Emphasis added.

32. Appenszlak, "Scena żydowska: Teatr Centralny: *Grzeszny Czu*."

33. Turkow's ability to organize large groups of supernumeraries within a limited area was especially esteemed, and he was even compared to the film director Ernst Lubitsch (1892–1947). See Appenszlak, "Teatr Centralny: *Sabataj Cwi*" [Centralny Theatre: *Shabtse Tsvi*], *Nasz Przegląd*, January 20, 1924.

34. On the brilliant acting of Z. Turkow's talented actors and their remarkable ensemble work, see, for instance, "Ostatnie występy W.I.K.T.u" [The last performances of the VYKT], *Nowy Dziennik*, July 10, 1924; M. K. [Mojżesz Kanfer], "Ostatnie występy W.I.K.T.u (dokończenie) [The last performances of the VYKT (conclusion)], *Nowy Dziennik*, July 12, 1924; Appenszlak, "Żydowski teatr artystyczny; *Dziesiąte przykazanie (Łoj sachmojd)*"; Appenszlak, "Scena żydowska: Żydowski Teatr Artystyczny (W.I.K.T.): *Ku złotej krainie* . . ." [Jewish stage: Jewish art theatre: In the golden land . . .], *Nasz Przegląd*, December 28, 1926.

35. M. K., "Teatr Goldfadenowski."

36. The European vaudeville is a comic play interspersed with songs set to popular tunes. In the United States the term is applied to a form of variety entertainment consisting of amusing short performances: singing, dancing, acts of skill, telling jokes etc., and is an analogue of the English music-hall (see Martin Banham, ed., *The Cambridge Guide to World Theatre* (Cambridge: Cambridge University Press, 1988), 1037; Phyllis Hartnoll, ed., *The Oxford Companion to the Theatre* (Oxford: Oxford University Press, 1978), 983.

37. On Z. Turkow's production of *Shulamis* see Mirosława M. Bułat, "From Goldfaden to Goldfaden in Cracow's Jewish Theatres," in Joel Berkowitz, ed., *Yiddish Theatre: New Approaches* (Oxford, UK: The Littman Library of Jewish Civilization, 2003), 150–151, and a schoolchild's "review" of the play in the Appendices.

38. Zygmunt Turkow, "Dlaczego wystawiłem *Sulamitę*" [Why I staged *Shulamis*], *Nowy Dziennik*, April 28, 1939. See also Z. Turkow's memoirs *Di ibergerisene tkufe*, 445–456. I wish to express my thanks to Prof. Michael C. Steinlauf for correcting and polishing this and subsequent quotations translated from Polish and Yiddish into English.

39. Ibid., 446.

40. Broder Singers were traveling performers, precursors to professional Jewish actors, who in the second half of the nineteenth century sang Jewish songs and acted short skits in the inns and taverns of eastern Europe.

41. See Shloyme Pryzament, *Broder zinger* (Buenos Aires: Tsentral-farband fun poylishe yidn in argentine, 1960). Reprinted as *Broder zinger*, with introduction by Zalmen Hirschfeld and Zygmunt Turkow (Amherst: National Yiddish Book Center, 2000).

42. On Z. Turkow's production of *Bar Kokhba* by A. Goldfaden, see Bułat, "From Goldfaden to Goldfaden in Cracow's Jewish Theatres," 151–153.

43. M. K. [Mojżesz Kanfer], "Wieczory teatralne: *Bar-Kochba* jako widowisko" [Nights at the theatre: *Bar Kokhba* as spectacle], *Nowy Dziennik*, June 20, 1939.

44. Ibid.

45. See H. W., "Dekoracje *Bar Kochby*" [The scenery for *Bar Kokhba*], *Nowy Dziennik*, July 1, 1939.

46. Other artists had analogous objectives, among them David Herman. It would be interesting to pursue the similarities and differences in the approach of these two talented individuals both addressing the same issues.

47. Appenszlak refers to the phenomenal success of S. An-sky's *Der dibek* (*The Dybbuk*), after which cabaret performances by the "Azazel" also became very popular.

CHAPTER 6

From *Boston* to *Mississippi* on the Warsaw Yiddish Stage[1]

Jeffrey Veidlinger

By the mid-1930s, Poland's Jewish community was already in decline; anti-Semitic riots had encompassed universities in Cracow, the National Democratic Party was gaining support for *numerus clausus* on Jewish admission to universities, and many Jews were suffering disproportionately from the economic crisis. The National Democratic Party of Poland (Endeks) and other rightist groups were invigorated by the rise of Nazism in neighboring Germany, and began their own campaign to rid Poland of its Jews. The Polish government itself would soon end its hostile relations with Nazi Germany with the conclusion of the January 1934 nonaggression pact. Soon after the promulgation of the April 1935 constitution, the Endeks would begin an active campaign to acquire political power, to encourage economic boycotts of the Jews, and to arouse anti-Semitic riots. The situation was hardly better with Poland's neighbors. To the west, Hitler was rapidly acquiring dictatorial power while gradually enacting anti-Jewish legislation. To the east, Stalin had already succeeded in closing over half the synagogues in Russia and was engaged in a policy of intimidation against those who continued to frequent the remaining houses of worship. The Zionist party had been virtually wiped out in the Soviet Union through mass arrests and intimidation, and use of the Hebrew language was criminalized.

In Warsaw, though, there was a group of Jewish artists dedicated to the fight against injustice and the oppression of humanity. Yet when they sought to expose violations of human rights, they did not seek examples in fascist Germany or Stalinist Russia, or within Poland itself, where the cultural heritage and physical existence of Polish Jewry was crumbling before their eyes. Instead, this group of Jewish artists looked across the ocean to America. When they sought material closer to home, they looked back in time to Tsarist Russia or Imperial Germany, but never hinted at problems at home or in the near abroad. Their blindness to domestic problems and atrocities in Nazi Germany and Soviet Russia was not entirely a result of censorship, although the theatre's ardent support for Communism meant that it was engaged in a cat-and-mouse game with Polish governmental censors throughout its existence. Memoirs of those who participated in the theatre also demonstrate that its plays were not primarily intended as allegories of political oppression in Poland. Rather, they were symptomatic of the concerns of Polish Jewish youth in the 1930s, seemingly oblivious to their own coming destruction.

Like many other theatres that cater to those who lack access to more conventional and open arenas of political expression, Yiddish theatre always abounded in social and political commentary. This was never more so than for Mikhl Weichert's (1890–1967) Yung Teater (Young Theatre), which functioned in Warsaw from 1933 to 1937, and in Vilna under the name Nay Teater (New Theatre) for another two years. Yung Teater was an outstanding example of Jewish youth confronting the modern age with an aesthetic attack upon what they regarded as social and moral injustice. Its aesthetic and political-revolutionary spirit was best reflected in its manifesto, which declared:

Yung Teater will first of all produce modern dramatic creations, both Yiddish and European; modern life with its peculiar rhythm, with its ideas and slogans, will find a living echo in the performances of Yung Teater. Yung Teater takes its first step into the public without outside help, propelled by its own striving and deep devotion to theatrical performance, believing in the creative strength of that part of the Jewish masses for whom theatre is not simply entertainment, but rather a medium for the struggle for human and social liberation.[2]

The theatre fell short of its goal of bringing about social liberation, but did succeed in introducing aesthetic innovations of contemporary avant-garde theatre to the Polish Yiddish stage. Inspired by Max Reinhardt's (1873–1943) "chamber theatre" (*Kammerspiel*) and Vsevolod Meyerhold's (1874–1940) "conditional theatre" (*uslovnyi teatr*), Yung Teater sought to break down the "fourth wall" between actors and audiences by disarranging the stage, reconstructing the performance space, and fostering intimacy between performer and spectator.

By the early twentieth century, Warsaw had become one of the centers of Yiddish theatre, with tens of thousands of theatre "patriots" who could be counted upon to fill any auditorium. Warsaw's role was cemented with the establishment of Di Yidishe Teater Gezelshaft (The Yiddish Theatrical Society), which was inspired by the work of Yitskhok Leyb Peretz (1852–1915). The Society encouraged writers such as Sholem Aleichem (1859–1916), Sholem Asch (1880–1957), and Peretz Hirschbein (1880–1948) to develop a serious repertoire of Yiddish plays that no longer relied exclusively upon the melodramas characteristic of early Yiddish theatre.

Along with the development of a serious Yiddish repertoire came professional Yiddish art theatres. In contrast to earlier traveling troupes, these theatres did not rely exclusively upon star power and sensationalism, but also on ensemble work and a commitment to the aesthetic value of the production as a whole. The director came to replace the lead actor as the heart of the production on the model of Constantin Stanislavsky's (1863–1938) Moscow Art Theatre. These theatres not only presented the newer Yiddish repertoire of Peretz and Asch, but also works from the European repertoire, including Molière, Maxim Gorky, and Friedrich von Schiller. Among the most successful of these art theatres were the Vilner Trupe (Vilna Troupe), which moved to Warsaw in 1917, and the Warsaw Yiddish Art Theatre (VYKT), formed officially in 1923. While Warsaw Yiddish theatres also certainly presented the type of popular entertainment that famously attracted New York audiences, art theatres ensured that consciously literary and experimental theatre also constituted a significant presence.[3]

Although the first VYKT collapsed in 1928 and most of the actors in the original Vilner Trupe abandoned Warsaw for New York in 1924, they had succeeded in creating an audience for Yiddish art theatre. By the late 1920s, Yiddish theatre in Warsaw was regularly selling out the two-thousand-seat Nowości Theatre, and by the early 1930s, would boast some five or six professional Yiddish theatres. Yet still lacking was a sense of security and permanence for Yiddish art theatre. Ensembles were haphazardly formed and rapidly dissolved before they had the chance to achieve institutional stability. Constant touring both of outside theatres into Warsaw and local theatres out of Warsaw meant there was little consistency. Further, without respectability, wealthy patronage, or state support, Yiddish actors lacked any formal training, other than that received from elder actors willing to take young students under their wings. Polish Yiddish art theatre, though, had a model in the most successful Yiddish Art Theatre of them all—the Moscow State Yiddish Theatre (Gosudarstvennyi Evreiskii Teatr, GOSET), which toured Europe in 1928 and became a sensation in Poland, even though it was left off their tour. The GOSET was also the only Yiddish theatre in the world to boast a theatre technicum, dedicated to training prospective actors, artists, and musicians in the theatrical arts.[4]

One of the most ardent supporters of this type of formal Yiddish theatre training in Warsaw was Mikhl Weichert. Weichert was born in 1890 in Staromiasto, Ukraine. At an early age, his family moved to Stanislav, where he studied in both a Polish folk school and a *kheyder* (Jewish elementary school). He then attended a Polish *gymnasium*, and continued private Hebrew and religious studies. As a student he became involved in Zionist circles, but also attended the rival Czernowitz conference of Yiddish enthusiasts in 1908. He studied jurisprudence at Lemberg (Lwów) University, but was more interested in the cultural activities of Lemberg than in his studies. After two years, he left for Vienna with hopes of studying at the Academy of Music and Graphic Arts. Having failed the German-language entrance examinations, though, Weichert instead pursued private instruction under the tutelage of the actor, director, and future manager of the Burgtheater, Albert Heine (1867–1949). At the same time, Weichert continued to take courses toward his degree at Vienna University. He received his doctorate in jurisprudence in 1916. He then left for Berlin, where he studied at Max Reinhardt's famed theatre school.

In 1917, Weichert began writing essays on the history of Yiddish theatre in the German-language journal *Der Jude* (The Jew). The following year, he moved to Warsaw to work for the German military press administration. Weichert quickly integrated himself into the circle of Yiddish theatre enthusiasts that had formed in the city, impressing his colleagues with his professionalism and formal training. In 1919, he got his first major assignment, directing Gerhart Hauptmann's (1862–1946) *Fuhrmann Henschel* (*Drayman Henschel*) for the Vilner Trupe. Weichert continued to receive sporadic jobs from the Vilner Trupe and other Yiddish theatres in Warsaw while working on the side as a German language teacher in a *gymnasium* and writing critical articles for the press on Yiddish theatre. Over the next several years, Weichert became a leading voice in Yiddish theatrical criticism. In 1921, he helped found the theatrical journal *Ringen* (Links). As a member of the Union of Jewish Artists, Weichert also sat on editorial boards of several Yiddish theatre journals.

In May 1928, Weichert achieved his first smash success, directing Sholem Asch's *Kidesh ha-shem* (*Sanctification of the Holy Name*) at the Vilner Trupe—a production that was performed about 250 times and featured music by Henech Kon (1890–1972), and scenic design and costumes by Vladislav Vayntroyb (1891–?). It was with this team that Weichert would form the Yung Teater. Vayntroyb in particular shared Weichert's European training and highbrow aspirations. Vayntroyb received formal training in Paris as a painter and set designer, under the tutelage of renowned Russian designer Leon Bakst (1866–1924), and had later been active in Yiddish cabaret in Warsaw.[5]

Weichert first attempted to create a dramatic school in 1922, when together with several Yiddish theatre activists he established a two-year program. The school, though, was plagued by financial and organizational difficulties. When the first crop of students graduated in 1924, most were unable to find jobs in any of the major Yiddish theatres in the world. In the spring of 1929, Weichert tried again. In May of that year, he announced the formation of a Yiddish dramatic school that would be united with a studio, "in which the students will participate in presenting modern original dramas."[6] This time he convinced the Warsaw office of the Yiddish School Organization to allow him to use one of its school buildings in the evening hours to house the studio. Soon after its foundation, the studio received a subsidy from the leftist cultural organization, Kultur-lige (Culture League), with which it was formally integrated as of January 1, 1931.

In contrast to the European theatre schools on which Weichert's program was modeled, few of his students came with high levels of education and few were of bourgeois background. Of the original twenty or so students who enrolled in the school, only two had finished a *gymnasium*; most were uneducated laborers or petty merchants who worked their way through the school, attending classes in the evenings after a full day's labor. The majority had already participated in one of the amateur theatre circles sponsored by the various Jewish youth groups that proliferated in interwar Poland. Most had been involved in leftist circles, but from a variety of different perspectives, including Communist, Bundist, and Labor Zionist.[7] As former student Fayvl Zigelboym wrote, the school attracted "young talent, who in addition to acting in the theatre, also sought a platform to cry out their protest against reaction and injustice."[8] They were "a young group of actors that was saturated with a revolutionary spirit."[9]

The goal of the studio was to train young actors in "the spirit of modern Yiddish mass culture and the principles of socialist *Weltanschauung*."[10] According to Weichert, "at every moment we were compelled not only to be a better theatre, but to be a new theatre with its own artistic formula and prominent repertoire."[11] On the model of the GOSET theatre school, it taught not only theatre skills, but also general studies. Classes included dance, music, make-up, costume, stage design, phonetics, dialectology, history of European theatre, history of Yiddish theatre, Jewish history, acoustics, psychology, hygiene, sexual education, physiology, and physical education; many were taught by Warsaw's leading Jewish luminaries, including historians Itzik (Ignacy) Schipper (1884–1943) and Raphael Mahler (1899–1977), composer Henech Kon, actress Leah Rotbaum, and linguist Noyekh Prylucki (1882–1941). The goal was not only to train students in the theatrical arts, but also to endow them with a general humanistic education. Weichert instructed his students in a version of the Stanislavsky system, encouraging them to bring to each role only their own personal experiences and feelings, and to forget all else they had seen before on the stage: "From one's self alone can one search for the path to a role," he declared.[12] The school was admired by Polish theatrical giants like director Leon Schiller (1887–1954) and the director of the Polish state theatre school, Alexander Zelwerowicz (1877–1955).

After three years of training, the students of the dramatic school presented a graduation theatrical evening at the Atheneum Theatre. The show consisted of three short plays, each demonstrating a different dramatic style: a short play based on one of Peretz's poems demonstrating the grotesque; Peretz Hirschbein's *Zaverukha* (A blizzard), demonstrating realism; and Ernst Toller's (1893–1939) *Masse Mensch* (*Man and the Masses*), demonstrating political satire and the theatre's ability to perform European art.[13] Weichert assembled the same creative team with which he had produced *Kidesh ha-shem* at the Vilner Trupe; Kon composed the music, and Vayntroyb created the costumes and set design. The hall was filled with luminaries from the Warsaw theatrical realm and drama critics. The production was praised for its technical achievement, particularly in the realms of diction and voice. The

Polish theatre critic, and later biographer of Leon Schiller, Zygmunt Tonecki, featured the theatre in the prestigious Polish literary paper *Wiadomości Literackie* (Literary news), which had previously remained aloof from developments in the Yiddish world. Despite the critical acclaim, the Kultur-lige decided to withdraw its support for the school after this performance. With its own funds spread so thinly already, the Kultur-lige felt itself unable to indulge Weichert in his endeavor. The students, nevertheless, persevered and persuaded Weichert to establish an independent theatre, which the ensemble of young enthusiasts named Yung Teater.

In order to establish the theatre, an organizing committee was created consisting of the theatre school's leading stars, Yosef Glikson, Avrom Greenspan, Fayvl Zigelboym, and Weichert. For a performance space, the troupe acquired a small hall at a local tailor's union, which they were able to rent for the weekends. Measuring a mere sixteen by five and a half meters, the hall seemed hardly large enough to be used for union meetings, let alone for theatre. Weichert, however, believed that he could use the space effectively. Although the troupe did not need to get paid—they all kept their day jobs—they still needed financial backing to rent the hall and to pay for advertising and other expenses. The troupe collected small sums of money from friends of the former dramatic studio, but were forced to raise the rest on their own. In order to accomplish this, several students together with Kon formed a *kleynkunst* (literally, "small-art") troupe that performed a type of Yiddish cabaret popular in Poland at that time.[14] The troupe that they formed adopted the name New Azazel, after the original Azazel that had entertained Warsaw Jewish literati since 1925. *Kleynkunst*'s political satire tended to appeal to elites; the New Azazel performed for the Warsaw Jewish Writers Union and toured towns around Warsaw, raising small sums of money that were nevertheless sufficient to fund the low-budget Yung Teater.

Yung Teater's first production, *Boston,* which premiered on February 3, 1933, was based on German author Bernhard Blume's (1901–1978) drama about the Sacco and Vanzetti affair, *In Namen des Volkes!* (In the name of the people!). Blume appeared in 1930 to be an emerging German playwright, whose work dealt with themes of class oppression and social justice. Blume's playwriting career, though, was cut short with the rise of National Socialism. In 1936, he and his Jewish wife emigrated to the United States. Lacking a significant audience for his playwriting, Blume pursued a career instead in academia, first at Ohio State University and then at Harvard University, where he held the Kuno Francke Professorship of German Art and Culture from 1956 to 1966. *In Namen des Volkes!* premiered in Leipzig in February 1930.

The play consisted of forty-four short scenes that depict the true story of the Sacco and Vanzetti affair, a sensational trial that made headlines around the world for nearly a decade. The play follows Nicola Sacco (1891–1927) and Bartolomeo Vanzetti (1888–1927), two Italian immigrants to America who were arrested in 1920 for their alleged participation in a murder-robbery. Despite well-supported alibis, they were found guilty by a jury, and after seven years of appeals, were sentenced to death for their alleged crimes. Many observers believed that the two were innocent and unjustly persecuted on account of their anarchist beliefs—an opinion still commonly held today. To many Americans and foreign observers, the trial served as an example of the excesses of the Red Scare and the embodiment of American injustice. Numerous literary works were inspired by the affair, including Upton Sinclair's (1878–1968) *Boston* (1928) and Howard Fast's (1914–2003) *The Passion of Sacco and Vanzetti* (1953), to name but a few. Although the victims were Italian, the trial resonated deeply within Jewish circles in America and around the world. Coming from a large immigrant community with leftist sympathies, many American Jews identified with the plight of Sacco and Vanzetti. It is therefore no surprise that many Yiddish writers found inspiration in the story as well.[15] Like most who followed the sensational trial, Weichert believed that the two were being scapegoated for their political beliefs, and denied true justice on account of their low socio-economic standing. He believed that Blume's play effectively demonstrated these points. In his words, "from the first scene . . . the political and social background of the trial is made clear."[16] Weichert changed the name of Blume's play to *Sacco and Vanzetti*, but at the last minute the censors forced him to change the name on the grounds that *Sacco and Vanzetti* was too openly political. The new name, *Boston*, did little to camouflage the content of the play. *Boston* was also the title of Upton Sinclair's 1928 novel about the Sacco and Vanzetti trial that was popular among Yiddish-speaking Poles in its 1930 Yiddish translation by Mark Fogelman. But, as Weichert himself noted, the Yiddish censor in Warsaw was not very meticulous.[17]

The small auditorium in the tailors' local union hall forced Weichert to work with space in creative ways. A stage would have taken up too much room, so Weichert presented each of the play's scenes in different spots throughout the auditorium, among the audience. In addition to solving the practical problem of space, this technique was also inspired by French cabaret and German Kleinkunst, both of which sought to break down the "fourth wall" between the audience and the performers, and to force the audience to become a part of the spectacle. The small performance space gave Weichert an excuse to put his doctrine of "contact performance," a variation of Reinhardt's "chamber theatre," into practice. In one of his earliest writings, "Bine un publikum" (The stage and the public), Weichert wrote of the need to "create a unified atmosphere" among the performers and audience: "one must feel as though a common spirit soars over the stage and the public; a warmth must be spread that can encompass all—those who are performing above as well as those who are listening below."[18] Weichert believed the best way to blur the boundary between the stage and the audience was through close contact: "the change in distance from the actor to the audience alters everything."[19] The actor, he continued, can no longer act only from the front, but must act from all sides, remembering always that he is a part of the auditorium. Further, the actor must adjust his voice, changing it from a loud stage voice to an ordinary conversational volume appropriate to the level of intimacy in the theatre. In the words of actor Yosef Glikson, "The hall truly heard how the actor breathed; saw every twitch of his face, every blink of the eye."[20]

Finally, the auditorium posed novel challenges for the sets, which could not be changed from the wings. In order to help configure the performance space, Weichert brought on board an architect who helped him envision the design. The benches for the audience were placed along the length of the auditorium rather than the breadth, with three rows on one side and two on the other. The empty space in the middle was used for a multitude of purposes in the play: it served as the street, the meeting hall, the apartment of Sacco's family, and the defense counsel's conference room. In what had been the front of the auditorium, but was now to the side of the audience, a small podium stood with a table and chair, which served as the police station, the judge's bench, the judge's office, and the governor's reception room. Opposite the podium were a few fence pickets placed over a doorstep that represented the prison. Finally, a small booth was placed along the third wall, which served as both a telephone booth and the spot from which the banker delivers his address. It also housed the light board for the play. There was no other scenery. In fact, the sets were so sparse that when the audience of distinguished invited guests showed up for the show's premiere, they all thought that they had been duped when they entered the auditorium. Not believing that a theatrical performance was actually going to take place in the empty meeting hall, the audience assembled on the street outside in bewilderment.

All action in the play was guided by simple lights, which illuminated the spot at which the next scene was to be played out. As the audience watched the illuminated spot, the other actors would silently enter and exit from two doors in the auditorium to place themselves for the next scene. This allowed for a rapid tempo to be maintained throughout the play: "one scene ended, the light was extinguished, and then together with the word of the actor there would be light in a second spot, in a second corner of the hall; the scenes ran like a kaleidoscope."[21] Each of the forty-four scenes followed successively with hardly a second's interruption. The only exceptions were the two intermissions between acts. Yet the play continued even then, as actors dressed as paperboys distributed "extra" newspapers among the audience with sensational headlines about the Sacco and Vanzetti trial.

Fayvl Zigelboym starred as Vanzetti, whom he portrayed as a conscientious worker and committed anarchist, in contrast to Fayvl Sivak's portrayal of Sacco as a simple, naïve family man who had dreamed of a better life in America. Much of the play centered on the trial, during which two jurors—representing the twelve—sat in the front of the hall looking disinterested and at times snoring loudly. The inherent theatricality of a courtroom drama was particularly appropriate for the small performance space, and also helped maintain the tempo. For this reason, Weichert would continually rely upon murder trials and court dramas for the repertoire of

Yung Teater. The only problem with the courtroom drama, though, was that it highlighted the plight of individuals rather than ideas and social classes. In order to bring out the social ramifications of the play, Weichert needed to bring in scenes from beyond the courthouse as well; these included contrasting scenes of the Sacco family's humble apartment, the governor's luxurious office, and of street protests.

The play was a tremendous success. Leon Schiller called it "the most interesting phenomenon of the current season in Warsaw."[22] However, at the twelfth performance a policeman showed up at the hall and ordered it closed. The problem, ironically, was not the content of the play, but that Weichert had obtained permission for only five performances. Weichert was able to convince the official in charge of the Warsaw Committee, who was a theatre aficionado himself, to allow the production to continue on its experimental merits. The play was so successful that the Polish actress Irena Solska (1875–1958) became interested in producing it. Weichert helped to develop it, but when the Polish version was submitted to the censors, it came back completely changed. When Solska presented even this diluted version, it aroused the anger of important governmental officials who rescinded her theatre's state subsidy. Yung Teater, as well, had no choice but to halt performances of the play.

For its next performance, the troupe was able to secure a new auditorium from a different union, which would allow them to perform on weekdays as well as on weekends. The troupe's new auditorium, located on Długa 19, could seat over 300 people, but the space was hindered by the presence of eight columns throughout the hall. Weichert realized that if he were to make the best use of the room, he would need to incorporate the columns into the play. "The columns in the middle of the hall," he wrote, "reminded me of my grandfather's stable in Pidhaiets. Suddenly it occurred to me to present a production about a wandering Yiddish troupe in the beginning of this century that performs in the stables of a rich man in a Galician shtetl. I called the production *Trupe Tanentsap: a Goldfaden shpil in a galitsish shtetl* (The Tanentsap Troupe, a Goldfaden play in a Galician shtetl)."[23] *Trupe Tanentsap* was an original play based on an actual traveling troupe that Weichert saw as a child. Weichert had always admired the early Yiddish theatre for its populism and folksiness. In an early article, "Dos alte un dos naye teater" (The old and the new theatre), Weichert chastised the new art theatres for distancing themselves from the audience. "This is the strength of the old theatre, the secret of its success. It always pays attention to the wild sounds of the masses, every slightest shiver of the thousands of heads, every wish and every desire satisfied. . . . [T]his harmony between the writer, the actor and the public to create has not yet come about in the new theatre."[24] In his nostalgia for the supposed ecstasies of premodern popular theatre, Weichert was recapitulating familiar arguments made by European theatre critics. The difference for Yiddish theatre, though, was that the Yiddish folk theatre was very much a matter of living memory rather than some semi-mythical theatre of yore. *Trupe Tanentsap* was Weichert's attempt to re-create the spontaneity of the old Yiddish theatre, to bring the public back into an active role, as he imagined they had had in the early Yiddish theatre.

The play revolved around a play-within-a-play as a fictional amateur troupe led by Rudolf Tanentsap performs Avrom Goldfaden's *Tsvey Kuni-Leml* (*The Two Kuni-Lemls*).[25] Weichert's theatrical space evoked a shtetl, with the auditorium set up to resemble a stable, with lanterns hanging from the eight poles. A makeshift stage of boards placed over beer barrels was erected behind a floral curtain at the front of the auditorium. As the audience sat down, Rudolf Tanentsap, dressed in a black frock coat and accompanied by his wife, emerged from the back and began greeting guests and taking tickets. The audience watches as Moyshe, a young tailor, enters the auditorium with Yenta, a young servant girl; they take two empty seats at the front. Soon after, an aristocrat, who is the head of the community and owner of the stable in which the production is taking place, enters and moves to the seats where the couple is sitting. A scandal erupts as the couple initially refuses to move, but with Tanentsap's intervention, they are persuaded to take new seats. Finally, Tanentsap takes the stage and introduces the troupe in Germanized Yiddish with puffery and grandstanding, characteristic of the early Yiddish theatre. During these formal remarks, a Lithuanian skeptic from the audience can be heard making the occasional snide comment.

The play-within-a-play begins as the troupe performs the first scene of *Tsvey Kuni-Leml*. Throughout the Tanentsap's performance, the "audience" members remain in character: Moyshe talks loudly throughout, ignoring the aristocrat's stares. At the end of the second scene, when the students in Goldfaden's play are supposed to sing a song in praise of the tsar, Weichert had some students bring in a portrait of Tsar Nicholas II. At this point from within the "audience," an "Austrian lieutenant" stands up and demands to know why the Russian tsar is being honored here in Austrian Galicia. A commotion ensues, during which Tanentsap quickly runs up to the portrait of Nicholas II, tears off his beard and hat, and tampers with the photo so that we see a bald head and sideburns characteristic of the Austro-Hungarian emperor, Franz-Joseph, instead. Tanentsap then turns to the orchestra and instructs them to play an Austrian patriotic song. The lieutenant and other officials in the audience stand up and salute. At the end of the act, the lights come on in the theatre to reveal a young Hasid hiding behind a pillar: "Look how the hypocrite comes to the theatre!" shouts Moyshe. In the midst of the fifth scene, though, a raucous noise erupts in the audience. The Hasid can no longer stand the performance and yells out, "Gevalt, fellow Jews! They are making a mockery of us! Heaven help us! Fellow Jews, why are you silent? This is blasphemy!" The aristocrat finds himself forced to agree, "He is right—why must such a mockery be made of Jews?"[26] A Litvak know-it-all gets up from the audience, stands on the stage and tries to take control of the situation by beginning a Talmudic analysis of the situation, but he is soon heckled by Moyshe, who just wants to see the rest of the play. Finally, the lieutenant and gendarmes conclude that the situation has gotten out of control and close down the performance. But first the director receives permission to say a few words. He tells the audience how the play ends, and then embarks upon a soliloquy bemoaning the difficult life of itinerant actors, and defending the merits of Yiddish theatre: "And what is our sin? We bring a little joy into the dark workshops and wet cellars. The Hasid does not need us; he has his rebbe. The German does not need us; he has his concerts. But the simple man, the artisan and the workers, the servant, the seamstress and the maid, they live, breathe and enjoy themselves with us."[27] This speech in particular was drawn from Weichert's own early articles on Yiddish theatre and represented his own faith in the populism of theatre. The director's soliloquy was also reminiscent of Goldfaden's curtain speeches, in which he would emerge from behind the curtain after a performance to explain the play to his audience.[28] The play's abrupt ending was also intended as an allegorical criticism of the censors who had closed down the performance of *Boston*.[29] The prominent Yiddish writer, dramatist, and critic, Itzik Manger, called the play one of the most innovative theatrical productions in Poland.[30]

For its next production, which premiered on March 23, 1934, Yung Teater once again presented a new play torn from the newspaper headlines. With the rise of Nazism in Germany and with what Weichert regarded as the decline of Polish humanitarian ideals at home, he was inspired by the captivating news story of the Soviet icebreaker *Krassin* that rescued an Italian polar expedition in distress. On May 24, 1928, polar explorer Umberto Nobile's seaplane crashed into an ice floe in the Svalbard Archipelago, the day after Nobile reached the North Pole. Nobile and eight other survivors were unable to make radio contact, and search and rescue operations dispatched in the following two weeks by Norway, Sweden, Finland, Russia, and Italy returned empty-handed. It was not until June 6 that an amateur Russian radio operator picked up the SOS from the *Italia*, beginning a massive international effort to rescue the survivors. The rescue effort, though, was poorly coordinated and inundated with political and diplomatic conflicts. It was not until July 12 that the Russian ice-breaker *Krassin* broke into the floe to rescue the survivors. For Weichert, this was an example of humanitarianism surpassing political differences, as well as a clear demonstration of the victory of Soviet Communism over Italian Fascism. The play was a stage adaptation of German Communist playwright Friedrich Wolf's radio play on the topic, but Weichert expanded Wolf's original nineteen scenes into fifty-two short scenes, utilizing the captain of the *Krassin*'s own memoirs in his adaptation.[31]

The play begins in complete darkness as the *"Giovinezza"* (the Italian Fascist anthem) is heard.[32] Then from various places around the hall, loudspeakers are illuminated one after another, each representing radio stations from around the world that called out for the *Italia*. Aboard an ice-breaker in the middle of the ocean, seamen see from a distance smoke coming out of a burning ship—it is the *Italia*. The Russian captain, Rudolf Samoilovich, radios Moscow to tell his superiors that he will be diverting to save the sinking ship. Moscow radios the Italian consulate in Leningrad, but is told to wait until the consulate can get in contact with Rome. While the formalities and bureaucratic delays take place, Samoilovich becomes impatient: "Ach, the formalities. And here human lives are hovering in danger!" [33] The rest of the play presents the tense, action-filled story of how the *Krassin* rescued the *Italia* in the Polar ice, ending with Samoilovich's rescue as all the loudspeakers start to play the Socialist anthem, the "Internationale."

One problem the troupe encountered was that the censors refused to allow the "Internationale" to be played on stage. To solve the problem, Kon recorded an album, which if spun slowly played the "Internationale," but if played quickly sounded like a foxtrot. With such a small auditorium it was easy to see if there were any officials in the hall by the end of the play. If so, the record would be spun quickly and the play would end with a foxtrot. For all remaining performances, the "Internationale" would be sounded.[34]

Weichert solved the problem of how to depict colossal ships and massive ice floes in a small auditorium with a shoestring budget by abolishing all separation between the audience and the performance space. All four walls of the theatre were decorated with scenes from the capitals of the world and particularly the Russian north. In a corner of the room lay the massive and stationary *Krassin*. The radio stations that appeared throughout the room were intended to illustrate how the entire world served a single ship. As in *Boston,* action took place at various locations in the hall, forcing the audience to twist and turn to watch each scene. Yung Teater also began touring the Polish provinces during the summer with *Krassin*, requiring the construction of a collapsible set, and further paring down of the staging.

The theatre's next production, which premiered in July 1934, was Weichert's version of Sholem Aleichem's *Di goldgreber* (The gold diggers), about a shtetl that goes berserk searching for gold, allegedly hidden in the cemetery by Napoleon and his army.[35] Weichert called his version of the play *Napoleon's Treasure*, alluding to folk beliefs in hidden treasure, dating to the Napoleonic era. Both Sholem Aleichem's original and Weichert's adaptation mock the futility of shtetl life and those who refuse to work for the betterment of their lives, trusting instead in fantastical dreams or messianic expectations. But where Sholem Aleichem's play champions the American work ethic (if not its moral grounding) by concentrating on the conflict between an American émigré who has returned to the shtetl and those who have remained, Weichert largely left out the American moralizing. Instead, his play centers on the character of Levi Mozgovoyer, a typical *luftmentsh* who wastes his time away searching for hidden treasure instead of contributing to society. The play had a clear social message, urging its audience members to give up their fantastical dreams and to concentrate instead on building institutions and working toward the social welfare. The play also allowed Weichert to depict the declining shtetls as he saw them, much as he had done with *Trupe Tanentsap*.

The play was praised by Nachman Mayzel (1887–1966), who wrote, "The internal enthusiasm among the actors quickly spread through the hall and infects the auditorium. Every performance is a celebration on the stage and a holiday among the public."[36] This less overtly political and experimental production was also welcomed by the press and audiences as a respite, both of whom preferred Sholem Aleichem to more oblique works. Nevertheless, Mayzel felt that Weichert had still gone too far in his uncomplimentary portrayal of the shtetl Jews: "The Jewish shtetl should not be portrayed as wild, isolated, and ugly.... Sholem Aleichem's children are still always cordial, kind, pert, and mischievous, but not idiots!"[37] Another reviewer noted that the characters lacked the depth and humor typical of Sholem Aleichem.[38] Nevertheless, "the interest in this performance," wrote one Yiddish paper, "is so strong, that even Polish theatregoers are visiting the production."[39] It was "an exceptional success. The full hall resounded with heartfelt laughter. The original staging, the exceptional acting by the actors, the folksy music and peculiar dance, the splendid sets and costumes charmed the hall."[40] The play was performed more than 150 times. Clearly audiences in Poland, as elsewhere, preferred Sholem Aleichem to the pedantic and experimental writers favored by politically conscious avant-garde directors and actors. Audiences came to the theatre for art and entertainment, not for political lessons on current events. It is ironic that Weichert himself had repeatedly made this point in his writings and in *Trupe Tanentsap*, but in his own theatre was unwilling to part with experimentalism and the avant-garde to please his audiences.

For the next production, Weichert chose an overtly Communist play by a Soviet writer, Vladimir Naumovich Bill'-Belotserkovsky (1884–1970), entitled *Zhizn' zovyot* (Life calls). The play premiered on November 30, 1934 under the Yiddish title *Dos lebn ruft*. This time Weichert decided to invite as a guest director Jacob Rotbaum (1901–1994), who had worked with the Vilner Trupe. The play, a standard in the Soviet canon of Socialist Realist drama, tells of Professor Chadov's plan to irrigate and fertilize the far reaches of Siberia by diverting the warm Kurushiwo current that travels along coastal Japan through the Gulf of Tartary. Meanwhile, Chadov's daughter Galina struggles to turn her industrial saboteur and drunkard husband into a Bolshevik worker. Realizing that he cannot be reformed, she falls in love with Kashirin, a conscientious worker, who is the director of a chemical trust in Siberia. At the play's climax, Galina tries to convince her father to give up his project, as the doctors advise that further work will kill him. Chadov chastises her with the morals of Soviet Bolshevism: "Is it possible that the instinct for possession—of an old piece of lumber like me—is dearer to you than a project that will bring life to the tundra and taiga and will give light and warmth to millions of people? [. . .] I now understand what a conservative institution the family is ... either you risk the life of your father or you lose the possibility of giving your country a new rich region."[41]

According to Weichert, Rotbaum's type of acting conflicted with the troupe's usual method, but in the end produced a successful production. Indeed, *Haynt* (Today) commented that Rotbaum's staging blended so well with the troupe that his presence is "like sugar that is dissolved in water." Despite some weak and immature acting, the review concluded that the play was "a good test for Yung Teater, which shows that the work of the artistic direction of Dr. Mikhl Weichert is necessary and positive."[42] It was performed over 100 times. According to *Haynt,* it "was a smash success . . . the public was most delighted."[43]

For its sixth production, Yung Teater again turned to recent headlines, and again to injustice in America—this time to the 1931 Scottsboro Affair in which nine black youths, the "Scottsboro Boys," were wrongly accused of raping two white women on a train in Alabama. Once again, a murder trial served as the setting of the drama. The play was written by Leyb Malach (1894–1936), a Polish Yiddish writer, who had left his broken family in the shtetl at the age of thirteen to support himself with odd jobs in Warsaw. He published his first poems in Warsaw Yiddish journals in 1915, and was admired as a self-educated writer. In 1922, he immigrated to Argentina, where he started writing dramatic works. He would later achieve some success as a travel writer and journalist, commenting on political, social, and economic life in Palestine, Europe, and America during the 1930s.[44] Malach had met Weichert in 1933 when, during a visit to Warsaw, he attended a performance of *Boston*. At the time, Weichert and Malach had discussed the possibility of Malach's penning a play for Yung Teater that would combine the theatre's social and artistic goals. The two discussed various current events that could serve as the basis for such a play and settled upon the Scottsboro Affair. The setting was changed from Alabama to Mississippi, the number of the accused was reduced by two, and the names were changed, but the play otherwise drew heavily from the newspapers. It premiered on March 19, 1935.

The play begins in a boxcar moving through the American South.[45] On board the car are several African Americans riding the rails in search of work and a better life. One of them, a fourteen-year-old boy named Tommy, is lying in the corner sick. Soon the train stops and the stowaways hear the conductor offering two women a place in an empty freight car until they reach the next station. Sure enough, Grace and Anne, two prostitutes, are brought aboard the same car in which the stowaways are hiding. When the train stops next, two white "boys" board the same boxcar. The black men separate from the whites and hover together in one corner while the white "boys" blow out the lanterns and begin taking advantage of the women. A struggle ensues and the white "boys" are thrown off the train. At the next stop, policemen board, having been tipped off by the white "boys," and discover a group of black men with two white women, who have obviously recently been violated. The African Americans are led off the train as a crowd calls for their lynching.

In the next act, the stark differences between the lifestyles of blacks and whites are emphasized by several different performance spaces and split stages. In the center of the hall is a circular podium that serves as center stage, and on which the most dramatic moments take place. However, the vast majority of the act is staged in a variety of locations throughout the theatre, and on divergent planes and heights.

At times, simultaneous parallel action takes place on different sites. Spotlights flash on each speaker, switching focus midway through sentences as the speech is interrupted by parallel conversations on the other side of the performance space. The constant movement thrusts the long act along. The act begins with a split stage: on one side we see the decrepit house in which Tommy's family resides, while on the other side we see the apartment of the two prostitutes. The former provides a picture of a loving family and hard work, while in the latter the prostitutes lie in bed in the middle of the day, begging a visitor for cigarettes. The "boys" from the train come to the prostitutes' apartment and are warmly welcomed. The prostitutes sit on the boys' laps as they laugh at the headlines of the paper: "Young Negroes Kidnap Two White Women in a Boxcar and Violate Them."

The prostitutes are further rewarded when representatives from the "White Lilies" society come to their door and offer them one thousand dollars as consolation for their sufferings and to help pay for the operation that may be necessary, as "the heavens must guard against Negroes being born."[46] On the other side of the stage, the sheriff comes to Tommy's family's house and tells them of Tommy's arrest. As Tommy's family reacts to this tragedy, we see Grace and Anne in their apartment, dancing to jazz on the radio, and singing about their sudden riches. The next segment takes us into the offices of the defense lawyer and the prosecutor, with the latter trying to intimidate the former by hinting that a defense of the African Americans will be perceived as unpatriotic and as a defense of anarchism and socialism. Meanwhile, the black defendants languish in jail and dream of satisfying their hunger. The discussions among the lawyers clearly indicate that the racial conflict is integrally related to the class conflict. When the inevitable guilty verdict is reached, we hear of mass worker demonstrations from San Francisco to Washington. In the final scene, the seven prisoners sit in jail listening to the working people demonstrate for their release outside. We realize that the martyrdom of the seven innocents has only strengthened the greater struggle for universal justice.

The production was greeted warmly by the press. Nachman Mayzel wrote that the play represents "without doubt, a new artistic accomplishment for the theatre."[47] He noted particularly the music, written by Kon, which utilized African-American motifs and livened up what could have been a pedantic performance. Ironically, since Kon was out of town during the rehearsals, the troupe had only ten days to learn and practice the music. Although plays by Malach had been produced in America before, this was the world premiere of *Mississippi* and the first production of Malach's to appear on the Polish stage. The talent of the young actors in the theatre, declared Mayzel, grew from production to production. "There is no doubt that this new sixth production will continue with no less success than all the previous productions," he concluded.[48] Nathan Buksboym wrote, "it is a production that deeply engraves the memory and will not allow you to forget it."[49] He commended Weichert for presenting the play at a gripping pace, and the actors for their ensemble performance. The premiere, he claimed, was met with "stormy applause."

The play was performed over 100 times and remained in the company's repertoire until its demise in 1937. The play has since been produced in Buenos Aires and in Hebrew translation in Tel Aviv.

The theatre's next production, Jacob Preger's *Simkhe Plakhte*, premiered on December 20, 1935. Preger, like Malach, had come to Warsaw from a broken family as a youth. At the age of twenty he started writing Yiddish poetry, and made his theatrical debut in 1927, when the Vilner Trupe produced his *Der nisoyen* (The temptation).[50] *Simkhe Plakhte* is based on a folkloric tale about a simple water-carrier who falls in love with a maid. She will not marry him, though, because of his low social standing. An orphan girl, who is a servant to a rabbi, takes pity on him and tells him that he could become a rabbi. She knits him a rabbinical outfit and he instantly becomes a rabbi. After helping a wealthy landlord find his horse, the new rabbi soon develops a following among the local Jews. He becomes the town's leading rabbi and a prominent figure, but is too dull-witted to take advantage of his position. Although he has been married to the orphan girl, he still pines for the maid. Near the end of the play he succeeds in divorcing the orphan, at which point his ruse is discovered and he reverts to being a simple water-carrier. The motif was common in the repertoire of *misnagdic* (anti-Hasidic) literature and early traveling Yiddish theatre troupes, which sought to mock the reverence with which followers of the Hasidic movement looked upon their *rebbes*.

Nachman Mayzel called the performance "a new artistic victory, a victory for the writer, the director and the collective, who have already crossed the line from being only students to being genuine performers."[51] *Haynt*, though, faulted Weichert for over-directing the play and for sometimes oversimplifying its characters.[52] The play also ignited a controversy in Warsaw over the use of crude language in the theatre. Preger used his gift for dialect, portraying the simple water-carrier as a ruffian with dialogue appropriate to his standing. Reviewers were divided over the effect of such language, and the play even elicited discussion about the usage of crude language in art. The play was later produced in the United States at the Yiddish Art Theatre by Maurice Schwartz under the title *Der vaser-treger* (The water carrier).

In 1936, while the company was visiting Vilna for the first time on one of its summer tours, the theatre's constitution was rescinded by the government. Although no official reason was given, the theatre's Communist orientation (and Jewish constitution) was clearly an important factor. Weichert returned to Warsaw to appeal the decision, while the troupe continued its tour under a new name. He made little headway until he secured a meeting with one top official who informed him that the theatre was closed for "three trifling reasons: your ensemble is Communist, your repertoire is Communist, and your acting is Communist."[53] Weichert responded that only one of the members of the ensemble was a member of the Communist Party, that the plays were all approved by the censors, and that acting cannot be Communist. While the theatre may appear Communist, he continued, it might also appear populist, unionist, Zionist, Orthodox, and assimilationist. He explained that he alone decided on the repertoire and the staging without following any one party line, but rather by allowing himself to be influenced by all the opinions around him. The official agreed to give a new constitution to the theatre, provided that it change its name to Yung Bine (Young Stage).

For its first revitalized production, Weichert decided upon Georg Büchner's (1813–1837) *Woyzeck* in a Yiddish translation by Itzik Manger (1901–1969). *Woyzeck* is based on the true story of Johann Christian Woyzeck, who was beheaded in 1824 for murdering his mistress in a fit of jealous rage. Büchner's Woyzeck is a victim of poverty and abuse; his crimes a product of his social environment, rather than an individual inclination toward criminal acts. Although Büchner died in 1836, leaving an unfinished manuscript of *Woyzeck,* the first known performance of the play did not occur until 1913. In the late 1910s and early 1920s, the play was embraced by the Expressionists—most famously by Alban Berg, whose 1923 opera *Wozzeck* became the most famous adaptation of Büchner's tale.

Weichert was unwell at the time of the production, so he hired a guest director, Kurt Katchen, a Jew from Grodno who had met Weichert while both were studying in Reinhardt's Berlin theatre school. Katchen remained in Germany, working with the Lessing Theater among others, until he was forced to flee eastward by the rise of fascism in Germany. This was Katchen's second time directing *Woyzeck*, the first having been in German. Katchen was less of an ensemble director and favored the star system, a novel form for Yung Teater; he himself even performed in the production. The play premiered October 9, 1936. Although the critics applauded the theatre for its bold attempt to stage a serious work of world drama, most ultimately thought it was unsuccessful. A reviewer for *Haynt* commented that the theatrical space was too small to stage such a work and that the actors, although ambitious and talented, were simply too inexperienced to fully explore all aspects of the work.[54] Although the play did tour the provinces and other cities, it was the theatre's least successful production.

In 1937, the theatre began production on what would be its final show, again under Weichert's direction. This time, Weichert secured Yekhezkel Dobrushin's (1883–1953) reworking of S. Y. Abramovich's (1835–1917) *Masoes Binyomin hashlishi* (*The Travels of Benjamin III*). Weichert had met with Dobrushin and Solomon Mikhoels (1890–1948), the director of the Moscow GOSET, in 1935, at a theatre festival in Moscow, where the play had first been performed in 1927. They agreed to send Weichert Dobrushin's script as well as the musical score, written by Lev Pulver (1883–1970). In late 1936, Weichert went to the Soviet embassy in Warsaw to pick up the script and score, which had been sent through official channels. The play tells of the adventures of two naïve shtetl bumpkins who set out in search of one of the Lost Tribes of Israel, only to find that they have been traveling in circles and have ended up in a neighboring village.

Once again, Weichert utilized the entire auditorium as a performance space. Several stations were set up throughout the auditorium, with each station functioning as the stage for one scene. Between scenes, the two adventurers, Benjamin and Senderl, would wander from one station to the next, emphasizing their journey and making the play resemble a medieval Christian Passion play. Ironically, this play, which was imported directly from the Soviet Union, was the least political of any of Yung Teater's plays. In Weichert's words, "It was a light and fluffy production, full of humor and joy—in those difficult and dark times, it was a welcome present."[55]

Nevertheless, not long after the play's Warsaw premiere, in May 1937, the theatre's charter was revoked again. This time, due to rising anti-Semitism in governmental circles, its charter to perform in Warsaw would not be renewed. The troupe moved to Vilna, where it continued to play under the new name "Nay Teater" (New Theatre) until 1939. In the coming years, most of the troupe would flee into the Soviet interior to escape the Nazi concentration camps. Others, like the talented actress Dvore Fakel, were less fortunate; she was murdered in Majdanek.[56] Weichert, for his part, became a figure of international renown. During the Second World War he headed the Yidishe Sotsiale Aleynhilf (Jewish Social Self-Help organization, often known by its Polish acronym, ŻSS, Żydowska Samopomoc Społeczna), which served as the main distribution office of foreign aid to Jewish communities in the *Generalgouvernement*. In October 1942, the organization was renamed the Jewish Aid Office for the Generalgouvernement (Jüdische Unterstützungsstelle für das Generalgouvernement, JUS) and brought under the direct control of the German authorities, leading to widespread accusations from the Jewish underground that Weichert had become a collaborator. Following the war, Weichert was arrested by the Polish authorities and tried by the Polish Committee of National Liberation as a traitor. Although he was found not guilty by the Polish court, he was subsequently tried again by a Jewish honor court, which found him guilty of collaborating with the enemy. Weichert was stripped of his public positions within the Jewish community and spent much of the rest of his life trying to justify his wartime actions.[57]

One of Nay Teater's last performances was Theodore Dreiser's *An American Tragedy*, which premiered in March 1939, directed by Jacob Rotbaum. Once again, the theatre used a true courtroom drama to demonstrate the fallacies of the American Dream. Dreiser's well-known 1925 novel presents a fictionalized version of a notorious 1910 murder case. The novel tells of Clyde Griffiths, who, like Woyzeck, conspires to murder his wife, in this case in order to marry a wealthier woman. As it had done so many times before, Yung Teater explored the tragic consequences of injustice and the socio-economic origins of crime. Once again the setting was the land regarded by so many Polish Jews as the "goldene medine" (golden land), America.

It is certainly tempting to view many of these plays as allegorical criticisms of Polish treatment of the Jews. Certainly their status as outsiders whose loyalty was regarded as suspect helped the young actors of Yung Teater—as well as their audiences—identify with the downtrodden, victimized characters they portrayed. Yet while their own social and political situation probably accounts for the empathy they felt toward Italian anarchists, African-American martyrs, and misfit sociopaths, there is little evidence that these characters were simply allegorical representations of themselves. Indeed, the theatre's lionization of Soviet scientists and explorers and aesthetic inclinations toward leftist theatre provide a clear indication of its loyalties. Ultimately, it stands as a testament to the vicissitudes of Jewish life in Poland that as late as March 1939, the tragedy that this group of Polish Jewish youth felt a need to warn its audiences about was an American Tragedy.

Appendix

Mikhl Weichert, "Bine un publikum," *Teater un drame*, vol. 1 (Vilna: Vilner farlag fun B. Kletskin, 1926), 12–16. "The Stage and the Public" from *Theatre and Drama*. Translated by Margot Valles.

A while back a story was making its way around Warsaw: During a dramatic performance one Saturday night, someone in the audience coughed conspicuously. This was soon followed by another cough. Soon, most of the audience was coughing. It turned into a racket, and the actor, a certain old thespian, lost his patience, stopped the play and turned to the public saying, "I will not act; I cannot act!"

This very same epidemic cough, which always causes a commotion, is also a well-known phenomenon in European theater. Directors and actors live in mortal fear of this cough. Indeed, they shudder the moment they hear that first lone cough from the audience. Especially on opening night, such a cough can spoil the whole show, to the point where even the Resurrection itself could not revive it.

What is the significance of this cough?

It is one of those means by which the masses who by chance find themselves together at the theater—we call them the audience—react *collectively* to what has just happened on stage. The clapping of the hands, the stamping of the feet, the shouting and whistling are all forms by which the satisfaction or dissatisfaction of the performance is expressed. Are the masses lost? Are they having trouble following the thread of the story? Are they not interested in it? Or, are they completely bored by the action on stage? They have particular ways of letting the actors know: The epidemic cough, small disturbances, and commotions. These are the spontaneous, unintentional reactions of a collective body. They inform the director that there is no *contact* being made between the stage and the public.

This is the essence, the *crux* of the matter. Threads must extend unconsciously from the actor to the onlooker, around whom they should slowly spin a web; a consecrated atmosphere should be created; it should feel like the same spirit hovers over both the stage and the public; warmth should spread out and take hold of everyone: those who perform above and those who watch beneath. Whoever has had the chance to see how the same ensemble can perform the very same show once for empty rows and another time for a packed hall knows how cold, plodding, grey and commonplace performances before a small audience can be, and how lively, exalted and festive they are before a full theater! The magic word here is: *contact.*

Consequently, both important and inconsequential directors alike since time immemorial have taken pains to engender this connection. Even while choosing their pieces they measure and weigh to what extent the public will "go along with it." And as they undertake to learn a new piece thoroughly, they pay close attention to each moment that will especially "excite" the audience. If artistic methods do not succeed despite the dramatic worth of the piece, or the artistic interpretation of the actor, then they search to find other more contemporary ways to create this exalted atmosphere *artificially*, other ways to create this contact. [. . .]

Thus, several years ago, an attempt was made to put the stage and the hall under the same light, to light the entire theater-space uniformly. Another time, the sets were expanded so that they encompassed not just the stage but everyone in the entire hall, so that not only the actors but also the public found themselves, for example, in a forest. One director, clearly not one of the greats, fell upon this very bright idea: Because the stage needed to appear as a forest, he left the stage, spraying the hall with perfume, so that the scent of the fragrant forest trees would be carried to the nose of each lady or gentlemen at his or her seat.

These and many other similar methods—I will mention only two more from the "Polish Theater" of Warsaw: the wide steps, which connect the auditorium to the stage and the barging in of costumed and masked actors from the audience onto the stage—go beyond connecting stage and public, go beyond making the relationship between actors and the public more intimate. These recent attempts want to put an end to the misconception that we are only accidental witnesses, looking inside our neighbors' homes through a crack in a wall—as in the bourgeois dramas championed by Diderot. They disparage the famous "fourth wall" and summon the illusion that the public is not separate from the actors, but conversely, the audience finds itself in the same place as the performers; *the audience is no longer a group of onlookers, but a group of participants.*

The Yiddish stage, as well, need not be ashamed of its attempts to connect the stage and the public. And, if they are not as sophisticatedly conceived and did not turn out as well as in the Gentile theaters, it is no great misfortune. The Yiddish actor, who is from the people, who fell directly from the cheapest seats onto the stage, is drawn to this exalted place. The action on the stage means little to him. Even before he has fully emerged from behind the curtain he feels like the Hundred-Eyed Giant on Olympus and a strange fire burns in him. The first word he utters, though still half-audible, will find a happy, resounding response from the audience. And when he stands on the stage and feels the sureness of the floor boards beneath his feet and the breathing of the hall envelops his body with a loving warmth—then he lets loose, engaging with the audience, tossing out rhymes and jokes that the public catches and hurls back onto the stage. Then he takes a deep bow, does a little jig, recites a couplet and the crowds can no longer control themselves: loudly, they tap their hands and feet in time with the music, they sing loudly and freely, like at their family's holiday table. The theater resounds with happiness, the rafter beams shake, and the audience takes great pleasure in it. *The boundary between the stage and the public is erased.*

Only in this kind of participatory theater can the Yiddish actor perform. Not only that, but the Yiddish actor shares the most serious moments of his life with the public. As soon as the show is over and everyone is either elated or depressed from the action on the stage, the "star" leaps up on to the stage, he tears off his false beard and wig, and holding these holy symbols of artistry in his right hand, bowing deep before the audience with his left, then placing himself akimbo, sturdy and square on the stage, he shoots off some fiery lines, or, as men call it in theater jargon, he recites a "speech" to the public. One time he requests a donation for a poor, sick "colleague," another time he awkwardly praises his patron. Again and again he criticizes the competition, and in the end he begs the "dear public" to be sure to come to the big Gala performance, as it will be the sensational, criminal, comical operetta: *The Tallis Kotn*, including a hundred-and-fifty musical numbers, which have been improved upon many times and will include the "Newest Zionist Tunes."

The *maskil* or even the half-educated intellectual, who sometimes winds up in such a place, unfortunately, is quite bothered by this and leaves with a broken heart. But he, in whose veins flows the *blood of the theater,* takes great pleasure in the activity of the Yiddish public. Not because he will be impressed by the high level of culture, but simply because he feels a bit of the "pure culture" of theater, an unadulterated piece of primitive theater. And, because he is strengthened in his belief that the masses, who take not only coarse and awkward appreciation but indeed *fresh* and *naïve enjoyment* in it, have a healthy flair for the theater and a rich treasury of unrealized potential for the theater of the future. And he is impressed because he has seen how large is the task and how difficult is the work of creating the theater of tomorrow.

Notes

1. A version of this article was published in Kathleen Cioffi and Bill Johnston, eds., "The Other in Polish Theatre and Drama," *Indiana Slavic Studies* 14 (2003), 141–163. I thank Slavica Publishers for permission to republish it.

2. Cited in Yosef Glikson, "Yung teater" [Young Theatre], in Itzik Manger, Jonas Turkow, and Moyshe Perenson, eds., *Poyln*, vol. 1 of *Yidisher teater in eyrope tsvishn beyde velt-milkhomes* [Yiddish theatre in Europe between the two world wars] (New York: Alveltlekher Yidisher Kultur-kongres, 1968), 127.

3. For more on Yiddish theatre in Poland, see Yitskhok Turkow-Grudberg, *Yidish teater in poyln* [Yiddish theatre in Poland] (Warsaw: Yidish Bukh, 1951); *Varshe—dos vigele fun yidishn teater* [Warsaw—the cradle of Yiddish theatre] (Warsaw: Yidish Bukh, 1956); and Anna Kuligowska-Korzeniewska and Małgorzata Leyko, eds., *Teatr Żydowski w Polsce* [Jewish theatre in Poland] (Łódź: Wydawnictwo Uniwersytetu Łódzkiego, 1998). In 1992, the journal *Pamiętnik Teatralny* [Theatrical memoirs] devoted a special issue to Jewish theatre in Poland. The best English survey of Yiddish theatre remains Nahma Sandrow's *Vagabond Stars: A World History of Yiddish Theatre* (New York: Harper & Row, 1977), which has several chapters dedicated to Yiddish theatre in Poland.

4. For more on GOSET, its theatre technicum, and its European tour, see Jeffrey Veidlinger, *The Moscow State Yiddish Theater: Jewish Culture on the Soviet Stage* (Bloomington: Indiana University Press, 2000).

5. Zalmen Zylbercweig, ed. *Leksikon fun yidishn teater* [Encyclopedia of the Yiddish theatre] (New York: Farlag Elisheva, 1931), 1:685; and Turkow, *Farloshene shtern* [Extinguished stars] (Buenos Aires: Tsentral-Farband fun Poylishe Yidn in Argentine, 1953) 2:100–107.

6. Mikhl Weichert, *Zikhroynes* [Memoirs] (Tel Aviv: Menorah, 1961), 2:228.

7. Ibid., 2:229.

8. Fayvl Zigelboym, "Yung teater—*Trupe Tanentsep*," in Mikhl Weichert, *Trupe Tanentsap: a Goldfaden-shpil in a galitsish shtetl* [The Tanentsap Troupe: A Goldfaden play in a Galician shtetl] (Tel Aviv: Menorah, 1966), 7.

9. Ibid., 8.

10. Cited in Zylbercweig, *Leksikon*, 2:946.

11. Weichert, *Zikhroynes*, 2:228–229.

12. Ibid., 2:231.

13. Ernst Toller's *Masse Mensch* was translated into Yiddish by Sara Brener in 1922 and published as *Mase mentsh* (Warsaw: Di Velt, 1922). For the text of *Zaverukha*, see Peretz Hirschbein, *Gezamlte dramen* [Collected dramas] (New York: Literarish Dramatishe Faraynen in Amerike, 1916), 1:93–120. Y. L. Peretz's poem can be found in his *Ale verk* [Complete works] (New York: CYCO, 1947), 1:42–43.

14. For more on *kleynkunst* see M. Nudelman, "Kleynkunst- un marionetn-teaters tsvishn beyde velt-milkhomes" [*Kleinkunst* and marionette theatres between the two world wars], in Manger, Turkow, and Perenson, *Poyln*, 148–168.

15. For more on the effects of the Sacco and Vanzetti case in Jewish public opinion, see Michael Alexander, *Jazz Age Jews* (Princeton: Princeton University Press, 2001). Among those Yiddish writers who composed poetry on Sacco and Vanzetti are Lamed Shapiro and H. Leivick. Nathan Asch, son of Yiddish playwright Sholem Asch, also wrote an English novel inspired by the trial, entitled *Payday*. The novel was translated into Yiddish by L. Hodes and published in Warsaw by the Kultur-lige.

16. Weichert, *Zikhroynes*, 2:239.

17. Ibid., 2:247.

18. Reprinted in Weichert, *Teater un drame* [Theatre and drama] (Warsaw: Yidish, 1922), 10–14.

19. Mikhl Weichert, "Di stsenishe lezung fun 'Boston' in 'yung-teater'" [The staged reading of "Boston" in "Yung Theater"], *Literarisher bleter* [Literary pages], 30 (July 28, 1933): 479–480.

20. Glikson, "Yung teater," 132.

21. Ibid.

22. Cited in Weichert, *Zikhroynes*, 2:247–248.

23. Ibid., 2:254–255.

24. Weichert, *Teater un drame*, 9.

25. Mikhl Weichert, *Trupe Tanentsap*. Weichert gives a detailed summary of the play in *Zikhroynes*, 2:251–265.

26. Weichert, *Trupe Tanentsap*, 72.

27. Ibid., 76.

28. See Sandrow, *Vagabond Stars*, 48.

29. Weichert, *Zikhroynes*, 2:265.

30. Itzik Manger, "Araynfir-vort" [Introduction] in Manger, Turkow, and Perenson, *Poyln*, 15.

31. Friedrich Wolf, "SOS . . . rao rao . . . Foyn-Krassin rettet Italia" in Johannes R. Becher et. al, *Frühe sozialistische Hörspiele* [Early socialist radio plays] (Frankfurt: A. M: Fischer Taschenbuch Verlag,1982), 41–66.

32. The play is described in detail in Weichert, *Zikhroynes*, 2:266–278. See also "Premyere fun 'Krasin' in 'yung teater' [Premiere of 'Krasin' in the Yung Teater]," *Haynt* [Today], March 23, 1934.

33. Weichert, *Zikhroynes* 2:268.

34. Ibid., 2:273–274.

35. The play, first written in 1907, was published serially in *Di tsukunft* [The future] (October, November, December) 1927. For an analysis of the play, see Delphine Bechtel, "America and the Shtetl in Sholem Aleichem's *Di Goldgreber*, The Golddiggers," *MELUS: The Journal of the Society*

for the Study of the Multi-Ethnic Literature of the United States 17, no. 3 (1992): 69–84. See also Jacob Weitzner, *Sholem Aleichem in the Theater* (Madison, NJ: Fairleigh Dickinson University Press, 1994), 39–73, where he discusses performances of the play, but notably leaves out the Yung Teater production.

36. Nakhman Mayzel, "'Yung teater' gefunen Sholem Aleykhems 'Oytser'" [Yung Teater finds Sholem Aleichem's "Treasure"], *Literarishe bleter*, 29 (July 20, 1934): 464.

37. Ibid.

38. Cited in Zylbercweig, *Leksikon*, 4: 3372–73.

39. "Fun di teateren" [From the theatres], *Haynt*, August 3, 1934.

40. "Fun di teateren," *Haynt*, July 27, 1934.

41. V. N. Bill'-Belotserkovskii, *Zhizn' zovyot: drama v chetyryokh deistviyakh* [Life calls: A drama in four acts] (Moscow: Khudozhestvennaya literatura, 1934), 51.

42. "Teater-notitsn" [Theatre notes], *Haynt*, December 11, 1934.

43. "Groyser erfolg fun 'Dos lebn ruft' in 'yung teater' [Great success of "Life calls" in "Yung Teater"], *Haynt*, December 11, 1934.

44. For more on Leyb Malach, see Zylbercweig and Mestel, *Leksikon*, 2:1333; and Leyb Malach, *Leyb Malakh* (Los Angeles: Leyb Malakh Bukh-komitet, 1949).

45. The play was published as *Misisipi: pyese in dray aktn* [Mississippi: Play in four acts] in *Leyb Malakh*, 253–314.

46. Ibid., 281.

47. Nakhman Mayzel, "Naye oyffirung in'm 'yung teater'" [New performance in "Yung Teater"], *Haynt*, April 2, 1935.

48. Ibid.

49. Nathan Buksboym, "Vegn L. Malakhs 'Misisipi'" [About Leyb Malach's "Mississippi"], reprinted in Malakh, *Leyb Malakh*, 330.

50. Zylbercweig and Mestel, *Leksikon*, 3:1888–1894.

51. Nakhman Mayzel, *Geven amol a lebn* [There once was a life] (Buenos Aires: Tsentralfarband fun Poylishn Yidn in Argentine, 1951), 347.

52. Y. M. Nayman, "Simkhe Plakhte," *Haynt*, December 27, 1935.

53. Weichert, *Zikhroynes*, 2:313.

54. Y. M. Nayman, "Teater-notitsn" [Theatre notes], *Haynt*, October 14, 1936.

55. Weichert, *Zikhroynes,* 2:323. See also Weichert, "Masoes Binyomin hashlishi fun Mendele Moykher Sforim " [The travels of Benjamin the Third by Mendele Moykher Sforim], *Haynt*, March 29, 1937.

56. Turkow, *Farloshene shtern*, 1:216–220.

57. See David Engel, "Who is a Collaborator? The Trials of Michal Weichert," in Slavomir Kapralski, ed., *Jews in Poland II* (Cracow: Judaica Foundation, 1999), 339–370; and Yehuda Bauer, *American Jewry and the Holocaust: The American Jewish Joint Distribution Committee, 1939–1945* (Detroit: Wayne State University Press, 1981), 317–322.

PART III

Authors, Actors, and Audiences

CHAPTER 7

Patriotn and Their Stars: Male Youth Culture in the Galleries of the New York Yiddish Theatre

Nina Warnke

"The gallery is dead, and the new second balcony is as similar to the former gallery as prohibition beer is to that frothy beer of the good old times." With these words, a *Forverts* reporter summed up his experiences at a Yiddish performance in New York in 1927. Instead of a gallery full of boisterous *patriotn*, there was a "second balcony" where young and old couples, families, and groups of friends sat—quietly, in an orderly fashion, and well dressed.[1] Another *Forverts* writer explained to those either too young or too new in the country that current fans (*onhenger*) or admirers (*farerer*) of stars had nothing in common with the former *patriotn*. Unlike contemporary fans, *patriotn* had been "devoted to their star with body and soul."[2] The Yiddish theatre of the 1920s, these journalists asserted, was much like the English-language theatres uptown, having irretrievably lost a vital element that had defined its performance culture for decades before World War I. One leader of a *patriotn* group, nicknamed "Gulash," was now even put on a par with the great stars of that era for his role in creating a vibrant theatrical culture: "One can say that together with [Sigmund] Mogulesco, [David] Kessler, [Jacob P.] Adler and others, Gulash was one of the pioneers of the Yiddish theatres. The stars built the Yiddish stage and Gulash with his *patriotn* was the expression of the love and gratitude of the masses."[3]

As in Russian, the Yiddish word *patriot* means not only the "patriot" of a country but a devotee, lover, or fan of a person or institution. In the context of the Yiddish theatre, *patriot* has been used to describe anyone who actively supported the institution or an actor. Bessie Thomashefsky, for example, tells of a *patriot* in Chicago in the 1880s who helped their newly arrived troupe financially and provided the necessary contacts to rent a theatre. Actors often spoke of their *patriotn* when they referred to their devoted fans—male and female—in general. But in the

"A farblondzheter patriot" (A lost *patriot*). A fan of David Kessler's mistakenly wanders into Boris Thomashefsky's "People's Theatre" and receives a "trimming" by Thomashefsky's *patriotn*. (*Der groyser kundes*, Nov 26, 1909) (From the library of the YIVO Institute for Jewish Research, New York.)

context of the New York Yiddish theatre before World War I, the term *patriotn* came to denote more specifically those fans who congregated in the gallery and were part of or at least associated with organized groups of *patriotn*: those who loved, supported, and were willing to defend their star with fists and bats. These organized *patriotn* and their hangers-on were exclusively young men.[4]

Although Yiddish theatre was generally described as family theatre, the space in the auditoriums was in fact stratified not only by income levels but also partially by gender and group identity. The gallery, with its tickets of fifteen to twenty-five cents, belonged to the *patriotn* and other male spectators while the balconies and floor, with prices from thirty-five cents to one dollar, were equally occupied by both genders and included families with small children, couples, or groups of friends. Actors tried to please everyone in this heterogeneous audience by offering historical operas, melodramas, songs and dances, laughter and tears, and some racy jokes. In fact, for decades, journalists appealed to the actors to give up the insinuating gestures, songs, and jokes, and to stop playing to the predilections of the male gallery audience, but to little avail. The actors needed their audience and especially their *patriotn*. They helped to keep an actor's personality cult alive, they were a performer's best advertisers, and they could make a show a success. *Patriotn*, too, were frequently admonished for their loud and rude behavior, their excessive applause, and their lack of artistic understanding, and were held responsible for the Yiddish theatre's lack of progress. The same Gulash who in the 1920s was celebrated as one of the builders of the Yiddish stage had twenty years earlier been called a *pogromtshik* for beating audience members.

Yiddish theatre audiences have fascinated contemporary observers as well as subsequent scholars. While anecdotes and descriptions of audiences abound, no in-depth study of the audience in regard to composition and behavior has been published to date. Contemporaries and scholars have regularly noted the intense interaction between actors and audience as well as the importance of the audience and of the *patriotn* in particular, in the theatrical culture of the turn of the last century. We need to contextualize individual incidences and anecdotes more fully in order to arrive at a more nuanced understanding of the inner workings of this culture. By focusing on the *patriotn*, I want to challenge the popular image of the Yiddish theatre audience as either naively absorbed in the action onstage and moved to spontaneous bursts of applause or as uniformly noisy and distracted. I also want to destabilize the notion that theatre-going was a unifying community experience when in fact it was at times fractured and divisive, and governed by intricate power relations. For this period, we need to take the *patriotn* and their interaction with the stars into account when we evaluate the success or failure of a particular play, actor, or group of actors.

Most of my information is culled from contemporary newspaper reports, and the reminiscences of actors and *patriotn* themselves, which reveal tantalizing glimpses of the lives and actions of *patriotn*. Although most sources tend to insist that *patriotn* were an independent force who acted of their own volition and thus determined the fate of plays and actors, a careful reading of these texts reveals complex power relations between the stars and their fans. Much of the world of the *patriotn* remains obscured, however, because of these texts' unreliable nature due to their narrative strategies or purposes. More often they raise enticing questions about the *patriotn*, their organizations, and their power, but do not always provide reliable answers.

Theatre Competition, Personality Cult, and the Beginnings of *Patriotizm*

In 1891, a decade after the onset of large-scale Jewish immigration from the Russian Empire, about 135,000 Jewish Lower East Side residents could choose to attend almost daily performances in three Yiddish playhouses. Most of the future stars of the New York Yiddish theatre arrived between 1886 and 1892—among them Adler, Kessler, Mogulesco, Keni Liptzin, Sigmund Feinman, and Boris and Bessie Thomashefsky—leading to an intense competition among the actors as they fought for preeminence in the burgeoning Jewish entertainment market. The origins of *patriotizm* can be traced back to this foundational, competitive period in the late 1880s and early 1890s, and to the personality cult that actors developed to ensure their own success.[5] In order to gain a competitive edge, companies ran concurrent productions with similar titles, tried to outdo each other with extravagant stagings, made creative use of publicity, rented ever-larger theatres, lured popular actors from each other, and at times denounced one another from the stage. During these years, fans occasionally began disturbing a rival company's productions. But the actors not only competed among themselves; they also attempted to break the power of the company dramatist who traditionally had control over the troupe. In 1888, only months after his arrival from Europe, actors staged the successful ouster of Avrom Goldfaden, the "father of Yiddish theatre." The popular playwright Shomer (Nokhem-Mayer Shaykevitsh), who like Goldfaden had directed his own troupe in eastern Europe, also lost his position as company playwright only a year after his arrival. The downfall of company director and playwright "Professor" Moyshe Hurwitz due to financial misconduct and the creation of a short-lived actors' union further weakened the traditional cohesiveness and hierarchical structure of the companies. Domination by the playwright-director was broken as actors began to establish themselves as actor-managers.[6]

Troupes poured enormous financial resources into their fight for predominance. They leased large theatres, and purchased expensive scenery and costumes at great financial risk; in fact, in the years around 1890, leases were frequently broken because companies found themselves unable to pay the rent. As stars seized considerable control of their theatres, they started to make use of the emerging Yiddish press as an additional conduit to promote themselves and their troupes. Actors' names and faces were no longer displayed only on the fronts of the theatres and in storefront windows, but in large ads that featured the star's portrait, an obvious departure from the established practice of publishing small ads or press releases about upcoming productions. Benefit nights for individual actors, in particular, became occasions for reinforcing and strengthening the fan base. Promotion of these events included illustrated ads and the promise that the audience would receive a songbook of the show's tunes and/or a photograph of the actor.[7]

While the competition among stars and troupes and their self-promotion certainly helped to strengthen the allegiances of certain fan populations, they alone do not account for the emergence of the *patriot* culture at that time. Two developments that resulted from the competitive struggle fostered the creation of this particular subset of the audience: the creation of amateur acting clubs and the troupes' move to large theatres with expansive galleries.

Emergence of the Dramatic Clubs

As Yiddish theatre became a mass phenomenon around 1890, a wide array of amateur dramatic clubs began to spring up that either were organized by a star actor or recruited one. Ads featuring the portrait of the star announced the founding and activities of these clubs, which carried names that claimed literary and educational aspirations, such as Zigmund Faynman's dramatisher farayn (Sigmund Feinman's Dramatic Club), Dora Vaysman's Educational League, Maks Karps dramatisher hibru yong men sosayeti Shiler (Dramatic Hebrew Young Men Society Schiller), or the Dramatisher untershtitsungs farayn Lira (Dramatic Mutual Aid Society Lyra), which succeeded in recruiting the recently arrived Jacob Adler as its teacher.[8]

Many of these clubs were organized by teenagers who invited their peers from work or school to join. Max Gabel, for example, was a fourteen-year-old suspender maker when he became a member of the East Side Dramatic Club in 1891; a year later he founded the Young Hebrews Dramatic Club, which the future actor Louis Hyman joined as a fifteen-year-old. The fourteen-year-old Abe Kogut, who would later be a star comedian and manager of a Yiddish vaudeville house before becoming a movie house manager, organized the David Kessler Dramatic Club around 1893 with several co-workers at his suspender shop. Most of them had been in the United States for a few years already and had become ardent fans of the Yiddish theatre in general, or of specific stars. When they started to attend the theatre or join the clubs, these youth had already entered the work force and thus had some disposable income, which they invested in their club activities and performances, or in theatre tickets. According to the actor Boaz Young, himself an early Adler *patriot* and member of an acting club, these clubs attracted many stage-struck youngsters who had become fans of a certain star. "For the amateur actor, the professional actor was a God and teacher; he imitates his speech, his make-up, and his gait on stage."[9]

Immigrant children lived suspended between their parents' cultural legacy, their poverty, and their own aspirations. Young boys, in particular, tried to carve out as much independence from their families as possible in order to explore their own options and to test possibilities beyond parental scrutiny.[10] They were looking for role models that pointed them to a future in the United States that their parents could not provide. Unless they had serious intellectual ambitions or were politicized, Yiddish actors were in fact the only heroes and role models recent immigrants could have in the early years of immigration. These dashing young actors who exuded power, glamour, and wealth (although at that time they had much less than it seemed) must have been beguiling to adolescents in search of their own future. These actors, after all, had transcended the limitations of their economic background and were the only widely-known figures within the immigrant community whose lives seemed filled with success, admiration, and enjoyment. It should come as no surprise that so many youths became enamored of the stage and dreamed of being actors.

Amateur theatricals played an important role throughout the immigrant period. Since dramatic clubs under the aegis of a star promised or at least suggested that members would study with or otherwise have access to the star, aspiring actors probably saw them as potential springboards to a professional career. In fact, a considerable number of performers of the next generation gained their first acting experience in dramatic clubs. Several clubs rented permanent rooms, which also offered books and newspapers, creating a social space for people to meet. But despite their popularity among immigrant youth, little is known about these clubs.[11] None of the stars whose names were attached to a club ever professed to having coached the amateurs or to having supported them financially. These clubs appear to have provided a structure that fostered the development and organization of the *patriotn* since they promised easy access to the stars and a locale to congregate: the members of the Dora Vaysman Educational League "educated," as one journalist wrote, from the gallery, and Bessie Thomashefsky mentioned that her husband's *patriotn* belonged to the Thomashefsky Dramatic Club.[12]

It is unknown to what degree these clubs also continued to engage in amateur theatricals, or if they turned exclusively into *patriot* organizations while other clubs may have devoted themselves primarily to amateur acting. Although early forms of *patriotizm* started in the late 1880s, *patriotn* began to operate in organized fashion in the early 1890s, at which point the term *patriot* emerged as well.[13] While in an article published in 1891 or 1892, Shomer still refers to *galiyoretshnikes* (gallery gods), by the time the volume *Di yidishe bihne* (The Yiddish stage) appeared in 1897, the institution of the *patriotn* as well as the term were firmly established—as the frequent complaints in the publication suggest.[14]

Yiddish "Gallery Houses": A Space for Male Working-class Youth

The fundamental architectural difference between the theatres leased in the first years of immigration and after 1888 lay not only in their overall size, but in their enormous galleries. Small halls that seated a maximum of 700 spectators were exchanged for houses that had served audiences since the first half of the nineteenth century, when the area on and around the Bowery was New York's primary entertainment district. By the 1870s and 1880s, as the city's theatrical center shifted briefly to Union Square before moving to Times Square around 1900, the Bowery theatres featured foreign-language troupes, cheap melodrama, and variety, which attracted primarily lower-class native and immigrant populations. The rapid increase of the Jewish immigrant population on the Lower East Side pushed many of the earlier immigrants and native-born populations to other neighborhoods, decreasing their need for entertainment in the area. The availability of existing houses, together with a change in leasing practices that reduced the risk for the lessees, made these buildings attractive options for the newcomers.[15]

The first foray into more sizable spaces came in 1888, when the recently renovated 1,400-seat Poole's Theatre (later, Union Theatre) was rented; it boasted a gallery that alone held 600.[16] In 1889, the 3,000-seat Thalia (the former Bowery Theatre) and in 1893, the 3,500-seat Windsor became the homes of Yiddish troupes. By the late nineteenth century, American middle-class audiences had been cowed into behaving passively and decorously, and the gallery had become the space of shop girls. But in the cheap English-language melodrama and variety houses that remained on the Bowery and across the country, and catered to an ethnically mixed working-class audience, the participatory and sometimes rowdy behavior of earlier decades was still the norm.[17] So too was the involvement and power of the gallery audience. In the early 1890s, this uppermost space in the so-called "gallery-houses" was occupied primarily by the city's newsboys, who turned their hard-earned pennies immediately into theatre tickets.[18] Another observer described the gallery audience in these houses as more heterogeneous:

... newsboys, factory hands, a few colored persons, an occasional Chinaman, and many Germans, some of whom bring their families. . . . This is the gallery audience, and they are as powerful as ever in determining the fate of a play or an actor. Woe to the aspirant who fails to please the 'gods of the gallery'! He is hissed and jeered with the same heavy fervor with which the favorite is applauded, and seldom succeeds in winning favor after he has failed at first.[19]

Although Jews are not mentioned in the ethnic composition of the audience, they could have been among the newsboys and factory hands. Their number was probably still relatively small, since large-scale Jewish immigration from eastern Europe had only begun in 1881, and for many the language remained a barrier. Of course, the phenomenon of an active gallery audience was not limited to the Bowery or provincial American theatres, but was part of male, working-class youth culture in central and eastern Europe as well. Jacob P. Adler, for example, told of his exploits as a stage-struck teenager in the gallery of the Russian theatre in Odessa.[20]

The acquisition of these enormous gallery-houses turned Yiddish theatre into mass entertainment, accessible to a large percentage of poor, disenfranchised immigrants who previously were rarely able to attend a performance. While tickets at the small Oriental Theatre cost between twenty-five cents and one dollar in 1885, gallery tickets could be purchased for fifteen cents in the early years, and were later raised to twenty cents and subsequently to twenty-five.[21] Thus Jewish gallery audiences and the *patriotn* in particular continued the long established tradition of male working-class youth frequenting the theatre. For some, joining the gallery audience and its culture was a matter of choice even if they could afford higher ticket prices. After 1900, spectators were often charged an extra ten cents if they wanted to sit in the front rows of the gallery. Their willingness—albeit grudging—to pay an extra dime indicates that spectators who could afford a thirty-five cent ticket on a lower balcony preferred to remain among their own in the gallery. Although some women may have joined the men in the gallery, the long wait at the ticket booth, the need to rush up long stairs with some 600 other spectators all competing to secure a good seat (since tickets were unnumbered), and the generally rowdy and sometimes volatile atmosphere probably kept most women away.[22] The gallery was considered a separate male space not only by its occupants but also by the architects: the Grand Theatre, which was built in 1902 for a Yiddish company, continued the tradition of a separate box office and entrance to the top gallery, and installed only restrooms for men on that level.[23]

The Social Sphere of *Patriotn*

Patriotn, like other members of the dramatic clubs, were primarily in their teens or early twenties. One contemporary source points to twelve- to fifteen-year olds as the typical age range for *patriotn*, while a few anecdotes tell of slightly older *patriotn* whose landlady or fiancée did not share the enthusiasm for the *patriot's* star, leading him to look for a different room to rent or to break off the engagement.[24] Most *patriotn* were single, although some were apparently married men who, according to one source, gave up not only food and sleep but their wives and children as well.[25] The actor and impresario Maurice Schwartz, who began associating with *patriotn* when he was around twelve, confirms the general age range.

Living and working conditions of immigrant youth made the street, the theatre, and other generally accessible spaces the preferred venues for socializing. An afternoon with *patriotn* and an evening in the theatre spared youths from returning to the cramped quarters of their family or the family with whom they boarded, whose members may have still been working in the home. Whether informally or in groups, clubs, or gangs, male youth congregated on street corners, at restaurants, or around candy stores. *Patriotn* circles provided a ready-made social network and daily sociability with like-minded companions. Boaz Young, for example, tells of *patriotn* meeting every evening after work either somewhere outside on Hester Street, or in a saloon run by a Mr. Spivak, where for three cents they could have a liver steak, bread, and some beer.[26] Schwartz, too, tells of enjoying meals together and once, for a special occasion, going to a bathhouse with some thirty other *patriotn*, where they feasted on expensive salami and pastrami sandwiches, beer, cigarettes, and cigars while swapping stories and performing for each other.[27] According to the actress Bertha Kalish, "[*patriotn*] went to the theatre right after work. There were stands where they sold hot dogs and other foods especially for them. They ate their meal at the stand and soon bought their fifteen-cent ticket for the gallery."[28] Since gallery tickets were unnumbered and sold directly before the performance, *patriotn* and other gallery spectators would have to gather early to get a ticket, which offered ample opportunity to share gossip, make plans, and reconfirm group affiliations or animosities. The proximity of the huge Windsor and Thalia Theatres, which were located directly across from one another on the Bowery, probably heightened the rivalry, as *patriotn* from both houses had plenty of time to exchange opinions and harass each other.

Many *patriotn* had nicknames that referred to the star they supported or a role they particularly admired or could imitate. Boaz Young recalls that he was called "Adler" because he kept praising the actor even before the latter arrived in New York. Similarly, other *patriotn* were called by the names of their admired stars: for example, Karp, Feinman, and Mrs. Goldstein, or Kimat Kessler (Almost Kessler) and Kimat Mogulesco for those who were particularly good at imitating their namesakes.[29] Two of Kessler's *patriotn* went by the names of "Meksl Virdzhinius" (Virginius after an early role of Kessler) and "Shloyme Boss." Likewise, Cashir was called "Meturef" after Gordin's eponymous hero, because this role made him an Adler *patriot*. Two other Adler boys were nicknamed "Small Shylock," and "Shmuel Gorgl" (after Lateiner's *Shloyme Gorgl*), while one of Max Rosenthal *patriotn* was called "Berele Sheygets," probably because they successfully imitated their stars in these roles.[30]

The *patriotn* scene consisted of core groups of so-called *geshvoyrene patriotn* (lit. sworn *patriotn*) who had sworn allegiance to their respective stars and those who loosely associated with them, but were not firmly committed to one particular actor. Informally, the *patriotn* and the stars referred to the members as *boyes* or "boys," such as Kessler's *boyes* or Adler's boys. The leaders of the *geshvoyrene* tended to be slighter older *patriotn* who served the star in semi-official or official functions. As *adyutantn* (adjutants) they had regular access to the star and were often personal confidants, whether as "body guards," dressers, personal assistants, or "sheriffs." "Sheriffs" wielded power in the gallery by assigning the best seats to their *patriotn* or pocketing an extra dime for others who wanted to sit in the front rows. Although "sheriffs" were presumably there to keep order, they often helped instigate conflict. The key position that *adyutantn* held could eventually lead to regular employment in the theatre. Among Adler's were Isidor Cashir, who in his early twenties ruled the gallery with an iron fist before becoming Adler's assistant *regisseur* and later a successful actor. Harry Harris, or Gulash, followed him as "sheriff" and subsequently served as a doorkeeper at various theatres. Khayim Parkh was Adler's dresser and later became his manager. As the actors' confidants, these *adyutantn* probably played a key role in organizing the *patriotn*; they would be the first to learn when an actor felt slighted or mistreated, and could then rally the troops.

Geshvoyrene, according to Schwartz, had to be ready and willing to fight for their actor and, of course, be completely loyal to their star. As one journalist put it, *patriotn* were for "preparedness" in case a fight broke out.[31] Scuffles, beatings, and fights could ensue as soon as someone spoke well of a rival or made a critical comment about the group's star. Despite being pressured, Schwartz himself never became a *geshvoyrener*, although he associated for a while with the Kessler boys before joining Adler's. Genuinely interested in the acting of a variety of performers, Schwartz could not commit to one star. He secretly went to performances of "rivals," hoping this infraction would not be detected by his *patriot* circle. But when an Adler boy informed on him, Kessler's *patriotn* cornered him and gave him an ultimatum: if he was ever seen on Adler's gallery again, he should no longer show his face to them.[32]

Loyalty toward one's star did not mean that *patriotn* would necessarily be blind to their actor's shortcomings. After all, *patriotn* were fierce critics of acting. But like fans of sports teams, they stood by their actors even if these "lost the competition." Unlike sports fans, however, *patriotn* could on occasion help cover up their actor's weakness. Thomashefsky's boys, for example, drowned out with their applause the final bars of a song because their star could not sing the high notes as well as Kessler had done in the same role.[33] *Patriot* groups would also form strategic alliances or make truces with rival groups if they felt it could benefit them and their stars. When Feinman played Othello for one of his benefits, a role that both Adler and Kessler had performed in 1893, his *patriotn* invited the Elias Rothstein and Moshkovitsh boys, with whom they were "at peace," to help counterbalance Kessler's and Adler's boys, who were expected to disrupt the performance. Indeed they did so by shushing and calling "Order! Order!" during Feinman's appearances.[34] If, as Schwartz suggests here, calls for order and shushing were typical devices to disrupt a performance and to drown out the applause for a rival, then outside observers who frequently referred to them as signs of the audience's desire for silence appear to have misinterpreted them.

Serious *patriotn*—whether *geshvoyrene* or not—would attend all nine weekly performances. Schwartz, who joined the *patriotn* in 1902, shortly after arriving in the United States, vividly describes the effect it had on his life. Probably like many of his peers, he decorated the corner around his bed with his star's pictures, cut out from old posters he collected at local stores.[35] Although "Schwartzl," as his buddies called him, entered the Baron de Hirsch Trade School and began working in his father's shop, being a *patriot* quickly became an all-encompassing social activity that interfered with both school and work. He quit both, left home, and lived briefly on the streets before returning home and resuming his job with his father. Schwartz was not the only one so caught up in being a *patriot* that he neglected his responsibilities. His friend Josef "Spufke" Shvartsberg, who would later become a playwright and a prompter in Schwartz's Yiddish Art Theatre, apparently also lived on the streets during his days as a *patriot*.[36] Bessie Thomashefsky tells of "Sam" who gave up his job as a carpenter because of his love for the theatre and who eventually became her husband's *adyutant*. She adds that for some, *patriotizm* became so consuming that it had a detrimental effect on their lives, while others outgrew this period to build stable lives and even successful careers, whether inside the theatre or beyond.[37] The prompter Ruvn Vaysman suggested somewhat facetiously that for many youngsters *patriotizm* became a holy obligation. "Their divine service," he wrote, consists of:

1) congregating in the gallery, making noise and clapping until they beat each other's sides and are finally taken to the police station;
2) neglecting their work and walking around in rags as befits true martyrs of art, and
3) spending summer nights until the early morning by the coffee house where their chosen actor has coffee or supper, swallowing their saliva until he comes out, and taking him home.[38]

For *patriotn*, the highlights of the year were the opening of a new season, the benefit held for their star, and possibly a ball in his or her honor. For these occasions, special preparations and expenses were necessary. In each case, they held meetings at which they collected money and made detailed plans for the event. At the season's opening, *patriotn* would fill the stage with flowers and plan for ovations to greet their star's first entrance.[39] Stars could also rely on their *patriotn* to help make their benefits a success. They were charged with selling tickets to the performance, and they enacted an elaborate spectacle at the benefit itself to celebrate their star. Again, meetings were held well in advance to plan for presents, flowers, or even a decorated carriage for the star to arrive in. Freshly bathed and decked out in their finest, the most devoted *patriotn* would abandon the shadows of the gallery on that night and purchase a front row seat for a dollar. They lined the floors with empty soda bottles to increase the noise from stamping their feet.[40] Those in the gallery showered the auditorium and stage with printed notes that compared the star, according to one account, to a "Shakespeare, a nightingale, a bird of paradise . . . After a benefit, when the star goes home, the *patriotn* follow him all the way home and there they stand outside and look with enthusiasm into the windows until the gaslights are turned off . . ."[41] For *patriotn*, the benefit was a celebration not only of their star but of themselves, and of their ability to support him or her. Their success at selling tickets and at creating a positive and festive atmosphere became their actors' success. How crucial their contribution was can be gleaned from the fact that the universally beloved Mogulesco did not have *geshvoyrene patriotn* because, as Schwartz asserts, he did not need them. His benefits, however, were not very successful.[42]

Patriotn also organized balls to which they tried to bring the star. According to one article, "They send a carriage with flowers to bring the star with great pomp and ceremony and then the march begins in which the star is usually the leader. The *patriotn* circle around him and watch his every move and turn with great enthusiasm. Their faces glow if they are able to exchange a few words, shake hands, or are in any other way able to come into contact with the star, and for weeks afterward they have something to tell the other *patriotn* and their acquaintances."[43] Schwartz recalls that he trembled before Feinman when he met the actor for the first time after his benefit, and for decades remembered the sound of "Hello, *boytshik*" when Feinman shook his hand.[44]

Function of *Patriotn* for the Stars

Actors realized that *patriotn* were an important asset; even minor actors tried to cultivate them. *Patriotn* were not only instrumental in making one's benefit a success, but having a group of loyal supporters could also help to secure an engagement for the coming season. When Yiddish music halls became the new vogue on the Lower East Side around 1905, even music hall performers had their *patriotn*.[45]

For an actor, the primary function of the *patriotn* was to applaud him or her during performance—upon every entrance and exit, after particularly important speeches—and to quiet down the audience during his or her scenes. And the next day, what could be better advertisement than dozens of excited *patriotn* returning to their shops after the opening of a new show, extolling the merits of its actors, singing the new songs, and sharing the gossip they picked up the previous night while standing in line before the performance, or hanging out in or around the cafés where the stars congregated after the show?

Even on the streets, *patriotn* fulfilled an important role: they promoted the stars and helped to reinforce the personality cult. A star with an entourage of *patriotn* on the way to the theatre or café provided yet another opportunity for self-enactment that would receive attention. And for the *patriotn* to be near their star and to be seen in public in his or her presence gave them a great sense of importance. Bessie Thomashefsky relates that after her husband performed the title role in *Uriel Acosta*, one of Adler's signature parts, Thomashefsky's boys waited for him at the stage door, lifted him onto their shoulders, and carried him to the Romanian Opera House where Adler performed, shouting: "Hurrah for Thomashefsky! May our star Boris Thomashefsky live long! Thomashefsky, the greatest Uriel Acosta! Thomashefsky, the only Uriel Acosta!" The procession went several times around the theatre until Adler's *patriotn* retaliated by pouring buckets of water on them.[46] They staged similar processions in 1894, when Thomashefsky became the actor-manager of the Windsor, the largest Yiddish theatre. Such public demonstrations became a frequent spectacle on the streets of the Lower East Side.[47]

Of course, *patriotn* were not a flawless promotional machine, but in the absence of any consistent promotion in the press, they played a crucial role that stars would not have wanted to miss. Throughout most of the 1890s, reviews were not a regular feature, and those that were published focused much less on the qualities of the actors than on the text. Even as the theatre became an increasingly important topic after 1900, features about stars remained conspicuously absent. Despite the occasionally positive reviews, the star-managers were more often criticized for the various perceived ills of the theatre than celebrated.

Power Relations between Actors and *Patriotn*: A Delicate Balance

If we believe most actors' memoirs, *patriotn* acted independently, beyond the control of the actors or, at least, beyond the control of the memoirist. *Patriotn,* too, tended to claim that they decided on their actions independently. We can certainly believe that actors lived in fear of the ability of their rivals' *patriotn* to disturb their own performances. But the question remains as to what degree actors controlled their *patriotn* or vice versa.

Patriotn would show their displeasure about plays and roles, and demand that their stars not purchase or perform them. Bertha Kalish, for example, recalls that Kessler had to appease his "boys" when he played Hershele Dubrovner in Gordin's *Got, mentsh un tayvl* (*God, Man, and Devil*, 1900) for the first time. They pressured Kessler to give up the role, probably because they did not want him to portray a negative character; stars, after all, were usually cast as heroes. While heroes were applauded, villains—no matter how well they played—were booed (for their role) as well as applauded (for their acting). The *patriotn* must have felt unsure how to respond. Kessler pleaded with them to let him continue performing the role, which quickly became one of his greatest successes.[48]

Despite assertions to the contrary, there are indications that actors had some control over their *patriotn.* Schwartz, for example, reports that Adler was able to direct his boys' applause during the performance. They knew his cues such as tapping his walking stick, stroking his beard, or glancing at the boxes, which demanded that they cease their applauding.[49] More important, actors could control the response of their *patriotn* to a potential rival actor. When Bessie Thomashefsky took over Mogulesco's signature role as Faytl Pavolye in Shomer's *Di emigrantn* (The emigrants), because he had lost his voice, Mogulesco promised to sit in a box to demonstrate his approval. Nonetheless, the theatre decided to play it safe and "hired a squadron of . . . paid claques."[50] Similarly, when Esther Rokhl Kaminska came in 1909 from Warsaw, for guest performances in New York, she asked Keni Liptzin to control her *patriotn*. Kaminska came to perform much of Liptzin's Gordin repertoire and knew that without Liptzin's explicit approval, her performances would be doomed.[51] If, as seems apparent, actors had some power to keep their *patriotn* from disturbing another actor's performance, then they must have been equally able to orchestrate or encourage disturbances or, at the very least, refrain from discouraging them.

In fact, actors were aware that the potential for violence was particularly high when they took on another's star role. Although brawls that got out of hand were not desirable, a noisy demonstration in which the new performer of the role hoped to emerge as the "winner" could only enhance his or her status. Apparently, neither the new nor the established performers of these roles discouraged their *patriotn* groups from provoking the competition in the gallery. During the brief period in the 1890s when Bertha Kalish and Regina Prager competed in prima donna roles, their respective *patriotn* did their best to "protect" their respective stars. During one of Prager's performances, Kalish's *patriotn* showed up in full force only to be greeted by Prager's boys who, like them, came prepared with bats, clubs, and metal pipes. Positioning themselves in the front rows of the gallery with their backs to the stage, Prager's fans faced their enemies in order to keep them in check. Whether it was due to Prager's sweet voice or the threatening armaments, apparently no fight broke out.[52] On occasion, however, as was the case when Adler played Kessler's role of Hershele Dubrovner in Gordin's *Got, mentsh un tayvl* in 1907, the situation spun so out of control that spectators in other parts of the auditorium fled the theatre.[53]

Patriotn, like actors themselves, had to be flexible in regard to who was friend and who was foe: last season's rival might be this season's partner. This adjustment, however, was never easy. In the mid-1890s, the three major male competitors—Adler, Thomashefsky, and Kessler—joined forces to create the so-called "star combination." During their joint performance of Gordin's *Di gebrider Lurye* (The brothers Luria), Kessler began imitating Thomashefsky—probably to the great delight of his boys. In retaliation, Thomashefsky threw two plates at his feet when stage directions called only for one. Not to be upstaged, Kessler spontaneously picked up and smashed some plates and Adler, who played an old rabbi, joined in the general demolition of the crockery until the curtain came down.[54] Although Bessie Thomashefsky does not mention the role of the *patriotn* in this instance, we can easily imagine that this impromptu stage action was accompanied—if not encouraged—by vociferous and volatile action of the *patriotn* of the three stars. Needless to say, the experiment ended here. The balance of power was kept more successfully in 1904, when Adler invited Kessler and Kalish to join him at the Grand Theatre. Jacob and Sarah Adler's *patriotn* had to work out a *modus operandi* with Kessler and Kalish's *patriotn* so that the applause would be evenly distributed. We can assume that the actors gave their respective boys some direction in how to conduct themselves. Of course, as we have seen, a perceived wrong visited by one actor on the other could easily upset this careful arrangement. In this case, Adler joined Kessler and Kalish in their Gordin repertoire, playing the roles of Morris Moshkovitsh, who had remained in the other troupe. The rivalry between Kessler and Adler was thus deflected as *patriotn* (and the press) compared the latter's performances to Moshkovitsh's.

On occasion, the rivalry occurred between the star and a supporting actor in the same play. Sarah Adler tells us that at the end of one scene in Gordin's *Emese kraft* (The true power), Gustav Schacht received so much applause and so many curtain calls from the entire house that Adler's presence on stage was overlooked. Adler's *patriotn* whistled and screamed in protest that their star was being upstaged—but to no avail. Between the acts, Isidore Cashier (Adler's *patriot* and gallery "sheriff") informed Adler that a riot was brewing. Sarah Adler does in fact assume that her husband was behind it, and threatens not to perform if he was "again creating a brawl with his *shleger* (fighters)."[55] This quote is noteworthy because it is the only admission in any of the memoirs that the violence in the gallery was, at least at times, directly orchestrated by the actors themselves. A riot did break out in the gallery: several were arrested, only to be promptly bailed out by Adler and his lawyer. But to put a permanent end to being upstaged by this young upstart, Adler removed Schacht from his role.

Fighting for Respect

For years, theatres made half-hearted attempts to regulate the atmosphere in the auditorium and to create a more orderly and less distracting environment. It is unclear, however, to what degree the theatres' announcements about enforcing order were followed through and succeeded in banning small children, latecomers, or the sale of refreshments in the auditorium. One such attempt was made in the summer of 1903, when Gordin, the "reformer of the Yiddish theatre," took over the directorship of the Thalia and assembled an impressive line-up of first-rate actors: Liptzin, Kalish, Kessler, Sigmund and Dina Feinman, Moshkovitsh, and Shmuel Tabatshnikov (Samuel Tobias). The leadership and actors promised a theatre dedicated to literary plays and artistic productions. To ensure quality performances and to control the audience, the management declared it would admit "no small children," would raise the curtain at 8:15 p.m. sharp and, in a veiled attack on the *patriotn* in particular, would demand the "greatest order" in the auditorium and on stage.[56] The season opening had in all likelihood been eagerly awaited and prepared in great detail by the *patriotn* of these many stars. The festive mood, however, changed when Gordin addressed the audience after the first act of his *Di shkhite* (The slaughter) and, apparently, spoke his mind about the *patriotn*. They, as well as other audience members, signaled their communal disapproval of the author's admonition of their behavior by demonstrating their power. For the remainder of the play, the *patriotn* went "on strike" by withholding their applause, and the rest of the house followed suit.[57] In this case, loyalty and devotion to the individual actors was broken because of what the *patriotn* perceived as an attack on their rights as spectators. Although we have no records of the discussions between *patriot* leaders and actors in the wake of this incident, we can imagine that the actors had to make some amends to appease their constituents. Both actors and *patriotn* had learned during the previous season that by forming strategic alliances against the management of a theatre, *patriotn* had the power to seriously affect business.

Withholding applause had also been the strategy six months earlier, when the festive holiday of the opening of the new Yiddish theatre on Grand Street ended in great disappointment and anger for the visitors to the gallery. The Grand was the first purpose-built Yiddish theatre and symbolized the economic progress of the immigrant community and the centrality of theatre within it. For days before the opening, *patriotn* gathered outside the building and some even slept on its fire escapes or the steps to the stage. When the doors to the gallery finally opened, throngs rushed up the many flights of stairs. There they quickly realized that only the first two rows offered partial views of the stage—at best, spectators could see the actors' heads.[58] The auditorium had been designed at the expense of the poorest audience members, without taking their needs and rights into account. The next day, they demanded that the gallery be closed and the second balcony be turned into a gallery—a demand the management refused. In response, according to Maurice Schwartz, the *patriotn* boycotted the theatre.[59]

The Grand's brief opening season was a financial disaster, which led the management to invite Adler to the theatre the following season. If we can believe Schwartz, the lackluster revenues were largely caused by the boycott of the *patriotn* and not, as Judith Thissen argues, primarily by the lack of a male star and the theatre's old-fashioned repertoire.[60] However, during the next season, when the theatre hired Adler with his large *patriot* base, the boycott was discontinued. While the *patriotn* may have contributed to the downfall of the company, their boycott did not change their situation. Ultimately, they had to make do with the Grand's gallery. But the frequent complaints to the press by gallery spectators about the Grand's "sheriff" pocketing additional money and the scuffles that broke out over seats can be explained by the limited visibility in the gallery and its few prime seats. In the fall of 1904, audiences had to pay an additional ten cents for the first row, and two cents for the second. According to the *Forverts*, the "sheriff" explained that he charged the extra fee because the management paid him only $4.50 a week.[61] In response to a similar complaint during the following season, Adler declared that neither he nor the management was aware of this practice and promised to fire the guilty parties if the abuse could be proven.[62] While other theatres had similar problems, the Grand was particularly notorious for its violence and unfair treatment of gallery spectators.

Conclusions

Patriotn were neither the independent agents some actors' memoirs made them out to be, nor could they be entirely co-opted by the stars. Unlike the claques in nineteenth-century France with whom they were sometimes compared, *patriotn* were not hired lackeys of the actors, even if their leaders often were. The free tickets that *geshvoyrene* appear to have received did not make them as accountable as might a regular paycheck. For stars this arrangement had its obvious benefits, although it resulted, at times, in unexpected or even undesired outcomes. The semi-independence of the *patriotn* allowed actors to cover up their own manipulations of their fans and to portray their actions and predilections as manifestations of the *vox populi*, which were beyond their control. *Patriotn* were useful agents in what actors called "theatre politics," the behind-the-scenes wrangling that all professed to being victims of at one time or other but in which none admitted to partaking. As the stars such as Adler, Kessler, and Thomashefsky were more and more often criticized by both the Hebrew Actors Union and the press for minimizing supporting roles, and for not letting younger actors take over lead roles, their large and powerful *patriot* bases served to reaffirm their star positions and to signal their undiminished popularity. For star-managers for whom the economic viability of their theatres was always a serious concern, both pleasing and using *patriotn* became an important strategy in navigating the theatre's fortunes. The balance between the two had to be carefully managed if the *patriotn* were to be the useful instruments that actors needed them to be. Although we can see glimpses of these power relations, much remains obscure about the negotiations between actors and *patriotn*.

Patriotn did not attend the theatre to have a cultural experience or even to be entertained by the play. *Patriotizm* was an encompassing and empowering peer-group experience that had more in common with the culture of sports fans or even gangs. Group belonging, and the sense of power and importance that arises from it, as well as competitiveness, appear to have been at the core of *patriot* culture. The fierce attachment and loyalty to their stars, as well as their boisterous participation in the action, had much in common with sports fans. But *patriotn* also had some parallels to gang culture: they shared a predilection for violence, an ability to organize fighters and recruit reinforcements, and, of course, a proclivity to turf warfare. *Patriotn* did not fight for literal control of a neighborhood block, but of an actor's aesthetic domain: his or her roles, visibility on stage, or the theatre in which their star performed. Only when these allies of the actors felt themselves slighted or attacked did they fight for their own turf: the rights of the gallery.

The culture of the *patriotn* ended around World War I: the immigrant community was rapidly dispersing into the outer boroughs, thus breaking up the group cohesion and making it difficult for them to congregate on a daily basis; the first generation of grand stars was aging and retiring; and the *patriotn*'s staging ground was being removed since the new theatres built or taken over in the 1910s and 1920 no longer featured the massive galleries. Male youth culture was increasingly directed at different entertainments, including the movies but also spectator sports, which provided a perfect continuum for young men looking for male role models in a competitive environment. What the immigrant press had sought for so long—a *laytish* (respectable) theatre—had finally come to pass. However, concurrent with the disappearance of the *patriotn*, the press began to publish weekly theatre pages for the first time which included reviews, personal interest stories about actors, gossip, and jokes—thus in some way substituting for one of the functions of the *patriotn*.

Within a decade, immigrants and their children wistfully looked back at the past as they began to feel the profound break between the pre- and post-World War I Yiddish culture. They began to memorialize the first generation of immigrants who had built the cultural infrastructure of American Jewish life during the three decades before Word War I. Foremost among the institutions they revisited was the Yiddish theatre. Much of what critics had derided around 1900 was being re-examined and reconstituted, giving new meaning to the early history of the New York Yiddish theater (and by extension, of immigrant life itself). From the safe distance of a generation, Goldfaden was performed again—even if in a modernist staging. Papers regularly printed memoirs of actors who wanted to create a personal and institutional legacy. Even the much-maligned audience received their share of nostalgic longing from actors and journalists alike. The Yiddish stage, they seemed to say, had irretrievably lost a vital element that had defined its performance culture for decades and had made it an "authentically" Jewish experience.

Appendix

Bertha Kalish, "Der patriot geyt," *Tog*, September 5, 1925.

In this chapter of her memoirs, entitled "Here comes the patriot,*" Bertha Kalish describes the initial responses of the* patriotn *after she arrived in New York at the end of 1896, and their power over the actors.*

After my first performance at the Thalia Theatre, everyone began to pass judgment: beside the newspapers, which heaped praise on me, the entire theatre world complimented me. People started comparing me: some said that I was much greater than Sophie Karp; others, that I didn't have as strong a voice as Madame Prager; and still others, that I would be strong competition for Madame Liptzin. The *patriotn* whom I won soon after my first performance argued that there was no comparison between these actresses and me, and that I could put all three into my pocket.

The crowd that would wait outside the theatre after the performance called me "young goddess" and followed me to Schreiber's Café on Grand Street, discussing me loudly so I could hear.

The theatre *patriotn* of that era were an institution of their own. They consisted of honest and sincere people, workers, who passionately loved the theatre. Many of these *patriotn* are well-to-do today and play an important role in Jewish life. I won't mention their names in case they are ashamed of that wonderful time when they helped build the Yiddish theatre with their enthusiasm.

Their power was remarkable. Both managers and actors had to contend with them. They could glorify or condemn; they could greatly enhance a performance, or they could destroy it. The playwright who had to contend with all parties in the theatre had to contend even more with the *patriotn*.

...

The *patriotn* led a curious life; they worked in the shops to earn their bread but fed their soul with theatre. They would go right from work to the theatre and had their dinner at a stand with hot dogs and other foods that was set up especially for them. Then they bought their fifteen-cent tickets for the gallery. Those who came early took the seats in the front row of the gallery; the ones who arrived later had to suffer in the back rows and often stand throughout the entire performance.

Kessler's *patriotn* were also my *patriotn*, and whenever Kessler and I finished a duet or final scene, the theatre resounded with applause prompted by the gallery.

Once the following happened: Kessler and I were supposed to appear in a new play and we rehearsed the entire week. On Thursday night Kessler suddenly fell sick and it was clear that he would not be able to perform on Friday. I was not informed of his illness, but [the management] telegraphed [Moyshe] Simonov in Boston to substitute for Kessler. Simonov came, read through his role and, beyond that, relied on the prompter. When the curtain was raised, I came on stage and sang my solo. Soon thereafter my hero and lover, David Kessler, was supposed to appear. How surprised was I when I suddenly saw an unfamiliar face before me. The gallery believed it was Kessler and gave him great applause. Meanwhile Simonov had time to come closer and introduce himself: "I am Mr. Simonov." When the applause quieted down and my hero uttered his first word, the gallery erupted in a storm. They immediately realized it was not Kessler, and Simonov could not even say his second word.

The situation became uncomfortable. The *patriotn* did not allow the play to go on. When Simonov turned to them, raised his head toward the gallery, and wanted to give a speech, they didn't let him. Only when Spachner [Kalish's husband and manager] went up to the gallery and started to argue on behalf of Bertha Kalish, did they allow Simonov to make his announcement.

[Simonov explained the situation and said] that it was no one's fault that Kessler fell ill and that he, Simonov, was a worker just like they in the gallery, and what did they have against him? Simonov's mention of "workers" moved the hearts of the *patriotn* and they gave him the privilege of performing the play.[63]

That's how the *patriotn* acted at the time, that's how they adored their stars, and that's how they influenced the Yiddish theatre.

Not just once but dozens of times did the *patriotn* stick up for me although I never asked them to. They generally did not wait to be asked but they also did not let themselves be influenced. The star was theirs whether he liked it or not.

Appendix 2

Sarah Adler, *Forverts*, June 2, 1938

In the context of describing the prosperity that Yiddish theaters experienced in the early 1890s, Sarah Adler mentions their first encounters with patriotn, *and describes one in particular, Gulash (Harris). By the 1920s he worked as a doorkeeper for the National Theatre.*

In Gulash's eyes, Adler was the greatest person in the world. When Gulash was young and strong, few people dared to say anything bad about Adler to his face. [Gulash] often got into fights, and when his opponent was stronger he did not hesitate to attack with a stick or club. After several such fights, Gulash began to always carry one or even two clubs. . . . It often happened that the victim grabbed his second club and beat him and he would walk around with battle wounds. But these 'battles' never taught him anything and he rarely backed off from a fight. [. . .]

Adler rarely witnessed Gulash's wars. He greatly enjoyed watching how Gulash began to boil with rage. But as soon as he felt that a fight was about to erupt, Adler cleared out. Most of the conflicts and fights occurred in front of the theatre cafes when Adler sat inside and chatted with other actors. In order to have some fun, the actors would send someone to pick a quarrel with Gulash. When the gofer was not a greenhorn it usually led to no more than an argument. But if the actor was able to find some fool or someone who did not know what was going on, it ended in an ugly scene. To enrage Gulash you needed only to tell him that Kessler, Thomashefsky, or Sonnenthal was a greater actor than Adler.

. . . [Gulash] did not follow Adler just for the fun of it all. My husband paid him a weekly salary for many years. I don't remember how much, but it was enough for Gulash to make a living.

Notes

1. Dzh. Greyson, "An ovent oyf der galeri fun a idishen teater" [An evening in the gallery of a Yiddish theatre], *Forverts* [Forward], April 2, 1927.

2. B. Balzam, "Zey zaynen nokh haynt patrioten fun di geshtorbene stars" [To this day they are *patriotn* of deceased stars], *Forverts*, June 16, 1929.

3. Sidni Gordon, "Vi azoy 'Gulash' iz barihmt gevoren als 'kenig fun teater patrioten'," [How "Gulash" earned fame as the "king of theatre *patriotn*"], *Forverts*, December 31, 1926.

4. "Patrioten in idishen teater," [*Patriotn* in the Yiddish theatre], *Forverts*, May 18, 1902.

5. Both Boaz Young and Abraham Cahan suggest that the origins of *patriotizm* can be traced to the arrival of the second troupe in New York in 1886. See Boaz Young, *Mayn lebn in teater* [My life in the theatre] (New York: YKUF, 1950), 62–63 and Abraham Cahan, *Bleter fun mayn lebn* [Pages from my life] (New York: Forverts Association, 1928), 2:389.

6. For a detailed account of the power struggle among troupes and actors, see Marvin L. Seiger, "A History of the Yiddish Theatre in New York City to 1892" (Ph.D. thesis, Indiana University, 1960), especially chapters 11–12.

7. See, for example, ads for Rudolf Marks's benefit in *Folksadvokat* [The people's advocate], February 21, 1890 and for Liptzin's benefit in *Folksadvokat*, December 12, 1890.

8. See, for example, advertisements in *Folksadvokat*, January 3, 1890 and June 27, 1890. For recruiting Adler, see advertisement in *Folksadvokat*, February 21, 1890.

9. Young, *Mayn lebn in teater*, 67.

10. See David Nasaw, *Children of the City: At Work and at Play* (New York: Oxford University Press, 1985).

11. The only studies of amateur dramatic clubs focused on those that had ambitions to stage literary works. See Dovid Ber Tirkel, *Di yugntlekhe bine* [The juvenile stage] (Philadelphia: Hebrew Literature Society, 1940) and "Progresiv dramatik klub" [Progressive Dramatic Club] in Zalmen Zylbercweig, ed. *Leksikon fun yidishn teater* [Encyclopedia of the Yiddish theatre] (New York: Farlag Elisheva, 1959), 3:1857–1866.

12. On Dora Vaysman's *patriotn*, see B. Balzam, "Vos iz gevoren fun di amolige idishe teater patrioten?" [What has become of the former theatre *patriotn*?] *Forverts*, November 4, 1928; for

Thomashefsky's boys, see Bessie Thomashefsky, "Besi Tomashevskis lebens-geshikhte" [Bessie Thomashefsky's life story], *Tog* [Day], December 23, 1935.

13. Boris and Bessie Thomashefsky's respective memoirs attest that *patriotn* operated in an organized fashion in the early 1890s. The journalist and editor Abraham Cahan suggests that early forms of *patriotizm* started in the late 1880s but recalled that the word was not used until some time after 1890. See Cahan, *Bleter fun mayn lebn*, 2:391.

14. Shomer, "Dos yudishe teater in amerika" [Yiddish theatre in America], *Der menshenfraynd* [The philanthropist], 2, no. 29, 461. The journal is undated but this issue is likely from late 1891 or early 1892. Khonen Minikes, ed., *Di idishe bihne* [The Yiddish stage] (New York: Ferlag fun Yehuda Katzenelenbogen, 1897).

15. Under the new "Commonwealth Plan" the proprietor received fifty percent of the box-office receipts in lieu of a pre-determined rent. Seiger, 287–288.

16. Poole's had been thoroughly renovated in 1886 to create a comfortable auditorium and seating with lots of leg room. At its opening the gallery seated 700; three years later when it housed the Yiddish troupe the number was reduced to 600. For its opening, see "Poole New Theatre," *New York Times*, September 4, 1886; for the subsequent seating capacity, see "Benefit in Puls teater," [Benefit in Poole's Theatre] *Folksadvokat*, June 28, 1889.

17. Richard Butsch, *The Making of American Audiences: From Stage to Television, 1750–1990* (Cambridge: Cambridge University Press, 2000), 136–138.

18. Julian Ralph, "The Bowery," *The Century*, Vol. XLIII (1891–1892), 235.

19. "The Bowery Theatres," *Harper's Weekly*, May 10, 1890, 370–371.

20. Jacob Adler, *A Life on the Stage*, trans. and ed. Lulla Rosenfeld (New York: Alfred Knopf, 1999), 24–26.

21. For ticket prices in 1885, see "A Quaint Hebrew Drama," *New York Sun*, February 22, 1885, reprinted in Yankev Shatski, ed., *Arkhiv far der geshikhte fun yidishn teater un drame* [Archive for the history of Yiddish theatre and drama] (Vilna and New York: YIVO, 1930), 431; for the price range in the galleries, see Young, 142. Even when gallery tickets were generally priced at twenty-five cents, matinee tickets could still be purchased for fifteen.

22. While this culture discouraged women from sitting in the gallery, one article does attest to a female presence there: a young married woman who presumably went by herself was accosted by the two men sitting next to her. When the "sheriff," apparently a friend of these men, refused to intervene on her behalf, she left the theatre in tears. "Ken der idisher teater zayn a lehrer fun onshtendigkayt?" [Can the Yiddish theatre teach decency?], *Forverts*, April 17, 1907.

23. See Judith Thissen, "Moyshe Goes to the Movies," Ph.D. thesis, Utrecht University, 2001, 189, note 223.

24. Ruvn Vaysman, "Masekhes teater" [Tractate theatre] in *Di idishe bihne*, n.p.

25. Balzam, "Zey zaynen nokh haynt . . ."

26. Young, 62.

27. Schwartz, February 22, 1941.

28. Bertha Kalish, "Der patriot geht" [Here comes the *patriot*], *Tog*, September 5, 1925.

29. Young, 62.

30. Sidney Gordon [Khayim Ehrenreich], "Farvos zaynen yetst nito keyn 'teater patrioten'" [Why there are no "theatre *patriotn*" today], *Forverts*, April 23, 1926.

31. Ibid.

32. Maurice Schwartz, "Moris Shvarts dertsehlt" [Maurice Schwartz recounts], *Forverts*, February 12, 1941 and March 1, 1941.

33. Balzam, "Zey zaynen nokh haynt . . ."

34. Schwartz, February 5, 1941.

35. Schwartz, February 8. 1941.

36. "Yoysef Shvartsberg," *Leksikon fun yidishn teater* (New York: Farlag Elisheva, 1963), 4: 2942.

37. Bessie Thomashefsky, *Mayn lebens geshikhte* [My life story] (New York: Varhayt Publishing Co., 1916), 212–215.

38. Vaysman, "Masekhes teater."

39. Gordon, "Farvos zaynen yetst nito. . . ."

40. "'Patrioten' fun idishe ektors," ["*Patriotn*" of Yiddish actors] *Forverts*, May 17, 1902. See also Schwartz's description of Feinman's *patriotn* preparing for his benefit in *Forverts*, February 1, 1941.

41. "Patrioten in idishen teater."

42. For Schwartz on Mogulesco, see February 1, 1941; for his unsuccessful benefits, see Young, 68.

43. "Patrioten in idishen teater."

44. Schwartz, February 5, 1941.

45. Schwartz, February 19, 1941. According to him, music hall performers gathered in cheaper cafes and were generally more accessible than the theatre stars. Music hall *patriotn* and theatre *patriotn* did not mix.

46. Bessie Thomashefsky, *Tog*, December 23, 1935.

47. Boris Thomashefsky, *Mayn lebens-geshikhte* [My life story] (New York: Trio Press, 1937), 308.

48. Kalish, "Der patriot geht." Kalish believes that his *patriotn* did not want him to play in literary dramas but Kessler had performed in both Gordin's and Leon Kobrin's repertoire before 1900. In a different context, Bessie Thomashefsky corroborates that around 1900 stars still tended to stay away from villainous roles. Bessie Thomashefsky, *Mayn lebens geshikhte*, 262.

49. Schwartz, March 15, 1941.

50. Bessie Thomashefsky, *Mayn lebens geshikhte*, 266. It is not surprising that Bessie was chosen to take Mogulesco's part. As a comic actress who had already played trouser roles, she was the company's best available choice. In fact, several of her future signature roles would be cross-dressing roles, among them Felix in Goldfaden's last play, *Ben Ami*.

51. "Ester Rokhl Kaminska," *Leksikon fun yidishn teater* (Mexico City: Farlag Elisheva, 1969), 6:5508.

52. Balzam, "Vos iz gevoren . . ."

53. "Patriotn makhen a mehume in Grand teater" [*Patriotn* create turmoil in Grand Theatre], *Forverts*, October 14, 1907.

54. Bessie Thomashefsky, *Mayn lebens geshikhte*, 238–240.

55. Sarah Adler, "Di lebens geshikhte fun Sara Adler" [Sarah Adler's life story], *Forverts*, March 30, 1939. Since Schacht was a supporting actor, his name did not appear in the ads, but he did receive very positive mention in reviews. See A. Cahan, "Y. Gordins 'emese kraft' in Grend teater" [J. Gordin's "True power" in Grand Theatre], *Forverts*, November 1, 1904, and H. Aleksandrov, "Di emese kraft" [The true power], *Der arbeter* [The worker], December 3, 1904.

56. See press release, "Thalia teater," *Forverts*, August 25, 1903.

57. "Di yidishe teatere" [The Yiddish theatres], *Forverts*, August 30, 1903. Unfortunately, the article does not provide any details about Gordin's speech.

58. "A New Jewish Theatre," *New York Times*, February 1, 1903.

59. Schwartz, February 26, 1941.

60. Judith Thissen, "Reconsidering the Decline of the New York Yiddish Theatre in the Early 1900s," *Theatre Survey* 44 (November 2003): 180.

61. "Fun folk tsum folk" [From the people to the people], *Forverts*, November 21, 1904.

62. "Di skandalen af der galerye" [The scandals in the gallery], *Forverts*, February 3, 1906, and "Adler fodert oyf" [Adler invites], *Forverts*, February 4, 1906.

63. An article in the *Forverts*, "A skandal in talia teater" [A scandal in the Thalia Theatre] (June 1, 1902), describes a similar situation, albeit with a very different ending: Simonov replaced the ailing Kessler in Zalmen Libin's *Der gebrokhener neyder* [The broken vow], in which Kalish had a leading part as well. According to the article, audience members left and demanded their money back but were refused. The police were called in to restore order. The *Forverts* sided with the audience, mentioning that Kessler often did not show up after a couple of performances in a new role.

CHAPTER 8

Liquor and Leisure: The Business of Yiddish Vaudeville

Judith Thissen

Throughout the late nineteenth century, a visit to one of the Yiddish theatres on the Bowery was the most popular form of commercial entertainment for New York's eastern European Jews. In the early 1900s, however, their entertainment preferences and practices changed dramatically. New forms of public recreation developed alongside the legitimate Yiddish theatre and the sponsored balls, picnic outings, and other non-commercial entertainments organized by *landsmanshaftn* (hometown societies) and trade unions. By 1910, moving-picture shows, Yiddish vaudeville theatres, and commercial dance halls dominated the local leisure landscape.

The main victim of this process of differentiation within the entertainment infrastructure was the so-called "legitimate" Yiddish dramatic theatre. The decline in the number of seats available for Yiddish performances gives a clear indication of its decline in market share and popularity. In 1900, there were three large Yiddish playhouses on the Bowery: the Thalia Theatre, the Windsor Theatre, and the People's Theatre. Together, they could accommodate up to 9,000 spectators. With the inauguration of a fourth Yiddish theatre on Grand Street in 1903, the total number of seats jumped from 9,000 to 11,000. Almost immediately, however, it turned out that the market for Yiddish drama had reached a level of saturation that was not sustainable commercially. Despite the fact that the Jewish population in New York City was growing explosively due to mass migration following the Kishinev pogroms of 1903, there was an overcapacity in terms of "Yiddish" seats. To adjust supply and demand, one out of the four Yiddish legitimate playhouses was rented out to an English-language company every season until a more lasting solution was worked out. In 1909, the Grand Street Theatre was given over to motion-picture interests. That same year, the old Windsor Theatre was demolished to make way for the entrance to the Manhattan Bridge. On the other hand, two new Yiddish playhouses opened their doors on Second Avenue in 1911–1912: David Kessler's Second Avenue Theatre and Boris Thomashefsky's National Theatre. Still, the balance remained negative. The total seating capacity declined from 9,000 in 1900 to 6,000 in 1912. In the same period, the city's immigrant Jewish population had more than tripled.[1]

The expansion of cheap, commercialized entertainment and the concomitant decline of legitimate Yiddish theatre was by no means an isolated phenomenon. All across the United States, ten-cent vaudeville and five-cent picture shows (nickelodeons) made inroads into everyday life around the turn of the century, providing working-class families with unprecedented access to public entertainment and offering exciting new pastimes for the middle classes. Yet if we explain the emergence of Yiddish music halls and *muving piktshur pletzer* ("moving-picture" houses, or cinemas) only in terms of a more general expansion of cheap amusements nationwide, we would fail to perceive the specific local conditions that spurred the exceptionally rapid transformation of the Jewish immigrant entertainment business in New York City. In presenting a detailed material analysis of the economic forces that shaped leisure business on the Lower East Side, I hope to illuminate profound changes in the recreational patterns of immigrant Jews within less than a decade, culminating in the triumph of the movies as the most popular form of entertainment.

Public Meeting Halls: Spaces and Practices

The genealogy of the entertainment revolution that took place on the Lower East Side is closely linked with the history of the district's public meeting halls. Between 1900 and 1905, the small neighborhood meeting hall in the heart of the Jewish quarter rapidly developed into the dominant site of cheap entertainment. Changing conditions in the meeting-hall business had created new challenges for the entrepreneurs who ran these halls, making ventures outside their regular realm of activities necessary, if not always as profitable as they had initially hoped.

Multi-purpose public halls and saloons with assembly rooms were central institutions of late nineteenth-century working-class culture and common in most immigrant neighborhoods.[2] In 1898, the *Trow's Business Directory* listed forty-six meeting halls on the Lower East Side, twenty-five of which were located in the center of the Jewish quarter (the area east of the Bowery and below East Houston Street). The majority of these establishments were converted tenement buildings and could accommodate up to 500 people at most. Typically, the main floor served as a multi-purpose hall that would be rented out to immigrant organizations and private persons for a wide variety of activities, such as mass meetings, masquerade balls, and weddings. The basement housed a saloon, kitchen, and dining room. The upper floors were divided into small assembly rooms and makeshift synagogues.

Most meeting halls were operated by small-time entrepreneurs, who hardly ever owned the building. They secured its lease for several years and paid an annual rent for the entire premises, which they subsequently subleased. The smaller assembly rooms were rented out per month, the main hall per day or night. The rental of assembly rooms, however, was not the core business. It generated income, but not enough to make a profit. Figures from the Golden Rule Hall on Rivington Street, for example, suggest that the income from rentals barely covered fixed expenses such as the annual rent.[3] The sale of liquor was almost certainly the main source of income for Samuel Friedman, who ran this well-attended hall during the 1890s. At the Golden Rule Hall and elsewhere, *landsmanshaftn*, trade unions, and other clubs often paid a nominal rental fee for the assembly rooms in which they gathered, on the understanding that their members would patronize the saloon in the building. It was standard practice on the East Side that when the receipts from the sale of drinks on the night of a ball or concert had been satisfactory to the management, the same organization could have the hall free of charge for its next function.[4] Similarly, poor couples could rent a hall for a modest price or obtain it for nothing to celebrate their wedding. Even then, it was understood that the hall keeper would make money on the wine and beer ordered by the guests, as well as from the hat checks sold at the entrance.[5] Only assembly rooms run by settlement societies did not serve liquor; all other meeting halls had a saloon function. In addition, many hall keepers operated a liquor and wine store on the premises or in the immediate vicinity.

Economically speaking, the trouble was that most Jews were moderate drinkers, unlike the district's older cast of Germans and Irish, who spent much of their leisure time around the bar. According to an 1898 report of the University Settlement Society, "the number of one saloon to every five hundred people" in the downtown Jewish quarter compared "well with many of the best suburban residence towns."[6] Those data were confirmed by a sociologist who found that "as the Jewish population of a given district increases, the number of 'gin mills' decreases ... [B]etween the [Russian Jew] and the saloon there is no affinity."[7] Obviously, this is a somewhat exaggerated observation because "discussing the affairs of the day over a glass of beer or wine" was not uncommon among Jewish workers, as a settlement worker observed.[8] Still, for the majority of East Side Jews, drinking was not a fact of everyday life, but an occasion for celebration, whether social or religious. In addition, many newly arrived immigrants could simply not afford to socialize around a glass of beer. As labor organizer Bernard Weinstein explains in his memoirs, greenhorns "didn't have a nickel" (the standard price for a glass of beer).[9] Slack seasons in the garment industry, which employed many immigrant Jews, also affected the turnover of retail businesses that catered primarily to a working-class clientele. In sum, then, operating a meeting hall was an insecure business, strongly subject to economic and seasonal fluctuation (winter being the best season).

Cutthroat competition was not uncommon and the leases of the halls frequently changed hands.

For the small-time meeting-hall managers, the situation became increasingly difficult at the end of the nineteenth century, when real-estate developers began to invest in large, modern meeting-hall buildings that offered a wide range of rooms, including halls that could accommodate up to 1,200 people. The older and much smaller meeting halls, almost all located in former tenement buildings in the central part of the Jewish quarter, could not compete with their new counterparts, such as Liberty Hall on East Houston Street or Progress Assembly Rooms on Avenue A.[10] There was still enough interest for the smaller assembly rooms on the upper floors of these older establishments, because the demand for this type of space was higher than the supply. But immigrant organizations and private persons showed little interest in the outdated halls on the ground floor and preferred to organize their annual balls or celebrate their weddings in a more fashionable hall that offered the latest conveniences, including such exciting novelties as an electric *khupe* (wedding canopy). Confronted with a decline in net earnings, the more enterprising hall keepers radically changed their strategy. Rather than renting the main hall out to third parties for non-commercial activities, they began to develop the space as a site for cheap commercial entertainment, often in close partnership with a "specialist." At the Golden Rule, for instance, one "professor" Ueberall ran a dancing academy on weekday evenings.[11] Around 1900, commercial dance halls began to spread all over the East Side, soon followed by the latest trend on the Bowery: the Yiddish music hall.

Early Yiddish Music Halls and Concert Saloons

The first Yiddish music hall, the Eldorado Theatre, opened in September of 1901. Four months later, there were three Yiddish music halls on the Bowery. On their heels, a number of East Side saloon- and hall keepers started offering free variety shows in the back rooms of their establishments or in the main hall. It is important to emphasize that in the early days there were considerable differences between the Yiddish music halls on the Bowery (the traditional entertainment zone) and the Yiddish concert saloons, which were located in the residential tenement district east of the Bowery.

The Yiddish music halls on the Bowery—the Eldorado Theatre, London Theatre, and People's Music Hall—were run by vaudeville actors who maintained strong ties with the Yiddish legitimate stage and borrowed many of its business practices. Unlike concert saloons, all three Bowery music halls charged admission for their shows. Tickets were the main source of income, although it should be noted that patrons could order refreshments at the bar inside the auditorium or in an adjoining saloon. This was also a common practice in the legitimate Yiddish playhouses and a much-welcomed source of additional income, just like the sale of confections. At the Eldorado Theatre, ticket prices ranged from fifteen to fifty cents at night; for matinee seats prices were set at ten, twenty, and thirty cents. The schedule was the same as in the nearby legitimate playhouses. For instance, the Eldorado Theatre presented a daily show at 8:15 p.m. and matinee performances on Saturdays and Sundays at 2:15 p.m. In addition to the box-office shows, the Bowery music halls also sold blocks of tickets at reduced prices for benefit performances. Abraham Tantzman, the manager of the Eldorado, promised "congregations, lodges, societies, and private persons very cheap benefit nights"—again a well-established practice in the Yiddish theatrical business.[12] Finally, it should be noted that from the outset some prominent Yiddish theatre managers were involved in vaudeville activities. The People's Music Hall was launched by Jacob Adler, Boris Thomashefsky, and Joseph Edelstein as a vaudeville subsidiary of the People's Theatre. In February 1902, they engaged Yudele Beltzer's double-brass dance quartet and a few talented youngsters, and presented their own vaudeville show in the small playhouse where Hurwitz's Rumanian troupe had played for years.

In sharp contrast with the Yiddish music halls on the Bowery, the concert saloons that had opened up in the heart of the Jewish quarter did not sell tickets at first. Until 1905–1906, all that was demanded of those who watched these "free" shows was that they spend five cents on a glass of beer or wine, preferably ordered in combination with some Hungarian meat patties, Romanian peppers, or other well-seasoned snacks that would further stimulate the consumption of drinks.[13] For obvious reasons, the saloon keepers did not empty the house after each performance. They allowed customers to sit as long as they liked or, more precisely, as long as they continued drinking and eating (most concert saloons served food). The particular circumstances under which saloonkeepers operated their variety houses prompted the practice of "continuous" shows, meaning that the first act was brought back on stage when the final act exited, so that customers could enter at any point during show.[14]

Within a few years, Yiddish vaudeville would become a major force on the local entertainment market. Initially, however, "the public kept far away from the Yiddish music halls," according to the first historian of the Yiddish stage, Bernard Gorin.[15] A fierce anti-vaudeville campaign by the *Tageblatt* and *Forverts*, in combination with bad management and lack of capital, were the main reasons for the slow start.[16] Of the three admission-charging Yiddish music halls that opened on the Bowery, only the People's Music Hall survived its first year. The smaller music halls in the heart of the Jewish quarter fared a little better. A few concert saloons went under, but most remained in business, even if it was not a particularly booming business. Vaudeville gave these halls something extra over the competition, and the free entertainment program bolstered the consumption of alcohol.

Regulating the Liquor Trade

A higher turnover in terms of liquor sales might well have been the strongest incentive for saloon- and hall keepers to offer vaudeville shows. Due to major changes in the liquor business following new legislation, their profit margin on beer had declined significantly. Large corporate brewers had gained control over the market and often held iron-clad contracts over their clients. Many independent saloon keepers feared that they had to "work their entire life for a brewer."[17] Brewery control began in 1896, with the introduction of the Raines Law, a New York State anti-vice bill that imposed severe restrictions on the liquor trade. Among other measures, the yearly license fee was raised to an excessive $1,200, and an $1,800 bond was required on all saloons, to be forfeited upon any violation of the law. To protect their own commercial interests, large breweries began to facilitate the payment of the license fee and stood surety for the bond. In return for this financial assistance, saloonkeepers were bound by contract to purchase all beers and ales from their backer at a fixed price.[18] As brewers reaped a substantial part of their clients' profits, saloon keepers saw their net earnings go down. To survive, they had either to sell more beer or to find additional sources of income (or both). Add to this the growing competition from large meeting halls and the fact that drinking in a commercial setting remained a relatively marginal affair among Jewish immigrants, and we begin to understand why so many meeting-hall managers ventured into the amusement business proper.

Five years after the introduction of the Raines Law, about twenty percent of the East Side saloons and meeting halls increased their profits by running commercial dances.[19] About a dozen meeting halls had been turned into concert saloons and offered vaudeville entertainment to attract more customers and keep them longer on the premises. For yet another group of saloon keepers, "the difference between bankruptcy and solvency was the prostitute," according to social historian Timothy Gilfoyle.[20] Throughout the nineteenth century, saloons had accommodated prostitutes in several ways, ranging from allowing them to solicit their customers to maintaining rooms for intercourse upstairs. One of the unanticipated results of the Raines Law was that prostitution in saloons became more prevalent.[21] The Raines Law prohibited Sunday sales of liquor except in hotels. Since hotels were defined as establishments that served meals and had at least ten beds, over 1,000 saloons, halls, and restaurants in New York simply subdivided their rear or upper floor space into small bedrooms and took out hotel licenses. The Victoria Hall at 80–82 Clinton Street was one of these so-called "Raines Law hotels." A few weeks after the bill was passed, the proprietor of the hall—a wholesale liquor dealer—turned the beer saloon in the front building into a hotel with bedrooms and a restaurant.[22] The tiny, noisy rooms did not attract many regular guests, but prostitutes and pimps went in and out. Meanwhile, the rear of the building continued to serve as a dance hall and banquet room with lodge rooms upstairs. A decade later, the hall would reopen as a Yiddish vaudeville house.[23]

A Surplus of Performers

A close look at the transformation of the meeting-hall business helps us to understand how Yiddish vaudeville could make its way into the traditional structures of public life on the East Side. However, in seeking to explain the emergence of Yiddish music halls, we also have to examine the changing conditions in the theatrical business. From the perspective of Yiddish theatre history, the major impetus behind the development of Yiddish vaudeville was the surplus of Jewish immigrant performers, which resulted in a desperate struggle for jobs and constant search for new opportunities to make a living on the stage.

Throughout the late nineteenth century, impresarios kept bringing in new talent from eastern Europe, while others crossed the Atlantic on their own initiative. Consequently, more and more Yiddish performers—actors, singers, dancers, musicians— were competing for work. By the late 1890s, employment had become more uncertain than ever and the payment, either by marks (shares in a theatre company, for which performers of greater stature were eligible) or salary, was often extremely low. Only a handful of top stars, actor-managers in particular, cashed in on the thriving theatrical business. Growing dissatisfaction with working conditions led to various unionization efforts among actors, chorus members, and musicians. In 1899, partly in response to the abuses of the star system, the actors of the Yiddish playhouses in New York City founded the Hebrew Actors' Union, which soon developed into a powerful organization. To secure its members a decent standard of living, the new union imposed rigid closed-shop rules. Any manager who desired to employ non-union staff was confronted with threats of a strike. More important, the union kept virtually all newcomers out of its ranks. Actors could apply for membership only if they had played several years outside New York City. Admission procedures were so difficult in actual practice that very few candidates passed. Other Yiddish theatre unions, such as the Hebrew Choristers Union, were organized along the same lines.[24]

The lockout measures had far-reaching consequences for would-be actors and newly arrived immigrant performers: both groups were relegated to the margins of the theatrical business. Since for most of them a career on the English-language stage seemed beyond reach, they had to look for opportunities outside New York City. Yet the road business was risky and unstable. Scores of troupes failed due to lack of capital and management experience.[25] Moreover, the well-established New York-based companies began to extend their control to the "provinces," in particular to nearby cities with large Jewish communities such as Philadelphia and Newark. To protect the interests of the existing road companies, Local 2 of the Hebrew

Actors' Union, with jurisdiction over traveling troupes, was established in 1902. Thus the job openings for newcomers were further reduced.

The almost inexhaustible supply of fresh faces, both amateur and professional, provided a key precondition for the emergence of Yiddish vaudeville. Many vaudevillians were still in their teens when they started out on the Yiddish music-hall stage.[26] The East Side music-hall business proved a fertile ground for their careers. Some of them achieved stardom far beyond the immigrant milieu in which they grew up, like Bella Baker, one of the "red-hot mamas" of American vaudeville, who started at age fourteen in a small music hall on Cannon Street.[27] Not everyone started from scratch. Several young vaudevillians had been trained in amateur dramatic clubs.[28] Others were *patriotn*—fanatical fans of particular stars—who grasped their chance to enter the theatre professionally and show their great passion for the Yiddish stage by imitating their idol (or a rival star) before music-hall audiences.[29] Yiddish vaudeville also absorbed a number of Yiddish theatre veterans. Almost all of them came from the road and excelled in comic roles.[30] The career of the character-comedian Abraham Tantzman (1857–1906) was typical of the experienced vaudeville actors. In eastern Europe, he had worked with Goldfaden and other Yiddish touring companies until 1889, when a New York theatre manager sent him tickets to come to America. After a brief engagement in New York, Tantzman and his wife, the actress Bertha Berlin, toured the United States from Chicago to California, where they won much praise with a production of Goldfaden's *Shulamis*. In 1901, at the age of forty-four, Tantzman returned to New York. Barred from the legitimate stage, he ventured into Yiddish vaudeville and launched the Eldorado Theatre. As we saw, the Eldorado closed down after one season. Five years later, however, when Yiddish vaudeville became a booming business in New York City, Tantzman was back in town again.

Yiddish Vaudeville Becomes a Booming Business

Three years after the opening of the Eldorado Theatre, many Jewish workers and their families had occasionally visited one of the East Side music halls, but Yiddish vaudeville had not become a major force on the local entertainment market. This situation changed in 1905. The rapid expansion of the potential audience due to mass immigration helped to create a firm market for cheap theatrical entertainment. The upsurge in patronage was further precipitated by the collapse of Moyshe Hurwitz's Windsor Theatre in November of 1904. Hurwitz's troupe had been the main provider of Yiddish operetta, a type of theatrical entertainment that in many respects—horseplay, slapstick, a wild mixture of genres, and an abundance of singing and dancing—closely resembled music-hall fare. Managers of concert saloons, who until then had offered free shows, were quick to capitalize on the increased demand for their product: they renovated their establishments and began to charge admission, ranging from ten to twenty-five cents. Their example was promptly copied. Suddenly there seemed to be a Yiddish vaudeville house on every corner. "Today every important street [on the East Side] has its glaring sign which announces 'Jewish Vaudeville House' or 'Music Hall,'" a settlement worker reported in late 1905.[31]

On Grand Street, two blocks from Adler's Grand Theatre, Julius Prince opened a 1,000-seat music hall above his father's liquor store with the help of the actor-impresario Morris Heine, Hurwitz's former partner at the Windsor Theatre. Other halls were directly rented out to Yiddish vaudeville entrepreneurs.[32] Abraham Tantzman rented the Golden Rule Hall, which had been transformed into a large dance hall in 1903. On Friday, September 1, 1905, he opened the Golden Rule Vaudeville House. Prospective customers were promised "first class variety: sketches and vaudevilles by the greatest dramatists and actors."[33] Shows were given every night, with matinee performances on Saturdays and Sundays (the bill changed on Friday night). Samuel Agid, an experienced Galician saloon keeper and restaurateur with a passionate commitment to Yiddish theatre, secured the lease of the Victoria Hall on Clinton Street and reopened it as Agid's Clinton Street Vaudeville House. He also acquired an interest in the Union Vaudeville Hall on Eldridge Street and the Bismarck Garden in Brooklyn. By the early 1910s, Agid was known as the "King of Jewish Varieties."[34]

While favorable market conditions spurred the demand for Yiddish vaudeville, widespread acceptance of Yiddish vaudeville as a suitable pastime did not come until the music halls began to charge admission, and thus dissociated their shows from the compulsory beer-drinking accompaniment. Most vaudeville entrepreneurs conveniently kept a liquor bar on the premises, but it seems that the policy of charging admission (rather than obliging customers to order a glass of beer) made the music halls more acceptable for a broad audience, women and children in particular.[35] In fact, time and again, the newly opened or renovated vaudeville houses sought to divorce themselves from the controversial image of the early concert saloons. The Grand Street Music Hall, for instance, was marketed as "a truly honest new Yiddish variety for Jewish families" and "a beautiful family place."[36] To further enhance the status of his establishment, Prince hired Morris Heine—the "founder of the Yiddish theatre in New York"—as stage manager.[37] As historian David Nasaw points out, through this type of advertising, "audience members, still unsure as to whether or not they should be paying their dimes and quarters to see variety acts in cheap theatres, were reassured that in doing so they were certifying their inclusion in a new and expanding respectable public for respectable amusements."[38] Prince's publicity campaign worked out very well. Jewish immigrants flocked to the Grand Street Music Hall to enjoy an evening's entertainment that cost not even half the price of a gallery seat in Adler's Grand Theatre, two blocks down the street.

Moving Pictures: From "a *tsimes* to the show" to Main Dish

Motion pictures were soon to conquer both Adler's Grand Theatre and the Grand Street Music Hall, but around 1905, they were still very much a novelty in the Jewish quarter. This is remarkable considering that American vaudeville managers had integrated the short-reel films of the early years into their programs soon after the first commercial presentation of Edison's vitascope at Koster and Bial's Music Hall in 1896. We may assume that many East Siders discovered the excitement of moving images in the vaudeville theatres on East Fourteenth Street and Union Square, at the Eden Musee waxworks or at Coney Island. On the Bowery and Grand Street, motion pictures could also be seen in penny arcades, which had peepshow devices such as the kinetoscope and mutoscope. And many eastern European Jews had been introduced to the Lumière cinématographe before they migrated to America. Several itinerant film exhibitors toured the Pale of Settlement, and many cities and towns in Russia had permanent movie theatres as early as 1904.[39]

It took over a decade before the cinema established itself firmly in the heart of the Jewish quarter. Until late 1907, Yiddish music halls in New York City remained limited outlets for films. Short film programs were presented by self-acclaimed "professors," who operated as itinerant film exhibitors, touring the local Yiddish vaudeville circuit with their own film projector and a set of moving pictures.[40] In the eyes of the managers, moving pictures were merely "a *tsimes* [sweet side dish] to the show," as the *Forverts* explained, and hence most of them did not invest in the new medium.[41] Others, however, did.

During the 1905–1906 season, the first nickelodeons—storefront theatres that offered a continuous show of short movies and illustrated songs for a nickel—opened in Manhattan. Within a few months, New York had more movie houses than any other American city. The largest concentration of them was found on Park Row and the Bowery.[42] On Saturday, these new entertainment venues allegedly attracted "great holiday crowds from the East Side."[43] Yet it would take another year before the first theatre specializing in moving pictures would open in the heart of the Jewish quarter. In the summer of 1906, Adolph Zukor, the future president of Paramount Pictures, operated a penny arcade with slot machines on Grand Street next to Jacob Adler's theatre, and "determined to take the chance" and transform the place into "a very attractive little theatre" for moving pictures. According to *Views and Films Index*, an early trade paper for film exhibitors, "the result was very gratifying. The place commenced to do a rushing business and is doing it yet. The films are changed frequently and the East Siders are willing to be kept interested."[44]

The following year, more Jewish entrepreneurs tried their luck in the film exhibition business.[45] Yiddish music-hall managers also became more interested in showing movies. The Golden Rule Hall was the first Yiddish music hall to switch to films as the main attraction. In November of 1906, following the untimely death of Abraham Tantzman, the lease of the main floor was taken over by Stephen J. Scherer, the owner of a photographic firm.[46] Under the new management, moving pictures dominated the bill. The new formula was a great success. *Views and Films Index* reported in August 1907 that the Golden Rule "had a record of 4,038 patrons to their theatre on Saturday, July 13th [. . .] and during the past weeks the average has been fourteen thousand tickets sold."[47] In December 1907, the weekly take of the Golden Rule had mounted to $1,800. With operating costs estimated at about $500, the house was reported to make a net profit of $1,300 per week.[48]

During the 1907–1908 season, nickelodeons were "spreading like mushrooms after the rain" on the East Side.[49] The boom was fueled by a severe economic depression that hit the United States in the winter of 1907. The thin purses that went with the recession forced many Jewish immigrants to look for cheaper forms of entertainment. The immediate effect of the crisis was a significant drop in theatrical attendance in the middle and upper segments of the entertainment market. The legitimate Yiddish playhouses lost "a considerable number of patrons" to the moving pictures, according to the *Forverts*.[50] Yiddish music halls also struggled to survive. The majority switched to moving pictures as their staple entertainment. Many vaudevillians lost their jobs but some continued to make a few dollars per week by entertaining the audience in between films (while the reels were changed) with skits, jokes, dances, and songs.

The nickelodeon business on the East Side witnessed phenomenal growth, attracting many newcomers who believed it to be a get-rich-quick scheme. At the end of 1908, the number of moving-picture outlets in the downtown Jewish quarter had climbed to about thirty-five, without counting those on the Bowery and East Fourteenth Street. On the corner of Essex and Rivington Streets alone, three of the nickel theatres were now offering moving-picture shows: the Golden Rule Vaudeville House, Steiner's Essex Street Theatre at 133 Essex Street, and the WACO Theatre at 118–120 Rivington Street. Film historian Ben Singer found that Jewish neighborhoods had the highest density of nickelodeons in Manhattan. It seems that immigrant Jews went more frequently to the movies than any other ethnic group in New York City.[51] The inexpensive picture shows provided them with a regular basis for leisure on a scale unmatched by the legitimate Yiddish theatre and Yiddish music halls.

Vaudeville in the Age of the Movies

As Jewish immigrants became committed filmgoers, the film exhibition business created ample opportunities for expansion. However, Yiddish music-hall managers failed to seize these opportunities. When the crisis was over, most music halls on the Lower East Side and in Brooklyn switched back to fully-fledged vaudeville shows. The lead in the local entertainment business was taken up by the film exhibitors who had started out during the nickelodeon boom. In sharp contrast with the music-hall managers, these entrepreneurs maintained ties neither with the liquor trade nor with meeting-hall business. In their theatres, one could purchase only soda water, ice cream, peanuts, and candy. More important, the majority of this new generation came from consumer-oriented trades and introduced business methods that were far more innovative and aggressive than those of the Yiddish music-hall managers. Eager to take advantage of the growing leisure market, the newcomers set up corporations and entered into partnerships with more affluent investors to expand their activities both on and beyond the Lower East Side.[52] They built new 600-seat "photo-play" houses and launched local chains that soon began to swallow the smaller independent movie theatres and music halls. The saloon- and hall keepers who operated the typical East Side Yiddish music hall lacked the necessary funds and expertise to compete in this increasingly professionalized leisure market. By the mid 1910s, most of them had stepped out of the film exhibition and vaudeville business.[53] In December of 1914, the death of Samuel Agid, the "King of Yiddish Varieties," marked the end of an era.

At 80–82 Clinton Street, where Agid had started his career by turning a former Raines Law hotel into a Yiddish vaudeville house, the brand-new Clinton Street movie theatre opened its door in 1917. During the following decade, the movies continued to gain popularity thanks to famous Hollywood stars, improved viewing conditions in picture palaces, and the introduction of talking pictures. While the feature-length film left little room on the program for non-filmic acts, new immigration laws put an end to the stream of Yiddish-speaking newcomers from eastern Europe who formed the natural audience for Yiddish vaudeville. Pushed to the margins of the local entertainment business, Yiddish vaudeville survived in neighborhood movie theatres such as the Clinton Theatre and Palestine Theatre, which combined live shows with Yiddish talkies and other Jewish theme films and catered primarily to a clientele of first-generation immigrants. By the 1930s, it had become an object of nostalgic reminiscence and a tourist attraction—a remainder of the Old-World-flavored immigrant culture that was rapidly fading away.

Appendix

Paul Klapper, "The Yiddish Music Hall," *University Settlement Studies* (New York: University Settlement Society), vol 2, no. 4 (1906): 19–23.

To the average Jewish immigrant, life is an extremely grave and serious proposition. From the cradle to his present moment, the struggle for existence amidst adverse conditions has forced him to the realization of this fact. Economic, social, and religious iniquities drive him to our shores. America, the panacea for all his ills, is his inspiration of courage and hope. But he is invariably doomed to disappointment. He is suddenly thrust into a new environment. A new language greets his ear. He is a stranger in the promised land. Assimilation is slow and discouraging. Everybody knows that he is a "greenhorn." He finds thousands like himself, competing for the same miserable positions. In the sweat-shop he must submit to the new tyranny of the "boss," and abide by the regulations of an arbitrary labor union, in order to eke out a mere pittance. The economic question eclipses all others. It becomes the glasses through which he views life in the "land of milk and honey." The natural reaction to this intensity of existence is very strong indeed. Recreation becomes essential. His soul craves for it. The saloon and the brothel have no attraction for a great body of Jewish immigrants. Their well-developed social instincts lead them rather to the cafe and the theatre. The Yiddish stage reflects very faithfully the Jewish temperament. The playwright produces his work because he has a lesson to teach, a moral to preach, a social question to solve. The drama is intensely realistic and portrays very forcibly the tragedies of daily life. Intermarriage of Hebrew and Gentile, the domestic triangle, the liberation of the downtrodden Jews in Russia, free love, anarchistic and socialistic propaganda are the topics of these plays. They are thoroughly "Ibsenisk," and necessitate deep thought and subtleties of argument. The humor, paradoxical as it may seem, serves only "to aggravate the tension by relieving it."

There is a lighter element among the Jewish theatre-going population that rebels against this seriousness. Their tastes are like those of our own comic opera and vaudeville habitués. About five years ago the possibilities of the present Jewish vaudeville first dawned upon an East Side saloon-keeper. He set aside the rear end of his establishment to this purpose. Here he constructed a small stage for the cheap talent he found. The rest of the place was utilized for chairs and tables where the patrons enjoyed their beer. The plan soon made its popularity manifest, and others, with more capital to invest, went into the vaudeville business, as it promised lucrative returns. To-day every important street on the lower East Side has its glaring electric sign which announces, "Jewish Vaudeville House" or "Music Hall." These vaudeville houses are generally reconstructed "dancin' halls." A flimsy wooden gallery, and a flimsier stage is erected. The scenery and the theatrical paraphernalia are crude and cheap. The places can be arranged to accommodate any number, ranging from three hundred to over fifteen hundred. But the point of maximum elasticity is never reached. The Law provides that places not built as theatres should not seat more than three hundred. The chairs in these places are often movable because there are times when it is absolutely essential to live up to the letter of the law. "But these occasions are few; it only takes a day or two to fix a new official," one of these new Frohmans explained. Many building regulations and safety provisions are neglected with impunity, because the proper inspector has been "fixed." Only the ravages of flame and the madness of a panic will tell how many of our brethren are to pay with their lives for this "fixing." In case of a future calamity, we may find some consolation in the fact that the various municipal departments concerned will surely institute the regular fiasco, "a rigorous investigation, in order to bring the culprits to justice." The performers are an ignorant lot,—the greater part, far more efficient in the intricacies of gambling, and still more experienced in the manifold forms of petty vice, than in acting. The rest are in the "vaudeville actin' business" because they are not fit for any profitable labor. Those with talent and a little refinement are absorbed by the regular Jewish theatres, where ability is essential. The inevitable result is that these music halls utilize the talent that is left,—the worst talent. The proprietors are often unduly censured for employing these people, but they really cannot help themselves, as we shall see. These vaudeville actors have a most exclusive union. They control every Jewish vaudeville house on the East Side. The patrons are union members, and refuse to frequent a particular house unless it employs "union labor." This organization dictates the policy of the vaudeville houses, fixes salaries, which range from twelve to fifty dollars a week, and allots a certain number of actors to each establishment, so that every member will be employed. The initiation fee is so high that is practically prohibitive for the poorer applicants. The "entrance examination" is so exacting, and the results judged with such careful scrutiny, that the applicant, however able, is often excluded at the end of the farce. Every conceivable injustice which labor unions may commit was practiced at one time or another by this vaudeville actors' union. The proprietor, therefore, is controlled, rather than controls, in matters relating to the performance. The character of these shows can easily be inferred from what has been said about the players. The evening program consists of a number of "turns" and the production of a short farce. The sketch, or farce, is a short play, portraying some phase of Jewish life, or caricaturing such American customs as seem strange and ludicrous to the immigrant. Those which base their plot on the recent Russian riots are extremely popular. Many in the audience have either experienced these incidents themselves, or have relatives that are to-day suffering the consequences of these anti-Semitic outbreaks. The climaxes are as melodramatic as the futile brain of the playwright can possibly make them. The villain is hissed vociferously, but he continues his nefarious plotting throughout the play. The hero, the unfortunate victim of all this, positive that poetic justice will be done, and that he will marry the girl in the end, is unmindful of all the dastardly plans.

Those actors who do a "turn" either sing and dance, or conduct a dialogue. In most of these numbers, there is a marked effort to imitate the poor English vaudeville actors; but the vulgarities are so exaggerated that they make the performance positively filthy. The songs are suggestive of everything but what is proper, the choruses are full of double meanings, and the jokes have broad and unmistakable hints of things indecent. All this is greeted with wild applause. What adds an element of pathos, is the number of young girls and children who are always to be found in the audience, thoroughly enjoying themselves, yet in ignorance of the true meaning of the songs in which they join. The children learn these ditties and often in all their glee, sing them in the streets. There are a number of small music halls that seldom, if ever, have enough patronage to pay for running expenses. Still, these places keep open, month after month, even in the summer, when the largest houses find business too slow to warrant a continuance of the performance. These places are the rendez-vous of well-known East Side Fagans [sic], and of those moral leeches that fatten on the virtue of innocent womanhood. How can we avoid the conclusion that these establishments are conducting gambling dens, or kindred vicious businesses? Can we prove this? Legally, no. But these facts nevertheless cannot be refuted, according to all outward appearances, these music halls in question, are run at a loss, and these notorious characters make them their "hangouts." A continuance of these low class vaudeville houses reflects on the moral standard of our immediate community. Our own Settlement, under the auspices of the Milton Club, has registered its sentiments on these matters, with the proprietors of these music halls, and with the vaudeville actors' union. The plea of those who commit these improprieties, is "the audience demands this; they enjoy it." This is most decidedly not so. It is true that many in the audience do get a certain pleasure out of this kind of a performance, but still there is no demand for it. Those houses that have set up a standard, and are earnestly living up to it, have packed houses; thus showing clearly that there is no clamor for the low character show. The union gave a very encouraging answer to the letter of protest which was sent to them. They promised faithfully that union regulations would demand decency on these stages, and that they would do all in their power to raise the moral tone of the shows. Thus far no improvement has taken place, and we must infer that either the union standard of a decent show is very low indeed, or else they have not lived up to their promise.

The radical Jewish press has had periodic qualms of conscience, and has intermittently attacked the character of these performances. The more conservative Jewish press, charmed by the metallic clink of the coin, and in fear of losing advertisements, deemed it a very politic move to close their eyes and shut their ears against all this. Yet they, more than anybody else, can render the most material aid towards creating a marked improvement. They can carry on a crusade of education, showing how bad and vicious these places are, and what a reflection they cast on the Jewish community.

We must not forget, however, that these places answer a need more or less urgent. Besides the cafe, there is no other place of amusement that would attract the young and giddy element. If these music halls were all conducted on absolutely proper lines, they would be a decided blessing to the neighborhood. It is a pity, therefore, that the old plan which some of the East Side Settlement workers started in this direction, was abandoned. They tried to establish a model German Bier-Garten and concert hall. The management was turned over to practical business men, as the theoretical Settlement workers feared that they would make a failure of the business end. But in doing so, they also gave over the supervision of the house to men who were far more anxious to make a business success of the venture, than to set a model of such a place for the neighborhood. A high-class music hall where the Eastsider can spend an enjoyable evening with his wife and children, is therefore, as far from a reality as ever.

Notes

1. For a detailed analysis, see Judith Thissen, "Reconsidering the Decline of the New York Yiddish Theatre in the Early 1900s," *Theatre Survey* 44 (2003): 173–97.

2. See, for instance, Roy Rosenzweig, *Eight Hours for What We Will: Workers and Leisure in an Industrial City* (Cambridge: Cambridge University Press, 1983), 35–64, 93–126, 183–190; Kathy Peiss, *Cheap Amusements: Working Women and Leisure in Turn-of-the-Century New York* (Philadelphia: Temple University Press, 1986), 17–21; and Harmut Keil and John B. Jentz, eds., *German Workers in Chicago: A Documentary History of Working-Class Culture from 1850 to World War I* (Urbana: University of Illinois Press, 1988), 175–182.

3. Office of the City Register, Pre-1917 Conveyances, Section II, liber 24 cp 23, Henry Weil to Simon Friedman (lease 1895); liber 101 cp 363, Thomas Field to Israel Suchman (lease 1902); liber 144 cp 128, Thomas Field to Israel Suchman (lease 1905); liber 209 cp 129, Thomas Field to Israel Suchman (sale, 1911). Pre-1917 Mortgages, Section II, liber 300 cp 435, Israel Suchman to Thomas Field (mortgage, 1911).

4. John M. Oskison, "Public Halls of the East Side," *Yearbook of the University Settlement Society of New York* (1899), 38.

5. Nathan Zwirin, "Mekhutonim un hol-kipers oyf yidishe khasenes" [In-laws and hall keepers at Jewish weddings], *Amerikaner*, 26 (June 1908); "Khasenes in yidishn kvartal" [Weddings in the Jewish quarter], *Forverts*, March 27, 1902.

6. The University Settlement Society counted about 150 saloons and other liquor outlets in the Eighth Assembly District, the area bounded by the Bowery and Rivington, Norfolk, and Division Streets. Raymond C. Spalding, "The Saloons of the District," *Yearbook of the University Settlement Society of New York* (1899), 34.

7. Edmund J. James, ed., *The Immigrant Jew in America* (New York: B. F. Buck and Co., 1907), 222.

8. Spaulding, "The Saloons of the District" (1899), 37–38.

9. Bernard Weinstein, *Fertsik yor in der yidisher arbeter bavegung* [Forty years in the Jewish labor movement] (New York: Jewish Socialist Verband, 1924), 106–107.

10. For a description of the halls, see Oskison, "Public Halls of the East Side" (1899), 39.

11. "Dancing teachers," *Trow's Business Directory* (1900–1901), 1070. Peiss, *Cheap Amusements*, 96.

12. Advertisement for the Eldorado Theatre, *Forverts*, October 5, 1901.

13. For a description of a typical music hall, see Nina Warnke, "Immigrant Popular Culture as Contested Sphere: Yiddish Music Halls, the Yiddish Press, and the Processes of Americanization, 1900–1910," *Theatre Journal* 48 (1996): 326.

14. The practice of the continuous show had been introduced by B. F. Keith in the 1880s. David Nasaw, *Going Out: The Rise and Fall of Public Amusements* (New York: Basic Books, 1993), 20.

15. Bernard Gorin, *Geshikhte fun idishn teatr* [History of the Yiddish theatre] (New York: Literarisher ferlag, 1918), 2:179.

16. For a detailed analysis, see Warnke, "Yiddish Music Halls."

17. "Vu zaynen ahingekumen di myuzik-hol 'stars'?" [What has become of the music-hall 'stars'?], *Forverts*, November 26, 1908.

18. Timothy J. Gilfoyle, *City of Eros: New York City, Prostitution and the Commercialization of Sex, 1790–1920* (New York: Norton, 1992), 243–247. See, for instance, the contracts between the lessees of 80–82 Clinton Street (later Agid's Clinton Vaudeville Theatre) and the Welz and Zerwech Brewery, Office of the City Register, Pre-1917 Conveyances, Section II, liber 83 cp 23 and liber 80 cp 323, August 24, 1900; and the lease for a hall at 143–145 Suffolk Street (later the Oriental Palace) which also contained a clause regarding a contract with Welz and Zerwech. Pre-1917 conveyances, Section II, liber 228 cp 479, March 5, 1914.

19. Verne M. Bovie, "The Public Dance Halls of the Lower East Side," *Yearbook of the University Settlement Society of New York* (1901), 31–32.

20. Timothy J. Gilfoyle, *City of Eros*, 244.

21. Ibid., 244–245. Raymond C. Spaulding, "The Saloons of the District" (1899), 37.

22. Office of the City Register, Pre-1917 Conveyances, Section II, liber 57 cp 137 and 185. Advertisement for the Victoria Hall, *Forverts*, October 12, 1900.

23. Office of the City Register, Pre-1917 Conveyances, Section II, liber 204 cp 490, Grosman to Samuel Agid, lease for five years starting May 1, 1911, renewal of lease dated April 24, 1906.

24. David Lifson, *Yiddish Theatre in America* (New York: Thomas Yoseloff, 1965), 130–135. Nahma Sandrow, *Vagabond Stars: A World History of Yiddish Theatre* (1977; Syracuse, NY: rpt. Syracuse University Press, 1996), 295–297.

25. Ibid., 296.

26. See, for instance, the biographies of Maurice Tuchband, Isidore Lillian, Jenny Atlas, Charlie Cohen, and Ella Wallerstein in Zalmen Zylbercweig, ed., *Leksikon fun yidishn teater* [Encyclopedia of the Yiddish theatre] (New York, Warsaw, and Mexico City: Farlag Elisheva, 1931–1969).

27. *Detroit Journal*, n.d., Bella Baker clipping file, Billy Rose Theatre Collection, New York Public Library.

28. For instance, Jenny Atlas, Max Gabel, and Abraham Kogut had played in the David Kessler Dramatic Club, of which Kogut was the founder. Samuel Weintraub and his wife had been a member of the Goldfaden Dramatic Society. "Di stars fun di yidishe muzik-hols" [The stars of the Yiddish music halls], *Forverts*, February 16, 1906; "Fun vanen nemen zikh unzere verayeti ektors?" [Where do our variety actors come from?], *Forverts*, February 24, 1906; Zylbercweig, *Leksikon fun yidishn teater*, 4:3046.

29. The coupletist Samulesko, for instance, had been a *patriot* of the great Yiddish comedian Sigmund Mogulesco. "Fun Mogulesko's dresing rum tsu der verayeti steydzsh" [From Mogulesco's dressing room to the variety stage], *Forverts*, February 27, 1906. See also, "Vu zaynen ahingekumen di myuzik-hol 'stars'?" [What has become of the music-hall 'stars'?], *Forverts*, November 26, 1908.

30. "Fun vanen nemen zikh unzere verayeti ektors?"

31. Paul Klapper, "The Yiddish Music Hall," *University Settlement Studies Quarterly*, 2/4 (1906): 20. See also, David Bernstein, "Di yidishe teaters un di yidishe myuzik-hols," [The Yiddish theatres and the Yiddish music halls] *Tsaytgayst* [Zeitgeist], September 8, 1905.

32. As a rule, the floors above the newly opened Yiddish vaudeville theatres remained in use as assembly rooms for *landsmanshaftn*, unions, and lodges. See advertisements for Yiddish music halls in the *Forverts* for the months of January–March 1906.

33. Advertisements for the Golden Rule Vaudeville House, *Forverts*, August 22, and September 1, 9, and 15, 1905.

34. "S. Agid," Zylbercweig, *Leksikon*, 1:9. Obituary for Agid, *New York Times*, December 17, 1914.

35. Unlike their American counterparts, Yiddish music halls had never been an exclusively male institution. Right from the outset, they attracted young couples, single women, and even families with children. Still, the introduction of an entrance fee, which dissociated Yiddish music-hall shows from compulsory beer-drinking and made them more respectable for Jewish immigrants of both sexes, did pay off with the increased attendance of women and children in particular.

36. Advertisements for the Grand Street Music Hall, *Forverts*, August 22 and September 9, 1905.

37. Advertisement for the Grand Street Music Hall, *Forverts*, August 11, 1905. Morris Heine (Haimovitch) had been a member of the Silberman-Karp troupe, the first professional Yiddish troupe to perform in New York (at the Oriental Theatre).

38. Nasaw, *Going Out*, 25.

39. Malgorzata Hendrykowska, "Film Journeys of the Krzeminski Brothers, 1900–1908," *Film History* 6 (1994): 206–218.

40. Advertisement for the Irving Music Hall, *Forverts*, September 5, 1905; advertisement for the People's Music Hall, ibid., September 15, 1905. The Irving Music Hall at 214–220 Broome Street was part of the New Irving Hall, one of the most popular meeting halls on the East Side.

41. "Vu zaynen ahingekumen di yidish myuzik hols?," *Forverts*, May 24, 1908.

42. Charles Musser, *The Emergence of Cinema: The American Screen to 1907* (Berkeley: University of California Press, 1990), 424.

43. "An Unexploited Field and Its Possibilities," *Views and Films Index*, October 6, 1906: 3.

44. Ibid.

45. Almost all of these moving-picture shows were located in (former) tenement buildings. Fire laws and building codes restricted their seating capacity to 299. Under the Aldermanic Standee Ordinance, another fifty persons were allowed to stand in the rear.

46. Obituary for Tantzman, *Forverts*, November 14, 1906.

47. *Views and Films Index*, August 3, 1907, 4

48. *Variety*, December 14, 1907, 12.

49. "Vu zaynen ahingekumen di yidishe myuzik hols?"

50. Ibid.

51. For the locations and figures, see Ben Singer, "Manhattan Nickelodeons: New Data on Audiences and Exhibitors," *Cinema Journal* 34 (1995): 5–35. For the distribution of moving-picture venues on the Lower East Side, see Judith Thissen, "Oy, Myopia!: A Reaction from Judith Thissen on the Singer-Allen Controversy," *Cinema Journal* 36 (1997): 104–106.

52. "Avarice and Amusement," *Views and Films Index*, October 26, 1907, 3. See also the biographies of the Hollywood moguls in Neal Gabler, *An Empire of Their Own: How the Jews Invented Hollywood* (New York: Doubleday, 1989).

53. The final blow as far the smaller Yiddish music halls were concerned was the new building code for theatres, which New York City adopted in 1914. This so-called Folks ordinance obliged small vaudeville theatres to apply for an expensive $500 theatrical license as well as to conform to very strict safety regulations. Only the large Yiddish music halls located in purpose-built theatres survived this rigid licensing process. Code of Ordinances of the City of New York (1914), Building code, article 24 (motion picture theatres) and article 25 (theatres and other places of amusement).

CHAPTER 9

"Gvald, Yidn, Buena Gente": Jevel Katz, Yiddish Bard of the Río de la Plata

Zachary M. Baker

During a visit to Buenos Aires in May 1996, I was among those present in the "live studio audience" for the 100th broadcast of the weekly Yiddish program on the Jewish community station Radio Jai. José Judkovski, the host of another of the station's regular programs, "Buenos Aires: Fervor y Tango," put in a guest appearance to mark that special occasion. In the course of his remarks, Judkovski commented that both his show and the Yiddish program endeavored to preserve important aspects of their community's cultural heritage. For Argentine Jews of a certain age and background, the coupling of Yiddish and tango seemed to be only natural.

A few years later, two books devoted to Jews and the tango were published in Buenos Aires: *El tango: una historia con judíos* (The tango: A history with Jews), by Judkovski, and *Tango judío* (Jewish tango), by Julio Nudler. Both authors stressed the notable contributions that Jewish performers and impresarios once made toward defining—and elaborating upon—a central element of Argentine cultural identity. However, they treated the tango's influence upon the Yiddish-speaking immigrant milieu in Argentina only *en passant*: "In the absence of tango lyrics reflecting themselves," wrote Nudler, "the Jews in the Thirties had their own troubadour, Jevel Katz—nicknamed for that reason *El Gardel Judío*" (a reference to the Argentine performer Carlos Gardel).[1] (Katz's name did not figure at all within the pages of Judkovski's book.[2]) Any discussion of a once-beloved performer of Yiddish tangos was deemed to be at best marginal to these books' main topic.

Nevertheless, it would be a mistake to overlook the impact that Jevel Katz—and by extension, the cohort of Yiddish performers to which he belonged—had on the Jewish immigrant communities of Argentina and Uruguay. As an index of this entertainer's popularity one need only mention his funeral, which was one of the most extraordinary public gatherings in the history of Jewish Buenos Aires. It took

Jevel Katz in the early 1930s. (From the archives of the YIVO Institute for Jewish Research, New York.)

place on a sultry Sunday morning in March of 1940. Between 25,000 and 40,000 mourners packed the streets of the city's Jewish district as the motorized procession passed, en route to Liniers cemetery on the outskirts of Buenos Aires. It was probably the most well-attended Jewish funeral in Argentina's history—all the more amazing for the fact that the outpouring was on behalf of a thirty-seven year-old Jewish immigrant who had resided in that country for only ten years.

Before emigrating, Jevel Katz was an impoverished young typographer in Vilna, employed by the famous Brothers and Widow Romm printing house. He sang his earliest compositions to guitar accompaniment, before gatherings of his fellow members of the Vilna Jewish Printers' Union. Beyond that he does not appear to have made a deep impression on his native city (which, however, did not prevent Katz from making Vilna the subject of a nostalgic ballad, after he settled in Buenos Aires). Katz departed for Argentina in May 1930, during that brief interval between the imposition of strict immigration quotas in the United States and a similar tightening up by an increasingly nationalistic Argentine regime. North America's loss was South America's gain.

Within a very short time he managed to transform himself into the most popular Yiddish performer in Argentina. Katz toured widely, entertaining his audiences with a medley of monologues, humoresques, couplets, parodies, nostalgic songs, and satires, in which he provided his own accompaniment on guitar, mandolin, harmonica, and accordion. Katz performed upwards of 650 original compositions (some of which, starting in 1939, were published in the daily Yiddish press). He also acted in Yiddish plays and was featured on radio programs. Katz's themes of nostalgia, privation, and struggle tugged at his audiences' heartstrings, though he also leavened his lyrics with copious doses of comic relief. It was this combination of nostalgic repertory and versatile performance style that caused the Yiddish journalist and theatre critic Samuel Rollansky (Shmuel Rozhanski, 1902–1995) to compare Katz with the Russian émigré composer and actor Alexander Vertinsky (1889–1957).[3]

In Rollansky's view, Jevel Katz was a performer *sui generis*. Neither a great writer nor a great actor (and a musical autodidact, to boot), he had a truly distinctive stage presence. Rollansky described Katz as a "non-star" who became a "superstar," a man who was on close terms with hundreds of individuals and who refused to stand on a pedestal or rest on his laurels.[4] When Jevel Katz died of a post-operative infection after undergoing a tonsillectomy, his eulogists observed that in a factionalized Jewish community he was the only public personality who stood above the fray, and was welcome wherever he went. Bentsion Palepade (1876–?), writing in the leftist newspaper *Di prese* (The press), contrasted Katz's appeal with that of the phenomenally popular tango singer Carlos Gardel (whose death in a 1935 airplane crash was still fresh in everyone's memory). He commented that while Gardel's love of tangos "were of interest just to young people, Jevel Katz [also] sang about present-day social issues, which elicited *everyone's* interest."[5]

Jevel Katz's repertory positively brimmed with Argentine content. His only book (or rather, booklet), *Argentiner glikn* (Good fortunes in Argentina, published in 1933)[6] contains several of his typical parodies, in which he set Yiddish (or Yiddish-Spanish) verses to the tunes of popular songs in Spanish. Appropriately, the very first song in *Argentiner glikn* bears the title "A rantshera (A *ranchera*[7])," and it spoofs the travails of a recently-arrived bachelor seeking to establish roots in the new land—and flee the habits of the old. As one of the verses puts it:

Tsu yidish hob ikh keyn pasyensye,
halt ikh shtendik di "La prense,"
un ven ikh halt ir far di okhes,
farshtey ikh dortn a kadokhes.

(For Yiddish I have no *paciencia*,
I always have in front of me *La prensa*,

And when I hold it in front of my *ojos*,
I understand it like a *kadokhes* [literally: "ague," "malaria," i.e., It's Greek to me).

The travails of the itinerant peddler are gently satirized in such songs as "Colchón" (Mattress) and the foxtrot "Mucho lujo" (Luxury) set to the tune of a perhaps forgotten number, "Me gustan las bocinas de los automóviles" (I like the sound of car horns). In addition to *rancheras* and foxtrots, *Argentiner glikn* includes Yiddish rumbas and tangos (a dance style with which Katz had probably become familiar in Poland[8]). Utilization of these musical genres can perhaps be viewed as vehicles (or reflections) of Argentinization, analogous to what the ethnomusicologist Mark Slobin describes as the "accommodation to the American song tradition" by Jevel Katz's counterparts in the United States.[9]

Several of the songs in *Argentiner glikn* are devoted to pastimes such as "Dados" (Dice) (elsewhere, Katz celebrated the games of poker, and as we shall see, dominoes). Other songs feature familiar locales, as with "A pik-nik in visente lopez (A picnic in Vicente Lopez)." Later on, he composed songs celebrating the settlements of Moisesville and Basavilbaso, along with the city of Buenos Aires, its Jewish neighborhoods and streets. For his primary audience, the Yiddish-speaking Jews of Argentina, Katz's appeals to local patriotism reassured them in their decision to uproot themselves and settle along the banks of the Río de la Plata. As in North America (to quote Slobin), ". . . popular culture, especially the music that lay at the heart of public and private entertainment, played a significant role in giving the immigrants a sense of identity, both in terms of where they came from and where they were headed."[10] Jevel Katz's songs were a significant manifestation of the popular culture that Jewish immigrants created as they negotiated their way through Argentine society.

On the other hand, the frequently ironic distance of Katz's lyrics tempered his listeners' sense of "at-homeness" in Argentina. Bearing in mind the unabashedly nostalgic Old Country numbers that Katz also sang at his concerts, one wonders how seriously his audience regarded these affectionate odes to the Jewish *barrios* or agricultural colonies that they now inhabited.[11] These "Argentine shtetl" songs employed the motifs of Jewish cultural and national pride very much in a tongue-in-cheek manner, as when Basivilbaso ["shtetele du mayns" (my little town)] is referred to as the "Kasrilevke of Entre Ríos," an affectionate reference to Sholem Aleichem's fictional town, well known for its population of busybodies. The song "Mozesvil" (Moisesville) makes use of a similar vocabulary when it is addressed as "mayn kleyn shtetele . . . mayn sheyn heymele" (my small town, my lovely home) and portrayed as "a yidishe medine . . . a shtolts far Argentine" (a Jewish state, the pride of Argentina).

The opening stanza of "Mozesvil" (Moisesville) extols the virtues of a town whose population is exclusively Jewish—a place where the pharmacist, bathhouse keeper, policeman, and judge are all Jews. The traditional eastern European tonalities of this song confirm its "Jewish" character. However, the lyrics convey a mixed message. On the one hand, the occupations of the Jews of the Moisesville colony are a combination of those found in the traditional *shtetlekh* that the colonists had left behind in Europe, and those marking a new departure in the direction of local autonomy, if not outright political sovereignty. But what kind of culture are these Argentine Jews nurturing? According to the song text, the Jewish youth of Moisesville greet one another in Spanish, their radios are tuned to stations that broadcast tangos, and a local dandy (*pundikl*)—also a Jew—whistles Spanish tunes through his moustache. Clearly, the Jews of Jevel Katz's "Mozesvil" have made great strides toward acculturating, even as the song's use of traditional Jewish melodies reflects Katz's intentions to "make [its] musical ethnic boundaries as clear as possible."[12] (For the lyrics to "Mozesvil" and other songs discussed in this chapter, see the Appendix.)

My first exposure to Jevel Katz's songs came during my visit to Buenos Aires in May of 1996. My hosts from the Fundación IWO (counterpart to the YIVO Institute for Jewish Research, in New York) took me to a musical revue bearing the macaronic title "Té con límene" (Tea with lemon), which included Spanish renditions of several of his most popular tunes. Early in the program, the players sang one of Katz's signature numbers, a song combining eastern European and Latin rhythms, "Mucho ojo" (figuratively: Watch out). The language of the opening stanza, which is set in the Old Country, is in pure Yiddish, unlike the rest of the song, which is written in a seamless mélange of Yiddish and Spanish, as when it rhymes "ojo" with "mazl-brokho." (The meter and melody of the opening line sound like a minor-key paraphrase of the popular Mexican song "Rancho grande.")

"Mucho ojo," in a series of seeming non-sequiturs, conveys a rake's progress in Argentina. Adhering to his Old Country rabbi's advice to keep his eyes wide open and look out for himself, the young male narrator thumbs his nose at the world, proclaiming, " I don't burn myself with a hot *mate* anymore; I say '*andá bañate* (go jump in the lake),' don't bother me!" He cheats at auctions and fools around with young women, all the while taking care to escape any possible repercussions. The narrator's brazen behavior perplexes the angels on high, who observe that the "troublesome Jews . . . sin like the goyim and then sway in the synagogue . . . as if there is no tomorrow." "Mucho ojo" utilizes several elements that Mark Slobin enumerates as typical of popular song in the immigrant era—"whimsy," "the simple urge to create a rhyme," "linguistic variety and hyperbole, along with cultural excess, reflect[ing] the disarray of immigrant life"—adding up to "a comment on the hurly-burly hodge-podge nature" of life in the new land.[13] This is a song that transcends the limitations of genre to which it might otherwise have been consigned, and its charms are fully evident at first hearing.

The Fundación IWO is trying its best to perpetuate Jevel Katz's legacy. When I visited its quarters in the Casa Simón Dubnow in 1996, it maintained a small shrine of Katz memorabilia in the lobby, including sheet music, a stylized portrait of the artist (garbed in his trench coat and felt hat), and the singer's very own, turquoise-green accordion.[14] A few years later, IWO launched a CD, *Homenaje a Jevel Katz* (Homage to Jevel Katz), including four recordings in Katz's own voice, plus renditions of ten of his songs by various singers, in both Yiddish (sung mostly by the actors Max Perelman and Max Zalkind) and Spanish (in watered-down and jazzed-up versions). In 2005, a 75-minute documentary, "Jevel Katz y sus paisanos" (Jevel Katz and his "landsmen"), directed by Alejandro Vagnenkos, was released in Argentina and exhibited at film festivals in Latin America and Spain. Among those who were interviewed for the film was Ester Szwarc, the Fundación IWO's education director.

Because he made only a handful of recordings, Katz was not able to rely upon them as a primary means of disseminating and popularizing his songs. The Yiddish segment of the Argentine record market would have been tiny during the 1930s—a decade when ethnic recordings of all kinds, including Yiddish recordings—flourished on the much larger North American scene.[15] That factor helps to explain the paucity of Jevel Katz's recordings. Instead, he derived most of his considerable popularity from live stage performances and radio broadcasts.[16]

We are fortunate to have a recording of one song in which Katz fully displays his versatility as a performer. In "Tucumán" he reenacts a train's progress across the Argentine *pampa*. From his crowded second-class carriage, the narrator looks out upon the ranches, the half-naked, dark-skinned children, and the gauchos with moustaches, until he finally arrives in Tucumán, in time for his next performance. The singer's rapid-fire delivery, replete with train whistles and chugs, and interrupted by harmonica interludes (which, the musicologist Francesco Spagnolo has suggested to me, are transpositions of Andean pan pipe melodies), produce an auditory effect that communicates the song's message as clearly as the words themselves remain incomprehensible to the casual listener. "Tucumán" was published in the daily Yiddish newspaper *Di idishe tsaytung* (The Jewish newspaper), where it appeared under the title "Mayn rayze keyn tukuman" (My trip to Tucumán) shortly after Katz's death, and is probably one of his later creations. Toward the end of the song, the composer reflects on his own celebrity with a degree of self-deprecation:

Gebrakht hot zi do an artist, vos iz a groyser parodist, a kontsertist, a humorist, ir kent im ale do gevis . . . er zol opshnaydn khotsh nit mies, men zol im klapn bravo bis, er zol nisht darfn geyn tsufis, fun tukuman, fun tukuman . . .

(It [the train] has brought here an artiste, who is a great parodist, a concertizer, a humorist, you all surely know him . . . may he not fall flat on his face, may he be applauded with cries of "Bravo, bis," and not need to slink away on foot from Tucumán, Tucumán . . .)

The economic privations suffered by Jews in such Buenos Aires districts as Barrio Once and Villa Crespo form a leitmotif in songs that Jevel Katz wrote during his first years in Argentina—which coincided with the worst phase of the global economic depression following the Wall Street stock market crash of 1929. One example of this is his song "Tango," in which, to the tune of "Secreto" (a song composed in 1932 by Enrique Santos Discépolo [1901–1951][17]), he compares the dancer's contortions with the immigrant's convoluted attempts to do business in a precarious environment:

Un azoy vi der tango
geyen mir a gang do
mit di gesheftn men dreyt vi men kon.[18]

(And so, like the tango,
we go about our errands and
we spin out our affairs as best we can.)

Another example is his song "Ikh zukh a tsimer" (I'm looking for a room), which humorously relates the bureaucratic and logistical gauntlet that the immigrant had to run in order to find housing, move in, and stay a step ahead of the landlord once the rent monies ran out. The setting is the Buenos Aires conventillo, with its close quarters and congestion, producing situations where one apartment abuts another where the radio is always blaring, a second apartment overlooks the hubbub of the marketplace, and a third one (lacking a wash basin and overrun with cockroaches) leads the singer's wife to temptation in the form of the handsome bachelor next door. The refrain provides a typical example of Katz's "castellanish," his mixture of Yiddish and Spanish lyrics set to a snappy Latin dance tune (overlaid—to my ears, at least—with Italianate, Verdian flourishes[19]):

Gvald, yidn, *buena gente*,
Ikh zukh a tsimer a *departamente*,
Ver es veys, entfert mir *urgente*,
Ikh muz zikh klaybn *inmediatamente*!

(Help, people, *buena gente*
I'm looking for a room, a *departamente*,
If you know of one answer me *urgente*,
I've got to move *inmediatamente*!)

Significantly, in the spirit of the music to which the refrain is set, Spanish words supply all of the rhymes.

A related theme of Katz's is the idleness and ennui that resulted from the often-unsuccessful quest to earn a few pesos. One of his best-known—and most subversive—parodies is set to the very familiar melody of "Avinu malkenu" (or "Ovinu malkeinu," reflecting the Ashkenazi pronunciation), a prayer for forgiveness that is chanted during High Holiday services. His listeners would automatically have associated its melody with the sacred realm, but this connection is undermined by Katz's narrative of the highly profane atmosphere surrounding a daylong domino game between four *luftmentshn*[20] sitting in the Bar León. The verses progress from a simple description of the narrator's contemplated moves with his domino tiles (venting his spleen at his hapless partner Simón all the while), to a rueful contemplation of his daughter's unlikely chances of landing a groom for lack of a dowry. The narrator's wife sits at home, under the illusion that he is wrapping up important business deals, while instead he's off playing dominoes, *nada más*!

Here, of all places, Katz chose *not* to use a Latin dance tune as the basis of his parody, instead relying on one of the most solemn of all liturgical compositions. The incongruous and dissonant juxtaposition of the sacred and the profane may have reflected Katz's commentary on the casual manner in which Jewish immigrants to Argentina were shedding the religious strictures that they had observed in Europe. To be sure, though, compositions of this sort have a long pedigree in the United States. As examples Mark Slobin cites broadsheet parodies of the *kiddush* blessing and something called "The Peddler's Haggadah." Such parodies were "an accepted practice at least as early as the 1890s."[21]

Still, was there a subtext to Jevel Katz's use of a very familiar liturgical melody to relate a narrator's reflections on his failure to provide his family with a livelihood? Is this "Ovinu malkeinu" a protest song, analogous to Rabbi Levi Yitskhok of Berdichev's impassioned lawsuit against the Almighty, "A din-toyre mit Got" (God on trial)?[22] Themes of deprivation, boredom, and even hopelessness do, after all, recur constantly in Katz's songs. Applying Mark Slobin's insight, "in the language and the unconscious gestures"—and the music of the "Ovinu malkeinu" parody—"we discover clues to social history,"[23] notably the message that life in this *goldene medine* is no bed of roses. Still, I would hesitate to place this composition on the same elevated plane or in the same thematic category as that of the Hasidic master. Where Levi Yitskhok chastised the Creator of the Universe in dire and accusatory (yet also reverent and loving) tones, the domino player in Katz's "Ovinu malkeinu" addressed his profane verses to an appreciative audience in a concert hall, whose members empathized with the narrator's predicament even as they chuckled at his foibles. In addition, by peppering his Yiddish stanzas with colloquial Spanish expressions Katz deliberately created a comic effect ("Mayn shutef Simón iz a groyser *chambón*," My partner Simón is a big oaf), which undercut the music's solemnity.

The popularity of "Ovinu malkeinu" is attested to by the fact that it is one of Jevel Katz's few compositions for which sheet music is extant and more than one recording in Yiddish exists (albeit sung by performers other than Katz). Of the two renditions that I have heard, the one by Max Zalkind plays it relatively straight—a solo singer with rather glossy accordion and instrumental accompaniment. The other recording, by David Itzcoff, is a full-dress cantorial number reminiscent of a bygone era, complete with both male and mixed choirs and an orchestra. The Itzcoff version was likely intended as a double parody, of both the original prayer and the operatic exaggerations of early twentieth-century eastern European *khazones*.

Just how aware was Jevel Katz of his reputation as "El Gardel Judío"? His song "Baynakht mit'n tramvay lakroze af koryentes" (At night, by tram to Lacroze along Corrientes) suggests an indirect answer to this question.[24] Katz follows the tram's route across the entire breadth of Argentina's federal capital, revealing the rich variety that the cityscape and its inhabitants have to offer. He animates the tram with quasi-human characteristics as it navigates first along Leandro Além, near the waterfront, past windows enticing passersby with their displays of red lights. Embarrassed by these lurid scenes, the tram then turns onto Corrientes, the "Broadway" of Buenos Aires, with its throngs of theatregoers. The driver is momentarily distracted by a pretty girl, and then steers the tram along Corrientes to Callao, the dividing line between the theatre district and the Jewish Once district. The tram stops at the corner of Pasteur, where the clash of immigrant and native cultures becomes evident. A Russian song, "Proshchai" (Farewell), emanates from the Café Internacional and the tram mutters:

Ikh farshtey keyn vort nit say vi say,
Ikh bin a higer, ikh farshtey a tango.

(I don't follow any of the words,
I'm a local, I understand a tango.)

The next stop is the immigrants' favorite hangout, the Bar León at the corner of Pueyrredón—where the domino players in "Ovinu malkeinu" whiled away the hours—and thence "farbay mercado, antshorener, vu es horeven di italyener" (past the Anchorena market, where the Italians toil). The tram continues along this artery "tsu kaning, tsu di yidn" (to Canning, to the Jews), and then stops at a railroad crossing to let a train pass:

Dervart zikh biz avek di ban,
git a genets der motorman,
git a drey dos hentl un fort aroys,
iber getseylemte linye shpringt di tramvay
kodoysh! kodoysh!

(Waiting till after the train has passed,
the motorman yawns,
turns the handle and moves forward,
at the crossing the tram jumps up,
kadosh! kadosh!)[25]

At this point the tram's headlights illuminate the great wall at the end of the line,

vu af eybik shlofn shoyn di toyte,
baveynt di tramvay yene yorn,
ven di ale, vos lign dort,
zenen af ir geforn,
azoy fil klientele hot zi forlorn,
s'iz fun zey gornisht nit gevorn,
s'iz tshakarita—TSHAKARITA!

(where the dead sleep on for eternity,
the tram laments those years
when all who lie there
were its riders,
so many customers has it lost,
they have come to naught,
it's Chacarita—CHACARITA!)

Now, it hardly seems coincidental that the route taken by Jevel Katz's tram is almost identical to the one traversed on February 6, 1936, by the cortège of Carlos Gardel. Simon Collier, in his biography of that great tango celebrity, tracks the procession from Luna Park "to its final destination, the Chacarita Cemetery, some seventy blocks away, up Calle Corrientes—or rather Avenida Corrientes as it now was, thanks to the widening it had undergone in recent years. The distance to be traversed was about five miles." In contrast to Jevel Katz, Collier largely ignores the distinctively Jewish presence along Corrientes although he does observe, "The [burial] commission had decided to transfer the singer's remains to a new, ornately carved mahogany coffin donated by the broadcasting magnate Jaime Yankelevich."[26] (Yankelevich is precisely the sort of impresario whom Judkovski and Nudler highlight in their books.)

In "Baynakht mit'n tramvay lakroze af koryentes" (At night, by tram to Lacroze along Corrientes), Katz thus seems to be paying his oblique respects to the legacy of Carlos Gardel.[27] Indeed, it is hard to believe that any of the habitués of Bar León at Pueyrredón—especially "an artist, a groyser parodist, a kontsertist, a humorist" such as Jevel Katz—would have permitted this deceased tango performer's final entourage to pass by its doors completely unnoticed.

Of course, "El Gardel Judío" was more than just that. As his songs reveal, Jevel Katz owed a tremendous debt to the performance traditions of Jewish eastern Europe, and especially to the literary and theatrical heritage of his hometown. Some of his more saccharine songs—such as his ode to Vilna or "Glokn in altn shtetl" (Bells in the old town)—express longing for the lives and families that immigrants left behind in Europe. Katz also tapped into their homesickness through his literary recitations, which were products of the Yiddish declamatory tradition of the *vort-kontsert*, as purveyed by such familiar European theatrical stars as the Vilna Troupe's Noah Nachbush (1886 or 1888–1970) and Habima's Chayele Grober (1898–1978). And one of his recordings, "A kinder maysele" (A children's story), is a rhymed Yiddish musical adaptation of the Grimm Brothers' tale "Hansel and Gretel." (The song's opening melody evokes that of the Yiddish drinking song, "Tayere Malke" [Dear Malke]). In his recordings, Katz at times sounds like a clone of Nachbush who has been transplanted to an exotic South American locale. Katz was, after all, a product of twentieth-century Vilna—a city that was steeped in the traditions of the Gaon, the Haskalah, the Jewish labor movement, Zionism, and Yiddishism.

At the same time, Katz's Argentine parodies and satirical songs, with their intensely local frames of reference, struck a profound chord with his audience, whose members had been set adrift by the tempestuous tides of twentieth-century Jewish history. These songs helped to anchor immigrants in their new surroundings, even as they underscored their very marginality in Argentina, a country that the Vilna-born composer observed from inside a coach, as his train raced across the country's vast plains en route to Tucumán, where yet another isolated audience of Jewish immigrants awaited the Yiddish bard of the Río de la Plata—and might send him packing if he did not satisfy their entertainment needs.

Most of the performers and impresarios whose names are noted by Nudler and Judkovski in their books about Jews and the tango were either born in Argentina or arrived there as children or adolescents. In contrast, Katz came to Argentina "fully formed," at a relatively advanced age, and fairly late in the annals of Jewish immigration from eastern Europe—in 1930. His songs provide a snapshot of Argentine Jewish immigrant life at a very specific juncture in that community's maturation and that country's history.

Jevel Katz's attributes as a popular entertainer, as Samuel Rollansky observed, amounted to a sum that was greater than its parts. Katz's trademark performance technique (drawing upon a wide gamut of the European music-hall and cabaret traditions), the repertory that he created, the many genres and musical styles that he mastered and then parodied, the timbre of his voice, his use of multilingual rhymes and onomatopoeia, his instrumental accompaniment—all of these together combined to create a truly unique, homegrown Argentine Yiddish product. For us today, probably the greatest value of Jevel Katz's songs lies in their interpretation and re-creation of the *ambiente* of the Yiddish-speaking immigrant community in Argentina, at the point when its members were poised on the cusp of *akreazhirn zikh* (*acriollarse*, acculturating to their Latin American surroundings).

It would of course be a mistake to regard the example of Jevel Katz in isolation from the Yiddish theatre of his day, locally and worldwide. His career and repertoire certainly lead one to ponder the spectrum of Yiddish performance practices encountered in realms of the Jewish Diaspora that were far removed from the "three capitals" of Moscow, Warsaw, and New York. While the Jewish theatre-going public in Argentina warmly embraced the numerous Yiddish performers who spent time there *af gastrol* (on tour) from the Europe and the United States,[28] the Argentine content and context of so many Katz numbers compellingly illustrate the presence of a once-flourishing popular culture within the Jewish immigrant communities of Argentina and Uruguay. An "archaeological excavation" of the forgotten Yiddish popular culture of Latin America—its theatrical heritage, its songs, and its press—would undoubtedly reveal both its close ties with the world of Yiddish theatre and letters internationally and the extent to which it was, simultaneously, bound intimately to its immediate geographical surroundings.[29]

The popularity that Jevel Katz derived from his musical compositions illustrates "the power of popular entertainment to play on the complexity of the linguistic, cultural, and musical situations in which the immigrants found themselves."[30] It was his synthesis of Yiddish, eastern European, and Latin, South American genres that resulted in something both unique, phenomenally popular (albeit within the confines of a small subculture) and, alas, altogether evanescent. Still, more than six decades after Jevel Katz wrote and performed his songs—Yiddish in form and Argentine in content—today's attentive listener can readily appreciate the formidable appeal that they once had to their intended audience.

What attributes did Latin and Anglo-American Yiddish popular culture share during the first half of the twentieth century, and in what ways did they diverge? What continuities exist today between the Yiddish-speaking immigrants' performance traditions in Argentina and those of their descendants? Anecdotal evidence suggests that the inter-generational connections are both deep and broad—especially in view of the celebrity that actors such as Norman Erlich (born in 1932) and Cipe Linkovsky (born in 1933) have achieved on the late-twentieth-century Argentine stage. The trajectories of the composer Osvaldo Golijov and the filmmaker Daniel Burman offer additional evidence of these cross-generational ties. So, rather than view Jevel Katz as a fascinating but isolated case, I suggest that were we to lift our gaze, we would discover the rich legacy that he and his generation of South American Yiddish performers have left to those who followed in their footsteps.

Appendix

Selected song texts by Jevel Katz

(1) "Mucho ojo"[31]
(a) Yiddish

In shtot vu ikh bin geborn a rebn hob ikh gehat, hot er mir far mayn forn gelernt ot dem pshat: —Forst in land in vaytn [. . .] kukn in ale zaytn un hobn gut an oyg.

(Refrain):
Hob *ojo*! hob *mucho ojo*!
hob okho, zay nit fartrakht!

ver es hot *ojo*—hot mazl-brokho,
un ver es hot nit—i' nit far mir gedakht!

Un ikh veys zikh vi tsu firn, ikh drey zikh gut in rod, mir kon men nisht makanirn, [*macana*] kh'bin [. . .] Mit a heyse *mate* brit men mikh mer nit op, ikh zog "*andá bañate*! fardrey mir nisht kayn kop!"

(Refrain):
Kh'hob zikh nisht lib tsu shemen far mayne gite fraynd, velkhe s'hobn lib tsu nemen, un gebn hot men faynt. Ikh gey af a *remate*, bay yederer ikh shtayg, un makh zikh tamevate [. . .] ikh koyf a fayg.

(Refrain):
Mit kayn puste mayses fardreyt men mir nisht keyn moyekh, ikh ze alts vos me darf nor, un vos me darf nisht oykh. Ikh bin mir moy [*muy*] *galante* tsu a meydl ven zi redt, un ikh nem mit a *purgante* ven ikh es af a banket.

(Refrain):
Un shpet ba nakht in *cine* a meydl ven ikh nem, veys ikh in argentine vi ir opfirn aheym: ikh loz ir geyn afrier un ikh gey bay der vant, tomer vart der tate in toyer mit a bezem in der hant.

(Refrain):
Der malakh-hadoyme iz umtsufridn arufgekumen tsu got, mit a tayne tsu di yidn, vos tsores er fun zey hot: me zindikt vi di goyim mit aveyres fil, es kumt do yomim-noroyim shoklt men zikh in shil!

(Refrain):
Kh'hob *ojo*, zogt got im, *ojo*! zey betn tsheklekh bay mir mit glik, ver s'hot kayn kvente kayn koriente—[*cuenta corriente*]

O-yenems tsetele vet kumen mir tsurik! Oy, oy, oy, *ojo*, kh'hob *mucho ojo*,

[. . .] zey betn brokhes, dem [. . .] oykh, [. . .] O-o-oy, *ojo*, *ojo*, *mucho ojo*, oy *ojo*, mayn guter fraynd, ver s'hot nor *ojo*—hot mazl-brokho, in ver es hot nit—i' nit far mir gedakht!

(b) English synopsis

A rabbi back in my home town gave me the following advice: You're moving to a far-away country—take care, look around, and keep your eyes open! Look here: I know how to maneuver; you can't lead me astray . . . I don't burn myself with a hot *mate* anymore; I say "*andá bañate*" [go jump in the lake], don't bother me!

(Refrain: Watch out! If you do, you'll be blessed with good fortune; if not, I don't want to imagine what will happen.)

I'm not shy around my freeloading friends. I go to an auction, outbid everyone, and then act ignorant and am told to go to hell. Don't bother me with your pointless stories; I see everything I need to see and everything I don't need to see, too.

I know how to behave around a girl when she speaks, and I bring along a *purgante* [laxative] when I eat at a banquet. Late at night I take a girl to the movies and I know how to get her home—I let her go ahead of me while I walk alongside the wall, in case her father is waiting with a broom in his hand.

The angel at the gates is dissatisfied with the troublesome Jews who are entering heaven; they sin like the goyim and then sway in the synagogue during the high holy days, as if there is no tomorrow.

(2) "Mozesvil"
(a) Yiddish[32]
Yidn, zayt itst freylekh, in a mazldiker sho,
in a vinkl argentine meshiekh iz shoyn do,
dort iz nishto keyn kristn, nor yidn kleyn un groys,
der apteyker un der beder un der komisar, der "khoys" [*juez*]—

(Refrain):
In mozesvil, mayn zis heymele,
mozesvile, mayn zis shtetele,
vu ikh hob di kindershe yorn farbrakht,
mozesvil, mayn zis heymele,
mozesvil, mayn zis shtetele,
bist a yidishe medine,
bist a shtolts far argentine,
mozesvil.

A yid iz dort afile der rebe, lebn zol;
a kooperative un a shule un a yidisher shpitol;
alts iz dortn yidish, keyn galekh iz nishto,
derfun iz dokh gedrungen, az meshiekh iz dort do—

(Refrain):
In mitn shtetl shteyt a plase [*plaza*] mit beymer gor a prakht,
shpatsirn dort di yungvarg a yeder af der nakht,
men zogt zikh "buenas noches," dos khayes geyt azh oys,
un nisht eyn mol take a shidekh dreyt zikh fun dem oys—

(Refrain):
A radio shpilt dort tangos farn oylem, vos shpatsirt,
dertseyln vayber mayses, vos in shtetl hot pasirt,
bay vemen s'vet zayn tnoyim un bay vemen s'vet zayn a bris,
bay vemen s'hot zikh fraytik tsugebrent der knish—

(Refrain):
Durkhn shtetl fort a "sulki,"[33] di reder shafn shtoyb,
kukn aroys yidn durkh der fenster-shoyb,
fort der kolonist Reb Khayem in shtetele arayn,
aynkoyfn af shabes un in mikve oykh tsu zayn—

(Refrain):
Af der "skine" [*esquina*, i.e., corner] shteyt a mentsh dort, a pundikl gevis,
mit gor-breyte "bombatshes" [*bombachas*, i.e., breeches worn by gauchos], "zapatizhes"
[*zapatillas*, i.e., slipper-like shoes] af di fis,

durkh di shvartse "bigotizhes" [*bigotillos*, i.e., mustachio] fayft er a shpanish lid,
megt ir dort zayn zikher, az der pundik iz a yid—

(Refrain):
Faran dort a "kadima" [the name of a Jewish club], faran a bibliotek,
kumen dortn staren un men leygt di kunst avek,
der oylem git retsenzyes, az es geyt a roykh,
vayl azelkhe staren gefint men dortn oykh.

(Refrain):

(b) English synopsis[34]

The messiah has come to a small corner of Argentina, where only Jews can be found: the pharmacist, bathhouse keeper, policeman, and judge (*juez*).

(Mozesvil, my beautiful town, you're a veritable Jewish state, the pride of Argentina!)

Here's the central plaza, where young people stroll, greet one another with "Buenas noches," and meet their future spouses. A radio plays tangos to passersby, who spread the latest gossip: Who's become engaged, who will be having a *bris*, and who burned a "knish" on Friday. A dandy [*pundik*] stands on a street corner in his saggy knee-pants and slippers, whistling a Spanish tune through his moustache – you can be sure, however, that he too is a Jew.

(3) "Ikh zukh a tsimer"
(a) Yiddish[35]

Ikh bin tsufridn in argentine,
es iz a goldene medine,
nor mit eyn zakh iz do tsores,
men darf arumzukhn do dires,
mit *garantías* fun *buena gentes*,
fun *sociedades* un *presidentes*,
un ven men kon tsu alts derkrikhn,
darf men itst a tsimer zukhn.

(Refrain):
Gvald yidn, *buena gente*,
ikh zukh a tsimer, a *departamente*,
ver es veys, entfert mir *urgente*,
ikh muz zikh klaybn *inmediatamente*.
Ikh bet bay yedn *recomendaciones*,
fun tsaytungen shnayd ikh *direcciones*,
ikh kuk af yedn roytn tsetl,
vu a shmate, vu a bletl—
dort bin ikh shoyn do fun frier,
un ikh kling shoyn bald in toyer,
un ikh zukh in ale gasn,
un ikh ken zikh nit tsupasn.

(Refrain):
Ale tog ding ikh *camiones*,
pak di kishns, di *colchones*,
un ikh klayb zikh fun baginen,
a tsimer vu ikh hob gefunen.
Mayne *muebles*, mayne zakhn,
vel ikh gikh af redlekh makhn,
zey zoln kenen aleyn forn,
di *camiones* ayntsushporn.

(Refrain):
Zaynen mayne *muebles* shoyn oysgeshtanen,
vu a tsimer iz faranen,
iz do ober yede dire,
hot far zikh an ander tsore;
do nishto keyn *instalado*,
do a shlak an *encargado*,
un tsores fun a radio,
un dortn filt zikh di *mercado*.

(Refrain):
Iz shoyn dort do "instalatsyes,"
iz do zhukes, mit *cucarachas*,
do muz ikh voynen mit mayn vayb bazunder,
vayl es tor nisht zayn keyn kinder.
Dort hob ikh a sufit a nasn,
keyn *pilete* nisht tsum vashn,
do felt mir a *bañadero*,
dort kukt mayn vayb afn *soltero*.

(Refrain):
Do tsebrokhn iz der "tush,"
un farlesht men fri di *luz*,
un dort di vayber krign zikh,
vayl es iz zey eng in kikh.
Dort hot men ongerirt di *plantas*,
do hengt men iber mayn kop mir "trantes,"
un dort iz andere gor tsores,
vayl es felt "*para señores*" . . .

(Refrain):
Ikh hob gehat a tsimer shoyn gor a gutn,
tsvey mit a fertl, halt der mitn,
mit ale *comodidades*,
mit a fuftsn *encargados*,
in same tsenter af medrano,

tsen kvadratn fun *subterráneo*,
fleg ikh forn yede *semana*,
af cordoba, in umzistn *baño*.

(Refrain):
Bay mir fun oybn der *azotea*,
gezen vi es fort um di *tranvía*,
s'iz geven a *patio* af tsum tantsn,
nisht geven keyn *mosquitos*, vantsn;
s'iz geven shoyn gut mit gor,
ikh hob gevoynt dort bald a yor,
ober hot men mir dortn nisht gevolt,
vayl ikh hob keyn dire-gelt getsolt.

(Refrain):

(b) English synopsis[36]

I'm satisfied with Argentina, it's a *goldene medine* (golden land), but there's one thing I'm having trouble with: it's hard to find an apartment. You need *garantías* from *buena gentes*, and from *sociedades* and *presidentes*—yet even after you've received them you still need to find a room.

(Help, people, *buena gente*, I'm looking for a room, a *departamente*, if you know of one answer me *urgente*, I've got to move *inmediatamente*.)

I ask everyone for recommendations and I clip addresses from newspapers . . . I've already been to this one . . . and as for that one I can't satisfy their requirements.

Starting at dawn I rent vans, pack my pillows and mattresses, and move my furniture to the room that I've found (I've put everything on wheels, to save on moving costs).

My furniture sits outside the place where I've found a room, but each apartment has its own drawbacks: this one has no conveniences, that one has a shrew of a concierge, the next one is near a radio that's distracting, and the noise from the marketplace is too loud outside of the other one.

Here's a place with "conveniences": it's infested with bugs, and besides I can't live there together with my wife because no children are allowed. The floor's wet, there's no washbasin or shower, and my wife looks longingly at the bachelor next door.

. . . I found a great place and lived there for a year but got evicted because I didn't pay my rent.

(4) "Ovinu malkeinu"[37]

Ovinu malkeinu,
gesheftn iz kleyne,
banketn iz oykh itst nito!
Tu ikh mikh on
un gey in "leon"
un ikh shpil mir dort a domino!

(Refrain):
A domino in fir hent,
a tuml, vi es volt gebrent,
mayn shutef Simón
iz a groyser *chambón*,
halevay volt ikh im nit gekent!
Ovinu malkeinu,
nu gey shoyn a shteyn nu,
vos trakhtstu dort, oy, azoy fil;
vos haltstu dort tayer,
di "tsveyer," di "drayer,"
du zest dokh, s'iz an ofene shpil.

(Refrain):
Farmakh dayne shteyner, men zet,
shlog nit op mayn shteyn, vos ikh bet,
ven du shpilst zikh nor oys,
dubl zeks geyt aroys,
dan makh ikh dir glaykh a banket.
Ovinu malkeinu,
ikh hob a tokhter a sheyne,
a bokher tsu ir kumt arayn.
A voyl yungerman,
nor er vart af nadan,
er meynt bay mir gliklekh tsu zayn!

(Refrain):
Nor a sent tsu gebn iz nishto,
a bintl naye tshvekes iz do,
nokh der khasene shoyn,
nem ikh im arayn
far a shutef tsu a domino.
Ovinu malkeinu,
mayn vayb Khaye Sheyne,
zi zitst dort in shtub, vart af mir,
zi darf a *tapado*,
un gelt in merkade [*mercado*],
zi halt mikh gor far a shtik gvir.

(Refrain):
Zi zet, ikh tuml, ikh rash,
kh'hob groyse gesheftn in gas,
gey dertseyl ir a mayse,
s'iz tsores do groyse,
men shpilt domino *nada más*.

(b) English synopsis[38]

Business is bad, there are no banquets anywhere, so I put on my clothes and go to "León," where it's crowded and stuffy, to play a game of four-handed dominoes. My partner Simón is a big oaf [*chambón*]; I wish we'd never met!

Your move—what's taking you so long? What's more important—the "two" or the "three"? Keep your tiles to yourself; anyone can see them . . . when you've finished "double-six" will get eliminated and I'll make a banquet in your honor.

I have a pretty daughter and she has a decent boyfriend who is waiting for a dowry and thinks I'll make him happy. But I don't have a penny to my name, just a bag full of new nails, so after the wedding I'll invite him to join me as my partner in dominoes.

Meanwhile, my wife Haya Sheyna sits at home and waits for me. She needs a coat and money for groceries, and thinks I'm a millionaire. She sees how much noise I make about my big business deals, so just try telling her that it's hard times and I'm playing dominoes, *nada más*!

Your move; what are you thinking about, you oaf?!

Notes

1. Julio Nudler, *Tango judío: del ghetto a la milonga* [Jewish tango: From the ghetto to the milonga] (Buenos Aires: Editorial Sudamericana, 1998), 17. (Milonga is the name of an Argentine and Uruguayan musical genre, and also denotes a venue where the tango is danced.) According to Nudler, Jews pass largely unmentioned in mainstream Argentine tango lyrics. In his preface, Nudler mentions his own distance from Jewish religious and cultural traditions, and this seems to be an occupational hazard among many of those who choose to write about Jewish history and culture in Latin America.

2. José Judkovski, *El tango: una historia con judíos* [The tango: A history with Jews] (Buenos Aires: Fundación IWO, 1998).

3. Vertinsky performed his own songs on stage and—like Katz—according to Gerald Janecek, "his popular performances were characterized by an elegant intimacy of style and a unique manner of singing marked by richly nuanced intonation and gestures to intensify the pathos of his often sentimental romantic subjects." From 1919 to 1943, Vertinsky resided abroad, "maintain[ing] his popularity as a purveyor of nostalgia among post-revolutionary émigrés." In this respect, too, he presents something of a parallel with Katz. Ultimately, he was permitted to return to Soviet Russia, where "he was received warmly by native audiences with an unquenched thirst for the emotion-laden, if occasionally bathetic, Vertinsky style . . ." See Janecek's entry on Vertinsky in Allan Ho and Dmitry Feofanov, eds., *Biographical Dictionary of Russian/Soviet Composers* (New York: Greenwood Press, 1989), 578–579. Additional information on Vertinsky may be found in the article on him by L. M. Shchemeleva, in P. A. Nikolaev, ed., *Russkie pisateli 1800–1917: Biograficheskii slovar'* [Russian writers, 1800–1917: A biographical dictionary] (Moscow: Sovetskaya entsiklopediya, 1989), 1:430–431. In contrast to Vertinsky, the option of a return to his native land would have been effectively foreclosed to Jevel Katz, even had he not succumbed at an early age.

4. Rollansky's observations, taken from several articles that he contributed to *Di idishe tsaytung* [The Jewish newspaper], are excerpted at length in the entry on Jevel Katz in the seventh (unpublished) volume of Zalmen Zylbercweig's *Leksikon fun yidishn teater* [Encyclopedia of the Yiddish theatre], cols. 6163–6167. See also Shmuel Rozhanski, "Geshtorbn der frehlikhster id in argentine, populerster un balibster artist in b. ayres" [The happiest Jew in Argentina, the most popular and beloved performer in Buenos Aires, has died], *Di idishe tsaytung*, March 10, 1940.

5. Bentsion Palepade, "Geshtorbn a institutsye: afn keyver fun Khevl Kats [An institution has died: By the graveside of Jevel Katz]," *Di prese* [The press], March 10, 1940, (emphasis added). Katz's songs were then being serialized in the rival, pro-Zionist daily, *Di idishe tsaytung*.

6. Khevl Kats, *Argentiner glikn: parodyes un kupletn* [Argentine luck: Parodies and couplets] (Buenos Aires: n.p., 1933).

7. The *ranchera* is a Mexican musical genre.

8. Cf. the folksinger Mariam Nirenberg's reflections on the wide range of dances—local, regional, and international—that she learned in a small Polish shtetl between the two world wars. See Mark Slobin, *Tenement Songs: The Popular Music of the Jewish Immigrants* (Urbana: University of Illinois Press, 1982), 28.

9. Slobin, 57. As Slobin writes with respect to Yiddish songwriters in the United States, "Our protagonists will be men who faced the task of formulating and delivering messages about Americanization to the Yiddish-speaking masses" (4).

10. Slobin, 2.

11. Irony was also a trait encountered frequently in North American Yiddish songs. See Slobin, 162.

12. Slobin, 193.

13. Slobin, 104–106.

14. By July 2006, when I revisited Buenos Aires, the Jevel Katz "shrine" had been relocated to the rebuilt headquarters of the Jewish community, the AMIA, on Pasteur Street. Some months earlier, however—in a typically Byzantine maneuver—the AMIA had evicted the Fundación IWO's offices and library from its building.

15. For a listing of American Yiddish recordings, see Richard K. Spottswood, *Ethnic Music on Records: A Discography of Ethnic Recordings Produced in the United States, 1893 to 1942* (Urbana: University of Illinois Press, 1990), vol. 3, *Eastern Europe*.

16. The newspaper *Di idishe tsaytung* began to publish Katz's song texts, together with simple music lines, only during the final year of his life. I am grateful to Dr. Gila Flam, director of the National Sound Archive, at the Hebrew University of Jerusalem, for supplying me with photocopies of a number of these songs.

17. Lyrics for "Secreto" may be found on the *isla_negra* website: http://isla_negra.zoomblog.com/archivo/2006/04/29/enrique-Santos-Discepolo-secreto.html (accessed May 19, 2007).

18. Katz, *Argentiner glikn* [page not numbered].

19. Upon hearing this song at the "Yiddish Theatre Revisited: New Perspectives on Drama and Performance" conference (University of Washington, Seattle, May 7–9, 2006), one member of the audience—attentive to the song's tempos—suggested that the music of its refrain actually derives from a Polish mazurka.

20. *Luftmentsh*, literally "person of air," is a Yiddish expression that is applied to someone lacking any visible means of support, even as he (and it usually is a he) hatches grand schemes for earning a livelihood. The classic literary example of a *luftmentsh* is Sholem Aleichem's character, Menakhem-Mendl.

21. Slobin, 101, 108.

22. Dr. Michael Thaler, upon hearing a recording of "Ovinu malkeinu" that I played at the "Thinking about Diaspora" conference at the University of California—Santa Cruz, in November 2000, suggested this reading.

23. Slobin, 143.

24. The text was published in *Di idishe tsaytung*, ca. 1939–1940. Although the lyrics indicate that the "music was adapted by [Jeremias] Ciganeri" (a violinist, conductor of the orchestra at the Teatro Mitre, and co-author, with Abraham Szewach, of Yiddish tangos), the music line is unfortunately absent on the photocopied newspaper clipping supplied to me by Dr. Gila Flam, of the National Sound Archive in Jerusalem.

25. In the Kedushah [Sanctification] prayer, which is recited while standing, the Jewish worshiper traditionally elevates his heels three times while chanting the words "Kadosh, kadosh, kadosh" [Holy, holy, holy (is the Lord of Hosts)].

26. Simon Collier, *The Life, Music, & Times of Carlos Gardel* (Pittsburgh, PA: University of Pittsburgh Press, 1986), 282.

27. Because the song was published in either 1939 or 1940 I am making the assumption that he wrote it after Gardel's untimely death.

28. Concerning the reception of touring Yiddish actors in Argentina see, for example, the memoir by Luba Kadison and Joseph Buloff (with Irving Genn), *On Stage, Off Stage: Memories of a Lifetime in the Yiddish Theatre* (Cambridge: Harvard University Library, 1992), 105–118. In addition, in his memoir Pesachke Burstein discusses his performances in South America from the 1940s and forward. See: Peysekhke Burshteyn [Pesachke Burstein], *Geshpilt a lebn* (Tel Aviv: n.p., 1980; English translation: *What a Life!* (Syracuse, NY: Syracuse University Press, 2003). Well before then Buenos Aires and Rio de Janeiro were regular stops on the Yiddish theatrical circuit, as the 1924 tour of Boris Thomashefsky demonstrates. While skimming the Argentine Jewish press of the 1930s, both in Yiddish and Spanish, I came across numerous articles about visiting stars such as Samuel Goldenburg (1886–?) and Stella Adler (1901–1992), not to mention the famous Polish cantor Gershon Sirota (1874–1943), who led High Holiday services in Buenos Aires in 1930.

29. By the same token, it is perhaps "no accident" that the popular Argentine Yiddish magazine *Penemer un penemlekh* ([Faces and countenances], which came out in the 1920s and 1930s) adopted *Caras y caritas* [Faces and masks] as its Spanish title—this being an obvious knock-off of *Caras y caretas* [Faces and masks], a popular Spanish-language magazine that was published from 1898 until the mid-1950s.

30. Slobin, 109.

31. I am grateful to Eliezer Niborski, formerly of Lyon, France, and now residing in Israel, for transcribing the Yiddish lyrics to this song, as performed by Jevel Katz. The source is the CD, *Homenaje a Jevel Katz* [Homage to Jevel Katz], produced by the Fundación IWO, in Buenos Aires (undated). Ellipses indicate where the phrasings are unclear.

32. "Azoy zingt Khevl Kats: Mozesvil" [Thus sings Jevel Katz: Mozesvil], in *Di idishe tsaytung*, undated, ca. 1939–1940). In the version sung by Max Zalkind, "zis" [sweet] is replaced by "sheyn" [beautiful] in the refrain (the phrase is not repeated), and the line "vu ikh hob di kindershe yorn farbrakht" [where I spent my childhood years] is omitted entirely, as are some of the stanzas in the published version. Katz lifted this phrase from the song "Mayn shtetele belz [My Hometown Belz]." "Mayn shtetele belz," with lyrics by Jacob Jacobs (1892–1972) and music by Alexander Olshanetsky (1892–1946), was registered for copyright in 1932. See Irene Heskes, *Yiddish American Popular Songs, 1895 to 1950* (Washington: Library of Congress, 1992), p. 334, entry 2432.

33. Sulky—a lightweight, two-wheeled, horse-drawn cart.

34. The translation is based on the version sung by Max Zalkind on the undated CD *Homenaje a Jevel Katz*.

35. "Azoy zingt Khevl Kats: Ikh zukh a tsimer" [Thus sings Jevel Katz: I'm looking for a room], in *Di idishe tsaytung* (undated, ca. 19392–1940).

36. The translation is based on the version sung by Max Perelman on the undated CD *Homenaje a Jevel Katz*, produced by the Fundación IWO, in Buenos Aires.

37. "Ovinu malkeinu: parodia de Jevel Katz," cantado por Jevel Katz, David Itzkof, Raul Tabachnik; música arreglada para piano y canto por Simón Tenovsky [Ovinu Malkeinu (Our Father, our King): Parody by Jevel Katz, sung by Jevel Katz, David Itzkof (Itzkoff), Raul Tabachnik; music arranged for piano and voice by Simón Tenovsky] (Buenos Aires: Julio Korn, ca.1936). Sheet music.

38. The translation is based on the version sung by Max Zalkind on the undated CD *Homenaje a Jevel Katz*, produced by the Fundación IWO, in Buenos Aires.

PART IV
Recoveries and Reconstructions

CHAPTER 10

Reconstructing a Yiddish Theatre Score: Giacomo Minkowski and His Music to *Alexander; or, the Crown Prince of Jerusalem*

Ronald Robboy

Aleksander, oder der kroynprints fun yerusholayim (Alexander; or, the crown prince of Jerusalem), an operetta with libretto by Joseph Lateiner (1853–1935), decisively launched the career of Boris Thomashefsky (1866–1939) as a star and matinee idol on New York City's Lower East Side.[1] It opened on Friday, December 23, 1892, and played through the weekend, through the remainder of the season and into the following one, and, indeed, into Thomashefsky's permanent repertoire.[2] So great was the adulation the role brought Thomashefsky that he claimed he would arrange trysts in an upper box between entrances. Occasionally, when the encounters became too passionate, he missed cues and would have to deliver his lines from his love perch high above the orchestra.[3] Even his estranged wife-turned-competitor, Bessie Thomashefsky (1873–1962), stated unequivocally: *Aleksander* had made him famous.[4] In it, she said, Thomashefsky was beauty personified.[5]

Abraham Cahan (1860–1951), the long-time editor of the New York daily *Forverts* (Forward) as well as a novelist, critic, and arbiter of immigrant cultural tastes, wondered, "Who among older New York Jews does not remember the stir aroused by Thomashefsky in the role of Alexander, Crown Prince of Jerusalem?" Cahan omits the tale of love among the loges, but offers a portrait of Thomashefsky as matinee idol (*"matini aydol,"* quotes in original) and object of feminine desire. "Women used to study his every scene, where and how he stood, to determine the best seat in a play."[6]

What was it about this potboiler that proved so incendiary? Well, there were the extravagant effects: the fortress aflame, the rearing white steed—and who can forget the silver armor?[7] All this was evidently thrilling, but so was Boris Thomashefsky himself: handsome, heroic and, in case the point has not been adequately made,

Boris and Bessie Thomashefsky, c. 1890. (From the archives of the YIVO Institute for Jewish Research, New York.)

an ardent lover, on stage and off. His famously over-the-top acting and fine singing voice were ideally suited for this work, as was his high-class *daytshmerish*, the pretentious Yiddish diction favored by many early actors, as well as some writers, in what has been described as a "conscious imitation of German."[8]

Beyond the lurid stories and tabloid copy, however, the question remains: what made these operettas and melodramas tick, and what kept audiences coming back?[9]

Potboilers of this variety constituted a large part of the Yiddish theatre repertoire, yet anecdotal descriptions of their performances, while entertaining (and occasionally reliable), are hardly sufficient to the task of understanding the complexity and scope of the Yiddish theatrical experience. A further hindrance to understanding these productions is the comparative lack of scholarly attention paid to one of their most important aspects: music. Yiddish theatre music—particularly from its earliest days until its popularization in sound recordings—has been little analyzed in terms of its content, performance practices, and significance for its audience.[10] Given the centrality of music to both Yiddish operetta and dramatic productions, it is essential that musical scores and libretti be subject to the same scrutiny allotted to the scripts, biography, and performance reviews that now form the bulk of Yiddish theatre criticism and historiography. In an effort to rectify this imbalance, this study focuses on the task of reconstructing *Aleksander*'s score, a process that coincides with another kind of reconstruction: that of the long-forgotten career of its improbably named composer, Giacomo Minkowski (1871–1941). Examination of Minkowski's career in turn illuminates some unexpected connections that *Aleksander* makes between European and American musical cultures, the twisting path to immigrant success, and the rapid but haphazard assimilation of eastern European Jewish talent into the Anglophone American mainstream.

When *Aleksander* opened in December of 1892, the Yiddish theatre was entering its so-called Golden Age. Two months earlier, the actor Jacob P. Adler (1855–1926) had premiered Jacob Gordin's (1853–1909) *Der yidisher kenig Lir* (*The Jewish King Lear*), a prototype of the "better," literary play, extolled by critics and intellectuals ever since as the antidote to exactly the kind of *shund* (trash) they saw in operettas such as *Aleksander*.[11] "Literary" plays were held to be champions of naturalism in plot and language; they maintained unity and consistency in terms of genre and thematic content, and allowed dramatic actors to probe tragic psychology and profound characterization. Operettas, by contrast, dispensed with high-toned naturalism, plausible narrative, thematic unity, consistent genre, and nuanced character study. They were able to do this, in no small part, by adding music, a sure-fire ingredient for abetting suspension of disbelief and for opening the door to all the showmanship its singers, dancers, and mugging comics could muster.

Though Jacob Adler was said to be a dramatic actor of spellbinding power, he was no song-and-dance man. *Aleksander* deliberately played to Thomashefsky's strengths both as musician and leading man, and offered a formidable box-office response to *Der yidisher kenig Lir*.

Aleksander, son of Queen Shlomis (Salome) and a brother of Aristobulus, is the crown prince. Disguised as a hunter in the Judean forest, Aleksander encounters Noyme (Naomi), a poor girl wandering alone, and the two fall in love. She is a ward of cantankerous old Menakhem, but we learn by turns that she, too, is in fact of royal birth.

Some of the characters are named after Hasmonean royalty, while others have canonical biblical names. Zilpe (Zilpah) the maidservant, and Naftole (Naphtali), Menakhem's manservant, are comic foils to the noble Noyme and Aleksander, their romance paralleling and parodying that of their masters. Part of the humor of the comic-servant love plot lies in the linguistic contrast they present to their betters. The royal couple speak a very high-sounding *daytshmerish*, while Zilpe and Naftole speak a flavorful Yiddish. *Daytshmerish* was affected as a mark of elevation and culture in much early Yiddish theatre, displacing the heavily Slavicized *zhargon*, or hybrid vernacular that was eastern European Yiddish. Thomashefsky was particularly prone to *daytshmerish*, and in her autobiography, Bessie Thomashefsky, who played Zilpe in the original production, offers a hilarious satire of her husband's bombastic *daytshmerish* as Aleksander.

Hier, mu-ter, izt mayne kro[n]ne, vaas nutst mir di kronne, ven di vahre kronne mir opgeshtorbn izt? Zi izt tod! O got, ale ketse lebn, ale hunde lebn, ale ferde lebn, ale mayze lebn—nor nikht mayne ehrlishe Noyme!

(*Hier* [here], Mater, *ist* my *Krone* [crown]. *Was* [what] use *ist* the *Krone* to me when the *wahre* [true] *Krone* has perished for me? She *ist* dead! O, God, cats all live, dogs all live, horses all live, mice all live—but *nicht* [not] my virtuous Naomi!)[12]

The comic servant Naftole's Yiddish, in contrast, is liberally salted with words taken from the Hebrew. These he deploys in one of his funniest recurring riffs, in which Naftole repeatedly refers to the Queen Mother as *mekhuteneste* (mother of the son-in-law). With this homely moniker, he punctures the pretensions of the *daytshmerish* royalty by underlining his own kinship to it.

Much of the deeper structure of the play revolves around linguistic contrasts between the comical delusions of power entertained by the Yiddish-speaking clown, and the state military prowess of the *daytshmerish*-speaking Jewish prince. When Noyme is traumatized by rejection from the foolishly suspicious Aleksander, she loses her power of speech altogether, and can only sing wordlessly. Filled with remorse, Alexander forswears speaking and is capable only of making asides to the audience, as well as singing the occasional song, of course, until he can redeem her love—and, incidentally, save his nation by defeating the scheming Edomites. In the interim, Naftole holds forth in a long comic scene in which he is held and interrogated by the Edomites. By turns clever and pathetic, craven and defiant, he offers a tour de force of Yiddish humor as the little man temporizes and matches wits with the Jews' enemies. Threatened with having his throat cut if he does not divulge the disposition of Aleksander's forces, Naftole tells his captors he is made too nervous by the sight of the *khalef* (kosher slaughterer's knife) brandished over him. After a slapstick negotiation, he manages to extract a promise from the Edomites not to interrupt him if he agrees to tell everything from the beginning. And with that, he launches in:

Tsum ershtn hot got bashafn himl un erd un di erd iz geven vist un ler un khoyshekh un finster, hot got gezogt es zol vern likhtik, iz gevorn likhtik.[13]

(The first thing, God created heaven and earth, and the earth was bleak and empty and dark and gloomy. God said, "Let there be light." And there was light.)

As the Edomites redouble their threats and Naftole renegotiates the terms of his interrogation, he manages to recite more of his Creation paraphrase until trumpets are heard and the day is saved by the German-speaking Jew, Aleksander, who leads his people to victory in the Land of Israel.

Each shift of language sees a corresponding shift of tone and slippage between dramatic and comedic genres. But if "tone" is nebulous and lacks a fixed point, its material counterpart lies in the physical sound, the acoustic dimension of the play and its language. Supporting, complementing, and creating its own counterpoint to that sonic world of language is the musical score. Indeed, the comic turns of Naftole and Zilpe draw on emerging conventions of the Yiddish theatre *kuplet*, the song-and-dance burlesqueries of music-hall patter and novelty song. But for the large choral numbers and for the arias—which is in fact what they are—as sung by the noble speakers of *daytshmerish*, the composer of *Aleksander*'s score turned to another, more prestigious model.

The Score

In 1998, I became the researcher for the Thomashefsky Project, and one of my initial tasks was to undertake a detailed descriptive inventory of Boris Thomashefsky's papers, held by the Jewish Division of the New York Public Library since 1939 but never catalogued or put in order. Among them, I identified a so-called Direction part to *Aleksander*'s musical score.[14] It was dated 1910, had belonged to the composer-conductor Joseph Brody (1877–1937), and had been used to lead the pit orchestra and chorus in at least one Thomashefsky production later in the 1910s.

Really only a sketch, it pared everything down, like a lead sheet, to one or two musical staves. A lead sheet typically reduces everything to a single line that includes the melody and lyrics, with alphabetic chord symbols above the line that tell what the harmonies are. Missing are non-melodic rhythmic textures, the bass line, explicit inner voices, and so on. In Yiddish theatre, a Direction part provides little or no harmonic information and often even omits lyrics. On the other hand, it can also include some stage directions, though never as thoroughly as would a script. According to the sparest mention on yet another promptbook, the operetta had *"muzik fun Minkovski"* (music by Minkowski),[15] whom Boris Thomashefsky briefly identified in his autobiography.

> To write music for the new operetta, I engaged Giacomo (Yankele) Minkowski, who at that time had just come over from Europe. A talented musician, Minkowski was a conservatory graduate, and he wrote successful music for *Aleksander*. To tell the truth, he had taken quite a bit from the famous cantors Nisn Belzer [Nisn Spivak, 1824–1906], Yerukhem Hakotn [Yeruchom Blindman, ca. 1798–1891], and Sulzer [Solomon Sulzer, 1804–1890], among others.

He also appropriated music from entirely older operas. But who cared, so long as the music was beautiful and complemented the action?[16]

But who was Giacomo Minkowski? He was apparently important enough to warrant billing for the operetta's opening: "Grose historishe oper fun Yozef Latayner. Muzik fun Minkovski. Oysgeshtatet fun rezhiser M. Finkel."[17] (Grand historical opera by Joseph Lateiner. Music by Minkowski. Production design (staging and effects) by the director, M. Finkel.)

Not even Thomashefsky's name, it should be noted, was considered important enough to this production to be included in the initial advertisements. Morris Finkel (1852–1904), on the other hand, was a powerful and dictatorial backstage presence. Though he began as an actor at the dawn of Yiddish theatre with Avrom Goldfaden (1840–1908) and then Sigmund Mogulesco (1858–1914), he was to become perhaps the first director, in the modern sense, in Yiddish theatre who was not also the public face of a company. His specialty was precisely this sort of historical drama, and despite Thomashefsky's swaggering account, one cannot help but wonder: was it actually Finkel who had "discovered" Minkowski?[18]

Following the success of *Aleksander*, the company staged two more operettas with "muzik fun Minkovski" over the next year: *Bas-sheva, oder der vintshnfingerl* (Bathsheba; or, the wishing ring) and *Kenig un boyer* (King and peasant). *Bas-sheva* opened on April 6, 1893, and played more or less continually through the season and into the next. The *Arbeter tsaytung* (Worker's paper) ad listed the same creative team as *Aleksander*: play by Lateiner, music by Minkowski, staged (*oysgeshtatet*) by Finkel.[19] At the beginning of the next season, *Kenig un boyer* opened on September 22, once again by the team of Lateiner and Minkowski, but now minus Finkel.[20]

Kenig un boyer was not remotely as successful as *Aleksander* or *Bas-sheva*, and Bessie Thomashefsky remarked that it was a flop due to competition from the neighboring Windsor Theatre.[21] If competition from the Windsor played a role, there were certainly also internal factors at play. Not only was Finkel's name not associated with the Lateiner-Minkowski team this time; he was soon to leave the Thalia Theatre altogether following a sort of palace coup.[22] Finkel's departure from the Thalia appears to have coincided with Minkowski's, which in Minkowski's case was not only a departure from the Thalia, but from Yiddish theatre altogether.

Though Zalmen Zylbercweig's *Leksikon fun yidishn teater* (Encyclopedia of the Yiddish theatre) does not provide Minkowski with an entry of his own, it does offer passing references to music by *someone* of that name. Zylbercweig mentions at least three operettas with "muzik fun Minkovski." Two are by Lateiner: *Khurbn yerusholayim* (The destruction of Jerusalem, 1890)[23] and *Kenig un boyer*.[24] The third, a play by Moyshe Zeifert, is *Der yidisher polkovnik* (The Jewish colonel, 1890), with music by "Mogulesko un Minkovski."[25]

Regarding *Khurbn yerusholayim* and *Der yidisher polkovnik*, I have not found anything to corroborate (or disprove) Zylbercweig's claim that our Minkowski—or some other Minkowski—wrote scores to either or both those works, though as we shall see, they would have been early in the young composer's life.[26] Of *Kenig un boyer*, Zylbercweig attributes to journalist Philip Krantz (1858–1922) the claim that, among other works, it used music from *Lakmé* and *Cavalleria Rusticana*.[27] It was only a year and a half after those operas' Metropolitan Opera premieres that *Kenig un boyer* appeared in September, 1893, so the timing is plausible for the music of the Met's performances to still have been in Minkowski's ear (or Krantz's). Alternatively, had Minkowski recently arrived from Europe, he might have heard the operas there, but the evidence suggests otherwise.

Pairing the names "Giacomo" and "Minkowski" sounded like an ironic Jewish joke, but Minkowski may also have been paying homage to Giacomo Meyerbeer (1791–1864), the German Jew, born Jakob Liebmann Meyer Beer, who had built an enormously successful and influential career writing operas in mid-nineteenth-century Paris.[28] But Thomashefsky's parenthetical tip-off that young Minkowski was really Yankele—not just Yankev (Jacob), but little Jakie—cemented the impression that the Italian name was a joke. Then the mystery deepened further still.

By early 2001, librarian Faith Jones, then at the Dorot Jewish Division of the New York Public Library, had been using the Thomashefsky Project's inventory as an aid in cataloging the Thomashefsky Collection. She asked me if I thought "muzik fun Minkovski" referred to the famous *khazn* (cantor) Pinchas Minkowski (1859–1924). I told her certainly not, and directed her to Thomashefsky's description of Yankele/Giacomo. She floored me a day or two later by producing a bibliographic record for Giacomo Minkowski's operetta *Die schönste Frau* (The fairest woman), published in Berlin in 1910.[29] Surely there were not *two* Giacomo Minkowskis?

In the absence of firm biographical information about Minkowski, I turned to his musical scores. Perhaps the work of reconstructing the score to *Aleksander* might also lead back to the man himself.

In the first act, Aleksander himself has a striking aria, a waltz, which is followed by an ambitiously operatic *scena*: a mix of quasi-recitative, declamation, and orchestral passage work—rapid figures of many notes, more abstract or ornamental than melodic in nature—leading up to a more formal duet for him and Noyme. But there were almost no lyrics in the bare-bones ex-Brody score, and the music itself was also fairly schematic.[30]

To complicate matters, it seemed that passages in the script would periodically unravel into enigmatic non sequiturs, until, matching promptbook against score, I realized that in some of the most opaque of these we were looking at just the first lines of musical verses or even of entire musical numbers. This was a promptbook, after all: the prompter fed only first lines to the singers.

Besides NYPL, the YIVO Archives, also in New York, has musical materials pertaining to *Aleksander* among the Sholem Perlmutter Music Collection, the David

Hirsch Collection, the Vilna Collection, and perhaps others, which proved useful in distilling relevant information. Especially helpful were some scores in the Vilna Collection that had been used in Lithuania and across Belarus,[31] as well as ones used in Warsaw and Odessa.[32] There are some important differences between these European *Aleksander* scores and the American parts, including a different overture as well as some orchestrational differences—notably, two trumpets in place of one cornet—but of crucial importance is that at least one of the Direction scores has comprehensive lyrics.[33] This particular score was arranged by Yitskhok Shlosberg (1877–1930), the preeminent Yiddish theatre conductor in Warsaw in the first decades of the twentieth century. It has been said of him that he spent "more time *arranging* an operetta than a composer in America would *composing* it."[34] In undertaking a reconstruction of the entire *Aleksander* operetta, these Shlosberg parts would be essential.

For orchestra parts, the Perlmutter Collection has an *Aleksander* set that is not only complete and particularly clean, but the parts—the actual pages of music that had been used by musicians in the pit—exactly match the ex-Brody score at NYPL, copied in the same hand and similarly dated. It was upon these that we at the Thomashefsky Project principally relied.[35] Musically, they are very similar to a set of Boris Thomashefsky's own parts, now at NYPL, in which a percussionist at the Thalia Theatre had signed his name on June 14, 1895, a mere two and a half years after the work's premiere.[36]

Michael Tilson Thomas had proposed a reconstruction technique, one we had already used for selections from several other operettas before we began work on *Aleksander*. It was elegant in its obvious simplicity. Once I had identified the set or sets of orchestra parts to be used, a music copyist would take each part successively—the clarinet, the bass, the first violin, etc.—and write it into the outlines of a full score.[37] When the last part was entered, the instrumental score was complete. Then I would fill in the vocal line(s) for lyrics, using a combination of Direction scores, promptbooks, and sometimes published play scripts or sheet music. In the case of *Aleksander* there were some intermediate steps. To make a case for how promising I thought the first-act scene was, I ferreted out lyrics and collated, point by point, the script and the score. I constructed a condensed sketch of the entire scene for Tilson Thomas, showing the full vocal parts, important harmonic information, and many orchestral cues.[38] Based on that sketch, the Project undertook a full realization for the Carnegie Hall program it presented in 2005.[39]

The scene begins with Aleksander's aria, "Vi gefloygn kum ikh vider" (As on wings do I return). A waltz, it has a plaintive principal theme in F minor. (See Fig. 1 in the Appendix.) It is answered by a shorter second section whose signature is an upward octave leap, followed by a gentle descent along playful, chromatically inflected switchbacks. (See Fig. 2.) A buoyant F-major trio follows. (The contrasting middle section common to waltzes, marches, and some other musical forms is called the trio, even though it does not necessarily have three of anything.) After the trio comes a return, though not to the principal theme *da capo* (that is, from the top), as one would expect, but in mirror image: *abcba*.

It passes first through the second theme, *b*, introduced by its signature octave, and then back to the principal theme, *a*. Trivial as this minor formal alteration may appear at first blush, it will in fact be mined for dramatic effect later in the scene.

Aleksander concludes his aria as the principal theme closes, and he exits just as Noyme enters. Her entrance is accompanied by a hushed, upper-register solo flute whose exotically modal arabesques signal a state of enchantment.

But if there is a sense of enchantment, there is also a foreshadowing of the traumatized swoon into which Noyme will soon fall, losing her voice and nearly losing her rightful place as royalty. In a plot twist identical to that of *Lucia di Lammermoor* (1835), by Gaetano Donizetti (1797–1848), Noyme will lose her senses after her lover has torn off his ring in the mistaken belief that she has forsaken him. (Lucia's iconic Mad Scene is also shadowed by a lone flute.) Noyme and Lucia share the fate of the nineteenth-century diva as victim, in which love's passion rules not only her mind, but her body and well-being.

Noyme was originally played by Sophie Karp (1859–1904),[40] a much beloved prima donna who had begun with Goldfaden in the earliest days in Romania. She was especially known for her sweet voice, but like Boris Thomashefsky, she was criticized for her *daytshmerish*, which Bessie Thomashefsky called Karp's "weakness."[41] In *Aleksander*, however, the two leads must have ideally complemented one another.[42]

After the flute solo, Noyme begins singing a short reprise of *"Dos paradiz var mir ofen"* (Paradise was open to me)—notice the *daytshmerizm* in the words *var* (was) and *paradiz* (paradise)—which she had introduced earlier in the act (see Fig. 3). It is her emblematic song of longing, reappearing throughout the operetta, sometimes in song, sometimes vocalized without words, and sometimes only in the orchestra as *melodram*. (*Melodram* employed musical score from the pit under the onstage dialogue, providing musical commentary or reinforcing the emotional content of what was being said.) The Paradise song is interrupted, from offstage, by Aleksander's signature octave leap initiating the second theme of his aria. Just as it had interrupted the usual form one would have expected in a waltz, conveying its ardor and urgency by preempting the principal theme, so it interrupts Noyme in her reverie.

From this point in the score, it is clear that a high-operatic *scena* is fully under way, strings leading in furious *agitato* figurations, and Noyme, in quasi-recitative, declaiming that she recognizes his voice. A stage direction has Aleksander run in (*loyft arayn*) and hold a long high note—a G, the top of Boris Thomashefsky's range—on the word *gelibte* (beloved), plunging down an octave for the final syllable (see Fig. 4). After Aleksander's entrance, the two lovers unite in a stately love duet, singing as one, "I must weep when we part" (see Fig. 6). Noyme counters, "Yet, when you come," and the two join in florid scales, alighting on a half cadence—"O, velkhe froyde!" (O, what joy!)—from which they launch into an ecstatic *cabaletta*, a brilliant closing allegro to an extended aria, amid intertwined vows of eternal devotion (see Fig. 5).

However glorious was the passionate close, it was Aleksander's high G on the word *gelibte* as he dashed onstage from the wings that, from a musico-dramatic standpoint, served as the climax of this scene. From the moment it became clear to me whose note that was, what he was singing, and how electrifying it must have been to his audience, I thought I had found a key to understanding the power of this operetta and what made it such a force in Thomashefsky's career, and Yiddish theatre in general, at that time.

Boris Thomashefsky's career as an artist began as *meshoyrer*, a choirboy, singing and training with the great *khazn* Nisn (Nisi) Belzer in Berdichev.[43] Many of the techniques of vocal production employed in eastern European *khazones*, or cantorial art, were not incompatible with those of the operatic stage: diaphragmatic support for the power and stability to project and fill public spaces without benefit of amplification; a fine control over pitch in rapid scales and ornaments; control over a wide dynamic range; and the ability to "place" the voice in chest or head as needed for coloristic effect. Thomashefsky reports that from an early age, he found the two arts—opera and *khazones*—inextricably connected. In fact, he first heard opera as a young boy, in Kiev, even before he had studied with Nisn Belzer, and he was infatuated with it.[44]

Coming to America, Thomashefsky made the transition from synagogue to stage while still in his youth, and by all evidence developed many of the skills required equally of *khazones* and opera as his voice came of age.[45] One should not be misled by the few extant recordings and films of his singing, all made when he was already in his sixties and which, because of the relatively primitive recording technology, masked the relative size and power of his voice. As a young man, when Thomashefsky first appeared in *Aleksander*, he must have been as intoxicating as any rock star. But he was singing opera, unabashed Italian opera, albeit in Yiddish.

The Composer

Still the question remains: who was Giacomo Minkowski, composer of *Aleksander*? On government documents his first name appears variously as Jacob, Giacomo (sometimes misspelled), initial J., even J. Giacomo, and his surname as Minkowsky.[46] The 1920 census reported Minkowski was born in Kiev in 1871,[47] although his 1941 obituary gave Odessa as a birthplace.[48] Minkowski first came to America in 1887,[49] and was naturalized five years later, in San Francisco, in the spring of 1892.[50] On July 11, 1892, having set out from San Francisco, one J. Minkowsky arrived in New York by way of the Isthmus of Panamá.[51] *Aleksander* opened the following December.

Minkowski's obituary reports that he received his musical training in Milan,[52] but it is unknown whether his formal training predates or postdates his writing the score for *Aleksander* for the New York Yiddish theatre in 1892–1893, at the age of about twenty-one.[53] As described above, Zylbercweig ascribes even earlier works to a "Minkovski" as the composer of Lateiner's *Khurbn yerusholayim*, which opened on January 1, 1890,[54] and Zeifert's *Der yidisher polkovnik*, which he says opened almost a year later, on December 25, 1890.[55] Giacomo Minkowski would have been very young for either of those—eighteen in the case of *Khurbn yerusholayim*—which raises the question: was the "Minkovski" of those two scores really our Giacomo? Or was it someone else?[56]

If he was not writing Yiddish theatre scores in 1890, however, he *was* publishing his own music by the next year. Consider the "New Oriental Waltzes," by J. Minkowsky, published in San Francisco in 1891 (see Fig. 6).[57] This is almost certainly our Giacomo, as we shall see from internal musical evidence. And it seems to place him still in San Francisco that year, not to leave until the summer of 1892, as the passenger list confirms.

In late 1899, the *New York Times* attributed a publicity article to the *San Francisco Call*, which said that Giacomo Minkowsky [sic] had the previous February been in San Francisco visiting relatives. It also announced that Giacomo was engaged to be married to a "San Francisco girl," Miss Wanda Galand, and that while there in San Francisco in early 1899, he'd had his first performances of his operetta *The Smugglers of Badayez*, for which he had previously won a prize in Vienna.[58] It was published in New York in 1899.[59]

In October of that same year, it was performed in Connecticut by The Bostonians.[60] One of America's leading light opera companies at the time, The Bostonians were working closely with Victor Herbert (1859–1924) on a premiere of his *The Viceroy* during the same weeks they were preparing Minkowski's *Smugglers*,[61] and Minkowski was reported to have entertained Herbert during a *Smugglers* rehearsal.[62]

Victor Herbert's operetta just previous to *The Viceroy* had been *The Ameer* (1899).[63] The librettist was Frederic Ranken (d. ca. 1907), who was Minkowski's librettist on *Smugglers*. How Ranken and Minkowski met, and when—and who introduced whom to Herbert—remains to be determined.

The Bostonians were reported to have scheduled New York performances of *Smugglers* the following spring, and then again in 1903.[64] In January, 1900, three performances are cited in Denver, Colorado.[65]

Though no music appears extant, Minkowski composed another operetta soon after this. *The 'Broidered Belt*, with a libretto by Curtis Dunham,[66] is a roman à clef about General Frederick Funston (1865–1917) and his suppression of the Filipino nationalist insurrection in the wake of the U.S. imperialist conquest.[67] Known in Great Britain as *Philipodia*, it was performed in London in June of 1902.[68] A synopsis of the plot concludes with the remark that New York and London critics found the music "even more melodious and catchy" than that of *The Smugglers of Badayez*.[69]

At the same time, in the earliest years of the twentieth century, Minkowski was publishing magazine articles on opera and voice. *Munsey's Magazine*, a popular New York monthly for a general readership, ran "Verdi and His Successors," in which he offered an appraisal of the Italian opera scene of the time, which, viewed from today, holds up well, but for his feeling that the only other Italianate composer he considered in Puccini's league was Isidore de Lara (1858–1935), an Englishman composing under an exotic pseudonym and now nearly forgotten. Were he "Italian by birth, as he is by musical sentiment," wrote Giacomo Minkowski of Isidore de Lara, he would be the legitimate inheritor of Verdi's mantle.[70] He does not mention, revealingly, that de Lara's birth name had been Cohen.[71] Other cited articles include "Character Revealed in the Color of the Voice" and "Opera Makers of To-day: How the Ancient Feud between the Italian School and the German School Has Ended in a Union of Methods on a Wagnerian Foundation."[72]

In 1908, the *Times* listed Mr. and Mrs. Giacomo Minkowski among those sailing aboard the *Pretoria* to Hamburg.[73] There in Germany, he published *Die schönste Frau*, which was performed in Berlin in 1910. The *New York Times* reported that, though "Minkowski's orchestration was found particularly pleasing by the fashionable audience," critics observed that the score was "a bit too ambitiously operatic to suit the taste of a public educated to the worship of Viennese waltz themes."[74] Evidently, Lower East Side audiences had higher expectations! I have found no documentation of any compositional activity following that of *Die schönste Frau*.

A conspicuous gap from 1894 to 1898 in Minkowski's known whereabouts suggests that he could have been in Europe, studying music, during some or all of that time. But when *Philipodia* was staged in London, a notice about it appeared in a German music journal, stating that Minkowski had been a student of Tchaikovsky![75] Perhaps he had met Pyotr Ilyich during his American tour of 1891? Tchaikovsky died in the fall of 1893, in Russia, not long after Minkowski vacated the Thalia Theatre. Is it possible Giacomo found his way to St. Petersburg during the last weeks of Tchaikovsky's life?

Minkowski's obituary offers additional information. From 1898 to 1908, he

> conducted a studio for voice-training in Carnegie Hall and also wrote music criticisms for The New York Evening Journal. In 1908 he opened a music school in Dresden, Germany, and remained there until 1915. During the next ten years he taught singing in San Francisco. In the late 1920s, and until recently, he had been teaching in Nice, France.[76]

Returning from Europe as France fell, he and his second wife, Martha Frieda, arrived in New York via Lisbon on June 21, 1940.[77] He died the next May.[78]

Our subject appears to have constructed a variety of possible histories of himself. Of those, Yiddish theatre experience represented only a brief episode in his career, and seemingly not one he was at pains to recall to the world; but neither, it seems, was he a man willing to throw away a good idea. A comparison of the introductory measures of J. Minkowsky's "New Oriental Waltzes"[79] (see Fig. 6) to those of the "Spanisches Lied"[80] from Giacomo Minkowski's *Die schönste Frau* (see Fig. 7) reveals unmistakable similarities. Note especially the way the bass line joins a parallel lower octave in the second measure of each. The "Spanisches Lied," composed nearly two decades later, is more sophisticated in the alteration it makes of its pattern, allowing it to precipitously collapse the figuration a measure earlier, in three measures instead of four. Nonetheless, the resemblance of one to the other is striking.

Compelling as that similarity may be, compare the melody itself of the "Spanisches Lied" (Fig. 8) beginning in the fourth measure, to that of Aleksander's *"Vi gefloygn kum ikh vider"* (Fig. 1). The melodic contours are identical, essentially note for note, for the entirety of the principal theme of each. The second theme of Aleksander's aria, the one with the signature octave leap, is slightly modified in the "Spanisches Lied"—the leap is omitted and a replaced by a sudden dynamic drop from *forte* to *piano*, and the chromatic notes eliminated—but otherwise it retains its basic shape and identity (see Fig. 9).

Much more, of course, can be done to fill in the blanks of a varied and peripatetic career, one that was quite unusual in the world of Yiddish theatre music. Though a great many actors crossed over into English-language stage acting and films in the United States, it was much rarer among composers. George Gershwin (1899–1937) is the poster child for a successful traversal from a Yiddish boyhood in Brooklyn to Tin Pan Alley. He was even famously offered work in Thomashefsky's theatre, though he declined, and in fact never took any work on Yiddish theatre's Second Avenue. A generation before the Thomashefskys gave Tilson Thomas to the world, the Gimpel family, who operated a storied theatre in Lemberg, Galicia, spawned their own renowned concert artists, including pianist Jakob Gimpel (1906–1989) and his violinist brother, the brilliant Bronisław Gimpel (1911–1979). Sam Medoff (1912–1991), son of a leading Yiddish theatre personality and Hebrew Actors' Union officer, was the popular arranger and leader of Yiddish swing groups on New York Yiddish radio in the 1940s, but changed his name to Dick Manning and went on to become music director for crooner Perry Como (1912–2001). In 1956, he shared credits on hits for Como with "Hot Diggity" and for Patti Page (b. 1927) with "Allegheny Moon." But the history of Yiddish theatre composers attempting to cross over is mostly one of relative failure and frustration. Alexander Olshanetsky (1892–1946), Sholom Secunda (1894–1974), and Abraham Ellstein (1907–1963), who are often compared to each other and whose work is usually viewed collectively as the apex of American Yiddish theatre song, all very much sought to break from Yiddish theatre, but were never very successful—

Secunda's "Bei Mir Bistu Schön," Olshanetsky's "I Love You Much Too Much" ("Ikh hob dikh tsufil lib"), or Ellstein's less-than-triumphant English-language operas notwithstanding. For a young musician to have made that transition during the 1890s, as Minkowski did, and as definitively as he did, was altogether extraordinary.

He bridged not just one divide, but several, as the recycled musical material all but certainly establishes that the early San Francisco "New Oriental Waltzes" and the fashionable Berlin operetta *Die schönste Frau*—and let us not forget *The Smugglers of Badayez*—were all created by one in the same, Giacomo (Yankele) Minkowski, the extraordinary and all but forgotten composer of *Aleksander, oder der kroynprints fun yerusholayim*.

Appendix

Music of Giacomo Minkowsky

Fig. 1. Principal theme from Aleksander's aria "Vi gefloygn kum ikh vider." Lyrics in italics show *daytshmerizmen*.

Fig 2. Secondary theme from "Vi gefloygn kum ikh vider," characterized by its opening octave leap.

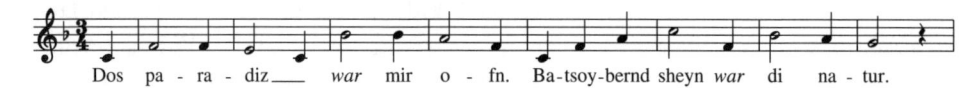

Fig 3. "Dos paradiz war mir ofen," Noyme's often-reprised song of longing.

Fig 4. Transcription of detail from the Brody manuscript of *Aleksander* showing agitated string passages accompanying Noyme's declamatory recitative as she recognizes Aleksander's voice, anticipating his entrance on his high note. (The Thomashefsky Project).

Fig. 5. A typically rhythmic *cabaletta*, ending the long scene for Aleksander and Noyme. (The Thomashefsky Project).

Fig. 6. Introduction to J. Minkowsky's "New Oriental Waltzes."

Fig. 7. Introduction and principal theme of Giacomo Minkowski's "Spanisches Lied," from *Die schönste Frau*.

Fig. 8. Secondary theme of the "Spanisches Lied."

Notes

 Much of the material here includes research originally conducted for the Thomashefsky Project (San Francisco). The author wishes to express thanks to them, and in particular to its president, Michael Tilson Thomas, and its executive director, Linda S. Steinberg, for permission to use that material here. A grandson of eminent Yiddish theatrical figures Boris and Bessie Thomashefsky, Tilson Thomas (b. 1944) has been music director of the San Francisco Symphony since 1995. With Steinberg, he founded the Thomashefsky Project in 1997 to celebrate his grandparents' legacy by locating, translating, or otherwise reconstructing Thomashefsky-related materials. The research could also not have been done without the generous cooperation and assistance of Chana Mlotek and her fellow archivists at the YIVO Institute for Jewish Research, and Michael Terry and his colleagues at the Dorot Jewish Division of the New York Public Library. An appointment as visiting scholar at the Department of Music, University of California, San Diego further provided access to essential resources at the Geisel Library, whose staff was unfailingly helpful. Lastly, the author is very much indebted to Joel Berkowitz and Barbara Henry, who, as editors, colleagues, and friends, encouraged the continued development of this study and offered so many insightful suggestions, large and small.

1. Boris Thomashefsky, *Mayn lebens-geshikhte* [My life story] (New York: Trio Press, 1937), 280–284. See also, for example, Nahma Sandrow, *Vagabond Stars: A World History of Yiddish Theater* (New York: Harper & Row, 1977), 112–113. This study will frequently draw on Thomashefsky's memoir for the when, where, and who of a crucially formative period in which he was a witness and often central participant. The reader is cautioned that Thomashefsky's reporting is often clouded by exaggerated and self-aggrandizing claims of his role in events.

2. Display advertisement for the Thalia Theatre, *Di arbeter tsaytung* [The worker's paper] (New York), December 23, 1892. It played the evenings of Friday, Saturday, and the following Monday (so-called blue laws prohibited Sunday performances at that time). See also theatrical ads in *Di arbeter tsaytung*, May 19, 1893, and September 1, 1893.

3. Boris Thomashefsky, *Mayn lebens-geshikhte*, 281–283.

4. Bessie Thomashefsky, *Mayn lebens geshikhte: di laydn un freydn fun a yidisher star aktrise* [My life story: The passions and joys of a Yiddish star actress], as told to A. [Elihu] Tenenholtz (New York: Warheit Publishing Co., 1916), 209.

5. Bessie Thomashefsky, *Mayn lebens geshikhte*, 211. Quoted in Zalmen Zylbercweig, *Leksikon fun yidishn teater* [Encyclopedia of the Yiddish theatre], 6 vols. (Warsaw: Farlag Elisheva, 1934), 2:813, 2:976.

6. Abraham Cahan, *Bleter fun mayn leben* [Pages from my life], vol. 2, *Mayne ershte akht yor in amerike* [My first eight years in America] (New York: Forverts Association, 1926), 396. Cahan's report sounds authoritative, but not only was he was writing some thirty years after the fact, he also acknowledged that he had never actually seen Thomashefsky as Aleksander—or in *any other role* in that early period of the latter's career, when his were the "handsomest pair of legs on the Yiddish stage," as Cahan was given to understand. "The East Side was filled with accounts of [Thomashefsky] and his success."

7. Joseph Lateiner (Yozef Latayner), *Aleksander, der kroynprints fun yerusholayim: historishe oper in 4 aktn*, n.d., ms. 210, Thomashefsky Collection, New York Public Library (NYPL); this promptboook had been used in productions since at least 1899. The plot and action of *Aleksander* are described in Sandrow, *Vagabond Stars*, 112–113. The most detailed plot synopsis appears in a long, humorous, but essentially accurate account in Bessie Thomashefsky, *Mayn lebens geshikhte*, 209–211. Her synopsis is quoted at length in Zylbercweig, *Leksikon*, 2:975. A vivid and valuable description of Boris Thomashefsky's style and presence in *Aleksander* appears in Lulla Rosenfeld, *Bright Star of Exile: Jacob Adler and the Yiddish Theatre* (New York: Thomas Y. Crowell Co., 1977), 273–274; but in her account of the rivalry between theatres at the time, Rosenfeld's chronology becomes scrambled, and *Aleksander* is mistakenly attributed to Hurvitz, i.e., "Professor" Moyshe Hurwitz (1844–1910), in the book's index (362). Though some of Rosenfeld's information may have come from old memories and family sources—she was a granddaughter of Jacob Adler—she appears to rely in large measure on Boris Thomashefsky, *Mayn lebens-geshikhte*, 280–284, 323–328; and Cahan, *Bleter fun mayn leben*, 2:395–396.

8. The phrase was added as a gloss by the translators of Max Weinreich, *History of the Yiddish Language*, trans. Shlomo Noble with the assistance of Joshua A. Fishman (Chicago: University of Chicago Press, 1980), 418; repr. in exp. ed. with Weinreich's extensive notes, 2 vols., ed. Paul Glasser (New Haven, CT: Yale University Press in cooperation with the YIVO Institute for Jewish Research, 2008), 2:418. *Daytshmerish* is "Eastern Yiddish remodeled on the lexical, morphological, and syntactic patterns of New High German." Dov-Ber Kerler, *The Origins of Modern Literary Yiddish* (Oxford: Clarendon Press; New York: Oxford University Press, 1999), 257.

9. *Aleksander*'s author, Joseph Lateiner, began as prompter and aspiring scriptwriter, alternately assisting and competing with Goldfaden from the earliest days in Jassy, Rumania, and in Odessa. He is considered the first professional prompter in Yiddish theatre; see Sholem Perlmuter, *Yidishe*

dramaturgn un teater-kompozitors [Yiddish playwrights and theatre composers], (New York: YKUF Farlag [Yiddisher Kultur Farband Farlag], 1952), 61–62. In New York from 1884 (Zylbercweig, *Leksikon*, 2:967), he earned the distinction of becoming the first professional Yiddish playwright in America; Zalman Reyzen, *Leksikon fun der yidisher literatur, prese un filologye*, 2nd ed., 4 vols. (Vilna: B. Kletskin, 1926–29), 2:50. Through the late 1880s and much of the 1890s, his assembly-line pastiches, often drawn from non-Jewish sources, remained in furious competition with those of "Professor" Hurwitz. The fruits of that rivalry more or less defined the mass-appeal Yiddish theatre that critics have ever since derided as *shund* (trash). "In a play by Lateiner, the clown always goes hand-in-hand with the prince, the way his serious drama is coupled with belabored, out-of-place humor ... so strange to us are the language, the sensations, the manner of speaking, the customs, the behavior of the people ... A king and a shepherd stand at the same rung, master and slave eat from the same dish. There is no night anywhere, no morning, no past, no future—everything is mixed up together, devil-may-care, and yet, Lateiner's audiences feel thoroughly at home in just this atmosphere." Perlmuter, *Yidishe dramaturgn un teater-kompozitors*, 64–65.

10. Notable exceptions are the considerable literature on Avrom Goldfaden (1840–1908), as well as a smaller but still significant literature on composer Joseph Rumshinsky (1881–1956), both too extensive to catalogue here. Several archives hold valuable collections of music manuscripts from the Yiddish theatre, but those at YIVO Institute, along with their finding aids, prepared by Chana Mlotek, provide the single most important set of resources for future research. Anecdotal portraits of some two dozen theatre composers appeared in Perlmuter, *Yidishe dramaturgn un teater-kompozitors*, 315–388. There is an implicit challenge in the remarks of Nachman Mayzel (1887–1966), literary historian and former editor of the prestigious Warsaw *Literarishe bleter* (Literary pages): "Alas, [from Goldfaden's first theatre in 1876] up to the present, no complete and exhaustive history has been written of Yiddish theatre in all its migrations, and we certainly have no broadly inclusive treatment of the role, of the significance, and of the origins of music in Yiddish theatre throughout the world." Nachman Mayzel, *Yidishe tematik, yidishe melodyes bay bavuste muziker: notitsn un materyaln* [Jewish subjects, Jewish melodies by well-known musicians: Notes and materials] (New York: YKUF Farlag, 1952), 62. A response to Mayzel's challenge finally appeared in Sandrow's *Vagabond Stars*, that "Music was an integral element in Goldfaden's theater and was to remain essential in the majority of Yiddish plays." Sandrow offers a short but penetrating discussion of what made it integral (63–66). Sandrow's remark opens Mark Slobin, "The Music of the Yiddish Theater: Manuscript Sources at YIVO," *YIVO Annual of Jewish Social Science* 18 (1983), 372–390, his groundbreaking inventory of an essential archival collection. The same author's *Tenement Songs: The Popular Music of the Jewish Immigrants* (Urbana: University of Illinois Press, 1982) is an indispensable volume, but it focuses on published sheet music rather than on manuscript sources drawn from actual theatre use. His *Yiddish Theater in America: David's Violin (1897) and Shloyme Gorgl (189–)*, ed. Mark Slobin, libretti by Joseph Lateiner, Nineteenth-Century American Musical Theater 11 (New York: Garland Publishing, 1994), likewise of inestimable importance, briefly discusses some manuscript sources and their difficulties (p. xv), but again relies on sheet music, this time to test strategies for reconstruction. Sheet music is also the subject of Irene Heskes's magnum opus, *Yiddish American Popular Songs 1895–1950: A Catalog Based on the Lawrence Marwick Roster of Copyright Entries* (Washington, DC: Library of Congress, 1992); the same can be said of her useful overview, "Music as Social History: American Yiddish Theater Music, 1882–1920," *American Music* 2, no. 4, Music of the American Theater (Winter, 1984): 73–87. For a concise but essential metahistory that surveys the literature and reframes the discussion by focusing upon the gap between the overwhelmingly musical Yiddish stage and its subsequent text-centered historiography, see Nina Warnke, "Yiddish Theater History, Its Composers and Operettas: A Narrative without Music," *Muzykalia* VII, Judaica 2 (2009), www.demusica.pl/cmsimple/images/file/warnke_muzykalia_7_judaica2.pdf; links to the complete contents

of *Muzykalia* VII, Judaica 2 (2009), including front and back matter, last modified 17 September 2011, may be viewed at http://www.demusica.pl/?Pismo_Muzykalia:Muzykalia_VII%2FJudaica_2.

11. Joel Berkowitz, *Shakespeare on the American Yiddish Stage* (Iowa City: University of Iowa Press, 2002), 39. As the Thalia Theatre ads demonstrate, *Aleksander* was not yet in production when *Der yidisher kenig Lir* opened, *pace* Ruth Gay and Sophie Glazer, "Jacob Gordin's Life," in Jacob Gordin, *The Jewish King Lear: A Comedy in America*, trans. Ruth Gay, with notes and essays by Ruth Gay and Sophie Glazer (New Haven, CT: Yale University Press, 2007), 117.

12. Bessie Thomashefsky, *Mayn lebens geshikhte*, 210–211. The satirized *daytshmerish* passage is elided from her synopsis quoted in Zylbercweig, *Leksikon*, 2:975.

13. Lateiner, *Aleksander*, ms. 210, NYPL, p. 70. Unless otherwise indicated, all translations are my own. But I must also acknowledge the skillful translation of the complete manuscript that Kalman Weiser made for the Thomashefsky Project, most resourcefully deciphering so much of the linguistic play and idiosyncratic cursive script.

14. Jos. Brody [sic], *Alexander: Direction*, score, 1910, ms. 721, Thomashefsky Collection, NYPL. Not cataloged by NYPL as of this writing. Though it has been microfilmed (master negative *ZZ-37360-10), there is no service copy. The Thomashefsky Project's survey of the NYPL Thomashefsky Collection originally identified this as musical ms. 327 in Ronald Robboy, "Musical Scores, Parts, and Sheet Music in the Thomashefsky Collection of the New York Public Library: A Preliminary Inventory: Alphabetical Index by Operetta" (working paper, The Thomashefsky Project, San Francisco, 1998).

15. Joseph Lateiner, *Aleksander: operete in 4 akten*, n.d., music by Minkovski [Minkowski], ms. 228, Thomashefsky Collection, NYPL.

16. Boris Thomashefsky, *Mayn lebens-geshikhte*, 280–281. Parentheses around Yankele are in the original. The name Giacomo, however, is somewhat mutilated in the Yiddish, appearing as Dzhakomi.

17. Advertisement for the Thalia Theatre, *Di arbeter tsaytung*, December 23, 1892. Even before *Aleksander* opened, the company appears to have understood that it was going to be something out of the ordinary. The first notice that the work was in preparation appeared nearly two months in advance of the opening; advertisement for the Thalia Theatre, *Di arbeter tsaytung*, November 4, 1892.

18. Finkel was also the author of a pamphlet, "Rules and Regulations for the Stage / Teater un bine regulament" (New York, 1886; in Yiddish), the first attempt to codify professional behavior for Yiddish actors, chorus members, prompters, and others who appeared on stage. See Sholem Perlmuter, "Der ershter statut farn yidishn teater in amerike un zayn farfaser Moyshe Finkel" [The first by-laws for the Yiddish theatre in America and its author, Moyshe Finkel], in Yankev Shatski, ed., *Arkhiv far der geshikhte fun yidishn teater un drame* [Archive for the history of Yiddish theatre and drama] (Vilna: YIVO, 1930), 422. The pamphlet is reprinted in its entirety, 423–430.

19. Advertisement for the Thalia Theatre, *Di arbeter tsaytung*, March 31, 1893.

20. The ad does boast that there will be "brilliant stage effects" (*brilyante oysshtatung*), which were Finkel's forte, but in place of Finkel's name we read that "various new ballet dances are arranged by the artist Bernard Bernshteyn."

21. Bessie Thomashefsky, *Mayn lebens geshikhte*, 221. Her appraisal is also summarized in Zylbercweig, *Leksikon*, 2:976.

22. Writing many years after the fact, the actor Boaz Young reported that the leader of the "insurrection" was the erudite comedic actor Rudolph Marks (1867–1930), who soon thereafter left the stage to pursue a career as an attorney. Boaz Young, *Mayn lebn in teater* [My life in the theatre] (New York: YKUF, 1950), 128.

23. Zylbercweig, *Leksikon*, 2:971, 3:2151.

24. Zylbercweig, *Leksikon*, 2:976.

25. Ibid., 2:1191

26. As it happened, *Khurbn yerhusholayim* was running in repertoire at the Romanian Opera House, the Thalia's competitor, during the initial weeks of *Aleksander*'s success (theatrical ad in *Di arbeter tsaytung*, February 24, 1893). This would have made it among the last productions at that legendary house, as the next month Mogulesco and others took their company, and Yiddish theatre, to the immense Windsor Theatre for the first time (paid announcement in *Di arbeter tsaytung*, March 17, 1893). Having his music playing concurrently by the two dominant companies would have been quite a feather in the young composer's cap.

27. Zylbercweig, *Leksikon*, 2:976. *Cavalleria Rusticana*, by Pietro Mascagni (1863–1945), and *Lakmé*, by Léo Delibes (1836–1891), both had their first Metropolitan Opera performances, running roughly concurrently, through the first three months of 1892; Key Word Search ("cavalleria rusticana"), MetOpera Database, Metropolitan Opera, last modified December 7, 2010, http://archives.metoperafamily.org/archives/frame.htm.

28. Among the many political, cultural, and educational titles published by Philip Krantz, the journalist who had identified other operas in the work of Minkowski (see above), is a monograph: *Meyerbeer: der opera kenig: zayn leben, zayne operen un muzikalishe oyftuungen* [Meyerbeer, the opera king: His life, his operas and musical achievements] (New York: Di internatsyonale bibliotek farlag, 1907).

29. Giacomo Minkowski, *Die schönste Frau* (*Operette* in three acts), libretto by Rudolph Lothar, with the use of some older material (*mit Benutzung eines alteren Stoffes*) (Berlin: Schlesinger'schen Buch- und Musikhandlung, 1910).

30. Brody [sic], *Alexander: Direction.*

31. [Giacomo Minkowski], *Aleksander oder Der kroynprints fun yerusholayim*, score and parts [ca. 1910], arr. Yitskhok Shlosberg, RG 7, folder 312, Vilna Music Collection, YIVO Institute, New York. Composer not identified.

32. [Giacomo Minkowski], *Aleksander oder Der kroynprints fun yerusholayim*, score and parts, 1912, arr. Yitskhok Shlosberg, RG 7, folder 9. Composer not identified.

33. [Giacomo Minkowski], *Aleksander oder Der kroynprints fun yerusholayim*, score (*"Directionstimme"*), 1912, arr. Yitskhok Shlosberg, copied by J. Losinski, RG 7,folder 9.1. Composer not identified.

34. Joseph Rumshinsky, "Yitskhok Shlosberg," in M[endel] Osherovitsh et al., eds., *Dos Rumshinski bukh: aroysgegebn lekoved zayn 50tn geburtstog* [The Rumshinsky book: Published in honor of his 50th birthday] (New York: 1931), 76 (emphases in the original). Slobin has similarly praised Shlosberg's "meticulously copied" work (*Tenement Songs*, 93).

35. Orchestra parts, *Alexander*, 1910, RG 289 / folder 35, Sholem Perlmutter Music Collection, YIVO Institute. At the conclusion of the first violin part, the copyist wrote "*Fine* Dec. 11 1910." The ex-Brody score at NYPL is marked "*Fine de la oper.* / Dec. 2nd 1910."

36. "Drums," from *Alexander Der Kronprinc fon Jerusalem*, orchestra part [ca. 1895], Thomashefsky Collection, NYPL. Not yet cataloged, but numbered as ms. 335 in Robboy, "Musical Scores," where the complete set comprises mss. 328–330, 333–338.

37. Peter Laurence Gordon, the copyist, also used these reconstructed scores as templates for orchestrations of other numbers he made for the Thomashefsky Project where no parts, or incomplete parts, were available.

38. Giacomo Minkowski, "Vi gefloygn kum ikh vider," from *Aleksander, oder der kroynprints fun yerusholayim*, sketch by R[onald] Robboy (working paper, The Thomashefsky Project, San Francisco, 2004).

39. *The Thomashefskys: Music and Memories of a Life in the Yiddish Theater*, [written and] hosted by Michael Tilson Thomas, produced by The Thomashefsky Project, directed by Patricia Birch, presented by Carnegie Hall, Zankel Hall at Carnegie Hall, New York City, April 16 and 17, 2005. Tilson Thomas has since performed it with major symphony orchestras across the United States.

40. Lateiner, *Aleksander*, ms. 228, Thomashefsky Collection, NYPL; in Boris Thomashefsky's hand, the original cast is listed among the dramatis personae. Corroborated in Bessie Thomashefsky, *Mayn lebens geshikhte*, 211.

41. Bessie Thomashefsky, *Mayn lebens geshikhte*, 132.

42. It was not so long after *Aleksander* that in an 1896 operetta by "Professor" Hurwitz, Sophie Karp introduced the immensely successful song *"Eli, Eli"* ("Eyli, eyli, lomo azavtoni" [My God, my God, why hast Thou forsaken me]), written by Hurwitz's chorus master, Yankev-Kopl Sendler (Jacob Koppel Sandler [ca. 1856–1931]). Though the song achieved quasi-liturgical, quasi-folk status nearly overnight, Karp herself was no longer alive by the time its origin became the subject of a closely followed lawsuit. Boris Thomashefsky, *"Di geshikhte fun 'eyli-eyli,'"* in Zalmen Zylbercweig ed., *Hintern forhang* [Behind the curtain] (Vilna: Kletskin, 1929), 29–30. See also, for example, "'Eili, Eili' Sandler's, Old Actors Testify," *New York Times*, April 30, 1925; this article, however, erroneously identified Sophie Karp as having still been singing the song as late as 1919.

43. Boris Thomashefsky, *Mayn lebens-geshikhte*, 29ff. Composer Joseph Rumshinsky, who also regarded Thomashefsky as a fine musician (*groyser menagn*), even a distinguished one (*menagn godl*), likewise recognized the importance of his early training with Nisn Belzer; Joseph Rumshinsky, *Klangen fun mayn lebn* [Sounds from my life] (New York: A. Y. Biderman, 1944), 477, 497.

44. Boris Thomashefsky, *Mayn lebens-geshikhte*, 8–27.

45. Boris Thomashefsky, *Mayn lebens-geshikhte*, 69–75. See also Boris Thomashefsky, "Der onfang fun yidishn teater in nyu york" [The beginning of Yiddish theatre in New York], in *Tomashevskis teater shriftn* [Thomashefsky's theatre writings] (New York: Lipshits Pres, 1908), 6–8.

46. Barbara Henry kindly brought these to my attention, and all following references to such documents are thanks to the facsimile images she generously provided me.

47. Department of Commerce–U.S. Bureau of the Census, "Fourteenth Census of the United States: 1920—Population," Supervisor's District 4, Enumeration District 204, Sheet No. 8189, State of California, County of San Francisco, Assembly District 32, Precinct 57, City of San Francisco, Ward 1, January 16, 1920, p. 21A, lines 13–14, Records of the Bureau of the Census, Record Group 29, microfilm roll T625_138, National Archives, Washington, DC, accessed at *1920 United States Federal Census*, Ancestry.com, http://search.ancestry.com/cgi-bin/sse.dll?h=95365046&db=1920usfedcen&indiv=try.

48. "Giacomo Minkowski: Composer, Music Teacher and Former Critic Dies at 69," *New York Times*, May 6, 1941. Comparing his age at the time of death given here, in May, with his age at other times of the year in other documents, it appears that he was born in June, 1871. At this writing, the Name Authority File of Library of Congress records published birth dates of 1871, 1872, and June 3, 1873, and officially recognizes a heading for "Minkowski, Giacomo, 1873–1941."

49. "Twelfth Census of the United States [1900]: Schedule No. 1—Population," Supervisor's District 1, Enumeration District 774, Sheet No. 12, State of New York, County of New York, Borough of Manhattan, New York City, Carnegie Music Hall [West 57th Street], June 14, 1900, United States Bureau of the Census, *Twelfth Census of the United States, 1900* (Washington, DC: National Archives and Records Administration, 1900), microfilm roll T623_1115, p. 12A, lines 7–8, accessed at *1900 United States Federal Census*, Ancestry.com, http://search.ancestry.com/cgi-bin/sse.dll?h=49273318&db=1900usfedcen&indiv=try.

50. Naturalized *April* 9, 1892, according to "List of Unites States Citizens," United States Department of Labor, Immigration Service passenger manifest of the *S.S. Andania* sailing from Cherbourg, August 1, 1924, and arriving at the port of Québec, August 9, 1924, sheet 3, line 1, National Archives and Records Administration, Washington, DC, *Manifests of Passengers Arriving at St. Albans, VT, District through Canadian Pacific and Atlantic Ports, 1895–1954*, Record Group 85, Records of the Immigration and Naturalization Service, microfilm serial M1464, roll 510, accessed at *Border Crossings: From Canada to U.S., 1895–1956*, Ancestry.com, provided in asscociation with the

National Archives, http://search.ancestry.com/cgi-bin/sse.dll?h=1399097&db=CanadianBC&indiv=try. But naturalized *June* 9, 1892, according to "List of United States Citizens," passenger manifest of the *S.S. Paris* sailing from La Havre, January 8, 1927, and arriving at the port of New York, January 12, 1927, line 29, *Passenger and Crew Lists of Vessels Arriving at New York, New York, 1897–1957*, National Archives Microfilm Publication T715, Records of the Immigration and Naturalization Service, National Archives, Washington, DC, microfilm serial T715, roll T715_3991, p. 157, line 29, accessed at New York Passenger Lists, 1820–1957, Ancestry.com, http://search.ancestry.com/cgi-bin/sse.dll?h=2003277321&db=nypl&indiv=try. *Postscript:* As we go to press, a German passenger manifest of 1888 has come to light listing a Jacob Minkowski, age 17, bound for Philadelphia from Hamburg via Liverpool aboard the *Kaffaria*; "Verzeichniss: der Personen, welche zur Auswanderung nach Nordamerika via Liverpool," Staatsarchive Hamburg, [inventory no.] 373-71, VIII B 1, Band 073, p. 598, line 1, (microfilm no. S_13153), accessed at Hamburg Passenger Lists, 1850–1934, Ancestry.com, with permission of the Staatsarchiv Hamburg, http://search.ancestry.com/cgi-bin/sse.dll?h=3121359&db=HamburgPL_full&indiv=try. The manifest states he was a resident of Belaya Tserkov (now Bila Tserkva, Ukraine). Anyone arriving in the United States in 1888 would not yet have been eligible for naturalization in 1892, which may have been why on subsequent documents he always declared he had arrived at least a year earlier. In another document recently made available, Jacob Minkowsky, also known as J. Giacomo Minkowsky, states that his father was named Mordecai; passport application for naturalized citizen, stamped by the Bureau of Citizenship, Department State, June 11, 1913, *Passport Applications, January 2, 1906–March 31, 1925,* NARA Microfilm Publication M1490, ARC Identifier 583830 / MLR Number A1 534, series M1490, roll 192, application no. 12593, National Archives and Records Administration, Washington, DC, accessed at *U.S. Passport Applications, 1795–1925*, Ancestry.com, provided in association with the National Archives, http://search.ancestry.com/cgi-bin/sse.dll?h=407541&db=USpassports&indiv=try. The father of Cantor Pinchas Minkowsky, who was likewise a cantor, was also named Mordecai. Cantor Mordecai (Motl Godis) Minkowsky (b.1840) and his more famous son were both from Belaya Tserkov.

51. Customs Form, List of Passengers, District of the City of New York, Port of New York, passengers originally embarked at San Francisco and sailing aboard the *S.S. Colombia* from Colón, Republic of Colombia, July 4, 1892, and arriving at New York, July 11, 1892, *Passenger Lists of Vessels Arriving at New York, New York, 1820–1897*, National Archives Microfilm Publication M237, Records of the U.S. Customs Service, Record Group 36, National Archives, Washington, DC, microfilm serial M237, roll M237_592, [p.1 (of 2)], line 2, accessed at *New York Passenger Lists, 1820–1957*, Ancestry.com, http://search.ancestry.com/cgi-bin/sse.dll?h=4036709235&db=nypl&indiv=try.

52. "Giacomo Minkowski," *New York Times*, May 6, 1941. The obituary incorrectly reports that he came to New York in 1898. (See n53, below.)

53. As this chapter goes to press, a passenger manifest has come to light listing a Jacob Minkowski, age 27, "citizen of the United States of America," returning from Italy in 1898; "List or Manifest of Alien Immigrants for the Commissioner of Immigration," List No. B(2), p. 14, line 20, *S.S. Salle*, sailing from Genoa, March 31, 1898, arriving at the Port of New York, April 12, 1898; Records of the Immigration and Naturalization Service (microfilm serial15, roll T715_18), National Archives, Washington, DC, http://search.ancestry.com/cgi-bin/sse.dll?h=4037206688&db=nypl&indiv=try.

54. Zylbercweig, *Leksikon*, 2:971.

55. Zylbercweig, *Leksikon*, 2:1191. This work was co-written by Mogulesco, which may have meant that Mogulesco adapted or reclaimed older music of Minkovksi.

56. Interestingly, Yitskhok Shlosberg, whose set of parts to *Aleksander* are so essential for reconstruction, made his own debut as a Yiddish theatre conductor (with Fishzon's troupe) in *Khurbn yersholayim,* "*muzik fun Minkovski*." Zylbercweig, *Leksikon*, 3:2151.

57. J. Minkowsky, "New Oriental Waltzes," score, (San Francisco: Broder & Schlam, 1891), in the Rudolph Collection, Paramount Theatre Music Library, Oakland, CA, accessed at the California

Sheet Music Project, Museum Informatics Project, University of California, Berkeley, http://www.mip.berkeley.edu/cgi-bin/csmp?001854.

58. "A Hitherto Hidden Genius," *New York Times*, November 19, 1899.

59. Giack [sic] Minkowski, *The Smugglers of Badayez: A Comic Opera in Three Acts*, libretto by Frederic Ranken (New York and London: Edward Schuberth & Co., 1899).

60. "A Hitherto Hidden Genius," *New York Times*. See also "Musical Matters at Home," *New York Times*, October 15, 1899, and October 29, 1899.

61. "Victor Herbert's New Opera: Putting the Finishing Touches on 'The Viceroy,'" *New York Times*, September 29, 1899.

62. Musical Matter at Home, *New York Times*, October 15, 1899.

63. Victor Herbert, *The Ameer* (comic opera in three acts), book by Frederic Ranken and Kirke La Shelle, (New York: Witmark, 1899). Herbert, who had been principal cellist of the Metropolitan Opera and then the conductor of the Pittsburgh Symphony, had not yet achieved the fame he was soon to gain with *Babes in Toyland* (1903), after which he turned to full-time composing; but he was already an important presence in American musical life.

64. "A Hitherto Hidden Genius," *New York Times*, November 19, 1899; "Comic Opera at the Grand," in "Another Musical Show for Broadway's Summer Season," *New York Times*, June 14, 1903.

65. The composer is identified as Miakovsky [sic]. "Opera Performances: Operas, Operettas, Concerts and Selected Musicals Performed in Denver: 1864–1900," Opera in Old Colorado, created and maintained by Charles L. Ralph, revised site accessed October 26, 2011, http://www.operaoldcolo.info/performances.pt1.html.

66. Curtis Dunham, *The 'Broidered Belt: A Comic Opera in Three Acts*, music by Giacomo Minkowsky [sic], promptbook, copyright 1901, Tams-Witmark/Wisconsin Collection, Mills Music Library, University of Wisconsin-Madison (described on WorldCat, Online Computer Library Center [OCLC], accessed May 2, 2006).

67. *The Scroll* 27, no. 1 (October, 1902): 114; in *The Scroll of Phi Delta Theta 27 (October, 1902–June,1903)*, ed. and managed by Hugh Th. Miller and Royall H. Switzler (Indianapolis: Phi Delta Theta Fraternity, 1903), books.google.com/books?id=sAQTAAAAIAAJ. General Funston had been a member of the fraternity.

68. The synopsis makes clear that the opera's hero, Lancelot, is a stand-in for Funston, whose capture of the Filipino leader Emilio Aguinaldo (1869–1964) by feigning surrender, and whose vocal advocacy of the most brutal means of suppression, had admirers and critics. He was also known for his intemperate, and even shocking, attacks upon domestic critics of American expansionism. The synopsis describes Lancelot's conflicts with his superiors and their commitment to "benevolent assimilation," which the operetta treats with great scorn and derision. A caustic appraisal of Funston appeared in Mark Twain, "A Defence of General Funston," North American Review 174 (May, 1902), http://www.jstor.org/stable/25119240. Funston was commander of the Presidio in San Francisco when the great earthquake struck in 1906, and his de facto declaration of martial law in the city also had its critics and admirers.

69. Attributed to the New York *Journal*, n.d., in *The Scroll* 27:114.

70. Giacomo Minkowsky, "Verdi and His Successors," *Munsey's Magazine*, March 1901, 852–855.

71. Michael Scott, "Raoul Gunsbourg and the Monte Carlo Opera," *Opera Quarterly* 3:4 (1985), 72, http://oq.oxfordjournals.org/cgi/reprint/3/4/70.

72. Giacomo Minkowsky, "Character Revealed in the Color of the Voice," *The Metropolitan Magazine*, November 1901, as listed in The Magazines, *New York Times*, October 26, 1901; Giacomo Minkowsky, "How the Ancient Feud between the Italian School and the German School Has Ended in a Union of Methods on a Wagnerian Foundation," *Munsey's Magazine*, [month?] 1903, transcribed

without further documentation at Mascagni.org, modified June 22, 2003, http://www.mascagni.org/articles/minkowsky-1903-munseys, and high-resolution images of the original article (4 pp.) may be downloaded at http://www.mascagni.org/book-reader/image/506087/1/300, http://www.mascagni.org/book-reader/image/506087/3/300, and http://www.mascagni.org/book-reader/image/506087/4/300.

73. "The Rush to Europe: Outgoing Liners Show Increased Passenger Traffic—The Homecomers," *New York Times*, May 23, 1908.

74. "'Die Schoenste Frau' Liked: Minkowski's New Operetta Produced In Berlin Clean and Melodious." *New York Times*, September 17, 1910.

75. "Umschau: Neue Opern," in *Die Musik* 1, No. 17 (I. June, 1902): 1606; in *Die Musik: Erster Jahrgang: Drittes Quartal* (Berlin and Leipzig: Schuster & Loeffler, 1902), http://books.google.com/books?id=WeAaAQAAMAAJ.

76. "Giacomo Minkowski," *New York Times*, May 6, 1941.

77. U.S. Department of Labor, Immigration Service, "List of Unites States Citizens," passengers aboard the *S.S. Washington* sailing from Lisbon, June 10, 1940, to the port of New York, June 21, 1940, *Passenger and Crew Lists of Vessels Arriving at New York, New York, 1897–1957*, National Archives Microfilm Publication T715, Records of the Immigration and Naturalization Service, National Archives, Washington, DC, microfilm serial T715, roll T715_6476, p. 37, lines 17–18, accessed at New York Passenger Lists, 1820–1957, Ancestry.com, http://search.ancestry.com/cgi-bin/sse.dll?h=1006870729&db=nypl&indiv=try.

78. "Giacomo Minkowski," *New York Times*, May 6, 1941.

79. Minkowsky, "New Oriental Waltzes," 3.

80. Minkowski, "Spanisches Lied," in *Die schönste Frau*, 32–35.

CHAPTER 11

Sex and Scandal in the *Encyclopedia of the Yiddish Theatre*

Faith Jones

The *Leksikon fun yidishn teater* (Encyclopedia of the Yiddish theatre) is the single most important reference work in its field. To date, no other work in any language comes close to providing its comprehensiveness of coverage or leads for further research on Yiddish theatre and its personalities. The work of primarily one person over the course of a half-century, the *Leksikon* plays a central role in enabling the study of Yiddish theatre. However, a dramatic controversy that played out during the first years of the work's production also illuminates the role that gender ideology played in the creation of Yiddish culture, and in the representation of Jews generally and of Jewish women in particular. In essence, a struggle was played out to ensure that women's biographies in the *Leksikon* would meet standards of decorum and respectability that were considered necessary for Jewish advancement in mainstream American society.

While much has been written about the particular pressures brought to bear on women to provide the respectable face of a culture or community, little of this theoretical material has been applied to the internal workings of Yiddish culture. In attempting to elucidate this idea, I look sideways to other events in Jewish culture, just before or around the same era as the *Leksikon* debate occurred, which show similar struggles enacted around women and questions of respectability. I find throughout these events that women were viewed through a mainstream, rather Christian lens, as innocent and in need of protection, yet particularly susceptible to moral lapses. Jews saw themselves as engaged in a battle against anti-Semitic beliefs, yet their efforts focused on internal regulation of Jewish behavior, tacitly endorsing rather than disputing those beliefs. In attempting to put aside this framework for discussing women and their presumed tendency to vice, I take a fresh look at a woman whose virtue was called into question in the initial draft of her

Zalmen Zylbercweig, editor of the *Leksikon fun yidishn teater* (Encyclopedia of the Yiddish theatre), reproduced by kind permission of Shirley I. Fair.

biography, and through this, attempt a historical assessment based on available evidence—taking an approach that the parties to the dispute could not.

The *Leksikon* Project[1]

In 1918, a young man named Zalmen Zylbercweig began collecting materials for a multi-volume *Pinkes fun yidishn teater* (Register of the Yiddish theatre), of which one volume would comprise a biographical dictionary, or *leksikon*, of Yiddish theatre personalities. Zylbercweig, a Polish Jew in his early twenties, had worked briefly as an actor, then as a translator of one-act plays from European languages to provide repertoire for theatre companies in Łódź, Poland. Eventually he earned his living as a journalist. Completely enamored of the theatre, but lacking talent as an actor, Zylbercweig saw his niche as a writer and chronicler of the Yiddish theatre, and set out to create a work that would allow the fleeting performance to leave a permanent record.

Very quickly the *pinkes* was put aside and Zylbercweig concentrated instead on the *leksikon*. While in New York in 1928, Zylbercweig got support for the project from the Hebrew Actors Union, which published a prospectus. This was a sixteen-page document mailed to newspapers and theatrical companies around the world who might be supportive of the *leksikon*.[2] The prospectus seems to have included a description of the book—then predicted to be a two-volume work—along with encomiums, endorsements from prominent theatre people, and a half-dozen sample entries. Zylbercweig also got backing from the Hebrew Actors Union to mail out a questionnaire to members, who were supposed to answer the questions and mail them back. These were to form the basis of their entries. The Union also began selling subscriptions to the book, just as for centuries writers of Hebrew *sforim* (religious books) had *pre-numerantn*, subscribers who paid for the book in advance, the income from which gave the writer the cash flow to produce the book.[3] With only this shaky financial footing, Zylbercweig set off on the path to produce the book. Eventually reaching six published volumes (a seventh was prepared but never published due to Zylbercweig's death), the *Leksikon* cost much more money and more years than Zylbercweig predicted. The entire project could easily have been halted before it even began by an uproar that ensued when he sent out that first prospectus.

The Scandal

In July 1928, the prospectus came under intense attack in the pages of an important Warsaw Yiddish journal, *Literarishe bleter* (Literary pages). This attack was a two-and-a-half-page, *ad hominem* screed by Jacob Shatzky (1893–1956), a historian of Jewish social and political movements, a literary critic, and an early historian of Yiddish theatre. *Literarishe bleter*—the premiere Yiddish cultural magazine of its time, serious of intent and with high standards—obviously saw a good fight emerging, and placed this article on the front page. First, Shatzky complains about the content of the biographies. Jacob Adler's, for example, includes various anecdotes about his Odessa forebears being important *maskilim* (intellectual adherents of the Jewish enlightenment). This, Shatzky says, is patently untrue.

The question arises: Sir, who is throwing sand in your eyes, or from whom do you allow it to be thrown? This is all *loy hoye veloy nivre* [complete nonsense]; rumors, made-up stories, simple lies.

> An editor has to have, in addition to forty one-act plays, a little intelligence, and must understand what it is to ask for an eyewitness account from an actor at all, much less a Yiddish actor.[4]

Shatzky continues this line of attack by mentioning various other points that, while not necessarily self-aggrandizing lies, are at least silly, meaningless details:

for example, he says, there is the story that the *Broder zinger* Israel Grodner was paid for his songs in tobacco. "Very important, don't you think?"[5]

The second complaint is about Zylbercweig's own skills. That Esther-Rokhl Kaminska is identified as having been born on Purim in 1870 is cause for Shatzky to sneer at an editor who can't be bothered to look up the date on which Purim fell in 1870. He goes further with stylistic complaints against Zylbercweig, such as material that is already of questionable value being repeated more than once. He says: "Reading the biographies that Zalmen Zylbercweig has laid out for us as samples, you can't escape the thought: maybe this isn't a dictionary but a parody of a dictionary? As a parody, it isn't bad."[6]

Finally, we get to the *pièce de resistance*, Shatzky's reaction to the sample entry on Keni Liptzin (1856–1918). Liptzin was a *grand dame* early on in Yiddish theatre and was long dead by the time the prospectus was circulated. Here is Shatzky's quote from that biography, and his reaction to it:

How she (that is, Miss Liptzin—JS) came to move from the countryside into the shtetl of Smile, in Kiev province, is not known; there is a theory that she married her father's coachman, and a bit (!) later ran away from him.

Regarding her employment in Smile there are various versions. Some say that she worked there as a seamstress; but certain actors report that her employment was of a completely different kind.

What exactly is this? What can one call this kind of writing? There is only one word for it: *vileness*.

Why is this even included? In the name of 'truth'? Let's see what kind of 'truth' Herr Editor Zylbercweig writes about the people on his committee.

[. . .] Everyone can do as he wishes, even translate fifty one-acters, if he's the only one responsible. But that is not the case here. The *Leksikon* is being advertised as a community undertaking. They are saving the Yiddish theatre from being forgotten. They are immortalizing the "*Leistungen*" [performances] of the Yiddish actors and actresses.

[. . .] Do they not see that this grandiose plan to create a biographical dictionary of Yiddish theatre has been undertaken by a person who, aside from ambition, possesses nothing: no qualifications at all, no knowledge, no method, no language, and no intelligence?[7]

Several points are notable here. First is that in the original article, which Shatzky quotes with such outrage, Zylbercweig displays a remarkably calm neutrality regarding Liptzin's possible prior career as a prostitute. He lays out both possibilities (seamstress vs. prostitute) and makes no moral judgment. It is not clear from Shatzky's account how this entry continued, because he does not quote further from it. Second, a lack of factual certainty is not the only reason for Shatzky's fury.

Keni Liptzin, photographed in an unidentified Gordin role. (From the archives of the YIVO Institute for Jewish Research, New York.)

Shatzky is not impressed with the inclusion of information about Israel Grodner's payment in tobacco. Both this and the Liptzin anecdote are provided in Zylbercweig's biographical entries without absolute proof, but with appropriately guarded language as to their historical basis. Shatzky's response to the tobacco story is dismissive, but his response to the Liptzin story is apoplectic. The difference in reaction must lie in the sexual nature of Liptzin's story.

Also of interest are Shatzky's own stylistic shortcomings. He tends to give negative opinions of literary inelegancies in ways that are themselves inelegant and even juvenile. In the first paragraph in the quotation above, where Shatzky is quoting Liptzin's biography as written by Zylbercweig, Shatzky adds an exclamation mark in parentheses to indicate that the use of the word "*shtikl*" (bit) is too informal or insufficiently precise. Later on, he quotes from a paragraph of the prospectus by putting the German word *Leistungen* in quotes (the Yiddish word for performances is *aroystretn*). In neither case does the interpolation flow seamlessly: his method is heavy-handed to the point of self-parody.[8]

The comment about forty one-act plays, later reprised as fifty one-act plays, is clearly aimed at Zylbercweig's early work generating repertoire for theatre companies. That these scripts were not of a high literary quality is certain. Nonetheless, many major figures worked extensively in lowbrow, formulaic, or derivative productions. Such activity was central to the economic viability of the Yiddish theatre. Highlighting Zylbercweig's work with this kind of repertoire is both snide and personalized.

And finally, Shatzky raises questions about the qualifications that should be necessary for a person editing such a dictionary. All the qualities he names are ones that, as he has implied throughout the article, Shatzky himself possesses. It is possible to infer an ulterior motive in this otherwise bewilderingly arrogant attack. It may also be that the editors of *Literarishe bleter* themselves discerned an unseemly egotism behind the article. In a note, the editors state that although they are publishing Shatzky's article with its strong criticisms, they do not believe in halting the *Leksikon* project, or in changing editorship; they only suggest that the editorial board attempt to improve the project, and continue with Zylbercweig as editor.

Zylbercweig immediately fought back against Shatzky's attack. In a reply just as long and just as hot-headed as Shatzky's article, Zylbercweig posits jealousy as the motivating force, as Shatzky had not been asked to join the *Leksikon*'s editorial board. Zylbercweig defends his facts, stating baldly that Liptzin almost certainly supported herself through prostitution as a young woman, and since she had left no children or close relatives to be hurt by a public disclosure, it was important to tell the truth. He even claims it shed light on her abilities as an artist to rise above her tainted past, particularly in her portrayal of genteel characters such as Mirele Efros. Zylbercweig provides additional details to rebut Shatzky's other criticisms, structuring his article as a numbered list of points: "6) Dr. Shatzky upbraids me for having written that Esther-Rokhl Kaminska was born on Purim 1870. I *purposely* mentioned Purim, because it is related to Miss Kaminska's name. She is called Esther because she was born on Purim."[9]

To this reply Shatzky rejoined with a short denial: "Zalmen Zylbercweig is very unhappy with my review of his work . . . and in order to weaken my criticisms, he uses the old method of personal attack."[10] Shatzky is apparently oblivious to his own transgressions in this regard. He goes on to claim he has no interest in working on the *Leksikon* and that everyone in the American theatre community was astonished that such a novice as Zylbercweig could possibly be taken seriously as the editor of such a publication. Shatzky even claims to have received several letters from actors and "the editor of a Yiddish newspaper in New York"[11] voicing their agreement with him. He then says the debate is at an end because he declines to discuss it further.[12]

This entire exchange—Shatzky's attack, Zylbercweig's hot-headed reply, and Shatzky's dismissive denial—originally published in *Literarishe bleter* in Warsaw, was picked up by the *Fraye arbeter shtime* (Free voice of labor) in New York, so that the dispute (as well as the scandal surrounding Liptzin) reached a very broad audience.

But in spite of Shatzky's unwillingness to debate the matter further, Zylbercweig had not finished. About a year later, Zylbercweig wrote a somewhat more restrained article in the *Fraye arbeter shtime* about the *Leksikon* and Shatzky's response. In this article he repeats Shatzky's attack on him—quoting at length from the offending article—but leaves out the very meat of the matter, what he had said about Liptzin that had so provoked Shatzky. Instead, Zylbercweig says that Shatzky was upset about certain things he had written about a certain person. "He knows the weakness of quite a few actors, and to a greater degree, actresses, who are always afraid that certain things shouldn't be published about them, things they do privately, even though private people nowadays do these things too."[13]

Zylbercweig gives many examples of biographies, mostly of non-Jews, in which negative attributes and actions are described. He defends his right to speak ill of the dead—the article is even called "Is Not Speaking Ill of the Dead a Custom or a Law?"—but he does not in this case exercise that right. This is the first inkling that Zylbercweig was being swayed by the criticisms leveled against him. Although it takes the form of a rebuttal, Zylbercweig in fact seems to have come to the conclusion that he must moderate socially-charged information such as that pertaining to sexual matters.

Finally, in 1931, the first volume of the *Leksikon* appeared. In the introduction to this volume, in addition to the usual thanks one might expect to find, he complains that he has "very often stumbled across a negative opinion on the part of certain Jewish actors and private people who make themselves out to be theatre lovers."[14]

While there were several kind reviews of volume one in the Yiddish press, Zylbercweig was probably surprised to find another attack awaiting him, this one from Alexander Mukdoyni (the nom de plume of Alexander Kappel, 1878–1958), a theatre historian and critic, in the *Morgn zhurnal* (Morning paper), a leading New York daily. Mukdoyni, like Shatzky, criticizes the *Leksikon* as being insufficiently scholarly, including too many dubious claims, and lacking sufficient bibliographies. Then he brings up the question of editorship: "Among us there are only two heads that could wear such a crown: there are only two among us, who are suitable to edit such a dictionary, and these are Dr. I. Shiper in Warsaw and Dr. J. Shatzky in New York."[15]

He adds that Zylbercweig has too close a relationship to the Hebrew Actors Union. The Union is not an academic body, he argues, and this close relationship will lead to abuses.

To this review Zylbercweig attempted a reply, but the *Morgn zhurnal* refused to publish it; it eventually ran in the Chicago literary monthly, *Shikage* (Chicago), a magazine with a much smaller circulation. Zylbercweig's reply is about half again as long as Mukdoyni's article, which was itself spread over many columns. Zylbercweig refutes each complaint of Mukdoyni's—that the women actors refuse to give correct birth dates, for example—in excruciating detail, in much the same manner as he had responded to Shatzky several years earlier.[16] However, he does not engage with the issue of his suitability as editor.

Three years later, in 1934, volume two, containing the ill-fated Keni Liptzin biography, was published, and here we see what became of Zylbercweig's interesting piece of news. Where the original biography in the prospectus had two paragraphs about the unhappy marriage from which she escaped and her entry into prostitution in Smile, in the published entry we see: "According to unconfirmed sources, Liptzin was forced into marriage with one of her father's employees, but after six months ran away and went to Smile where she worked as a seamstress."[17]

The gradual withdrawal from his original defense of full disclosure of painful or embarrassing details, which began with his guarded *Fraye arbeter shtime* article, here comes to completion.

But if Zylbercweig thought his troubles were at an end, he was mistaken. Mukdoyni pounced again with a review in the *Morgn zhurnal*. This time he is markedly less subtle. He begins by complaining about the biographies of minor actors and playwrights of mediocre talent, particularly saying there are far too many bibliographic details given. He again complains that Zylbercweig is entirely the wrong person to edit such a work. Then Mukdoyni goes on to complain that his major articles about certain actors were not included in the bibliographies at the end of the entries for those actors. He makes an extended attack on Jacob Mestel, Zylbercweig's assistant editor, for no apparent reason, claiming that Mestel doesn't know Yiddish and can't write a coherent sentence. Since, other than in the signed introductions, there is no indication of what material was written by Mestel, once more the dispute gives off a whiff of some past quarrel or hidden agenda. And finally, there is the issue of the entry on Mukdoyni himself. As a theatre critic, he was also included in the *Leksikon*. His only comment on this entry is that the *Leksikon* has gone out of its way to make sure the bibliography included several articles that accused him of plagiarism, in the course of a war between rival theatre groups. "I had meant to write a chapter about this in my memoirs [which he was then writing], but had forgotten about it completely. So the *Leksikon* deserves my thanks."[18]

Again the *Morgn zhurnal* refused to let Zylbercweig reply; this time he answered in the *Nyu-yorker vokhnblat* (New York weekly). By this time his replies were somewhat more tempered. The article was entitled "D"r Mukdoyni, meyk op yur maynd" (English written in Yiddish characters), and it was again rather long. In this article, Zylbercweig points out Mukdoyni's inconsistency and personal motives. If Mukdoyni is irritated at the inclusion of too many bibliographical details, Zylbercweig asks, why does he make an exception for his own articles?[19]

Mukdoyni's response could not have been more vicious. Entitled "Menakhem-Mendl Edits an Encyclopedia," after Sholem Aleichem's famous nebbish protagonist who loses every penny he has in one bird-brained scheme after another, this article brought the dispute to a new *ad hominem* low. Near the end of the (of course lengthy) rebuttal, after comparing each new piece of evidence against Zylbercweig to one or another of the fictional Menakhem-Mendl's qualities (an inability to understand facts or statistics, the tendency to jump to conclusions, etc.), Mukdoyni asks in an aggrieved tone, "Why is it that one isn't supposed to say even a truthful and polite word about a work that has been created by two undesirable dilettantes, by two lexicographically inexperienced people?"[20]

That same week, Mukdoyni sent Zylbercweig a personal note of regret that he could not come to the banquet (presumably one being held in honor of Zylbercweig and Mestel for the completion of the second volume), and that he hoped Zylbercweig would not take his criticisms personally.[21] Under the circumstances, it is hard to see how else Zylbercweig could have taken them; but the following week's answer to Mukdoyni's rebuttal to Zylbercweig's refutation of Mukdoyni's original article, was written by Jacob Mestel. This was a short letter primarily serving to prove that several bibliographical points of Mukdoyni's were wrong: Mestel, clearly stung by being considered less than professional in his research skills, seems to have set out specifically to prove their worth.[22]

Mestel's letter, published on March 15, 1935, in the *Nyu-yorker vokhnblat*, was for a while the resting point of the dispute. It is not clear what happened between March 1935 and January 1936, but in this interim Mukdoyni, and perhaps the rest of the theatre community, suddenly seem to have grasped that the *Leksikon* was probably the only major reference work that would ever be published on the Yiddish theatre, and that its existence was in danger. It is also possible, given the level of personal ego investment that characterizes the exchange up to this point, that Mukdoyni was feuding with the Hebrew Actors Union at that time, and saw in their financial abandonment of the *Leksikon* a stick with which to beat them. Here, then, is the opening of Mukdoyni's January 1936 take on the *Leksikon*, as published in the *Morgn zhurnal*:

Theatre Casualties
(Behind the Encyclopedia of Yiddish Theatre)

    Behind every Yiddish book published in the last few years there is a hard, heart-rending drama: every Yiddish writer endures the suffering of the damned before he sees his book make its appearance on this earth. He has to be his own publisher, underwriter, and even his own accountant.

    And the bigger the Yiddish book, the bigger and more difficult and more bitter the drama.

    And it would be very sensible for every critic, before sitting down to review a book, to have a chat with the writer about how his book came to lie between two covers.

    In some cases the history of a Yiddish book before it makes its debut in print is more thrilling than the book itself.

    A great number of people and bookstores have, on their shelves, two huge volumes, two fantastic volumes of the *Encyclopedia of the Yiddish Theatre*.

    But nobody knows the awful drama playing out behind the two big, gorgeous volumes; nobody knows, even though everyone is aware that these days a Yiddish book is an orphan, an abandoned orphan in the Jewish world, without a savior or a relative.

    A theatre encyclopedia has been necessary for many years. This is clearly a by-product of the Yiddish theatre. The Yiddish theatre itself only knows how to handle its cash-box, but its history, the sources for its history, it does not know how to handle. No Yiddish theatre has an archive, a library of the plays that it has produced, or a file of the actors who have appeared during the years of its existence.

    Just as a herring merchant conducts his business, so the theatre businesses conduct theirs in our Jewish world.[23]

And so on at, of course, some length. Mukdoyni goes on to extol the virtues of the young, energetic man who took it upon himself to create the *Leksikon*, only to find the actors in America (clearly there was no money in the 1930s in Europe for such an undertaking) indifferent to the plan. The Hebrew Actors Union, Mukdoyni sneers, issued a call for supporters to send donations for the *Leksikon*. But in the end, when the proceeds from volume one failed to cover the costs of producing volume two, Zylbercweig was left to raise the money himself.

And our confident hero borrows money right and left, he mortgages his house, the roof over his own head and that of his family in Palestine, a house he built with the sweat of his own brow before he started work on the encyclopedia.

    In a split second, the second volume literally eats up the house and the borrowed money and screams "Hey, hey, give me more, give me more money."[24]

Mukdoyni's guarded reference to his own earlier judgment of the book (in the article's third paragraph) is the only indication this article gives that anyone other than the Hebrew Actors Union bears any blame for the matter. With this Zylbercweig must have been pleased: certainly pleased enough, in 1941, to include the entire exchange, ending with Mukdoyni's song of praise, in his collection *Teater mozaik* (Theatre mosaic) as a bizarre sort of "I told you so." Zylbercweig, too, was not above letting his ego out in public. But this resolution was certainly not the end of the financial problems of the *Leksikon*; nor was the feud entirely forgiven and forgotten. A year after Zylbercweig's death, when the newspaper columnist Mordkhe Yardeni attempted to encourage the Yiddish cultural community to find the finances to bring out the final, seventh volume of the *Leksikon*, which languished in page proofs in a print shop in Mexico City, he reminded his readers of the attacks Shatzky and Mukdoyni brought against the *Leksikon*.[25]

Sexual Deviancy: Jewish, Theatrical, and Female

At this point in our discussion of the Shatzky/Mukdoyni/Zylbercweig debate, it might be useful to step back to consider some contextual forces that may have been at work. The confluence in this debate of Jews, women, prostitution, and theatre created an environment in which the people under discussion were laden with meanings far beyond the simple facts of their own lives or work. Stereotypes of women and actresses were embraced, even when they contradicted each other. For example, both sides in the dispute believed that women, and especially actresses, lie about their ages and cannot be trusted to provide accurate material with which to complete the historical record. Male scholars such as themselves, however, were seen as justified in obscuring, if not falsifying, the historical record in the service of protecting a given woman's reputation from the taint of sexual impropriety. In some ways Shatzky seemed to argue that men were obligated to bury such a fact, although he must have been aware that in raising the point in a widely-disseminated journal he actually brought it to broader notice than the encyclopedia article alone would have. Shatzky's outrage was only putatively about protecting Liptzin's reputation. What it was really about can be guessed at by looking at beliefs, events, and cultural phenomena that formed an unspoken backdrop to the self-contained drama of the *Leksikon* dispute.

Since at least the eighteenth century there was a widespread belief in English-speaking cultures that actresses often engaged in some form of prostitution. As Tracy C. Davis has shown, this correlation was extremely weak in reality, probably far lower than the correlation between prostitution and other female-dominated professions such as laundresses or domestic servants in England during the 19th century.[26] The correlation remained in the popular imagination, according to Davis, because of similarities of economic status and social visibility between prostitutes and actresses: "Women performers defied ideas of passive middle-class femininity and personified active self-sufficiency."[27] They were visible in the public realm and offered themselves up for the male gaze; they worked late hours, in the same geographic locales that brothels and streetwalkers operated; and were required to be physical and personable. They also made an unfeminine amount of money in using these talents: "no other occupations could be so financially rewarding for single, independent Victorian women of outgoing character, fine build, and attractive features."[28] These similarities in social standing defied cultural norms of the time, and created a myth of the actress-prostitute that was retained well beyond the Victorian era.[29] This popular image created a tension at the very heart of the debate among Shatzky, Mukdoyni, and Zylbercweig.

If actresses were linked with prostitution in the English mind, in the eastern European one the link was further complicated by associations between Jews and prostitution. Jewish involvement in the sex trade was a reality: Jews made up a disproportionate number of pimps and madams in many eastern European localities for which statistics are available. These numbers do not indicate, however, that Jews dominated the sex trade, although that was a common perception.[30] For Jews from eastern Europe, living in an English-speaking country such as the United States, there were two strong associative links between Keni Liptzin and prostitution before the insinuation had even been made.

Bringing these general ideological currents into the realm of Yiddish theatre were several incidents that were recent and well known to the parties to the Liptzin dispute. At least as early as 1902, New York Yiddish journalists began crusading against the moral tone of Yiddish music halls, particularly as they were likely to produce a corrupting influence on women in the audience. The concert halls in Manhattan's Tenderloin district were located near centers of prostitution; the homes of most audience members, who lived on the Lower East Side, were also located in an area notorious for bordellos. Among their concerns were that women in the audience might become sexually excited by suggestive songs or lyrics.[31] At the heart of this matter was the belief that the music halls undermined Jewish life: "Yiddish journalists' attack on the moral fabric of audience and performers was their response to transformations in immigrant social behavior which, in their view, threatened the cohesiveness of the Jewish immigrant community as they knew it."[32]

Thus, from at least 1902 on, Yiddish theatres were constrained by social and journalistic pressures to ensure their productions and performers were untainted and would not lead to the moral decline of women in the audience.

Farther from home, but still well within the fold of the international Yiddish theatre community, the Buenos Aires Yiddish theatre (not, as in New York, just the music halls) was attacked from within the Jewish community for allowing pimps and prostitutes to freely patronize the theatres. This battle raged for almost twenty years until, in 1926, after pimps intervened to prevent a play decrying prostitution from being performed, a large public outcry and threats of boycotts finally caused

A Yiddish theatre audience, New York, 1920s. (From the archives of the YIVO Institute for Jewish Research, New York.)

the theatres to ban pimps and prostitutes from entering their premises. This entire debate would have been well known to journalists who covered the Yiddish theatre, including Zylbercweig, Shatzky, and Mukdoyni, as many of the debates were carried out in the international Jewish press.[33]

One particularly important issue in these communal attempts to regulate morality in and around Jewish theatres is that of how the Jewish communities involved were viewed, or how they believed they were viewed, by the non-Jewish elite in their respective countries. While there was a strong link between a certain group of immigrant Jews and the Buenos Aires sex trade, the sex trade was never exclusively or even primarily Jewish. Yet it was among Jews that the most extensive community response to prostitution occurred. One historian posits the more precarious situation of Jews within Argentinean society as a primary reason for this response.

Other communities with much higher indices of prostitution in Buenos Aires were the French, the Spanish, and the Italian: their Romance languages were related to Spanish; they were Catholic; and their countries of origin were familiar in Argentina. Though concerned about the bad reputation criminals might give to the whole group, the leaders of the French, Spanish, and Italian institutions were not as adamant as the Jewish ones, for they had much less at stake.[34]

In the United States, self-regulation of sexual morality was carried out just as thoroughly, but in a less publicly acknowledged forum, particularly during the Progressive Era.[35] These efforts often focused on Jewish women who were seen as being in some way analogous to actresses and prostitutes: for example, in the investigation of Macy's department-store clerks. These women were seen as working in public view, rather than in the private confines of a factory or office; the stores were located in the Tenderloin, putting employees in contact with prostitution. Like theatres, the department stores were glamorous (in their display of luxury goods) and were gender-mixed workplaces. Because of these and other factors, female department-store employees were seen as likely to have their moral character debased through their work, engaging in either prostitution or other kinds of sexual deviancy such as mixed-race relations. This issue became a particularly Jewish one because immigrant Jews were seen as bringing into America a variety of moral ills. This idea of Jewish deviancy then was expanded to include all Jews, even those who had already attained a privileged, almost-white status. As Val Marie Johnson has noted, even

> the most elite Jewish men were at times demonized through a racialized identity that excluded them from full citizenship. The success and assimilation of northwestern European Jews, both immigrant and U.S. born, and the mass migration of working-class eastern European Jews in the late nineteenth century intensified anti-Semitism and the inbetweenness of more privileged Jews. These processes and the anxieties around them meant that native-born Jews of predominantly German heritage and eastern European Jewish immigrants were, respectively, prominent leaders in and targets of New York City antiprostitution campaigns.[36]

As a result of these fears of contamination with the image of immigrant Jews, the Jewish elite strove to refute the basis for this image. Percy Straus, a member of the family that owned Macy's, entered into a "mission to refute the association of immigrant Jews with sexual immorality."[37] As only one of several investigations into workers' moral conduct, Straus authorized an investigation of women clerks at his store during 1913 and into 1914. As Johnson shows, not only was Straus involved in policing other Jews, but many of the women under investigation were conscious of the need to police themselves: they refused to work in stores where they would have to serve men; gossiped about and derided fellow workers who did not meet their standards of purity; and refused to live on the Lower East Side, with its abundance of prostitution and Jews who were viewed as morally debased. Johnson views these activities as "strategies of intensive self-management."[38] Also of note is that the saleswomen, in the view of the Macy's investigators and the women themselves, were balanced on a knife-edge of respectability at all times: though originating as delicate innocents, they were curiously susceptible to temptation (through contact with luxury goods and men at Macy's), and could in short order become hopelessly corrupted, even to the extent of corrupting others who lay in their path. This is why some women avoided others, and avoided locales that they viewed as potential sites of contamination. For a woman to fall was easy and irreparable. None of these assumptions devolved to men.

The Macy's investigation took place in the Progressive Era, showing that the anxiety of uptown Jews to retain their relative privilege was already a factor in Jewish communal responses to perceived moral threats at that time. As the 1920s unfolded, with its increase in anti-Semitism, the Jewish community's reactive strategies intensified.[39] A good example of this increased nervousness can be found in responses to the 1923 Broadway production of Sholem Asch's *Got fun nekome* (*God of Vengeance*, 1907).

Theatrical representation of prostitutes was a staple on the stage long before the 1920s, but it was during this decade that several such plays grabbed headlines and honed an atmosphere of moral vigilance, which regulated representations of sexually debased women. As Katie N. Johnson has pointed out, within just a few months of Eugene O'Neill winning the 1922 Pulitzer Prize for his brothel drama, *Anna Christie*, Sholem Asch's *Got fun nekome* was charged with obscenity and found guilty.[40] Where one stage prostitute won plaudits and prizes, Asch's lesbian prostitute created a scandal both inside and outside the Jewish community. Although it had played in Yiddish and other languages both in New York and Europe, and had been produced off-Broadway in English, it was when the production moved to Broadway that notice was taken of it. As critics have pointed out,[41] the first public complaint lodged against Asch's play was by a rabbi on the basis that it was anti-Semitic; yet when this was taken up by the press and eventually the court, the objection was turned on its head. Far from being perceived as anti-Jewish, it was seen as too Jewish, promoting a worldview that was, in the words of one reviewer, "alien stuff, and, because alien, offensive."[42] In defending himself in court, the producer claimed that *Got fun nekome* was in fact a hyper-moral play, serving to show how sin is always punished. (In the play, the pimp is "punished" by his daughter's lesbianism and her choice to join her lover in prostitution.) It was probably the lesbian love affair which in the end doomed *Got fun nekome*, but in the view of mainstream America, it was sexual deviance of a particularly Jewish kind. The play offered none of the punishment of the prostitute or taming of her sexuality that could have made it acceptable. In contrast with *Anna Christie*, *Got fun nekome* "incorporates virtually none of the staple elements of the brothel genre: there's no white slave in need of rescue, no hero to rescue her, no heterosexual love story, and no self-sacrificing whore."[43]

A few years later, and very shortly before the first Shatzky attack on the *Leksikon* appeared in *Literarishe bleter*, another unrepentant whore was driven off Broadway. Mae West's *Sex* (1926) featured a prostitute who has every opportunity to cast off her sexual deviance through marriage to a suitably genteel fellow, but who decides finally to return to her independent life. Not only was West found guilty of obscenity, she actually served jail time.[44] Although there was no Jewish content this time, it may have been seen as a reprise of the *Got fun nekome* case.

For a prostitute to be allowed on the stage in American society, she had to be redeemed through marriage or self-sacrifice. Neither *Sex* nor *Got fun nekome* allowed for this reading.

The problem, then, for Shatzky and later Zylbercweig, was to find a rhetorical strategy by which a long-dead Liptzin could be redeemed from her morally debased condition as a woman who might have, just once, slipped off the knife-edge of respectability. Problematically, Liptzin had married several times but had no children: her redemption through middle-class marriage and family was impossible. Shatzky's response to this was to deny emphatically that rumors of her prostitution could be given any possible credence. He couches this as a slander based on a lack of proper historical verification, displacing the loaded sexual matter onto a question of scholarship. His extended attacks on writing style, word choice, footnotes, and other minutiae of the *Leksikon* were both an expression of his wounded ego, as an expert who had not been asked to be involved in the project, and a stand-in for the accusation at the heart of the matter: that in suggesting the possibility of a Jewish actress-prostitute, Zylbercweig had exposed aspects of Jewish life that would be better kept under wraps. Because this was the ultimate point, Shatzky was not as concerned with Liptzin's reputation in and of itself, and therefore was not shy about printing his diatribe in a wide-circulation journal. Rather, his goal was to discredit a Jewish publication that did not conform to presenting a view of Jews that was consistent with the respectability they hoped to attain in mainstream culture. Mukdoyni, in Act II of the Liptzin debate, picked up Shatzky's line of attack.

Zylbercweig's response took a different approach to the same problem. To redeem Liptzin, he promoted a view of her artistic work as hyper-moral, thus retrospectively cleansing her own past. This attempt is very like the defense made of *Got fun nekome* at its trial, but it is even less convincing. The narrative of a fallen woman given a second chance through virtuous action harks back to one of the central stories of the Christian Bible, demarcating a line between Jewish and non-Jewish theology; the trope sits uneasily in a Jewish cultural context. Zylbercweig's reaction to Shatzky's objections is initially defiant, but as time goes on he gradually moderates his stance, tacitly bowing to Shatzky's position. This may have been a result of the ever-increasing anti-Semitism of American society and a general reading of the desires of his audience to elide evidence of Jewish moral lapses.

In another similarity to the *Got fun nekome* case, the Liptzin debate shows Jewish men engaged in a struggle over the depiction of Jewish women, who stand in for the Jewish people as a whole in matters of sexual purity and deviance. When Shatzky and Zylbercweig sought to clear Liptzin of the stain of prostitution, they implicitly subscribed to the proposition that a Jewish prostitute was a stain on the entire Jewish people. For a majority culture, a "deviant" fringe element like actors or prostitutes could exist without staining the mainstream, or might even offer a safely contained space for deviance that helped to uphold a mythology of purity elsewhere for the rest of society. For a minority group already suspected of degeneracy, however, each and every member of the group had to be a worthy representative in the eyes of mainstream culture. Like the New York Yiddish music-hall brouhaha of 1902, and the Macy's investigation of Jewish saleswomen's susceptibility to vice, the in-group response of Jews to the potential for bad publicity was harder on women than on men. If women were seen to be repositories for sexual purity, they also could stray more easily and more disastrously, sometimes simply by listening to a lurid song in a music hall. Played out against a background of the image of the actress-prostitute, the considerable reality and even larger mythology of the Jewish sex trade, and the rising anti-Semitism of the 1920s, the Liptzin debate encapsulated a host of minority preoccupations and a range of possible responses to them. As in the Buenos Aires situation and the *Got fun nekome* case, the struggle within the Jewish community to find appropriate ways to deal with Jewish prostitution strained the ingenuity of an immigrant group attempting to both retain its cultural specificity and attain mainstream approbation.

Was She or Wasn't She?

It is still of interest to try to ascertain the truth of Liptzin's possible work as a prostitute in Smile, Ukraine, for a few years in the 1870s or so, and to do so without falling into either defensive or laudatory mode. Hard evidence is unlikely to become available. Yet Jewish prostitution in the towns and cities of Ukraine is well documented. Edward Bristow has found evidence that licensed prostitution in Ukraine was to a large extent run by Jewish brothel keepers and procurers; the extent to which Jews worked prostitutes is less well documented, but he found hundreds of individual cases. Even very small towns had brothels, sometimes all run by Jews.[45] Bristow also shows repeatedly that many women worked in prostitution for a few years, then moved on to other economic activity, particularly if they were able to save their earnings to supply themselves with start-up capital for a store or another such undertaking.[46] Therefore one cannot dismiss the possibility that Liptzin supported herself in this way. She was a single young woman without family protection, having not only fled her husband but presumably incurred the wrath of her parents in doing so. If she did not have a trade (and there is no indication she was trained for one, such as being apprenticed), her best-paying option could well have been prostitution.

On the other hand, there are many reasons to be suspicious of any glib association of a woman as unconventional as Liptzin with prostitution. As an actress she was said to decide on her own roles and spend her own money producing plays she preferred over audience favorites.[47] She had at least three husbands, including the first from whom she fled and a second who died, and she never had children.

Given the automatic association of actresses with sex, and the tendency to impute to independent women deviant sexuality of various kinds, it is entirely possible the prostitution rumor derives from situational assumptions rather than known fact.

Yet Zylbercweig was a careful reporter of many kinds of stories in the *Leksikon*. Statements of fact that can be checked are usually correct. He had an unusually broad vision of what made appropriate material for inclusion in history, including gossip.[48] The story of Israel Grodner's payment in tobacco, derided by Shatzky, provides an intriguing glimpse of informal economic activity. When Zylbercweig insisted, in his first response to Shatzky, that Liptzin was indeed a prostitute—information he can have gleaned only from personal conversations with people who had worked with Liptzin—he displays a regard for anecdotal evidence and oral lore that was well before his time. Zylbercweig's historiographic method allows for a more complicated vision of women's lives than pure documentation would provide. It is also the case that Zylbercweig valued women far beyond what was normal among Yiddish historians of his day: fully 28 percent of the biographies in the *Leksikon* are of women.[49] Given the delicacy of the subject matter, it seems unlikely that Zylbercweig would have identified any woman as a prostitute unless his information came from multiple sources, who had some compelling knowledge of the woman in question, or whose information came directly from her. In all, while acknowledging there can be no certainty at this historical remove, there are good reasons to believe that the Liptzin story is true.

True or not, however, the controversy over its proposed inclusion and its eventual suppression in the published *Leksikon* stands as a vivid example of the role gender plays in Yiddish theatre historiography, and in turn, of the treatment of women's sexuality in Jewish historiography more broadly.

Appendix

Jacob Shatzky, "An Example of a Theatre Encyclopedia," *Literarishe bleter* 28 (1928).

Note: We make space here for Dr. Shatzky's article about the projected "theatre encyclopedia." However, we believe that we should not head down the path of destroying this important undertaking. Since the work is at its very beginning, people in America should create a responsible editorial board and work with Z. Zylbercweig to move the work of the encyclopedia forward, so that the end product will be equal to the task we will entrust it with. We believe that Z. Zylbercweig, who took the initiative on this project, would willingly go forward with an editorial board of professionals.

Editors of the *Literary Pages*

Recently a prospectus for the "Encyclopedia of the Yiddish Theatre" was published. This is a chapbook 16 pages long, in quarto format, the same size as Reisen's encyclopedia.[50] This prospectus is meant to give us a sense of how the encyclopedia, about which the theatre pages of the Yiddish press in New York have been buzzing, will appear.

The prospectus consists of reprints of articles and notices about the "significance of an encyclopedia of performers and lovers of the theatre," or about the fact that this is a work that "will be of great utility" and so on. One of the articles even says of the yet-unborn encyclopedia that "when you open a book of this sort, you are quickly enveloped (!)[51] in that very (that is, a theatrical—JS)[52] atmosphere."

Another one writes accurately that an encyclopedia cannot be produced nowadays by an individual, but collectively—but he quickly makes an exception for the Yiddish language environment, because he is "personally" acquainted with the editor, Mr. Zalmen Zylbercweig, and this knowledge allows him, it seems, to believe that the young "very energetic and exceptionally talented author-instigator" will see the project through. And in the same manner, with one or two exceptions, the rest of the articles are written by irresponsible people who have not the slightest inkling what is meant by an encyclopedia.

But why should we take the word of the experts, or even of the editor and his autobiographical essay where he describes how he came to have the idea for the encyclopedia? Let us become better acquainted with the examples that are published in the prospectus. These examples should give us a sense of how the biographies of Yiddish theatre people will be written. In brief, you can tell from the biographies (the beginnings of which are published in the prospectus, "the rest, in the encyclopedia") what the theatre encyclopedia will contain.

The prospectus includes the following four incomplete biographies: Keni Liptzin, Esther-Rokhl Kaminska, Jacob P. Adler, and Abraham Fishzon.

Let us begin with the men. About Adler it is said, for example, that their house (in Odessa) was a *beys va-ad la-khakhomim* [a gathering place for wise men] where "the greatest (!) maskilim of the day used to gather." Or that a certain Dr. Kenigshatz was a teacher in the "Evreiskaya kazennoe uchilishche" [Jewish state rabbinical academy] where Adler studied.

The question arises: Sir, who is throwing sand in your eyes, or from whom do you allow it to be thrown? This is all *loy hoye veloy nivre* [complete nonsense]. Rumors, made-up stories, simple lies.

An editor has to have, in addition to forty one-act plays, a little intelligence, and must understand what it is to ask for an eyewitness account from an actor at all, much less a Yiddish actor.

What follows, in pure newspaper lingo, is a biography of "Yankele"[53] and how his father wanted him to be a doctor, and later set him up as a merchant, and so on and so forth.

Reading the biographies that Zalmen Zylbercweig has laid out for us as samples, you can't escape the thought: maybe this isn't a dictionary but a parody of a dictionary? As a parody, it isn't bad. It's like Vardi's parody of a lesson on David Frischmann[54]: "When Frischmann was five years old, he said to his wife" etc.

In Abraham Fishzon's biography, for example, you find such "momentous" historical facts as that the *Broder zinger* Israel Grodner was paid for his "*khiburim*" (!)[55] with . . . tobacco. Very important, don't you think?

But the Yiddish actresses have meet an even worse fate at the hands of the compiler of "*diese*"[56] biographies.

Esther-Rokhl Kaminska. Born on Purim, 1870. A very well-educated editor it is who can't be bothered to figure out the date of Purim in 1870, or who knows that Adler had a "doctor" as a teacher in the Odessa Yiddish school.

But I don't need to give you my commentary when you can see an example of the style and biographical construction yourself:

"The father of E. R. (Kaminska—JS), who was already old and feeble (!), was among the retired community employees (!), having been at one time a cantor-ritual slaughterer, and in old age required to put aside his *avoydes-hakoydesh* [holy service]" (!). Not enough that he's old and "feeble" and "retired," but it has to be repeated in a second sentence again in a different form the way it's done in newspaper articles where they're trying to fill up column inches.

Then follows the story, which without it, God forbid, you wouldn't understand Kaminska's talent, about how her father was able to live off what rich customers gave him, and so on.

Then comes a classic sentence: "Of all six children, only a brother remained in the house at the time when E. R. (Esther Rokhl) was growing up. Things were not good there . . . Only once in a blue moon could they afford to eat meat etc." And finally, Esther Rokhl Kaminska "grew up to be a healthy, well-developed girl and played with the non-Jewish girls in the countryside" and so on.

How do you like such "good" style by an editor, and what do you say about his historical skill, how he looks in the pots and pans of the "great" artists and set it down for posterity in an "encyclopedia." What is this? I read and can't believe my eyes! Is it possible to find such a style and such content in a biography of a non-Jewish actress? What is this: folly or ignorance? Do you think that this is just pure philistinism, "illiterate" Yiddish, and an open demonstration of talentlessness, ignorance, and third-rate journalistic style? No, there's something else going on that's a lot worse than ignorance! Let me first quote for you: In the biography of Keni Liptzin there are, among other biographical "blossoms" and stylistic absurdities these two paragraphs:

How she (that is, Miss Liptzin—JS) came to move from the countryside into the shtetl of Smile, in Kiev province, is not known; there is a theory that she married her father's coachman, and a bit (!) later ran away from him. Regarding her employment in Smile there are various versions. Some say that she worked there as a seamstress; but certain actors report that her employment was of a completely different kind.

What exactly is this? What can one call this kind of writing? There is only one word for it: *vileness*.

Why is this even included? In the name of 'truth'? Let's see what kind of 'truth' Herr Editor Zylbercweig writes about the people on his committee. Probably he wouldn't tell the "truth" about living people, but slander he is willing not only to impart freely, but a few examples from the prospectus shows that he has already spread them around.

Shouldn't the editor of an encyclopedia have if not intelligence (which only God can give him), then tact—and knowing what should be included and what is unimportant.

Doesn't the young man "with knowledge and energy" (as one of the main admirers of the encyclopedia advertises him) understand that there are *historical facts* that are necessary for biography, and scandalous facts that are only necessary to make a journalistic "hit"? Where is the editorial sense, moderation, clear vision? What is involved in writing a biography of an actor or actress?

The examples in the encyclopedia are dreadful, truly scandalous. Everyone can do as he wishes, even translate fifty one-acters, if he's the only one responsible. But that is not the case here. The *Leksikon* is being advertised as a community undertaking. They are saving the Yiddish theatre from being forgotten. They are immortalizing the "*Leistungen*" [performances] of the Yiddish actors and actresses.

Truly a historical mission!

And in the committee I see a few names of intelligent actors. What are they doing there? Do they also believe that a biographical dictionary should be composed of insinuations, gossip, total falsehoods, and bad writing? Do they also believe that an encyclopedia should be turned into a collection of letters to the editor, written in that tone and style! Do they not see that this grandiose plan to create a biographical dictionary of Yiddish theatre has been undertaken by a person who, aside from ambition, possesses nothing: no qualifications at all, no knowledge, no method, no language, and no intelligence? Why do they stay silent? Why do our better theatre writers, who have, thank God, not given their blessing to the encyclopedia before it appears, also say nothing? It is necessary to warn the audience that, judging by the examples (and usually the better examples are given in advance, so that they can move the "merchandise"), the encyclopedia of Yiddish theatre will be a book that will not do the Yiddish language and culture any credit.

Notes

1. For a complete biographical sketch of Zylbercweig and the publication history of the *Leksikon*, see Faith Jones, "The Fate of Yiddish Dictionaries: Zalmen Zylbercweig and the *Leksikon fun yidishn teater*," *Journal of Modern Jewish Studies* 5 (November 2006): 323–342.

2. I have not located a copy of this prospectus in any of the major Judaica libraries in New York. Information about it is gleaned from the sources described below.

3. This was also common in certain eras in non-Jewish European cultures. See Christa Jansohn, "The Making of a National Poet: Shakespeare, Carl Joseph Meyer, and the German Book-Market in the Nineteenth Century," *The Modern Language Review* 90 (1995): 545–555. Quaint as it seems now, paying for a book in advance of its publication was an accepted publishing practice. My thanks to Dror Abend-David for this information.

4. Yankev Shatski, "A muster fun a teater-leksikon" [An example of a theatre encyclopedia], in *Teater mozaik* [Theatre mosaic], ed. Zalmen Zylbercweig (New York: Biderman, 1941), 68–69. Originally published in *Literarishe bleter* (Warsaw) 28 (1928).

5. Ibid., 69.

6. Ibid., 69.

7. Ibid., 70–72. Although it is tempting to quote this article at even greater length because of its histrionic and rhetorical pleasures, I have here only given the paragraphs that give the best example of Shatzky's style and argument, and that the reader will need in order to understand the further events of this brouhaha. The full text can be found in the appendix to this article.

8. About Zylbercweig's writing style I can only say that it seems to me perfectly competent and suitable to his audience. Shatzky's writing does not seem to me markedly more graceful than Zylbercweig's.

9. Zalmen Zylbercweig, "Shteyner in veg" [Stones in the road], in *Teater mozaik*, 76. Originally published in *Literarishe bleter* 30 (1928). Here Shatzky is not entirely wrong, though. Most researchers using the *Leksikon* would probably appreciate being given both the calendar date and the observation regarding the source of Kaminska's name.

10. Yankev Shatski, "Tsu vos kas ken brengen: mekoyekh Z. Zilbertsvayg un zayn 'leksikon'" [Where anger leads you: Regarding Z. Zylbercweig and his encyclopedia], in *Teater mozaik*, 78. Originally published in *Literarishe bleter* 37 (1928).

11. Ibid., 79.

12. An amusing coda to the contention that the *Leksikon* was poorly edited is found in the history of Shatzky's own editorship of a different biographical dictionary. The *Leksikon fun der nayer yidisher literatur* [Encyclopedia of new Yiddish literature] was a mammoth, eight-volume project undertaken by the Congress for Jewish Culture in New York after World War II. Shatzky was co-editor, although he lived long enough to see only one volume into print. This volume was roundly criticized for its lack of confirmed dates and bibliographical details, and for the sheer number of errors it contained. In one case there are two entries for the same person. (For a discussion of these matters, see Shimeon Brisman, *A History and Guide to Judaic Encyclopedias and Lexicons* [Cincinnati: HUC, 1987].) In fact, such errors are a common part of all multi-volume reference works, even those published under much more auspicious circumstances than any Yiddish book enjoys. Shatzky was more wrong to condemn Zylbercweig than to make similar mistakes of his own.

13. Zalmen Zylbercweig, "Iz akhrey moys kedoyshim emer a minhag oder a din?" [Is not speaking ill of the dead a custom or a law?], in *Teater mozaik*, 80. Originally published in *Fraye arbeter shtime* (New York), November 22, 1929.

14. Zalmen Zylbercweig, Introduction to *Leksikon fun yidishn teater* (New York: Farlag Elisheva, 1931), 1:11.

15. A. Mukdoyni, "A teater-leksikon" [A theatre encyclopedia], in *Teater mozaik*, 89. Originally published in *Morgn zhurnal* (New York), February 27, 1931.

16. Zalmen Zylbercweig, "Ven a kritiker aylt zikh" [When a critic rushes], in *Teater mozaik*, 95–104. Originally published in *Shikage*, June 1931.

17. *Leksikon fun yidishn teater* (Warsaw: Farlag Elisheva, 1934), 2:1108.

18. A. Mukdoyni, "Der teater-leksikon," in *Teater mozaik*, 104–112. Originally published in *Morgn zhurnal*, February 15, 1935.

19. Zalmen Zylbercweig, "D"r Mukdoyni, meyk op yur maynd," in *Teater mozaik*, 116. Originally published in *Nyu-yorker vokhnblat*, March 1, 1935.

20. A. Mukdoyni, "Menakhem Mendl redaktirt a leksikon" [Menakhem-Mendl edits an encyclopedia], in *Teater mozaik*, 125. Originally published in *Nyu-yorker vokhnblat*, March 8, 1935.

21. A. Mukdoyni, "A brivl fun D"r Mukdoyni " [A letter from Dr. Mukdoyni], in *Teater mozaik*, 126–127.

22. Yankev Mestel, "A brivl tsu D"r Mukdoyni" [A letter to Dr. Mukdoyni], in *Teater mozaik*, 127–128. Originally published in *Nyu-yorker vokhnblat*, March 15, 1935.

23. A. Mukdoyni, "Teater-korbones" [Theatre casualties], in *Teater mozaik*, 129–130. Originally published in *Morgn zhurnal*, January 10, 1936. While Mukdoyni laments the lack of proper documentation of Yiddish theatre, from a contemporary standpoint, what seems most remarkable is the obsessive activity on the part of so many people to fully document and describe a form of cultural expression that had, at that point, operated on a mass scale for only a few decades. While I have no particular explanation for this phenomenon, I see it as connected to the larger project of modern, post-1905 Yiddish language activists to valorize every aspect of Jewish culture (as opposed to the earlier tendency of maskilic Jews to promote assimilation). My ideas about this are influenced by Barry Trachtenberg, *The Revolutionary Roots of Modern Yiddish, 1903–1917* (Syracuse, NY: Syracuse University Press, 2008).

24. Ibid., 132.

25. Mordkhe Yardeni, "Zalmen Zilbertsvayg," in *Vort un klang* [Word and sound], (New York: Farlag Malke, 1979): 399–402. Originally published in *Algemeyner zhurnal* (New York), July 27, 1973.

26. Tracy C. Davis, *Actresses as Working Women: Their Social Identity in Victorian Culture* (London and New York: Routledge, 1991), 78–80.

27. Ibid., xiv.

28. Ibid., 84.

29. See the Introduction to Katie N. Johnson, *Sisters in Sin: Brothel Drama in America, 1900–1920* (Cambridge: Cambridge University Press, 2006), for a variety of novels and plays involving actress-prostitutes in the early 20th century.

30. See Edward J. Bristow, *Prostitution and Prejudice: The Jewish Fight Against White Slavery, 1870–1939* (Oxford: Clarendon Press, 1982), Chapter 2, for detailed statistics on eastern European prostitution.

31. Nina Warnke, "Immigrant Popular Culture as Contested Sphere: Yiddish Music Halls, the Yiddish Press, and the Processes of Americanization, 1900–1910, *Theatre Journal* 48 (1996): 330–331.

32. Ibid., 328.

33. Victor A. Mirelman, "The Jewish Community versus Crime: The Case of White Slavery in Buenos Aires," *Jewish Social Studies* 46 (1984): 145–168. While Mirelman lauds the mainstream Buenos Aires Jewish community for forcing members of the sex trade out of the theatres, he does not note the inherent contradiction. The reason pimps liked to bring prostitutes to the theatres was not for their employees' entertainment, but as a means of advertising their attractiveness and availability. This advertising was aimed at the same mainstream Jewish community Mirelman describes as nobly and virtually uniformly attempting to fight Jewish trafficking in women.

34. Ibid., 165.

35. Dates for this era are disputed by historians, but at least the years 1890–1913 are usually included, with some dating it up to 1920.

36. Val Marie Johnson, "'Look for the Moral and Sex Sides of the Problem': Investigating Jewishness, Desire, and Discipline at Macy's Department Store, New York City, 1913," *Journal of the History of Sexuality* 18 (2009): 465.

37. Ibid., 466.

38. Ibid., 467.

39. Leonard Dinnerstein, "Antisemitism in Crisis Times in the United States: the 1920s and 1930s," in Sander L. Gilman and Steven T. Katz, eds., *Anti-Semitism in Times of Crisis* (New York: New York University Press, 1991), 212–226. Dinnerstein notes such incidents as the immigration restrictions of 1921 and 1924, the imposition of quotas on Jews entering universities, the rise of Henry Ford's *Dearborn Independent* (which often accused Jews of sexual vice), and other efforts to either keep Jews out of the United States altogether, or to limit their influence on civic life.

40. Katie N. Johnson, *Sisters in Sin*, 196–197. The verdict was eventually overturned on appeal.

41. Alisa Solomon, *Re-Dressing the Canon: Essays on Theatre and Gender* (New York: Routledge, 1997), 117–118; Harley Erdman "Jewish Anxiety in 'Days of Judgement': Community Conflict, Antisemitism, and the God of Vengeance Obscenity Case," *Theatre Survey* 40 (1999): 51–74.

42. Quoted in Solomon, 118.

43. Katie N. Johnson, *Sisters in Sin*, 197.

44. Kirsten Pullen, *Actresses and Whores: On Stage and in Society* (Cambridge: Cambridge University Press, 2005), 13–19.

45. Bristow, *Prostitution and Prejudice*, 56.

46. Ibid., 66 and throughout the book.

47. *Leksikon fun yidishn teater* (Warsaw: Farlag Elisheva, 1934), 2:1113.

48. Research on this paper has brought to my attention the need for further investigation of the role of gossip in Yiddish-speaking culture. Gossip seems to play a particular role with regards to women, often as a way of enforcing norms of behavior, as with the Macy's saleswomen who used it to reinforce group beliefs and conduct by gossiping about those whom they felt did not live up to certain moral standards. The gossip regarding Keni Liptzin, whether true or not, can be seen as belonging to the long-standing convention of calling women whores if they stray too far from accepted behavior (see Anna Clark, "Whores and Gossips: Sexual Reputation in London, 1770–1825,"

in Arina Angerman, Geerte Binnema, Annamieke Keunen, Vefie Poels, and Jacqueline Zirkzee, eds., *Current Issues in Women's History* [New York: Routledge, 1989], 231–248). But this is not the only role gossip can play. As Susan Cotts Watkins and Angela D. Danzi show, gossip networks have also been harnessed by Jewish (and other) women to change their situations and share knowledge when more traditional sources of information are unable to meet the demands of changing social situations (Susan Cotts Watkins and Angela D. Danzi, "Women's Gossip and Social Change: Childbirth and Fertility Control among Italian and Jewish Women in the United States, 1920–1940," *Gender and Society* 9 [1995]: 469–490). Among the small number of articles addressing gossip in Jewish settings is one in which both the negative valence of gossip and women's particular tendency to gossip are unexplored assumptions seemingly shared by researchers and subjects (Lewis Glinert, Kate Miriam Loewenthal, and Vivienne Goldblatt, "Guarding the Tongue: a Thematic Analysis of Gossip Control Strategies among Orthodox Jewish Women in London," *Journal of Multilingual and Multicultural Development* 24 [2003]: 513–524). Another article discusses an unsuccessful attempt by a kibbutz magazine to initiate a discussion on the role of gossip in its community (Ori Bet-Or, "Gossip, Community, and the Kibbutz Magazine," *Kibbutz Trends* 22/23 [1996]: 55–63). In one study, Yiddish is identified as the preferred language for gossip among elderly, multilingual care-home residents in Israel. (Eliezer Ben-Rafael, "A Sociological Paradigm of Bilingualism: English, French, Yiddish, and Arabic in Israel," in Eliezer Ben-Rafael and Hanna Herzog, eds., *Language and Communication in Israel* [New Brunswick, NJ: Transaction, 2001]: 175–206). While each is useful, none of these studies comes close to explaining the understanding of gossip that informed the Liptzin affair. In guessing as to the fury behind Shatzky's attack on "rumors, made-up stories, simple lies" and "insinuations, gossip, total falsehoods" (see appendix to this article), in relation to both male and female subjects, I can only speculate that gossip as a means of cultural and informational transmission was in the process of being rejected as Jews became modern and Westernized.

49. This is in marked contrast to all other Yiddish biographical dictionaries, which fall below ten percent and, in some cases, go as low as one percent biographies of women.

50. Zalmen Reyzen, ed., *Leksikon fun der yidisher literatur, prese un filologye* [Encyclopedia of Yiddish literature, newspapers, and philology] (Vilna, 1928–1930).

51. Here Shatzky's exclamation mark may indicate that he disapproves of the word used to mean "enveloped" (*beheucht*, literally "breathed on"), which is German rather than standard Yiddish.

52. This is the notation Shatzky used to insert his editorial comments into quotations from the prospectus.

53. Yankele is a diminutive of Jacob.

54. This probably refers to David Vardi (1893–?), an actor who performed a solo comedy act. David Frischmann (1859–1922) was a writer and translator.

55. "Khiburim" means "texts" in Hebrew and in a Hebrew-inflected Yiddish. Here, the exclamation mark might indicate that Shatzky found the use of the Hebrew word an affectation, or too grand to describe the work of a folksinger.

56. "These" in German.

CHAPTER 12

Joy to the Goy and Happiness to the Jew: Communist and Jewish Aspirations in a Postwar *Purimshpil*

Annette Aronowicz

The play *Homens mapole* (*Haman's Downfall*) was performed in many different cities in Europe and the Americas between 1945 and 1949.[1] Its author, Dr. Haim Sloves, was both a Communist and a writer committed to Jewish causes, and the play provides us with a glimpse into the mentality of a Jewish Communist of this type and of this period. The play also makes us ponder the relationship between religion and politics, for Communism in *Homens mapole* is both an argument for a political alliance between the Jews and the Soviet Union and something much more diffuse—not an argument at all, but blending into a religious sensibility. *Purimshpiln*, the traditional folk plays retelling the story of the Jews' triumph over their archenemy Haman (Homen), have always been a blend of religion and politics.[2] I will describe this blend as it appears in *Homens mapole*. Before doing so, however, a few words about its author should shed light on how the two parts of the equation—Jewish tradition and Communist allegiance—functioned offstage in his own life.

Haim Sloves (1905–1988) had two great passions from early youth. The first, which he developed in the Yiddish secular school he attended in his native Białystok, Poland, was for Yiddish language and culture. As Sloves describes it in a much later autobiographical sketch, the young teachers at his school inspired in their students a life-long love for Yiddish literature. They did not merely study it, but learned it in the way a Talmud student would pore over a page of Gemara, but, claims Sloves, with much greater enthusiasm.[3] This passion for secular Yiddish culture was to remain with him for the rest of his life, fueled rather than dampened by that culture's decline in the postwar years.

His second great love was for the Communist cause. Sloves joined the Red Army at the tender age of fifteen, when the army passed through Białystok on its way back to Moscow.[4] His native city had previously been occupied by the pro-tsarist Whites, who had engaged in various acts of violence against the Jews. The Communists, who had put a stop to this anti-Jewish violence when they took over the city, inspired him to renounce all his other plans. In his autobiographical sketch, Sloves describes the intense excitement of hearing Lenin's speech on Red Square.[5] It led him to become the secretary of the Jewish section of the Polish Komsomol (Communist Youth League), which in turn earned Sloves four years in prison, during which his commitment to the cause only grew stronger. Soon after his release in 1926, unable to continue his studies in Warsaw, Sloves emigrated to Paris. He pursued his education, eventually earning a doctorate in law at the Sorbonne. By the time Sloves got this degree in 1935, he had been a member of the French Communist Party for six years and was active in its Yiddish-language sub-section.

His Jewish activism was to intensify during the period of the Popular Front and during the war itself, but was inseparable from his Communist commitment. Sloves organized a World Congress for Yiddish Culture in 1937 in Paris, and helped found a long-lasting international organization, the Yidishe Kultur Farband (YKUF). This organization, whose center was in New York, disseminated a very influential periodical, *Yidishe kultur*, and concerned itself with Jewish education. Both the congress and YKUF allied themselves ideologically with the Soviet Union. During the war, Sloves joined the French Communist Resistance and co-edited an underground Yiddish newspaper.

It is, in fact, as part of that resistance that *Homens mapole* needs to be seen. The original version was completed just before the Germans entered Paris in June of 1940. Sloves describes being suddenly gripped, in the face of dire circumstances, by the traditional *bitokhen* (trust) of the Jewish people in the future. The form that this took was that of the purimshpil, the traditional folk play in which Jews customarily thumbed their noses at the tyrants who wished to destroy them. Sloves set to writing and managed to send a copy to a friend in New York.[6] At war's end, upon returning from Lyon where he had been in hiding, Sloves considerably shortened the play, modifying a few of the central characters in the process. *Homens mapole* was his debut as a performed Yiddish playwright. Sloves continued writing plays that reflected both of his allegiances, Jewish and Communist, into the 1960s.

Sloves's adherence to the Communist cause, so interwoven with his commitment to Jewish culture, did not remain static, however. In the later 1950s and early 1960s, he began to distance himself from the Party.[7] Sloves's last two books look critically at the Soviet Union and the blind allegiance to it of Jews like himself.[8] His disillusionment was a slow process, and even at his most critical, Sloves never became anti-Communist, nor was his passion for the movement replaced by another. *Homens mapole,* however, belongs to the immediate postwar years, when the two commitments were still inseparable.

Communism as political ideology is most evident in one of the play's subplots. Although Sloves follows the events of the Book of Esther closely, he inserts a war that the great villain Haman decides to wage against Greece. Claiming that winning this war will provide the Persians and Medeans with *Lebensraum*, slaves, riches, and natural resources, he eventually persuades King Ahasuerus to send 600 battleships and 800,000 soldiers to the front.[9] Since Haman had originally told Ahasuerus that the Jews were the ones trying to destroy the Persian Aryans, the king is, for once, understandably confused: "Di grikhn zaynen oykh yidn?" he asks. (The Greeks are also Jews?) No, no, Haman responds. They are Aryans, and even kosher Aryans, but they need to be punished for having allowed themselves to become instruments in the hands of the Jews.[10]

This subplot threads its way into every act of the play, through references to the progress of the military campaign, through Haman's boasting of his great prowess, and through the people's complaints about what the costs of war.[11] Finally, as news reaches Ahasuerus's ministers that 590 out of the 600 battleships have been sunk and that 750,000 of the 800,000 Persian soldiers have been killed, the king's ministers ask Mordechai, the Jewish hero, to head the court's opposition to Haman.[12] In the fourth and final act, two Persian generals, Marsana and Parsana, come back and explain their defeat in the following way:

MARSANA. S'iz gegangen a shney, vey, vey. (Snow fell, woe, woe.)
PARSANA. S'hot genumen a frost—un nit opgelozt.[13] (A frost came and did not let go.)

These references to snow and frost made it clear, for anyone who might have had any doubts, that Greece was a stand-in for the Soviet Union.

For Sloves, this subplot not only declared his political allegiance, but also functioned as a badge of honor. He had been in a small minority when he joined the Communist cause in 1920, at the age of fifteen, when the Red Army liberated Białystok from the White occupation and its attendant pogroms.[14] But in the immediate postwar period, Communism gained enormous prestige in both non-Jewish and Jewish eyes. Both Party membership and sympathizers' ranks swelled. In France and Italy, the Communist Party became a very important part of the political landscape, part of the government itself. This increased prestige had everything to do with the Red Army's valiant stand against Hitler's forces, at an enormous cost in lives. In France and in other countries occupied by the Germans, the Communist Resistance had played a central and early role.

For Jews, there were additional reasons to see the Soviet Union in a positive light. When no other country was admitting Jewish refugees, it had allowed 200,000 Polish Jews who were fleeing the Nazis to enter its borders. Its very defeat of the German army meant that the Jews of eastern Europe were not totally destroyed. It was also the Communist Resistance that had let in Jews, as opposed to other underground movements that refused them.[15] All of this seemed to vindicate the Jewish Communists' claim that it was the Soviet cause that stood for justice. Many years after the war, when Sloves had long distanced himself from Party activities, he still held that the Jews were bound to the Soviet Union by a bond of blood.[16] Even in his final disillusionment, expressed in his last book, *A shlikhes keyn moskve* (A mission to Moscow, 1985), in which Sloves fully acknowledges how much he had been fooled, he begins by mentioning the Soviet Union's saving of Jewish lives during the war and the gratitude it naturally evoked.[17]

The Communist dimension of the play, however, turns out to be much more than a matter of a subplot advocating a certain political alliance. This added dimension, however, is difficult to pinpoint, for at least two reasons. It is less a matter of a thinly veiled allusion and more a matter of the very spirit of the purimshpil, potentially overturning the conventional order of the world. Second, Communist ideology blends with some very widespread attitudes of the times, not limited to the Communists themselves. In order to pinpoint this more diffuse Communist sensibility in the play, we need to take a detour.

It is well known that both the Soviets and the French either failed or refused to acknowledge that the Nazis targeted the Jews specifically. To the Soviets, the Jews were "Soviet victims of Nazi aggression," as the memorial at Babi Yar reads. As for the French Communist Party, the French historian Annie Kriegel characterizes its attitude to the Jews murdered in World War II as "Victims of Hitler's racism? No: unfortunate citizens of countries momentarily defeated and occupied by the Germans."[18] Annette Wieviorka, another French historian, tells us that the French as a whole shared this attitude. She explains that the French Republican ideal was such that to focus on the Jews as a specific people, with their own specific destiny, would be to exclude them from the community of citizens, to make them other than French.[19] Both the Communists and the Republicans glorified the Resistance and cast under a shadow all who had not taken up arms against the enemy. The vast majority of Jews, having gone to their deaths unarmed, either go unmentioned or are subsumed under the category of political deportee.[20]

At first, it would seem that *Homens mapole* pits itself against this kind of universalism, which rejects all allegiance outside that of the individual to the State (the Party being the representative of a State). Sloves's play is, after all, glaringly particularistic in language and in plot, a fact that several reviewers had noted with disappointment. A French reviewer, writing in *Lettres Françaises* in 1946, questions why the play needed to be written in Yiddish at all. "This will to particularism seems shocking to many," he concludes.[21] A few years later, in 1949, when the Cold War had definitely begun, a Yiddish newspaper, *Unzer shtime* (Our voice), reported a Jewish Communist official's disapproval of the play, after having seen it performed in Wrocław; it was too nationalistic. It was bad, he said, for the Jews to insinuate that all enemies who rise up against them shall suffer the fate of Haman.[22] This "will to particularism" and nationalism is corroborated by several insistent repetitions, within the play, of the kind of destruction Haman had intended for the Jews—their elimination down to the last man, woman, and child. The Greeks, on the other hand, were only to be enslaved, Haman tells Ahasuerus.[23]

Yet *Homens mapole* does downplay Jewish suffering, deflecting attention to the Resistance fighter instead. It accomplishes this merely by being a play based on the Book of Esther, in which Jews are threatened with annihilation, but the catastrophe is completely averted. In the biblical text, Ahasuerus's first decree commanding the destruction of the Jews is followed by a second decree, in which he allows the Jews to attack their enemies before they can be attacked, which they do successfully. In Sloves's play, Ahasuerus simply annuls his first decree and has Haman hanged.[24] This means that with the exception of one line very early in the play, in which Mordechai bemoans the deaths of all his relatives back in Jerusalem (save Esther), killed when Haman invaded, there is no mention of Jewish deaths.[25] The focus of the play is altogether on an impending threat and successful resistance, a resistance inseparable from the Persian court's own, of which Mordechai is made the head.

Especially in the last two acts, Mordechai emerges as a Resistance hero. "Tamos nafshi im plishtim," he declaims to the King's ministers when they ask him to become their leader in their fight against Haman. "Let me die with the Philistines."[26] This line identifies him with the great biblical hero, Samson, sacrificing his life in one last act that brings down the enemy. His resistance is echoed by that of the entire populace, which marches on the palace in the last scenes of the play, demanding Haman's death.[27]

As much as Communist and French Republican ideology might be responsible for the peculiar dissonance of the play's plot with the actual experience of the Jews, we cannot take them to be the sole factors in skewing that experience. Other causes could account for it, coinciding with this or that ideological directive but independent of them as well. The first is simply the lack of perspective, as the play appeared so soon after the war that it was impossible to take in the enormity of what had happened. It took another fifteen to twenty years before the vocabulary that we are now used to—words such as Holocaust and Shoah, indicating the unique status of Jewish fate under the Nazis—gained currency. Sloves, like most Yiddish writers of the period, used the word *khurbn* (destruction) or *brokh* (catastrophe) when talking of Jewish suffering during the war. This placed it in a broad historical context of disaster but did not distinguish it in kind from other destructions. The very debate as to whether the gas chambers and crematoria gave a qualitatively different meaning to what happened to the Jews had not yet started. Given this, the lack of emphasis in *Homens mapole* on Jewish suffering per se, as distinct from the suffering of others, could be read as the incapacity to assimilate the specific features of the Jewish catastrophe at such close range to the events.

A second factor that precluded emphasis on Jewish suffering might be tied to the imperative to rebuild, to renew. The historian Tony Judt, in his study *Postwar*, tells

Mordechai (Oscar Fessler) does battle with Haman (Leon Szpigelman) in the original 1946 Paris production of *Homens mapole*, directed by Oscar Fessler. (From the archives of the YIVO Institute for Jewish Research, New York.)

us that the majority of peoples in the lands recently occupied by the Germans were more interested in putting uncomfortable or unpleasant memories behind them and getting on with their fractured lives. "All over Europe," he says, "there was a strong disposition to put the past away and start afresh."[28] Seen from this perspective, the minimal attention given to the destruction of Jews within the play expressed a vital need to escape. The Israeli novelist Aharon Appelfeld, who saw various theatrical performances in transit camps in the immediate aftermath of the war, portrays this negatively: "What did these troupes express? Essentially it was the latent, instinctive desire to live and to restore us to life; on another level, it was a kind of protest against suffering and sorrow; but above all it was forgetfulness . . . anything so as not to be alone with oneself."[29] This same phenomenon is evaluated much more positively elsewhere. "What was the response of the Jews in the displaced persons camps? They rebuilt their lives, both physically and spiritually."[30] Most reviewers of *Homens mapole* saw it as a sign of the latter. "A veln lebn" (A desire to live) is the title of an early review of the play in Paris, representative of many others.[31] The play moved onlookers precisely because it seemed a choice for life. To be sure, this "focus on the positive" coincides with obligatory Socialist Realist optimism, meant to remind the masses of their essential optimism.[32] Both Judt's and Appelfeld's remarks, however, suggest that forgetting the suffering presented itself as a kind of imperative, independent of any ideological mediation. It was, as Appelfeld put it, a kind of instinct.

To this point we have noted that in *Homens mapole*, Communism means two things. It positions Sloves and his group in the political camp of the Soviet Union, and minimizes or sidesteps the enormous suffering of the Jews in the name of a certain kind of universalism. In this more diffuse form, Communist ideology merges with many other factors, both conscious and unconscious, to produce a play that celebrates a victorious resistance, rather than one that mourns the countless, powerless victims. But there is yet a third way that Communism is present in the play, evident in its very form.

Homens mapole is a purimshpil—not only because it recounts the story of the book of Esther, but because Sloves self-consciously sought to recreate the folk genre. Practically no adjective recurs more frequently in the reviews than "folkshtimlekh" —in the popular style. The formal characteristics of the purimshpil were all the more prominent given the ambitions of both its author and its several directors in different locales to create avant-garde theatre. As is well known, the twentieth century avant-garde often went back to folk forms, in a reaction against the neoclassical and realistic theatre of the preceding centuries. One only has to read an interview with Oscar Fessler, the director *of Homens mapole*'s Paris production, to see how much attention he devotes to both the folk theatre and avant-garde conceptions of theatre art. Fessler often speaks of the similarities between the Commedia dell'Arte and the purimshpil. Under his direction, the characters too have double roles, playing both actors in a Jewish troupe and the characters of the Book of Esther. He speaks of the curtain that remains open for the duration of the performance and the changing of the props in front of the audience, as well as of the interchangeability of the props. Fessler speaks of the coordination of all the arts. Thus the actors' costumes were to be the same color as the set designs, and the movements on stage were to be in a triangle, symbolic of *hamentash*, the three-cornered pastry of Purim. The purpose of all theatre, he states, is to lift the spectator from his humdrum daily existence into a Sabbath-like, holy-day atmosphere.[33] The other chief directors of the play, Benjamin Zemach in the United States and Zygmunt Turkow in Latin America and Poland, were similarly influenced by the Russian and German avant-garde.[34]

The focus on these formal elements, on recreating the synergy of word, music and dance, and color on stage resulted, if one is to believe the many reviews, in the impression of a people's coming back to life. The music, the humor, and the colors suggested a communal rebirth. Reviewers speak of the play as of a light emerging from the darkness, as a black curtain lifting, as a sudden change on a child's face from tears to laughter.[35] One is reminded of the release of vital energies associated with the holiday of Purim itself—energies that are pent up during the year, but allowed full expression on this one day. Sloves's play stays clear, at least in his final version, of the scatological humor and sexual innuendo often associated with this release of energy in many popular purimshpiln.[36] But his intent, as he says in the preface to the published text of the play, is to reproduce the folkplay's *shprudlekhkayt*—its exuberance.[37]

Sloves does so in a number of ways. Music and dance play prominent roles, even though the play is neither a musical nor a folk operetta, as some purimshpiln were, but consists mainly of spoken prose. Folk songs break into the plot here and there, as in the wedding scene when Esther sings a lament, or when the King's ministers sing a silly ditty about being Aryans.[38] Dancing takes place at the end of various scenes and, in the French production, as the dancers change sets between acts. Both music composition and choreography were the work of professionals, and practically all the reviews focused on these aspects of the play, finding in them a good portion of the play's charm.

Much of the play's exuberance also came from its parodic humor; as is the norm in purimshpiln, much liberty is taken with the retelling of the biblical story of Esther. The parodic elements of Sloves's play, as in the traditional purimshpil, center on the character of Mordechai. In *Homens mapole*, we are first introduced to the great hero of the Jewish people as he stumbles on the stage *begilufndik*, drunk.[39] Mordechai is a matchmaker, as in so many purimshpiln. Yet even in his more solemn moments, Mordechai does not lose something of his goofy, irreverent character. He does not bow to Haman because, as he says, he is *Mordkhe ha-tsadik*—Mordechai the Righteous—and it just would not do.[40] This is not the silent, righteous character of the Bible. Even when he is engaged in a mortal combat with Haman, who has just drawn his sword with an enormous swastika handle, Mordechai counters the foe, in the French staging, with his matchmaker's emblematic umbrella.[41]

The humor, as most reviewers noted, is rife with the grotesque, with incongruous juxtapositions, and with illogic. Early in the first act, we find out that the palace guard, Parshandasa, is not really Persian. He is Mordechai's *landsman*, another Jew from Jerusalem. Mordechai wants news of the family, including the grandmother. The guard explains that since Haman's decrees about Jewish grandparents were enacted, they have had to prove in court that the grandmother was childless. Her own children were witness to that fact.[42] In another scene, King Ahasuerus, the great ruler of twenty-seven provinces, marries Esther under a Jewish canopy and the herald asks Mordechai to officiate since "di orelim kenen nisht, nebekh, keyn sheytl ivri" (the uncircumcised, alas, do not know a stitch of Hebrew).[43] In a similar reversal of logic, the *Persian* generals returning from the front are accused of

King Ahasuerus (Moshe Kineman) and the Herald (Yashar [Jakub Aronowicz]) in the original Paris production of *Homens mapole*, 1946. (From the archives of the YIVO Institute for Jewish Research, New York.)

Ensemble photograph of a revival of *Homens mapole* features the original Fessler production's characteristic triangular, hamentash shape on stage. Paris, 1948 or 1949. (From the archives of the YIVO Institute for Jewish Research, New York.)

being *goyishe kep* because they do not know who Mordechai is.[44] *Goyishe kep* is a term of opprobrium reserved for Jews who know as little about Jewish tradition as non-Jews (*goyim*). As a final example, in the last scene, Haman, knowing that he will be hanged, asks to say the *vidui*, the confession of sins. Mordechai accommodates and starts in the following manner: "Poyshe yisroel—vos hostu geton oyf peysekh tsum seyder?" (Offender of Israel—what have you done during the Passover Seder?) Haman replies: "Um peysekh tsum seyder, hob ikh gefresn broyt, in di vokhedike kleyder." (During the Passover Seder, I gobbled up bread in my weekday clothes.)[45]

This grotesque element of *Homens mapole*, its confusing all normal logic, recalls another characteristic of Purim—the principle of *na'afokh hu*—"it was turned upside down." Purim is the holiday of reversals because from the bottom, the Jews suddenly rose to the top, and from the top, Haman suddenly fell to the bottom: thus "Homens mapole," Haman's downfall. To symbolize this reversal of the normal order of things, all sorts of prohibitions are lifted on Purim. Drunkenness, crossdressing, theatre, and the lampooning of sacred texts and of venerated contemporaries, are all permitted and even encouraged. This goes back to the release of vital energies hitherto suppressed, but at the same time, it also demonstrates that the prevailing social order is pure convention.[46] It is not set in stone and could be utterly different from our usual experience.

Was not this the experience of a people who had just lived through the war? They had witnessed an unimaginable horror—the social order dissolving before their eyes to make room for the machinery of death. Then, they witnessed the restoration of life. Must not the conventions of society—what we usually take to be written into the very nature of things—have seemed very flimsy indeed, revealing a world of reversals? Itche Goldberg, the editor of *Yidishe kultur*, a journal originally associated with the Jewish Communists, describes *Homens mapole* in the following way: "In a world that has become insane, the absurd is the only measure of logic, of real wisdom, the true (crooked) mirror of a (crooked) world."[47] Y. Weinfeld, writing only a few months after the play's premiere in Paris, saw the grotesque elements of Sloves's play as revealing some secret about the cosmos that could not be expressed in any other way.[48]

The fact that everything could be otherwise, that everything is possible, can lead to a kind of existential despair, but it can also be a source of hope, for what one sees now is not the sum of what can be. What many saw then, in 1945–1946, must have been much the way Tony Judt describes it: "Europe in the aftermath of the Second World War offered a prospect of utter misery and desolation. Everyone and everything [. . .] seems worn out, without resources, exhausted."[49] Into this comes the logical illogic of *Homens mapole*. If our logic does not suffice, it leaves an opening. "God sits in the heavens and laughs," literary critic Stanley Fish tells us, is the verse from Psalm 2 often connected to the holiday of Purim.[50] We are not in control, and knowing that paradoxically frees us to imagine change and to wait for it.[51]

This is what I would like to refer to as the religious moment in the play. The parodic dimension of the purimshpil and the grotesque humor that Sloves emphasized made room for hope as an affirmation of life, despite the sorrow, and even in the midst of it. The very performance of this play, requiring, for its Paris production as well as for the others, several months of practice, an extensive cast, the renting of space, the pooling of many resources and talents, was itself a renewed commitment to life, and to the life of the Jewish people. If things are not cast in stone, then the reconstruction of the Jewish people, on a new and better basis, was also possible.

It is precisely here that Sloves's Communist commitment re-emerges. For did not Communism promise a world without oppression, a brand-new world? Mordechai's last speech announces this world in a half-playful, half-serious way:

"From today onward, there is no more Aryan descent in Persia and Medea! All will be equally privileged—the Jews exactly in the same way as the nations of the world. Everyone will make a living! Wine will pour from bottles, coins will sound in pockets, there will be joy to the nations and happiness to the Jews."[52] Max Rosenfeld, in his translation, captures the ditty-like nature of the passage in Yiddish; "Our country will again be a land of milk and honey, dates and figs, bread and meat, and plenty to eat! Roast duck and beer and good wine to fill you with cheer! No trouble and no fights, sunny days and peaceful nights!"[53] The speech ends with the following words: "Es vet zayn sosn bay goyim un simkhe bay yidn!" (There will be joy for the goyim and happiness for the Jews.")[54]

This language is not markedly Communist. It is simply a proclamation that a better life is coming. In the hope for such a world, Communism and the transcendence of "God sits in the heavens and laughs" blend into each other. Both are beyond the order we know, opening human beings to the realm of possibility.

This convergence was brief. By 1948, *na'afokh hu*, it was turned upside down. The Cold War affected community Yiddish theatres of the sort in which *Homens mapole* had been played, making it difficult, if not impossible, for Communists and anti-communists to cooperate in joint enterprises. The unity the play both called for and expressed translated into bitter struggles, in the Yiddish world, between the "progressives" and "reactionaries." Communism no longer blended into a generalized hope, but represented once again a separate and fiercely contested ideological commitment. Sloves wrote six more plays in Yiddish, the last one in the early 1960s. Five of the six were performed, but they are written in a different key. Gone is the exuberance of *Homens mapole* and, from 1948 on, gone too is a Communist allegiance that merged effortlessly with a Jewish one.[55] It has become something for which one must argue.

Appendix

Correspondence relating to *Homens mapole* (*Haman's Downfall*)

This letter is a response to one that Sloves must have included with the manuscript of *Haman's Downfall* to Nokhem Buchwald, in June 1940, just before the German occupation of Paris. Buchwald was the theatre critic of *Morgen frayhayt* (Morning freedom), the Yiddish Communist daily of New York, and he was closely involved in Yiddish art theatre in New York, especially Artef, and its successor, the Ensemble Players. The letter details some of the backstage operations involved in trying to get the play performed. Maurice Schwartz was the director of the Yiddish Art Theatre, and very well known as both an actor and a director. No doubt Schwartz turned to Buchwald because the latter had more resources than the fledging, amateur Ensemble Players. The correspondence between Buchwald and Sloves does not resume until 1944. After the Germans occupied Paris, Sloves left for the Free Zone and settled in Lyon, where he lived under false papers and as a member of the Communist Resistance. He was the co-editor of the Yiddish Communist underground newspaper *Unzer vort* (Our word).

New York, September 8, 1940
Respected colleague H. Sloves!

Forgive me that I did not answer your last letter right away. But there is a reason for it, as you will soon see.

I received your play and read it immediately. I was living outside of New York this summer. So I immediately wrote a letter, full of enthusiasm, to Maurice Schwartz. This is an excerpt from that letter:

> I have read over the play and what can I tell you? I am truly enchanted. Not only will the public enjoy it, but it is joyful from beginning to end, and it is a play for theatre, a treasure for every creative director, and it is the kind of popular money-making play that can draw any spectator, from the most refined taste to those ordinary ones who pack the *shund* theatres. When I read the play, I imagined what would come out of it in your theatre and how you would enjoy the central role—a theatrical figure filled with folk humor, filled with the qualities of Hotsmakh[56], and with the tradition of the harlequin. And a number of other roles are like that too. The text is entertaining through and through, and written in wonderful folk-style [*folkshtimlekh*] language. I have dreamt of such a purimshpil for years. I consider this play a treasure for you and that at the moment it is the finest and the best that the art-theatre can wish for.

In such a tone did I write to Maurice Schwartz. He, naturally, became interested, and I sent him the manuscript. A few days later, I received a telegram from him saying that he wants to see me. It was during the terrible heat wave, when New York is a city without air, but I went into the city and had a long conversation with Schwartz. He liked the play and he assured me that if he had received it earlier, he would have started the season with it. I showed him your letter, in which you authorize me to negotiate about the play, and he claimed that according to the letter I had a legal right to underwrite a contract for you. We agreed on the conditions—not at all bad, given the situation his theatre is in. He must perform the play within a year and a half, no later than December 15, 1941. In the weeks that the play is being performed, the honorarium is to be $130/week, if it is played nine times a week, as is customary here. If not, you will get 20 dollars a performance Friday, Saturday and Sunday night, 15 dollars for Friday and Saturday during the day and 10 dollars for weekday evenings. Everything was arranged and, a while later, Schwartz sent me the contract form. But Waden, his attorney, explained to him that according to your letter I am not a legitimate representative of the author and that if I want to be, I need to get a formal authorization from you beforehand.

I immediately sent you a telegram with the request that you would send me the authorization. But in a few days' time, I received the telegram back from the telegraph office, because the address was in the Occupied Zone and no telegrams were received there. I had to wait until I got your address. When I received your last letter, I immediately sent its contents to Schwartz, with an urgent request that he give me a separate 50 dollars on your behalf. Schwartz did not give it, thinking up all sorts of excuses. Through other people, we are trying to collect approximately this sum for you, and perhaps we will succeed. After Schwartz's way of behaving, my desire to underwrite a contract with him cooled. What do you need it for? He does not give you an advance and he holds the right to the play for a year and a half, which means that my hands are tied, and that I can't negotiate with anyone else.

I think we should do the following: You send me the authorization immediately. What to write I do not need to teach you; you are a lawyer, after all, and I am only a theatre critic. Write in Yiddish or English or in French that you give me the right to negotiate with any theatre official about your play and that I am authorized to underwrite a contract for you. It can easily be imagined that Schwartz will badly need your play after this season because the show he is starting with has an excellent chance of failing. If he turns to me after the play, I will obtain an advance for you beforehand. I will insist on a minimum of 150 dollars, and will, of course, send you this money right away. If he again will not need the play for that season, for what reason in hell (in a Schwartz yor) should I underwrite a contract with him, without receiving a penny? If we do need to wait until December 1941, we can wait without being bound! Why should I give the right to Schwartz to block access to the play, if you do not gain anything materially from it?

So this is the situation as of now. I am sure that your play will be performed, if not now than a year from now. Maybe it will indeed be performed by Schwartz. Meanwhile, I can't produce even a dollar as an advance. If the interest that the play has aroused is a consolation to you, be consoled. If, on the other hand, you awaited immediate real results, this is, understandably, a disappointment. From my side, I have done all that I could, and I am ready to plow the earth with my nose so that that the play can be performed and that you can be materially compensated as you should be.

As concerns the few dollars that we are trying to collect for you, you have probably heard about it from other friends.

So stay healthy and strong and send me the power of attorney. Since we have already decided this, it might be a good idea that you write to Dr. Mukdoyni[57] that you have given me the power of attorney to negotiate about the play. Otherwise, there may be some confusion, especially since Mukdoyni and I are not on the best of terms.
With friendship,
N.Buchwald
I am also sending you my home address
N. Buchwald
215 E. 12th Street
New York, N.Y.

Letter in English to Sloves from Nokhem Buchwald

215 E. 12th Street
New York, N.Y.
November 13, 1944
My dear Sloves:—

Your friends, including myself, were overjoyed at the news contained in your postcard dated September 27 that you were alive and well. I received your card only the other day and I immediately communicated its contents to those who knew you from Paris. They were all very happy and asked me to convey to you their warmest greetings.

I want you to know that we made every effort to communicate with you during the dark days of the German occupation. But letters were returned with the stamp of the Vichy authorities without further explanation. Naturally we were very much worried and we feared the worst.

I have both good and bad news about your play, "The downfall of Haman." For a time it looked as if Maurice Schwartz could produce it and that you would earn a considerable sum in royalties. But unfortunately nothing came of it. Schwartz was interested in the play only to the extent of preventing others from producing it.

A few months ago, a new non-professional group, including a few former Artef players, was formed, and upon my recommendation your play was accepted for production under the direction of Benjamin Zemach of the Habima. Zemach and myself put in a good deal of work on revising the script. We had to cut it considerably because it was too long and also because the outlook in 1944 is different from 1940 when you wrote the play. As a result, we eliminated the scenes that contain your prognostications of a people's revolt in Germany against Hitler and kept the plot more or less within the limits of the biblical story of Esther. In the opinion of qualified judges, the play gained by such a revision.

Unfortunately, the prospect of royalties from the play is not very bright. The group is non-commercial and will produce the play under difficult circumstances. I shall try to obtain from you some money as royalties, but the sum will be very small, probably no more than a hundred dollars.

However, it is too early to speculate upon this matter. The play will have its opening at the end of January or early in February.

I am, naturally, interested in the new plays you have written. If at all possible, send me the scripts.

I hope to hear from you soon and often.

Best regards from everybody.

Cordially yours

N. Buchwald

Letter from Nokhem Buchwald to Sloves

The manuscript that Sloves originally sent to Buchwald was much longer than the version of the play that appeared in book form in 1949, and, as Buchwald's letter makes clear, it was also longer than the staged versions performed in the 1945 New York production or the 1946 Paris production. The director of the New York version was Benjamin Zemach and the director of the Paris version was Oscar Fessler. Zemach was well known at the time and Fessler, the student of Granovsky mentioned in the letter, was not. Sloves, as he states in his introduction to the book, did significantly transform the Mordechai and Esther characters in his postwar rewriting, but whether this was due to Buchwald or to the general mood after the war is not clear. He left quite a few of the political allusions in, although he shortened this part as well.

December 4, 1945

Dear Comrade Sloves,

[...] You see, about *Haman's Downfall*, I have my doubts. I don't know what will come out of it from that student of Granovsky, and I am sure that his staging version can be just as charmingly creative, and quite different from that of Zemach. I want to acknowledge, though, that I worry not so much about the director as about the author. Your formulation: "the primitive, exuberant purimshpil element" is characteristic of your entire approach to the play and is, in my opinion, a crutch for the serious flaws of the original. Certainly exuberance is a quality, and our show was at the height of exuberance. Certainly the purimshpil is an important cultural inheritance. Otherwise, we would not have been so taken with the very idea of staging a purimshpil. And folk charm is certainly a quality. And tradition too. But with all that exuberance in your original text, with the treasure of folk humor and puns, you did not, excuse my harsh opinion, pass the traditional purimshpil through the critical examination of a modern Jew of our kind. I am by no means ready to deify traditional garbage, and you should not do it either. Jewish spiciness—yes, but vulgarity, obscenity, a lawless [*hefker-petrushka*] approach to the characters—not this! There is a primitivism that is wonderfully beautiful and naïve, and there is a primitivism that gives off a stinking odor. My greatest objection to your original was that you were already too loyal to the "spirit" of the traditional purimshpil, including its most vulgar, most inadmissible features and manners. When Mordechai—the symbol of the Jewish people—is presented as a crook, a pimp, a gangster [*dzulik*] . . . who is ready to trick his niece for the sake of his career, this rings true to the traditional purimshpil, because it was a lawless world and the characters spoke what fell into the mouth of the "primitive" author and they operated with the "exuberance" of bad rhymes [*shtram-gram makh mir a letnik*]. When Esther comes out as a lusty female this is completely consonant with the "tradition." And so, where are we, the guardians among the cultural activists? Where are we, the selectors of the fine gold and the discarders of the garbage and poison in the tradition? Is it not clear that uncritical and nonselective traditionalism can lead our spirit who knows where?

I have therefore permitted myself to perform an operation on your original which you may have noticed and received with displeased surprise. I worked over your original for the sake of the fine gold—much fine gold both from the traditional purimshpil and from the talented remake—and for the sake of the fine gold I have tried to eliminate the garbage. Concluding from the necessity of shortening the text, which was twice the required length, and concluding from the political allusions, which no longer had any weight because the political reality automatically rejected and discredited them, I tried to save the honor of the purimshpil and, of course, the honor of the traditional Jewish symbolic figures, Mordechai and Esther. In the reworked text, they may not accord with the garbage of the "tradition," but they do accord with Jewish heroism. And what, I ask you is more preferable, the traditionalism of the "exuberant"-vulgar purimshpil texts or the traditionalism of Jewish sacrifice and nobility?

Had you seen our performance of *Haman's Downfall*, you would have had the same impression as the thousands of spectators and the few connoisseurs and people of refined taste had: that this is a purimshpil with all the details and all the charm, naïveté, playfulness and exuberance of the purimshpil of old. Nobody noticed that the garbage, the immorality, the obscenity, the empty illogical mish-mash of the "authentic" purimshpil were missing. The connoisseurs were delighted by the folk style, by the "Commedia dell'Arte" quality of the show. And we didn't on account of this quality sacrifice the values of the Mordechai-Esther symbols.

Of course we cannot expect that your director would take over either our version of the play, or our music, or our operatic technique. Of course, the text must be cut to the specifications of the conception and desires of your director and his staging idea. But we would like that in cutting the text, you cut with the same critical knife with which we cut: that you cut exuberance and spiciness where Jewish values are concerned. The traditional purimshpil is not an idol and we do not need to bow to it. It is a source from which we can draw either crystal-pure water or stinking mud. We must let go the mud.

Forgive me for the outburst but I was seized with anxiety at the very thought that Mordechai and Esther will in your reworking would come out the same as in the original. This would be a catastrophic mistake. It would also be a mistake, if you were, for the sake of "exuberance," leave the unnecessary "clever" puns. In what concerns the rhyme, this is clearly in accord with the tradition and if you could have carried through with the rhymed form throughout, this would have been an interesting matter. But since rhymes are a craft and often one must pay a high price for them, it isn't worth spending so much energy on them, in my opinion, and it is right only here and there to salt and pepper the text with the folk rhyme.

The following is Sloves's Foreword to *Homens mapole*, published as a book in Paris by the publishing house Oyfsnay, in 1949.

Haman's Downfall is not the renewal of an old Ahasuerus play. To restore a past genre is no doubt interesting, instructive, and important, but it is a subject that matters especially to researchers and to refined aesthetic tastes.

Haman's Downfall is altogether something different: It digs its way to the sources of the many-generations-old Yiddish theatre tradition, which is capable of fertilizing our theatre creativity today and of pouring new life into it because of its vigorous folk style (*folkshtimlekhkayt*) and its organic connection with the Jewish theatre temperament.

It is certainly one of the paradoxes of our theatre history that this very style, the so-called purimshpil, for many years practically the only expression and embodiment of secular theatrical enjoyment among Jews, soaking up, in its generations-long form, all that is in the folk style from the life of the masses, all the charm and flavor of the Yiddish word and of Yiddish movement, has had the least influence on our modern theatre movement and has remained outside the frame of modern Jewish playwriting.

Our literature has grown based on a blessed continuity—from generation to generation and from folk creations to the highest forms of artistic expression. But there is an enormous break in the line of development of our theatre. A rich heritage, many centuries old, was neglected and thrown away. And perhaps in this lies the main reason, notwithstanding all the achievements of our modern theatre, that we are still all looking for the secret of a truly Jewish theatre style.

Haman's Downfall is an attempt to bring into the contemporary Yiddish theatre the forgotten, artistic values of the theatre style of old. It is an attempt at a synthesis between the old Jewish form and today's modern content, on the basis of a sound, always Jewish folk style. This synthesis is sought less in dramaturgic formulas and stage designs than in the enlivening spirit of exuberant folk creativity, in the breath coming deep from the people transmitted to us by the purimshpil tradition.

The necessity of such a refreshing breath makes itself felt most especially today when the greater part of Yiddish playwriting is stuck in the smoke and mist of a mystique foreign to the folk tradition.

The current published text of *Haman's Downfall* is distinctly different from the first version of the play, which was finished in June 1940.

Between the two versions lie years of work and experience and most importantly—the flood of blood over the world and the terrifying destruction of our people [*unzer groylekher folks-khurbn*]. The hell fires of the crematoria disturbed not only the happiness of victory and the carefree nature of bright laughter, but also threw a new light on a number of characters in the play, a light that almost completely transformed them.

What has remained unchanged and in many ways even deepened is the love of folk creativity, the tremor of respect for and wonder at the unconquerable life force and wonderful optimism of our people.

Today more than ever, this people is like the black earth that nourishes, and at the same time, like the bright sun, toward which every living plant of authentic art draws near.

Notes

1. The play was performed in New York, Paris, Los Angeles, Wrocław, Brussels, Rio de Janeiro, and Buenos Aires. Sloves, in "Ha-tarbut ha-yehudit be-tsarfat" [Jewish culture in France], *Fri yisroel* [Free Israel], August 10, 1952, also claimed that it was performed in Romania and South Africa. I did not find archival material on the latter countries. The record of the other performances can be found either at the YIVO Institute for Jewish Research in New York City (file RG 1128) or at the Medem Library in Paris, under his name. By far the most complete archives are at YIVO, sent there by Sloves himself. Although the play's chief run occurred between 1945 and 1949, it was revived in 1957 in Buenos Aires and again in 1962, in the same city. In the latter case, it was performed in Spanish translation in the theatre faculty of the university. Both of these revivals were due to the move of the talented director of the French version, Oscar Fessler, to Argentina.

2. Purimshpiln could also be based on many other biblical themes, or even on non-biblical themes altogether. Many Hasidic communities, for instance, enact stories either based on Hasidic tales or on biblical accounts other than the Book of Esther. See Shifra Epstein, "Drama on a Table: The Bobover Hasidim Piremshpiyl," in Harvey E. Goldberg, ed., *Judaism Viewed from Within and From Without: Anthropological Studies* (Albany: State University of New York Press, 1987), 195–215; Jean Baumgarten, "Un Purimshpil à Kyriat Vishnitz de Bnai Braq (1996)," *Perspectives* 10 (2003): 127–142; Shari Troy, "On the Play and the Playing: Theatricality as Leitmotif in the Purimshpil of the Bobover Hasidim" (Ph.D. thesis, City University of New York, 2002). A standard study of the genre of the purimshpil is Khone Shmeruk, *Makhazot mikra'im be-yidish 1697–1750* [Yiddish biblical plays, 1697–1750] (Jerusalem: Israel Academy of Sciences and Humanities, 1979).

3. Sloves, *In un arum: eseyen* [In and around: Essays] (New York: YKUF, 1970), 300.

4. Ibid., 303.

5. Ibid., 304.

6. Ibid., 307. The friend was Nokhem Buchwald, theatre critic for *Morgen frayhayt,* the Yiddish Communist daily of New York, who edited the play and had it performed in New York in 1945.

7. For more details about the evolution of Sloves's relation to the Soviet Union, see his *A shlikhes keyn moskve* [A mission to Moscow] (New York: YKUF, 1985); Annette Aronowicz, "Spinoza among the Jewish Communists," *Modern Judaism* 24, (2004): 1–35; Aronowicz, "Haim Sloves, the Jewish People, and a Jewish Communist's Allegiances," *Jewish Social Studies* 9 (2002): 95–142.

8. Sloves, *Sovyetishe yidishe melukheshkayt* [Soviet Jewish state-building] (Paris: Haim Sloves, 1979); Sloves, *A shlikhes keyn moskve*, 1985

9. Sloves, *Homens mapole* (Paris: Oyfsnay, 1949), 29–30.

10. Ibid., 29.

11. Ibid., 24, 60, 65–66, 69–70, 85–86.

12. Ibid., 65–72.
13. Ibid., 85.
14. Sloves, *In un arum,* 303.
15. For an account of Jewish participation in the French Communist Resistance, see Annette Wieviorka, *Ils étaient juifs, résistants, communists* (Paris: Editions Denoël, 1984); Renée Poznanski, "On Jews, Frenchmen, Communists, and the Second World War," in Jonathan Frankel, ed., *Dark Times, Dire Decisions: Jews and Communism* (Oxford: Oxford University Press, 2004), 168–198.
16. Jonathan Boyarin, *Polish Jews in Paris* (Bloomington: Indiana University Press, 1991), 71.
17. Sloves, *A shlikhes keyn moskve,* 13–15.
18. Annie Kriegel, *Réflexion sur les questions juives* (Paris: Hachette, 1984), 68.
19. Annette Wieviorka, *Déportation et génocide* (Paris: Plon, 1992), 411, 431.
20. Annie Kriegel, *Communisme au miroir français* (Paris: Gallimard, 1974), 183.
21. Pol Gaillard, untitled review, *Lettres françaises,* May 10, 1946.
22. "Komyunistishe atake kegn Dr. H. Sloves 'Homens mapole'—a shedlekhe pyese. Vos vet itst zayn?" [A Communist attack against Dr. H. Sloves's *Haman's Downfall*—an evil play. What will happen now?] *Unzer shtime* [Our voice], November 2, 1949. This is a French Yiddish newspaper's report of a prior article in the Communist Yiddish newspaper of Warsaw, *Folks-shtime* [The people's voice], October 28, 1949.
23. *Homens mapole,* 59, 72, 73, 97 (for destruction of the Jews); 30 (enslavement of the rest of the world).
24. Purimshpiln in general made no reference to the violence the Jews unleashed on their enemies at the end of the Book of Esther. In leaving this scene out, Sloves followed folk tradition.
25. Ibid., 17.
26. Ibid., 72.
27. Ibid., 100.
28. Tony Judt, *Postwar: A History of Europe Since 1945* (New York: Penguin Press, 2005), 52, 61.
29. Aharon Appelfeld, "After the Holocaust," in Berel Lang, ed., *Writing and the Holocaust* (New York: Holmes and Meier, 1988), 87.
30. Morris M. Faierstein, "Abraham Joshua Heschel and the Holocaust," *Modern Judaism* 19, (1999): 255.
31. "'Homens mapole'—a veln lebn" [*Haman's Downfall*—A desire to live], *Naye prese* [New press], February 5, 1946.
32. Jeffrey Veidlinger, who examines the impact of Socialist Realism on Yiddish theatre, makes a similar observation about the immediate postwar period, arguing that the resurgence of hope was not merely ideological: "The victorious campaign of the Red Army during 1944 genuinely impressed upon Soviet citizens a new hope. The unbounded enthusiasm that overtook Soviet Jewish culture as the Red Army marched toward Berlin was not merely mandated by the state, but in fact seems to have genuinely permeated the thinking and attitude of many Soviet Jews after their country's victory over Nazi forces. Soviet Jewish writers celebrated the triumph of the Jewish people over Nazism and the perseverance of the Jewish nation." See *The Moscow State Yiddish Theatre* (Bloomington: Indiana University Press, 2000), 245–246.
33. Moshe Litwin, "Vi azoy mir hobn tsugegreyt dem spektakl" [How we got the show ready], *Naye prese,* February 19, 1946.
34. Each of the major directors of *Homens mapole* had been a student of some of the great Russian and German avant-garde directors. Fessler, for instance, had apprenticed in Max Reinhardt's studio and also worked, in Berlin, with Erwin Piscator, Bertolt Brecht, and Alexander Granovsky. Zygmunt Turkow, director of the Buenos Aires and Wrocław productions, and one of the founders of VYKT, the interwar Warsaw Yiddish Art Theatre, claimed to have been influenced by Vsevolod

Meyerhold and Piscator. Benjamin Zemach, the director of the New York and Los Angeles productions, had been one of the founders of Habima, the avant-garde Hebrew-language art theatre in the Soviet Union (which eventually moved to Israel) and had worked under Evgenii Vakhtangov.

35. "'Homens mapole'—a veln lebn," *Naye prese*, February 5, 1946; "Homens mapole," *Unzer shtime*, Feb. 2, 1946; "Encore une fois Haman-le-Terrible" [Haman the terrible one more time], *Droit et Liberté*, February 20, 1946; Y. Weinfeld, "Homens mapole," *Parizher shriftn* [Parisian writings] (1946), 83.

36. There is a difference in this respect between the first version of the play, written in 1940, and the one published in 1949, the latter being the source of the subsequent performances. Esther, in the earlier versions, is portrayed as a floozy, who had had a bad reputation back in Jerusalem, the city from which she and Mordechai originally hail. When she claims that she does not want to marry King Ahasuerus because she is in love with a young man, Mordechai lists all her previous lovers. Sloves, typescript of *Homens mapole*.

37. *Homens mapole*, 6.

38. Ibid., 52–53, 58.

39. Ibid., 13.

40. Ibid., 56.

41. Photograph, YIVO, Box 1, file 17.

42. *Homens mapole*, 18–19.

43. Ibid., 62.

44. Ibid., 87.

45. Ibid., 98–99.

46. Many scholars see Purim as a Jewish analogue of carnival, in the sense made famous by Mikhail Bakhtin, *Rabelais and His World* (Bloomington: Indiana University Press), 1984.

47. Itche Goldberg, *Eseyen* (New York: YKUF, 1981), 327.

48. Weinfeld, "Homens mapole."

49. Judt, *Postwar*, 13.

50. Stanley Fish, "Reading and Carnival: On the Semiotics of Purim," *Poetics Today* 15 (1994): 68.

51. My colleague, Barbara Henry, suggested that this insight calls to mind a wonderful quotation from Antonin Artaud, "No More Masterpieces," in *The Theatre and Its Double*, trans. Mary Caroline Richards (New York: Grove Press, 1958), 79: "We are not free and the sky can still fall on our heads. And the theatre has been created to teach us that first of all."

52. *Homens mapole*, 101–102.

53. Chaim Sloves, *Haman's Downfall. A Purim Shpil in Four Acts*, trans. Max Rosenfeld, in David S. Lifson, ed. *Epic and Folk Plays of the Yiddish Theatre* (Rutherford, N.J: Fairleigh Dickinson University Press, 1975), 223–224.

54. *Homens mapole*, 102

55. The six plays were as follows: *Nekome–nemer* [Avengers] 1947; *Di Yoynes un der valfish* [The Jonahs and the whale], 1947; *Di tsayt fun gezang* [The time of song], 1950; *Borekh fun Amsterdam* [Baruch of Amsterdam], 1956; *Di milkhome fun got* [The war of God], 1963; *Tsen brider zaynen mir gevezn* [We were ten brothers], 1963. Only *Tsayt fun gezang* remained in manuscript form; the rest were published as books. The dates given here are the dates of writing, not publication. For a discussion of the bitter recriminations between Jewish communists and non-Communist Jews, as well as some of the cracks that appeared in the Jewish Communist symbiosis, see Annette Aronowicz, "Haim Sloves, the Jewish People, and a Jewish Communist's Allegiances."

56. A lovable trickster, one of the central characters of Avrom Goldfaden's operetta *Di kishefmakherin* (The sorceress.) For more details about this character and play, see Chapter 13.

57. Alexander Mukdoyni (1878–1958), the noted New York Yiddish writer and theatre critic.

CHAPTER 13

No Raisins and Almonds in the Land of Israel: A Tale of Goldfaden Productions Featuring Four Hotsmakhs, Three Kuni-Lemls, Two Shulamits, and One Messiah

Donny Inbar

Enthusiastic Amateurs, Hotheaded Saboteurs

In December 1914, a performance in Tel Aviv of Avrom Goldfaden's (1840–1908) opera *Shulamis* was interrupted by a group of hotheaded high school students from Gymnasia Herzliyah, who were intent on committing acts of sabotage. The Yiddish poet Yehoash (Solomon Bloomgarden, 1870–1927) recounted in his memoirs how the stridently secular students had first attacked a poor woman working in her garden on the Sabbath, then prevented Socialist activist and author Chaim Zhitlovsky (1865–1943) from making a speech in Yiddish, and finally entered the theatre, where "They launched a 'chemical obstruction' in a theatre where the Yiddishists—who have as much chance in Tel Aviv as the Hebraists in Chicago—were producing a play in Yiddish [Goldfaden's *Shulamis*]."[1]

As the Hebrew press reported, the Turkish police were summoned, and the young vandals arrested.[2] This rowdy episode in the history of Goldfaden productions in Palestine is not representative, however, of the vast majority of productions staged there.[3] Goldfaden enjoyed a largely mainstream status, and the diverse artistic approaches taken with his plays serve as fascinating test cases in resurrecting a "moldy" traditional repertoire. The Israeli reception of Goldfaden also illustrates how his vitality as a cultural symbol at times exceeded the popularity of the plays themselves.

It is essential, however, to distinguish between the alleged hostility with which the Hebraist *yishuv* (the Jewish Zionist community in pre-statehood Palestine) treated the Yiddish language, and its simultaneously warm embrace of Yiddish culture. In 1929, Chaim Nachman Bialik (1873–1934) was one of the first to clarify this duality of language and culture:

From the Yiddish language Hebrew received its intimacy and vitality; [. . .] In Eretz Israel[4] Hebrew ceased to be a holy tongue; namely it lost the narrow focus on limited areas of life and has metamorphosed into a vernacular. On the other hand, Yiddish lost the ground of life from under its feet, and now it seeks refuge—as Hebrew had formerly done—in literature. Hebrew has become the language of life, Yiddish—of ideology. *Language is only one component—though an important one—of culture.*[5]

Goldfaden, widely known as "the father of the Yiddish theatre," enjoyed an unlikely friendship and mutual admiration with Eliezer Ben Yehuda (1858–1922), the man remembered as "the father of modern Hebrew." Their camaraderie gave rise to the first Hebrew translation of the complete text of a Yiddish play, Goldfaden's *Der fanatik oder di tsvey Kuni-Lemls* (*The Fanatic, or The Two Kuni-Lemls*), which was published in 1900 as a booklet by the press attached to Ben Yehuda's newspaper, *Ha-tsvi* (The stag).[6] The newspaper also ran an extensive advertising campaign for the Hebrew *Two Kuni-Lemls*, especially during the Purim season, and the play was eventually produced by the students of the Mikve Yisrael agricultural school on the holiday of Tu Bishvat in 1902. A quarter of a century later, this translation was used for the first semi-professional Goldfaden production by "The Association of Eretz-Israeli Actors" in October 1927. Two decades on, this archaic translation was reprinted under even more unlikely circumstances, when it was one of a series of booklets distributed to Israel Defense Force soldiers in 1949–1950, shortly after the end of the War of Independence. The first dozen booklets in this series were devoted to war historiography, but the "dessert" was this stalwart Hebrew *Kuni-Lemls* translation.[7] One can only speculate on the motivations of the military's education department for including a near-forgotten Yiddish comedy in soldiers' rations of instructive martial pamphlets.

Bewitched

The Goldfaden play that has proved to be a favorite among both professional theatre artists and their audiences in Eretz Israel is *Di kishefmakherin* (The sorceress, 1879). Palestinian/Israeli theatres have averaged one professional production of *Di kishefmakherin* per decade for the past seventy years, making it one of the most frequently produced plays of any kind in Israel. At least twelve Israel Prize laureates, as well as two of the theatres honored with this prestigious award, have been involved in Goldfaden productions.[8]

The special magic that *Di kishefmakherin* has cast on Israelis, rendering it the "default" Hebrew Goldfaden, calls for a separate discussion. The secret of the play's appeal lies both in its form and musicality, and in its relative lack of ideological partisanship. *Di kishefmakherin* is not particularly secularist, or nationalis-

Ha-mekhashefa (The sorceress), by Avrom Goldfaden, produced in Hebrew at the Ohel Theatre, Palestine, 1946. Reproduced by permission of the Israeli Documentation Center for the Performing Arts.

tic, or Zionist, but rather celebrates the collaboration of the "lowly" traditional Jewish peddler Hotsmakh with the stalwart maskilic lover Markus. The lamb and the wolf of the Haskalah dwell together on stage in song and dance, and their collaboration outlives any dated ideological matrix of the Haskalah. *Di kishefmakherin* was one of the final plays of Goldfaden's early cycle of Jewish Enlightenment satires, and is known by a multitude of Yiddish titles, including *Di makhsheyfe, Di tsoyberin,* and *Koldunye.* It is a musical fairytale that draws on folkoric archetypes in its tale of the orphan girl Mirele's abduction by the evil sorceress, Bobe Yakhne. After being sold by the sorceress to a gypsy, Mirele ends up in Turkey, where the unlikely team of Markus the maskil and Hotsmakh the Hasidic peddler rescue her, and return her home for a happy ending.

The first professional Hebrew-language production, as *Ha-mekhashefa,* was performed at The Eretz-Israeli Comedy in 1935, and it established the high standards with which Goldfaden was to be staged from that point on. The producer was Dr. Miriam Bernstein-Cohen (1893–1991), a physician from Kishinev who had studied acting with Stanislavsky and Nemirovich-Danchenko. She and her husband, Michael Gor, who directed *Ha-mekhashefa* and played Hotsmakh, were among the founders of the first professional theatre in Eretz Israel.[9] The repertoire of 1935 included Brecht and Weill's *Threepenny Opera,* Gogol's *The Government Inspector*, and Hašek's *Good Soldier Schweik* (performed at the Habima and the

Ohel, the two established repertory theatres). Bernstein-Cohen's memoirs make clear that the company's attitude to the play was neither patronizing nor apologetic: "We considered it our privilege and honor to revive an original Jewish musical play by the founder of the Jewish Theatre. [. . .] This was a bold attempt to present a musical."[10]

Ben Ze'ev Liber, an immigrant from Germany who founded the magazine *Ha-khayim ha-llalu* (This life: an illustrated Eretz-Israeli weekly), was full of praise in his review, which remarked on "the utmost importance of Goldfaden's primeval theatrical talent for the benefit of our theatre in Eretz Israel. [. . .] The Eretz-Israeli Comedy should compliment itself for having made the first step in this direction." Unlike the two known approaches to such material—either the "primitive-naïve" or the "Muscovite propagandist," he wrote, the Eretz-Israeli Comedy chose a third path, and treated the play as a full-scale professional operetta, including jazzy musical arrangements and tap-dancing.[11]

The play's translator, Nathan Alterman (1910–1970), already an established lyricist and promising poet in his own right, made a number of unorthodox choices in his translation. The first was the insertion of a comically nuanced modern Israeli motif into one of the market songs, which turned it into a humoristic musical jingle for home-grown oranges:

Bo, bo, bo'u, dvash ve-khalav
Mitz ein kamohu, mitz tapukhey zahav
Ha-boker rak higi'a.
Yashar me-herzliya
Hine ha-pri rakh ve-tari
Bi, adoni, shte ve-tavri.[12]

(Come, come, come for milk and honey
Golden orange juice, best value for your money
Arrived this morning here.
Straight from Herzliyah
The fruit is juicy, you can tell
Have a sip, sir, and get well!)

His other major change, however, was reversed before the opening: Alterman sought to Hebraize Markus's "assimilated" name into Mordechai, probably unaware of the special status of the maskilic hero named "Markus."[13] More far-reaching artistic choices would be made by later Hebrew translators of *Ha-mekhashefa;* these would so overshadow Alterman's earlier work that his version was not included in his collected works, and is presumed to be no longer extant.[14]

The Ohel Theatre, the theatre of the Labor movement (under David Ben Gurion's auspices), first produced Goldfaden in 1947. Once again, it was *Ha-mekhashefa.*

Their translator, Abraham Levinson (1891–1955), is credited with coining a phrase that has become an enduring Hebrew idiom.

One of Mirele's sobbing arias opens with "Oy, ir yidn bney rakhmonim" (Oh, you Jews, sons of the merciful), which, in fact, consists of as much Hebrew as it does Yiddish. "Oy" has Slavic roots; "ir" and "yidn" both come from the Germanic component of Yiddish; and "bney" (sons of) and "rakhmonim" (merciful) both derive from Hebrew. In 1935, Alterman had translated it faithfully as "*Yehudim bney rakhmanim.*" But in the shift from Ashkenazi to the so-called "Sephardi" pronunciation, which entails a shift in stress from the penultimate to the ultimate syllable, the original Goldfaden flavor was at risk.[15]

Levinson, therefore, took some liberties, and in accordance with the biblical mode of doubling a verb and changing the second verb's vocalization and stress for greater emphasis (*Shafot eshpot* [Judging I will judge], *Som tasim* [Put, you will put], *Halokh telekh* [Go, go thee]), he adapted the line to read *Yehudim, rakhmu rakhemu*. The approximate English equivalent would be: Jews, have mercy, mercy. This version worked a magic as forceful as Bobe Yakhne's, and proved so memorable that all future translations of *Di kishefmakherin* would contain either delicate variations or outright plagiarisms of the line. Allusions to the play, the song, or an equivalent play on words with the same doubled format were to appear in several other Goldfaden productions.[16]

Yehudim rakhmu, rakhemu became a Goldfaden trademark in Israel, and, arguably, even the trademark of Yiddish theatre itself for Israeli audiences. The idiom has become so deeply rooted in Israeli culture that even in the summer months of 2005, during public debate over the unilateral Israeli withdrawal from the Gaza strip, both proponents of territorial compromise and fervent right-wing Orthodox settlers often used the phrase *Yehudim rakhmu, rakhemu*. On the internet and in opinion pieces in the Israeli press, the phrase was employed in both a straightforward manner, and to convey a cynical, mocking attitude.[17] A year earlier, in 2004, a radical sculptor, Motti Mizrahi, commissioned rock star Berry Sakharof to perform a hard-rock rendition of the song, in a complex triple exhibit-performance event that involved Yigal Amir (Yitzhak Rabin's assassin), the music of Egyptian classical singer Um Kultum, images of Mordechai Vanunu (who publicized Israel's atomic secrets), and the inevitable *Yehudim rakhmu, rakhemu*.[18]

Framing a Goldfaden Potpourri and Resurrecting a Generic Shtetl

Moshe Halevi, the Ohel artistic director who mounted the 1947 Hebrew production of *Di kishefmakherin*, set yet another stylistic standard for future Goldfaden productions in Israel. He added a framing device to Goldfaden's original play, and produced it as a play-within-a-play involving a traveling Jewish company, its director and actors, a hotel owner, and a policeman, as well as an onstage "audience."

This was inspired both by Mikhl Weichert's (1890–1967) 1934 production of *Trupe Tanentsap* (The Tanentsap troupe) in Poland, and several Sholem Aleichem tales on Yiddish theatre.[19] Though produced shortly after the end of World War II, Halevi's production refrained from indulging in sentimentality, guilt, and eulogies, and emphasized life rather than mourning. This convention was to become a staple in subsequent Goldfaden productions, and those that strayed too far from it flopped. The framing device combined an apologetic statement about the primitive and naïve nature of the original "folk" play, with a call for poetic license for a light-hearted or parodic style. It also provided an opportunity to present medleys of Goldfaden favorites from other plays. A sub-genre evolved that also tied an additional festive ribbon to the event, presenting several Goldfaden productions as anniversary celebrations of "the eightieth jubilee of the founding of Goldfaden's theatre," "the ninetieth anniversary of *Di kishefmakherin*," or "the hundred and twenty-fifth anniversary of Yiddish theatre in Europe," and so forth. Each Goldfaden production was regarded as a unique and rare event, notwithstanding the frequency of these productions.[20]

Following the Ohel's 1947 smash hit *Ha-mekhashefa,* the other two repertory theatres of the time, Habima and the young Cameri Theatre of Tel Aviv, attempted to create their own variation on this popular theme. But despite commissioning renowned directors of genuine Yiddish theatre, Dovid Licht (1904–1975) and Zygmunt Turkow (1896–1970), they had little success. Licht's bizarre 1953 *Ma'ase be-nasikh* (A tale of a prince), an adaptation of Goldfaden's *Kaptsnzon et Hungerman,* left very little of the original play and got carried away with its frame story.[21] It was savaged by many of the critics, yet ran for forty-five performances. Turkow's 1950 production was a recreation of his 1938 adaptation of Sholem Aleichem's *Blondzhende shtern* (*Wandering Stars*) for the Warsaw Yiddish Art Theatre (Varshever Yidisher Kunst-Teater, or VYKT). The stage production, about an actor nicknamed Hotsmakh and a flea-bag traveling Yiddish theatre reminiscent of Goldfaden's own, closed after only eleven performances.[22] Both guest directors, it seems, offered eulogies for a *dead* Jewish theatre rather than a celebration of its ongoing life. In a traumatized, post-Holocaust Israeli society, celebration had proved key to the success of most other Goldfaden productions, including those created by Holocaust survivors who had made *aliya* (immigrated) to Israel. The translator of *Blondzhende shtern* was the poet Abraham Shlonsky (1900–1973), who, having ferociously advocated a "divorce between Hebrew and Yiddish" in the early 1920s, later became one of the most enthusiastic promoters of Yiddish culture in Hebrew translation. He contributed an impassioned and highly charged rhymed prologue and epilogue to the Hebrew translation, which departed from the Sholem Aleichem original by stressing the idea of rebirth rather than endings:[23]

Petakh davar
Kahal nikhbad, ha-lo tislakh salo'akh

Im nedakdek ha-yom ve-lo nukhal lidlog
Al nosakh mesuyam bo nohagim lifto'akh
Makhazot be-hakdama, ma she-korin prolog.

Ve-ha'inyan hu ze: ha-pa'am kan mutseget
Pinat khayim akhat, khayim asher eynam
Asher hayu ei-az. Rak hatkhala ileget
Tmima, af neloza, kmo ilgut ha-am.

Ha-am, asher he'ez limrod bi-shkhol, be-oni,
U-ve-akmimut khayav asher avlu me'od,
Lomar od lenafsho: hitna'ari va-roni
U-shmei khalom lifros le-khokhavav lindod.

(Prologue
Dear audience, forgive us if you would
If we stick to the protocol and, pray,
Don't skip over the practice and include
The opening, called the prologue of the play.

And this is all it is: tonight we bring to you
A piece of life, a life that is no more,
But that once was; a lame beginning was it, true,
Crooked and naïve, just like the innocent people of yore.

Defiant against poverty and gloom, the nation cries,
"End our crooked ways, there is no time to ponder!"
It dares to call and herald thus: "rejoice, arise!"
And spread a sky of dreams, where stars could wander.)

Sof davar
Ve-Hotsmakh ba, ve-Hotsmakh met,
Ve-khakh, alo va-redet masakh bimat ha-zman gazar:
Shikhekha ve-zikaron korot ha-am gam hem nidmu
Ke-lehaka nodedet, adei amar ha-kets, ha-kets!)[24]
U-ve-khesed ha-moledet anakhnu ha-gilgul ha-akharon.)[25]

(Epilogue
And Hotsmakh came and died, the curtain of the stage
Of time went up and down, the mem'ry and oblivion of a nation
Just like a wand'ring troupe, the people's annals, the crumbled pages,
'Til at the wake they heard, awake! And hark, new generation,
We, in the homeland, are the last reincarnation.)

An almost identical spirit animates the prologue added to the 1959 stage adaptation of *Di tsvey Kuni-Leml*, by Moshe Sakhar and director Israel Becker. Becker (1917–2003) was by then a member of the Habima National Theatre ensemble, and the screenwriter and star of the 1948 Yiddish film *Lang ist der Weg* (Long is the road).

Be-miskhak he-erev nenatsel
khezyonot ha-yeduim mikvar. Mi-pilel shegam be-yisrael
Pizmono shel Goldfaden yushar.
Bi-shat khipus ha-toda'a
Al tabit be-za'am le-akhor
Ki me'az davar lo hishtana
Zot nir'e lavan al pnei shakhor.
Kuni-Leml, Kuni-Leml,
Mi-kabtsansk ad yisrael,
Hu yatsig lanu ha-erev
Khizayon al katriel.[26]

(In tonight's performance we'll exploit
Well-known visions of yesteryear
Goldfaden's ditty, who'd have thought
Would be sung in Israel, right here?
When an identity is sought
Looking back in anger just won't do
What has really changed now? Naught.
We'll show it black on white for you.
Kuni-Leml, Kuni-Leml
From *Kabtsansk* to Israel
He'll perform for us this evening
A good old *Kasrilevker* tale.)

The prologue and epilogue of *Kokhavim to'im* (*Wandering Stars*) and the introduction to *Kuni-Leml* share a belief that the Yiddish cultural world that had been exterminated was alive in Israel. The lyrics repeat the message of reincarnation and vitality of both the people and their cultural legacy, as they proudly embrace "Yiddish" life and theatre. Not only do they re-emphasize the link between Yiddish past and Hebrew present, but they insert allusions to "respectable" western theatre. Shlonsky invokes Shakespeare, and Sachar makes a direct reference to *Look Back in Anger*, a mere three years after Osborne's modernist political play had opened in London.[27] Where Turkow's production used Sholem Aleichem's novel in an attempt to re-create Goldfaden's theatre, Sachar and Becker used the world of Sholem Aleichem and S. Y. Abramovitsh to complement Goldfaden's world, and to create a sort of a generic theatrical shtetl, fusing Abramovitsh's Kabtsansk and Sholem Aleichem's Kasrilevke.[28] It is also significant that the above additional lyrics were written and performed in 1950 and 1959, the period in which David Ben Gurion's government tried, unsuccessfully, to ban performances in Yiddish in the young State of Israel. But the productions also predate the 1961 Adolph Eichmann trial, which is said to have triggered Israelis' readiness to discuss the Holocaust openly.[29] Apparently, reversing negative evaluations of Diaspora life and re-embracing *yidish-kayt* were also necessary preludes to facing the horrors of the Holocaust.

The Hebrew *Kuni-Leml* production, which ran about 400 times, was made into a hit musical motion picture in 1966.[30] The original 1880 anti-Hasidic satire is a comedy of errors, in which an enlightened student disguises himself as his beloved's lame, half-blind, dim-witted Hasidic groom, and everything seems to go wrong, before it all ends happily. This first Israeli film musical also inspired two popular sequels: *Kuni-Leml be-tel aviv* (Kuni-Leml in Tel Aviv, 1976) and *Kuni-Leml be-kahir* (Kuni-Leml in Cairo, 1983).[31] All three were released on DVD between 2002 and 2005.

Laughter, Tears, and Commercials

About twenty-five years later, as a young director, I satirized the Shlonsky-Turkow-Becker-Sachar heroic pathos in an anarchistic fringe production entitled *Bi-tskhok va-dema yehuda nafla; bi-tskhok va-dema yehuda takum: melodrama kora'at* (With laughter and tears hath Judea fallen; With laughter and tears will Judea arise: A smashing melodrama).[32] This was an adaptation of Goldfaden's rarely produced six-act drama of 1891, *Meshiekhs tsaytn?!* (The Messianic era?!).[33] The play, one of Goldfaden's last, is a desperate attempt at contemporary relevance by a playwright whose dramatic services were no longer sought after. It attempts to encapsulate the entirety of modern Jewish history into a single work. The plot of Goldfaden's *Meshiekhs tsaytn?!* encircles the Jewish globe to include the traditional shtetl, assimilation in Russia, the tough reality of New York, white slavery in Argentina, and utopian Zionist Palestine. The tangled plot involves a plethora of melodramatic devices and special effects. The finale of our 1985 parody encompassed a similarly ambitious number of cherished Jewish and Zionist clichés and kosher sacred cows:

Bo'u yehudim lismo'akh
Bo'u yehudim livkot
Mukhrakhim ha-yom lishko'akh
Ve-lizkor ve-lo lishkot.
Ki zehu yom khagenu
Lakhen ha-lev nishbar
Ve-hakamim le-horgenu

Yamtinu ad makhar.
Bi-tskhok va-dema
At bokha o tsokheket?
Be-dema u-vi-skhok
Ha-shtika zo'eket.
Bi-tskhok va-dema
Harimu ha-raglayim
Ve-la-shana ha-ba'a bi-yerusholayim.[34]

(Fellow Jews, we're celebrating
Fellow Jews, it's time to cry
For today we are forgetting
And rememb'ring till we die.
This holiday now fills us
With broken hearts, oy vey,
And those who plot to kill us
Should wait just one more day.
With tears and laughter
Are you laughing or crying?
With giggling and *krekhtsn*
Even silence is sighing.
With tears and laughter
Hold hands and drink *l'chaim*
So that next year we'll be together in *yerusholayim* [Jerusalem]).

Veteran journalist Michael Ohad of *Ha'aretz* was both shocked and delighted by our aggressive parody—though its attack on cherished Goldfaden traditions was in no way as hostile as the stink-bomb lobbed by Herzliya hooligans at the amateur *Shulamis* production of 1914:

Bi-tskhok va-dema [. . .] is not a civilized production, and definitely not an aesthetic one. It is a play that jabbers and rattles, it is cheap and vulgar – and utterly enjoyable. It is different from any *Shulamis*, any *Sorceress* and *Kuni-Leml* that we've seen in Israel. [. . .] Donny Inbar and his brilliant cast's inventions (the Sabras are always excellent when they are allowed to shout, run around, and exaggerate) could suffice for half a dozen normative comedies. [. . .] Is this thing Goldfaden?! It's a party of drunken students who pull a handful of brilliant inventions out of their sleeve, and when they don't mock *The Messianic Era*, they mock themselves.[35]

Though not using the traditional framing device, the play was presented as a self-conscious play-within-a-play, inspired by Michael Green's *A Guide to Coarse Acting* (1964) and subsequent *Plays for Coarse Actors* (1978, 1980, 1985) and

Michael Frayn's *Noises Off* (1982). And since we considered nineteenth-century melodrama the equivalent of a modern-day soap opera, several commercial breaks were included in the elaborate plot. One of those commercials, which featured two actors inside human-size beer cans, was inspired by a running campaign for Israeli *Goldstar* beer and its ceaseless slogan *tnu la-gever goldstar* (Give the man a Goldstar). In the version of *Bi-tskhok va-dema* the star on the beer can was, naturally, master Goldfaden:

Zot ha-bira she-dofeket et ha-rosh
Ve-oti hi memastelet pi shalosh.
Zot ha-bira ha-akheret
Be-rama she-lo nigmeret
Ve-shotim ota im kas ve-gam im kosh.
Tnu la-gever Goldfaden
Mi-kol ever Goldfaden
Eize gever, Goldfaden
Hu mit'hapekh ba-kever Goldfaden.
Goldfaden, ve-ze tosesssssss!)[36]

(It's the cool beer that will always get you high
Gulp another six-pack, man, and don't be shy.
It's the beer that you keep pouring
Down your throat and ask for more in
Greater numbers till you either drop or fly.
Real men all drink Goldfaden
Real men all think Goldfaden
He's a rave, ol' Goldfaden
In his grave he rolls, Goldfaden. Goldfaden, it has a buzzzzzzzz!)

Shulamis, Shula, and the Asterisk

Since this survey of Goldfaden productions in Eretz Israel opened with the early crisis of *Shulamis*, it will conclude with a discussion of later productions of this operetta and the additional problems that the play raised. When The Ohel Theatre was set to produce its second Goldfaden ten years after the success of *Ha-mekhashefa*, artistic director Moshe Halevi chose to stage *Shulamis*, thus initiating a major debate over style. Unlike *Di kishefmakherin*, *Shulamis* is set in post-biblical times in the Judean desert and in Bethlehem, and a choice had to be made: should the Hebrew *Shulamit* be enacted "authentically" in the Zionist-Israeli sense, namely in Orientalist or "Bedouin" style? Or would its authenticity lie in its portrayal of the anachronistic manner in which the Jews of Goldfaden's era imagined the people of the desert? Halevi reached a compromise by combining the tried-and-true

Shulamit, by Avrom Goldfaden, produced in Hebrew at the Ohel Theatre, Israel, 1957. Reproduced by permission of the Israeli Documentation Center for the Performing Arts.

framing device of a Yiddish provincial theatre troupe, with a cast dressed in mock-biblical robes (actually ragged bed sheets), thus providing for an abundance of imaginative and comic situations.[37]

At the same time, an independent producer, George Val, was working on his own production of *Shulamit* for his theatre, Do-Re-Mi. Two simultaneous productions of the same play are a rare sight in Israel, whose potential audience tends to be too small to support two rival productions.

Val, a new immigrant from Romania (where Goldfaden's theatre was born in 1876), chose the stylistic path of orientalizing *Shulamis*.[38] Val's team was commissioned to write a brand-new "Israeli" score for the production, which was titled "The First Israeli Operetta." *Shulamis* effectively served two seemingly opposing purposes: by striking a sentimental and Diasporic note, the producer and creative team sought to exploit the nostalgic box-office potential of this beloved Yiddish operetta. But by adopting the dignified Zionist appellation "first Israeli operetta," they declared its status as both a brand-new, non-Diasporic work of art, and simultaneously reaffirmed ties to the heroic history of the Jewish people in the Land of Israel. The humble *Shulamis* served here as a theatrical *Altneuland* (*Old New Land*), a bridge between the ancient and the modern.

The unsubsidized production was to compete with the established Ohel's "sequel" to its previous hit, *Di kishefmakherin*. Whereas Val's popular composer, Moshe Wilensky, was now introducing "the first Eretz-Israeli *operetta*," the Ohel

Shoshana Damari as Shulamit, Do-Re-Mi Theatre production of Avrom Goldfaden's *Shulamit*, Israel, 1957. Reproduced by permission of the Israeli Documentation Center for the Performing Arts.

commissioned Mark Lavry, who, since the first 1935 *Ha-mekhashefa,* had composed *Dan ha-shomer* (Dan the guard), considered "The First Israeli opera." Both productions recruited champions and stars for this battle. It is noteworthy that Val's production, while priding itself on being the first authentic Israeli operetta, was boasting of (or drawing its legitimacy from) its strong ties with a Yiddish play of the Diaspora.

Goldfaden's *Shulamis* is based on a maskilic adaptation of a Talmudic tale about a Jewish maiden and a warrior who fall in love in the desert, in post-biblical Eretz Israel. They make a pledge to marry each other, with the well and a wild cat as their witnesses. Later, when the young man forgets his oath, disasters occur until the lovers are reunited.[39] In an effort to create an exotic "oriental" atmosphere, the casting choice of the Do-Re-Mi team for the role of Avisholem's slave (Tsingitang in the original) could be said to be in line with the colonialist sentiments of the Ashkenazi ruling class. An "authentic" Yemenite popular entertainer, Se'adia Damari, was cast in the role, whereas the title role went to a popular female vocalist, Shoshana Damari, none other than Se'adia's younger sister, and already a star in Israeli show business.[40]

The unprecedented double productions entailed another significant event: an enthusiastic—even heated—argument in the press about the right and wrong approaches to interpreting Goldfaden. The debate prompted headlines such as "And [it came to be that] Two Theatres were Holding One Shulamit . . ."[41] or "Shulamis vs. Shula."[42] The debate transcended the issue of the competing productions and focused now on the fundamental question of Jewish-Israeli identity: which sort of authenticity was more authentic.[43] In the footsteps of two earlier "public trials" held for the Hebrew productions of An-sky's *Der dibek* (*The Dybbuk*) and *The Merchant of Venice, Shulamis* now entered the ideological arena.[44]

Critics and commentators in the Israeli press relished the opportunity to discuss the fundamental significance of such stylistic choices, well beyond these specific productions. The debate as to whether the post-biblical content of the play or the theatrical Russian-Romanian context of Goldfaden's theatrical enterprises was more relevant here engaged most of the reviewers. (Only one critic, writing in Yiddish, covered only the Ohel's "traditional," if parodic, production, and ignored its "Sabra" rival.) Some reviewers suggested that the Do-Re-Mi production appealed primarily to new, non-Ashkenazi immigrants, whereas others found it more suited to the younger generation of Israeli-born spectators. There was criticism of both the parodic aspects of Ohel's production ("[Ohel's] Shulamit is a *yenta*") and of the commercialization of tragedy. (Damari reportedly emphasized the comic aspects of the opera throughout the production, and the production is over-influenced by the popularity of army entertainment troupe's sketch comedy.) The title "the first original Israeli operetta" did find favor with several critics, who praised the endeavor (especially since it was performed by a commercial, unsubsidized establishment), yet the outcome was still the object of criticism. No firm conclusions can be drawn from the unusually rich assortment of reviews and debates, but clearly, the opportunity for such a debate was favored by all.

However, the most dramatic aspect of the dichotomy between the two productions concerned one of the play's songs: "Rozhinkes mit mandlen" (Raisins and Almonds), one of the most popular Yiddish songs of all time, and probably the one Goldfaden song that has survived the test of time better than any other.[45]

In dem beys hamikdesh, in a vinkl kheyder,
Zitst di almone, Bas Tsiyon aleyn.
Ir ben-yokhidl, Yidele, vigt zi keseyder,
Un zingt im tsu shlofn a lidele sheyn:
Unter yideles vigele
Shteyt a klor-vays tsigele.
Dos tsigele is geforn handlen
Dos vet zayn dayn baruf.
Rozhinkes mit mandlen
Shluf zhe yidele shluf.[46]

(In a little corner of the old temple
Sits Zion's daughter, the widow, alone.
Her only son, Yidele, she softly cradles,
Wiping a tear while she's singing a song:
Under your cradle, Yidele, you know
There's a kid whose fleece is white as snow.
The little kid has gone to the market
That's your trade to keep.
Dealing in raisins and almonds
Sleep, my Yidele, sleep.)

Even Goldfaden himself clung to this scenario sentimentally in his final play, *Ben-Ami*.[47] This lullaby, whose lyrics were insired by a Yiddish folksong, was the only song of the original Goldfaden score whose tune was retained in the Do-Re-Mi production.[48]

"Raisins and Almonds" is a lullaby in which a mother, sitting among the ruins of the Holy Temple in Jerusalem, prophesies that her son will become a trader in the marketplace, and then at the stock exchange, and will ride railroads on his way to new worlds. It was absolutely anachronistic for a biblical piece, as Goldfaden himself was aware, as is evident from his footnote to the script: "Though this song does not really belong in this place, I still put it in here because the public knows it and likes it so much."[49] The Do-Re-Mi team decided on a radical solution. They simply wrote brand-new anachronism-free lyrics, while keeping the original tune. Thus "Raisins and Almonds," traditionally sung by Avisholem, became another solo for the heroine, in the form of "Shulamit's Dream":

Parkha ha-tsipor al knaf ga'agu'a
Kara ha-midbar la va-ta'an homa.
Avnei ha-bazelet, imru la madu'a
Lo ye'asfena bekhir khaloma.

Khalomi, khalomi, ha-yitgashem?
Alumai, alumai, le-mi etnem?
Mi yankheni elekha?
Mi ya'ir et leili?
Bosheshu pe'amekha
Ana hoshia eli.
Bo'a, bo'a dodi[50]

(The bird has flown on the spread wings of yearning
The desert had called and she cooed in a dream.
O, pray, lava rocks, and answer, she's burning,
Why her cavalier would not come to redeem?

O, my dream, my dream, will it come true?
O, my youth, my youth belongs to you.
Who'll deliver and carry?
Who will light my dark night?
Oh, your feet, they still tarry.
Lord, please answer my plight
Beloved, appear in my sight.)

Shoshana Damari, playing Shulamit, was already famed as the Yemenite vocalist who sang "Rozhinkes mit mandlen" in fluent Yiddish to Holocaust refugees in Cyprus, and to American Jews.[51] In an interview in 1998, Damari recalled: "We wandered [in 1948] in camps and hospitals . . . [Rozhinkes mit mandlen] in Yiddish is the single song that I'd never managed to sing through, because their emotional excitement rose to such heights that they'd always ask us to stop."[52] The "exotic" Damari was, furthermore, strongly identified as *the* biblical Shulamit from the Song of Songs, and, by extension, with the Land of Israel itself.[53] Yet ironically, in the Land of Milk and Honey, Shulamit had to abandon the original lyrics to "Rozhinkes mit mandlen." The original was exchanged for a libretto steeped in Eretz-Israeli, biblical, messianic, and oriental allusions, to including such characteristic motifs as the Lava Rocks of Tiberias, cooing doves, the feet of the messenger, the lover of Song of Songs, and the pillar of fire.

Arguably, however, the rival Ohel's "traditional" interpretation of this same song embraced a far more radical approach than that of the Do-Re-Mi. For while the Zionist ethos could easily embrace the anachronisms for which Goldfaden had apologized, it could not tolerate the future mercantile profession that the mother wishes for her son. To become a trader at the fair, to make profitable deals in the stock exchange, and then to journey to the Golden Land? The message in the original folksong, based on the Yiddish idiom "toyre iz di beste skhoyre" (Torah is the best merchandise), definitely did not suit the Zionist socialist vision. This may have been the reason that Yakov Lerner's first faithful Hebrew translation of the play in 1921 made one single omission: he did not include the second verse of the song, which refers to the stock exchange and making money.[54] In fact, all of the Hebrew versions of "Rozhinkes mit mandlen" ignore the "problematic" issue of a mother's wishing her son to become a merchant. All Hebrew translators to this day have chosen not to confront the song's un-socialist, prosaic aspirations. Shmuel Fischer offers a free adaptation in which "Raisins and almonds / Will bloom in your garden." In Haim Hefer's, the white kid "To all children / From his way will bring / Raisins and almonds." Yoram Tehar-Lev preferred an obscure syntactical reference to the issue: "The kid has gone to the market / He will take you with him / Raisins and almonds / Sleep your slumber, my son." Ehud Manor came the closest to the "reactionary" petit-bourgeois original when he, while neither wishing nor even discussing actual trading at the fair, at least set it in a market stall: "Underneath you a white kid stands / Who's returned from the old marketplace / You, too, will get there / And will find there a stall / Raisins and almonds / Good night, little son."[55]

Apparently, of all the issues involving Yiddish culture in general, and Goldfaden's repertoire in particular, the idea of an innocent Jewish boy's launching a career in trade proved to be the most intolerable for the theatre of the labor movement. For three decades, the theatre of the Zionist Federation of Unions presented a rich assortment of plays from the Yiddish repertoire (Abramovitsh, Sholem Aleichem, H. Leivick, I. J. Singer, I. L. Peretz), regardless of Ben Gurion's declared mission to banish Yiddish from the country.

Shimshon Meltzer (1909–2000), translator of the play for the Ohel production, inverted Lerner's omission by adding a final verse to the lullaby that reversed both the mother's wishes for a trading career for her son, and the course of his journey to capitalist America.[56] The path that started in ancient Eretz Israel in the first verse now ended in modern Eretz Israel in the last. The bourgeois banker who trades in stocks turns into a total rejection of materialism; commerce in grain is transformed into harvesting in sunny fields; trading in raisins and almonds is replaced by the healthy reaping of vines and almonds;[57] and the innocent white kid from the *yarid* (fair) is transformed into a kibbutznik. Meltzer's equation of *toyre un skhoyre* (Torah and merchandise) is replaced by A. D. Gordon's socialist-Zionist philosophy that connected Torah and labor (*dat ha-torah ve-ha-avoda*).[58]

Thus, by this inconspicuous additional verse, the supposedly old-fashioned and unpretentious Ohel production actually engendered a more radical aspect to *Shulamit*.

> Akh yom yavo, timas be-khol revakh
> Tashuv titga'age'a al erets avot.
> Tashuv el artsekha be-shir u-ve-shevakh
> Ba-nir, ba-katsir u-va-kerem la'avod.
> Ki ha-gdi le-olam nishar gdi
> Va-ata hu ha-gdi, yekhidi!
> Ha-gdi el ha-kerem pose'a
> Lilkot tsimukim u-shkedim.
> Torah ve-amal hu yode'a
> Numa, bni, numa nim.[59]

> (But the day will come, all profits you'll reject, son,
> Once more for your forefathers' land you will yield.
> With song your homeland you'll come to erect, son,
> To nurture the vineyards and harvest the fields.
> For the kid forever is a kid
> And you are my one and only kid.
> To the vineyard the kid is now riding,
> Raisins and almonds to reap.
> Torah and toil he's uniting,
> Sleep, my son, go to sleep.)

As the founder of the Yiddish Studies Department at the Hebrew University in Jerusalem, Professor Dov Sadan, wrote in 1947:

> And in a natural way, here now [in Palestine] Goldfaden also arose from his grave and removed the burial stone placed upon him, and tens of thousands of spectators, old and young, from the Diaspora as well as yishuv natives, delight in the abundance of sights and sounds. For Goldfaden was the herald of our life [here]; [therefore] it would be arbitrary to separate his three foundations: the spirit of The Haskalah, his love for the folksy, and the love of Zion.[60]

Sadan was almost right. Excepting the twin *Shulamit* debacle, Israeli Goldfaden productions repeatedly proved that the playwright's work was cherished regardless of the noble Jewish or Zionist values productions might choose to emphasize. Goldfaden drew audiences to theatres and to cinemas for one more reason: the spirit of the theatrical.[61]

Appendix

Chronology of Goldfaden Productions in Palestine and Israel

Unless otherwise noted, text and music are Goldfaden's originals. Notes indicate language of performance. In some cases, such as Godik's 1970 *Sorceress*, the musical director was credited as the composer.

Amateur and semi-professional productions:
Shulamis. (In Yiddish). Moritz Schönberg and Zvi Kleiner (dir.). Jaffa. Passover, 1894.
Rabbi Yozelman. (In Yiddish). Rehovot. Purim 1898 or 1899.
Shnei Yoktan Yokshan [*The Two Kuni-Lemls*]. (In Hebrew). Mikve Israel (agricultural school students). Tu Bishvat, 1902.
Bar Kokhba. (In Yiddish), ca. 1908. (Hebrew Teachers Union in Eretz Israel: anti-Yiddish campaign).
Akhasveyresh-shpil. (In Yiddish), c. 1909.
Shulamis. (In Yiddish). Jaffa 1914.
Songs from *Bar Kokhba*. (In Hebrew). (Student and adult choirs, Rosh Pina, dir. Baruch Ben Yehuda). ca.1915.
Bar Kokhba. (In Hebrew). No Information.

The Sorceress
Ha-mekhashefa. Nathan Alterman (trans., lyrics); Michael Gor (dir.); Mark Lavry (musical dir.); Genia Berger (design); Naomi Leaf and N. Cogan (choreography). Eretz-Israeli Comedy, Palestine. Opened: November 1935.
Sholem Aleichem, *Katri'elim* [*Kasrilevkers*]. Baruch Chemerinsky, adapt. [from *Alt-nay kasrilevke*], dir.); Mark Lavry (musical dir.); Emanuel Luftglass (design); Fanny Luvitch (chor.). Habima Theatre, Palestine. 1939. The play included a skit about *The Sorceress* and a number of songs from Goldfaden's play.
Ha-mekhashefa. Abraham Levinson (trans and additional scenes); Moshe Halevi (dir.); Mark Lavry (musical dir.); Paul Levi (des.); Yehudit Orenstein (chor.). Ohel Theatre, Federation of Unions, Palestine. Opened 8 June 1946.
Di kishefmakherin. (In Yiddish). A production starring Chayale Ash in the role of Bobe Yakhne that ran for two years in the 1950s.
Ha-mekhashefa. Ezra Lahad (trans.); Joseph Milo and Haim Hefer (adap.); Haim Hefer (lyrics); Joseph Milo (dir.); Noam Sheriff (music, orchestrations); Shmuel Bak (scen.); Hagar Amrani (costumes); Gene Hill Sagan (chor). Giora Godik productions. Opened May, 1970.
Itzik Manger. *Shlosha Hotsmakh* [Three Hotsmakhs (*Hotsmakh-shpil*)]. Yakov Shabetai (trans.); Shmuel Bunim (dir.); Dov Seltzer (music dir.); Audrey Bergner (design). Cameri Theatre of Tel Aviv. Opened 5 November 1977.
Avrom Goldfaden (and Itzik Manger). *Ha-mekhashefa.* Yakov Shabetai (adap., trans.); Etti Reznik (dir.); Adi Weiss (musical dir.); Dov Ben David (scen.); Yehudit Greenspan (cost., props). Orna Porat National Theatre for Children and Youth. Opened 1984.
Di makhsheyfe. Shmuel Bunim (dir.); Poldi Shatzman (musical dir.); Audrey Bergner (scen.); Pini Moshe (cost.); Valentine Menuchin (chor.). (In Yiddish). Yiddishpiel, Israel. Opened 1992.

Ha-mekhashefa. Michael Gurevitch (adap., dir.); Yakov Rotblit (Lyrics trans.); Ori Widislavsky (musical dir.); Frieda Klapholtz-Avrahami (design); Marina Beltov (chor.). Habima National Theatre. Opened October 21, 2000.

Itzik Manger. *Shlosha Hotsmakh* [Three Hotsmakhs (*Hotsmakh-shpil*)]. Yakov Shabetai (trans.); Albert Cohen (dir.); Dov Seltzer (musical dir.); Anat Maruk (design). Yoram Lewinstein Acting Studio, Tel Aviv. Opened February 22, 2003.

Bar Kokhba
Bar Kokhba. Teater A.N.A. Goldfaden. David Hart, Nathan Wolfovitch, Israel Segal (theatre directors). (In Yiddish). Tel Aviv, 1950–1951.

Wandering Stars
Sholem Aleichem, *Kokhavim nodedim [Wandering Stars]*. Mark Razumny (adap.); Zygmunt Turkow (adap., dir.). Itzik Manger (lyrics); Avrom Goldfaden (additional lyrics); Avrom Shlonsky (trans., additional prologue, epilogue and additional lyrics); A [Georg] Halperin (music); Paul Levi (design). Cameri Theatre of Tel Aviv. Opened 30 April 1950.

Kaptsnzon et Hungerman (Beggarson and Hungerman)
Ma'ase be-nasikh [A tale of a prince]. Dovid Licht (adap., dir.); Shimshon Meltzer (trans.); Joseph Kaminsky (music); Arie Navon (design). Habima National Theatre. Opened January 25, 1953.

Shulamis
Shulamis. Teater A.N.A. Goldfaden. David Hart, Nathan Wolfovitch, Israel Segal (theatre directors). (In Yiddish). Tel Aviv, 1950–1951.

Shulamit: komedia muzikalit be–7 tmunot [Shulamit: A musical comedy in seven scenes.] Shimshon Meltzer (trans.); Moshe Halevi (dir.); Mark Lavry (musical dir.); Arie Navon (design); Yehudit Orenstein (chor.). Ohel Theatre, Federation of Unions, Israel. Opened 31 August 1957.

Yigal Mosenzon. *Shulamit: agada musikalit bi–2 ma'arakhot, 10 tmunot, likhvod yovel ha–80 le-te'atrono shel Goldfaden, ha-opereta ha-yisraelit ha-rishona* [Shulamit: A musical fable in two acts and ten scenes, commemorating the 80th jubilee of Goldfaden's theatre, the first Eretz-Israeli operetta]. Moshe Wilensky ([original] music); Menachem Golan (dir.); Yechiel Mohar (lyrics); Genia Berger (design); Gertrud Kraus (chor.). Do-Re-Mi Theatre (George Val, prod.). Opened 22 August 1957.

The Two Kuni-Lemls
Shnei Kuni-Leml. (In Hebrew; Semi-professional production). Nakhman Zibel (dir.); Gabriel Grad (music dir.); Hitakhadut mesakhakei Eretz Yisrael [Association of Eretz Israeli actors]. 6 October 1927.

Di beyde Kuni-Leml. Teater A.N.A. Goldfaden. David Hart, Nathan Wolfovitch, Israel Segal (theatre directors). (In Yiddish). Tel Aviv, 1951.

Shnei Kuni-Leml. Moshe Sakhar (trans., lyrics); Israel Becker (dir.); Shaul Berezovsky (music); Shaul Avrahami (scenery); Avrom David (chor). Do-Re-Mi Theatre (George Val, prod.). Opened 7 August 1959. Revived 1962.

Mordekhai Navon (prod.); Israel Becker (dir.); Alex Maimon (screenplay); Avrom Goldfaden (original play); Moshe Sakhar (play, lyrics); Shaul Berezowsky (music). *Shnei Kuni-Leml*. Motion Picture, Israel, 1966. (DVD: Shoval Films, Globus United, 2004.)

Roll Films, Yair Pradelsky, Israel Ringel (prod.); Joel Silberg (screenplay, dir.); Dov Seltzer (music); Amos Ettinger (lyrics). *Kuni-Leml be-tel aviv* [Kuni-Leml in Tel Aviv]. Motion Picture, 1976. (DVD: 2005.)

Roll Films, Yair Pradelsky, Israel Ringel (prod.); Joel Silberg (screenplay, dir.); Kobi Oshrat (music). *Kuni-Leml be-kahir* [Kuni-Leml in Cairo]. Motion Picture, 1983. (DVD: 2005.)

Tsvey Kuni-Leml. Motti Averbuch (adap., dir.); Avi Benjamin (music); Yossi Ben Ari (design); Shlomi Golan (chor.). (In Yiddish). Yiddishpiel Theatre. Opened 2001.

Avrom Goldfaden / Sing, My People!

Zygmunt Turkow (play, solo performer). *Avrom Goldfaden* [Later, given a new title: *Zing, mayn folk!* (Sing, my People!)]. A one-man play (in Yiddish). Israel, 1968–1969.

The Messianic Era?!

Donny Inbar (play, dir.; parody of Avrom Goldfaden's *Meshiekhs tsaytn?!* [The Messianic Era?!]. *Bi-tskhok va-dema yehuda nafla; bi-tskhok va-dema yehuda takum: melodrama kora'at* [With Laughter and Tears Hath Judea Fallen; With Laughter and Tears Will Judea Arise: A Smashing Melodrama]. Anat Topol (co-writer); Ori Widislavsky (music); Yoram Barzilai (scen.); Meira Sheffi (cost.); Daniela Michaeli (chor.). Acco Fringe Festival (later Yuval Theatre). Opened September 1985.

Goldfaden's Dream

Jacob Rotbaum. *Goldfaden kholem* (In Yiddish). Avrom Goldfaden and Itztik Manger (original materials); Helen Kaut Hauson (dir.); Uzi Esner (musical dir.); Daniela Michaeli (chor); Miki Ben Canaan (scen.); Anat Mesner (cost.). (In Yiddish). Yiddishpiel Theatre. Opened 1995.

Notes

1. Yehoash [Solomon Bloomgarden], *The Feet of the Messenger* [Translation of *Fun nyu-york biz rehovot*], trans. Isaac Goldberg (New York: Arno Press [1923] 1977), 30–32.

2. Abraham Adar, "Te'atronim, lehakot, sakhkanim u-vama'im" [Theatres, troupes, actors and directors]; Jacob Rabbi, "Ha-gimnazia herzliah ke-merkaz tarbut shel tel aviv ha-ktana" [Gymnasia Herzliah as a cultural center of little Tel Aviv], in A. A. Yaffe, ed., *Esrim ha-shanim ha-rishonot* [The first twenty years: Literature and arts in Tel Aviv 1909–1929] (Tel Aviv: Ha-Kibbutz Ha-Meu'had, Tel Aviv Foundation of Literature and Art, 1980), 63–64, 240–241.

3. Several other Yiddish (and later Hebrew) amateur performances of Goldfaden plays were mounted between 1894 and the first decades of the twentieth century, in Jaffa, Tel Aviv, and several *moshavot* (villages). A Gymnasia Herzliyah graduate mounted a concert of *Bar Kokhba* songs in Hebrew (which he had learned at the Gymnasia) in the *moshava* Rosh Pina in the Galilee in 1915. Yehoash Hirshberg, "Hitpatkhut ha-gufim ha-mevatsim be-muzika" [The development of musical performance organizations], in Zohar Shavit and Moshe Lissak, eds., *Toldot ha-yishuv ha-yehudi be-erets yisrael me'az ha-aliya ha-rishona* [History of the Jewish community in Eretz Israel since the first Aliya] (Jerusalem: Mossad Bialik and The Israeli Academy of Sciences, 1989), 268–269.

4. Hebrew for "the Land of Israel," a term in use long before the founding of the State of Israel in 1948. In this chapter, "Eretz Israel" and "Eretz-Israeli" will be used when referring to pre-and post-1948 productions, texts, etc. "Palestine" refers to the same territory under successive Ottoman and

British rule from the late nineteenth century to 1948, and "Israel" to the same geographical entity after 1948.

5. Chaim Nachman Bialik, "Ha-tarbut ha-yehudit he-khadasha be-erets yisrael" [The new Jewish culture in Eretz Israel]; speech given in Beit Ha-am, Berlin, Tishrei, 1929. Chaim Nakhman Bialik, *Dvarim she-be'al pe* [Spoken Matters]. Tel Aviv: Dvir, 1935, 146–147. Emphasis mine.

6. Avrom Goldfaden (adapted by Mar-Dror [pseudonym of Mordechai Ezrachi,] trans.), *Ha-kanai o shnei Yoktan Yokshan: makhaze tskhok (opereta) be-arba'a ma'asim* [The fanatic or two Yoktan Yokshans: A funny play (operetta) in four acts] (Jerusalem: Ha-Zvi Printing Press, 1900).

7. Avrom Goldfaden (translated by Mar-Dror), *Shnei Kuni-Leml: opereta be-arba ma'arachot, me'et (. . .) yotser ha-te'atron ha-yehudi* [Two Kuni-Lemls: An operetta in four acts by (. . .) the creator of Jewish theatre]. [A reprint of *Shnei Yoktan Yokshan*] (Tel Aviv: Sifriyat Kis La-chayal ha-Ivri [A Pocket Library for the Hebrew Soldier], no. 13, I. Minkovsky, 1949–1950).

8. Information and statistics based on the official Israel Prize database, http://www.education.gov.il/pras-israel/.

9. Bernstein-Cohen was the daughter of the leader of the Jewish community in Kishinev at the time of the 1903 pogrom. She taught drama, translated plays and belletristic literature, introduced several plays from the world classical and modern repertoire to the Hebrew stage, and acted and directed in most Palestinian and Israeli theatres. Among her many roles, she was the first Hebrew Nora, in Ibsen's *A Doll's House*. Bernstein-Cohen introduced to the Hebrew stage plays by Ibsen, Strindberg, Goldoni, Ostrovsky, and others. Miriam Bernstein-Cohen, *Ke-tipah ba-yam: zikhronot* [Like a drop in the sea: Memoirs] (Ramat Gan: Masadah, 1971). Additional biographical information for several Israeli artists discussed here was complemented by Shimon Lev-Ari, *Madrikh 100 shana la-te'atron ha-ivri, 1889–1989* [A guide to a hundred years of Hebrew theatre, 1889–1989] (IDCPA, The Documentation Center for The Israeli Performing Arts, http://www.tau.ac.il/arts/idcpa/Mavo.html).

10. Bernstein-Cohen, 180–181.

11. Ben-Ze'ev Lieber, "Goldfaden ba-komedia ha-erets yisraelit" [Goldfaden in Eretz-Israeli comedy], in *Ha-khayim ha-llalu: shavu'on erets-yisraeli metzuyar* [This life: An illustrated Eretz-Israeli weekly] (Tel Aviv, 28 November 1935).

12. Lyrics from Lavry's manuscript. All English translations are my own.

13. Chone Shmeruk has discussed the persistence of that the archetypal maskilic protagonist—Markus/Max—in Haskalah drama, beginning with Isaac Euchel's *Reb Henokh, oder vos tut men dermit?* [Reb Henokh or what to do with it?, 1793)] and Aaron Wolfssohn's *Laykhtzin un fremelay* [*Silliness and Sanctimony*, 1796]. The maskilic "Markus" is a deliberate *inversion* of the traditional purimshpil's Mordechai-Mondrish, who is typically portrayed as a hunchback, and an ugly and vulgar panderer, who trades in his orphaned niece as if she were merchandise. See Chone Shmeruk, *Makhazot mikrai'im be-yidish, 1697–1750* [Yiddish biblical plays, 1697–1750] (Jerusalem: The Israel Academy of Sciences and Humanities, 1979); Chone Shmeruk, "Ha-shem ha-mashma'uti Mordekhai-Markus: gilgulo ha-sifruti shel ide'al khevrati" [The significant name Mordekhai-Markus: The literary transformation of a societal ideal], *Tarbitz* 1 (1959).

14. I am grateful to musical director Mark Lavry's daughter, Ms. Efrat Lavry-Zaklad (a musician herself) in Haifa, and to Dr. Gila Flam, Director of the Music Archive at the National Library in The Hebrew University, Jerusalem, for their generous assistance and permission to browse through Lavry's personal archive, and for retrieving the manuscripts of his musical arrangements for the 1935 production, which included most of Alterman's lyrics. These manuscripts, and a single copy of the production's playbill, are the only apparent remnants of Alterman's translation.

15. The feeble compromise reached was to artificially stress the last word, *rakhmanim*, on its ultimate syllable (*nim*), according to the pronunciation of modern Israeli Hebrew. The 1935 version was sung with the stress shifted to the penultimate syllable in the Ashkenazi way, but the vowel was

pronounced "*ma*" in the Sephardi manner, rather than "*mo*" as is customary for Ashkenazi pronunciation. It is Levinson's ingenious linguistic solution, rather than Alterman's earlier imperfect verbal compromise, which should be credited with creating the unexpected potency that the song was to enjoy. For a discussion of the special challenges presented by the transposition of the Hebraic components of Yiddish to a modern vernacular Hebrew context, see Gershon Shaked, *Mendele, lefanav ve-akharav* [Mendele, before and after] (Jerusalem: The Magnes Press, Hebrew University, 2004), 135–136.

16. Among them were an adaptation of Goldfaden's *Kabtsnzon et Hungerman* [Beggarson and Hungerman] at the Habima National Theatre and an adaptation of *Meshiekhs tsaytn?!* [The Messianic era?!] at the Acco Fringe Festival. Both productions are discussed below.

17. In 2005, Daniel Bloch, former Executive Editor of *Davar* [The matter], criticized excessive subsidies for the settlements: "[. . .] seriously. Jews, have mercy, mercy. The Shtetl is burning." http://www.notes.co.il/daniel/8765.asp. David Weisberg, in a forum on the Gush Katif settlement block in the Gaza strip, attacked the self-righteous leftists: "Jews, have mercy, mercy. Once this [expression] meant 'save us from terror,' but now it refers to 'save us from our own destroyers [from within].'" http://www.katif.net/inc/viewreply.inc.php?id=7218. An anonymous settler supporter on Culmosnet newsgroup in response to an anti-settlers' posting by Yoram Hamizrahi opens with curses and threats, and ends with "Jews, have mercy, mercy!" (exclamation mark at the end of the plea). www.blabla4u.com; a satirical attack on Sephardi spiritual leader Rabbi Ovadia Yosef, who is accused of misleading and swindling his flock, ends with "Jews have mercy, mercy, and may the redeemer of Zion arrive." www.freechoice.co.il, www.bananot.co.il.

18. The official flyer can be found at http://web.beitberl.ac.il/~bbsite/midrasha/galeriot/archive-telaviv/previous.htm.

19. Mikhl Weichert, *Trupe Tanentsap: a Goldfaden shpil in a galitsish shtetl* [The Tanentsap Troupe: A Goldfaden play in a Galician shtetl] (Tel Aviv: Hamenorah, 1966); Sholem Aleichem, *Blonzhende shtern [Wandering Stars]* (New York: Hebrew Publishing Co., 1920); Sholem Aleichem, "Shimele," *He-asif* (Warsaw: 1889), 47–61; Sholem Aleichem, "Kasrilevker teater" [*Kasrilevke's Theatre*], *Alt-nay kasrilevke [Old-New Kasrilevke]* (New York: Morgn Freiheit, 1901).

20. Goldfaden events were produced in Eretz Israel in 1935, 1947, 1949 (book), 1950, 1951–1952 (three, in Yiddish), 1953, 1955 (Yiddish), 1957 (two simultaneous), 1959 (play and a children's book), 1962, 1966 (film and Yiddish script), 1970, 1977 (play and film), 1983 (film), 1984, 1985, 1992 (Yiddish), 1994 (script), 1995 (Yiddish), 2000, 2001 (Yiddish), 2003, 2004–2005 (DVDs).

21. Goldfaden's original play is a farce about a provincial maiden who insists on calling herself Carolina, like a character from one of the trashy novels she reads, and marrying only a clone of "German" literary suitors. She falls into the hands of an impostor, and the comic situation turns, at its conclusion, into a melodrama. Avrom Goldfaden, *Kaptsnzon et Hungerman, oder di kaprizne kalemoyd* [Beggarson and Hungerman, or The capricious bride] (Warsaw: Boymritter and Son-in-Law Printers, 1887). Avrom Goldfaden. *Ma'ase be-nasikh* [A tale of a prince], adapted and directed by Dovid Licht, opened at the Habima National Theatre on January 25, 1953. It was translated by Shimshon Meltzer, with music by Joseph Kaminsky, and sets by Arie Navon.

22. Sholem Aleichem's novel (published as a serial 1909–1910, and in book form in 1920) is a saga about the thwarted love of two shtetl children, who join Yiddish troupes in eastern Europe, travel to the ends of the earth, and become the first Yiddish dramatic star and a world-renowned classical singer before they are reunited in the New World. Directed by Turkow and adapted by Turkow and Mark Razumny, *Kokhavim nodedim [Wandering Stars]* opened at the Cameri Theatre of Tel Aviv on April 30, 1950. Additional personnel: Itzik Manger (lyrics); Abraham Shlonsky (trans., additional prologue, epilogue and additional lyrics); A [Georg] Halperin (music), and Paul Levi (design).

23. Since the prologue that preceded the 1959 stage production of *Di tsvey Kuni-Leml* shares several components, I will discuss all three lyrics together.

24. Abraham Shlonsky, *Dagesh kal* [Light stress], ed. Arie Aharoni (Tel Aviv: Keren Tel Aviv le-sifrut ve-omanut, Sifriyat Po'alim, Yad Shlonsky, 1993), 43–45.

25. Ibid..

26. *Shnei Kuni-Leml* [Di tsvey Kuni-Leml—*The Two Kuni-Lemls*], Lyrics: Moshe Sakhar, Music: Shaul Berezowsky, Do-Re-Mi 1959 program.

27. "We are such stuff / As dreams are made on," William Shakespeare, *The Tempest;* John Osborne's *Look Back In Anger* opened at The Royal Court Theatre in London in 1956. Shlonsky was considered one of the leading translators of Shakespeare, and his 1946 Hebrew version of *Hamlet* is still considered one of the best. John Osborne's *Look Back in Anger* transformed British (and in many ways Western) theatre in its modern approach to postwar social upheaval, class-conscious British society, and working-class realism.

28. Another "generic" and parodic shtetl was created in the 1985 adaptation of *Meshiekhs tsaytn?!*, in which the shtetl in Act I was called *Shtutl* as a play on words: *shtetl* (Yiddish) + *shtut* (Hebrew for "nonsense"). As most of Goldfaden's plays are set indoors, his depiction of the shtetl itself is far more limited than that of prose writers, whose literary "camera" can zoom out and wander around a broader space, thus painting a rich landscape. Theatre artists compensated for the dearth of Goldfaden's shtetl material by borrowing from the great masters, particularly in the cinematic version of *Kuni-Leml*.

29. On the ban on Yiddish theatre in the early years of Israel and the struggle with the police, see Nathan Wolfovitch, "Hershele me-ostropoli be-veit ha-mishpat" [Hershele Ostropolyer in court], originally published in the Israeli Yiddish daily *Letste nayes*, 20 July 1951]; Hebew translation and introduction by Rachel Rozhansky in *Ha'aretz* (literary supplement), April 2, 2004; and Nahma Sandrow, *Vagabond Stars* (New York: Harper & Row, 1977), 377–380. Several references to the transformation in the Israeli acceptance of the Holocaust and the opening-up to the traumas of World War II among the Israelis can be found in Tom Segev, *The Seventh Million: The Israelis and the Holocaust* (New York: Owl Books, 2000).

30. Mordechai Navon, (prod.), Israel Becker (dir.), Alex Maimon (screenplay), Avrom Goldfaden (original script), *Shnei Kuni-Leml* [*The Two Kuni-Lemls*]. Feature film, Israel, 1966 (DVD: Shoval Films, Globus United, 2004).

31. Roll Films, Yair Pradelsky, Israel Ringel (prod.); Joel Silberg (screenplay, dir.); Dov Seltzer (music); Amos Ettinger (lyrics), *Kuni-Leml be-tel aviv* [Kuni-Leml in Tel Aviv]. Feature film, Israel, 1976 (DVD: 2005); Roll Films, Yair Pradelsky, Israel Ringel (prod.); Joel Silberg (screenplay, dir.); Kobi Oshrat (music), *Kuni-Leml be-kahir* [Kuni-Leml in Cairo], Feature film, Israel, 1983 (DVD: 2005).

32. Donny Inbar, *Bi-tskhok va-dema yehuda nafla; bi-tskhok va-dema yehuda takum: melodrama kora'at* [With laughter and tears hath Judea fallen; With laughter and tears will Judea arise: A smashing melodrama], adapted from Goldfaden's *Meshiekhs tsaytn?!* Anat Topol (co-writer); Ori Widislavsky (music); Yoram Barzilai (sets); Meira Sheffi (costumes); Daniela Michaeli (choreography). Premiered September 1985 at the Acco Fringe Festival (later Yuval Theatre).

33. Avrom Goldfaden, *Meshiekhs tsaytn?!* [The Messianic era?!] (Cracow: Farlag Yosef Fischer, 1900).

34. Inbar, *Bi-tskhok va-dema yehuda nafla.*

35. Michael Ohad, "Tnu la-gever Goldfaden" [Give the man a Goldfaden], in *Ha'aretz.* September, 1985.

36. Inbar, *Bi-tskhok va-dema yehuda nafla.*

37. Avrom Goldfaden, *Shulamit: komedia muzikalit be-7 tmunot* [Shulamit: A musical comedy in seven scenes]. Shimshon Meltzer (translator); Moshe Halevi (director); Mark Lavry (musical director); Arie Navon (design); Yehudit Orenstein (choreography). Ohel Theatre, Federation of Unions, Israel. Opened August 31, 1957. Halevi's reflections on his artistic approach are in the program.

38. Yigal Mosenzon, *Shulamit: agada muzikalit bi-2 ma'arakhot, 10 tmunot, likhvod yovel ha-80 le-te'atrono shel Goldfaden, ha-opereta ha-yisraelit ha-rishona* [Shulamit: A musical fable in two acts and ten scenes, commemorating the 80th jubilee of Goldfaden's theatre, the first Israeli operetta]. Moshe Wilensky ([original] music); Menachem Golan (dir.); Yechiel Mohar (lyrics); Genia Berger (design); Gertrud Kraus (choreography). Do-Re-Mi Theatre (George Val, prod.). Opened August 22, 1957.

39. Avrom Goldfaden, *Shulamis, oder bas yerusholayim* [Shulamis, or The daughter of Jerusalem] (Warsaw: Boimritter and Ganshar, 1886). Eliyahu, Mordekhai Werbl, *Edim ne'emanim o khulda u-vor* [Faithful witnesses, or a weasel and a well] (Vilna: Yossef ben Menachem of Rom, 1852–1853).

40. Earlier that year Se'adia Damari created a special production for The Ohel: *Ha-mevaser* [The herald], with text by Damari and music by Nachum Nardi. It opened on April 17, 1957.

41. Nachman ben Ami, "Ve-hekheziku shnei te'atronim be-Shulamit akhat" (And two theatres seized one Shulamis), *Ma'ariv* (date missing). The headlines echo a Talmudic phrase about two opponents holding one prayer shawl. Many of the clippings cited here were collected by the Israeli Documentation Center for the Performing Arts (IDCPA) at Tel Aviv University, from artists' personal clippings albums, many of which are undated.

42. A review by Ephraim Katz (newspaper and date are missing), who refuses to take sides and recommends viewing both productions. Clipping from IDCPA.

43. Such a debate has often been raised in relation to the "authentic" way in which classical plays should be mounted: for example, should *Julius Caesar* be played in togas, in the "authentic" ancient Roman style, or rather in Elizabethan garb, the way this play was traditionally performed in William Shakespeare's time? Both conflicting fashions are authentic, in their own way.

44. Feingold, 216–7; Ora Ahimeir and Haim Beer, eds., *1900–2000: Me'a shnot tarbut be-erets yisrael* [1900–2000: One hundred years of Hebrew culture in Eretz Israel] (Tel Aviv: Am Oved/Yedioth Ahronoth, 2000), 268.

45. The Music Archive at the national Library of the Hebrew University holds close to ten different Hebrew translations of the song. Among the translators are Haim Hefer, Ehud Manor, Shmuel Fischer, Dan Almagor, Avi Koren and Yoram Tehar-Lev.

46. Goldfaden, *Shulamis*, Act I:4, 41–42.

47. Ezra, the artist-protagonist, alludes to the "widowed daughter of Zion by the ruins of the Temple in Jerusalem." Avrom Goldfaden, *Ben Ami: folksshtik in dray aktn mit prolog un epilog* [Ben Ami: A folk play in three acts with a prologue and an epilogue] (Unpublished typescript, New York Public Library), 26.

48. On the origin of "Rozhinkes mit mandlen," see Irene Heskes, *The Music of Abraham Goldfaden, Father of the Yiddish Theatre* (USA: Tara Publications, 1990), 4–5; Leo Wiener, *The History of Yiddish Literature in the Nineteenth Century* (New York: Hermon Press,1899: rpt. 1972), 54–55; David G. Roskies, *The Jewish Search for a Usable Past* (Bloomington: Indiana University Press, 1998), 105. Musicologist A. Z. Idelsohn lists all the "borrowed" origins of the play's music in *Jewish Music in its Historical Development* (New York: Tudor Publishing Company, 1929: rpt. 1948), 452. The original tune of the folksong can be found in Ruth Rubin, ed., *The Treasury of Jewish Folksong* (New York: Schocken, 1964), 16–17.

49. Goldfaden, *Shulamis, oder bas yerusholayim*, Act 1, scene3. It is interesting to note that S. Y. Abramovitsh, who otherwise kept his distance from Goldfaden—even though they had both studied in Avrom Ber Gottlober's house in Zhitomir—has a single allusion to Goldfaden in his Hebrew short story "Ha-se'ara" [The hair], in *Khagim u-zmanim* [Holidays and festivals]. Abramovitsh's allusion combines references to the female personification of the widowed and exiled Israel, the female "protagonist" in the Song of Songs, and his own Hebrew translation of the original folk version of the lullaby that Goldfaden adapted into "Rozhinkes mit mandlen." See *Kol kitvey Mendele*

Mokher Sfarim [The complete works of Mendele Mokher-Sforim] (Tel Aviv: Dvir, 1947: rpt. 1958), 461.

50. Mosenzon, *Shulamit: agada musikalit.*

51. Gila Flam, "Ha-shir ha-yidi ve-shiluvo ba-shir ha-yisraeli, o: madua ne'elam shir ha-ahava?" [The Yiddish song and itsi into the Israeli song, or: Why has the love song disappeared?], in *Ha-agala ha-mele'a* [The full wagon: A hundred and twenty years of culture in Israel], ed. Israel Bartal (Jerusalem: The Magnes Press, Hebrew University, 2002), 260.

52. The 1998 interview with Damari was reprinted in *Ha'aretz* after her death. Noam Ben Zeev, "Mivkhan ima" [Maternal test-case], in *Ha'aretz*, February 15, 2006. Damari performed and re-recorded "Rozhinkes mit mandlen" in Yiddish in an evening produced by the Habima National Theatre and Galei Zahal, IDF Radio, *Be-yidish ze nishma yoter tov: mofa pumbi, mekhva la-zemer ha-yidi* [It sounds better in Yiddish: A public celebratory performance of Yiddish song], Habima National Theatre, January 10, 1987. CD issued on NMC records.

53. The most notable song was "Shulamit" (Alterman and Wilensky), written for Damari in 1946, eleven years prior to the Goldfaden production, Li-La-Lo Theatre. See Gilad Ben Shakh, "Shoshana Damari: mi-kalaniyot ad or" [Shoshana Damari from (her songs) "Anemones" to "Light"] Hed Artzi, Kol Israel, 1994, (vol. 1), CD compilation.

54. Avrom Goldfaden, *Shirim u-makhazot* [Poems and plays], ed. Reuven Goldberg (Jerusalem: Dorot, Mossad Bialik, 1970), 140–141, fn. 2.

55. Unpublished texts from Meir Noy's manuscripts at the Music Archive at the National Library, The Hebrew University, Jerusalem. Tehar-Lev's version has been recorded by the Ge'vatron Kibbutz choir and released on its Yiddish song CD. Emphasis mine.

56. Meltzer was a poet in his own right and one of the most respected translators from Yiddish; Meltzer translated I. L. Peretz, Dovid Pinski, and other high-profile Yiddish works.

57. "The harvest of the grape in the native regions of the Vine," in Benjamin Disraeli's words. Benjamin Disraeli, *Tancred or The New Crusade* (London: Longmans, Green and Co., 1871), 389–390.

58. Aharon David Gordon (1856–1922) was a spiritual mentor of the Zionist labor movement, which emphasized self-realization through pioneering settlement on the land of Israel. His philosophy was known as *"Tora ve-avoda"* [Torah and labor].

59. Goldfaden, *Shulamit: komedia musikalit be-7 tmunot,* translated by Shimshon Meltzer.

60. Dov Sadan, *Avnei miftan: masot al sofrei yidish* [Cornerstones: Essays on Yiddish writers] (Tel Aviv: I. L. Peretz Publishing House, 1961), 1:21.

61. Special thanks to Messrs. Shimon Lev-Ari and Shai Marcus at the IDCPA, The Israeli Documentation Center for the Performing Arts, Tel Aviv University; Dr. Gila Flam, director of the Music Archive at the National Library, The Hebrew University, Jerusalem; as well as to Messrs. Paul Hamburg (UCB library), Yeshaya Metal (YIVO library), Zachary M. Baker (Stanford library), Michael Terry (New York Public Library). Additional gratitude to Ms. Efrat Lavry-Zaklad (Mark Lavry's daughter) in Haifa; to actors Mike Burstein (Los Angeles); and Chayale Ash (San Jose), and to Professor Thomas F. Shannon (UC Berkeley) for their help in this research. My greatest gratitude to my parents, Siona and Shmuel Bodansky, for their active involvement in this research, which makes them full partners in it.

Notes on Contributors

ANNETTE ARONOWICZ is the Robert F. and Patricia G. Ross Weis Professor of Judaic Studies at Franklin & Marshall College. She is the author of *Freedom from Ideology: Secrecy in Modern Expression* (1987); *Jews and Christians on Time and Eternity: Charles Peguy's Portrait of Bernard Lazare* (1998), and the translator of *Nine Talmudic Readings* by Emmanuel Levinas (1991).

ZACHARY BAKER is Assistant University Librarian for Collection Development and the Reinhard Family Curator of Judaica and Hebraica Collections, Stanford University Libraries. He is the compiler of an annotated bibliography of The Lawrence Marwick Collection of Copyrighted Yiddish Plays for the Library of Congress.

JOEL BERKOWITZ is Director of the Sam and Helen Stahl Center for Jewish Studies and Professor of Foreign Languages and Literature at the University of Wisconsin-Milwaukee. He previously taught at the University at Albany, Oxford University, and at several colleges in the City University of New York system. He received his Ph.D. in theatre from the City University of New York Graduate School, and served as a Fulbright postdoctoral fellow in Jerusalem. He is the author of *Shakespeare on the American Yiddish Stage* (2002), editor of *Yiddish Theatre: New Approaches* (2003), and co-editor, with Jeremy Dauber, of *Landmark Yiddish Plays: A Critical Anthology* (2006).

MIROSŁAWA BUŁAT is a Lecturer in Theatre Studies at Jagiellonian University, Cracow, where she also completed her doctoral dissertation on Cracow's Yiddish theatre. She is the author of *Krakowski Teatr Żydowski: Krokewer Jidisz Teater:*

między szundem a sztuką (The Cracow Yiddish Theatre: Between *Shund* and Art, 2006), and has published articles, reviews, and reports on the Yiddish theatre, as well as translations from Yiddish into Polish.

JEREMY DAUBER is Atran Associate Professor of Yiddish Studies at Columbia University and the director of its Institute for Israel and Jewish Studies. He is the author of *Antonio;s Devils: Writers of the Jewish Enlightenment and the Birth of Modern Jewish Literature* (2004) and *In the Demon's Bedroom: Yiddish Literature and the Early Modern* (2010), and is co-editor (with Joel Berkowitz) of *Landmark Yiddish Plays* (2006). Jeremy is also the co-editor of *Prooftexts: A Journal of Jewish Literary History.*

BARBARA HENRY is Associate Professor of Russian Literature and an affiliate in the Jewish Studies Program at the University of Washington, Seattle. Her monograph, *Rewriting Russia: Jacob Gordin's Yiddish Drama*, on Gordin's adaptations of Russian literature for the Yiddish stage, was published by the University of Washington Press in 2011.

DONNY INBAR is associate director for arts and culture at the Israel Center of the Jewish Community Federation in San Francisco. He received his Ph.D. from the Graduate Theological Union in Berkeley, for his dissertation, *A Closeted Jester: Abraham Goldfaden between Haskalah Ideology and Jewish Show Business*. An Israeli theatre director, translator and editor, Inbar has adapted and directed Goldfaden's *Days of the Messiah* for the Israeli stage and teaches Jewish and Israeli culture at Bay Area universities.

FAITH JONES is a librarian and teaches library science at the University of British Columbia. Her translations of Yiddish poems and stories have appeared in anthologies and magazines, and she serves as Yiddish editor for *Bridges: A Jewish Feminist Journal*. Her scholarly articles have appeared in journals such as *Canadian Jewish Studies* and *Judaica Librarianship*.

ALYSSA QUINT teaches Yiddish literature at Columbia University. She is the co-editor of *Arguing the Modern Jewish Canon* (Harvard University Press: 2008) and has published articles in *The Forward*, *Tablet*, and several academic journals.

RONALD ROBBOY is a cellist in the San Diego Symphony as well as a composer and musical investigator. He was Senior Researcher for conductor Michael Tilson Thomas's Thomashefsky Project, and as one of the West Coast's initiators of the klezmer revival in the United States, he was the leader of The Big Jewish Band and other experimental performance groups.

JUDITH THISSEN is Assistant Professor in Media History at Utrecht University, Netherlands. Her essays on the social history of Jewish immigrant entertainment in New York City have been published in *Theatre Survey*, *KINtop*, *Cinema Journal* and in several edited anthologies including *Going to the Movies: Hollywood and the Social Experience of Cinema* (2007), *The Art of Being Jewish in Modern Times* (2008) and *Kinoöffentlichkeit/Cinema's Public Sphere, 1895-1920* (2008).

JEFFREY VEIDLINGER is Professor of History, Alvin H. Rosenfeld Chair in Jewish Studies, and Director of the Borns Jewish Studies Program at Indiana University. He is the author of *The Moscow State Yiddish Theater: Jewish Culture on the Soviet Stage* (2000), and *Jewish Public Culture in the Late Russian Empire* (2009). He is currently working on a book entitled, *In the Shadow of the Shtetl: Jewish Memory in Eastern Europe*.

NINA WARNKE is Assistant Professor of European Studies and Jewish Studies and Executive Director of Vanderbilt Visions and Commons Seminars at Vanderbilt University. Her recent articles include "Theater as Educational Institution: Jewish Immigrant Intellectuals and Yiddish Theater Reform," in *The Art of Being Jewish in Modern Times* (2007), "Operetta," in *The YIVO Encyclopedia of Jews in Eastern Europe* (2008), "Yiddish Theater History, Its Composers, and Operettas: A History Without Music," in *Musykalia VII, Judaica 2* (2009) at http://www.demusica.pl.

SETH L. WOLITZ is Gale Professor of Jewish Studies and Professor of French, Slavic, and Comparative Literature at the University of Texas at Austin. Among his many published works, some of the most recent are the catalogue, *Futur Antérieur*, on eastern European Jewish Avant-garde Art, for the major exhibit in Paris at the Musée d'art et d'histoire du judaisme (2009); "Goldfaden: Theatrical Space and Historical Place for the Jewish Gaze," *Jewish Theatre: Tradition in Transition and Intercultural Vistas*, Tel Aviv University, (2009); "*Yoysef Shor* Between Two Worlds," (2007); "Inscribing An-Sky's Dybbuk in Russian and Jewish Letters," (2006); "The Ashkenazic Gaze: Creating the Jewish Art Book" (2005); "Fixity of Place and Freedom of Theatrical/Mental Space: Parallels East and West" (2005); "Subaltern Theater: Parallels in Jewish And Bengali Theater," in *Ethnicity & Identity: Global Performance,* (2005); *The Hidden Bashevis Singer* (ed., 2002); and *The Renaissance in Kosher Cuisine: From Ethnicity to Universality* (1999). Prof. Wolitz is a member of the Editorial Board of *Assaph* and served as President of the Modern Languages Association's Yiddish Section.

Bibliography

Compiled by Zachary Baker, Joel Berkowitz, Barbara Bułat, Mirosława Bułat, Barbara Henry, and Leonard Prager

This bibliography had its genesis in the bibliography for an earlier volume of essays: *Yiddish Theatre: New Approaches,* edited by Joel Berkowitz (Oxford, UK: Littman Library of Jewish Civilization, 2003). The editors are grateful to the Littman Library for permission to use the previous bibliography as the foundation for a revised and expanded version.

This new version retains the core of the previous version, but makes a number of changes and additions. First, nearly a decade separates the publication of these two volumes. In the interim, a number of important scholarly works—books, journal articles, dissertations, book chapters—have been published on a wide array of topics related to Yiddish theatre, drama, and performance.

Second, the Littman bibliography was a hybrid phenomenon, attempting to capture citations to significant scholarship in the field, but also providing citations to other scholarship cited by the contributors to that particular volume. The revised version eliminates references to supporting materials outside the field of Yiddish theatre studies, and attempts to cast a wide net by including scholarly articles, academic and popular histories and works of criticism, and book-length memoirs of Yiddish theatre personnel.

In order to optimize this resource, the editors have recruited a small team of bibliographers with a command of most of the languages in which Yiddish theatre scholarship has been published. The original team consisted of Joel Berkowitz (Yiddish, English, German, Romance languages), Mirosława Bułat (Polish), Barbara Henry (Russian), and Leonard Prager (Hebrew). When our friend and colleague Leonard Prager passed away in December 2008, Zachary Baker agreed to join the other members of this group to review and stay up to date with scholarship published in Hebrew.

Abend, Dror. *"Scorned My Nation": A Comparison of Translations of the Merchant of Venice into German, Hebrew, and Yiddish.* Berlin: Peter Lang, 2003.

Abramsky, G. *Bamot-yiskhak o gey-khizayon* [The high places of laughter or the valley of vision]. Bucharest?: Salon 'Pomo Verde,' n.d.

Adler, Jacob. *A Life on the Stage.* Translated by Lulla Adler Rosenfeld. New York: Knopf, 1999.

Adler, Lois. "Alexis Granovsky and the Jewish State Theatre of Moscow" *The Drama Review* 24, Jewish Theatre Issue (Sept. 1980): 27–42.

Adler Rosenfeld, Lulla. *Bright Star of Exile: Jacob Adler and the Yiddish Theatre*. New York: Thomas Y. Crowell, 1977.

Adler, Tsili, with Yakov Tikman. *Tsili Adler dertseylt* [Celia Adler recounts], 2 vols. New York: Tsili Adler Fondeyshn un Bukh-komitet, 1959.

80 yor yidish teater in rumenye [80 years of Yiddish theatre in Romania]. Bucharest: n.p., 1956.

Alter, Iska. "Jacob Gordin's *Mirele Efros*: King Lear as a Jewish Mother." *Shakespeare Survey* 55 (2002): 114–27.

———. "When the Audience Called 'Author! Author!'": Shakespeare on New York's Yiddish Stage." *Theatre History Studies* 10 (1990): 141–162.

Altshuler, Mordechai. *Ha-te'atron ha-yehudi be-vrit ha-mo'atsot: mekhkarim—iyunim—te'udot* [The Jewish theatre in the Soviet Union: Research, references, documents]. Jerusalem: Hebrew University, 1996.

Anderson, Mark M. "'[. . .] nicht mit großen Tönen gesagt': On Theater and the Theatrical in Kafka." *Germanic Review* 78 (Summer 2003): 167–176.

Apchinskaya, Natal'ya V. *Teatr Marka Shagala: Konets 1910-kh-1960-e gody* [The theatre of Marc Chagall: Late 1910s–1960s]. Vitebsk: UO: "VGTU" (Vitebskii Gosudarstvennyi Tekhnologicheskii Universitet), 2004.

Apter-Gabriel, Ruth. *Shagal: khalomot u-makhazot: avodot mukdamot ve-tsiurey-ha-kir la-te'atron ha-yidi be-rusya* [Chagall: Dreams and plays: Early works and wall drawings for the Yiddish theatre in Russia]. Jerusalem: Israel Museum, 1993.

Apter-Gabriel, Ruth, ed. *Tradition and Revolution: The Jewish Renaissance in Russian Avant-Garde Art, 1912–1928*. Jerusalem: Israel Museum, 1988.

Aptroot, Marion. "Creating Yiddish Dialogue for 'The First Modern Yiddish Comedy.'" In Justin Cammy, Dara Horn, Alyssa Quint, and Rachel Rubinstein, eds., *Arguing the Modern Jewish Canon: Essays on Literature and Culture in Honor of Ruth R. Wisse*, 427–444. Cambridge, MA: Center for Jewish Studies, Harvard University, 2008.

———. "Satire and the Performing Arts in a Late Eighteenth Century Yiddish Polemic." In Walter Röll and Simon Neuberg, eds., *Jiddische Philologie: Festschrift für Erika Timm*, 227–242. Tübingen: Max Niemayer Farlag, 1999.

Aronowicz, Annette. "*The Downfall of Haman:* Postwar Yiddish Theater Between Secular and Sacred." *AJS Review* 32 (2008): 369–388.

———. "Haim Sloves, the Jewish People, and a Jewish Communist's Allegiances." *Jewish Social Studies* 9 (Fall 2002): 95–142.

———. "*Homens mapole*: Hope in the Immediate Postwar Period." *Jewish Quarterly Review* 98 (Summer 2008): 355–388.

———. "Spinoza Among the Jewish Communists." *Modern Judaism* 24 (2004): 1–35.

Astro, Alan. "Metatheater and Allegory in Mordkhe Alpersohn's 'Di arendators fun kultur.'" *Yiddish* 13 (2003): 43–55.

Avishar, Shmuel. *Ha-makhaze ve-ha-te'atron ha-ivri ve-ha-yidi* [Hebrew and Yiddish drama and theatre]. Jerusalem: Reuven Mas, 1996.

Azarkh-Granovskaya, Aleksandra V. *Vospominaniya. Besedy s V. D. Duvakinym* [Reminiscences. Conversations with V. D. Duvakin]. Moscow and Jerusalem: Mosty kul'tury, Gesharim, 2001.

Baker, Zachary. "The Lawrence Marwick Collection of Copyrighted Yiddish Plays at the Library of Congress." *Association of Jewish Libraries: Annual Convention* 35 (2000): 116–120.

———. "Yiddish in Form and Socialist in Content: The Observance of Sholem Aleichem's Eightieth Birthday in the Soviet Union." *YIVO Annual* 23 (1996): 209–231.

——— and Steven W. Siegel. *Bibliography of Eastern European Memorial (Yizkor) Books*. New York: Jewish Genealogical Society, 1992.

Bal Makhshoves [Isidor Eliashev]. *Geklibene shriftn* [Collected writings], 5 vols. Warsaw: Kooperativ "Bikher," 1929.

Bar-Dayan, H. *Le-reshito shel makhaze ha-haskala—al opera komit be-yidish* [The beginnings of the Haskalah play: On a Yiddish comic opera]. Jerusalem: Second World Congress of Jewish Studies, 1957.

Bar-Yosef, Hamutal. "Ha-hitkablut shel Leonid Andreyev ba-sifrut u-ba-te'atron be-ivrit u-ve-yidish." *Khulyot* 8 (2004): 329–343. Translated as "The Reception of Leonid Andreev in Hebrew and Yiddish Literature and Theatre," *Symposium* 58 (Fall 2004): 139–151.

Baron, John Herschel. "Music as Entertainment and Symbol in the Yiddish Cinema from the 1920s and 1930s." In Bernhard R. Appel, Karl Wilhelm Geck, and Herbert Schneider, eds., *Musik und Szene: Festschrift für Werner Braun zum 75. Geburtstag*, 413–428. Saarbrücken: Saarbrücker Druckerei und Verlag, 2001.

Baumgarten, Jean. *Introduction à la littérature yiddish ancienne*. Paris: Cerf, 1993. Translated as *Introduction to Old Yiddish Literature* by Jerold C. Frakes. New York: Oxford University Press, 2005.

———. *Le Yiddish*. Paris: Presses Universitaires de France, 1990.

———. "Un Purimshpil à Kyriat Vishnitz de Bnai Braq (1996) [A Purimshpil in Kyriat Vishnitz in Bnei Braq (1996)]." *Perspectives* 10 (2003): 127–142.

———. "Yiddish Oral Traditions of the Batkhonim and Multilingualism in Hasidic Communities. *Bulletin du Centre de recherche français à Jérusalem* 6 (Spring 2000): 99–120.

Bayerdörfer, Hans-Peter. "'Geborene Schauspieler': Das jüdische Theater des Ostens und die Theaterdebatte im deutschen Judentum" ["Born actors": The Jewish theatre of the east and the debate on theatre in German Jewry]. In Otto Horch and Charlotte Wardi, eds., *Jüdische Selbstwahrnemung* [Jewish self-perception], 195–215. Tübingen: Max Niemeyer Verlag, 1997.

Beam, Patricia S. "Aesthetic Movements in the Yiddish Theatre." M.A. thesis, University of North Carolina at Chapel Hill, 1971.

Bechtel, Delphine. "America and the Shtetl in Sholem Aleichem's *Di goldgreber* [The golddiggers]." *MELUS* 17 (Fall 1991–1992): 69–84.

———. "Yiddish Theatre and Its Impact on the German and Austrian Stage." In Jeanette R. Malkin and Freddie Rokem, eds., *Jews and the Making of Modern German Theatre*, 77–98. Iowa City: University of Iowa Press, 2010.

Beck, Evelyn Torton. *Kafka and the Yiddish Theater*. Madison: University of Wisconsin Press, 1971.

Beckerman, Aaron. *F. Bimko: der dramaturg un realist* [F(ishl) Bimko: The playwright and realist]. New York: n.p., 1944.

———. *Goylem als velt derleyzer: vegn Leyviks goylem* [The golem as savior: on Leivick's *Golem*]. Warsaw: S. Goldfarb, 1926.

Beckermann, Ruth, ed. *Die Mazzesinsel. Juden in der Wiener Leopoldstadt 1918–1938* [The island of matzah: Jews in Vienna's Leopoldstadt, 1918–1938]. Vienna: Löcker Verlag, 1984.

Beizer, Mikhail. *The Jews of St Petersburg: Excursions through a Noble Past*. Philadelphia: Jewish Publication Society, 1989.

———. "The Petrograd Jewish Obshchina (Kehillah) in 1917." *Jews and Jewish Topics in the Soviet Union and Eastern Europe* 3 (Winter 1989): 5–29.

Belenkii, M. S. *Literarishe portretn* [Literary portraits]. Moscow: Sovetskii Pisatel', 1989.

Belkin, Ahuva. *Beyn shtey arim; ha-makhaze ha-ivri* Simkhat purim [Between two cities; The Hebrew play "The joy of Purim"]. Lod: Makhon Haberman le-mekhkarey sifrut, 1997.

———. "Citing Scripture for a Purpose: The Jewish *Purimspiel* as a Parody." *Assaph* C/12 (1997): 45–59.

———. "Kapoyerdiker kapoyer: der yidisher karnaval-teater" [Inverted inversion: Yiddish carnival theatre]. *Oksforder yidish* 3 (1995): 449–472.

---. *Ha-purim shpil: iyunim ba-te'atron ha-yehudi ha-amami* [The Purimshpil: Studies in Jewish folk theatre]. Jerusalem: Mosad Bialik, 2002.

---. "Ritual Space as Theatrical Space in Jewish Folk Theatre." In Edna Nahshon, ed., *Jewish Theatre: A Global View*, 15–24. Leiden: Brill, 2009.

---. "Salvation Now? Ideology and Parody in Abraham Goldfaden's *Messiah Time?!*" In Ahuva Belkin, ed., *Jewish Theatre: Tradition in Transition and Intercultural Vistas. Assaph: Studies in the Theater* (2008): 115–130.

Belling, Veronica Penkin. "From the Bowery to Brakpan: A Bibliographic Guide to Yiddish Theatre Worldwide." *Proceedings of the 39th Annual Convention of the Association of Jewish Libraries.* Brooklyn, NY, June 20–23, 2004, 1–9.

---. "The Golden Years of Yiddish Theatre in South Africa, 1902–1910." *Jewish Affairs* 55 (2000): 7–14.

---. "The History of Yiddish Theatre in South Africa from the Late Nineteenth Century to 1960." M.A. thesis, University of Cape Town, 2003.

---. "A Short-Lived Revival: Yiddish Theatre in South Africa, 1945–1960." In Joseph Sherman, ed., *Yiddish After the Holocaust*, 92–116. Oxford, UK: Boulevard Books, 2004.

---. "'A Slice of Eastern Europe in Johannesburg': Yiddish Theatre in Doornfontein, 1929–49." *Jewish Culture and History* 9 (Autumn/Winter 2007), 194–207.

---. *Yiddish Theatre in South Africa: A History from the Late Nineteenth Century to 1960*. Cape Town: Isaac and Jessie Kaplan Centre for Jewish Studies and Research, 2008.

---. "Yiddish Theatre in South Africa: An Overview." *Jewish Affairs* 61 (December 2006), 5–16.

Bellis, Shlomo. "Alter Kacyzne (Katsizne)." *Yiddish* 2 (1975): 50–53.

Ben-Ami, R. *Habima*. Chicago: L. M. Shteyn, 1937. Translated into English as *Habima* by A. H. Gross and I. Soref. New York: Thomas Yoseloff, 1957.

Ben-Shach, Jane Respitz. "The False Messiah in Yiddish Literature: A Comparison between Two Dramatic Works." M.A. thesis, McGill University, 1990.

Bennett, Bernice I. "A Study of the Yiddish Theater in America: With Selected Individuals Who Have Influenced and Contributed to the Growth and Development of American Theater." M.A. thesis, Emerson College, 1963.

Beregovsky, M. *Arfy na verbakh: prizvanie i sud'ba Moiseya Beregovskogo* [Harps upon the willows: The calling and destiny of Moyshe Beregovski]. Moscow: Evreiskii universitet v Moskve; Jerusalem: Gesharim, 1994.

Berg, Hetty. "Jiddisch theater in Amsterdam in de achttiende eeuw" [Yiddish theatre in Amsterdam in the eighteenth century]. *Studia Rosenthaliana* 26 (1992): 10–37.

---. "Thalia and Amsterdam's Ashkenazi Jews in the Late 18th and Early 19th Centuries." In Jonathan Israel and Reinier Salverda, eds., *Dutch Jewry: Its History and Secular Culture (1500–2000)*, 191–199. Leiden: Brill, 2002.

Berger, Sidney L. "The Theme of Persecution in Selected Dramas of the Yiddish Art Theatre." Ph.D. thesis, University of Kansas, 1964.

Berkovitsh, Yisroel. *Bukarester yidisher melukhe-teater: finf un tsvantsik: 1948–1973* [Bucharest State Yiddish Theatre: twenty-five (years): 1948–1973]. Bucharest: n.p., 1974.

---. *Hundert yor yidish teater in rumenye* [One hundred years of Yiddish theatre in Romania]. Bucharest: Criterion, 1976.

Berkowitz, Joel. "Avrom Goldfaden's Theatre of Jewishness: Three Prooftexts." In Glenda Abramson and Hilary Kilpatrick, eds., *Religious Perspectives in Modern Muslim and Jewish Literatures*, 258–282. London: Routledge, 2006.

---. "The Brothel as Symbolic Space in Yiddish Drama." In Nanette Stahl, ed., *Sholem Asch Reconsidered*, 34–49. New Haven: Beinecke Rare Book and Manuscript Library, 2004.

---. "The Many Languages of Yiddish Drama." In Joseph Roach, ed., *Changing the Subject: Marvin Carlson and Theater Studies, 1959–2009*, 238–260. Ann Arbor: University of Michigan Press, 2009.

---. "The 'Mendel Beilis Epidemic' on the Yiddish Stage." *Jewish Social Studies* 8 (Fall 2001): 199–225.

---. *Shakespeare on the American Yiddish Stage*. Iowa City: University of Iowa Press, 2002.

---. "*Shtetl* and *Shtot* in Yiddish Haskalah Drama." In Antony Polonsky, ed., *Polin: Studies in Polish Jewry*, vol. 17: The Shtetl: Myth and Reality, ed. Antony Polonsky, 213–232. London: Littman Library of Jewish Civilization, 2004.

---. "The Tallis or the Cross? Reviving Goldfaden at the Yiddish Art Theatre, 1924–26." *Journal of Jewish Studies* 50 (Spring 1999): 120–138.

---. "This is Not Europe, You Know: The Counter-Maskilic Impulse of American Yiddish Drama." In Edward S. Shapiro, ed., *Yiddish Culture in America: Essays on Yiddish Culture in the Golden Land*, 135–165. Scranton, PA: University of Scranton Press, 2008.

---. "A True Jewish Jew: Three Yiddish Shylocks." *Theatre Survey* 37 (May 1996): 75–98.

---. "Wicked Daughters, Wilting Sons: Jacob Gordin's King & Queen Lear." *Assaph: Studies in the Theatre* (June 1997): 125–148.

---, ed. *Yiddish Theatre: New Approaches*. London: Littman Library of Jewish Civilization, 2003.

--- and Jeremy Dauber. "Translating Yiddish Comedies of the Jewish Enlightenment." *Metamorphoses* 9 (Spring 2001): 90–112.

--- and Jeremy Dauber, eds. Introduction to *Landmark Yiddish Plays: A Critical Anthology*, 1–72. Albany, NY: State University of New York Press, 2006.

Berman, L. *In loyf fun di yorn: zikhroynes fun a yidishn arbeter* [As the years go by: Memoirs of a Jewish worker]. Warsaw: Memuarn-komitet baym Dvinsker "Bund" Brentsh 75 Arbeter-ring in Amerike, 1936. Rpt. New York, 1945.

Bernardi, Jack. *My Father the Actor*. New York: W. W. Norton, 1971.

Bertolone, Paola. *L'esilio del teatro: Goldfaden e il moderno teatro yiddish* [The exile of theatre: Goldfaden and the modern Yiddish theatre]. Rome: Bulzoni, 1994.

--- and Laura Quercioli Mincer. *Café Savoy: teatro yiddish in Europa* [Café Savoy: Yiddish theatre in Europe]. Rome: Bulzoni, 2006.

Bez, Khayim. "Vegn akht yidishe drames" [About eight Yiddish dramas]. Introduction to *Di yidishe drame fun 20stn yorhundert* [Yiddish drama in the 20th century], 2 vols. 1: 9–78. New York: Alveltlekher Yidisher Kultur-kongres, 1977.

Bialik, Ilana. "Audience Response in the Yiddish Shund Theatre." *Theatre Research International* 13 (Summer 1988): 97–105.

---. "Ekronot shel ha'atakat makhazot le-yidish ba-te'atron ha-'shund' (lefi 'Dos yidishe harts' me'et Yosef Latayner)." [Principles of copying plays for the Yiddish "shund" theatre (According to Joseph Lateiner's *The Jewish Heart*)]. *Bama* 107 (1987): 15–22.

Bialin, A. H. *Moris Shvarts un der yidisher kunst teater* [Maurice Schwartz and the Yiddish Art Theatre]. New York: Itshe Biderman, 1934.

Biletsky, Y. H. *H. Leyvik, ha-dramaturgiya ha-khezyonit* [H. Leivick's visionary dramaturgy]. Tel Aviv: Ha-kibuts ha-meyukhad, 1979.

Bilov, S., and A. Veledinsky. Introduction to Avrom Goldfaden, *Geklibene dramatishe verk* [Selected dramatic works], 3–64. Kiev: Melukhe-farlag, 1940.

Binevich, Evgenii. "Evreiskii teatr v odesse. Annotirovannaya bibliografiya" [Jewish theatre in Odessa: An annotated bibliography]. Preprints 47 and 48, Obshchestvo "evreiskoe nasledie" [Jewish Heritage Society], http://www.jewish-heritage.org.

---. "Evreiskii teatr v peterburge. Annotirovannaya bibliografiya russkoyazychnykh povremennykh izdanii" [Jewish theatre in St. Petersburg: An annotated bibliography of articles in Russian-language periodical publications]. Preprint 46, Obshchestvo "evreiskoe nasledie" [Jewish Heritage Society], http://www.jewish-heritage.org.

———. *Evreiskii teatr v peterburge. Opyt istoricheskogo ocherka* [Jewish theatre in St. Petersburg: An experiment in historical essay]. St. Petersburg: Evreiskii obshchinnyi tsentr sankt-peterburga, 2003.

———. "Evreiskii teatr v rossii, 1896–1904 [Jewish theatre in Russia, 1896–1904]. Preprint 44, Obshchestvo "evreiskoe nasledie" [Jewish Heritage Society], http://www.jewish-heritage.org.

———. "Gastrolery v peterburge" [Touring performers in St. Petersburg]. Preprint 9, Obshchestvo "evreiskoe nasledie" [Jewish Heritage Society], http://www.jewish-heritage.org.

———. *Istoriya evreiskogo teatra v rossii: 1875–1918* [History of the Jewish theatre in Russia: 1875–1918]. Baltimore: Seagull Press, 2009.

———. "Istoriya evreiskogo teatra v rossii, 1876–1883. Annotirovannaya bibliografiya russkoyazychnykh povremennykh izdanii" [The history of Jewish theatre in Russia, 1876–1883: An annotated bibliography of articles in Russian-language periodical publications]. Preprint 38, Obshchestvo "evreiskoe nasledie" [Jewish Heritage Society], http://www.jewish-heritage.org.

———. "Nachalo evreiskogo teatra v rossii [The beginnings of Jewish theatre in Russia]. Preprint 3, Obshchestvo "evreiskoe nasledie" [Jewish Heritage Society], http://www.jewish-heritage.org.

———. "'Svoi' teatr v peterburge" ["Our own" Petersburg theatre]. Preprint 39, Obshchestvo "evreiskoe nasledie" [Jewish Heritage Society], http://www.jewish-heritage.org.

———. "Stabilizatsiya iz istorii evreiskogo teatra" [Stabilization in the history of the Jewish theatre]. Preprint 45, Obshchestvo "evreiskoe nasledie" [Jewish Heritage Society], http://www.jewish-heritage.org.

Bliakher, Shabtse. *Eyn un tsvantsik un—eyner* [Twenty-one plus—one]. New York: Vilner Farlag, 1962.

Blumert, Rut. "Mi-Shmuel ad Shmuel ad . . . Shmuel (pegisha im ha-'kleyne mentshelekh' be-vitsua)" [From Samuel to Samuel to . . . Samuel (Meeting the "Little People" in Performance)]. *Bama* 98–99 (1984): 147–151.

Borovoy, S., ed. *Mendele un zayn tsayt: materyaln tsu der geshikhte fun der yidisher literatur in XIXtn yorhundert* [Mendele and his era: Materials toward the history of 19th-century Yiddish literature]. Moscow: Emes, 1940.

Botoshanski, Jacob. *Nokh der forshtelung: groteskn un bilder funem idishn aktyorn-lebn* [After the performance: Grotesques and images from the lives of Yiddish actors]. Buenos Aires: Farlag Shlayfer, 1926.

Boymvol, Rokhl. *Daniyel Finklkroyt: a yidish aktyor, 1894–1971* [Daniel Finkelkraut: a Yiddish actor, 1894–1971]. Jerusalem: Farlag "Eygns," 1974.

Bradley, Catherine Isabel. "The Development of Yiddish Theatre in Czarist Russia: a Study of the Interaction Between Majority and Minority Cultures." M.A. thesis, Missouri State University, 2006.

Bredstein, Andrey. "Nokhem-Meyer Shaykevitsh: Another Classic of Yiddish Theater?" In Leonard J. Greenspoon, Ronald A. Simkins, and Brian J. Horowitz, eds., *The Jews of Eastern Europe*, 203–216. Creighton, NE: Creighton University Press, 2005.

Brenner, David A. "'Making Jargon Respectable': Leo Winz, Ost und West and the Reception of Yiddish Theatre in Pre-Hitler Germany." *Leo Baeck Institute Year Book* 42 (1997): 51–66.

Brenner, Michael. *The Renaissance of Jewish Culture in Weimar Germany*. New Haven: Yale University Press, 1996.

Brook, Vincent. "Forging the New Jew: Ulmer's Yiddish Films." In Bernd Herzogenrath, ed., *The Films of Edgar G. Ulmer*, 71–85. Lanham, MD.: Scarecrow Press, 2009.

Bronsztejn, Szyja. "Teatr" [Theatre]. In Szyja Bronstein, *Z dziejów ludności żydowskiej na Dolnym Śląsku po II wojnie światowej* [From the history of the Jews of Lower Silesia after World War II], 75–77. Wrocław: Wydawnictwo Uniwersytetu Wrocławskiego, 1993.

Bruce, Iris. *Kafka and Cultural Zionism: Dates in Palestine.* Madison: University of Wisconsin Press, 2007.

Buchalski, Simao. *Memorias da minha juventude e do teatro idiche no Brasil* [Memories of my youth and of the Yiddish theatre in Brazil]. São Paolo: Editora Perspectiva, 1995.

Bukhvald, Nokhem. *Teater* [Theatre]. New York: Farlag-komitet Teater, 1943.

Bułat, Mirosława. "'Cwiszn cwej teaters'—na pograniczu dwóch teatrów: źródła jidysz w badaniach nad kontaktami międzykulturowymi w polskim teatrze—kilka przypomnień, szereg uzupełnień" ["Tsvishn tsvey teaters" (Between two theatres): Yiddish sources on the intercultural contacts of the Polish theatre: A few reminders, several additions]. In Ewa Geller and Monika Polit, eds., *Jidyszland: polskie przestrzenie* [Yiddishland: Polish spaces], 121–141. Warszawa: Wydawnictwa Uniwersytetu Warszawskiego, 2008.

———. "Historia teatru żydowskiego w Krakowie: rekonesans badawczy" [History of the Jewish theatre in Cracow: A research reconnaissance]. In Krzysztof Pilarczyk, ed., *Żydzi i judaizm we współczesnych badaniach polskich. Materiały z konferencji Kraków 21–23 XI 1995* [Jews and Judaism in contemporary Polish research: Conference proceedings, Cracow, November 21–23, 1995], 413–428. Kraków: Księgarnia Akademicka, 1997.

———. "'Izraelita' o teatrze żydowskim w Warszawie w latach 1883–1905" [*The Israelite* on the Jewish theatre in Warsaw, 1883–1905]. In Marta Meducka and Regina Renz, eds., *Kultura Żydów polskich XIX–XX wieku* [Culture of the Polish Jews in the 19th and 20th centuries], 181–195. Kielce: Kieleckie Towarzystwo Naukowe, 1992.

———. "'Jung Teater' i 'Naj Teater' w Krakowie" ["Young Theatre" and "New Theatre" in Cracow]. *Pamiętnik Teatralny* 3–4 (1996): 511–539.

———. *Krakowski Teatr Żydowski (Krokewer Jidisz Teater): między szundem a sztuką* [The Cracow Yiddish Theatre (Krokever Yidish Teater): Between "shund" and art]. Kraków: Wydawnictwo Uniwersytetu Jagiellońskiego, 2006.

———. "'Od Goldfadena do Goldfadena': (utwory Abrahama Goldfadena na żydowskich scenach Krakowa)" ["From Goldfaden to Goldfaden": (Avrom Goldfaden's works on Cracow's Jewish stages]. In Krzysztof Pilarczyk and Stefan Gąsiorowski, eds., *Materiały z konferencji Kraków 24–26 XI 1998* [Conference proceedings, Cracow, November 24–26, 1998]. Volume 2 of *Żydzi i judaizm we współczesnych badaniach polskich* [Jews and Judaism in contemporary Polish research], 295–311. Kraków: Polska Akademia Umiejętności, 2000.

———. "Teatry jidyszowe w Wilnie i ich występy gościnne w Krakowie w latach 1918–1939: (wprowadzenie do tematu)" [Yiddish theatres in Vilna and their guest performances in Cracow, 1918–1939: (Introduction to the subject)]. In Mirosława Kozłowska, ed., *Wilno teatralne* [Theatrical Vilna], 349–71. Warszawa: Ogólnopolski Klub Miłośników Litwy; "Interlibro," 1998.

———. "Tracing Yiddish Theatre in Cracow Before 1914." In Armin Eidherr and Karl Müller, eds., *Jiddische Kultur und Literatur aus Österreich* [Austrian Yiddish culture and literature], 44–56. Klagenfurt: Theodor Kramer Gesellschaft and Drava Verlag, 2003.

———. "Trójjęzyczny teatr żydowski w Polsce 'w lustrze' publicystyki Michała Weicherta na łamach *Literarisze Bleter*: (wprowadzenie)" [The trilingual Jewish theatre in Poland in the mirror of Mikhl Weichert's articles and reviews in *Literarishe Bleter*: (Introduction)]. In Eleonora Udalska and Anna Tytkowska, eds., *Żydzi w lustrze dramatu, teatru i krytyki teatralnej* [Jews in the mirror of drama, theatre, and theatre criticism], 269–279. Katowice: Wydawnictwo Uniwersytetu Śląskiego, 2004.

———. "W poszukiwaniu teatru 'żydowskiego': Zygmunt Turkow" [In search of the "Jewish Theatre": Zygmunt Turkow]. In Jacek Popiel, ed., *Antreprener: księga ofiarowana profesorowi Janowi Michalikowi w 70. rocznicę urodzin* [Entrepreneur: Festschrift for Professor Jan Michalik on the occasion of his 70th birthday], 585–605. Kraków: Wydawnictwo Uniwersytetu Jagiellońskiego, 2009.

Burko, Faina. "'Habima' and the Moscow Yiddish Chamber Theater in the Early Twenties." *Proceedings of the Ninth World Congress of Jewish Studies*, Division D, 2:233–240. Jerusalem: World Union of Jewish Studies, 1986.

———. "The Soviet Yiddish Theatre in the Twenties." Ph.D. thesis, Southern Illinois University at Carbondale, 1978.

Burshteyn, Peysekhe. *Geshpilt a lebn* [A life performed]. Tel Aviv: n.p., 1980.

———. *What a Life!: The Autobiography of Pesach'ke Burstein, Yiddish Matinee Idol.* Syracuse, NY: Syracuse University Press, 2003.

Bützer, Evi. *Die Anfänge der jiddischen purim shpiln in ihrem literarischen und kulturgeschichtlichen Kontext* [The origins of the Yiddish purimshpil in literary and cultural contexts]. Hamburg: Helmut Buske Farlag, 2003.

Buzgan, Khevel. *Hantbukh far aktyorn* [Handbook for actors]. Warsaw: M. Karpinovitsh, 1937.

Cahan, Abraham. *Bleter fun mayn lebn* [Pages from my life], 5 vols. New York: Forverts, 1926–1931.

Caplan, Debra. "Oedipus, Shmedipus: Ancient Greek Drama on the Modern Yiddish Stage." *Comparative Drama* 44/45 (Spring 2011), 405–422.

Cassedy, Steven, ed. *Building the Future: Jewish Immigrant Intellectuals and the Making of "Tsukunft."* New York: Holmes & Meier, 1999.

———. *To the Other Shore: The Russian Jewish Intellectuals Who Came to America.* Princeton: Princeton University Press, 1997.

Cohen, Nathan. "Isaac Bashevis-Singer's Attitude to the Yiddish Theater as Shown in His Works." In Edna Nahshon, ed., *Jewish Theatre: A Global View*, 49–61. Leiden: Brill, 2009.

Cypkin, Diane. "Second Avenue: The Yiddish Broadway." Ph.D. thesis, New York University, 1986.

Dalinger, Brigitte. "Begegnungen mit dibbukim. Chassidische Mystik im modernen Wiener Theater zwischen 1880 und 1938" [Encounters with dybbuks: Hasidic mysticism in the modern Viennese theatre between 1880 and 1938]. *Menora* 11 (2000): 229–250.

———. "Ein 'unterirdisches Dasein'; jiddisches Theater in Europa vor 1914" [An "underground existence": Yiddish theatre in Europe before 1914]. *Das Jüdische Echo* 45 (1996): 180–186.

———. "'Galizianer' in Wien; zur Darstellung 'östlicher Juden' im jiddischen Theater und Film." ["Galitzianers" in Vienna; on the phenomenon of "Eastern Jews" in Yiddish theatre and film.] In Armin A. Wallas, ed., *Jüdische Identitäten in Mitteleuropa: literarische Modelle der Identitätskonstruktion* [Jewish identities in central Europe: Literary models of identity construction], 35–46. Tübingen: Max Niemeyer Farlag, 2002.

———. "Jiddische Dramen aus Wien" [Viennese Yiddish dramas]. In Armin Eidherr and Karl Müller, eds., *Jiddische Kultur und Literatur aus Österreich* [Austrian Yiddish culture and literature], 57–71. Klagenfurt: Theodor Kramer Gesellschaft and Drava Verlag, 2003.

———. "Jiddisches Theater—ein Grenzgänger zwischen den Sprachen und Kulturen; Gastspiele jiddischer Truppen in Böhmen, Mähren und der Slowakei von 1910 bis 1938" [Yiddish Theatre—crossing borders between languages and cultures; Yiddish touring companies in Böhmen, Mähren, and Slovakia, 1910–1938]. *Maske und Kothurn* 47 (2002): 89–100.

———. "'Jüdaly mit dem Wandersack' bricht' auf nach Tel Aviv.' Zionismus und populäres jiddisches Theater" ["Jüdaly and his Travelling Bag" goes "to Tel Aviv": Zionism and Yiddish popular theatre]. *Das Jüdische Echo. Zeitschrift für Kultur und Politik* [The Jewish Echo. Journal for Culture and Politics] 47 (Oct. 1998): 250–256.

———. "Jüdisches Theater in Wien" [Jewish theatre in Vienna]. M.A. thesis, University of Vienna, 1991.

———. "Poczatki teatru żydowskiego w Wiedniu" [The beginnings of the Yiddish theatre in Vienna]. In Anna Kuligowska-Korzeniewska and Małgorzata Leyko, eds., *Teatr żydowski w Polsce* [Yiddish theatre in Poland], 332–341. Łódź: Wydawnictwo Uniwersytetu Łódzkiego, 1998.

———. "Te'atron yehudi be-Vinah, be-Berlin u-ve-Prag: hofa'ot orakh ve-hitkablutan [Jewish theatre in Vienna, Berlin, and Prague: guest performances and their reception]," *Bama* 166 (2002): 48–58.

———. *"Verloschene Sterne." Geschichte des jüdischen Theaters in Vienna* ["Extinguished stars": A history of the Jewish theatre in Vienna]. Vienna: Picus Verlag, 1998.

Dauber, Jeremy Asher. *Antonio's Devils: Writers of the Jewish Enlightenment and the Birth of Modern Hebrew and Yiddish Literature*. Palo Alto, CA: Stanford University Press, 2004.

———. "What's So Funny about Yiddish Theater? Comedy and the Origins of Yiddish Drama." In Justin Cammy, Dara Horn, Alyssa Quint, and Rachel Rubinstein, eds., *Arguing the Modern Jewish Canon: Essays on Literature and Culture in Honor of Ruth R. Wisse*, 535–550. Cambridge, MA: Center for Jewish Studies, Harvard University, 2008.

Davis, Jim. "The East End." In Michael R. Booth and Joel H. Kaplan, eds., *The Edwardian Theatre: Essays on Performance and the Stage*, 201–219. Cambridge: Cambridge University Press, 1996.

Dell, Harry. *Impresario*. New York: n.p., 1967.

Demetz, Peter. "Speculations about Prague Yiddish and its Disappearance; From Its Origins to Kafka and Brod." In Mark H. Gelber, ed., *Confrontations/Accommodations: German-Jewish Literary and Cultural Relations from Heine to Wassermann*, 237–247. Tübingen: Niemeyer, 2004.

Denk, Dovid. *Hinter di kulisn* [Behind the scenes]. New York: Farlag Vokhnblat, 1959.

———. *Shvarts af vays* [Black on white]. New York: n.p., 1963.

Dimov, Osip. *Vos ikh gedenk* [What I remember], 2 vols. New York: CYCO, 1943.

Dinah Roytkop. Tel Aviv: Farlag Kaf-alef Elul, 1976.

Dinezon, Yankev. *Zikhroynes un bilder: shtetl, kinderyorn, shrayber* [Memories and scenes: Shtetl, childhood, writers]. Warsaw: Farlag Akhiseyfer, n.d.

Dobrushin, Yekhezkel. *Binyomin Zuskin*. Moscow: Melukhe-farlag, 1939.

———. *Di dramaturgye fun di klasiker* [The dramaturgy of the classic writers]. Moscow: Emes, 1948.

———. *Mikhoels der aktyor* [Mikhoels the actor]. Moscow: Emes, 1940.

The Drama Review 24: Jewish Theatre (1980).

Dressler, Roland. *Von der Schaubühne zur Sittenschule. Das Theaterpublikum vor der vierten Wand* [From entertainment stage to school of manners: The theatre audience before the fourth wall]. Berlin: Henschel Verlag, 1993.

Druxman, Michael B. *Paul Muni: His Life and His Films*. South Brunswick, NJ: A. S. Barnes, 1974.

Dvorzhetski, M., M. Tsanin, and Ruvn Rubinshteyn, eds. *Yankev Mansdorf in zayn dor* [Jacob Mansdorf in his generation]. Johannesburg: Culture Federation of Histadrut Ivrit and Jacob Mansdorf Fund, n.d.

Dzigan, Shmuel. *Dzhigan: der koyekh fun yidishn humor* [Dzigan: The power of Jewish humor]. Tel Aviv: n.p., 1974.

Eglash-Siegel, Kari, "Mishpoke [sic]: Immigration, the Jewish Family and the Yiddish Theater." M.S.M. thesis, Hebrew Union College-Jewish Institute of Religion, 2001.

Ehrenreich, Khayim. *Figurn un profiln af der yidisher bine* [Figures and profiles on the Yiddish stage]. Tel Aviv: Khayim Erenraykh Bukh-komitet, 1976.

Eidherr, Armin. "'Auf stillem Pfad . . .': Jiddische Schriftsteller in Wien" ["On a silent path . . .": Yiddish authors in Vienna]. *Literatur und Kritik* [Literature and criticism] 273–4 (1993): 47–55.

Entin, Boris, ed. *Polveka evreiskogo teatra: 1876–1926. Antologiya evreiskoi dramaturgii* [A half-century of Jewish theatre: 1876–1926. An anthology of Jewish dramaturgy]. Moscow: Dom evreiskoi knigi, 2003.

Entin, Yoel. "Di forgeshikhte funem yidishn teater" [The prehistory of the Yiddish theatre]. In *Suvenir tsu Yankev Gordins tsen-yerik yubileyum* [Souvenir of Jacob Gordin's tenth anniversary], 15–22. New York: n.p., 1901.

———. "Leon Kobrin der dramaturg" [The playwright Leon Kobrin]. Introduction to Leon Kobrin, *Dramatishe shriftn* [Dramatic writings], xi–xxxvii. New York: n.p.: YKUF, 1952.

———. *Di zayln fun der nayer idisher literatur: nayn lektsyes vegn Mendele Moykher-Sforim, Sholem Aleykhem, un Y. L. Perets* [The pillars of the new Yiddish literature: nine lectures on Mendele Moykher-Sforim, Sholem Aleichem, and Y. L. Peretz]. New York: Idish-natsyonaler Arbeter Farband, 1923.

Epstein, Melech. *Profiles of Eleven: Profiles of Eleven Men who Guided the Destiny of an Immigrant Society and Stimulated Social Consciousness Among the American People*. Detroit: Wayne State University Press, 1965.

Epstein, Shifra. *"Daniyel-shpil" ba-khasidut bobov* [The *Daniel Play* of the Bobover Hasidim]. Jerusalem: Magnes Press, 1998.

———. "Drama on a Table: The Bobover Hasidim Piremshpiyl." In Harvey E. Goldberg, ed., *Judaism Viewed From Within and From Without: Anthropological Studies*, 195–215. Albany: State University of New York Press, 1987.

———. "Ha-'purim shpil' ha-rishon shel khasidey bobov be-nyu-york akharey ha-sho'a" [The first Purim play of the Bobover Hasidim in New York after the Shoah]. *Khulyot* 3 (1996): 317–325.

Erdman, Harley. "Jewish Anxiety in 'Days of Judgement': Community Conflict, Antisemitism, and the *God of Vengeance* Obscenity Case." *Theatre Survey* 40 (May 1999): 51–74.

Erenraykh, Khayim. *Figurn un profiln af der yidisher bine* [Figures and profiles on the Yiddish stage]. Tel Aviv: Khayim Erenraykh Bukh-komitet, 1976.

Erik, Max. *Etyudn tsu der geshikhte fun der haskole* [Studies toward the history of the Haskalah]. Minsk: Melukhe-farlag far Vaysruslendisher Kultur, 1934.

———. *Di geshikhte fun der yidisher literatur fun di eltste tsaytn biz der haskole tkufe* [The history of Yiddish literature from olden times to the Haskalah period]. Warsaw: Kultur-lige, 1928.

———. *Konstruktsye-shtudyen: tsu der konstruktsye fun Der goldener keyt un Bay nakht afn altn mark: batrakhtungen vegn patos* [Construction studies: On the construction of *The Golden Chain* and *At Night in the Old Marketplace*: Contemplations on pathos]. Warsaw: Arbeter Heym, 1924.

———. *Sholem Ash (1900–1930)*. Minsk: Vaysrusisher Visnshaft-akademye, 1931.

———. *Vegn sotsyaln mehus fun Aksenfelds shafn* [On the social nature of Aksenfeld's works]. *Tsaytshrift* 5 (1931): 125–169.

———. ed., *Sh. Etinger: geklibene verk* [S. Ettinger: Collected works]. Kiev: Farlag fun der Ukraynisher Visnshaft-akademye, 1935.

Erlich, Victor. "Vispianskis hashpoe af *Bay nakht afn altn mark*" [Wyspiański's influence on *At Night in the Old Marketplace*]. *Yivo bleter* 28 (Autumn 1946): 81–99.

Eynes, Avrom. *Fun lublin biz rige: goles-oprikhtn fun idishn aktyor* [From Lublin to Riga: Wanderings of a Yiddish actor]. Riga: self-published, 1940.

Fass, Moshe. "Theatrical Activities in the Polish Ghettoes During the Years 1939–1942." *Jewish Social Studies* 38 (Winter 1976): 54–72.

Feder, Samy. "The Yiddish Theatre of Belsen." In Rebecca Rovit and Alvin Goldfarb, eds., *Theatrical Performance during the Holocaust: Texts, Documents, Memoirs*, 156–158. Baltimore: Johns Hopkins University Press, 1999.

Feffer, Heather L. "From Second Avenue to the Synagogue: the Vital Connection Between Theater and Worship as Illustrated in the Life and Music of Abe Ellstein." M.S.M. thesis, Hebrew Union College-Jewish Institute of Religion, 1996.

Feingold, Ben-Ami. "Historical Dramas on the Inquisition and Expulsion." *Haifa University Studies in Jewish Theatre and Drama* 1 (Autumn 1995): 9–30.

——— "Te'atron yidish: kol he-avar lefanav" [Yiddish Theatre: The entire past lies before it]. *Te'atron* 11 (2003): 21–25.

Filler, Susan M. "The Music of Yiddish Theater and Its Influence on Broadway." In Leonard J. Greenspoon, ed., *I Will Sing and Make Music: Jewish Music and Musicians Throughout the Ages*, 167–179. Omaha, NE: Creighton University Press, 2006.

Finkelshteyn, Leo. *Dortn un do: vegn dem dertseyler un dramatiker F. Bimko* [There and here: About the novelist and dramatist F(ishl) Bimko]. Toronto: Farlag Gershon Pomerants Esey-bibliotek, 1950.

———. *Tsvishn di shures fun Leyviks Goylem* [Between the lines of Leivick's *Golem*]. Warsaw: B. Kletskin, 1925.

Fisher, Krysia, Michael C. Steinlauf, and Henryk Greenberg, eds. *Ida Kaminska: Grande Dame of the Yiddish Theater.* New York: YIVO Institute for Jewish Research, 2001.

Fishman, David Eliyahu. "Ha-mediniut klapey yidish be-rusiya ha-tsarit." [The policy toward Yiddish in Czarist Russia]. *Khulyot* 3 (1996): 255–269.

Fishman, Jacob, B. Levin, and B. Stabinovitsh, eds. *Finf un tsvantsik yor folks-bine* [Twenty-five years of the Folksbiene]. New York: Posy-Shoulson Press, n.d.

Fishman, Jacob, B. Levin, B. Stabinovitsh, Louis Mann, and Beynush Steyvin, eds. *Fertsik yor folks-bine* [Forty years of the Folksbiene]. New York: n.p., 1955.

Fishman, Joshua. "Yiddish in Israel: The Press, Radio, Theatre, and Book Publishing." *Yiddish* 1 (1974): 4–23.

Fletcher, Anne. *Rediscovering Mordecai Gorelik: Scene Design and the American Theatre*. Carbondale: Southern Illinois University Press, 2009.

Foreman, Marlene Phyllis. "Remembrances of Cincinnati's Yiddish Theatre." M.A. thesis, University of Cincinnati, 1972.

Frankl, Yekhiel. "Te'atron u-fe'ilut amanutit akheret be-geto lodzh" [Theatre and other artistic activities in the Łódź ghetto]. *Bama* 103 (1986): 12–42; 104 (1986): 38–60.

Freeden, Herbert. *Jüdisches Theater in Nazideutschland* [Jewish theatre in Nazi Germany]. Tübingen: Mohr, 1964.

Freeman, Moyshe. "Idish teater in filadelfia" [Yiddish theatre in Philadelphia]. In Moyshe Freeman, *Fuftsik yor geshikhte fun idishn lebn in filadelfia* [Fifty years of the history of Jewish life in Philadelphia], 2:189–249. Philadelphia: Kultur, 1934.

Freie Jüdische Volksbühne. Pressestimmen [Free Jewish People's Theatre Organization: Press commentaries]. Vienna: Gründungskomitee der Jüdischen Künstlerbühnen, 1921.

Frost, Matthew. "Marc Chagall and the Jewish State Chamber Theatre." *Russian History* 8 (1981): 90–107.

Fuftsn yor "vilner trupe" [Fifteen years of the Vilna Troupe]. Łódź: Lodzher Teater-komitet, 1931.

Fuks-Mansfeld, Renata G. "West- en Oost-Jiddisch op het toneel in Amsterdam aan het einde van de achttiende eew" [Western and eastern Yiddish in Amsterdam at the end of the eighteenth century]. *Studia Rosenthaliana* 26 (1992): 91–96.

———. "West-und Ostjiddisch auf Amsterdamer Bühnen gegen Ende des achtzehnten Jahrhunderts" [Western and eastern Yiddish on the Amsterdam stage at the end of the eighteenth century]. In Astrid Starck, ed., *Westjiddisch. Mündlichkeit und Schriftlichkeit/Le Yiddish occidental: Actes du Colloque de Mulhouse* [West Yiddish. Speech and writing/West Yiddish: Mulhouse conference proceedings], 112–118. Aarau: Sauerländer, 1994.

Furnish, Ben. *Nostalgia in Jewish-American Theatre and Film, 1979–2004*. New York: Peter Lang, 2005.

Gadberry, Glen W. "Nazi Germany's Jewish Theatre." *Theatre Survey* 21 (1980): 15–32.

Gaines, Frederick Eugene. "The Effect of Collective Theatre Practices on the American Playwright." Ph.D. thesis, University of Minnesota, 1982.

Gąssowski, Szczepan. *Państwowy Teatr Żydowski imienia Ester Rachel Kamińskiej: przeszłość i teraźniejszość* [The Ester-Rokhl Kaminska State Jewish Theatre: Past and present]. Warszawa: Wydawnictwo Naukowe PWN, 1995.

Gay, Ruth. "Inventing a Yiddish Theater in America." In Jacob Gordin, *The Jewish King Lear: A Comedy in America*, edited and translated by Ruth Gay, 73–106. New Haven: Yale University Press, 2007.

———. "Jacob Gordin's Life." In Gordin, *The Jewish King Lear*, 107–138.

———. "Why Do We Smile?" In Gordin, *The Jewish King Lear*, 67–72.

Geizer, Matvei M. *Mikhoels: Zhizn' i smert'* [Mikhoels: Life and death]. Moscow: Zhurnalistskoe agentstvo "Glasnost.'" Soyuza zhurnalistov RF, 1998.

Gelegnhayts shrift tsu Ruvn Guskins 10 yoriger tetikayt [Occasional writing for Reuben Guskin's 10 years of activity]. New York: Hebrew Actors Union, 1930.

Gerasimova, Inna. *Vystavka "Evreiskii teatr v Belarusi"* [Exhibition catalogue: Jewish theatre in Belarus]. Minsk: Museum of the History of Jewish Culture in Belarus, 2007.

Gershtein, Anna. "Notes on the Jewish State Theater of Belorussia." *Jews in Eastern Europe* 27 (1995): 27–42.

Gładysz, Izabela. "Życie kulturalne Żydów w Lublinie w latach 1918–1939" [The cultural life of Jews in Lublin, 1918–1939]. In Tadeusz Radzik, ed., *Żydzi w Lublinie. Materiały do dziejów społeczności żydowskiej Lublina* [The Jews in Lublin: Materials on the history of the Jewish community of Lublin], 201–213. Lublin: Wydawnictwo Uniwersytetu Marii Curie-Skłodowskiej, 1995.

Glatshteyn, Yankev. *In tokh genumen: eseyen 1948–1956*, 2 vols. [Sum and substance: Essays]. New York: Farlag fun Idish Natsyonaln Arbeter Farband, 1947 and 1956.

Glazer, Sophie. "Reading *The Jewish King Lear*." In Jacob Gordin, *The Jewish King Lear: A Comedy in America*, edited and translated by Ruth Gay, 139–160. New Haven, CT: Yale University Press, 2007.

Glickman, Nora. "Max Berliner and Cipe Lincovsky: Two Great Actors of the Yiddish/Spanish Theatre in Argentina." *Modern Jewish Studies* 14 (2004): 50–56.

Goldberg, Isaac. *The Drama of Transition: Native and Exotic Playcraft*. Cincinnati: Stewart Kidd, 1922.

Goldberg, Judith N. *Laughter Through Tears: The Yiddish Cinema*. Rutherford, NJ: Fairleigh Dickinson University Press, 1983.

Goldberg, Reuven. "Ida Kaminska (5.9.1899–21.5.1980)." *Bama* 86 (1981): 54–64.

———. "Kharuzo shel Goldfaden" [Goldfaden's rhyme]. *Proceedings of the Eighth World Congress of Jewish Studies*, Division C, 325–330. Jerusalem: World Union of Jewish Studies, 1982.

———. "Me'a shnot te'atron yehudi be-romanya" [A century of Jewish theatre in Romania]. *Shevet romanya* 4–5 (1979): 16–32.

———. "Yidish teater" [Yiddish theatre]. *Yivo bleter* 44 (1973): 304–310.

Goldberg, Y., ed. *Unzer dramaturgye* [Our dramaturgy]. New York: YKUF and Yekhiel Levenshteyn Bukh Komitet, 1961.

Goldberg, Ze'ev. "Ha-deramah 'Doktor Almasado' le-Avraham Goldfaden" [Avrom Goldfaden's drama *Doctor Almasado*]. *Masad* 4 (2006): 33–46.

Goldenberg, Mikhail. *Zhizn' i sud'ba Solomona Mikhoelsa* [The life and fate of Solomon Mikhoels]. Baltimore: Vestnik, 1995.

Goldfaden, Avrom. *Oysgeklibene shriftn: Shulamis un Bar Kokhba* [Selected writings: *Shulamis* and *Bar Kokhba*], ed. Shmuel Rozhansky. Buenos Aires: YIVO, 1963.

Goldfarb, Alvin. "Theatre and Drama and the Nazi Concentration Camps." Ph.D. thesis, City University of New York Graduate Center, 1977.

———. "Theatrical Activities in Nazi Concentration Camps." *Performing Arts Journal* (Autumn 1976): 3–11.

Goldman, Berek I. "Cultural Activities Among Jews in the Displaced Persons Camps in Germany, Austria, and Italy After World War II." Ph.D. thesis, Jewish Teachers Seminary and People's University, 1970.

Goldman, Eric A. *Visions, Images, and Dreams: Yiddish Film Past and Present*. Ann Arbor: UMI Research Press, 1979.

———. "The Yiddish Cinema in America: a Celebration of Jewish Life." In Edward S. Shapiro, ed., *Yiddish in America: Essays on Yiddish Culture in the Golden Land*, 81–108. Scranton, PA: University of Scranton Press, 2008.

Gordin, Abba. *Yidish lebn in amerike: in shpigl fun F. Bimkos verk* [American Jewish life as reflected in F. Bimko's work]. Buenos Aires: Yidish Shrayber Farayn H. D. Nomberg, 1957.

Gordin, Jacob. *Ale shriftn* [Complete writings], 4 vols. New York: Hebrew Publishing Co., 1910.

Gordon, Mel. "Granovsky's Tragic Carnival: Night in the Old Market." *The Drama Review* 29 (Winter 1985): 91–94.

Gorelik, Mordecai. *New Theatres for Old*. New York: Samuel French, 1940.

Gorin, B. *Di geshikhte fun idishn teater* [The history of the Yiddish theatre], 2 vols. New York: Literarisher Farlag, 1918; repr. New York: Max N. Mayzel, 1923.

Got, Jerzy. "Aus dem Theaterleben in der Provinz von Galizien im 18. und 19. Jahrhundert" [On Galician theatrical life in the 18th and 19th centuries]. *Studia Austro-Polonica* 5 (1996): 439–457.

Gotesfeld, Khone. *Brodvey un tel-aviv* [Broadway and Tel Aviv]. New York: Khone Gotesfeld Bukhkomitet, 1951.

———. *Tales of the Old World and the New*. New York: Thomas Yoseloff, 1964.

———. *Vos ikh gedenk fun mayn lebn* [What I remember]. New York: Fareynikte Galitsyaner in Amerike, 1960.

Gotlib, Yankev. *H. Leyvik, zayn lid un drame* [H. Leivick: His poetry and drama]. Kaunas: Pasaulis, 1939.

Gottlieb, Jack. *Funny, It Doesn't Sound Jewish: How Yiddish Songs and Synagogue Melodies Influenced Tin Pan Alley, Broadway, and Hollywood*. Albany, NY: State University of New York Press, 2004.

Gould, Lea Shampanief. "Artef Players Collective: A History." M.A. thesis, Cornell University, 1953.

Gourfinkel, Nina. "Les théâtres hébraïque et yiddish à Moscou" [Hebrew and Yiddish theatres in Moscow]. In Denis Bablet and Jean Jacquot, eds., *L'Expressionisme dans le théâtre européen* [Expressionism in the European theatre]. Paris: CNRS, 1984.

Granach, Alexander. *Da geht ein Mensch: Autobiographischer Roman von Alexander Granach* [There goes a man: autobiographical novel by Alexander Granach]. Stockholm: Neuer-Verlag, 1945. Translated into English by Willard Trask as *There Goes an Actor*. Garden City, NY: Doubleday, 1945) and into Yiddish by Jacob Mestel as *Ot geyt a mentsh* [There goes a man]. New York: YKUF, 1948. Reissued as *From the Shtetl to the Stage: The Odyssey of a Wandering Actor*. New Brunswick, NJ: Transaction Publishers, 2011.

Greenbaum, Alfred Abraham. "The Belorussian State Jewish Theater in the Interwar Period." *Jews in Eastern Europe* 2 (2000): 56–75.

Greenberg, Eliezer. *Tsentrale motivn un grunt-problemen in H. Leyviks shafn* [Central motifs and fundamental issues in H. Leivick's work]. New York: CYCO, 1961.

Gris, Noah. "A yidisher teater-trupe in pariz in yor 1896" [A Yiddish theatre troupe in Paris in 1896]. *Yivo bleter* 44 (1973): 261–265.

Grober, Khayele. *Mayn veg aleyn* [My own way]. Tel Aviv: Farlag Y. L. Perets, 1968.

Groiser, David. "Translating Yiddish: Martin Buber and David Pinski." In Joseph Sherman and Ritchie Robertson, eds., *The Yiddish Presence in European Literature: Inspiration and Interaction*, 45–72. Legenda Studies in Yiddish 5. London: Modern Humanities Research Association, 2005.

Gronski, Ryszard Marek. *Proca Dawida: kabaret w przedsionku piekiel* [David's slingshot: A cabaret in hell's antechamber]. Warszawa: Warszawskie Wydawn. Literackie, 2007.

Grözinger, Elvira. *Die jiddische Kultur im Schatten der Diktaturen: Israil Bercovici—Leben und Werk* [Yiddish culture in the shadow of dictatorship: Israel Bercovici—life and work]. Berlin: Philo, 2002.

Guinsberg, J. *Aventuras de uma língua errante: Ensaios de literatura e teatro ídiche* [Adventures of a wandering tongue: Essays on Yiddish literature and theatre]. São Paulo: Perspectiva, 1996.

Gur, Yisrael. "Makhazehu ha-yidi shel Aharon Tseytlin al Brener" [Aaron Zeitlin's Yiddish play on Brenner]. *Bama* 87–88 (1981): 24–49.

———. "Ba-inyan ha-'Yidish kunst teater'" [Regarding the Yiddish Art Theatre]. *Bama* 87–88 (1981): 149–150.

———. "Goldfaden ve-Gordin" [Goldfaden and Gordin]. *Bama* 87–88 (1981): 189–204.

———. "Me'a shnot te'atron yehudi" [A century of Jewish theatre]. *Bama* 87–88 (1981): 146–48.

Gutfreind, Ieda. *A imigração judaica no Rio Grande do Sul: da memória para a história* [Jewish immigration to Rio Grande do Sul: From memory to history]. Leopoldo: Editora Unisinos, 2004.

Haberman, Avraham Me'ir. "Al makhazot kedumim be-yehudit ashkenazit" [On early plays in Judeo-German]. *Mozna'im* 50 (1980): 228–230.

Haenni, Sabine. "The Immigrant Scene: The Commercialization of Ethnicity and the Production of Publics in Fiction, Theater, and the Cinema, 1890–1915." Ph.D. thesis, University of Chicago, 1998.

Hanak-Lettner, Werner and Brigitte Dalinger. *Being Shylock: Ein Experiment am Yiddish Art Theatre, New York 1947*. Vienna: Jüdisches Museum, 2009.

Hannowa, Anna. "Jakub Rotbaum, czyli dwa teatry [Jakub Rotbaum, or two theatres]: Interview with Jakub Rotbaum." *Teatr* 49, no. 7/8 (1994): 48–55; 49, no. 9 (1994): 40–46.

———. *Jakub Rotbaum: Świat zaginiony. Malarstwo, rysunki* [Jakub Rotbaum: The world that has perished. Paintings, drawings]. Wrocław: Ośrodek Badań Twórczości Jerzego Grotowskiego i Poszukiwań Teatralno-Kulturowych, 1995.

———. "Wileńskie lata Jakuba Rotbauma" [The Vilna years of Jakub Rotbaum]. In Mirosława Kozłowska, ed., *Wilno teatralne* [Theatrical Vilna], 331–349. Warszawa: Ogólnopolski Klub Miłośników Litwy; "Interlibro," 1998.

Hansman, Sylvia, and Susana Skura. "Curatorship, Patrimonialization, and Memory Objects: Exhibition of Yiddish Theater Posters Created in Argentina." *Modern Jewish Studies* 14 (2004): 57–86.

———. Susana Skura, and Gabriela Kogan. *Oysfarkoyft, Localidades Agotadas: Afiches del Teatro Ídish en la Argentina* [Sold out: Argentinian Yiddish theatre posters]. Buenos Aires: Del Nuevo Extremo, 2006.

Hapgood, Hutchins. *The Spirit of the Ghetto*. 1902; repr. Cambridge, MA: Harvard University Press, 1967.

Harendorf, S. Y. *Teater karavanen* [Theatre caravans]. London: Fraynt fun Yidish Loshn, 1955.

———. "Yidish teater in England" [Yiddish theatre in England]. *Yivo bleter* 43 (1966): 225–248.

Harshav, Benjamin, ed. *The Moscow Yiddish Theater: Art on Stage in the Time of Revolution*. New Haven, CT: Yale University Press, 2007.

Henry, Barbara. *Rewriting Russia: Jacob Gordin's Yiddish Drama*. Seattle and London: University of Washington Press, 2011.

———. "Jacob Gordin's Dialogue with Tolstoy: *Di Kreytser Sonata* (1902)." In Edna Nahshon, ed., *Jewish Theatre: A Global View*, 25–48. Leiden: Brill, 2009.

———. "Tolstoy on the Lower East Side: *Di Kreytser Sonata*." *Tolstoy Studies Journal* 17 (2005): 1–19.

Hernik-Spalińska, Jagoda. "Żydowskie towarzystwa teatralne w Wilnie w świetle dokumentów (1928–1938)" [Yiddish theatrical societies in Vilna in the light of documentary evidence (1928–1938)]. *Pamiętnik Teatralny* 44 (1995): 288–292.

Heskes, Irene. "Music as Social History: American Yiddish Theater Music, 1882–1920." *American Music* 2 (1984): 73–87.

Heuberger, Georg. *Schtarker fun ajsn: Konzert- und Theaterplakate aus dem Wilnaer Getto, 1941–1943* [Stronger than iron: Concert and theatre posters from the Vilna ghetto, 1941–1943]. Frankfurt am Main: Jüdisches Museum, 2002.

Hirschbein, Peretz. *Mayne kinder-yorn* [My childhood years]. Warsaw: Literarishe Bleter, 1932.

———. *In gang fun lebn: zikhroynes* [In the course of a lifetime: Memoirs]. New York: CYCO, 1948.

Hoberman, Ida. "Ha-te'atron ha-yehudi be-moskva, he-segav ve-khisulo—90 shana le-holadeto shel Shlomo Mikhoels" [The Jewish theatre in Moscow, its achievments and its closure—The 90th anniversary of the birth of Solomon Mikhoels]. *Iton 77 le-sifrut u-le-tarbut* 20 (1980): 28–29.

Hoberman, J. *Bridge of Light: Yiddish Film Between Two Worlds*. New York: Museum of Modern Art and Schocken Books, 1991.

———. "Der Ershter [sic] Talkies: *Uncle Moses* and the Coming of the Yiddish Sound Film." *Film Comment* 27 (November 1991): 32–41.

———. "A Face to the Shtetl: Soviet Yiddish Cinema, 1924–36." In Richard Taylor and Ian Christie, eds., *Inside the Film Factory: New Approaches to Russian and Soviet Cinema*, 124–150. London: Routledge, 1991.

Hödl, Klaus. "From Acculturation to Interaction: A New Perspective on the History of the Jews in Fin-de-Siècle Vienna." *Shofar* 25 (2007): 82–103.

———. "Jüdische Popularkultur im 19. Jahrhundert am Beispiel des jiddischen Theaters" [Popular Culture in the 19th Century: the Example of the Yiddish Theatre]. In Christine Haug, Franziska Mayer, and Madleen Podewski, eds., *Populäres Judentum—Medien, Debatten, Lesestoffe* [Popular Judaism: Media, Debates, Readings], 47–63. Tübingen: Max Niemeyer Verlag, 2009.

Hoffman, Warren. *The Passing Game: Queering Jewish American Culture*. Syracuse, NY: Syracuse University Press, 2009.

Hohman, Valleri J. *Russian Culture and Theatrical Performance in America, 1891–1933*. New York: Palgrave Macmillan, 2011.

Holberg, Amelia S. "Betty Boop: Yiddish Film Star." *American Jewish History* 87 (December 1999): 291–312.

Horovits, Norbert. "Yidish teater fun der sheyres-hapleyte" [The Yiddish theatre of Holocaust survivors]. In Meyer Balaban, ed., *Fun noentn over* [From the recent past], 113–182. New York: Congress for Jewish Culture, 1955.

Horowitz, Mayer. "Bibliography of Yiddish Translations of English Literature." *Jewish Book Annual* 11 (1952–1953): 136–153.

Howe, Irving. *World of Our Fathers*. New York: Harcourt Brace Jovanovich, 1976.

——— and Eliezer Greenberg, eds. *Voices from the Yiddish*. Ann Arbor: University of Michigan Press, 1972.

Idelsohn, Abraham Z. *Jewish Music: Its Historical Development*. New York: Henry Holt, 1929; repr. New York: Dover, 1992.

Inbar, Donny. "A Closeted Jester: Abraham Goldfaden Between Haskalah Ideology and Jewish Show Business." Ph.D. thesis, Graduate Theological Union, 2007.

Iris, Shmuel. *Ot azoy hot men geshpilt teater* [That's how theatre was performed]. Buenos Aires: A Gezelshaftlekher Komitet, 1956.

Isenberg, Noah. "Perennial Detour: The Cinema of Edgar G. Ulmer and the Experience of Exile." *Cinema Journal* 43 (Winter 2004): 3–25.

Ivanov, Vladislav. *GOSET: Politika i iskusstvo. 1919–1928: monografiya* [The State Jewish Theatre: Politics and art. 1919–1928: A monograph]. Moscow: GITIS, RATI, 2007.

———. "Petrogradskie sezony evreiskogo kamernogo teatra" [The Petrograd seasons of the Jewish Chamber Theatre]. *Moskva* 2 (1998): 571–597.

———. *Russkie sezony teatra Gabima* [Habima's Russian seasons]. Moscow: Artist. Rezhisser. Teatr, 1999.

Jasionek, Eliza. "Franz Kafka und das Theater" [Franz Kafka and the theatre]. *Studia Germanica Gedanensia* 8 (2000): 109–130.

Jones, Faith. "Cumulative Index to Zalmen Zylbercweig's *Leksikon fun Yidishn Teater*." http://www.nypl.org/research/chss/jws/leksikonindex.html.

———. "The Fate of Yiddish Dictionaries: Zalmen Zylbercweig's *Leksikon fun Yidishn teater*." *Journal of Modern Jewish Studies* 5 (November 2006): 323–342.

Kachuk, Rhoda S. "Entering *King Lear* with Shakespeare and His Yiddish Adapter." In Robert F. Willson, Jr., ed., *Entering the Maze: Shakespeare's Art of Beginning*, 145–153. New York: Peter Lang, 1995.

———. "The First Two Yiddish Lears." In Krystyna Kujawińska Courtney and John Mercer, eds., *The Globalization of Shakespeare in the Nineteenth Century*, 55–67. Lewiston, NY: Mellen, 2003.

Kadison, Luba, and Joseph Buloff. *On Stage, Off Stage*. Cambridge, MA: Harvard University Press, 1992.

Kagan, Berl. *Leksikon fun yidish-shraybers* [Encyclopedia of Yiddish writers]. New York: R. Ilman-Kohen, 1986.

Kaganoff, Nathan M., Susan Landy, and Bruce Rosen. *Catalog of the Abram and Frances Pascher Kanof Collection of Yiddish Theatre and Motion Picture Posters Found in the Library of the American Jewish Historical Society*. Waltham, MA: The Library, 1972.

Kahan, R. Shoshana. *In fayer un flamen: togbukh fun a yidisher shoyshpilerin*. [In fire and flames: The diary of a Yiddish actress]. Buenos Aires: Tsentral-Farband fun Poylishe Yidn in Argentine, 1949.

Kalban, Avraham. "Shlomo Mikhoels be-tashkent" [Solomon Mikhoels in Tashkent]. *Bama* 81–82 (1979): 138–139.

Kalinowski, Daniel. "Franz Kafka o teatrze żydowskim" [Franz Kafka on the Jewish theatre]. In Eleonora Udalska and Anna Tytkowska, eds., *Żydzi w lustrze dramatu, teatru i krytyki teatralnej* [Jews in the mirror of drama, theatre and theatre criticism], 313–330. Katowice: Wydawnictwo Uniwersytetu Śląskiego, 2004.

Kaminska, Esther-Rokhl. *Briv* [Letters], ed. Mark Turkow. Vilna: B. Kletskin, 1927.

Kaminska, Ida. *My Life, My Theater*. Translated by Curt Leviant. New York: MacMillan, 1973. Translated into Polish by Joanna Krakowska-Narożniak as *Moje życie, mój teatr* [My life, my theatre]. Warsaw: Krąg, 1995.

Kaplan, Beth. *Finding the Jewish Shakespeare: the Life and Legacy of Jacob Gordin*. Syracuse, NY: Syracuse University Press, 2007.

Karner, Doris A. *Lachen unter Tränen: Jüdisches Theater in Ostgalizien und der Bukowina* [Laughter through tears: Jewish theatre in Eastern Galicia and Bukovina]. Vienna: Edition Steinbauer, 2005.

Karpinovitsh, Avrom. "Zikhroynes fun a farshnitener teater heym" [Memoirs of an annihilated home of theatre]. *Oksforder yidish* 2 (1991): 241–254.

Katchansky, Miriam. "Avraham Goldfaden, avi ha-te'atron be-yidish, ve-'Khibat-tsion'" [Avrom Goldfaden, father of the Yiddish theatre, and the "Lovers of Zion" Movement]. *Khulyot* 8 (Fall 2004): 347–358.

———. "Hibat-Zion and Yiddish: the Multi-dimensional Encounter Between Movement, Language, and Culture." Ph.D. thesis, Jewish Theological Seminary of America, 2002.

Katsis, Leonid F. "The Russian Jew Osip Mandelstam and Jewish Kiev." *East European Jewish Affairs* 40 (August 2010): 159–172.

———, M. Kaspina, and D. Fishman. *Idish: Yazyk i kul'tura v sovetskom soyuze. Sbornik statei* [Yiddish: Language and culture in the Soviet Union. Collected essays]. Moscow: Rossiiskii Gosudarstvennyi Gumanitarnyi Universitet, 2009.

Kaufman, Dahlia. "The First Yiddish Translation of Julius Caesar." In David Goldberg, ed., *The Field of Yiddish*, 5th Collection, 219–242. New York: YIVO and Northwestern University Press, 1993.

———. "Ha-targumim le-ivrit u-le-yidish shel 'Uriel Akosta' le-Karl Gutskov" [Translations of Karl Gutzkow's *Uriel Acosta* into Hebrew and Yiddish]. *Proceedings of the Eighth World Congress of Jewish Studies*, Division C, 331–336. Jerusalem: World Union of Jewish Studies, 1982.

———. "Targumey makhazot le-ivrit u-le-yidish mi-sof ha-me'a ha-18 ve-ad li-shenat 1883" [Hebrew and Yiddish drama translations from the late 18th century to 1883]. Ph.D. thesis, Hebrew University, 1983.

Kaufman, Rhoda Helfman. "The Yiddish Theatre in New York and the Immigrant Community: Theatre as Secular Ritual." Ph.D. thesis, University of California, Berkeley, 1986.

Kaufman, Tania Neumann. "O teatro îdiche; âncora e plataforma da identidade judaica (Décadas de 1930 a 1940)" [The Yiddish theatre: Anchor and platform of Jewish identity in the 1930s]. In Helena Lewin and Diane Kuperman, eds., *Judaísmo: memória e identidade*, 1:229–247. Rio de Janeiro: Universidade do Estado do Rio de Janeiro, 1997.

Keller, Mary Louise. "Interpreting the Agency of Possessed Women in a Postcolonial Comparative Study: Toward a Concept of Instrumental Agency." Ph.D. thesis, Syracuse University, 1998.

Kelman, Ari V. "The Acoustic Culture of Yiddish." *Shofar* 25 (Fall 2006): 127–151.

———. *Station Identification: A Cultural History of Yiddish Radio in the United States*. Berkeley: University of California Press, 2009.

Kerler, Dov-Ber, ed. *The Politics of Yiddish. Winter Studies in Yiddish*, vol. iv. Walnut Creek, CA: AltaMira Press, 1998.

Klein, Albert and Raya Kruk. *Alexander Granach: Fast Verwehte Spuren* [Nearly covered traces]. Berlin: Edition Hentrich, 1994.

Kirshenblatt-Gimblett, Barbara. "*Contraband*: Performance, Text and Analysis of a *Purim-shpil*." *The Drama Review* 24, Jewish Theatre Issue (September 1980): 5–16.

Klier, John D. "From Elisavetgrad to Broadway: The Strange Odyssey of Iakov Gordon." In Marsha Siefert, ed., *Extending the Borders of Russian History: Essays in Honor of Alfred J. Rieber*, 113–125. Budapest: Central University Press, 2003.

Klinger, Y. H., ed. *Hundert yor yidish teater, 1862–1962* [One hundred years of Yiddish theatre, 1862–1962]. London: Yidishe Kultur-gezelshaft, 1962.

Klos, Max. *Baym shayn fun rampe-likht* [By the glow of the footlights]. Buenos Aires: Stilos, 1972.

Kobrin, Leon. *Erinerungen fun a yidishn dramaturg* [Recollections of a Yiddish playwright], 2 vols. New York: Komitet far Kobrins Shriftn, 1925.

———. *Mayne fuftsik yor in amerike* [My fifty years in America]. Buenos Aires: Farlag Yidbukh, 1955.

Kohanski, Aleksander. "The Yiddish Theater in New York: Season 1932–1933." M.A. thesis, Graduate School for Jewish Social Work, 1933.

Kohlbauer-Fritz, Gabriele. "Jiddische Subkultur in Wien" [The Yiddish subculture in Vienna]. In Peter Bettelheim and Michael Ley, eds., *Ist jetzt hier die "wahre Heimat"? Ostjüdische Einwanderung nach Wien* [Is this the "true Homeland?" East European emigration to Vienna], 89–115. Vienna: Picus Verlag, 1993.

Kolganova, Ada A., ed., *Solomon Mikhoels: Issledovaniya, arkhivy, bibliografiya. Pervye Mikhoelsovskie chteniya* [Solomon Mikhoels: Research, archives, bibliography. First Mikhoels readings]. Moscow: Ministerstvo Kul'tury RF, Ros. gos. b-ka po iskusstvu, Kul'turnyi tsentr im. Solomona Mikhoelsa, 1999.

———, ed. *Tret'i mezhdunarodnye Mikhoelsovskie chteniya: Natsional'nyi teatr v kontekste mnogonatsional'noi kul'tury: arkhivy, biblioteki, informatsiya, mezhdunar. nauch. konf.* [Third international Mikhoels readings: National theatre in the context of multinational culture: Archives, libraries, information, an international academic conference]. Moscow: Ministerstvo Kul'tury RF, Ros. gos. b-ka po iskusstvu, Kul'turnyi tsentr im. Solomona Mikhoelsa, 2004.

———, ed. *Natsional'nyi teatr v kontekste mnogonatsional'noi kul'tury: Arkhivy, biblioteki, informatsiya: doklady chetvertykh Mikhoelsovskikh chtenii* [National theatre in the context of multinational culture: archives, libraries, information: Proceedings of the fourth Mikhoels reading]. Moscow: Fair-Press, 2006.

——— and N. I. Bykov, eds. *Sud'ba evreiskogo teatra v Rossii. XX vek: Issledovaniya, arkhivy, bibliografiya: vtorye Mikhoelsovskie chteniya* [The fate of the Jewish theatre in Russia. 20th century: research, archives, bibliography: Second Mikhoels readings]. Moscow: Ministerstvo Kul'tury RF, Ros. gos. b-ka po iskusstvu, 2001.

Konigsberg, Ira. "'The Only 'I' in the World': Religion, Psychoanalysis, and *The Dybbuk*." *Cinema Journal* 36 (Summer 1997): 22–42.

———. "*Our Children* and the Limits of Cinema: Early Jewish Responses to the Holocaust." *Film Quarterly* 52 (Autumn 1998): 7–19.

Korin, Moshé. "Recuerdos del teatro idish" [Recollections of the Yiddish theatre]. In Ricardo Feierstein and Stephen A. Sadow, eds., *Encuentro: Recreando la Cultura Judeoargentina* 2, 57–62. Buenos Aires: Editorial Milá, 2004.

Korn, Yitskhok. *Yidish in rumenye: eseyen* [Yiddish in Romania: Essays]. Tel Aviv: Farlag Abukah, 1989.

Kornblith, Z. *Di dramatishe kunst* [The dramatic art]. New York: Itshe Biderman, 1928.

Korzeniewski, Bohdan and Zbigniew Raszewski. *Teatr żydowski w Polsce do 1939* [Yiddish theatre in Poland to 1939]. Special issue of *Pamiętnik Teatralny.* Warsaw: Polska Akademia Nauk/Institut Sztuki, 1992.

Kotlerman, Ber Boris (see also Kotlerman, Boris). *In Search of Milk and Honey: The Theater of "Soviet Jewish Statehood" (1934–49).* Bloomington, IN: Slavica, 2010.

Kotlerman, Boris (see also Kotlerman, Ber Boris). "The Prewar Period of the Birobidzhan State Jewish Theater, 1934–1941." *Jews in Eastern Europe* 1 (2001): 29–59.

———. "Der sovetisher 'Bar-Kokhba' in hebreyishe malbushim" [The Soviet *Bar Kokhba* in Hebrew dress]. *Khulyot* 10 (Fall 2006): 447–458.

———, ed. *Te'atron yidish: sifrut tarbut u-le'umiyut* [Yiddish theatre: Literature, culture, and nationalism]. Ramat-Gan: Bar-Ilan University Press, 2009. Published as a special issue (no. 41) of *Bikoret u-farshanut* [Criticism and interpretation]. Contents: (1) *Between Yiddish and Hebrew.* Dorit Yerushalmi, "Te'atron yidish ke-tashtit omanutit le-te'atron ha-ivri: mabat al ha-te'atron shel bama be-tekufat ha-yishuv" [Yiddish theater as an artistic infrastructure of Hebrew theatre: A new perspective on theatre directors in the Yishuv period]: 7–39. Rachel Rojanski, "'Anu sakhkanim yehudim me-ha-golah': ha-ma'avak le-kiyumo shel te'atron repertuari be-yidish be-yisrael, 1950–1952" ['We are Jewish actors from the Diaspora': The struggle for a Yiddish repertory theatre in Israel (1950–1952)]: 41–64. Shelly Zer-Zion, "Ha-'Vilner trupe'—prolog la-historiyah shel 'Habimah'" [The Vilna Troupe: Prologue to the history of Habima]: 65–92. Ariela Krasney, "'Rav shel purim': te'atron shel yom ekhad" ['Purim Rabbi': A one-day theatre]: 93–110. (2) *Between Yiddish and Politics.* Ber Boris Kotlerman, "Makhazotav shel Perets Markish: halikhah al khevel dak ben 'yehudi' le-'sovyeti'" [The plays of Peretz Markish: Balancing between "Jewish" and "Soviet"]: 111–129. Natan Cohen, "Te'atron ve-politikah (1937): ha-pulmus be-itonut ha-yehudit be-varshah be-davar ibudo shel Manger le-'Di kishefmakherin'" [Theatre and politics: The debate in the Warsaw Jewish press regarding Itsik Manger's adaptation of *The Sorceress* (1937)]: 131–140. Thomas Soxberger, "Ha-ma'avak le-ma'an te'atron yidish ekhuti be-vinah" [Yiddish theater in

Vienna and its critics]: 141–153. (3) *Between Yiddish and Yiddish*. Goultschin, Moshe. "Yidish ben ha-se'ifim: Byalik, Perets ve-Sutskever" [Yiddish at the crossroads: Bialik, Peretz, and Sutzkever]: 155–171. Donny Inbar, "Sheloshah Kuni Lemel—sod ha-hisardut: al gilgulim she-hafkhu satirah khevratit botah le-nostalgiyah ha-mishtabakhat be-tkinut politit" [Three Kuni-Lemls, the secret of survival: Metamorphoses that turned a harsh social satire into nostalgia, adorned in the political]: 173–196.

Kotlyarova, Mariya. *Plecho Mikhoelsa: vospominaniya aktrisy GOSETa* [Mikhoels's shoulder: Reminiscences of a GOSET actress]. Moscow: Bibliotechka gazety "Tarbut" (Samara), 2003.

Kovarsky, H. "An-skis 'dibek' in balaykhtung fun der psikologye" [An-sky's *Dybbuk* in the light of psychology]. *Yivo bleter* 4 (Oct. 1932): 209–222.

Kozłowska, Mirosława. "'Swoi' i 'obcy': dramat żydowski na polskich scenach w Wilnie 1906–1940" ["Us" and "them": Jewish drama on Polish stages in Vilna, 1906–1940]. In Wojciech Kaczmarek and Joanna Michalczuk, eds., *Dramat obcy w Polsce w XIX i XX wieku* [Foreign drama in Poland in the 19th and 20th Centuries], 65–76. Lublin: Wydawnictwo Katolickiego Uniwersytetu Lubelskiego, 2004.

Kozłowski, Józef. "'Tkacze' G. Hauptmanna na scenie żydowskiej na przełomie XIX i XX w." [Hauptmann's "Weavers" on Jewish stages at the turn of the 19th and 20th centuries]. *Biuletyn Żydowskiego Instytutu Historycznego* 4 (1976): 95–101, 124.

Krasiński, Edward. "Teatralia izraelskie" [Theatrical miscellany from Israel]. *Pamiętnik Teatralny* 45 (1996): 223–233.

Krasney, Ariela. *Ha-badkhan* [The wedding jester]. Ramat Gan: Bar-Ilan University Press, 1998.

Kruk, Stefan. "Teatr żydowski w Lublinie w latach 1916–1917. (Na podstawie teatraliów zawartych w 'Myśli Żydowskiej')" [Jewish theatre in Lublin, 1916–1917 (Based on articles and reviews published in the weekly "Jewish Thought")]. *Biuletyn Żydowskiego Instytutu Historycznego* 3/4 (1982): 49–63, 138.

Kuligowska-Korzeniewska, Anna. "'. . . jedno oko się śmieje, a w drugim widać łzy': o teatrze w getcie łódzkim" [". . . one eye laughs, and the other tears": On the theatre in the Łódź ghetto]. *Tygiel Kultury* 4/6 (2004): 138–143. Also available electronically: http://spplodz.nazwa.pl/tygiel/4_6_2004/aktual/22ram.htm.

———. "Łódź teatralna: polska, niemiecka i żydowska" [Theatrical Łódź: Polish, German, and Jewish]. *Tygiel Kultury* 1/3 (2005): 59–63; 4/6 (2005): 226. Previously published in *Tygiel Kultury* 3 (1996): 71–74. Also available electronically: http://spplodz.nazwa.pl/tygiel/1_3_2005/aktual/7ram.htm and http://spplodz.nazwa.pl/tygiel/4_6_2005/aktual/51ram.htm.

———. "Die polnisch-deutsch-jüdische Theaterlandschaft in Lodz: Zusammenarbeit und Rivalität" [The Polish-German-Jewish theatre landscape in Łódź: Cooperation and rivalry]. Translated by Wolfgang Jöhling and Jürgen Hensel. In Jürgen Hensel, ed., *Polen, Deutsche und Juden in Lodz 1820–1939: eine schwierige Nachbarschaft* [Poles, Germans and Jews in Łódź, 1820–1939: A difficult community], 301–306. Osnabrück: fibre, 1999.

———. "Polska 'Szulamis': dramat żydowski na scenach polskich na przełomie XIX i XX wieku" [The Polish "Shulamis": Jewish drama on Polish stages in the late 19th and early 20th centuries]. In Wojciech Kaczmarek and Joanna Michalczuk, eds., *Dramat obcy w Polsce w XIX i XX wieku* [Foreign drama in Poland in the 19th and 20th centuries], 45–63. Lublin: Wydawnictwo Katolickiego Uniwersytetu Lubelskiego, 2004. Previously published in *Kwartalnik Historii Żydów* 1 (2003): 35–51. Translated into English as "The Polish *Shulamis*: Jewish Drama on the Polish Stage in the Late 19th-Early 20th Centuries." In Edna Nahshon, ed., *Jewish Theatre: A Global View*, 81–97. Leiden: Brill, 2009.

———. "Sześciojęzyczny teatr lwowski" [The six-language Lwów Theatre]. *Tygiel Kultury* 4/6 (2005): 138–147. Also available electronically: http://spplodz.nazwa.pl/tygiel/4_6_2005/aktual/32ram.htm.

———, ed. *Teatralna Jerozolima: przeszłość i teraźniejszość: praca zbiorowa* [Theatrical Jerusalem: The past and the present]. Warszawa: Oficyna Wydawnicza "Errata", 2006.

——— and Małgorzata Leyko, eds. *Teatr żydowski w Polsce* [Yiddish theatre in Poland]. Łódź: Wydawnictwo Uniwersytetu Łódzkiego, 1998.

Kurtze, Ralf. *Das jiddische Theater in Berlin um die Jahrhundertwende* [The Yiddish theatre in Berlin at the turn of the century]. Köln: Teiresias, 2001.

Lahad, Ezra. "Al akharon mi-mishpakhat Turkov" [On the last of the Turkow family]. *Bama* 113–114 (1988): 5–9.

———. "Ha-badkhanim" [The jesters]. *Bama* 95–96 (1983): 43–68.

———. "Ha-badkhanim be-yisrael (mavo ve-bibliografia)" [Jesters in Israel (Introduction and bibliography)]. *Tatslil* 11 (1980): 51–58.

———. "'Ha-lahaka ha-vilna'it' bat-shivim (kolel reshimat ha-hatsagot she-hutsgu al-yedey ha-lahaka ba-shanim 1935–1961)" [The Vilna Troupe at 70 (with a list of all the plays they staged from 1935 to 1961)]. *Bama* 111 (1988): 5–29.

———. *Ha-makhazot be-yidish ba-makor u-ve-tirgum: bibliografia / Dramatishe verk af yidish; originele un iberzetste, a bibliografye* [Original and translated Yiddish plays: A bibliography]. Haifa: privately published, 2001. (An 87-page "Mafteyakh ha-makhazot" [Key to the plays] was printed separately.)

———. "Hatsaga be-yidish be-kahir" [Yiddish performance in Cairo]. *Etmol* 5 (1979): 19.

———. "Makhazot amami'im be-yidish—makhazot Avraham Goldfaden" [Yiddish folk plays—Avrom Goldfaden's plays]. Vol. 4 of Moshe Gorali, ed., *Amli—mekhkarim bibliografi'im be-musikah* [AMLI studies in music bibliography]. Haifa: Haifa Music Museum and Library, 1970.

———. "Zikhronotav shel Moshe Zayfert (1851–1922) (le-toldot ha-teatron ha-yehudi)" [Memoirs of Moyshe Zeifert (1851–1922) (Toward a history of the Jewish theatre)]. *Khulyot* 8 (2004): 361–362.

Landis, Joseph C., ed. *Memoirs of the Yiddish Stage*. Flushing, NY: Queens College Press, 1984.

———. "Peretz, Asch, and *God of Vengeance*." *Yiddish* 10 (1995): 5–17.

Larrue, Jean-Marc. "Alacrité et identité: le cas du théâtre yiddish à Montréal." Maria S. Horne, Jean-Marc Larrue, and Claude Schumacher, eds., *Théâtre Sans Frontières/Theatre Without Frontiers/ Teatro Sin Fronteras*. Liège, Belgium: AITU Press, 2002.

———. *Le théâtre yiddish à Montréal*. Montreal: Éditions Jeu, 1996.

La Taille, Blandine de. *La théâtralité dans le théâtre yiddish: "Le jeu de Hotsmakh"*. Paris: JAB conseil, 2009.

Lawrence, Jerome. *Actor: The Life and Times of Paul Muni*. New York: Putnam, 1974.

Lebediker, Der [Khayim Gutman]. *Di ferte vant* [The fourth wall]. Warsaw: Farlag Akhiseyfer, n.d.

Leneman Helen. "More than the Love of Men: Ruth and Naomi's Story in Music." *Interpretation: A Journal of Bible and Theology* 64 (April 2010), 146–160.

Leiter, Cary. *Yiddish Theatre/Modern American Theatre: The Importance of the Yiddish Theatre in the Evolution of the Modern American Theatre*. VDM Verlag Dr. Müller, 2010.

Lerner, Warren Zollery. "The Yiddish Theatre and Drama." M.A. thesis, University of Nebraska, 1933.

Lestchinsky, Jacob. *Dos idishe ekonomishe lebn in der idisher literatur* [Jewish economic life in Yiddish literature]. Leipzig: Idisher sektsye bam komisariat far folkbildung, 1922.

———. "Di yerides fun der yidisher prese un fun yidishn teater" [The decline of the Yiddish press and the Yiddish theatre]. In Lestchinsky, *Dos natsyonale ponem fun goles-yidntum* [The national image of diaspora Jewry], 193–212. Buenos Aires: Farlag Poaley-Tsion-Hitakhdut, 1955.

Levi, Shimon. [see also Levy]. "Al da'at ha-makom ve-al da'at ha-kahal: he'arot al ha-te'atron ha-ivri va-te'atron yidish" [On the wisdom of the place and wisdom of the crowd: studies on Hebrew and Yiddish theatre], *Davka* 4 (2008): 48–51.

Levin, Dov. "Shnat prikha ve-shirat ha-barbur: ha-te'atron ha-yehudi be-lita ha-sovyetit 1940–1941" [Year of flowering and swan song—The Jewish theatre in Soviet Lithuania, 1940–1941]. *Bama* 72 (1977): 64–75; 73 (1977): 56–73.

Levin, Rut. "Lo rak Manger ve-Tselan" [Not just Manger and Celan]. *Davka* 4 (2008): 29–31.

Levintal, Naftali. "Tsura shel tefila: al ha-kesher shel Kafka im ha-olam ha-yehudi" [A form of prayer: On Kafka's connection to the Jewish world]. *Dimui* 13 (1996): 6–13.

Levitan, Olga. "Ha-te'atron ha-erets-yisraeli ba-shanim 1904–1914: ben ivrit le-yidish" [Theatre in Eretz Israel, 1904–1914: Between Hebrew and Yiddish]. *Bama* 172 (2005): 42–58.

———. "Theater in the Land of Israel: Between Hebrew and Yiddish (1904–1914)." *Theatralia* 7 (2005): 139–150.

Levitina, Viktoriya. *Evreiskii vopros i sovetskii teatr* [The Jewish question and the Soviet theatre]. Jerusalem: self-published, 2001.

Levy, Shimon [see also Levi]. "Yiddish and Hebrew Theatre: On Dramatic Space and Audience." In Ahuva Belkin, ed., *Jewish Theatre: Tradition in Transition and Intercultural Vistas. Assaph: Studies in the Theater* (2008): 101–114.

Leyko, Małgorzata, ed. *Łódzkie sceny żydowskie: studia i materiały* [Łódź Jewish theatres: Studies and materials]. Łódź: Wydawnictwo Uniwersytetu Łódzkiego, 2000.

———. "Rola polskojęzycznej prasy żydowskiej w reaktywacji scen żydowskich w Polsce po 1945 roku" [The role of the Polish-language Jewish press in the reactivation of Jewish theatres in Poland after 1945]. In Eleonora Udalska and Anna Tytkowska, eds., *Żydzi w lustrze dramatu, teatru i krytyki teatralnej* [Jews in the mirror of drama, theatre and theatre criticism], 297–309. Katowice: Wydawnictwo Uniwersytetu Śląskiego, 2004.

———. "Zamknięta karta: teatr żydowski w Łodzi" [A closed chapter: Jewish theatre in Łódź]. *Kronika Miasta Łodzi* (2007): 99–107.

———. "Zapomniane sceny, zapomniani artyści" [Forgotten stages, forgotten artists]. *Tygiel Kultury* 2 (1996): 129–130.

Lifson, David S. *The Yiddish Theatre in America*. New York: Thomas Yoseloff, 1965.

———. "Yiddish Theatre." In Maxine Schwartz Seller, ed., *Ethnic Theatre in the United States*, 549–587. Westport, CT: Greenwood Press, 1983.

Likhter, Pini. "Ha-te'atron ha-yidish be-varsha" [The Yiddish theatre in Warsaw]. *Bama* 101–102 (1985), 125–129.

Lima, Robert. "Rites of Passage: Metempsychosis, Possession, and Exorcism in S. An-Sky's *The Dybbuk*." In Robert Lima, *Stages of Evil: Occultism in Western Theater and Drama*, 117–136. Lexington, KY: University Press of Kentucky, 2005.

Linert, Andrzej. *Teatr w kręgu "Ha-Szacharu": z kroniki żydowskich występów teatralnych w Bielsku i Białej w latach międzywojennych* [Theatre in the circle of "Ha-Shahar": From the chronicle of Jewish performances in the towns of Bielsko and Biała in the interwar period]. Bielsko-Biała: Urząd Miejski; Cracow: Wydział Zarządzania i Komunikacji Społecznej Uniwersytetu Jagiellońskiego, 2004.

———. "Życie teatralne Żydów Bielska i Białej w latach międzywojennych" [Jewish theatrical life in the towns of Bielsko and Biała in the interwar period]. In Eleonora Udalska and Anna Tytkowska, eds., *Żydzi w lustrze dramatu, teatru i krytyki teatralnej* [Jews through the mirror of drama, theatre and theatre criticism], 173–184. Katowice: Wydawnictwo Uniwersytetu Śląskiego, 2004.

Lipsky, Louis. *Tales of the Yiddish Rialto: Reminiscences of Playwrights and Players in New York's Jewish Theatre in the Early 1900s*. New York: Thomas Yoseloff, 1962.

Liptzin, Sol. *Eliakum Zunser: Poet of his People*. New York: Berhman House, 1950.

———. *A History of Yiddish Literature*. Middle Village, NY: Jonathan David, 1972.

Litka, Piotr. "O teatrze żydowskim i Idzie Kamińskiej [On Jewish theatre and Ida Kamińska]: Interview with Szymon Szurmiej." *Kwartalnik Filmowy* 23 (2002): 292–295, 394.

Littman, Adam Stuart. "From the Shtetl to the Screen: the Develoment of Yiddish Theatre in Performance." M.A. thesis, University of Nevada, Las Vegas, 2004.

Litvakov, Moyshe. *Finf yor melukhisher idisher kamer-teater* [Five years of the State Yiddish Chamber Theatre]. Moscow: Farlag Shul un Bukh, 1924.

Livnat, Aviv. "*Der vaser gezang*: On Drama and Musical Interpretation in Aaron Zeitlin's Play *Jacob Jacobson*." In Ahuva Belkin, ed., *Jewish Theatre: Tradition in Transition and Intercultural Vistas. Assaph: Studies in the Theater* (2008): 161–172.

Loev, Moisei. *Ukradennaya muza: Vospominaniya o kievskom gosudarstvennom evreiskom teatre imeni Sholom-Aleikhema. Khar'kov—Kiev—Chernovtsy 1925–1950* [Stolen muse: Memories of the Sholem Aleykhem Kiev State Jewish Theatre. Khar'kov—Kiev—Czernowitz, 1925–1950]. Kiev: Dukh i Litera (Institut Iudaiki) 2003.

Loewy, Ronny, ed. *Das jiddische Kino* [The Yiddish cinema]. Frankfurt: Deutsches Filmmuseum, 1982.

Lyubomirski, Y. *Af di lebnsvegn* [On life's journey]. Moscow: Farlag Sovetskii Pisatel', 1976.

———. *Melukhisher yidisher teater in ukrayne* [State Yiddish theatre in Ukraine]. Khar'kov: Literatur un Kunst, 1931.

———. *Mikhoels*. Moscow: Izdat. "Iskusstvo," 1938.

Malachy, Thérèse. "Shalom Aleichem ou la comédie juive." *Perspectives* 10 (2003): 103–112.

Malkin, D. B. *Dzhigan albom in vort un bild: 35 stsenishe tetikayt fun Shimen Dzhigan* [Dzigan album in word and image: 35 years of Shimen Dzigan's stage activity]. Tel Aviv: n.p., 1964.

Mamana, June. "From the Pale of Settlement to 'Pacific Overtures': The Evolution of Boris Aronson's Visual Aesthetic." Ph.D. thesis, Tufts University, 1997.

Manger, Itsik, Jonas Turkow, and Moyshe Perenson, eds. *Yidisher teater in eyrope tsvishn beyde veltmilkhomes* [Yiddish theatre in Europe between the World Wars], 2 vols. New York: Congress for Jewish Culture, 1968.

Marc Chagall and the Jewish Theater. New York: Guggenheim Museum, 1992.

Marc Chagall: die Russischen Jahre, 1906–1922 [Marc Chagall: The Russian years, 1906–1922]. Frankfurt am Main: Schirn Kunsthalle Frankfurt, 1991.

Margalit, Me'ir. "Eyney-yeled yokdot (mi-zikhronotav shel ha-sakhkan Meir Margalit she-supru ve-huklatu al-yad Dr. Dov Levin)" [A child's burning eyes (from the memoirs of the actor Me'ir Margalit as told and recorded by Dr. Dov Levin)]. *Bama* 101–102 (1985): 130–133.

Margolis, Rebecca. *Jewish Roots, Canadian Soil: Yiddish Cultural Life in Montreal, 1905–1945*. Montreal: McGill/Queen's University Press, 2011.

———. "Yiddish Literary Culture in Montreal, 1905–1940." Ph.D. thesis, Columbia University, 2005.

Marks, Richard G. *The Image of Bar Kokhba in Traditional Jewish Literature: False Messiah and National Hero*. University Park: Pennsylvania State University Press, 1994.

Marmor, Kalmen. *Yankev Gordin*. New York: YKUF, 1953.

———. *Yoysef Bovshover*. New York: Kalmen Marmor Yubiley-komitet, 1952.

Massino, Guido. "Franz Kafka, *Der Meshumed* by Abraham Sharkanski and *Elisha ben Avuyah* by Jacob Gordin." *Journal of the Kafka Society of America* 20 (June–December 1996): 30–41.

———. *Franz Kafka, Jizchak Löwy und das jiddische Theater: "dieses nicht niederzudrückende Feuer des Löwy"* [Franz Kafka, Isaac Löwy and the Yiddish theatre: "This irrepressible fire of Löwy's"]. Frankfurt am Main: Stroemfeld/Nexus, 2007.

———. "Jizchak Löwy, l'amico russo' di Franz Kafka" [Isaac Löwy, Franz Kafka's "Russian friend"]. *Rassegna Mensile di Israel* 62 (1996): 279–300.

Mayer, Morris. *Idish teater in london, 1902–1942* [Yiddish theatre in London, 1902–1942]. London: M. Mayer [1943].

Mazo, Joseph H. "The Rise of the Yiddish Theatre." M.A. thesis, University of Washington, 1963.

Mazower, David. *Yiddish Theatre in London*. London: Jewish Museum, 1987; rpt. 1996.

Mazur, Daria. *Dybuk*. Poznań: Uniwersitet im. Adam Mickiewicza, 2007.

Medovoy, George. "The Federal Theatre Project Yiddish Troupes." Ph.D. thesis, University of California, Davis, 1975.

Meducka, Marta. "Z życia teatralnego Żydów w województwie kieleckim w latach 1918–1939" [On the theatrical life of Jews in the Kielce voivodeship, 1918–1939]. In Marta Meducka and Regina Renz, eds., *Kultura Żydów polskich XIX-XX wieku* [Polish Jewish culture in the 19th and 20th centuries], 165–180. Kielce: Kieleckie Towarzystwo Naukowe, 1992.

Mayzel, Nachman (also Meisel). *Avrom Goldfaden: der foter fun yidishn teater* [Avrom Goldfaden: The father of the Yiddish theatre]. Warsaw: Farlag Groshn Bibliotek, 1935.

———. *Geven a mol a lebn: dos yidishe kultur-lebn in poyln tsvishn beyde velt-milkhomes* [Once upon a life: Yiddish cultural life in Poland between the world wars]. Buenos Aires: Tsentral-farband fun Poylishe Yidn in Argentine, 1951.

Meisels, Abish. *Von Sechistow bis Amerika / Fun sechisstow bis amerika. Eine Revue in 15 Bildern / A rewi in 15 bilder* [From Sechistow to America. A revue in 15 scenes]. Edited and translated by Brigitte Dalinger and Thomas Soxberger. Vienna: Picus Verlag, 2000.

Melman, Marian. "Teatr żydowski w Warszawie w latach międzywojennych" [Jewish theatre in Warsaw in the inter-war period]. In Marian Marek Drozdowski, ed., *Warszawa II Rzeczypospolitej* [Warsaw of the 2nd Republic], 1:381–400. Warsaw: Państwowe Wydawnictwo Naukowe, 1968.

Mendelovitch, Bernard. "Memories of London Yiddish Theatre." Seventh Annual Avrom-Nokhem Stencl Lecture in Yiddish Studies. Oxford: Oxford Centre for Postgraduate Hebrew Studies, 1990.

Mendl Elkin: tsu zayn zekhtsik-yorikn geboyrntog [Mendl Elkin: On his sixtieth birthday]. New York: Yubiley Komitet, 1937.

Merkur, Volf. *Merkuriozn* [Mercurios]. Philadelphia: Nebekhaleyn, 1948.

Messer, Alexandre. "Les Kaminski dans le théâtre yiddish de Pologne" [The Kaminskys in the Polish-Yiddish theatre]. In Patricia Hidiroglou, ed., *Entre héritage et devenir: la construction de la famille juive*, 267–281. Paris: Publications de la Sorbonne, 2003.

Mestel, Jacob. *70 yor teater repertuar* [70 years of theatre repertoire]. New York: YKUF, 1954.

———. *Literatur un teater* [Literature and theatre]. New York: YKUF, 1962.

———. *Undzer teater* [Our theatre]. New York: YKUF, 1943.

Michalik, Jan, and Eugenia Prokop-Janiec, eds. *Teatr żydowski w Krakowie: Studia y materiały* [Yiddish theatre in Cracow: Studies and materials]. Translated by Anna Ciałowicz. Cracow: Uniwersytet Jagielloński, 1995.

Michel, Chantal Catherine: "Cinéma identitaire ou miroir du regard d'autrui?" [Cinema of identity or mirror of others' views?]. M.A. thesis, Université Paul Valéry, Montpellier III, 1998.

———. "Der Soziale Aufstieg im Jiddischen Kino. Konflikt zwischen jüdischer Identität und Assimilation" [Social advancement in Yiddish film: the conflict between Jewish identity and assimilation]. Ph.D. thesis, Freie Universität Berlin, 2010.

———. "Zwischen *Shtetl* und *'goldener Medine'*: Das jiddische Kino im Spiegel der Presse" [Between 'Shtetl' and 'Golden Land': The Yiddish cinema in the mirror of the press]. *Jiddistik Mitteilungen—Jiddistik in Deutschsprachigen Ländern* 35 (April 2006), 1–15.

Mide, A. *Epizodn fun yidishn teater* [Episodes from the Yiddish theatre]. Buenos Aires: Asociacion judeo argentina de estudios historicos, 1954.

Mikhoels, Solomon Mikhailovich. *Artiklen, shmuesn, redes* [Articles, conversations, speeches]. Buenos Aires: Heymland, 1961.

Miller, James. *The Detroit Yiddish Theater, 1920 to 1937*. Detroit: Wayne State University Press, 1967.

Mincer, Laura Quercioli. "The Laughing Jew: a Yiddish Theatre in Contemporary Italy." *Theatralia* 7 (2005): 151–160.

———. "La tradizione rivisitata nel teatro yiddish di Moni Ovadia" [Tradition revisited in Moni Ovadia's Yiddish theatre]. *La Rassegna mensile di Israel* 66 (2000): 145–154.

Minikes, Khonen Y., ed. *Di idishe bine* [The Yiddish stage]. New York: Katzenelenbogen, 1897.

Mladek, Klaus. "Radical Play: Gesture, Performance, and the Theatrical Logic of the Law in Kafka." *Germanic Review* 78 (2003): 223–250.

Mlotek, Eleanor, ed. *Mir trogn a gezang: the New Book of Yiddish Songs*. New York: Workmen's Circle Education Department, 1972.

——— and Joseph Mlotek, eds. *Perl fun yidishn lid / Pearls of Yiddish Song*. New York: Workmen's Circle Education Department, 1988.

———. *Lider fun dor tsu dor / Songs of Generations: New Pearls of Yiddish Song*. New York: Workmen's Circle Education Department, 1997.

Mohrer, Fruma and Marek Web, eds. *Guide to the YIVO Archives*. Armonk, NY: M. E. Sharpe, 1998.

Moje, Dani. "Az hi meta al ha-bama" [Then she died on the stage]. *Sinematek* 53 (1990): 6–7.

———. "Khadash ba-arkhion: Rivka Fefer" [New in the archives: Rivka Fefer]. *Bama* 117–118 (1989): 99–101.

Moon, Michael. "Tragedy and Trash; Yiddish Theater and Queer Theater, Henry James, Charles Ludlam, Ethyl Eichelberger." In Daniel Boyarin, Daniel Itzkovitz, and Ann Pellegrini, eds., *Queer Theory and the Jewish Question*, 266–284. New York: Columbia University Press, 2003.

Moraly, Yehuda. "Défense et illustration d'Abraham Goldfaden, le 'père du théâtre yiddish' (1840–1908)" [A defense and illustration of Abraham Goldfaden, the "father of Yiddish theatre" (1840–1908)]. *Revue d'histoire du théâtre* 60 (2008): 273–286.

Morevski, Avrom. *Ahin un tsurik* [There and back], 4 vols. Warsaw: Farlag Yidish Bukh, 1960. Translated and edited by Joseph Leftwich as *There and Back*. St. Louis: Warren H. Green, 1967.

Moskovskii teatr Gabima direktor-osnovatel' N. L. Tsemakh: Turne Evropa-Amerika, direktsiya turne: M. Kashuk [Moscow's Habima theatre, founder-director N. L. Tsemakh: Director for their European-American tour: M. Kashuk.]. Riga: Tipografiya "Hasafa," 1926.

Moskovskoe Gosudarstvennoe Evreiskoe Teatral'noe Uchilishche; Rossiiskii Gosudarstvennyi Arkhiv Literatury i Iskusstva; Moskovskii Gosudarstvennyi Evreiskii Teatr [Moscow State Jewish Theatre School; Russian State Archive for Literature and Art; Moscow State Jewish Theatre]. Translated as *Jewish Theatre Under Stalinism: Moscow State Jewish Theater (GOSET) and Moscow State Jewish Theater School (MGETU)*. Amsterdam: IDC Publishers, 2005.

Mukdoyni, A. [Alexander Kapel]. *In varshe un in lodzh (mayne bagegenishn)* [In Warsaw and in Łódź (My encounters)]. Buenos Aires: Tsentral-farband fun Poylishe Yidn in Argentine, 1955.

———. *Teater*. New York: A. Mukdoyni Yubiley-komitet, 1927.

———. *Yitskhok Leybush Perets un dos yidishe teater* [Yitskhok Leybush Peretz and the Yiddish theatre]. New York: YKUF, 1949.

Murphy, Daniel J. "Yiddish at the Abbey Theatre, Dublin." *Bulletin of Research in the Humanities* 81 (Winter 1978): 431–435.

Nadir, Moyshe [Isaac Reiss]. *Mayne hent hobn fargosn dos dozige blut* [My hands shed that very blood]. New York: Farlag Verbe, 1919.

Nahshon, Edna. "Ma'ane lashon me'al bimat ha-yidish: Shaylok u-vato ba-te'atron ha-omanuti shel Moris Shvarts" [A sharp tongue on the Yiddish stage: *Shylock and his Daughter* in Maurice Schwartz's Yiddish Art Theatre]. *Zmanim* 99 (2007): 46–53.

———. "Nashim ba-te'atron ha-idi ha-mahapakhani be-artsot ha-brit ba-shanim 1925–1940" [Women in the revolutionary Yiddish theatre, 1925–1940]. *Bama* 151 (1998): 65–71.

———. "The Pulpit and the State: Rabbi Joseph Silverman and the Actors' Church Alliance." *American Jewish History* 91 (March 2003): 5–27.

———. *Yiddish Proletarian Theatre: The Art and Politics of the Artef, 1925–1940*. Westport, CT: Greenwood Press, 1998.

Nahshon, Gad. "Al te'atron ha-yidish" [On the Yiddish theatre]. *Kivunim* 13 (1981): 183–185.

Nakhtumi, Avrom. *In shotn fun doyres* [In the shadow of generations]. Buenos Aires: Tsentralfarband fun Poylishe Yidn in Argentine, 1948.

Niger, S. [Shmuel Charney]. *Dertseylers un romanistn* [Storytellers and novelists]. New York: CYCO, 1946.

———. *Fun mayn togbukh* [From my diary]. New York: Congress for Jewish Culture, 1973.

———. *H. Leyvik, 1888–1948*. Toronto: Leyvik Yoyvl-komitet, 1951.

———. *Kritik un kritiker* [Criticism and critics]. Buenos Aires: Argentina Division of the Congress for Jewish Culture, 1959.

———. *Mendele Moykher-Sforim: zayn lebn, zayne gezelshaftlekhe un literarishe oyftu-ungen* [Mendele Moykher-Sforim: His life and social and literary accomplishments]. Chicago: L. M. Shteyn, 1936.

———. *Sholem Ash: zayn lebn zayne verk* [Sholem Asch: His life and work]. New York: S. Niger Book Committee of the Congress for Jewish Culture, 1960.

———. *Y. L. Perets: zayn lebn, zayn firndike perzenlekhkayt* [Y. L. Peretz: His life, his guiding personality]. Buenos Aires: Argentina branch of the World Jewish Culture Congress, 1952.

———, ed. *Perets Hirshbayn (tsu zayn zekhsikstn geboyrntog)* [Peretz Hirschbein: On his sixtieth birthday]. New York: CYCO, 1948.

——— and Yankev Shatski, eds. *Leksikon fun der nayer yidisher literatur* [Encyclopedia of the new Yiddish literature], 8 vols. New York: Alveltlekher Yidisher Kultur-kongres, 1956–1981.

Nink, Beáta. "Literaturnye obrazy idish v stsenicheskom voploshchenii moskovskogo Evreiskogo Gosudarstvennogo Teatra (GOSET)" [Yiddish literary images in the Moscow State Jewish Theatre's (GOSET) stage productions]. *Studia Russica* 21 (2004): 227–234.

Novershtern, Abraham [see also Nowersztern]. "Between Dust and Dance: Peretz's Drama and the Rise of Yiddish Modernism." *Prooftexts* 12 (1992): 71–90.

———. *Kesem ha-dimdumim: apokalipsa u-meshikhiyut be-sifrut yidish* [The lure of twilight: Apocalypse and messianism in Yiddish]. Jerusalem: Magnes Press, 2003.

———. "Mekholot ha-mavet, ha-drama shel Y. L. Perets 'Baynakht afn altn mark' ve-reyshut ha-modernizm be-yidish" [The dance of death: On Peretz's *At Night in the Old Marketplace* and the beginnings of modernism in Yiddish]. *Khulyot* 1 (1993): 93–123.

Odell, G.C.D. *Annals of the New York Stage*, 15 vols. New York: Columbia University Press, 1927–1949.

Orot u-tselalim: khayey ha-yehudim be-rusiya ba-avodeyhem shel Sara Shor u'Meir Akselrod [Brushstrokes of history: Jewish life in Russia in the works of Sarah Schorr and Meir Axelrod]. Jerusalem: Hebrew University, Yad Vashem, 1995.

Orshanski, Ber. *Teater-shlakhtn* [Theatre battles]. Moscow: Tsentraler Felker-farlag fun F.S.S.R., 1931.

Osherovitsh, M. *Dovid Kesler un Muni Vayzenfraynd* [David Kessler and Muni Weisenfreund]. New York: n.p., 1930.

———, Z. H. Rubinshteyn, and Zalmen Zylbercweig, eds. *Dos Rumshinski-bukh* [The Rumshinsky book], 2 vols. New York: Trio Press, 1931.

Ot Biblii do postmoderna. Stat'i po istorii evreiskoi kul'tury [From the Bible to the postmodern: Articles on the history of Jewish culture]. Moscow: Tekst, 2009.

Otte, Marline. *Jewish Identities in German Popular Entertainment, 1890–1930*. Cambridge: Cambridge University Press, 2006.

Oyslender, Nokhem. *Yidisher teater, 1887–1917* [Yiddish theatre, 1887–1917]. Moscow: Melukhefarlag, 1940.

Oyslender, Nokhem and Uri Finkel. *A. Goldfadn: materyaln far a biografye* [A. Goldfaden: Materials toward a biography]. Minsk: Institut far Vaysruslendisher Kultur, 1926.

Palepade, Bentsion. *Beyn hashmoshes* [At dusk]. Buenos Aires: n.p., 1951.

———. *Zikhroynes fun a halbn yorhundert idish teater* [Memoirs of a half-century of Yiddish theatre]. Buenos Aires: n.p., 1946.

Paskin, Sylvia, ed. *When Joseph Met Molly: A Reader on Yiddish Film*. Nottingham: Five Leaves Publications, 1999.

Patt, Sarah. *Lebn un shafn: 60 yor arbet far yidisher kultur un kunst in amerike* [Life and work: 60 years' work for Yiddish culture and art in America]. Tel Aviv: Farlag Oyfkum, 1971.

Pawlina-Meducka, Marta. "Teatr i jego rola w życiu społeczności żydowskiej przed 1939 rokiem" [Theatre and its role in Jewish life before 1939]. In Marta Pawlina-Meducka, *Kultura Żydów województwa kieleckiego (1918–1939)* [Jewish culture in Kielce province (1918–1939)], 122–152, 187–191. Kielce: Kieleckie Towarzystwo Naukowe, 1993.

Peretz, Y. L. *Briv un redes* [Letters and speeches], ed. Nachman Mayzel. Vilna: Farlag B. Kletskin, 1929.

"Perhift" Players of the Jewish Community Center Celebrating 40 Years of Yiddish Theater in Milwaukee, 1921–1961. Milwaukee: Jewish Community Center, 1961.

Perkof, Yitskhok. *Avrom Goldfadn: mayne memuarn un zayne brif* [Avrom Goldfaden: My memoirs and his letters]. London: Jouques Print Works, 1908.

Perlmuter, H. *An aktyor in oyshvits* [An actor in Auschwitz]. Tel Aviv: Farlag Hamenorah, 1972.

———. *Bine-maskes bay katsetler: yidish teater nokhn khurbn.* [Concentration camp inmates' stage masks: Yiddish theatre after the Holocaust]. Tel Aviv: Farlag Hamenorah, 1974.

Perlmuter, Sholem. *Yidishe dramaturgn un teater-kompozitors* [Yiddish playwrights and theatre composers]. New York: YKUF, 1952.

Philipp, Michael. *Nicht einmal einen Thespiskarren: Exiltheater in Shanghai, 1939–1947* [Not even a Thespis cart: Exile theatre in Shanghai, 1939–1947]. Hamburg: Hamburger Arbeitstelle fur deutsche Exilliteratur, 1996.

Picon, Molly, and Jean Bergantini Grillo. *Molly!* New York: Simon & Schuster, 1980.

Picon-Vallin, Béatrice. *Le Théâtre juif soviétique pendant les années vingt* [Soviet Jewish theatre during the 1920s]. Lausanne: La Cité-L'Âge d'Homme, 1973.

Pilowski, Arye L. "Le-kheker ha-makhaze be-yidish be-shalkhey ha-18 u-va-me'a ha-19—al shney kitvey yad shel ha-komedia ha-maskilit *Reb Henokh oder vos tut men damit?*" [Research on the Yiddish drama of the end of the 18th and the 19th Centuries—On two manuscripts of the Maskilic comedy *Reb Henokh or What Do You Do With It?*]. *Dapim le-mekhkar be-sifrut* 4 (1988): 87–100.

Pinski, D. *Dos idishe drama: Eyn iberblik iber ihr entviklung* [Yiddish drama: A survey of its development]. New York: Drukerman, 1909.

Pladott, Dinnah. "The Yiddish Theatre as a Species of Folk Art: Joseph Lateiner's *The Jewish Heart* (1908)." In Mark Gelber, ed., *Identity and Ethos: Festschrift for Sol Liptzin on Occasion of his 85th Birthday*, 69–87. New York: Peter Lang, 1986.

"Pokłosie zeszytu 'Teatr Żydowski w Polsce do 1939'" [Gleanings from the volume *Yiddish Theatre in Poland until 1939*]. *Pamiętnik Teatralny* 44 (1995): 255–262.

Pollak, Oliver B. "The Yiddish Theater in Omaha, 1919–1969." In Leonard Jay Greenspoon, ed., *Yiddish Language and Culture Then and Now*, 127–163. Omaha, NE: Creighton University Press, 1998.

Portnoy, Edward. "Freaks, Geeks, and Strongmen: Warsaw Jews and Popular Performance, 1918–1930." *TDR* 50 (Summer 2006): 117–135.

———. "Modicut Puppet Theatre: Modernism, Satire, and Yiddish Culture." *TDR* 43 (Fall 1999): 115–134.

Prager, Leonard. "A Catalog of Yiddish Play Manuscripts and Typescripts at the American Jewish Archives, Cincinnati." *Yiddish Theatre Forum* 2 (30 April 2003). http://www2.trincoll.edu/

~mendele/ytf/ytf02002.htm (part 1 of 2) and http://www2.trincoll.edu/~mendele/ytf/ytf02003.htm (part 2 of 2).

———. "Of Parents and Children: Jacob Gordin's *The Jewish King Lear.*" *American Quarterly* 18 (Autumn 1966): 506–516.

———. "Shakespeare in Yiddish." *Shakespeare Quarterly* 19 (Spring 1968): 149–158.

———. *Yiddish Culture in Britain: A Guide.* Frankfurt am Main: Peter Lang, 1990.

———. "Yiddish Theater in Cairo." *Israeli Academic Center in Cairo: Bulletin* 16 (1992): 24–30.

Prager, Leonard and Brad Sabin Hill. "Yiddish Manuscripts in the British Library." *British Library Journal* 21 (Spring 1995): 93.

Prilutski, Noyekh. "Farvos iz dos yidishe teater oyfgekumen azoy shpet?" [Why did Yiddish theatre appear so late?]. *Yivo bleter* 26 (September–October 1945): 96–104.

———. *Yidish teater* [Yiddish theatre], 2 vols. Białystok: A. Albek, 1921.

———. *Zamlbikher far yidishn folklor, filologye un kultur-geshikhte* [Anthologies of Yiddish folklore, philology, and cultural history]. Warsaw: Nayer Farlag, 1912.

Prizament, Shloyme. *Broder zinger* [Broder Singers]. Buenos Aires: Tsentral-farband fun Poylishe Yidn in Argentine, 1960.

Pulaver, Moyshe, ed. *Ararat.* Tel Aviv: Farlag Y. L. Perets, 1972.

Quint, Alyssa. "The Botched Kiss: Abraham Goldfaden and the Literary Origins of the Yiddish Theatre." Ph.D. thesis, Harvard University, 2002.

———. "The Botched Kiss and the Beginnings of the Yiddish Stage." In Benjamin Nathans and Gabriella Safran, eds., *Culture Front: Representing Jews in Eastern Europe*, 79–102. Philadelphia: University of Pennsylvania Press, 2008.

———. "Ha-makhaze 'Bar Kokhba' me-et Avraham Goldfaden" [Avrom Goldfaden's play *Bar Kokhba*]. *Khulyot* 6 (Fall 2000): 79–90.

———. "The Currency of Yiddish: Shloyme Ettinger's *Serkele* and the Reinvention of Shylock." *Prooftexts* 24 (Winter 2004): 99–115.

———. "Naked Truths: Avrom Goldfaden's *The Fanatic or the Two Kuni-Lemls.*" In Justin Cammy, Dara Horn, Alyssa Quint, and Rachel Rubinstein, eds., *Arguing the Modern Jewish Canon: Essays on Literature and Culture in Honor of Ruth R. Wisse*, 551–578. Cambridge, MA: Center for Jewish Studies, Harvard University, 2008.

———. "'Yiddish Literature for the Masses'?: A Reconsideration of Who Read What in Jewish Eastern Europe." *AJS Review* 29 (2005): 61–89.

R.W., ed. "Artyści i pisarze o teatrze żydowskim" [Polish artists and writers on Yiddish theatre]. *Pamiętnik Teatralny* 44 (1995): 278–287.

Rapel, Zina. *Fir doyres idish teater: di lebns-geshikhte fun Zina Rapel* [Four generations of Yiddish theatre: The autobiography of Zina Rapel], 2 vols. Buenos Aires: self-published, 1944.

Ravitsh, Melekh. "Alter Katsizne (1885–1941)." *Yiddish* 8 (1992): 80–86.

———. *Mayn leksikon* [My encyclopedia], 4 vols. Montreal and Tel Aviv: A Komitet, 1945–1982.

Reyzen, Zalmen. *Fun Mendelson biz Mendele* [From Mendelssohn to Mendele]. Warsaw: Farlag Kultur-lige, 1923.

———. *Leksikon fun der yidisher literatur, prese un filologye* [Encyclopedia of Yiddish literature, the press, and philology], 4 vols. Vilna: B. Kletskin, 1926–1929.

———. "Zilbertsvaygs 'Leksikon fun yidishn teater'" [Zybercweig's *Encyclopedia of the Yiddish Theatre*]. *Yivo bleter* 2 (1931): 251–266.

Rich, Frank, and Lisa Aronson. *The Theatre Art of Boris Aronson.* New York: Knopf, 1987.

Rivesman, Mark. "The Past and the Future of Yiddish Theatre." Translated by Benjamin and Barbara Harshav. In *Marc Chagall and the Jewish Theatre.* New York: Solomon Guggenheim Foundation, 1992.

Rivkin, B. [Bernard Weinrib]. *H. Leyvik, zayne lider un dramatishe verk* [H. Leivick: His poems and dramas]. Buenos Aires: Farlag Yidbukh, 1955.

Rivo, Sharon Pucker. "In Search of Jewish Identity." In Bernd Herzogenrath, ed., *Edgar G. Ulmer: Essays on the King of the B's*, 105–118. Jefferson, NC: McFarland & Co., 2009.

Roback, A. A. *The Story of Yiddish Literature*. New York: Yiddish Scientific Institute, 1940.

———. *Supplement to the Story of Yiddish Literature*. Cambridge, MA: Sci-Art Publishers, 1940.

Robertson, Ritchie. "Kafka's Encounter with the Yiddish Theatre." In Joseph Sherman and Ritchie Robertson, eds., *The Yiddish Presence in European Literature: Inspiration and Interaction*, 34–44. Legenda Studies in Yiddish 5. London: Modern Humanities Research Association, 2005.

Robinson, Valleri Jane. "Beyond Stanislavsky: The Influence of Russian Modernism on the American Theatre." Ph.D. thesis, Ohio State University, 2001.

Rojanski, Rachel. "The Struggle for a Yiddish Repertoire Theatre in Israel, 1950–1952." *Israel Affairs* 15 (January 2009): 4–27.

Romano, Marisa. "Franz Kafka als Kritiker und Kenner des jiddischen Theaters und der ostjudischen Kultur" [Franz Kafka as a critic of, and authority on, Yiddish theatre and Eastern European Jewish culture]. In Armin Eidherr and Karl Müller, eds., *Jiddische Kultur und Literatur aus Österreich*, 115–130. Klagenfurt: Theodor Kramer Gesellschaft and Drava Verlag, 2003.

Rome, David, ed. *The Yiddish Theatre: The Adler*. Montreal: National Archives, Canadian Jewish Congress, 1987.

Romeyn, Esther. *Street Scenes: Staging the Self in Immigrant New York, 1880–1924*. Minneapolis: University of Minnesota Press, 2008.

Roskies, David. "The Last of the Purim Players: Itzik Manger." *Prooftexts* 13 (September 1993): 211–235.

———. "The Medium and Message of the Maskilic Chapbook." *Jewish Social Studies* 41 (Summer/Fall 1979), 275–290.

Rotman, Diego. "Ha-te'atron yidish be-yisrael, 1948–1988" [Yiddish theatre in Israel, 1948–1988]. *Zemanim* 99 (2007): 38–45.

Rotte, Joanna Helen. "The Principles of Acting According to Stella Adler." Ph.D. thesis, City University of New York, 1983.

Rovit, Rebecca and Alvin Goldfarb, eds. *Theatrical Performance During the Holocaust: Texts, Documents, Memoirs*. Baltimore: Johns Hopkins University Press, 1999.

Rozhansky, Shmuel, ed. *Gedrukte vort un teater in argentine* [The printed word and theatre in Argentina]. Buenos Aires: n.p., 1941.

———. *Nusekh haskole: antologye: lider, dertseylungen, dialogn un teater-shpil* [Enlightenment mode: Anthology: Songs, stories, dialogues, and plays]. Buenos Aires: Yoysef Lifshits-fond, 1968.

———. *Oysgeklibene shriftn [fun Avrom Goldfaden]* [Selected writings (of Avrom Goldfaden)]. Buenos Aires: YIVO, 1963.

———. *Oysgeklibene shriftn [fun Dovid Pinski]: dertseylungen, drames, eseyen, memuarn* [Selected writings (of Dovid Pinski): Stories, dramas, essays, memoirs]. Buenos Aires: Yoysef Lifshits-fond, 1961.

———. *Oysgeklibene shriftn [fun Moyshe Broderzon]: lider, dramoletn, mayselekh* [Selected writings (of Moyshe Broderzon): Poems, dramatic sketches, stories]. Buenos Aires: Yoysef Lifshits-fond, 1959.

———. *Oysgeklibene shriftn [fun Shloyme Etinger]: komedye, mesholim, katoveslekh* [Selected writings (of Shloyme Ettinger): Comedies: fables, satires]. Buenos Aires: Yoysef Lifshits-fond, 1957.

———. *Teater, veltrayzes, zikhroynes [fun Peretz Hirshbeyn]* [Peretz Hirschbein: Theatre, travels, memoirs]. Buenos Aires: Yoysef Lifshits-fond, 1967.

Rozier, Gilles. *Moyshe Broderzon: Un écrivain yiddish d'avant-garde* [Moyshe Broderzon: A Yiddish avant-garde writer]. Saint-Denis: Presses Universitaires de Vincennes, 1999.

———. "Les Paradoxes de l'engagement: Haïm Slovès (Białystok, 19 juin 1905–Paris, 8 septembre 1988" [The paradoxes of engagement: Haim Sloves]. *Archives Juives* 30 (1997): 71–84.

———. "'When *Purim-shpiler* meets Columbine': Characters of *Commedia dell'arte* and *Purimshpil* in the Works of Moyshe Broderzon." In Joseph Sherman and Ritchie Robertson, eds., *The Yiddish Presence in European Literature: Inspiration and Interaction*, 7–12. Legenda Studies in Yiddish 5. London: Modern Humanities Research Association, 2005.

Rubel, Elinor. "Itsuv khalal ha-te'atron be-hatsagot akhadot shel lahakat 'Yung teater,' 1932–1937, varsha" [The design of theatre space in several "Yung Teater" productions in Warsaw, 1932–1937]. *Bama* 130 (1992): 42–66; 132.

———. "Lahakat ha-yung teater" [The Yung Teater troupe]. M.A. thesis, Hebrew University, Jerusalem, 1990.

Rumshinsky, Joseph. *Klangen fun mayn lebn* [Sounds from my life]. New York: Itshe Biderman, 1944.

Ruvn Guskin: lekoved zayn 30 yoriker tetikayt in der yidisher aktyorn yunyon un 60 yorikn geboyrntog [Ruvn Guskin: In honor of his 30 years of work on behalf of the Yiddish Actor's Union, and his 60th birthday]. New York: n.p., 1948.

Safran, Gabriella. "Dancing with Death and Salvaging Jewish Culture in *Austeria* and *The Dybbuk*." *Slavic Review* 59 (Winter 2000): 761–781.

———. "Jews as Siberian Natives: Primitivism and S. An-sky's *Dybbuk*." *Modernism/modernity* 13 (2006): 635–655.

———. *Wandering Soul:* The Dybbuk's *Creator, S. An-sky*. Cambridge, MA: Harvard University Press, 2010.

——— and Steven J. Zipperstein, eds. *The Worlds of S. An-sky: A Russian Jewish Intellectual at the Turn of the Century*. Palo Alto, CA: Stanford University Press, 2006.

Sagi-Bizaui, Eyal. "Kol ha-yidish me-kahir" [The voice of Yiddish from Cairo]. *Davka* 4 (2008): 36–38.

Sánchez, Rosa. "Difusión y recepción de obras teatrales de Shólem Aléijem en ámbitos sefardíes" [Dissemination and reception in Sephardic regions of Sholem Aleichem's theatrical works]. *Theatralia* 7 (2005): 175–185.

Sanders, Ronald. *The Downtown Jews: Portraits of an Immigrant Generation*. New York: Harper & Row, 1969.

Sandrow, Nahma. "'A Little Letter to Mama': Traditions in Yiddish Vaudeville." In Myron Matlaw and Ray B. Browne, eds., *American Popular Entertainment*, 87–95. Westport, CT: Greenwood Press, 1979.

———. *Vagabond Stars: A World History of Yiddish Theatre*. New York: Harper & Row, 1977; repr. New York: Limelight Editions, 1986; and Syracuse, NY: Syracuse University Press, 1999.

Sauber, Mariana. "Le Théâtre yiddish et sa langue" [Yiddish theatre and its language]. *Temps Modernes* 41 (1984): 557–567.

Schaffer, Carl. "Leivick's *The Golem* and the Golem Legend." In Patrick D. Murphy, ed., *Staging the Impossible: The Fantastic Mode in Modern Drama*, 137–149. Westport, CT: Greenwood Press, 1992.

Schechter, Joel. *Messiahs of 1933: How American Yiddish Theatre Survived Adversity Through Satire*. Philadelphia: Temple University Press, 2008.

———. "Messiahs of 1933: Radical Yiddish Theatre at ARTEF (a Speculative Theatre History)." *Studies in Theatre & Performance* 25 (2005): 79–81.

Schedrin, Vassili. [See also "Shchedrin, Vasilii"]. "Equation of GOSET: History of Yiddish Theatre in the USSR." In Leonard Jay Greenspoon, ed., *Yiddish Language and Culture Then and Now*, 93–108. Omaha, NE: Creighton University Press, 1998.

Scherman, M. *Istoricul teatrului evreesc din România, 1876–1952* [History of Jewish theatre in Romania, 1876–1952]. Tel Aviv: Tip. Al. Moses, 1953.

Schiff, Ellen. "Sinners, Scandals, Scoundrels, and Scamps on the American Jewish Stage." *American Jewish History* 91 (2003): 83–96.

Schildkraut, Joseph. *My Father and I*. New York: Viking, 1959.

Schmuck, Hilmar. *Jüdischer Biographischer Index* [Jewish biographical index], 4 vols. Munich: K. G. Saur, 1998.

——— and Pinchas Lapide, eds. *Jüdischer Biographischer Archiv* [Jewish biographical archive]. Munich: K. G. Saur, 1995.

Schneider, David. "Critical Approaches to Modern Yiddish Drama." In Dov-Ber Kerler, ed., *History of Yiddish Studies*, 103–115. *Winter Studies in Yiddish*, vol. iii. Chur: Harwood Academic Publishers, 1991.

Schrire, Gwynne. "Abiding 'Yiddishkayt'; Remembering Rochel Turok." *Jewish Affairs* 51 (1996) 42–48.

Schwartz, Julian. *Literarishe dermonungen* [Literary recollections]. Bucharest: Kriterion, 1975.

Schweig, M. *Fapte și idei* [Facts and ideas]. Bucharest: n.p., 1931.

Schudt, Johann J. *Judische Merckwürdigkeiten vorstellende was sich Curieuses und Denckwürdiges in den neuen Zeiten* [Jewish oddities: Presenting that which is curious and memorable in recent times]. 4 vols. Frankfurt: n.p., 1714–1718.

Schweid, Mark. *30 yoriger yubileyum* [30th jubilee]. New York: n.p., 1949.

Secunda, Victoria. *Bei mir bist du schon: The Life of Sholom Secunda*. New York: Magic Circle Press, 1982.

Segal, Milli, and Brigitte Ungar-Klein, eds. *10 Jahre Jiddisches Theater in Wien: Dokumentation* [10 years of Yiddish theatre in Vienna: Documents]. Vienna: Jüdisches Institut für Erwachsenenbildung, 2004.

Seidman, Aaron. "The First Performance of Yiddish Theatre in America." *Jewish Social Studies* 10 (1948): 67–70.

Seidman, Naomi. "The Ghost of Queer Loves Past: Anky's 'Dybbuk' and the Sexual Transformation of Ashkenaz." In Daniel Boyarin, Daniel Itzkovitz, and Ann Pellegrini, eds., *Queer Theory and the Jewish Question*, 228–245. New York: Columbia University Press, 2003.

———. "Staging Tradition: Piety and Scandal in *God of Vengeance*." In Nanette Stahl, ed., *Sholem Asch Reconsidered*, 51–61. New Haven: Beinecke Rare Book and Manuscript Library, 2004.

Seiger, Marvin. "A History of the Yiddish Theatre in New York City to 1892." Ph.D. thesis, Indiana University, 1960.

Serpe, Zvika. "'Between Two Worlds': 'The Dybbuk' and the Japanese Noh and Kabuki Ghost Plays." *Comparative Drama* 35 (Fall 2001): 345–376.

Shalit, Levi. *Meshiekh-troymen in Leyviks dramatishe poemes* [Messianic dreams in Leivick's dramatic poems]. Munich: Eynzam, 1947.

Shandler, Jeffrey. "Postvernacular Yiddish: Language as a Performance Art." *TDR: The Drama Review* 48 (Spring 2004): 19–43.

Sharon, Rachel. "Te'atron lo ozvim (ra'ayon im sakhkanit ha-yidish Lea Shlanger)" [You don't leave the theatre (Interview with the Yiddish actress Leah Shlanger)]. *Bama* 138 (1994): 95–98.

Shatski, Yankev [Jacob Shatzky]. "Di ershte geshikhte fun yidishn teater" [The first history of Yiddish theatre]. *Filologishe shriftn* (1928): 215–264.

———. "Geshikhte fun yidishn teater" [The history of Yiddish theatre]. In R. Abramovitch et al., eds., *Algemeyne entsiklopedye* [General encyclopedia] (11 vols.), 2:389–414. Paris: Dubnov-Fond, 1934–1966.

———. "The History of Purim Plays." In Philip Goodman, ed., *The Purim Anthology*, 357–367. Philadelphia: Jewish Publication Society of America, 1949.

———. "Der kamf kegn purim-shpil in praysn in 18tn y[or]h[undert]" [The struggle against Purim plays in 18th-century Prussia]. *Yivo bleter* 15 (January–February 1940): 28–38.

———. "Purim-shpiln un leytsim in amsterdamer geto" [Purim plays and clowns in the Amsterdam ghetto]. *Yivo bleter* 19 (March–April 1942): 212–220.

———. "Teater-farvaylungen bay di ashkenazim in holand" [Theatrical entertainments of the Ashkenazim in Holland]. *Yivo bleter* 21 (May–June 1943): 302–322.

———. "Yidisher teater in varshe in der ershter helft fun 19tn y[or]h[undert]" [Yiddish theatre in Warsaw in the first half of the 19th century]. *Yivo bleter* 14 (January–February 1939): 1–9.

———, ed. *Arkhiv far der geshikhte fun yidishn teater un drame* [Archive for the history of Yiddish theatre and drama]. Vilna: YIVO, 1930.

———, ed. *Goldfaden-bukh* [Goldfaden book]. New York: Idisher Teater Muzey, 1926.

———, ed. *Hundert yor Goldfadn* [One hundred years of Goldfaden]. New York: YIVO, 1940. See also *Yivo bleter* 15 (May–June 1940): Special Goldfaden issue.

Shayn, Yoysef [Joseph Schein]. *Arum moskver yidishn teater* [Around the Moscow Yiddish theatre]. Paris: n.p., 1964.

Shchedrin, Vasilii [See also "Schedrin"]. *Istoriya Gosudarstvennogo evreiskogo teatra na idish (GOSET) v Moskve, 1919–1948: dokumental'nye istochniki po istorii GOSETa v moskovskikh arkhivokhranilishchakh* [The history of the Moscow State Yiddish Theatre (GOSET), 1919–1948: Documentary sources on the history of GOSET from Moscow archives]. Moscow: n.p., 1994.

Sherling, Yuri. *Paradoks*, vol. 1, *Odinochestvo dlinoyu v zhizn'*, vol. 2, *Ego velichestvo myatezhnyi shut* [Paradox, vol. 1, Loneliness for life, vol. 2, His Majesty the rebellious jester]. Rostov on the Don: Feniks, 2007.

Shiper, Yitskhok. *Geshikhte fun yidisher teater-kunst un drame* [The history of Yiddish theatre art and drama], 3 vols. Warsaw: Kultur-lige, 1923–1928.

Shipow, Sandra. "Depression-era Trends in Popular Culture as Reflected in the Yiddish Theatre Career of Molly Picon." *Theatre Studies* 30 (1983), 43–55.

Shmeruk, Khone. "Drama ve-te'atron be-yidish—yesodot ve-reyshit (ra'ayon im profesor Khone Shmeruk im tseyt sifro 'Makhazot be-yidish 1697–1750'" [Drama and theatre in Yiddish—Foundations and genesis (Interview with Professor Khone Shmeruk on the publication of his book *Yiddish Plays 1697–1750*]. *Ha-universita* 25 (1981): 53–56.

———. "Lashon otentit, mesirat dibur otentit: ivrit ve-yidish" [Authentic language and authentic reported speech: Hebrew and Yiddish]. *Ha-sifrut* 30–31 (1981): 82–87 (with Itamar Even-Zohar).

———. "Ha-makhaze ha-'khasidi' shel Y. L. Perets" [I. L. Peretz's "Hasidic" play]. In Rachel Elior, Yisrael Bartal and Khone Shmeruk, eds., *Tsadikim ve-anshey ma'ase—mekhkarim be-khasidut polin* [Righteous men and men of great deeds: studies in Polish Hasidism], 293–315. Jerusalem: Mosad Bialik, 1994.

———. *Makhazot mikra'im be-yidish, 1697–1750* [Yiddish Biblical plays, 1697–1750]. Jerusalem: Israel Academy of Sciences and Humanities, 1979.

———. "Mark Shagal ve-ha-te'atron ha-kameri ha-yehudi be-moskva (be-shuley ta'arukhat Shagal be-muzeon yisrael)" [Marc Chagall and the Moscow Yiddish Chamber Theatre (on the occasion of a Chagall exhibition at the Israel Museum]. *Bama* 137 (1994): 83–92.

———. "Mordekhai und Ester: 'opereta komit' be-yidish mi-shalkhey ha-me'a ha-yod'khet" [Mordechai and Esther: Yiddish "comic opera" from the end of the eighteenth century]. *Areshet* 6 (1981): 241–256.

———. "Di Moyshe Rabeynu bashraybung—an umbavuste drame fun 18tn yorhundert" [The Moses story—an unknown drama from the 18th century]. *Di goldene keyt* 14 (1964): 296–320.

———. "Ha-noded u-mivne ha-makhaze 'Ba-layla ba-shuk ha-yashan' le-Y. L. Perets" [The wanderer and the structure of I. L. Peretz's play *At Night in the Old Marketplace*]. *Ha-Sifrut* 1:3–4 (1968–1969): 501–528.

———. "Nusakh bilti yadua shel ha-komedia ha-anonimit 'Di genarte velt'" [An unknown variant of the anonymous play *The Deceived World*]. *Kiryat sefer* 54 (1979): 802–816.

———. "Perets ha-dramatikan—iyun be-'Bay nakht afn altn mark'" [Peretz the dramatist—Studies in Peretz's *At Night in the Old Marketplace*]. *Molad* 23 (September 1965): 300–307.

———. *Peretses yiesh-vizye: interpretatsye fun Y. L. Peretses bay nakht afn altn mark un kritishe oysgabe fun der drame* [Peretz's vision of despair: An interpretation of Y. L. Peretz's *At Night in the Old Marketplace* and a critical edition of the drama]. New York: YIVO, 1971.

———. "Ha-shem ha-mashma'uti Mordkhe-Markus—gilgulo ha-sifruti shel ide'al khevrati" [The significant name Mordkhe-Markus: The literary reincarnation of a social ideal]. *Tarbits* 29 (1959–1960): 76–98.

———. "The Stage-Design of Peretz' *Bay nakht afn altn mark*." *Scripta Hierosolymitana* 19 (1967): 39–57.

———. "Tevye der milkhiker—le-toldoteha shel yetsira" [Tevye the dairyman—Evolution of the character]. *Ha-sifrut* 26 (1978): 26–38.

———. "Le-toldot ha-sifrut ha-'shund' be-yidish" [On the history of "shund" in Yiddish]. *Tarbits* 52 (1983): 325–350.

———. "'Tsezeyt un tseshpreyt' le-Shalom Alekhem ve-ha-hatsagot shel ha-makhaze ba-safa ha-polanit be-varsha ba-shanim 1905 ve-1910" [Polish performances of Sholem Aleichem's *Scattered and Dispersed* in Warsaw, 1905 and 1910]. In Ezra Mendelson and Khone Shmeruk, eds., *Kovets mekhkarim al yehudey polin—sefer le-zikhro shel Paul Glikson* [Studies on Polish Jewry: Paul Glikson memorial volume], 79–95. Jerusalem: Ha-merkaz le-kheker yehudey polin ve-tarbutam ve-ha-makhon le-yahadut zmaneynu, 1987.

———. "Uwagi o zeszycie 'Teatr żydowski w Polsce do 1939'" [Commentary on the volume *Yiddish Theatre in Poland to 1939*]. *Pamiętnik Teatralny* 44 (1995): 594–596.

Shmuelevitsh-Hoffman, Miriam. "Di khavley leyde funem Yoysef Pap yidishn teater" [The birth pangs of the Joseph Papp Yiddish Theatre]. *Oksforder yidish* 3 (1995): 809–832.

Shoef, Corina. "The Impossible Birth of a Jewish Theatre." *New Theatre Quarterly* 17 (2001): 67–73.

———. *Kakh nolad te'atron: ha-teatron ha-yehudi ve-ha-ivri be-shalhey ha-me'a ha-19* [Thus was a theatre born: The Jewish and Hebrew theatre at the end of the 19th century]. *Iyunim be-tekumat yisrael: me'asef le-va'ayot ha-tsionut, ha-yishuv ve-erets-yisrael* [Studies in the founding of Israel: a collection on issues in Zionism, the Yishuv, and the State of Israel] 10 (2000): 477–489.

Shomer-Bachelis, Rose. *Vi ikh hob zey gekent: portretn fun bavuste idishe perzenlekhkaytn* [As I knew them: Portraits of renowned Jewish personalities]. Los Angeles: n.p., 1955.

———. and Miriam Shomer-Tsunzer. *Unzer foter Shomer* [Our father Shomer]. New York: YKUF, 1950.

Shtatskikh, Aleksandra. *Teatral'nyi fenomen Marka Shagalla* [The theatrical phenomenon Marc Chagall]. Vitebsk: Muzei Marka Shagalla, 2001.

Shternberg, Jacob. *Vegn literatur un teater* [On literature and theatre]. Tel Aviv: H. Leyvik-farlag, 1987.

Shternshis, Anna. *Soviet and Kosher: Jewish Popular Culture in the Soviet Union, 1923–1939*. Bloomington: Indiana University Press, 2006.

Shteynberg, Arn. "Yedidi mi-dvinsk: Shlomo Mikhoels" [My Dvinsk friend: Solomon Mikhoels]. *Khulyot* 9 (2005): 378–387.

Shulman, Elazar. *Sfat-yehudit ashkenazit ve-sifruta* [The Jewish Ashkenazi language and its literature]. Riga: Eli Levin Press, 1913.

Shulman, Eliyohu. "Sholem-Aleykhems debyut in amerike" [Sholem Aleichem's American debut]. *Yivo bleter* 4 (December 1932): 419–431.

Shunami, Shlomo. *Bibliography of Jewish Bibliographies*, 2nd ed. Jerusalem: Magnes Press, 1965.

Siegel, Ben. *The Controversial Sholem Asch*. Bowling Green, OH: Bowling Green University Popular Press, 1978.

Silverman, Lisa. "Max Reinhardt between Yiddish Theatre and the Salzburg Festival." In Jeanette R. Malkin and Freddie Rokem, eds., *Jews and the Making of Modern German Theatre*, 197–218. Iowa City: University of Iowa Press, 2010.

———. "The Transformation of Jewish Identity in Vienna, 1918–1938." Ph.D. thesis, Yale University, 2004.

Simon, Shloyme. *H. Leyviks goylem* [H. Leivick's *Golem*]. New York: Idish lebn, 1927.

Singer, Isaac Bashevis. "Yiddish Theater Lives, Despite the Past." *Yiddish* 6 (1985): 149–155.

Skura, Susana and Leonor Slavsky. "El teatro idish como patrimonio cultural judío argentino" [The Yiddish theatre as Argentinian cultural legacy]. In Ricardo Feierstein and Stephen A. Sadow, eds., *Encuentro: Recreando la Cultura Judeoargentina* 2, 41–50. Buenos Aires: Editorial Milá, 2004.

Slobin, Mark and H. I. Minikes. "Vilna to Vaudeville: Minikes and *Among the Indians* (1895)." *The Drama Review* 24, Jewish Theatre Issue (Sept. 1980): 17–26.

———. "The Music of the Yiddish Theatre: Manuscript Sources at YIVO." *YIVO Annual* 18 (1983): 372–390.

———. *Tenement Songs: The Popular Music of the Jewish Immigrants*. Urbana: University of Illinois Press, 1982.

Sloves, Khaim. *In un arum: eseyen* [In and around: Essays]. New York: YKUF, 1970.

Smith, Sandra Weathers. "Spectators in Public: Theatre Audiences in New York City, 1882–1929." Ph.D. thesis, University of California, Berkeley, 2001.

Solomon, Alisa. *Re-Dressing the Canon: Essays on Theatre and Gender*. London: Routledge, 1997.

Solomovici, Tesu. *Teatrul evreiesc din România* [Yiddish theatre in Romania]. Bucharest[?]: Editura Tesu, 2005.

Sosnovskia, Ella. "Ha-te'atron ha-ivri ve-ha-te'atron ha-idi be-moskva be-shnot ha-esrim" [The Hebrew theatre and the Yiddish theatre in Moscow in the 1920s]. *Bama* 134 (1993): 80–82.

Soxberger, Thomas. "Jiddische Literatur und Publizistik in Wien" [Yiddish literature and journalism in Vienna]. M.A. thesis, University of Vienna, 1994.

Sprenger, Peter. "Kafka und der 'wilde Mensch': Neues von Jizchak Löwy und dem jiddischen Theater" [Kafka and *The Wild Man*: Latest news on Isaac Löwy and the Yiddish theatre]. *Jahrbuch der Deutschen Schiller-Gesellschaft* 39 (1995): 305–323.

———. *Populäres jüdisches Theater in Berlin von 1877 bis 1933* [Popular Jewish theater in Berlin from 1877 to 1933]. Berlin: Haude & Spener, 1997.

———. *Scheunenviertel-Theater. Jüdische Schauspieltruppen und jiddische Dramatik in Berlin (1900–1918)* ["Barn Quarter" theatre: Yiddish theatre troupes and Yiddish drama in Berlin, 1900–1918]. Berlin: Fannei & Walz, 1995.

Staerk, W. "Die Purim-Komödie *Mekhires Yoysef*" [The Purim comedy *The Sale of Joseph*]. *Monatsschrift für Geschichte und Wissenschaft des Judentums*, NS 30 (1922): 294–299.

Starck, Astrid. "Alsatian Yiddish Theater at the Turn of the Century." In Dagmar C.G. Lorenz and Gabriele Weinberger, eds., *Insiders and Outsiders: Jewish and Gentile Culture in Germany and Austria*, 100–108. Detroit: Wayne State University Press, 1994.

Starck-Adler, Astrid. "Introduction au théâtre yiddisch alsacien au XIXe siècle" [Introduction to 19th-century Alsatian Yiddish theatre]. *Yod* 31–2 (1992): 145–157.

Stavish, Corinne B. "There's Nothing Like that Now: The Yiddish Theatre in Chicago—Personal Perspectives." M.A. thesis, Northeastern Illinois University, 1979.

Steinlauf, Michael C. "Cul-de-sac: The 'Inner Life of Jews' on the Fin-de-Siècle Polish Stage." In Benjamin Nathans and Gabriella Safran, eds., *Culture Front: Representing Jews in Eastern Europe*, 119–142. Philadelphia: University of Pennsylvania Press, 2008.

———. "Fear of Purim: Y. L. Peretz and the Canonization of Yiddish Theater." *Jewish Social Studies* 1/3 (Spring 1993): 44–65.

———. "I.L. Perec i 'nowy' teatr żydowski" [I.L. Peretz and the "New" Jewish theatre]. Translated by Agata Tomaszewska. *Biuletyn Żydowskiego Instytutu Historycznego w Polsce* 3 (1991): 21–27.

———. "Jews and Polish Theater in Nineteenth Century Warsaw." *Polish Review* 32 (1987): 439–458.

———. "Polish-Jewish Theater: The Case of Mark Arnshteyn." Ph.D. thesis, Brandeis University, 1988.

———. "Sources for the History of Jewish Theatre in Poland." *Gal-Ed: On the History of the Jews in Poland* 15–16 (1997): 83–103.

———. "Ha-te'atron ha-yehudi be-polin" [Jewish theatre in Poland], in Israel Bartal and Yisrael Gutman, eds., *Kiyum ve-shever: yehudey polin le-doroteyhem* [The broken chain: Polish Jewry through the ages], vol. 2, 327–349. Jerusalem: Merkaz Zalman Shazar, 2001.

Stencl, A. N., ed. *Yoyvl almanakh, loshn un lebn 1956* [Jubilee almanac of the Loshn un Lebn (Language and Life) Society, 1956]. London: n.p., 1956.

Strauss, Jutta. "Aaron Halle-Wolfssohn: A Trilingual Life." D.Phil. thesis, University of Oxford, 1994.

———. "Aaron Halle-Wolfssohn. Ein Leben in drei Sprachen" [Aaron-Halle Wolfsohn: A life in three languages]. In Anselm Gerhard, ed., *Musik und Ästhetik im Berlin Moses Mendelssohns* [Music and aesthetics in Moses Mendelssohn's Berlin], 57–75. Tübingen: Max Niemeyer, 1999.

Strube, Miriam. "When You Get to the Fork, Take It: From Ulmer's Yiddish Cinema to Woody Allen." In Bernd Herzogenrath, ed., *The Films of Edgar G. Ulmer*, 87–107. Lanham, MD: Scarecrow Press, 2009.

Szeintuch, Yechiel. "Aharon Tseytlin ve-ha-te'atron be-yidish: al makhazotav beyn shtey milkhamot ha-olam" [Aaron Zeitlin and the Yiddish theatre: His plays in the interwar period]. In Aaron Zeitlin, *Brener, Esterke, Vaytsman der Tsveyter: shlosha makhazot* [Brenner, Esterke, Weizmann the Second: three plays], 11–53, ed. Yechiel Szeintuch. Jerusalem: Magnes Press, 1993.

———. "Al shney makhazot histori'im mi-toldot yehudey polin be-yetsirato shel Aharon Tseytlin" [On two historical plays from the history of Polish Jewry in Aaron Zeitlin's writings]. In Khone Shmeruk and Shmuel Werses, eds., *Beyn shtey milkhamot ha-olam: perakim shel khayey ha-tarbut shel yehudey polin li-leshonoteyhem* [Between the two world wars: Chapters in the cultural life and languages of Polish Jewry], 182–207. Jerusalem: Magnes Press, 1997.

———. *Beyn sifrut le-khazon: tkufat varsha be-yetsirato ha-du-leshonit shel Aharon Tseytlin* [Between literature and vision: The Warsaw period in the bilingual writings of Aaron Zeitlin]. In Ezra Mendelson and Khone Shmeruk, eds, *Kovets mekhkarim al yehudey polin—sefer le-zikhro shel Paul Glikson* [Collected essays on Polish Jewry: volume in memory of Paul Glikson, 117–142]. Jerusalem: Ha-Merkaz le-Kheker Yehudey Polin ve-Tarbutam ve-ha-Makhon le-Yahadut Zmaneynu, 1987.

———. Introduction to *Bi-reshut ha-rabim u-vi-reshut ha-yakhid: Aharon Tseytlin ve-sifrut yidish: pirkey mavo ve-igrot muarot be-livui te'udot le-toldot tarbut yidish be-polin beyn shtey milkhamot ha-olam* [Aaron Zeitlin and Yiddish literature in interwar Poland: An analysis of letters and documents of Jewish cultural history], 21–97. Jerusalem: Magnes Press, 2000.

———. "Madrikh le-makhazot Yitskhak Katzenelson be-geto varsha" [A guide to Yitzhak Katzenelson's plays from the Warsaw ghetto]. *Bama* 135 (1994): 81–106.

———. "Meymad ha-retsinut bikhtavav ha-humoristi'im shel Yosef Tunkl (Der Tunkeler)" [The dimensions of seriousness in the humorous writings of Yoysef Tunkl (Der Tunkeler). In Yekhiel Szeintuch, ed., *Der seyfer fun humoreskes un literarishe parodiyes: an opklayb fun humoristishe shriftn vegn di mizrekh-eyropeyishe yidn* [The book of humoresques and literary parodies: A collection of comic writings on Eastern European Jews], 13–68. Jerusalem: Magnes Press, 1990.

---. "Di tsvantsiker un draysiker yorn in Aron Tseytlins shafn" [The 1920s and 1930s in Aaron Zeitlin's literary works]. In *Proceedings of the Eighth World Congress of Jewish Studies*, Division C, 363–368. Jerusalem: World Union of Jewish Studies, 1982.

---. "'Di yidishe melukhe' oder 'Vaytsman der tsveyter' le-Aharon Tseytlin" [Aaron Zeitlin's The Jewish State or Weizmann the Second]. *Khulyot* 2 (1994):141–149.

---, ed. *Yitskhak Katsenelson: ketavim she-nitslu mi-geto varsha u-mi-makhane vitel* [Yitzhak Katzenelson's rescued manuscripts from the Warsaw ghetto and the Vitel concentration camp]. Jerusalem: Magnes Press and Ghetto Fighters' House, 1990.

Szydłowska, Mariola. "'Rozsiani i rozrzuceni': w dokumentach galicyjskiej cenzury teatralnej" ["Scattered and Dispersed" in the records of Galician censors]. *Pamiętnik Teatralny* 44 (1995): 269–270.

Taub, Michael. "Social Issues in Peretz's Short Dramas." *Yiddish* 10 (1995): 18–24.

---. "Yiddish Theatre in Romania: Profile of a Repertoire." *Yiddish* 8 (1991): 59–68.

Taytlboym, Avrom. *Fun mayne vanderungen* [From my travels]. New York: Biderman, 1935.

---. *Teatralia*. Warsaw: Yatshkovskis Bibliotek, 1929.

Teater-almanakh: london 1939–1943 [Theatre almanac: London, 1939–1943]. London: M. Markov, 1943.

Teater-bukh [Theatre book]. Kiev: Kultur-lige, 1927.

Teatro IFT: Cincenta Aniversario [IFT Theatre: Fiftieth Anniversary]. Argentina: La Asociación, 1982.

Teatrul Evreiesc De Stat București: 1948–1968. [Jewish State Theatre of Bucharest: 1948–1968]. Bucharest[?]: Teatrul Evreiesc de Stat din Bucuresti, 1968.

Thissen, Judith. "Film and Vaudeville on New York's Lower East Side." In Barbara Kirshenblatt-Gimblett and Jonathan Karp, eds., *The Art of Being Jewish in Modern Times*, 42–56. Philadelphia: University of Pennsylvania Press, 2007.

---. "Jewish Immigrant Audiences in New York City, 1905–14." In Melvyn Stokes and Richard Maltby, eds., *American Movie Audiences: From the Turn of the Century to the Early Sound Era*, 15–28. London: BFI Publishing, 1999.

---. "Jüdische Einwanderer aus Osteuropa und der frühe Film in New York: Eine kulturelle Brücke über dem Atlantik" [Eastern European Jewish immigrants and early film in New York: A cultural bridge over the Atlantic]. *Kintop* 10 (2001), 61–72.

---. "'*Leshono habo' bimuving piktshurs* (Next Year at the Moving Pictures): Cinema and Social Change in the Jewish Immigrant Community." In Richard Maltby, Melvyn Stokes, and Robert C. Allen, eds., *Going to the Movies: Hollywood and the Social Experience of Cinema*, 113–129. Exeter: University of Exeter Press, 2008.

---. "Moyshe Goes to the Movies: Jewish Immigrants, Popular Entertainment, and Ethnic Identity in New York City (1880–1914)." Ph.D. thesis, University of Utrecht, 2001.

---. "Reconsidering the Decline of the New York Yiddish Theatre in the Early 1900s." *Theatre Survey* 44 (November 2003): 173–197.

Thomashefsky, Bessie. *Mayn lebens geshikhte* [My life story]. New York: Varhayt, 1916.

Thomashefsky, Boris. *Mayn lebens-geshikhte* [My life story]. New York: Trio Press, 1937.

---. *Tomashevski's teater shriftn* [Thomashefsky's theatre writings]. New York: Lipshits Press, 1908.

Tiefenthaler, Sepp L. "Das jiddische Theater in Amerika" [The Yiddish theatre in America]. In Brigitte Scheer-Schäzler, ed., *Go West, Moses: Aufsätze zur jüdisch-amerikanischen Literatur und Kultur von Sepp L. Tiefenthaler* [Essays on Jewish-American literature and culture by Sepp L. Tiefenthaler], 31–40. Trier: Wissenschaftlicher Verlag, 1993.

Tirkel, Dovid Ber. *Di yugntlekhe bine* [The juvenile stage]. Philadelphia: Hebrew Literature Society, 1940.

Toffel, Gil. "'Come See, and Hear, the Mother Tongue!': Yiddish Cinema in Interwar London." *Screen* 50 (Autumn 2009): 277–298.

Troy, Shari S. "On the Play and the Playing: Theatricality as Leitmotif in the Purim Play of the Bobover Hasidim." Ph.D. thesis, City University of New York, 2001.

Trunk, Yekhiel Yeshaye. *Sholem-Aleykhem: zayn vezn un zeyne verk* [Sholem Aleichem: The man and his work]. Warsaw: Farlag "Kultur-Lige," 1937.

Tsanin, M., ed. *Briv fun Sholem Ash* [Letters of Sholem Asch]. Bat-Yam: Beyt Sholem Ash, 1980.

Tsen yor artef [Ten years of Artef]. New York: Tsenyorikn Yubiley, 1937.

Tseytlin, Elkhonen. *Bukh un bine: notitsn un refleksn iber literatur un teater* [Book and stage: Notes and reflections on literature and theatre]. Warsaw: E. Tsaytlin, 1939.

Tsinberg, Yisroel. *Di geshikhte fun der literatur bay yidn*, 10 vols. Vilna: Tomor, 1929–1966. Translated as Israel Zinberg, *A History of Jewish Literature*, 12 vols., translated and edited by Bernard Martin. Cleveland: Press of Case Western Reserve University, 1972–1978.

Tsuker, Nekhemye. *Fir doyres idish teater: di lebns-geshikhte fun Zina Rapel* [Four generations of Yiddish theatre: The biography of Zina Rapel], 2 vols. Buenos Aires: Nekhemye Tsuker, 1944.

———. ed. *Zeks yor beser idish teater* [Six years of better Yiddish theatre]. Buenos Aires: n.p., 1951.

Tucker, Percy. *South African Jews in the Theatre*. Houghton: South African Jewish Board of Deputies, 2006.

Turigliatto, Roberto, and Hans Winterberg, eds. *Il cinema Jiddish*. Turin: S.A.N., 1981.

Turkow, Jonas. *Farloshene shtern* [Extinguished stars]. Buenos Aires: Tsentral-farband far Poylishe Yidn in Argentine, 1953.

———. *Vegvayzer far dramatishe krayzn* [Guide for drama clubs]. Warsaw: Rekord, 1924.

Turkow, Zygmunt. *Fragmentn fun mayn lebn* [Fragments from my Life]. Buenos Aires: Tsentral-farband far Poylishe Yidn in Argentine, 1951.

———. *Di ibergerisene tkufe* [The interrupted era]. Buenos Aires: Tsentral-farband far Poylishe Yidn in Argentine, 1961.

———. *Shmuesn vegn teater* [Conversations on the theatre]. Buenos Aires: Farlag Unzer Bukh, 1950.

———. *Teater-zikhroynes fun a shturmisher tsayt* [Theatre memoirs from a tempestuous time]. Buenos Aires: Tsentral-farband far Poylishe Yidn in Argentine, 1956.

Turkow-Grudberg, Yitskhok. *Af mayn veg (shrayber un kinstler)* [My way (Writers and actors)]. Buenos Aires: Tsentral-farband fun Poylishe Yidn in Argentine, 1964.

———. *Geven a yidish teater: dos yidishe teater in poyln tsvishn beyde velt-milkhomes* [There was a Yiddish theatre: Yiddish theatre in Poland between the world wars]. Tel Aviv: I. Turkow, 1968.

———. *Goldfaden un Gordin*. Tel Aviv: S. Grinhoyz, 1969.

———. *Di mame, Ester Rokhl* [My mother, Esther Rokhl]. Warsaw: Yidish Bukh, 1951.

———. *Sholem Ashes derekh in der yidisher eybikayt* [Sholem Asch's path in Jewish eternity]. Bat-Yam: Bet Shalom Ash, 1967.

———. *Sovyetishe dramaturgye* [Soviet dramaturgy]. Warsaw: Yidish Bukh, 1955.

———. *Varshe: dos vigele fun yidishn teater* [Warsaw: The cradle of Yiddish theatre]. Warsaw: Yidish Bukh, 1956.

———. *Yidish teater in poyln* [Yiddish theatre in Poland]. Warsaw: Yidish Bukh, 1951.

———. *Y. L. Perets—der veker: tsu der 50-ter yortsayt* [Y. L. Peretz, the alarm: on the 50th anniversary of his death]. Tel Aviv: Farlag Y. L. Perets, 1965.

———. *Zigmunt Turkov*. Tel Aviv: Dfus Orli, 1970.

Valencia, Heather. Introduction to S. J. Harendorf, *Der kenig fun lampeduse/The King of Lampedusa*, edited and translated by Heather Valencia, vii–xxi. London: Jewish Music Institute/International Forum for Yiddish Culture, 2003.

Vanvild, M. [Shloyme-Leyb Kava]. *Pseydo-kunst un pseydo-kritik* [Pseudo-art and pseudo-criticism]. Łódź, 1921.

Vaserman, Yankev. *Dos teater un der sotsyalizm* [Theatre and socialism]. Warsaw: Y. Vaserman, 1921.

Vaynrib, B. "An umbakante yidishe komedye fun poyzner gegnt" [An unknown Yiddish comedy from the Posen district]. *Yivo bleter* 2 (1931): 358–166.

Vays, Aaron, "Te'atron ve-sifrut yidish be-galitsia ha-mizrakhit ba-shanim 1939–1941" [Yiddish theatre and literature in Eastern Galicia, 1939–1941]. *Bekhinot* 8–9 (1980): 113–128.

———, Evgenii Binevich, Yulii Shterenberg, and Ira Meleshkina. *Stranitsy istorii evreiskogo teatra v Galitsii: Sbornik statei* [Pages from the history of the Jewish theatre in Galicia: Collected essays]. L'vov: Khesed Ar'e, 2002.

Veidlinger, Jeffrey. "From Boston to Mississippi on the Warsaw Yiddish Stage." In Kathleen Cioffi and Bill Johnston, eds., *The Other in Polish Theatre and Drama*. *Indiana Slavic Studies* 14 (2003): 141–163.

———. "How the Weasel and the Well Became the Heavens and the Earth: Soviet Yiddish Drama in the 1930s." In Katherine Bliss Eaton, ed., *Enemies of the People: the Destruction of Soviet Literary, Theater, and Film Arts in the 1930s*, 91–112. Evanston, IL: Northwestern University Press, 2002.

———. "Let's Perform a Miracle: The Soviet Yiddish State Theater in the 1920s." *Slavic Review* 57 (Summer 1998): 372–397.

———. *The Moscow State Yiddish Theater*. Bloomington: Indiana University Press, 2000.

———. "The Moscow State Yiddish Theater as a Cultural and Political Phenomenon." In Jonathan Frankel and Dan Diner, eds., *Dark Times, Dire Decisions: Jews and Communism*. *Studies in Contemporary Jewry* 20, 83–98. New York: Avraham Harman Institute of Contemporary Jewry/Oxford University Press, 2004.

Veksel'man, M. I. *Evreiskie teatry (na idish) v Uzbekistane, 1933–47 gg.: Ocherki istorii* [Essays on the history of Yiddish theatres in Uzbekistan, 1933–47]. Jerusalem: "Filobiblon," 2005.

Viner, Meir. *Tsu der geshikhte fun der yidisher literatur in 19-tn yorhundert* [Toward the history of Yiddish literature in the 19th century], 2 vols. New York: YKUF, 1945.

Voskoboinik, Ts. *Moskovskii evreiskii teatr Shalom* [The Moscow Jewish Theatre "Shalom"]. Moscow: Moscow Jewish Theatre "Shalom," 1994.

Vovsi-Mikhoels, Natalia. *Avi Shelomo Mikhoels* [My father Solomon Mikhoels]. Tel Aviv: Ha-kibbutz Hame'ukhad, 1982. Russian edition: *Moi otets Solomon Mikhoels*. Tel Aviv: Iakov Press, 1984. Translated into French by Erwin Spatz as *Mon père Salomon Mikhoels: souvenirs sur sa vie et sur sa mort*. Montricher, Switzerland: Les Éditions Noir sur Blanc, 1990.

Walden, Joshua. "Leaving Kazimierz: Comedy and Realism in the Yiddish Film Musical *Yidl mitn Fidl*." *Music, Sound, and the Moving Image* 3 (Autumn 2009): 159–193.

Waldinger, Albert. "Jacob Gordin and the Liberation of the American Yiddish Theater." *Yiddish* 11 (1998): 72–80.

———. "Jewish Groundlings, Folk Vehemence and *King Lear* in Yiddish." *Yiddish* 10 (1996): 121–39.

Waldman, Berta. *O teatro idiche em São Paulo: memória* [The Yiddish theatre in São Paulo: A memoir]. São Paulo: Casa Guilherme de Almeida, 2010.

Wallas, Armin A. "Jiddisches Theater. Das Gastspiel der Wilnaer Truppe in Wien 1922/23" [Yiddish theatre: The Vilna Troupe's Vienna tour, 1922–23]. *Das Jüdische Echo* 44 (1995): 179–192.

Warembud, Norman. *Great Songs of the Yiddish Theater*. New York: Quadrangle/New York Times, 1975.

Warnke, Nina. "*God of Vengeance:* The 1907 Controversy Over Art and Morality." In Nanette Stahl, ed., *Sholem Asch Reconsidered*, 63–77. New Haven: Beinecke Rare Book and Manuscript Library, 2004.

———. "Going East: The Impact of American Yiddish Plays and Players on the Yiddish Stage in Czarist Russia, 1890–1914." *American Jewish History* 92 (2005): 1–29.

———. "Immigrant Popular Culture as Contested Sphere: Yiddish Music Halls, the Yiddish Press, and the Processes of Americanization, 1900–1910." *Theatre Journal* 48 (1996): 321–335.

———. "Of Plays and Politics: Sholem Aleichem's First Visit to America." *YIVO Annual* 20 (1991): 239–76.

———. "Reforming the New York Yiddish Theater: The Cultural Politics of Immigrant Intellectuals and the Yiddish Press, 1887–1910." Ph.D. thesis, Columbia University, 2001.

———. "Theater as Educational Institution: Jewish Immigrant Intellectuals and Yiddish Theater Reform." In Barbara Kirshenblatt-Gimblett and Jonathan Karp, eds., *The Art of Being Jewish in Modern Times*, 23–41. Philadelphia: University of Pennsylvania Press, 2007.

———. "Yiddish Theater History, Its Composers and Operettas: A Narrative without Music." *Muzykalia* VII, Judaica 2 (2009), 1–11. http://www.demusica.pl/?Pismo_Muzykalia:Muzykalia_VII%2FJudaica_2

Waszkiel, Marek. "Z dziejów żydowskiego teatru lalek w Polsce" [On the history of Yiddish puppet theatre in Poland]. *Pamiętnik Teatralny* 44 (1995): 293–303.

Waterman, Ray. "Proltet: the Yiddish-speaking Group of the Workers' Theatre Movement." *History Workshop Journal* 5 (1978): 174–178.

Węgrzyniak, Rafał, ed. "Jung Teater w Wilnie: materiały do dziejów teatru żydowskiego w Wilnie (1935–1939)" [Yung Teater in Vilna: Materials related to the history of the Yiddish theatre in Vilna (1935–1939)]. *Pamiętnik Teatralny* 44 (1995): 459–489.

———. "Repertuar Teatru Młodych (Jung Teater) 1933–1937" [The repertoire of the Yung Teater (1933–1937)]. *Pamiętnik Teatralny* 44 (1995): 271–277.

———. "Teatr sąsiadów: przyczynki do historii scen żydowskich w Polsce" [Neighbors' Theatre: Contributions to the history of the Jewish stage in Poland]. *Dialog* 52 (2007): 216–225.

———. "Trupa Weicherta albo Zeittheater w jidisz" [Weichert's troupe or Zeittheater in Yiddish]. *Dialog* 51 (2006): 123–141.

Weichert, Mikhl. *Teater un drame* [Theatre and drama]. 2 vols. Warsaw: Farlag Yiddish, B. Kletskin, 1922–1926.

———. *Zikhroynes* [Memoirs], 4 vols. Tel Aviv: Hamenorah, 1960–1970.

Weinreich, Beatrice, and Uriel Weinreich. *Yiddish Language and Folklore*. Amsterdam: Mouton, 1959.

Weinreich, Max. *Bilder fun der yidisher literatur-geshikhte fun di onheybn biz Mendele Moykher-Sforim* [Scenes from Yiddish literary history from the beginning to Mendele Moykher-Sforim]. Vilna: Farlag Tomor, 1928.

———. "Tsu der geshikhte fun der elterer Akhashveyresh-shpil" [Towards the history of the older Ahasuerus play]. *Filologishe shriftn* 2 (1928): 425–452.

———. ed. *Ale ksovim [fun Shloyme Etinger]* [Complete works (of Solomon Ettinger)], 2 vols. Vilna: B. Kletskin, 1925.

Weinryb, Bernard D. "Aaron Wolfsohn's Dramatic Writings in Their Historical Setting." *Jewish Quarterly Review* 48 (July 1957): 35–50.

———. "An Unknown Hebrew Play of the German Haskalah." *Proceedings of the American Academy of Jewish Research* 24 (1955): 165–170.

Weitzner, Jacob. *Ha-drama shel Shalom-Alekhem u-mimushav ha-bimati*. [Sholem Aleichem's plays and their staging.] Jerusalem: Hebrew University, 1982.

———. *Mekhirat Yosef ba-te'atron ha-yehudi ha-amami* [The sale of Joseph in the Jewish folk theatre]. Tel Aviv: Farlag Y. L. Perets, 1999.

———. "'Mekhirat Yosef.' Purim-shpil be-rovno, polin lifney milkhemet ha-olam ha-shnia" [*The Sale of Joseph*: A Purimshpil in Rovno, Poland before World War Two]. *Dimui* (1996): 16–21.

———. *Sholem Aleichem in the Theater*. Northwood: Symposium Press, 1994.

Werb, Bret. "Cantorial Elements in Rumshinsky's Early Songs." *Journal of Synagogue Music* 35 (Fall 2010), 35–58.

Werses, Shmuel. "Beyn bidyon le-metsiut ba-makhaze shel Mendele 'Di takse'" [Between invention and reality in Mendele's play *The Tax*]. *Khulyot* 10 (2006): 11–30.

———. "Mi-khilufey lashon le-khilufey mashma'ut: ha-makhaze 'Melukhat Sha'ul'" [From change of words to change of meaning: the play *Saul's Kingdom*]. *Khulyot* 6 (2004): 55–78.

———. "Beyn shney olamot: 'Ha-dibuk' le-Sh. Anski be-gilgulav ha-tekstuali'im" [Between two worlds: The textual transformations of S. An-sky's *Dybbuk*]. *Sifrut* 35–36 (1986): 154–194.

Wiener, Leo. *The History of Yiddish Literature in the Nineteenth Century*. New York: C. Scribner's Sons, 1899.

Winchevsky, Morris. *Erinerungen*. Edited by Kalmen Marmor. New York: Farlag "Frayhayt," 1927.

———. *Geklibene verk* [Collected works]. Edited by Sh. Agurski, M. Levitan, K. Marmor, and M. Erik. Minsk : Farlag fun der Vayrusisher Visnshaft-akademye, 1935.

———. *A tog mit Yankev Gordin* [A day with Jacob Gordin]. New York: M. Mayzel, 1909.

Wishnia, Kenneth. "'A Different Kind of Hell': Orality, Multilingualism, and American Yiddish in the Translation of Sholem Aleichem's *Mister Boym in Klozet*." *AJS Review* 20 (1995): 333–358.

———. "Yiddish in 'Amerike': Problems of Translating Multilingual Immigrant Texts—Morris Rosenfeld's 'Rent Strike' (1908)." *Yiddish* 10 (1996): 140–160.

Wiśniewski, Tomasz. "Teatr żydowski w Białymstoku" [Yiddish theatre in Białystok]. *Pamiętnik Teatralny* 44 (1995): 263–268.

Wittke, Carl. "The Immigrant Theme on the American Stage." *Mississippi Valley Historical Review* 39 (September 1952): 211–232.

Wolitz, Seth L. "The Americanization of Tevye or Boarding the Jewish *Mayflower*." *American Quarterly* 40 (December 1988): 514–536.

———. "Forging a Hero for a Jewish Stage: Goldfadn's *Bar Kokhba*." *Shofar* 20 (2002): 53–65.

———. "Goldfaden: Theatrical Space and Historical Place for the Jewish Gaze." In Ahuva Belkin, ed., *Jewish Theatre: Tradition in Transition and Intercultural Vistas. Assaph: Studies in the Theater* (2008): 59–72.

———. "Performing a Holocaust Play in Warsaw in 1963." In Claude Schumacher, ed., *Staging the Holocaust: The Shoah in Drama and Performance*, 130–146. Cambridge: Cambridge University Press, 1998.

Wolting, Stephan. "Das jüdische Theater" [The Jewish theatre]. In Stephan Wolting, *Bretter, die Kulturkulissen markierten: das Danziger Theater am Kohlenmarkt, die Zoppoter Waldoper und andere Theaterinstitutionen im Danziger Kulturkosmos zur Zeit der Freien Stadt und in den Jahren des Zweiten Weltkriegs* [Theatres and the backstage of cultural life: The Gdansk Theatre on the coal market, the Sopot Woods Opera and other theatrical institutions in the Gdansk cultural milieu from the early days of the free town of Gdansk to the end of World War II], 330–336. Wrocław: Wydawnictwo Uniwersytetu Wrocławskiego, 2003.

Yabolokoff, Herman. *Arum der velt mit yidish teater* [Around the world with Yiddish theatre], 2 vols. New York: n.p.,1968–1969. Translated and adapted into English by Bella Mysell Yablokoff as *Der payatz*. Silver Spring, MD: Bartleby Press, 1995.

Yachnin, Paul. "The Jewish King Lear: Populuxe, Peformance, and the Dimension of Literature." *Shakespeare Bulletin* 21 (Winter 2003): 5–18.

Yardeyni, Mordkhe. *Vort un klang* [Word and sound], 3 vols. New York: Farlag Malke, 1979.
Yedidya, Yitskhaki. "Miskhakey purim ve-tarbut ha-te'atron be-yidish" [Purim games and Yiddish theatrical culture]. *Iton 77 le-sifrut u-le-tarbut* 292 (2004): 8–9.
Yerushalmi, Dorit and Shimon Levy, eds. *"Al na tegarshuni": iyunim khadashim be-"ha-dibuk"* ["Do not drive me out": new studies on *The Dybbuk*]. Tel Aviv: Safra, 2009.
Yeshurun, Yefim. *100 yor moderne yidishe literatur: bibliografishe tsushtayer* [100 years of modern Yiddish literature: Bibliography]. New York: Workmen's Circle Book Committee, 1965.
Yizkor Book Project, JewishGen. http://www.jewishgen.org/yizkor/.
Yizkor (Holocaust memorial) books [in the New York Public Library]. http://www.nypl.org/research/chss/jws/yizkorbooks_intro.cfm.
Yo, Mikhail [Meir Yaffe]. *Teater pesimizmen* [Theatre pessimisms]. Riga: Bilike Bikher, 1938.
Young, Boaz. *Mayn lebn in teater* [My life in the theatre]. New York: YKUF, 1950.
Yuditski, Avrom. "Vegn inhalt fun Volf Kamrashes pyese 'Kohol in shtetl'" [On the contents of Wolf Kamrash's play *Kohol in shtetl*]. *Shriftn* (Kiev, 1928), 1:331–336.
Yugend-Green, Julie Lynn. "Yiddish Theatre: From the Purim Play Through the Jewish King Lear." M.S.M. thesis, Hebrew Union College-Jewish Institute of Religion, Brookdale Center, 1994.
Zable, Arnold. *Wanderers and Dreamers: Tales of the David Herman Theatre*. South Melbourne: Hyland House, 1998.
Zakin, M., G. Gelman, and Victor Kohn, eds. *30 yor ift* [30 years of IFT]. Buenos Aires: IFT [Argentinian Yiddish People's Theatre and Art Society], 1962.
Zalmen Zilbertsvayg yoyvl-bukh [Zalmen Zylbercweig jubilee book]. New York: Yubiley-komitet, 1941.
Zatzman, Belarie. "Yiddish Theatre in Montreal." *Canadian Jewish Studies* 6 (1998): 89–97.
Zer-Zion, Shelly. "The Birth of Habima and the Yiddish Art Theatre Movement." In Ahuva Belkin, ed., *Jewish Theatre: Tradition in Transition and Intercultural Vistas. Assaph: Studies in the Theater* (2008): 73–88.
Zieliński, Konrad. "Życie teatralne ludności żydowskiej na Lubelszczyźnie w latach pierwszej wojny światowej" [Jewish theatrical life in the Lublin region during World War I]. *Annales Universitatis Mariae Curie-Skłodowska, Sectio F: Historia* 52/53 (1997/1998): 301–327.
Zivanovic, Judith. "GOSET: Little-Known Theatre of Widely Known Influence." *Educational Theatre Journal* 27 (May 1975): 236–244.
Zohar, Tsvi. "Avi ha-te'atron ha-yehudi (80 shana le-te'atrono shel Avraham Goldfaden)" [Father of the Jewish theatre (the 80th anniversary of Avrom Goldfaden's theatre)]. *Orlogin* 13 (1957): 216–228.
Zohn, Hershel. *The Story of the Yiddish Theatre*. Las Cruces, NM: Zohn, 1979.
Zolotarov, Hillel [also Solotaroff, Zolotareff]. "Di idishe bine" [The Yiddish stage] and "Fun nayem idishen teater" [From the new Yiddish theatre], in *Geklibene shriften* [Collected writings], ed. Joel Entin, 3 vols, 2: 161–201. New York: Dr. H. Solotaroff Publication Committee, 1924.
———. "Der onfang fun der yidisher drame in rusland" [The beginnings of Yiddish drama in Russia]. In *Suvenir tsu Yankev Gordins tsen-yerikn yubileyum* [Souvenir of Jacob Gordin's tenth anniversary], 23–30. New York: n.p., 1901.
Zuskina-Perel'man, Alla. *Puteshestvie Venyamina: Razmyshleniya o zhizni, tvorchestve i sud'be evreiskogo aktera Venyamina Zuskina* [The travels of Benjamin: Thoughts on life, creativity, and the fate of the Jewish actor Benjamin Zuskin]. Moscow: Mosty kul'tury, 2002. Translated into Hebrew by Tirtsah Yoel-Viner as *Masa'ot Binyamin Zuskin*. Jerusalem: Carmel, 2006.
Zylbercweig, Zalmen. *Avrom Goldfaden un Zigmunt Mogulesco*. Buenos Aires: Farlag Elisheva, 1936.
———. *Hantbukh fun yidishn teater* [Handbook of the Yiddish theatre]. Mexico City: Zalmen Zylbercweig Yoyvl-komitet baym Yivo in Los Angeles, 1970.

———. *Hintern forhang* [Behind the curtain]. Vilna: B. Kletskin, 1928.

———, ed. *Leksikon fun yidishn teater* [Encyclopedia of the Yiddish theatre], 6 vols. New York, Warsaw, and Mexico City: Farlag Elisheva, 1931–1969.

———. *Teater-figurn* [Theatre people]. Buenos Aires: Farlag Elisheva, 1936.

———. *Teater mozaik* [Theatre mosaic]. New York: Itshe Biderman, 1941.

———. *Di velt fun Ester-Rokhl Kaminska* [The world of Esther-Rokhl Kaminska]. Mexico: n.p., 1969.

———. *Di velt fun Yankev Gordin* [The world of Jacob Gordin]. Tel Aviv: Farlag Elisheva, 1964.

———. *Vos der yidisher aktyor dertseylt* [What the Yiddish actor says]. Vilna: B. Kletskin, 1928.

———, Harry Lang, and A. Babitsh, eds. *Eliyohu Tenenholts yoyvl-bukh* [Elia Tenenholtz jubilee book]. Los Angeles: Eliyohu Tenenholts Yoyvl-komitet, 1955.

Acknowledgments

Many people and organizations made this book possible, and it is a great pleasure to acknowledge their contributions here. This volume emerged from a conference, "Yiddish Theatre Revisited: New Perspectives on Drama and Performance," held in May 2006 in Seattle at the University of Washington, and we are grateful for the funding and administrative support of the Samuel and Althea Stroum Jewish Studies Program, the Ellison Center at the Russian, East European, and Central Asian Studies Program, the Department of Slavic Languages and Literatures, and the Chaim Schwarz Foundation for Yiddish Culture. We would like to extend special thanks to Paul Burstein, Galya Diment, Allison Dvaladze, Lydia Gold, Steve Hanson, Marta Mikkelsen, Dvorah Oppenheimer, Toni Read, Rochelle Roseman, and Shosh Westen, for their support, encouragement, good cheer, and astonishing agility in negotiating the hairpin turns and complicated evasive maneuvers required by Jackson School paperwork. We would also like to thank all of the speakers in "Yiddish Theatre Revisited": Annette Aronowicz, Zachary Baker, Mirosława Bułat, Jeremy Dauber, Donny Inbar, Faith Jones, Dov-Ber Kerler, David Mazower, Edna Nahshon, Sharon Pucker Rivo, Alyssa Quint, Ron Robboy, Gabriella Safran, Nahma Sandrow, Judith Thissen, Jeffrey Veidlinger, Nina Warnke, and Seth Wolitz. Your scholarship and collegiality made the conference as enjoyable as it was intellectually stimulating and productive, and those of you who have contributed to this volume have done so in the same spirit.

Kathy Wildfong of Wayne State University Press has been an unflagging advocate for this book, and we are extremely grateful to her and to her excellent team at Wayne State. Our thanks go as well to the two anonymous readers of our manuscript; their excellent suggestions have been incorporated into the final volume.

Thanks are also due to our team of able bibliographers who tracked down publications with us on Yiddish theatre in Polish and Hebrew. Thank you, Zachary Baker, Barbara Bułat, Mirosława Bułat, and Leonard Prager (z"l).

We are very grateful to the staff of YIVO, especially to Gunnar Berg, Jesse Aaron Cohen, and Lyudmila Sholokhova. Jesse's patient assistance, as we ordered file after file after file of photos from YIVO's colossal archive, has furnished our book with some exceptionally beautiful images, and we are delighted to be able to reproduce them here. Our thanks go as well to the Israeli Documentation Center for the Performing Arts, for permission to reproduce images 14, 15, and 16 of Goldfaden productions at the Ohel and Do-Re-Mi theatres; and to Shirley I. Fair, for permission to reproduce her photo of Zalmen Zylbercweig.

For permission to reproduce previously published versions of select chapters that appear in this volume, we would like to thank Slavica Publishers, for permission to reproduce Jeffrey Veidlinger's "From Boston to Mississippi on the Warsaw Yiddish Stage," a version of which appeared in Kathleen Cioffi and Bill Johnston, eds., *The Other in Polish Theatre and Drama,* Indiana Slavic Studies 14 (2003), 141–163; the University of Washington Press, for permission to print a version of Barbara Henry's chapter, published by the UWP in *Rewriting Russia: Jacob Gordin's Yiddish Drama* (2011); The University of Pennsylvania Press, for permission to reprint a version of Annette Aronowicz's chapter, which appeared in the *Jewish Quarterly Review* 98.3 (Summer, 2008): 355–388, as "*Homens mapole*: Hope in the Immediate Postwar World"; and to Jagiellonian University, for permission to reproduce a version of Mirosława Bułat's chapter, previously published as "W poszukiwaniu teatru 'żydowskiego': Zygmunt Turkow" in a special edition of the journal *Antreprener: Księga ofiarowana Profesorowi Janowi Michalikowi w 70. rocynicę urodyin*, edited by J. Popiel. We are also grateful to Connie Webber and Ludo Craddock of the Littman Library for Jewish Civilization for giving their blessing to use the bibliography from Joel Berkowitz's *Yiddish Theatre: New Approaches* as the foundation for the revised, significantly expanded version here.

Barbara would like to thank her husband, Wolfram Latsch, not only for providing professional-quality, in-house German-language translations and linguistic counseling on the fly, but for always being consistently awesome, and our son, Noah, for being his funny self. Thanks also to Wolf and Noah for showing remarkable forbearance as Joel and I collapsed with laughter over impenetrable jokes about Abe Cahan's hatwear and Moyshe-Leyb Halpern's furniture.

Joel's work on this volume spans his employment at two universities, and he is grateful to colleagues at both for their support in countless ways during the preparation of this volume. Special thanks to Barry Trachtenberg at the University at Albany; one could not ask for a finer colleague and friend. And on the home front, my sons Reuben and Nathan, and my wife Esther, are an ongoing source of love, laughter, and discovery.

Acknowledgments

This volume is dedicated to the memory of our colleagues John Doyle Klier (1944–2007) and Leonard Prager (1925–2008). Both made pioneering contributions to the study of Yiddish theatre, though both scholars are better known for their work in related areas: John as a noted historian of Russian Jewry, Leonard as a scholar of Yiddish literature in many genres, a bibliographer, and editor. Both were also widely beloved. We count ourselves among the many people whose lives and work were enhanced by knowing John and Len, both of whom were unfailingly gracious and generous with their time and erudition. Those of us who study Yiddish theatre and drama continue to benefit from their insights, and for those of us who knew them, their memory is indeed for a blessing.

Index

Page numbers in italics refer to illustrations.

Abramovitsh, S. Y., 56, 118, 302, 303, 311, 319n49; *Der priziv,* 118–119; *Di klyatshe,* 39n43; *Dos yidele,* 56; *Khagim u-zmanim:* "Ha-se'ara," 319n49; *Kitser masoes Binyomin hashlishi,* 152–153
Adler, Jacob P., 14, 87, 94, 95, 161, 164, 165, 167, 169, 170, 173, 174, 175, 176, 177, 179–180, 188, 192, 193, 227, 243n7, 253, 269
Adler, Sarah, 174–175, 179–180; recalling fan culture, 179–180
Adler, Stella, 222n28
Aeschylus, 2
Agid's Clinton Street Vaudeville House (New York), 192
Agid, Samuel, 192, 195
Aguinaldo, Emilio, 249n68
Akiva (rabbi), 129
Aksenfeld, Yisroel, 60n28; *Man un vayb, shvester un bruder,* 60n28
Alekhin, Arkadii, 75
Aleksander, oder der kroynprints fun yerusholayim (Alexander, or the crown prince of Jerusalem) (Lateiner and Minkowski). *See under* Lateiner, Joseph, and Minkowski, Giacomo
Alexander III (tsar), 99

Almagor, Dan, 319n45
Alterman, Nathan, 298, 299, 313, 316n14, 316–317n15
Altneuland (Herzl), 306
Ambrożewiczówna, Maria, 131
Amir, Yigal, 299
Amrani, Hagar, 313
Andreev, Leonid, 12, 121, 122; *Rasskaz o semi poveshennykh,* 121, 122–123, 125
An-sky, Sholem (Sholem Rapoport), 128, 308; *Der dibek,* 116, 128, 308, 135n47
Apelbaum, Moyshe, 118, 119, 123
Appelfeld, Aharon, 280, 281
Appenszlak, Jakub, 123–124, 131–132, 135n47; and the Jewish Association for the Advancement of Fine Arts, 123; and the Jewish Theatre Society (Warsaw), 123
Arbeter tsaytung (New York), 230
Aristophanes, 73
Artaud, Antonin, 294n51
Artef (New York), 89, 92, 114n9, 286, 289
Asch, Nathan, 157n15
Asch, Sholem, 12, 118, 137, 138, 139, 157n15, 265; *Got fun nekome,* 265–266, 267; *Kidesh ha-shem,* 139, 140; *Motke ganev,* 118; *Onkl Mozes,* 125
Ash, Khaye'le, 313

Ashendorf, Yisroel, 63n65, 128, 129
Association of Eretz Israeli Actors (Tel Aviv), 296, 314
Atheneum Theatre (Warsaw), 140
Atlas, Jenny, 199n26, 200n28
Averbuch, Motti, 315
Avrahami, Shaul, 314
Aynhorn, Arn, 121
Azazel (Warsaw), 132, 134n15, 135n47, 141

Babi Yar, 278
Bak, Shmuel, 313
Baker, Bella, 191
Bakst, Leon, 139
Balk, Zygmunt, 126
Barish, Jonas, 36n3, 42
Baron de Hirsch Trade School, 170
Bartal, Israel, 37–38n22
Barzilai, Yoram, 315
Baudelaire, Charles, 95
Becker, Israel, 302, 314
Beltov, Marina, 314
Beltzer, Yudele, 188
Belzer, Nisn (Nisi Belzer, Nisn Spivak), 229, 234, 247n43
Ben Ari, Yossi, 315
Ben Canaan, Miki, 315
Ben David, Dov, 313
Ben Gurion, David, 298, 303, 311
Benjamin, Avi, 315
Ben-Yehuda, Baruch, 313
Ben-Yehuda, Eliezer (Eliezer Yitzkhok Perlman), 296
Bercovici, Israel, 90; poetic form and register, 92, 93, 97–98, 99, 100, 103, 104, 105, 106–113, 114n10; translation of *Uriel Acosta:* borrowings from existing translations, 97
Berezowsky, Shaul, 314, 318n26
Berg, Alban, 152; *Wozzeck,* 152
Berger, Genia, 313, 314
Berger, Ludwig, 133n13
Bergner, Audrey, 313
Berkowitz, Joel, 83n33, 134n19
Berlin, Bertha, 191
Bernstein-Cohen, Miriam, 297, 298, 316n9
Bernstein, S., 56; "Magazin far yidishe lider far dem yidishn folk," 56, 63n60

Berstl, Julius, 121, 123; *Der lasterhafte Herr Tschu,* 121, 123, 124
Bialik, Chaim Hachman, 295–296
Bill'-Belotserkovsky, Vladimir, 148; *Zhizn' zovyot,* 148
Bismarck Garden (New York), 192
Bloch, Daniel, 317n17
Blume, Bernhard, 141; *In Namen des Volkes! (Boston),* 141, 142–144, 145, 147
Bonaparte, Napleon (emperor), 147
Bostonians, The (Boston), 235
Bowery Theatre (New York), 167. *See* Thalia Theatre
Brecht, Bertolt, 94, 293n34; *Galileo,* 94; *Threepenny Opera,* 297
Bristow, Edward, 267
Broder, Berl (Margulies), 43–46, 56, 63n63; "Dos lid fun dem shames," 44–45; "Ikh bidne," 44–48, "Ikh broder Berl," 45–46
Broder singers, 43–54, 58, 59nn8–10, 59n11, 63n63, 63n65, 254, 269; *Di broder zingers,* 63n65
Broderzon, Moyshe, 120, 131, 132, 134n16
Brody, Joseph, 229; Brody score to *Aleksandr, oder der kroynprints fun yerusholayim,* 231, 232, *239,* 246n35
Büchner, Georg, 13, 152; *Woyzeck,* 13, 152
Buchwald, Nokhem, 286–291, 292n6
Buksboym, Nathan, 150
Buloff, Joseph, 222n28
Bund, 212
Bunim, Shmuel, 313
Burgtheater (Vienna), 139
Burman, Daniel, 213
Burstein, Peysachke, 222n28
Butkevich, Anatolii, 75, 77

Cahan, Abraham, 10, 180n5, 181n13, 225, 243n6
Cahn, Yehuda Leib, 58n3
Cameri Theatre (Tel Aviv), 300, 313, 314, 317n22
Canaan, Miki Ben, 315
Caras y caretas (Buenos Aires), 222n29
Carnegie Hall (New York), 232
Casa Simón Dubnow (Buenos Aires), 206
Cashier, Isidore, 175
Cavalleria Rusticana (Mascagni), 231, 246n27

Ceaușescu, Nikolae, 92
Chemerinsky, Baruch, 313
Chernyshevsky, Nikolai, 82n19; *Chto delat'?,* 82n19
Ciganeri, Jeremias, 221n24
Cioffi, Kathleen, 156n1
Cogan, N. 313
Cohen, Albert, 314
Cohen, Charlie, 199n26
Collier, Simon, 211
Commedia dell'Arte, 119, 261
Communist Party, 276, 277, 278
Como, Perry, 237
Congress for Jewish Culture (New York), 272n12

Damari, Se'adia, 308, 319n40
Damari, Shoshana, *307,* 308, 310, 320nn52–53
Danzig, Moshe, 57; "Der kukuk," 57; *Di litvetshke: farsheydene yidishe lider af prost yidisher shprakh,* 57, 63n62
Daszewski, Cwi-Hersz, 121, 122
Davar (Tel Aviv), 317n17
David, Avrom, 314
David Kessler Dramatic Club (New York), 165, 200n28
Davis, Tracy C., 261–262
daytshmerish (Yiddish stage dialect), 92, 97, 226, 227–228, 229, 233, 238, 243n8
Dearborn Independent, 273n39
Dik, Isaac Meir, 52, 61n41
Dinezon, Jacob, 41–42, 43, 60n26; "Di ershte yidishe drama," 60n26; "Di yidishe sphrakh un ir shrayber," 42
Discépolo, Enrique Santos, 208; "Secreto," 208, 221n17
Disraeli, Benjamin, 320n57
Dobrushin, Yekhezkel, 152
Donizetti, Gaetano, 233; *Lucia di Lammermoor,* 233
Do-Re-Mi theatre (Tel Aviv), 306, *307,* 308, 309, 311, 314
Dostoevsky, Fyodor, 12; *Brat'ya Karamazovy,* 121
Dramatic Mutual Aid Society Lyra (New York), 165
Dreiser, Theodore, 153; *An American Tragedy,* 153–154

Dumas, Alexandre, 12
Dunham, Curtis, 235; *The 'Broidered Belt (Philipodia),* 235–236

East Side Dramatic Club (New York), 165
Edelstein, Joseph, 188
Edison, Thomas Alva, 193
Eichmann, Adolph, 303
Eldorado Theatre (New York), 187, 188, 191
Elisavetgradskii vestnik (Elisavetgrad), 71, 72–73, 77
Eliseum theatre (Warsaw), 125
Ellstein, Abraham, 237, 238
Ensemble Players (New York), 286
Epstein, Didye, 126
Erdeli, Alexander, 71, 82nn20–21
Eretz-Israeli Comedy (Tel Aviv), 297–298, 313
Erlich, Norman, 213
Esner, Uzi, 315
Ettinger, Amos, 315
Ettinger, Solomon, 5, 12, 37n19, 118, 119; *Serkele,* 12, 118, 119, 131
Euchel, Isaac, 28, 316n13; *Reb Henokh, oder vos tut men dermit?,* 28, 316n13

Fakel, Dvore, 153
Fainerman, Isaak (Teneromo), 75, 77, 83n38, 83n40
Fainzilberg, Rozalia, 83n50
Fast, Hoard, 142; *The Passion of Sacco and Vanzetti,* 142
Feinman, Dina, 175
Feinman, Sigmund, 164, 165, 170, 172, 175, 182n40; Sigmund Feinman's Dramatic Club (New York), 165
Feller, Albert, 126
Fessler, Oscar, *280,* 281, 289, 292n1, 293n34
Fidleman, Alexander Sender, 52; *Shirey asaf,* 52
Finkel, Morris, 230, 245n18, 245n20
Fischer, Shmuel, 311, 319n45
Fish, Stanley, 285
Fishzon, Abraham (Avrom), 52, 59n11, 248n56, 269
Flam, Gila, 221n16, 221n24, 316n14
Fogelman, Mark, 142
Folksadvokat (New York), 180n7
Folksblat (Łódź), 116
Folks-shtime (Warsaw), 293n22

Ford, Henry, 273n39
Forverts (New York), 161, 188, 176, 179–180, 183n63, 193, 194, 225
Franz-Joseph I (emperor), 145
Frayn, Michael; 305; *Noises Off,* 305
Fraye arbeter shtime (New York), 257, 258
Frieda, Martha, 236
Friedman, Samuel, 186
Frischmann, David, 269, 274n54
Frohman, Charles, 196
Frug, Shimon, 60n26
Fundación IWO (Buenos Aires), 206, 207, 221n14
Funston, Frederick, 235, 249nn67–68

Gabel, Max, 165, 200n28
Galand, Wanda, 235
Galileo, Galilei, 94
Gar, Evgenii, 83n50
Gardel, Carlos, 202, 204, 211, 222n27
Gentzler, Edwin, 105, 115n24, 115n36
Gershwin, George, 237
Gilfoyle, Timothy, 189
Gimpel, Bronislaw, 237
Gimpel, Jakob, 237
Ginsburg, Saul M., 52, 60n29
Ginzburg, Horace (baron), 50
Glikson, Yosef, 141, 143
Godik, Giora, 313
Gogol, Nikolai, 121; *Revizor,* 121, 297
Golan, Menachem, 314
Golan, Shlomi, 315
Goldberg, Itche, 285
Goldenburg, Samuel, 222n28
Golden Rule Hall (New York), 186, 187, 192, 193, 194
Golden Rule Vaudeville House (New York), 192, 194
Goldfaden, Avrom, 1, 4–5, 8, 11, 19–20, 21n1, 41, 42, 54–56, 57, 58, 61–62n47, 62n48, 62nn55–56, 73, 94, 95, 105, 117, 118, 119, 120, 125, 126–130, 131, 134n19, 144, 145, 146, 164, 178, 182n50, 191, 230, 233, 243n9, 244n10, 294n56, 295–312, 313, 314, 317n20, 318n28, 319n49
Goldfaden, Avrom, Works of:
  Film adaptations: *Kuni-Leml be-tel aviv; Kuni-Leml be-kahir,* 303, 314, 315, 318n28
  Play adaptations: 303–305, 315, 316n7; *Avrom Goldfaden/Sing, My People!* 315; *Goldfaden kholem,* 315; *Bi-tskhok va-demayehuda nafla; bi-tskhok va-dema yehuda takum: melodrama kora'at,* 303–305, 315, 317n16, 318n28
  Plays: *Akhasveyresh-shpil,* 313; *Bar Kokhba,* 125, 129–130, 313, 314, 315n3; *Ben-Ami,* 182n50, 309, 319n47; *Der dibek,* 128; *Der fanatik oder di tsvey Kuni-Leml,* 12, 94, 117, 118, 119, 120, 145, 296, 302–303, 304, 313, 314, 315, 316n7, 317n23, 318n26; *Di Broder zinger,* 125–26, 128; *Di kishefmakherin (Di makhsheyfe; Di tsoyberin; Ha-mekhashefa; Koldunye),* 20, 120, 134n15, 294n56, 296–297, *297,* 298–301, 304, 305, 308, 313, 314; "Oy, ir yidn bney rakhmonim," 299, 317n17; *Di mume Sosye,* 4; *Di yidene,* 4; *Kaptsnzon et Hungerman,* 300, 314, 317n16, 317n21; *Loy sakhmoyd (Dos tsente gebot),* 117, 118, 120, 131–132, 134n18; *Meshiekhs tsaytn?,* 303, 304, 315–317n16, 318n28; *Ni me, ni be, ni kukuriku,* 128; *Rabbi Yozelman,* 313; "Rozhinkes mit mandlen," 309–312, 319n45, 319nn48–49, 320n52; *Shmendrik,* 94; *Shulamis,* 20, 73, 82n26, 125, 126–128, 132–133, 135nn37–38, 191, 295, 304, 305–312, *306, 307,* 313, 314, 319n47, 319n49
  Poetry: 62n49; *Di yidene: farsheydene gedikhte un teater in prost yudishen,* 41; "Dos pintele yid," 55; *Dos yudele: yudishe lider af prost yudishe shprakh,* 41, 54–55, 56, 57, 62n48; *Tsitsim u'frakhim,* 55, 62n55
Goldfaden Dramatic Society (New York), 200n28
Goldfaden, Khana Rivke, 55
Goldoni, Carlo, 316n9
Golijov, Osvaldo, 213
Gor, Michael, 297, 313
Gordin, Jacob, 5–6, 10, 11, 64–78, 173, 174, 175, 182n48, 227; emigration, 64–65, 77, 79n1; fictive biography, 64–65, 76, 79n3, 82n21; "letter to Russian Jewry," 67, 78–79, 81nn10–12; police surveillance of, 77, 81n15, 83n40, 83n49; pseudonyms, 65,

66, 67–68, 71–72, 75–77, 78, 80n5, 82n22; realist "reformer" of Yiddish stage, 10, 64, 65, 74–75, 78, 175, 227; Spiritual-Biblical Brotherhood, 66–67, 69, 70, 71, 74, 75, 77, 79n3, 80n4, 80n6, 81n9, 81n11, 81n15, 82n21, 82n30, 83n40, 83n49; and Stundism, 66, 67–70, 81nn14–15

Gordin, Jacob, Works of:
Journalism: "Dovol'no! Dovol'no!, 75–76; "Letter to readers," 76; 80n5
Novel: *Liberal i narodnik,* 82n19
Plays: *Der yidisher kenig Lir,* 227, 245n11; *Di gebrider Lurye,* 174; *Di shkhite,* 175; *Elisha ben Avuya,* 69; *Emese kraft,* 174; *Got, mentsh un tayvel,* 173, 174; *Khasye di yesoyme,* 72; *Safo,* 69
Stories: "Der shvimender orn," 64; "Evreiskie siluety:" 70–71, 75; "Tipy shtundistov": 67–70, 71, 74; "Antip Bosoi," 69; "Ivan Chaika," 68; "Panas Tolyupa," 68–69; "Petr Kukuev and Roman Kirichenko," 69–70

Gordon, Aharon David, 311, 320n58
Gordon, Judah Leib, 48, 57, 39n43; "Le-mi ani amel?," 39n43
Gordon, Mikhl, 48, 49–50, 56, 60n26, 63n63; "Der get," 50; "Der litvak," 50–51; *Di bord un dertsu andere sheyne yidishe lider,* 56, 63n59; "Di bord," 50
Gordon, Peter Laurence, 246n37
Gorin, Bernard, 188
Gorky, Maxim, 10, 138
GOSET. *See* Moscow State Yiddish Theatre
Got fun nekome (Asch). *See* Sholem Asch
Gottlober, Avrom Ber, 5, 54, 55, 62nn51–52, 319n49
Grad, Gabriel, 314
Granach, Alexander, 123
Grand Street Musical Hall (New York), 176, 192, 193; boycott by fans, 176
Grand Theatre (New York), 168, 184, 174, 192, 193
Granovsky, Alexander, 58, 92, 114n4, 120, 134n15, 289, 293n34
Green, Michael, 304; *A Guide to Coarse Acting,* 304–305; *Plays for Coarse Actors,* 305
Greenspan, Avrom, 141
Greenspan, Yehudit, 313

Grimm Brothers, 212; "Hansel and Gretel," 212
Grober, Chayele, 212
Grodner, Israel, 48, 254, 269
Gross, Terry, 21n3
Groyser kundes, Der (New York), *162*
Gurevitch, Michael, 314
Gutzkow, Karl, 8, 11, 87, 90, 98; *Uriel Acosta:* 11–12, 87–113, 114n4, *121;* censorship of, 89; centrality to international repertoire, 94, 95; centrality to Yiddish repertoire, 87, 89, 91, 92, 94, 95; dramatic form, 89, 93–94; and Enlightenment values, 88–89, 93; poetic form and register, 90, 91, 92, 93–94, 95, 96–97, 98, 100–101, 103, political resonance of, 93, 94, 99. *See also* Bercovici; Hofshteyn; Lerner; Morevski
Gymnasia Herzliyah (Tel Aviv), 295, 304

Ha'aretz (Tel Aviv), 304, 320n52
Ha-khayim ha-llalu (Tel Aviv), 298
Habima (Tel Aviv), 94, 212, 289, 293–294n34, 297, 300, 302, 313, 314, 317n16, 317n21, 320n52
Hakotn, Yerukhem (Yeruchom Blindman), 229
Halevi, Moshe, 299, 300, 305, 313, 314, 318n37
Halkin, Shmuel, 92
Halperin, A. (Georg), 314, 317n22
Halperin, Henryk, 126
Halévy, Fromental, *La juive,* 73, 94
Hamizrahi, Yoram, 317n17
Harris, Harry ("Gulash"), 161, 163, 169, 179–180
Hart, David, 314
Hašek, Jaroslav, *Good Soldier Schweik,* 297
Ha-shakhar (Vienna), 60n23
Hasidism, 28, 29–30, 31–32, 57, 37n14, 37–38n22, 38n36; Hasid as Ostjude, 29–30
Haskalah (Jewish enlightenment), 4, 7, 8–9, 20, 27, 29–30, 32, 51, 55, 66, 212, 297, 312, 36n11, 39n43, 316n13; Haskalah drama, 8–9, 20–21, 27–35, 36nn2, 8, 10, 118, 316n13; as theme in Yiddish drama, 89, 93–94; *Di genarte velt* (anonymous), 8, 27, 30, 31–35, 37n15, 37n20, 37–38n22, 38n28; *Di hefker-velt* (Levinson), 8–9, 27, 30, 32–35, 38nn31–32, 39n39; *Laykhtzin*

Haskalah (*continued*)
   un fremelay (Wolfssohn), 28, 29, 31, 32, 36n8, 36n10, 37n19, 316n13; *Serkele* (Ettinger), 12, 118
Ha-tsvi (Jerusalem), 296
Hauptmann, Gerhart, 139; *Fuhrmann Henschel,* 139
Hauson, Helen Kaut, 315
Haynt (Warsaw), 148, 149, 151, 152
Hebrew Actors' Union, 177, 190, 198, 237, 253, 258, 259, 261; exclusionary practices of, 190–191, 197
Hebrew Choristers Union, 190
Hefer, Haim, 311, 313, 319n45
Heine, Albert, 139
Heine, Morris, 192
Heskes, Irene, 244n10, 319n48
Herbert, Victor, 235, 249n63; *The Ameer,* 235; *Babes in Toyland,* 249n63; *The Viceroy,* 235
Herman, David, 124, 135n46
Hirschbein, Peretz, 137, 140; *Zaverukha,* 140
Hitler, Adolf, 136
Hofshteyn, Dovid, 89, 97; translation of *Uriel Acosta:* date, 92; limitations of Soviet Yiddish, 92, 97; poetic form and register, 93, 97, 100, 102, 103, 104, 105, 106–113, 114n9
Holz-Mänttäri, Justa, 115n24
Homens mapole (*Haman's Downfall*) (Sloves), *see* Sloves, Haim
Hugo, Victor, 12; *Les Misérables,* 121; *Notre-Dame de Paris,* 121
Hurwitz, Moyshe, 164, 188, 191, 192, 243n7, 243–244n9, 247n42
Hyman, Louis, 165

Ibsen, Henrik, 10; *A Doll's House,* 316n9
Idelsohn, A. Z., 319n48
Idishe tsaytung, Di (Buenos Aires), 207, 220n4, 221n16, 221n24
Inbar, Donny, 303–305, 315; *Bi-tskhok va-demayehuda nafla; bi-tskhok va-dema yehuda takum: melodrama kora'at,* 303–305, 315
Irving, Henry, 83n33
Israel Defense Force, 296
Itzcoff, David, 210

Jacobs, Jacob, 222n32
Janacek, Gerald, 220n3
Jewish Association for the Advancement of Fine Arts (Warsaw), 123
Jewish Social Self-Help organization (Warsaw), 153
Jewish Theatre Society (Warsaw), 123
Johnson, Katie N., 265
Johnson, Val Marie, 264
Johnston, Bill, 156n1
Jones, Faith, 231
Jude, Der (Berlin and Vienna), 139
Judkovski, José, 202, 211, 212
Judt, Tony, 279, 281, 285

Kadison, Luba, 222n28
Kalish, Bertha, 168, 173, 174, 175, 183n63; on fan culture, 178–179, 182n48
Kaminska, Esther-Rokhl, 117, 122, 173, 254, 256, 257, 269, 270
Kaminska, Ida, 117, 131, 132
Kamiński, Józef, 131, 132
Kaminsky, Avrom Yitskhok, 117
Kaminsky, Joseph, 314, 317n21
Kaminsky theatre (Warsaw), 125, 131
Kanfer, Mojżesz, 129
Kanfer, Stefan, 21n3
Kaplan, Beth, 79–80n3
Karaite Judaism, 66
Karp, Max, 165, 169; Max Karp's Dramatic Hebrew Young Men Society Schiller (New York), 165
Karp, Sophie, 178, 233, 247n42
Katchen, Kurt, 152
Katz, Bella, 126, 128
Katz, Ephraim, 319n42
Katz, Jevel, 8, 14–15, 202–222, *203;* funeral of, 202–203
Katz, Jevel, Works of:
   Documentary film: *Jevel Katz y sus paisanos,* 207
   Recording: *Homenaje a Jevel Katz,* 207, 222n31, 222n38
   Songs: *Argentiner glikn:* "A kinder maysele," 212; "A pik-nik in visente lopez," 205; "A rantshera," 204–205; "Baynakht mit'n tramvay lakroze af koryentes," 210–211; "Colchón," 205; "Dados," 205; "Glokn in

altn shtetl," 211; "Ikh zukh a tsimer," 208, 216–218; "Me gustan las bocinas de los automóviles," 205; "Mozesvil," 205–206, 215–216, 222n32; "Mucho ojo," 206, 213–215; "Ovinu malkeinu," 208–210, 218–220, 221n22, 222n37; "Tango," 208; "Tucumán (Mayn rayze keyn tukuman)," 207
Kaufman, Dalia, 114n4
Kessler, David, 14, 87, 161, 162, 164, 169, 170, 173, 174, 175, 177, 179, 180, 182n48, 183n63, 185; David Kessler Dramatic Club, 165, 200n28
Khad-gadye (Łódź, Warsaw), 134n16
Kineman, Moshe, *283*
Klapholtz-Avrahami, Frieda, 314
Klapper, Paul, 195
Kleiner, Zvi, 313
Kleinman, Fryc, 128, 130
Knizhki nedeli (St. Petersburg), 70, 72, 82n19
Kobrin, Leon, 182n48
Kogut, Abraham, 165, 200n28
Kol mevaser (Odessa), 54
Komsomol (Communist Youth League), 276
Kon, Henech, 139, 140, 147, 150
Koren, Avi, 319n45
Koster and Bial's Music Hall (New York), 193
Kranc, Sz., 121, 122
Krantz, Philip, 231, 246n28
Kraus, Gertrud, 314
Kriegel, Annie, 278
Krochmal, Nachman, 33
Kropivnitsky, Mark, 73, 82n30
Kultum, Um, 299
Kultur-lige (Warsaw), 139, 141, 157n15
kuplet (rhyming verse), 229
Kuzmitsky theatre (Elisavetgrad), 73

Lahad, Ezra, 313
Lakmé (Delibes), 231
landsmanshaftn (hometown societies), 184, 186, 200n32
Lang ist der Weg (Fredersdorf and Goldstein), 302
Lara, Isidore de (Isidore Cohen), 236
Lateiner, Joseph, 169, 225, 230, 235, 243n9

Lateiner, Joseph, Works of:
Plays: *Aleksander, oder der kroynprints fun yerusholayim,* 17–18, 225–235; 237–238, 245n11, 245n17; *Bas-sheva, oder der vintshnfingerl,* 230; *Kenig un boyer,* 230, 231; *Khurbn yerusholaim,* 230–231, 235, 246n26, 248n56; *Shloyme Gorgl,* 169
Lavry, Mark, 308, 313, 316n14; *Dan ha-shomer,* 308
Lavry-Zaklad, Efrat, 316n14
Leaf, Naomi, 313
Lebensohn, Avraham Dov, 57; *Emet ve-emunah,* 57
Lebensohn, Mikhah Yosef, 48
Leivick, H. (Leivick Halpern), 19, 23n18, 157n15, 311; *In di teg fun Iyov,* 23n18; *In treblinka bin ikh nit geven,* 23–24n18; *Maharam fun rotenburg,* 23n18; *Mit der sheyres-hapleyte,* 23–24n18
Leksikon fun yidishn teater, see Zylbercweig
Lenin, Vladimir (Vladimir Ulyanov), 276
Lerner, Yakov, 311
Lerner, Yehuda Yoysef, 10, 11, 89; conversion, 11; translation of *Uriel Acosta:* 87–105, 114n4, 114n7, 115n24; political resonance of, 99–100; use of biblical elements, 94, 98, 99, 102, 104; use of varied Yiddish register, 91, 93, 95–96, 97; use of Hebrew, 90, 96, 98, 100, 101–103; use of localizing Jewish elements, 94, 95, 96–97, 98–99, 100, 102–103, 104–105; use of Slavic elements, 90–91, 95, 96, 97
Lessing Theater (Berlin), 152
Letste nayes (Tel Aviv), 318n29
Lettres Françaises (Paris), 278
Lev-Ari, Shimon, 316n9
Levi, Paul, 313, 314, 317n22
Levi, Yehoshua ben, 34
Levinson, Abraham, 20, 299, 313
Levinson, Israel Ber, 27, 32–33, 34, 38n29, 38n32; *Di hefker-velt,* 8–9, 27, 30, 32–35, 38nn31–32
Lewenstein, Yoram, 314
Lewicka, Luba, 126
Li-La-Lo Theatre (Tel Aviv), 320n53
Liber, Ben Ze'ev, 298
Liberty Hall (New York), 187

Libin, Zalmen, 183n63; *Der gebrokhener neyder,* 183n63
Licht, Dovid, 300, 317n21
Lilienblum, Moyshe Leyb, 80n4
Lillian, Isidore, 199n26
Linetski, Yitskhok Yoel, 47, 54, 56–57, 58, 63n66; *Der beyzer marshalik: satirishe folkslider, 47,* 60n21; "Der kurtszeiker shrayber," 57; *Di vibores,* 57; *Dos mishlakhes: kartines fun yidishn lebn,* 56–57
Linkovsky, Cipe, 213
Lipski, 126
Liptzin, Keni, 16–17, 164, 173, 175, 178, 254, *255,* 256, 258, 266, 269, 270; controversial biography, 16–17, 254, 256, 258, 261, 262, 266, 267–268, 270, 273–274n48
Literarishe bleter (Warsaw), 244n10, 253, 257, 265, 268, 271n9
London Theatre (New York), 187
Lubitsch, Ernst, 134n33
Luftglass, Emanuel, 313
luftmentsh, 147, 209, 221n20
Luvitch, Fanny, 313

Mahler, Raphael, 140
Maimon, Alex, 314
Malach, Leyb, 149, 151, 158n44; *Mississippi,* 149–151
Malachi, A. R., 61–62n47
Malevich, Kazimir, 133n14
Mallarmé, Stéphane, 95
Manger, Itzik, 146, 152, 313, 317n22; *Hotsmakh-shpil (Shlosha Hotsmakh),* 313, 314, 315
Manor, Ehud, 311, 319n45
Manning, Dick (Sam Medoff), 237; "Allegheny Moon," 237; "Hot Diggity," 237
Marek, Peysakh S., 52, 60n29
Marekhovski, Moshe (Boslever marshalik), 46, 48
Margolies, A., 59n11
Mariinsky Theatre (Odessa), 89, 94
Marks, Rudolf, 180n7, 245n22
Maruk, Anat, 314
Masliansky, Zvi, 80n4
May Laws (Temporary Laws), 73
"Mayn shtetele belz" (unattributed), 222n32

Mayzel, Nachman, 147–148, 150, 151, 244n10
Meltzer, Shimshon, 311, 314, 317n21, 320n56
Mendelssohn, Moses, 28, 36n8
Menuchin, Valentine, 313
Mesner, Anat, 315
Mestel, Jacob, 258, 259
Metropolitan Opera (New York), 231
Meyerbeer, Giacomo (Jakob Meyer Beer), 231, 246n28
Meyerhold, Vsevolod, 137, 293–294n34
Michaeli, Daniela, 315
Mikhoels, Solomon, 87, 92, 114n4, 152
Milo, Joseph, 313
Milton Club (New York), 197
Minkowski, Giacomo (Jacob Minkowsky), 8, 17, 225, 227, 229–231, 234–238, 247–248nn48–50
Minkowski, Giacomo (Jacob Minkowsky), Works of:
Opera scores: *Aleksander, oder der kroynprints fun yerusholayim,* 225–235; 237–238, 245n11, 245n17; arias, "Dos paradiz var mir ofen," 233, *238;* "Vi gefloygn kum ikh vider," 232–233, 237, *238;* as *shund,* 227; synopsis, 227–229; use of *daytshmerish,* 226, 227–228, 229, 233; use of *melodram,* 233; *Bas-sheva, oder der vintshnfingerl,* 230; *The 'Broidered Belt (Philipodia),* 235–236; *Die schönste Frau,* 231, 236, 237, 238; *The Smugglers of Badayez,* 235, 236, 238
Songs: "Spanisches Lied," 237, *241–242;* "New Oriental Waltzes," 235, 237, 238, *241*
Minkowski, Pinchas, 231, 247–248n50
Mirelman, Victor A., 273n33
Mizrahi, Motti, 299
Mlotek, Chana, 41, 60n23
Mlotek, Eleanor Gordon, 58–59n3
Mlotek, Yosef, 41
Mogulesco, Sigmund, 161, 164, 171, 173, 182n50, 200n29, 230, 246n26, 248n56; *Der yidisher polkovnik* (attributed), 230–231
Mohar, Yechiel, 314
Molière (Jean-Baptiste Poquelin), 29, 138; *L'Amour médecin,* 121; *L'Avare,* 121; *Tartuffe,* 29, 37n19

Molodowsky, Kadia, 19, 24n19
Moment, Der (Warsaw), 116
Morevski, Avrom, 87, 89; poetic form and register, 91, 97, 103, 104, 105; translation of *Uriel Acosta*: 89, 91–92, 93, 95, 97, 98, 100, 103, 104, 105, 106–113, 114n4, 115n24
Morgen frayhayt (New York), 286, 292n6
Morgn zhurnal (New York), 258, 259, 272n23
Moscow State Yiddish Theatre (GOSET), 87, 92, 134n15, 138, 152, 156n4
Mosenzon, Yigal, 314
Moshe, Pini, 313
Moshkovitsh, Morris, 170, 174, 175
Mukdoyni, Alexander (Alexander Kappel), 8, 16–17, 257–261, 262, 263, 266, 272n23, 288, 294n57
Munsey's Magazine (New York), 236
Muravanshik, Yeshayahu, 46; "Der goy," 46

Nachbush, Noah, 212
Nahshon, Edna, 92
Nardi, Nachum, 319n40
Nasi, Doña Gracia Mendes, 19
Nasaw, David, 192
Nasz Przegląd (Warsaw), 123, 131–132
National Democratic Party of Poland (Endeks), 136
National Socialism (Nazism), 136, 141, 145, 153
National Theatre (New York), 185, 179
Natanson, Duber, 38nn32–33
Navon, Arie, 314, 317n21
Nay Teater (Vilna), 137
Nedelya (St. Petersburg), 67, 81n11, 81n15, 134n30
Nemirovich-Danchenko, Vladimir, 297
New Azazel (Warsaw), 141
New York Public Library, 229, 231, 232
New York Times, 235, 236
Neyman, Yekhezkel-Moyshe, 118
Niborski, Eliezer, 222n31
Nicholas II (tsar), 145
Niger, Shmuel, 60n26, 62n56
Nirenberg, Mariam, 221n8
Nobile, Umberto, 146
Nowości Theatre (Warsaw), 138
Nowy Dziennik (Warsaw), 132–133

Noy, Meir, 320n55
Nudler, Julio, 202, 211, 212, 220n1
Nyu-yorker vokhnblat (New York), 259

Odesskie novosti (Odessa), 71, 73, 81n12
Ohad, Michael, 304
Ohel Theatre (Tel Aviv), *297,* 298, 300, 305, *306,* 308, 311, 312, 313, 314, 319n40
O'Neill, Eugene, 265; *Anna Christie,* 265
Olshanetsky, Alexander, 222n32, 237, "I Love You Much Too Much" ("Ikh hob dikh tsufil lib"), 238
Orenstein, Yehudit, 313, 314
Oriental Theatre (New York), 167
Orna Porat National Theatre for Children and Youth (Tel Aviv), 313
Osborne, John, *Look Back in Anger,* 302, 318n27
Oshrat, Kobi, 315
Ostrovsky, Alexander, 121, 316n9; *Bez viny vinovatye,* 121, 122
Oyslender, Nokhem, 59n10, 62n49

Page, Patty, 237
Palepade, Bentsion, 204
Palestine Comedy (Eretz Israeli Comedy) (Tel Aviv), 297, 298
Paperna, Avraham, 54
Parkh, Khayim, 169
Pat, Yankev, 118; *In goldn land,* 118
Penemer un penemlekh (*Caras y caritas*) (Buenos Aires), 222n29
People's Music Hall (New York), 187, 188
People's Theatre (New York), *162,* 184
Perelman, Max, 207
Peretz, I. L., 60n26, 137, 138, 140, 311, 320n56
Perl, Joseph, 31, 33, 37–38n22; *Über das Wesen der Sekte Chassidim,* 31, 37–38n22
Pinski, Dovid, 6, 19, 118, 320n56; *Der oytser,* 118
Piscator, Erwin, 293–294n34
Plato, 9
Poe, Edgar Allan, 95
Polinskaya, Esther, 73
Polish Committee of National Liberation (PKWN), 153
Poole's Theatre (New York), 167, 181n16. *See also* Union Theatre

Portnoy, Eddy, 61n43
Pradelsky, Yair, 315
Prager, Regina, 174, 178
Preger, Jacob, 151; *Der nisoyen,* 151; *Simkhe Plakhte (Der vaser-treger),* 151
Prese, Di (Buenos Aires), 204, 220n4
Prince, Julius, 192
Progress Assembly Rooms (New York), 187
Progressive Era, 264, 265, 273n35
Prylucki, Noyekh, 140
Pryzament, Shloyme, 63n65, 128
Pulver, Lev, 152
purimshpil, 275, 289–291, 292n2, 293n24
Pushkin, Alexander, *Povesti Belkina,* 69; *Stantsionnyi smotritel',* 69

Rabin, Yitzhak, 299
Rabinovich, Isaac, 134n15
Raines Law, 189, 195
Ranken, Frederic, 235; *The Ameer,* 235
Razsvet (St. Petersburg), 81n10
Razumny, Mark, 126, 314, 317n22
Red Army, 275, 277
Reinhardt, Max, 137, 142, 152, 293n34
Reisen, Zalmen, 43; *Encyclopedia of Yiddish Literature,* 43
Reznik, Etti, 313
Ringel, Israel, 315
Ringen (Warsaw), 139
Rolland, Romain, 121, 123; *Les Loups,* 121, 123–124
Rollansky, Samuel (Shmuel Rozhanski), 204, 212, 220n4
Romanian Opera House (New York), 246n26
Rosenberg, Yisroel, 95; translation of *Uriel Acosta,* 95
Rosenfeld, Lulla, 243n7
Rosenfeld, Max, 286
Rosenthal, Max, 169
Roskies, David, 49, 319n48
Rotbaum, Jacob, 315, 148–149, 153
Rotbaum, Leah, 140
Rotblit, Yaacov, 314
Rothstein, Elias, 170
Royal Court Theatre (London), 318n27
Rozengart, S., 126
Rozhansky, Rachel, 318n29
Rubin, Ruth, 319n48

Rubin, Sholom, 94; translation of *Uriel Acosta,* 94
Ruf, Avigdor Barkhiye, 52, 61n43; *Der shiker: oder di makhloykes tsvishn Reb Trinkman un dem shnaps,* 52, *53,* 61n43
Rumshinsky, Joseph, 244n10, 247n43
Russkii evrei (St. Petersburg), 81n10
Rymer, Luba, *88*

Sabbatai Zevi, 121, 122
Sacco, Ferdinando, 13
Sacco, Nicola, 13, 141–142, 143, 157n15
Sakhar, Moshe, 302, 314, 318n26
Sadan, Dov, 312
Sagan, Gene Hill, 313
Sakharof, Berry, 299
Samoilovich, Rudolf, 146–147
Samulesko, Deiv (David Samuels), 200n29
Sandrow, Nahma, 156n3, 244n10, 318n29
Schacht, Gustav, 174–175, 182n55
Scherer, Stephen J., 194
Schiller, Friedrich von, 56, 138; *Über naïve und sentimentalische Dichtung,* 56
Schiller, Leon, 140, 141, 144
Schipper, Itzik (Ignacy), 140
Schönberg, Moritz, 313
Schreiber's Café (New York), 178
Schroeder, Joergen, 89
Schwartz, Maurice, 120, 151, 168, 169, 170, 171, 172, 173, 176, 182n40, 182n45, 286, 287, 288, 289; Maurice Schwartz's Yiddish Art Theatre (New York), 120, 151, 170, 286
Scottsboro trials, 13, 149
Second Avenue Theatre (New York), 185
Secunda, Sholom, 237, "Bei Mir Bistu Schön," 238
Segal, Israel, 314
Segalovitsh, Zusman, 121
Segev, Tom, 318n29
Seltzer, Dov, 313, 314, 315
Sendler, Yankev-Kopl (Jacob Koppel Sandler), 247n42; "Eli, Eli," 247n42
settlement societies (New York), 186, 197, 198
Shabetai, Yakov, 313, 314
Shakespeare, 95, 127, 171, 302; *Hamlet,* 129; *Julius Caesar,* 319n43; *Measure for Measure,* 133n13; *The Merchant of Venice,*

73–74, 83n33, 129, 308; *Othello,* 170; *Romeo and Juliet,* 94; *The Tempest,* 318n27
Shapiro, Lamed, 157n15
Shatzman, Poldi, 313
Shatzky, Jacob, 8, 16–17, 62n49, 253–261, 262, 263, 265, 266, 268, 271nn7–8, 272n12, 273–274n48, 274nn51–52, 274n55; "An Example of a Theatre Encyclopedia," 268–271, 271n7; *Leksikon fun der nayer yidisher literature,* 272n12
Sheffi, Meira, 315
Sheriff, Noam, 313
Shikage (Chicago), 258
Shiper, Itzhak (Yitskhok), 258
Shlonsky, Abraham, 300, 302, 314, 318n27; translation of *Blondzhende shtern,* 314, 317n22; translation of *Di kishefmakherin,* 300–301
Shlosberg, Yitskhok, 232, 248n56
Shmeruk, Chone, 37n15, 37n18, 316n13
Sholem Aleichem (Sholem Rabinovitsh), 12, 38n32, 41, 42, 61n39, 62n53, 87, 90, 118, 126, 128, 137, 147–148, 157n35, 205, 221n20, 259, 300, 302, 303, 311, 313, 317n22; *Dos yidishe folksbibliotek,* 38n32, 61n39
Sholem Aleichem (Sholem Rabinovitsh), Works of:
 Essays: *Shomers mishpet,* 42; novels: *Blondzhende shtern,* 87, 114n2, 125, 126, 300–301, 302, 314, 317n22
 Plays: *Di goldgreber,* 147–148, 157n35
 Stories: *Alt-nay Kasrilevke,* 128, 313; Menakhem-Mendel (character), 221n20, 259; *Tevye der milkhiker,* 118
Shomer (Nokhem Shaykevitsh), 42, 164, 166, 173; *Di emigrantn,* 173
shund (trash), 9–10, 227, 244n9
Shvartsberg, Josef, 170
Silberg, Joel, 315
Simonov, Moyshe, 179, 183n63
Sinclair, Upton, 142; *Boston,* 142
Singer, Ben, 194
Singer, I. B., 102
Singer, I. J., 311
Sirota, Gershon, 222n28
Sivak, Fayvl, 143

Skolnik, Jonathan, 93
Śliwniak, Józef, 120, 131, 132
Slobin, Mark, 205, 206, 209, 221n9, 244n10, 246n34
Sloves, Haim, 18, 275–276, 277–278, 287–291, 292n7, 294n55; organization of World Congress for Yiddish Culture, 276; organization of Yidishe Kultur Farband, 276
Sloves, Haim, Works of:
 Essays: *A shlikhes keyn moskve,* 278, 292n7
 Plays: *Di Yoynes un der valfish,* 24n22; *Homens mapole,* 18, 275–292, *280, 283, 284;* historical context, 276–278, 279–285, 292, 293n32; ideological elements, 18, 276, 278–279, 281, 285–286; productions, 292n1, 294n36; as *purimshpil,* 275, 276–277, 278, 279, 281–285, 289–290; reviews of, 281, 282, 293n22; titles of, 294n55
Smolenskin, Peretz, 60n23
Socialist Realism, 82n19, 92, 148, 293n32
Socrates, 73
Solska, Irena, 144
Song of Songs, 310, 319n49
Sonnenthal, Adolf, 180
Spachner, Leopold, 179
Spagnolo, Francesco, 207
Spinoza, 93
Stadt Theatre (New York), 94
Stalin, Joseph, 136
Stanislavsky, Constantin, 138, 297; Stanislavsky system, 140
Steiner's Essex Street Theatre (New York), 194
Straus, Percy, 264–265
Strindberg, August, 316n9
Sulzer, Solomon, 229
Szeintuch, Yechiel, 133n1
Szewach, Abraham, 221n24
Szpigelman, Leon, *280*
Szwarc, Ester, 207
Szyfman, Arnold, 123

Tabatshnikov, Shmuel (Samuel Tobias), 175
Tageblatt (New York), 80n4, 188
Tantzman, Abraham, 188, 191, 192, 194, 200n46
"Tayere Malke" (unattributed), 212

Tchaikovsky, Pyotr, 74, 236; *Evgenii Onegin*, 74
Teater A. N. A. Goldfaden (Tel Aviv), 314
Teatro Mitre (Buenos Aires), 221n24
Teglikher herald, Der (New York), 82n31
Tehar-Lev, Yoram, 311, 319n45, 320n55
Thaler, Michael, 221n22
Thalia Theatre (New York), 167, 169, 175, 178, 183n63, 184, 230, 232, 236, 246n26
Thissen, Judith, 176
Thomashefsky, Bessie, 161, 164, 166, 170, 173, 174, 181n13, 182n48, 182n50, 225, *226,* 228, 230, 233, 242, 243n7
Thomashefsky, Boris, 17–18, 162, 164, 166, 170, 174, 177, 180, 180–181n12, 181n13, 185, 188, 222n28, 225, *226,* 228, 229–230, 231, 232, 237, 242, 243n1, 243n6, 247nn42–43; as lothario, 17–18, 225–226; personal papers, 229, 232; as singer, 226, 227, 233–234
Thomashefsky Dramatic Club, 166
Thomashefsky Project, 229, 231, 232, 242, 245n14
Tilson-Thomas, Michael, 232, 237, 242, 246n39
Toller, Ernst, 140; *Masse Mensch,* 140, 157n13
Tolstoy, Lev, 69, 75, 83nn38–39; *Chto takoe iskusstvo?,* 69
Tonecki, Zygmunt, 141
Topol, Anat, 315
Tsentral Theatre (Warsaw), 117; repertoire, 121–122
Tsukunft, Di (New York), 64, 157n35
Tuchband, Maurice, 199n26
Turgenev, Ivan, 82n19; *Dvoryanskoe gnezdo,* 82n19
Turkow, Zygmunt, 12, 63n65, 116, 117, *121,* 134nn33–34; 281, 293n34, 300, 302, 314, 315, 317n22; adaptation of foreign works, 122–123, 124–125; evolving ideas on Jewish theatre, 117–118, 122, 124–125, 127, 128, 129–131; modernizations of Yiddish classics, 119–120, 126–132; and Suprematism, 120, 130, 132, 133n14; Tsentral Theatre repertoire, 117, 121–124, 129, 133n7; VYKT 1924–25 company, 116, 117, 118, 119–120, 121–124, 129; second 1926–28 company, 117, 118, 120, 129; third 1938 company, 117, 125–131
Turkow-Grudberg, Yitskhok, 58
Tymoczko, Maria, 105, 115n36

Ueberall, "Professor," 187
UFA (Universum Film AG, Berlin), 125
Union of Jewish Artists (Warsaw), 139
Union Theatre (New York), 167
Union Vaudeville Hall (New York), 192
University Settlement Society (New York), 186, 199n6
Unzer shtime (Warsaw), 278
Unzer vort (Paris), 286
Uriel Acosta (Gutzkow). *See under* Gutzkow, Karl. *See also* Bercovici, Israel; Hofshteyn, Dovid; Lerner, Yehuda Yoysef; Morevski, Avrom; Rosenberg, Yisroel

Vagnenkos, Alejandro, 207
Vakhtangov, Evgenii, 293–294n34
Val, George, 306, 308
Vanunu, Mordechai, 299
Vanzetti, Bartolomeo, 13, 141–142, 143, 157n15
Vardi, David, 269, 274n54
Varshavski, Mark, 55, 62n53; "Aleph beys (Oyfn pripetshik)," 55
Varshavski, Meir, 55
Varshever Yidisher Kunst-Teater (VYKT), 8, 12–13, 116, 138, 293n34, 300; first 1924–25 company, 116, 117, 118, 119–120, 121–124, 129, 138; second 1926–28 company, 117, 118, 120, 129; third 1938 company, 117, 125–131; reviews, 131–133. *See also* Turkow, Zygmunt
Vayntroyb, Vladislav, 139, 140
Vaysman, Dora, 165, 180n12; Dora Vaysman's Educational League, 165, 166
Vaysman, Ruvn, 171
Veidlinger, Jeffrey, 92
Veinberg, Pyotr, 94; Russian translation of *Uriel Acosta,* 94, 95, 97
Verdi, Giuseppe, 236
Vertinsky, Alexander, 204, 220n3
Victoria Hall (New York), 189, 192
Views and Films Index (New York), 193, 194

Vilna Gaon, 212
Vilner Trupe (Vilna Troupe), 87, 89, 91, 116, 138, 139, 140, 148, 151, 212
Viner, Meir, 31, 33, 35, 37n15, 37n19
Volksbühne Theater (Berlin), 123
Voskhod (St. Petersburg), 81n10

WACO Theatre (New York), 194
Warnke, Nina, 80n4, 244n10
Warsaw Jewish Writers Union, 141
Warsaw Yiddish Art Theatre. *See* Varshever Yidisher Kunst-Teater (VYKT)
Wasserstein, Ella, 199n26
Weill, Kurt, *Threepenny Opera,* 297
Weichert, Mikhl, 13, 116, 137, 138–155, 158n57, 300
Weichert, Mikhl, Works of:
  Essays: "Bine un publikum," 142, 154–156; "Dos alte un dos naye teater," 144
  Play: *Trupe Tanentsap,* 144–146, 147, 148, 157n25, 300
Weinstein, Bernard, 186
Weintraub, Samuel, 200n28
Weintraub, Władysław Zew (Khayim Volf), 123
Weisburg, David, 317n17
Weiser, Kalman, 245n13
Weiss, Adi, 313
Wengeroff, Pauline, 52
West, Mae, 265; *Sex,* 265, 266
Widaomości Literackie (Warsaw), 141
Widislavsky, Ori, 314, 315
Wieland, Christoph Martin, 95
Wiener, Leo, 41, 49, 52, 54, 61n31, 61n39, 319n48
Wieviorka, Annette, 278
Wilensky, Moshe, 306, 314
Windsor Theatre (New York), 167, 169, 184, 191, 192, 230, 246n26
Wolf, Friedrich, 146; *Krassin* (adaptation), 146–147
Wolfssohn, Aaron, 5, 28, 29, 36n6, 38n8, 316n13; *Laykhtzin un fremelay,* 28, 29, 31, 32, 36n8, 36n10, 37n19, 316n13
Wolfovitch, Nathan, 314, 318n29

Yankelevich, Jaime, 211
Yardeni, Mordkhe, 261
Yashar (Jakub Aronowicz), *283*

Yehoash (Solomon Bloomgarden), 295
Yiddish Art Theatre (New York), 120, 151, 286
Yiddishism, 212
Yiddish School Organization (Warsaw), 139
Yiddishspiel (Tel Aviv), 313, 315
Yiddish State Theatre (Bucharest), 90
Yiddish theatre
  actors, surplus of, 16, 190–191, 164
  amateur New York dramatic clubs, 164, 165–166, 168, 180n11; Dora Vaysman's Educational League, 165, 166; Dramatic Mutual Aid Society Lyra, 165; East Side Dramatic Club, 165; Max Karp's Dramatic Hebrew Young Men Society Schiller, 165; Sigmund Feinman's Dramatic Club, 165; Thomashefsky Dramatic Club, 166; Young Hebrews Dramatic Club, 165
  antitheatrical tendencies, 3, 9, 27–28, 31, 42
  association with immorality, 17, 31, 42, 189–190, 197–198, 262–263, 266–267, 273n33
  audiences: character of, 6, 9, 12, 14, 16, 156, 161, 163–164, 167, 175–176, 195–196, 197, 200n35, *263;* decline of in 1920s, 177–178, 195; expansion of in 1880s–90s, 163–164, 166–167, 175–176, 191
  avant-garde, 12–14, 137–156
  badkhonim (wedding jesters), 48–49, 51, 52, 53, 54, 60nn27–28, 61n39; David the Badkhn from Bober, 46; Khonen Badkhn, 52; Mordkhe Mane, 52, 61n44; Peysekh Eliyohu the Badkhn, 52
  biblical themes in, 94, 98, 99, 102, 104, 276–277, 279, 282–285
  Broder singers, 43–54, 60n27, 125–126, 128, 135n40
  business practices, 181n15
  cabaret (*kleynkunst*), 212, 132, 134n15, 135n47, 139, 141, 142
  censorship of, 3, 20, 22n4, 58, 63n64, 73, 82n25, 144, 153, 303, 308, 318n29
  competition with cinema, 184–185, 193–194
  competition with music hall (vaudeville), 184–185; cross-dressing, 182n50; *daytshmerish* (Yiddish stage dialect), 226, 227–228, 229; development of "better" plays, 10, 11–12, 227

Yiddish theatre (*continued*)
  fan culture (*patriotn*), 14, 161–180, 180n5, 191, 200n29; effect on box-office, 175–176; establishment of clubs, 164, 165; organizational structure, 169–170, 181n13; value to actors, 163, 164, 170–171, 172–173, 176–177, 178–179, 180n6; violence of *patriotn,* 175, 179–180, 181n22, 183n63
  fans: Abe Kogut, 165; "Adler," 169; "Berele Sheygets," 169; "Feinman," 169; "Gulash" (Harry Harris), 161, 163, 169, 179–180; Isidore Cashier, 175; Josef "Spufke" Shvartsberg, 170; "Karp," 169; Khayim Parkh, 169; "Kimat Kessler," 169; "Kimat Mogulesco," 169; Louis Hyman, 165; Max Gabel, 165; "Meksl Virdzhinius," 169; "Meturef," 169; "Mrs. Goldstein," 169; "Sam," 170; "Shloyme Boss," 169; "Small Shylock," 169; "Shmuel Gorgle," 169
  folk poetry (*folksdikhtung, folkslider*), 40–58; and European art song, 58n1; folkloric character of, 58n3; performance venues, 59n11, 59n13, 60n24, 60n27; publications, 61n39, 62n54
  Hebrew Actors' Union, 177, 190, 198, 237, 253, 258, 259, 261; exclusionary practices of, 190–191, 197
  Hebrew Choristers Union, 190
  historical legends regarding, 1–2, 21n3, 95
  historiography, 2, 16–17, 251, 252, 272n23
  after the Holocaust, 18–19, 20, 23n18, 303, 310
  in Israel, 19, 20, 24n24, 296, 299, 302–315; attempted banning of, 303; in Palestine, 19, 20, 24n24, 295, 296–301
  music hall (vaudeville), 172, 184–185, 135n36; actors in, 190–191, 196–197; business practices, 15–16, 185–190, 192–193, 195, 196, 197, 200nn32–45; fan culture of, 182n45; music of, 229, 244–245n10; origins, 187–188, 191–192; regulations concerning, 189–190, 201n53; ticket prices, 188, 192
  New York Yiddish theatre district, 166
  and non-Jewish theatre, 3, 4, 7, 11–12, 15, 82n31, 89, 94, 105, 116
  operetta, 18, 191, 225, 227
  performed in transit camps, 280–281
  political views expressed in, 13, 18, 19, 137, 142–144, 148–149, 151–152
  and *purimshpil,* 1, 9, 19, 28, 36n6, 119, 275, 276–277, 278, 279, 281–285, 289–290
  rapid development of, 3–5, 6
  self-inventing tendencies, 2, 7–8, 14
  as *shund,* 9–10, 156, 227
  suitability of Yiddish language to drama and theatre, 3, 20, 91, 124, 227–228
  ticket prices, 162, 167–168, 176, 181n21
  women, representation of, 16–17, 251, 265, 266–267

Yidishe kultur (New York), 285
Yidishe Kultur Farband (YKUF, New York), 276
Yidishe Teater Gezelshaft, Di (Warsaw), 137
yishuv (Jewish Zionist community in Palestine), 295
YIVO (Institute for Jewish Research), 231–232; David Hirsh Collection, 231–232; Sholem Perlmutter Music Collection, 231–232; Vilna Collection, 232
Yoram Levinstein Acting Studio (Tel Aviv), 314
Yosef (rabbi), 34
Yosef, Ovadia, 317n17
Young, Boaz, 165, 168, 169, 180n5, 245n22
Young Hebrews Dramatic Club (New York), 165
Yung Bine (Warsaw). *See* Yung Teater
Yung Teater (Warsaw), 13–14, 137, 139–154; actor-training program, 12, 139, 140–141; censorship of, 144, 153; political sympathies of, 142–144, 148–149, 151–152, 154; re-named Yung Bine, 152; renamed Nay Teater (Vilna), 153
  Productions: *An American Tragedy,* 153–154; *Boston,* 142–144, 145, 147; *Di goldgreber,* 147–148; innovative staging, 142–143, 144–147, 149–150, 153, 154–156; *Krassin,* 146–147, 157n32; *Masoes Binyomin hashlishi,* 152–153; *Mississippi,* 149–151; *Simkhe Plakhte,* 151; *Trupe Tanentsap,* 144–146, 147, 148, 157n25, 300; *Woyzeck,* 152; *Zhizn' zavyot* (*Dos lebn ruft*), 148
Yung Yidish, 134n16

Yuval Theatre (Tel Aviv), 315
Yuzhnyi krai (Khar'kov), 78, 81n10

Zalkind, Max, 207, 222n32, 222n38
Zbarzher, Velvl (Zbarzher-Ehrenkrants), 48, 49, 56, 59n11, 60n23–24, 61n32, 61–62n47, 63n63, 128; "Der goldener zeyger," 49; *Khazon le-mo'ed,* 60n23; *Kokhevey yitskhak,* 60n23; *Mikal no'am,* 56, 61n32
Zibel, Nakhman, 314
Zeifert, Moyshe, 230, 235; *Der yidisher polkovnik* (Zeifert, Mogulesko, and Minkowski), 230, 235
Zelwerowicz, Alexander, 140
Zemach, Benjamin, 281, 289, 293–294n34
Zhitlovsky, Chaim, 295
Zigelboym, Fayvl, 140, 141, 143

Zionism, 212; in theatre, 311–312
Zukor, Adolph, 193
Żuławski, Jerzy, *Koniec Mesjasza,* 121, 122
Zunser, Elyokum, 48, 49, 51, 52, 54, 56, 61n31, 61n39, 61–62n47; "Der freylekher mentsh," 49; "Tsu dem tsen rubl bilet," 49, 61n33
Zylbercweig, Zalmen, 8, 16–17, 60n27, 80n5, 230, 235, *252,* 252–263, 266, 268–271; theatrical background, 252, 256, 269, 270; *Leksikon fun yidishn teater,* 16–17, 230, 252–261, 265, 266–267, 268–271, 271n1; controversies regarding, 16–17, 253, 255–259, 265, 268–271; representation of women in, 17, 251–252, 256, 257, 258, 261, 268, 270, 274n49; *Pinkes fun yidishn teater,* 252; *Teater mozaik,* 261